SMITHSONIAN INSTITUTION
BUREAU OF AMERICAN ETHNOLOGY
BULLETIN 189

RIVER BASIN SURVEYS PAPERS

FRANK H. H. ROBERTS, JR., *Editor*

Inter-Agency Archeological Salvage Program

NUMBERS 33–38

U.S. GOVERNMENT PRINTING OFFICE
WASHINGTON : 1964

For sale by the Superintendent of Documents, U.S. Government Printing Office
Washington D.C., 20402 • Price $3.75 cloth

LETTER OF TRANSMITTAL

SMITHSONIAN INSTITUTION,
BUREAU OF AMERICAN ETHNOLOGY,
Washington, D.C., September 28, 1962.

SIR: I have the honor to transmit the accompanying manuscripts, entitled "The Paul Brave site (32SI4), Oahe Reservoir area, North Dakota," by W. Raymond Wood and Alan R. Woolworth; "The Demery site (39CO1), Oahe Reservoir area, South Dakota," by Alan R. Woolworth and W. Raymond Wood; "Archeological investigations at the Hosterman site (39PO7), Oahe Reservoir area, Potter County, South Dakota, 1956," by Carl F. Miller; "Archeological investigations at the Hickey Brothers site (39LM4), Big Bend Reservoir, Lyman County, South Dakota," by Warren W. Caldwell, Lee G. Madison, and Bernard Golden; "The Good Soldier site (39LM238), Big Bend Reservoir, Lyman County, South Dakota," by Robert W. Neuman; "Archeological investigations in the Toronto Reservoir area, Kansas," by James H. Howard, and to recommend that they be published as a bulletin of the Bureau of American Ethnology.

Very respectfully yours,

FRANK H. H. ROBERTS, Jr.,
Director.

DR. LEONARD CARMICHAEL,
Secretary, Smithsonian Institution.

EXPLANATION OF THE INTER-AGENCY ARCHEOLOGICAL SALVAGE PROGRAM

The Inter-Agency Archeological Salvage Program is a cooperative plan of the Smithsonian Institution; the National Park Service and the Bureau of Reclamation, Department of the Interior; and the Corps of Engineers, Department of the Army. It was formulated, through a series of interbureau agreements, for the purpose of recovering archeological and paleontological remains that would otherwise be lost as a result of the numerous projects for flood control, irrigation, hydroelectric power, and navigation improvements in the river basins of the United States. Various State and local agencies have assisted in the work. To carry out its part of the joint undertaking, the Smithsonian Institution organized the River Basin Surveys as a unit of the Bureau of American Ethnology. The National Park Service has served as liaison between the various agencies and has provided the Smithsonian Institution with all of the necessary information pertaining to the location of proposed dams and other construction and their priorities. It has also had responsibility for budgeting costs of the program, funds for which are provided in the annual appropriations of the Department of the Interior. The operations of the River Basin Surveys, Smithsonian Institution, have been supported by funds transferred to it from the National Park Service. Through agreements with the National Park Service, money has also been made available to State and local agencies to supplement their own resources and aid them in their contributions to the program.

The River Basin Surveys Papers, of which this is the ninth bulletin, are issued under the scientific editorship of Frank H. H. Roberts, Jr., director of the Bureau of American Ethnology.

PUBLISHER'S NOTE

A separate edition is published of each paper in the series entitled "River Basin Surveys Papers." Available copies of Papers 1–38 can be had upon request to the Publications Office, Smithsonian Institution, Washington, D.C., 20560.

RIVER BASIN SURVEYS PAPERS PUBLISHED PREVIOUSLY

No. 1. Prehistory and the Missouri Valley Development Program: Summary Report on the Missouri River Basin Archeological Survey in 1948, by Waldo R. Wedel. Bull. 154, pp. xv–xviii, 1–59, pls. 1–12, fig. 1. 1953.

No. 2. Prehistory and the Missouri Valley Development Program: Summary Report on the Missouri River Basin Archeological Survey in 1949, by Waldo R. Wedel. Bull. 154, pp. 61–101, pls. 13–15. 1953.

No. 3. The Woodruff Ossuary, a prehistoric burial site in Phillips County, Kansas, by Marvin F. Kivett. Bull. 154, pp. 103–141, pls. 16–28, figs. 2–3. 1953.

No. 4. The Addicks Dam site:
  I. An archeological survey of the Addicks Dam Basin, Southeast Texas, by Joe Ben Wheat. Bull. 154, pp. 143–252, pls. 29–47, figs. 4–23. 1953.
  II. Indian skeletal remains from the Doering and Kobs sites, Addicks Reservoir, Texas, by Marshall T. Newman. Bull. 154, pp. 253–266, figs. 24–28. 1953.

No. 5. The Hodges site:
  I. Two rock shelters near Tucumari, New Mexico, by Herbert W. Dick. Bull. 154, pp. 267–284, pls. 48–54, figs 29–30. 1953.
  II. Geology of the Hodges site, Quay County, New Mexico, by Sheldon Judson. Bull. 154, pp. 285–302, figs. 31–35. 1953.

No. 6. The Rembert Mounds, Elbert County, Georgia, by Joseph R. Caldwell. Bull. 154, pp. 303–320, pls. 55–56, figs. 36–40. 1953.

No. 7. Archeological investigations in the Oahe Dam area, South Dakota, 1950–51, by Donald J. Lehmer. Bull. 158, 190 pp., 22 pls., 56 figs., 6 maps. 1954.

No. 8. Excavations in the McNary Reservoir Basin near Umatilla, Oregon, by Douglas Osborne. With appendixes by Marshall T. Newman, Arthur Woodward, W. J. Kroll, and B. H. McLeod. Bull. 166, 250 pp., 40 pls., 6 figs., 19 maps. 1957.

No. 9. Archeological investigations in the Heart Butte Reservior area, North Dakota, by Paul L. Cooper. Bull. 169, pp. 1–40, pls. 1–12, figs 1–2. 1958.

No. 10. Archeological investigations at the Tuttle Creek Dam, Kansas, by Robert B. Cumming, Jr. Bull. 169, pp. 41–78, pls. 13–24. 1958.

No. 11. The Spain site (39LM301), a winter village in Fort Randall Reservoir, South Dakota, by Carlyle S. Smith and Roger T. Grange, Jr. Bull. 169, pp. 79–128, pls. 25–36, figs 3–4. 1958.

No. 12. The Wilbanks site (9CK–5), Georgia, by William H. Sears. Bull. 169, pls. 37–45, figs 5–9. 1958.

No. 13. Historic sites in and around the Jim Woodruff Reservoir area, Florida-Georgia, by Mark F. Boyd. Bull. 169, pp. 195–314, pls. 46–55, figs. 10–11. 1958.

No. 14. Six sites near the Chattahoochee River in the Jim Woodruff Reservoir area, Florida, by Ripley P. Bullen. Bull. 169, pp. 315–357, pls. 56–73, figs. 12–13. 1958.

No. 15. Historic sites archeology on the Upper Missouri, by Merrill J. Mattes. Bull. 179. pp. 1–24.

No. 16. Historic sites archeology in the Fort Randall Reservoir, South Dakota, by John E. Mills. Bull. 176, pp. 25–48, pls. 1–9, figs. 1–2, map 1. 1960.

No. 17. The excavation and investigation of Fort Lookout Trading Post II (39LM57) in the Fort Randall Reservoir, South Dakota, by Carl F. Miller. Bull. 176, pp. 49–82, pls. 10–18, figs. 3–14, map 2. 1960.

No. 18. Fort Pierre II (39ST217), a historic trading post in the Oahe Dam area, South Dakota, by G. Hubert Smith. Bull. 176, pp. 83–158, pls. 19–30, maps 3–4. 1960.

No. 19. Archeological investigations at the site of Fort Stevenson (32ML1), Garrison Reservoir, North Dakota, by G. Hubert Smith. (Introduction by Robert L. Stephenson and an appendix by Carlyle S. Smith.) Bull. 176, pp. 159–238, pls. 31–54, figs. 15–20, maps 5–6. 1960.

No. 20. The archeology of a small trading post (32MN1) in the Garrison Reservoir (Kipp's Post), South Dakota, by Alan R. Woolworth and W. Raymond Wood. Bull. 176, pp. 239–305, pls. 55–65, figs. 21–25, map 7. 1960.

No. 21. Excavations at Texarkana Reservoir, Sulphur River, Texas, by Edward B. Jelks. Bull. 179, pp. xiii–78, pls. 1–17, figs. 1–9. 1961.

No. 22. Archeological investigations at the Coralville Reservoir, Iowa, by Warren W. Caldwell. Bull. 179, pp. 81–148, pls. 18–29, figs. 10–24. 1961.

No. 23. The McNary Reservoir: A study in plateau archeology, by Joel L. Shiner. Bull. 179, pp. 151–266, pls. 30–46, figs. 25–40, maps 1–7. 1961.

No. 24. The Sheep Island site and the Mid-Columbia Valley, by Douglas Osborne, Alan Bryan, and Robert H. Crabtree. Bull. 179, pp. 269–321, pls. 47–56, figs. 41–43. 1961.

No. 25. Archeology of the John H. Kerr Reservoir Basin, Roanoke River, Virginia-North Carolina, by Carl F. Miller. (Appendix by Lucile E. Hoyme and William M. Bass.) Bull. 182, 447 pp., pls. 1–110, figs. 1–65, maps, 1–8. 1962.

No. 26. Small sites on and about Fort Berthold Indian Reservation, Garrison Reservoir, North Dakota, by George Metcalf. Bull. 185, pp. 1–56, pls. 1–11, figs. 1–5, 1 map. 1962.

No. 27. Star Village: A fortified historic Arikara site in Mercer County, North Dakota, by George Metcalf. Bull. 185, pp. 57–122, pls. 12–17, figs. 6–16, 3 maps. 1962.

No. 28. The dance hall of the Santee Bottoms on the Fort Berthold Reservation, Garrison Reservoir, North Dakota, by Donald D. Hartle. Bull. 185, pp. 123–132, pl. 18, figs. 17–18. 1962.

No. 29. Crow-Flies-High (32MZ1), a historic Hidatsa village in the Garrison Reservoir area, North Dakota, by Carling Malouf. Bull. 185, pp. 133–166, pls. 19–26, figs. 19–25. 1962.

No. 30. The Stutsman Focus: An aboriginal culture complex in the Jamestown
        Reservoir area, North Dakota, by R. P. Wheeler. Bull. 185, pp. 167–
        233, pls. 27–36, figs. 26–38. 1962.
No. 31. Archeological manifestations in the Toole County section of the Tiber
        Reservoir Basin, Montana, by Carl F. Miller. Bull. 185, pp. 235–255,
        pls. 37–45, figs. 39–40, 1 map. 1962.
No. 32. Archeological salvage investigations in the Lovewell Reservoir area,
        Kansas, by Robert W. Neuman. Bull. 185, pp. 257–306, pls. 46–57,
        figs. 41–43. 1962.

CONTENTS

PAGE

No. 33. The Paul Brave site (32SI4), Oahe Reservoir area, North Dakota, by W. Raymond Wood and Alan R. Woolworth_____ IX

No. 34. The Demery site (39CO1), Oahe Reservoir area, South Dakota, by Alan R. Woolworth and W. Raymond Wood_____ 67

No. 35. Archeological investigations at the Hosterman site (39PO7), Oahe Reservoir area, Potter County, South Dakota, 1956, by Carl F. Miller_____ 139

No. 36. Archeological investigations at the Hickey Brothers site (39LM4), Big Bend Reservoir, Lyman County, South Dakota, by Warren W. Caldwell, Lee G. Madison, and Bernard Golden_____ 267

No. 37. The Good Soldier site (39LM238), Big Bend Reservoir, Lyman County, South Dakota, by Robert W. Neuman_____ 291

No. 38. Archeological investigations in the Toronto Reservoir area, Kansas, by James H. Howard_____ 319

List of reports, articles, and notes relating to the salvage programs published in other series_____ 371

Index_____ 393

SMITHSONIAN INSTITUTION
Bureau of American Ethnology
Bulletin 189

River Basin Surveys Papers, No. 33
The Paul Brave Site (32SI4), Oahe Reservoir Area, North Dakota

By W. RAYMOND WOOD and ALAN R. WOOLWORTH

CONTENTS

	PAGE
Preface	XIII
Introduction	1
Archeology of the site	2
Site description	2
Excavation methods	2
Features	4
Excavation unit 1 (house 1)	4
Excavation unit 2 (house 2)	7
Excavation unit 3 (house 3)	9
Excavation unit 4	11
Excavation unit 5	11
Excavation unit 6	11
Excavation unit 7	11
Excavation unit 8 (house 4)	12
Human burials	12
Artifacts	14
Pottery types	14
Riggs ware	16
Fort Yates ware	20
Unclassified wares	21
Miniature vessels	22
Body sherds	23
Miscellaneous objects of baked clay	24
Work in stone	25
Work in bone	35
Work in antler and teeth	45
Work in shell	48
Vegetal remains	50
Unmodified bone and shell	50
Discussion	51
Structures	51
Artifact complex	52
Other sites	57
Robert Zahn site (32SI3)	57
Havens site (32EM1)	60
Conclusions	61
Literature cited	63

TABLES

		PAGE
1.	Description of features	13
2.	Seven species of fossil shells examined	50
3.	Species identified at Paul Brave	51
4.	Pottery frequencies at Thomas Riggs and Paul Brave sites	55
5.	Comparison of traits at Paul Brave and Thomas Riggs sites	58

ILLUSTRATIONS

PLATES
(All plates follow page 66)

1. *a*, Aerial view of the Paul Brave site and environs.   *b*, House 2.
2. *a*, Feature 70 in House 3.   *b*, Burned timbers in House 3.
3. Pottery rim sherds.
4. Crosshatched rim sherds.
5. Pottery examples A–D, and cord-impressed rim sherds.
6. Pottery disks, body sherds, and vessels.

TEXT FIGURES

	PAGE
1. Pottery design elements	17
2. Pottery design elements	18
3. Projectile points	26
4. End scrapers and knives	28
5. Chipped and ground stone artifacts	33
6. Baked clay effigies and scapula hoes	36
7. Worked bone	37
8. Worked bone	39
9. Bone awls	40
10. Worked bone	41
11. Objects of antler and animal teeth	47
12. Shell beads and disks	49

MAPS

1. Paul Brave site and environs	3
2. Site map, showing excavations	5
3. House 1, excavation 1	6
4. House 2, excavation 2	8
5. House 3, excavation 3	10

PREFACE

In 1947 an archeological field party, sponsored by the University of North Dakota and the State Historical Society of North Dakota, carried out excavations in the upper limits of the Oahe Reservoir, in North Dakota. Test excavations were made at the Paul Brave site (32SI4), also known as the Fort Yates site. The elevation of this prehistoric village is between 1,600 and 1,610 feet. The site will be flooded by the Oahe Reservoir when backwater reaches the maximum pool level of 1,620 feet. The work in 1947 was directed by Dr. Gordon W. Hewes, then with the University of North Dakota. The limited excavations in 1947 indicated the desirability of further and more intensive work at the site, and in 1955 the State Historical Society of North Dakota sponsored a second party for full-scale excavation.

Funds were made available for this archeological salvage work through a cooperative agreement with the National Park Service. Between July 6, 1955, and August 30, 1955, excavation was carried out under our supervision when we were both staff archeologists with the State Historical Society. The assistance of Oriol Pi-Sunyer, then a graduate student at Harvard, is gratefully acknowledged. The genial and competent crew members contributed further to the summer's accomplishments. These were Stephen W. Robinson and Robert P. Barr, of Grand Forks, N. Dak., and Russell B. Lawrence and Robert F. Gipp. of Fort Yates, N. Dak.

The overburden at the site necessitated the use of a bulldozer, which was rented from the Standing Rock Tribal Council, and operated by Jack McLaughlin of Shields, N. Dak. The use of this machine implemented the removal of the nearly 3 feet of sterile overburden from the house floors. The River Basin Surveys, Smithsonian Institution, provided the field party with cameras and other equipment necessary to document features found in the excavations. We took aerial photographs on a flight early in September 1955.

We wish to thank Robert L. Stephenson, Charles H. McNutt, and Warren Caldwell for constructive criticism of this report. Joseph P. E. Morrison identified the shell material from the site. Russell Reid, superintendent of the State Historical Society of North Dakota, assisted in the identification of the baked clay animal figurines from the site and aided the investigators in many other ways. Photographic plates were prepared with the assistance of Bernard Weinreich, Bismarck photographer. The maps and line drawings were prepared by Wood.

Permission to excavate on the Standing Rock Indian Reservation was generously granted by the Standing Rock Tribal Council. Members of the Paul Brave estate gave their permission to excavate site 32SI4. Superintendent J. W. Wellington extended every effort to make the summer comfortable and successful, and Tribal Chairman David Black Hoop aided the excavators in many ways. This assistance made the summer of 1955 a profitable and enjoyable one, and it is gratefully acknowledged.

The field notes, maps, and artifacts from the site were returned for study and preservation to the State Historical Society Museum in Bismarck, and they are on file in that institution. Some of the field records and collections made in 1947 are also in the collections at that museum, and the rest are at the University of North Dakota, in Grand Forks. All of the 1947 material at the Museum was reanalyzed and is incorporated in the present study.

W. RAYMOND WOOD
ALAN R. WOOLWORTH

THE PAUL BRAVE SITE (32SI4), OAHE RESERVOIR AREA, NORTH DAKOTA [1]

By W. Raymond Wood and Alan R. Woolworth

INTRODUCTION

The purpose of this study is to present a detailed descriptive statement of the archeology of one of the early village sites in the northern part of the Middle Missouri area. The Middle Missouri area consists of the Missouri River Valley and the lower reaches of its tributaries between Bismarck, N. Dak., and southeastern South Dakota (see Lehmer, 1954, p. 140). The Paul Brave site is significant because it was occupied at the time when the first village or town dwellers were establishing themselves in the northern part of this area. The derivation of these early village people and the subsequent settlement patterns of the Northern Plains are topics of interest to the anthropologists and historians of the region.

Since 1906, when George F. Will and Herbert J. Spinden reported work at the Double Ditch (Bourgois) Mandan site, north of the city of Bismarck, N. Dak., archeological interest in the northern Middle Missouri area has increased. Some of the stages in the history of the area have been blocked in roughly, particularly by George F. Will and Thad. C. Hecker (1944). Details, however, are scant, and the present study provides a base from which a more adequate definition of the early village people may be made. The lack of any real fund of comparative data precludes any sweeping conclusions, although a few tentative generalizations are justified on the basis of excavations at the Paul Brave site.

Preliminary statements of the archeology of Paul Brave have appeared in several publications. The first reference to the site is in Will and Hecker (ibid., p. 89), where it is described as an unnamed "Archaic Mandan" site on tribal land north of the Paul Brave estate. Test excavations in 1947 resulted in two brief articles by the excavator, Gordon W. Hewes. The first of these (1949 a) describes the excavations in summary form, discusses some of the significant finds and tentatively places the site in time. A second article (1949 b) is

---

[1] Submitted September 1959; some revision April 1961.

1

a preliminary classification of the pottery from the excavations, with notes on extra-site distributions. In addition, there are references to Paul Brave in the report on the Thomas Riggs site, 39HU1 (Hurt, 1953). In Hurt's report Paul Brave is referred to as the "Fort Yates site." In the present study, site 32SI4 is designated as the Paul Brave site to avoid duplication in terms, since the term "Fort Yates" has been used in other contexts.

ARCHEOLOGY OF THE SITE

SITE DESCRIPTION

The Paul Brave site is located in the N½N½NE¼ of sec. 8, T. 129 N., R. 79 W., Sioux County, N. Dak. It is on the west bank of the Missouri River 6 miles downstream from the town of Fort Yates, and about 6 miles upstream from the North and South Dakota boundary. The site is on a rolling terrace that overlooks the Missouri River flood plain, this terrace averaging 20 feet above the flood plain. To the south, the land rises in a series of low hills that abut against the Missouri River bluffs, about one-half of a mile distant (map 1; also pl. 1, a). Fire Heart Butte, a high, flat-topped butte, is about 4 miles to the southeast.

At the time the site was investigated in 1955, it was found that at least 14 oval house depressions were distributed over an area of about 4 acres. These depressions were as much as 65 feet long and were 2 to 3 feet deep. They were filled with a lush vegetation that contrasted with the short, dry grass on higher points in the village area. The site is said to have been cultivated (Will and Hecker, 1944, p. 89), but activity does not seem to have obscured the surface indications of the larger subsurface features. The village may have been larger originally, because Will and Hecker (1944, p. 89) also noted house floors exposed in the terrace edge facing the river. This terrace was checked in 1955. A number of artifacts were recovered from the surface, but there was no indication of house floors. There is no evidence that the site was fortified, but it is partially isolated from the remainder of the terrace by a narrow swale south of the village (map 2; also pl. 1, a).

EXCAVATION METHODS

Preliminary testing determined that the houses were built in shallow pits. Three houses were chosen for excavation after the depth of the house floors and the house walls had been determined. These houses were evenly distributed over the site, and none of them had been tested previously. The entire site was mantled by a deposit of light-buff aeolian soil. This mantle was as much as 4 feet deep over some of the houses, but high points within the village were buried

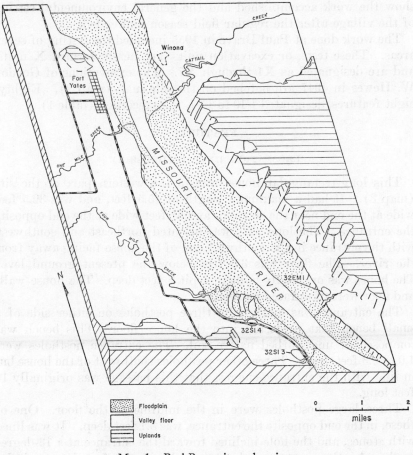

MAP 1.—Paul Brave site and environs.

only about a foot. A bulldozer was used to strip this overburden from the three houses down to house fill, which was excavated by conventional hand methods. House fill was a dark, mottled, and relatively soft mixed earth that contrasted with the lightly colored sandy native soil. The depth of the bulldozer cut was regulated to approximate the depth of the former village occupational level.

Three other bulldozer cuts were made in the eastern part of the site to expose cache pits and other features, and to check for deeper occupational levels. No evidence was observed that indicated any occupation prior to that represented by the houses. House floors were carefully exposed, and all postholes, fireplaces, pits, and other features were cored. The structures were mapped radially by use of a plane table, open-sight alidade, and steel chain after excavation. Photographs were taken of the excavated houses, features, significant finds, and progress of the work. Several aerial photographs were taken to show the work accomplished and the general environmental setting of the village after the regular field season had ended.

The work done at Paul Brave in 1955 included the testing of seven areas. These tests, or excavation units, are herein termed X units, and are designated as X1 through X7. The excavations of Gordon W. Hewes in 1947 are hatched on the site map (map 2). Eighty-eight features, designated F10 to F97, were recorded (table 1).

FEATURES

EXCAVATION UNIT 1 (HOUSE 1)

This long-rectangular house was in the western part of the site (map 3). It had a maximum length of 45.5 feet, and was 32.5 feet wide at the end near the entrance and 31 feet wide at the end opposite the entrance. The long axis was oriented northeast and southwest, with the entrance in the southwest end of the house facing away from the river. The floor was 3.6 feet below the present ground level. The house was originally built in a pit 2 feet deep. The house walls and floor were of unfaced native soil.

The entrance was marked by three postholes on either side of a small bench that projected into the house floor. This bench was composed of undisturbed native soil. The entrance postholes were 1.0 to 2.3 feet deep. Three other postholes southwest of the house but in line with the entrance suggest that this passage was originally 14 feet long.

Three large postholes were in the midline of the floor. One of these, in the end opposite the entrance, was 3.1 feet deep. It was lined with stones, and the hole inclined toward the entrance at a 13-degree angle. Another post near the rear wall was 1.6 feet deep and also inclined toward the entrance. Midway between the end post and the entrance was a post 3.0 feet deep. Another post, not located along the midline of the floor, leaned toward the end post. It may have served as a brace.

There were 20 postholes along each of the long walls of the house, from 0.9 to 2.1 feet deep, averaging 1.5 feet deep. There were no posts in the house ends. On either side of the midline of the floor, there was an intermediate row of posts. In each row were five posts, spaced 8 to 10 feet apart (posts I to X, map 3).

The fireplace, F19, was centered on the midline of the house, off-set toward the entrance. It was circular and basin shaped, and contained ash, mixed earth, and a burned floor. Another basin-shaped pit, F81, may also have been a fireplace, owing to the fact that its floor was burned, but there was little depth to the burning. Perhaps it was used sparingly or for only a brief time as a fireplace.

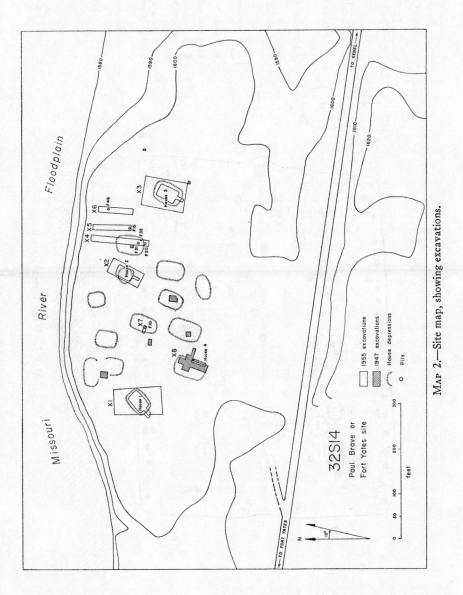

MAP 2.—Site map, showing excavations.

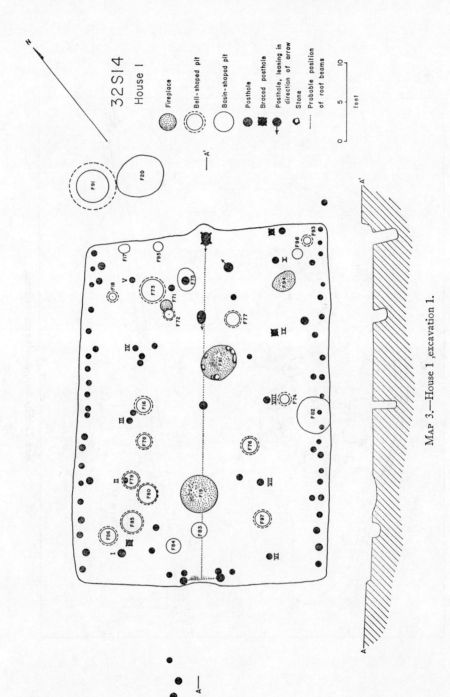

MAP 3.—House 1, excavation 1.

A number of large stones were along the edge of this pit. At the rear of the house was an area of burned earth (F94), which appeared to be a surface hearth. A small, basin-shaped fireplace (F71) contained white ash, and the underlying soil was burned.

Fourteen bell-shaped pits of various sizes were in the house floor. They tended to be in a line with the intermediate rows of posts. These pits were small, averaging less than 2 feet in depth. Six basin-shaped pits contained mixed earth and refuse. One of these (F82), may have been dug after the house was abandoned, since the wall postholes observed in the pit floor were not visible within the pit fill. A layer of charcoal blanketed the floor of the house, and many of the postholes contained the charred remains of posts. Apparently the house was destroyed by fire.

EXCAVATION UNIT 2 (HOUSE 2)

This long-rectangular house was in the north-central part of the site (map 4; pl. 1, b). It had a maximum length of 37.5 feet, was 24.0 feet wide near the entrance, and 26.0 feet wide at the rear. The long axis of the house was nearly north and south, with the entrance in the south end facing away from the river. The house floor lay 2.8 feet below the surface, and the house was built in a pit 1.4 feet deep. The house floor and walls were of unfaced native soil.

The entrance was marked by four postholes, two on each side of a small bench of native soil that projected into the house floor. These postholes were 1.1 to 2.4 feet deep. An entrance was indicated by 11 postholes that outlined a passage 18 feet long and 4 to 5 feet wide. The postholes began at a point about 10 feet from the house wall. Despite a careful search, no postholes could be located between the house wall and that point. A hole 1 foot in diameter and 0.8 of a foot deep was in the midline of the entrance, but it probably was not a part of that feature.

Two large postholes were in the midline of the house. The post-hole in the rear wall was 0.9 foot in diameter and 2.1 feet deep and was filled with white ash. Midway between the end posthole and the entrance was a posthole 0.9 foot in diameter and 3.2 feet deep containing the remains of a cedar post that was braced with stones. The long walls of the house were lined with 12 postholes each and, although auxiliary posts occurred, the two rows were mirror images of each other in spacing and placement. These postholes were 0.8 to 2.4 feet deep, averaging 1.5 feet. All house posts observed were cedar, and all were vertical. There were no postholes along the end walls.

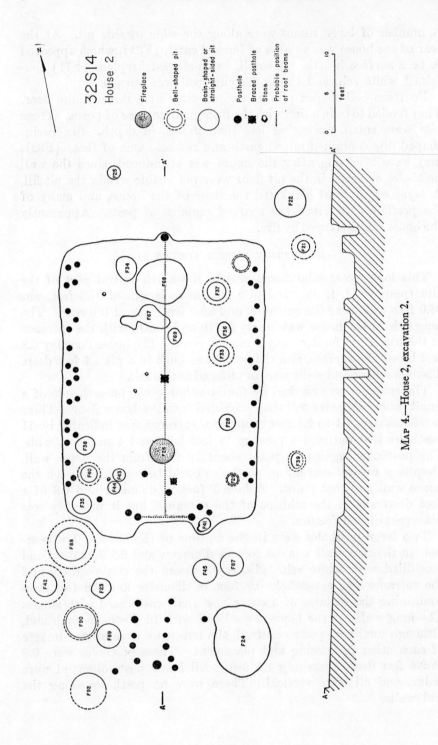

MAP 4.—House 2, excavation 2.

The fireplace (F26) was offset toward the entrance, and was centered on the midline of the house. It was filled with compact white ash and mixed earth and was lined with burned earth. East of the entrance, in a shallow recess in the house wall, a large unmodified stone slab was on the house floor. The material is a conglomerate, and similar stone occurs along the river bluffs south of the site. Five bell-shaped pits and several basin-shaped pits filled with mixed earth and refuse were in the house floor. An irregularly shaped pit (F67) was near the rear wall of the house. A thin layer of charcoal and burned earth marked the floor level, and the tops of most of the posts were charred, a condition indicating that the house was leveled by fire.

EXCAVATION UNIT 3 (HOUSE 3)

This long-rectangular house was in the eastern part of the site (map 5). It was 46.0 feet long, 32.5 feet wide at the end near the entrance, and 29.0 feet wide at the back end. The long axis of the house was oriented north and south, and the entrance was in the south end, facing away from the river. The house floor was 2.8 feet below the present surface. The structure was originally built in a pit more than 1 foot deep. The floor and walls were of unfaced native soil.

The entrance was marked by four postholes, two on each side of a small bench of native soil that projected into the house. These postholes were 0.9 to 1.3 feet deep. Two postholes south of the house but in line with the entrance suggest that the passage was 15 feet long and 4 to 5 feet wide.

There were two large postholes along the midline of the house. A posthole 3.0 feet deep and 1.6 feet wide in the rear wall contained a vertical cedar post 0.9 foot in diameter that was braced with stones. In the house center, midway between the entrance and the end posthole, was a posthole 0.9 foot wide and 1.9 feet deep. Secondary supports were provided by two rows of postholes located between the house midline and the walls. They consisted of two rows of five posts each, spaced from 8 to 10 feet apart (posts I to X, map 5). Several of them were lined with stones. There were no postholes along the end walls.

The fireplace was centered on the midline of the house, offset toward the entrance. It contained compact white ash, mixed earth, and was lined with burned earth. Three miniature pottery vessels were found embedded in the ash. Two of these vessels are illustrated (pl. 6, f–g). An oval, basin-shaped pit (F53) and a small rectangular pit (F63) had lightly fired floors and may also have served as fireplaces. Three smaller fireplaces (F64, F65, and F66) contained ash, and were lined with burned earth.

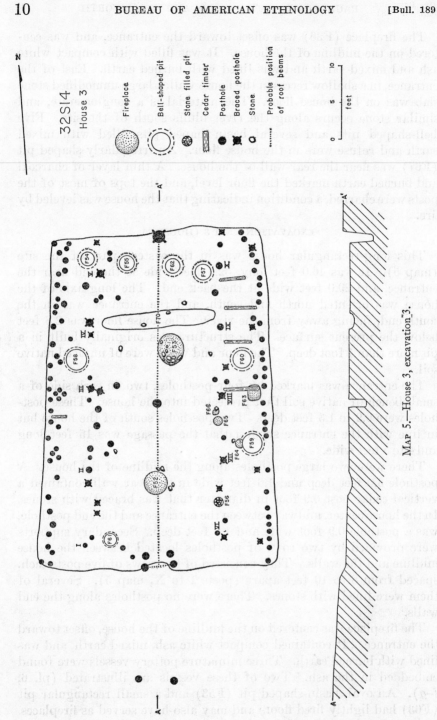

MAP 5.—House 3, excavation 3.

A unique feature near the rear wall of the house was a long straight trench with rounded ends and a shallow U-shaped cross section. Its long axis was perpendicular to the long axis of the structure. The feature (F70) contained a few bone fragments and two stones (pl. 2, *a*). There were a few bison skull fragments near the rear wall in the house, but there was no other evidence of a household shrine.

Eight bell-shaped floor pits were along the house walls. Basin-shaped pits, present in the other dwellings, were lacking in this structure. Five charred timbers on the house floor, at right angles to the house walls, were probably fallen wall posts (pl. 2, *b*). They were cedar timbers ranging in length up to 4.8 feet. The inner ends of the timbers were about 5 feet from the line of wall posts, suggesting that the wall was at least 5 feet high. The timbers averaged about 0.3 foot in diameter, although they may originally have been larger. The evidence indicates that this house, as well as the other two excavated houses, was destroyed by fire.

EXCAVATION UNIT 4

Unit 4 was in the northeastern part of the site, east of House 2. It was a trench oriented north and south, 130 feet long and 14 feet wide, attaining a maximum depth of 5 feet. Near the south end of the unit was a house depression (F12) the floor of which was 4.2 feet below the present surface. Three pits were exposed near the south end of the house. F32 was profiled; this bell-shaped pit could not be associated with the house. F31 was a small bell-shaped pit in the floor of the house, and F30 was a pit of indeterminate form on the south edge of the house.

EXCAVATION UNIT 5

Unit 5 was east of House 2 and northwest of House 3. It was a trench oriented north and south, 85 feet long and 14 feet wide, with a maximum depth of 5 feet. A bell-shaped pit (F15) was in the south end of the unit.

EXCAVATION UNIT 6

Unit 6 was east of House 2 and northwest of House 3. It was a trench oriented north and south, 75 feet long and 14 feet wide, attaining a maximum depth of 5 feet. A bell-shaped pit (F46) was in the north end of the unit.

EXCAVATION UNIT 7

Unit 7 was a test pit approximately in the center of the village area, 5.6 feet north and south and 17 feet east and west. It is an extension of a test pit excavated by Hewes in 1947. The 1947 excavation was a 5-foot square. In 1955 this unit was extended to the west and revealed a house wall. The wall was of unfaced native soil, sloping up from the floor at an angle of 20 degrees to the former village level. The house pit was 1.8 feet deep, and at the wall the overburden was 2 feet deep. Four postholes along the wall contained the remains of cedar posts or soft mixed earth. The holes varied in diameter from 0.5 to 0.8 foot, and were 1.3 to 2.4 feet deep. No other features of interest were noted on the trench floor.

EXCAVATION UNIT 8 (HOUSE 4)

Unit 8 revealed the floor of a long-rectangular house. The structure was excavated in 1947, and the following description was paraphrased from Hewes' original report (1949 a, pp. 22–23).

The largest and deepest house depression at the site was cross-trenched, and the greater part of the floor was ultimately cleared. The floor lay at a depth of about 4 feet below the present surface. The upper foot of the overburden was sterile, including only recent deposits of humus, but the remaining fill included sherds, bone and flint tools, and animal bone. The structure was approximately rectangular, 65 feet long and 35 feet wide, with four rows of postholes. (The floor plan of the house is apparently similar to that of House 1 and House 3.) Three fireplaces, devoid of refuse, were on the floor. The only other significant features were three large piles of bison bone, chiefly cranial parts and horn cores, intermingled with rough stone. Near the floor center, about 50 inches below the surface of the house depression, were two large broken pottery vessels resting mouth down on the floor. These two vessels were illustrated in Hewes' original report (1949 b, pl. 5, lower right, t-u). The house fill above the floor contained such refuse as bone, sherds, and tools, but the floor was free of such detritus. Hewes was inclined to interpret this feature as a ceremonial structure, rather than a household dwelling unit. In size, at least, the house stands apart from the smaller structures excavated in 1955, and Hewes' interpretation is convincing.

HUMAN BURIALS

There is a low rise of ground south of the site, and this rise is intercepted along its north edge by a road (map 2). In 1956, George Haiser reported to the excavators that, prior to World War II, several human burials were gouged from the south bank of the road by road-cutting operations. It is possible that this rise of ground may have served as a cemetery for the village, since there were no human remains in the site. The burial positions and the disposition of the remains from the road cut are not known.

Other evidence of activity in the low rises south of the site was encountered. Survey parties in 1955 found circular shell disk beads on a hill about 1,000 yards south of the site. These objects might be grave offerings brought to the surface by animal activity, and they are similar to beads from the excavated houses and features. Unfortunately the brief field season did not permit further exploration of the area south of the site.

TABLE 1.—*Description of features*

Feature No.	X No.	Depth	Length and width	Identification
		Feet	*Feet*	
10	7	1.8	No data	Rectangular house.
11	2	1.4	Length, 37.5 N-S width, 24.0-26.0 E-W.	Rectangular house (house 2).
12	4		Floor 4.2 below surface	Rectangular house.
13	1	2.0	Length, 45.5 N-S width, 31.0-32.5 E-W.	Rectangular house (house 1).
14	3	1.0	Length, 46.0 N-S width, 39.0-32.5 E-W.	Rectangular house (house 3).
15	5	3.8	Orifice diam., 4.0; diam., 6.0	Bell-shaped pit, floor slightly fired.
16	1	1.4	Orifice diam., 1.8; diam., 2.2	Bell-shaped pit in House 1.
17	1	.6	Diameter 1.3 E-W 1.1 N-S	Basin-shaped pit in House 1.
18	1	1.0	Orifice diam., 0.9; diam., 1.5	Bell-shaped pit in House 1.
19	1	.6	Diameter, 5.0	Primary fireplace in House 1.
20	1	1.0	Diameter, 5.2 N-S, 6.8 E-W	Basin-shaped pit north of House 1.
21	2	2.6	Orifice diam., 2.4; diam., 3.2	Bell-shaped pit northeast of House 2.
22	2	.3	Diameter, 4.0	Basin-shaped pit northeast of House 2.
23	2	1.4	Diameter, 4.4	Basin-shaped pit south of House 2.
24	2	1.7	Diameter, 9.2 N-S, 7.5 E-W	Irregularly shaped pit south of House 2.
25	2	.6	Diameter, 1.8	Basin-shaped pit north of House 2.
26	2	.8	Diameter, 3.0	Primary fireplace in House 2.
27	2	1.1	Orifice diam., 1.8; diam., 2.2	Bell-shaped pit in House 2.
28	2	.4	Diameter, 2.0	Basin-shaped pit in House 2.
29	2	1.2	Orifice diam., 1.4; diam., 1.6	Bell-shaped pit in House 2.
30	4		Indeterminate	Pit of indeterminate form.
31	4	2.0	Orifice diam., 2.6; diam., 3.2	Bell-shaped pit in F12.
32	4	3.9	Orifice diam., 2.0; diam., 5.6	Bell-shaped pit.
33	2	2.0	Orifice diam., 1.8; diam., 3.3	Bell-shaped pit in House 2.
34	2	2.7	Diameter, 3.1 N-S, 2.5 E-W	Straight-sided pit with round bottom in House 2.
35	2	2.1	Diameter, 3.3	Straight-sided pit with flat bottom in House 2.
36	2	1.8	Diameter, 2.0 N-S, 1.8 E-W	Straight-sided pit with flat bottom in House 2.
37	2	2.6	Orifice diam., 2.5; diam., 3.5	Bell-shaped pit in House 2.
38	2	1.6	Orifice diam., 2.5; diam., 2.8	Bell-shaped pit in House 2.
39	2	2.0	Orifice diam., ca. 1.2; diam., 2.2	Bell-shaped pit east of House 2.
40	2	1.0	Orifice diam., 2.1; diam., 2.6	Bell-shaped pit in House 2.
41	2	1.4	Length 1.7; width 1.2; thickness 0.2	Flat conglomerate stone on floor of House 2.
42	2	2.7	Orifice diam. 3.0; diam., 5.0	Bell-shaped pit southwest of House 2.
43	2	.4	Diameter, 1.6	Basin-shaped pit in House 2.
44	2	.4	Diameter, 1.6	Basin-shaped pit in House 2.
45	2	1.2	Diameter, 3.0	Basin-shaped pit southeast of House 2.
46	6	2.6	Orifice diam., 4.5; diam. 6.5	Bell-shaped pit.
47	3		Length, 4.8; thickness, 0.3	Charred cedar post in House 3.
48	3		Length, 3.4; thickness, 0.3	Charred cedar post in House 3.
49	3		Length, 4.1; thickness, 0.3	Charred cedar post in House 3.
50	3		Length, 3.4; thickness, 0.3	Charred cedar post in House 3.
51	3		Length, 1.5; thickness, 0.2	Charred cedar post in House 3.
52	3	.6	Diameter, 3.0	Primary fireplace in House 3.
53	3	.6	Diameter, 4.0 N-S, 3.4 E-W	Basin-shaped pit containing stones; bottom slightly fired.
54	3	1.7	Orifice diam., 2.0; diam., 2.6	Bell-shaped pit in House 3.
55	3	1.5	Orifice diam., 2.0; diam., 2.6	Bell-shaped pit in House 3.
56	3	1.0	Diameter, 1.3	Straight-sided pit with rounded bottom in House 3, filled with fragments of sandstone.
57	3	2.1	Orifice diam., 2.2; diam., 2.8	Bell-shaped pit in House 3.
58	3	2.0	Orifice diam., 2.7; diam., 3.0	Bell-shaped pit in House 3.
59	3	2.6	Orifice diam., 3.0; diam., 3.4	Bell-shaped pit in House 3.
60	3	2.5	Orifice diam., 2.5; diam., 3.0	Bell-shaped pit in House 3.
61	3	2.0	Orifice diam., 1.6; diam., 2.0	Bell-shaped pit in House 3.
62	3	1.8	Orifice diam., 1.8; diam., 2.4	Bell-shaped pit in House 3.
63	3	.5	Diameter, 1.9 N-S; 1.7 E-W	Basin-shaped pit, rectangular in outline, with slight firing on bottom.
64	3	.3	Diameter, 1.0 N-S; 0.6 E-W	Basin-shaped fireplace containing ash, charcoal, burned earth.
65	3	.4	Diameter, 1.0	Basin-shaped fireplace containing ash, charcoal, burned earth.

TABLE 1.—*Description of features*—Continued

Feature No.	X No.	Depth	Length and width	Identification
		Feet	*Feet*	
66	3	0.2	Diameter, 0.9_____	Basin-shaped fireplace containing ash, charcoal, burned earth.
67	2	1.1	Length, 7.2 E–W; width, 3.0 N–S_____	Irregularly shaped pit in House 2.
68	2	1.8	Diameter, 5.6 N–S; 6.5 E–W_____	Oval, basin-shaped pit in House 2.
69	2	.4	Diameter, 2.0 N–S; 1.6 E–W_____	Basin-shaped pit in House 2.
70	3	1.0	Length, 15.4 E–W; width, 2.0_____	Long straight trench in House 3.
71	1	.3	Diameter, 1.2_____	Basin-shaped fireplace, with ash, burned earth; House 1.
72	1	.8	Orifice diam., 1.5; diam., 1.7 _____	Bell-shaped pit in House 1.
73	1	2.3	Orifice diam., 2.8; diam., 3.2_____	Bell-shaped pit in House 1.
74	1	1.3	Orifice diam., 1.2; diam., 1.8_____	Bell-shaped pit in House 1.
75	1	2.1	Diameter, 2.5 N–S; 3.0 E–W_____	Basin-shaped pit with posthole in bottom; House 1.
76	1	1.4	Orifice diam., 1.8; diam., 2.1_____	Bell-shaped pit in House 1.
77	1	1.2	Orifice diam., 1.8; diam., 2.0_____	Bell-shaped pit in House 1.
78	1	1.7	Orifice diam., 1.8; diam., 2.0_____	Bell-shaped pit in House 1.
79	1	1.8	Orifice diam., 2.0; diam., 2.4_____	Bell-shaped pit in House 1.
80	1	1.3	Orifice diam., 2.4; diam., 2.6_____	Bell-shaped pit in House 1.
81	1	1.3	Diameter, 4.1 N–S; 4.9 E–W_____	Basin-shaped pit containing stones on pit wall; floor is slightly fired; House 1.
82	1	.7	Diameter, 5.0_____	Basin-shaped pit with postholes in bottom; House 1.
83	1	1.0	Diameter, 2.0_____	Basin-shaped pit in House 1.
84	1	1.6	Diameter, 1.8_____	Straight-sided pit with round bottom in House 1.
85	1	2.2	Orifice diam., 2.6; diam., 3.0_____	Bell-shaped pit in House 1.
86	1	1.4	Orifice diam., 2.0; diam., 2.4_____	Bell-shaped pit in House 1.
87	2	1.0	Diameter, 3.0_____	Basin-shaped pit southeast of House 2.
88	2	2.2	Orifice diam., 4.3; diam., 6.2_____	Bell-shaped pit southwest of House 2.
89	2	.8	Diameter, 2.8_____	Basin-shaped pit southwest of House 2.
90	2	2.0	Orifice diam., 3.2; diam., 4.0_____	Bell-shaped pit southwest of House 2.
91	1	2.3	Orifice diam., 4.2; diam., 6.0_____	Bell-shaped pit north of House 1.
92	2	2.0	Diameter, 4.5_____	Basin-shaped pit south of House 2.
93	1	1.0	Orifice diam., 1.0; diam., 1.2_____	Bell-shaped pit in House 1.
94	1	.2	Diameter, 2.3 N–S; 3.3 E–W_____	Shallow depression, floor of burned earth; House 1.
95	1	.8	Diameter, 1.2_____	Basin-shaped pit in House 1.
96	1	.4	Diameter, 1.4_____	Basin-shaped pit in House 1.
97	1	1.1	Orifice diam., 1.8; diam., 2.2.	Bell-shaped pit in House 2.

ARTIFACTS

POTTERY TYPES

Several pottery types from the Paul Brave site are described below. These types differ in certain respects from types previously described by Gordon W. Hewes for some of the same pottery (1949 b, pp. 61–67). This study utilizes the pottery types defined at the Thomas Riggs site (Kleinsasser, 1953), but adds certain types that were lacking at Thomas Riggs. This reclassification was deemed necessary for several reasons. Pottery wares and types have been defined for a number of complexes in the Middle Missouri area since Hewes initially defined his types from the Paul Brave site. These classifications seem to have adopted rim form as the primary sorting criterion. Types or subtypes have been established within each ware for vessels or sherds bearing different decorative techniques. It is difficult to compare Hewes' types with those established by other workers, since Hewes did not use rim form as the primary criterion in his classification of Paul Brave pottery. The classification below uses the concepts of types and wares defined by Lehmer (1954, p. 41), which are in current use in the Middle Missouri area. Wares are defined as groups of types which share a majority of basic characteristics including paste, vessel shape, surface finish, and rim form. Types included within a ware are groups of vessels or rim sherds decorated or modified in a consistent manner.

The paste, surface finish, and form of the pottery from Paul Brave are described below to apply to all ceramics from the site.

PASTE:

    Method of manufacture: Probably lump modeled with paddle and anvil.

    Temper: The material is uniformly decomposed or calcined granite. The amount and size of tempering varies with the size of the vessel. In the smaller vessels and in miniatures, temper is small and sparse, while in larger vessels it is coarser and more abundant. Particles of quartz, mica, and feldspar are visible in sherd cross sections; particles are 0.5 to 3.0 mm. in diameter.

    Texture: The surfaces are medium fine to coarse, with the quality of the paste decreasing as vessel size increases. The majority of sherds are rough on the exterior because of irregular smoothing, and many are crackled on the interior. The core is compact to contorted, with evenly distributed temper.

    Hardness: 3.0 to 3.5, the majority 3.0 (calcite).

    Color: Buff, through light and dark grays to black, with the majority a dark gray.

    Source clay: A plastic clay, light gray in color, was used to make the pottery. It is free of sand but contains silt.

SURFACE FINISH: Vessel interiors and the upper parts of the vessel exteriors are usually horizontally smoothed. Shoulders were malleated vertically with a grooved paddle, but more frequently the resulting grooves were smoothed over. Rim sherds may be vertically stamped, but ordinarily are smoothed. Only three rims are horizontally stamped. The bases of the vessels are impressed in a random fashion. Some vessels are lightly polished, and their surfaces reflect some light (pl. 6, *e*, *h*).

FORM:

    Lip: Rounded, pointed, or flat, depending upon the presence and type of decoration.

    Rim: Two rim forms occur. The Riggs Ware includes those types with vertical, straight to outflaring rims. The Fort Yates Ware includes those types with S-shaped rims.

    Neck: Ordinarily constricted, except on vessels with straight, vertical rims.

    Shoulder: Rounded and steeply sloping.

    Body: All vessels appear to be globular, with round bases and wide mouths. In the restorable vessels, vessel height is about equal to maximum diameter.

    Appendages: Loop handles predominate, with strap handles present but rare. Handles are welded to the lip and riveted to the shoulder. Vertical, triangular tabs are common on the lip. Usually these elements have a central incision.

WARES AND COMPONENT TYPES:
  Riggs Ware:
    Component types:
      Riggs Plain Rim
      Riggs Cross-Hatched Rim
      Riggs Incised Rim
      Riggs Pinched Rim
  Fort Yates Ware:
    Component types:
      Fort Yates Cord Impressed Rim
      Fort Yates Cross-Hatched Rim
  Unclassified:
      Example A
      Example B
      Example C
      Example D

RIGGS WARE

Riggs Plain Rim

(Pl. 3, *b, d–h;* pl. 6, *e*)

SAMPLE: 619 rim sherds, representing about 381 vessels, and one restored vessel.

DECORATION:

Lip: On 237 sherds there are oblique or vertical tool impressions on the lip or on the outer edge of the lip. Circular and oval punctates and tool-impressed crosshatched lines, as well as fingernail impressions, occur on some lips (pl. 3, *e–g*). Three rims bear oblique cord-impressed lines, and seven rims have closely spaced castellations (pl. 3, *d*). The remaining rims have plain lips (pl. 3, *h*).

Rim: Plain, with some horizontal smoothing over grooved paddle impressions. A few rims have horizontal paddle impressions unmodified by smoothing. A single decorated rim is included in this type (fig. 1, *c*).

Shoulder: Sherds of 13 vessels are incised with various designs, most of which are rectilinear. Four design motifs are present:

  (1) Incised chevrons of three or four lines alternate with a triangular "bear foot" element (fig. 1, *a-b*). The restored vessel bears this design, executed by a stab-and-drag technique (pl. 6, *e*).
  (2) Incised "drooping corn stalks" or oblique incisions are superimposed over horizontally incised lines (fig. 1, *f-g*).
  (3) Panels of opposed diagonals occur (fig. 2, *b-c*).
  (4) Sherds from two vessels have incised, concentric circles on the upper shoulder (fig. 2, *d*).

FORM:

Lip: Round, pointed, or flat, depending upon the presence and type of decoration. Thickness, 4 to 10 mm., averaging 6 mm.

Rim: Straight and vertical to somewhat outflared. Heights are 10 to 70 mm., averaging about 35 mm.; thickness, 5 to 12 mm., averaging 7 mm.

Size: The projected orifices of 12 rim sherds indicate diameters between 120 and 346 mm.:

120	240	308
140	243	320
156	264	334
228	286	346

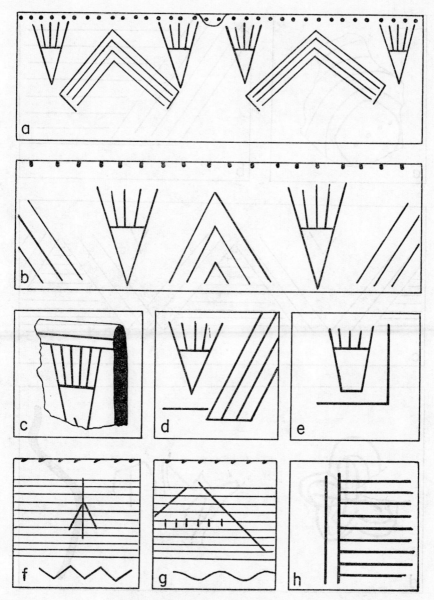

FIGURE 1.—Pottery design elements.

Appendages: Sherds from seven vessels have loop handles extending from the lip to the upper shoulder. One of them has a vertical, triangular tab with an apical incision. There are two loop handles and two incised tabs on the restored vessel (pl. 6, *e*). Twenty-three vertical tabs, roughly triangular, are of various sizes. Three of them are apically incised. Three horizontally projecting lugs occur on vessel lips.

Reconstructed vessel: A globular vessel with two loop handles and two incised tabs has a shoulder design made with the stab-and-drag technique

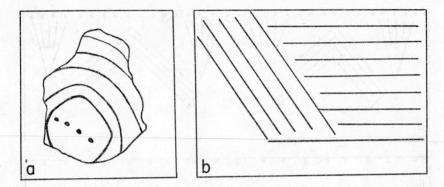

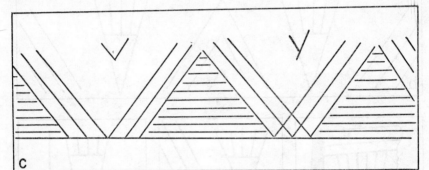

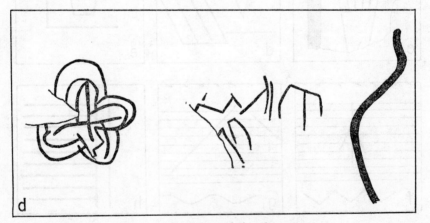

FIGURE 2.—Pottery design elements.

(pl. 6, e). When filled to the neck it contains about three-quarters of a pint of water. It has the following dimensions:

	Mm.
Height (excluding appendages)	75
Maximum diameter (at shoulder)	103
Orifice diameter (inner lip)	85
Lip thickness	7
Rim height	8
Thickness of base	2

Miscellaneous: One straight rim sherd with a plain, flat lip has a cylindrical hole 15 mm. from the lip (pl. 3, *b*). The hole was punched from the exterior while the clay was still moist, and the raised edges on the interior smoothed down. The edges of the hole are not worn.

PREVIOUS ILLUSTRATIONS AND DESCRIPTIONS: Sherds of this type are described by Hewes as "Type 9" and as "Type 11" from Paul Brave, and illustrated by several sherds (1949 b, pp. 64–67; pl. 5, lower right, *t–u*; pl. 6, left, *i*; pl. 6, right, *m, o, r*). The present type includes those sherds described by Hewes as "Fort Yates Plain."

Riggs Cross-Hatched Rim
(Pl. 4, *a–b, f*)

SAMPLE: 54 rim sherds, representing 43 vessels.

DECORATION:

   Lip: Oblique tool impressions occur on six sherds, and crosshatched tool impressions appear on two sherds. Rims from one vessel are indented along the lip with oval punctates; the remaining lips are plain.

   Rim: The rim is filled with crosshatched lines between the lip and the neck. On 11 sherds there is a horizontally incised line encircling the rim below the lip.

   Shoulder: The four decorated shoulders have horizontally incised lines. Two of them have a "drooping corn stalk" and one of them has an incised triangle over the horizontal lines (pl. 4, *f*).

FORM:

   Lip: Predominantly flat, with some round lips. Thickness, 7 to 9 mm.

   Rim: Straight to somewhat outflared. Height is between 30 and 43 mm.: thickness, 6 to 8 mm.

   Neck: The rim joins the shoulder in a smooth curve.

   Shoulder: Rounded and steeply sloping.

   Size: The orifices of two vessels, projected from large rim sherds, were 130 and 190 mm. in diameter.

   Appendages: Small triangular tabs are on the lips of four sherds. The crest of each tab is incised. Sherds of one vessel with an incised tab has, in addition, two plain vertical tabs.

PREVIOUS ILLUSTRATIONS AND DESCRIPTIONS: Sherds of this type are included in the pottery described by Hewes as "Type 9, Fort Yates Fine Incised," and one sherd is illustrated (1949 b, pp. 64–65, pl. 6, right, *n*).

COMMENTS: The type originally defined by Hewes as "Fort Yates Fine Incised" includes rims that were straight and flaring as well as S-shaped rims. The straight or flaring rims bearing crosshatched designs are herein described as "Riggs Cross-Hatched Rim," and the S-shaped rims with the same decoration are herein classed as "Fort Yates Cross-Hatched Rim."

Riggs Incised Rim
(Pl. 3, *c*)

SAMPLE: 6 rim sherds, representing 6 vessels.

DECORATION:

   Lip: One sherd is obliquely tool impressed. The remaining lips are plain.

   Rim: Four to seven horizontally incised lines occur, with oblique lines interrupting the horizontals (pl. 3, *c*).

FORM:

    Lip: Round to somewhat flat. Thickness, 4 to 6 mm.

    Rim: Straight to somewhat outflared. Height, 28 to 32 mm.; thickness, 6 to 8 mm.

Riggs Pinched Rim
(Pl. 3, *i*)

SAMPLE: 26 rim sherds, representing 22 vessels.

DECORATION: Vessels are plain except for the finger pinching.

FORM:

    Lip: May be round, flat, or pointed. The lips are wavy, a condition induced by pressing the moist clay with the thumb and forefinger offset, one inside and one outside the vessel. The resulting undulation of the lip, when observed from above, is similar to that of Stanley Wavy Rim (Lehmer, 1954: 43–44; pl. 12).

    Rim: Straight to somewhat outflared. Height, 12 to 52 mm.; thickness, 5 to 7 mm.

    Neck: Some constriction on outflaring rims.

    Appendages: One loop handle, originating in the mid-rim, is attached to the upper shoulder. The handle projects straight out from the rim, and defines a right angle before it joins the shoulder.

PREVIOUS ILLUSTRATIONS AND DESCRIPTIONS: A sherd of this type is illustrated in Will and Hecker (1944, pl. 13, the left sherd in the fifth row from the top) as "Archaic Mandan."

FORT YATES WARE

Fort Yates Cord Impressed Rim
(Pls. 3, *a*; 5, *c–j*)

SAMPLE: 136 rim sherds, representing 106 vessels.

DECORATION:

    Lip: None.

    Rim: Three to six evenly spaced, horizontally applied cord-impressed lines encircle the vessel rims. The diameter of the cord used varies from 2 to 3 mm., with the majority 2 mm. in diameter. Sixty-six sherds have triangular elements. On 7 sherds, the apex of the triangle is angular; on 25 sherds the apex is rounded, forming a curvilinear design. The triangles are formed by either two or three lines. A sherd from one vessel (pl. 5, *h*) has six horizontal lines of cord-wrapped stick impressions, and two oblique lines. One sherd has a red stain, probably ocher, on both the interior and exterior (pl. 5, *e*).

FORM:

    Lip: Predominantly flat, but may be round. Thickness, 6 to 8 mm.

    Rim: Outflaring, with a recurving lip, resulting in an S-shaped rim. Height, 26 to 42 mm.; thickness, 7 to 12 mm.

    Neck: Constricted, with the rim joining the shoulder in a smooth curve.

    Shoulder: Rounded and steeply sloping.

    Size: The orifices of three vessels, projected from large rim sherds, were 130, 176, and 260 mm. in diameter.

    Appendages: A small, triangular tab is present on one rim (pl. 5, *f*). A single sherd appears to be part of a small strap handle with two vertical cord-impressed lines (pl. 3, *a*).

PREVIOUS ILLUSTRATIONS AND DESCRIPTIONS: Sherds of this type were originally defined by Hewes as "Type 10, Fort Yates Cord Impressed," and two sherds are illustrated (1949 b, pp. 65–66, pl. 5, lower right, *v*, pl. 6, right, *q*).

COMMENTS: The present type description largely duplicates the original type description by Hewes. Pottery of this type is similar to the type "Aldren Cord Impressed" at the Thomas Riggs site (Kleinsasser, 1953, p. 27; fig. 29, *1–3*, *6*). The sherds designated as "Fort Yates Cord Impressed" from the Thomas Riggs site (Kleinsasser, 1953, p. 27; fig. 29, *P/16*, *4–5*), however, do not fit the type description of Hewes and should be renamed (Wheeler, 1954, p. 8; 1955, p. 398).

Fort Yates Cross-Hatched Rim
(Pls. 4, *c–e*; 6, *h*)

SAMPLE: 30 rim sherds, representing 15 vessels, and one restored vessel.
DECORATION:

Lip: None.

Rim: Between the lip and the neck the rims are incised with crosshatched lines. A horizontal incised line encircles the rim below the lip on sherds from several vessels (pl. 4, *e*). On six rims there are punctates spaced 10 mm. apart on the rim below the crosshatched lines.

Shoulder: The shoulders of two sherds are horizontally incised.

FORM:

Lip: Predominantly flat, with some round; thickness, 6 to 8 mm.

Rim: Outflaring, with a recurving lip, resulting in an S-shaped rim. Height, 21 to 41 mm.; thickness, 6 to 10 mm.

Neck: Constricted, with the rim joining the shoulder in a smooth curve.

Shoulder: Rounded and steeply sloping on large sherds. Some smaller sherds suggest a shoulder more nearly flat.

Size: A partially restored vessel, 90 mm. high, has a maximum diameter of about 130 mm. When filled to the neck it contains 1 pint of water (pl. 6, *h*). The orifice of one vessel, projected from a large rim, was 168 mm. in diameter.

Appendages: Scars on two rims indicate the presence of tabs on the lip. One sherd retains a tab with an apical incision.

PREVIOUS ILLUSTRATIONS AND DESCRIPTION: Several sherds of this type are included in the pottery described by Hewes as "Type 9, Fort Yates Fine Incised," and one sherd is illustrated (1949 b, pp. 64–65, pl. 6, left, *k*).

COMMENTS: See the statements under the type "Riggs Cross-Hatched Rim" above.

UNCLASSIFIED WARES

Example A
(Pl. 5, *a*)

SAMPLE: 16 rim sherds, representing 12 vessels.
DECORATION:

Lip: Oblique tool impressions occur on two rims.

Rim: One of the rims with a decorated lip is crosshatched. Another rim has two horizontally applied cord-impressed lines on the interior lip, oblique cord impressions on the outer lip, and five horizontal cord-impressed lines on the exterior mid-rim. The remaining rims are plain.

FORM:

> *Lip:* Round.   Thickness, 3 to 5 mm.
>
> *Rim:* Outflaring, with a protruding ridge centered on the rim exterior and channeled on the rim interior. Height, 37 to 55 mm.; thickness, 5 to 9 mm.
>
> *Neck:* Constricted, with the rim joining the shoulder in a smooth curve.
>
> *Appendages:* Three rims have small, vertical, plain tabs.

PREVIOUS ILLUSTRATIONS AND DESCRIPTIONS: Several sherds of this example were described by Hewes as "Type 6," and one rim is illustrated (Hewes, 1949 b: pp. 62–63; pl. 6, left, *h*).

Example B
(Pl. 5, *b*)

SAMPLE: 1 rim sherd.

DECORATION:

> *Lip:* Oblique indentations.

FORM:

> *Lip:* Round, with a thickness of 6 mm.
>
> *Rim:* Inflaring near the lip.
>
> *Appendages:* The scar of a triangular, horizontal lug is on the outer rim 12 mm. below the lip.

COMMENTS: This rim form is known only from Paul Brave.

Example C
(Pl. 5, *c*)

SAMPLE: 1 rim sherd.

DECORATION:

> *Rim:* Oval indentations occur on the lower rim.

FORM:

> *Lip:* Round, with a thickness of 6 mm.
>
> *Rim:* S-shaped, with a height of 27 mm.
>
> *Neck:* Constricted.

COMMENTS: This rim form, and the particular design involved, is known only from Paul Brave.

Example D
(Pl. 5, *d*)

SAMPLE: 3 rim sherds from 2 vessels.

DECORATION: None.

FORM:

> *Lip:* Round, with a thickness of 6 to 7 mm.
>
> *Rim:* S-shaped, with heights 25 to 30 mm., and 8 to 9 mm. thick.
>
> *Neck:* Constricted, with the shoulder joining the rim in a smooth curve.
>
> *Shoulder:* Rounded.

COMMENTS: These rims are similar in form to those of Fort Yates Ware, and may be a plain variant of that ware.

MINIATURE VESSELS

Three minature vessels were in the hard ash of the primary fireplace in House 3. Evidently they had been subjected to an intense secondary firing, for the pots were soft and crumbly. They were treated with a mixture of acetone and ambroid. This treatment gave the vessels a light-reflecting quality that they lacked before. Two of them are complete, and both have the following dimensions: height, 68 mm.; maximum diameter, 87 mm.; orifice at inner lip, 75 mm.; neck diameter, 74 mm. The size of the incomplete specimen would be much the same. The surfaces are irregularly smoothed, and the shoulders are steeply sloping. Two of them have outflaring rims (pl. 6, f) and the other has a constricted neck and a nearly vertical rim (pl. 6, g). Each of the pots contains slightly more than a quarter of a pint of water when filled to the neck.

A vessel fragment indicating an orifice of 56 mm., with an outflaring rim 8 mm. high, has a steeply sloping and irregularly smoothed shoulder. Another fragmentary miniature is decorated with incised lines (fig. 2, d). This vessel has an estimated orifice diameter of 80 mm., with an outflaring rim 11 mm. high. The surface is irregularly smoothed. Fragments of two other vessels have outflaring rims. One of them shows the scar of a handle that was welded to the lip and riveted to the upper shoulder. Bowls may be indicated by three small sherds, two of which have indented lips.

BODY SHERDS

The majority of sherds from the site are simple-stamped or smoothed. Some 514 sherds are classed as simple-stamped and bear the characteristic grooves resulting from the malleating of the moist clay with a grooved paddle. The 845 smooth sherds are irregularly smoothed, and only a few of them might be classed as polished. The polished sherds have a low light-reflecting surface. Many of the smoothed sherds show irregularities which suggest that the surface was originally simple-stamped.

The 54 decorated body sherds are incised or trailed on the shoulder, which is usually smooth but which may reveal partially obliterated traces of vertical simple-stamps. The decoration may consist of either fine line incising or deep trailing, sometimes in combination with punctates. The width of the lines varies from 0.5 to 6.0 mm., and cross sections are either V-shaped or U-shaped. One of the more common designs consists of alternating "bear tracks" and chevrons (fig. 1, a-b, d). In only one instance do the "tracks" have more than five "digits" (fig. 1, c). A design termed the "drooping corn stalk" is incised on shoulders that are covered with horizontally incised lines and a wavy or zigzag lower border. Oblique incised lines and punctates also occur on the same background (fig. 1, f–g). Other fragmentary designs consist of oblique, vertical, and horizontal lines in several combinations (fig. 1, h; fig. 2, b-c). Broad-trailed concentric circles occur on the shoulder of one large rim sherd, and on one body sherd.

One of these has four punctates in the center (fig. 2, *a*). Two separate designs that are not duplicated in the collections are incised on the shoulder of a small vessel (fig. 2, *d*).

Nineteen body sherds differ from the majority of sherds at the site in being cord-roughened. These sherds are from vessels that were first malleated with a paddle wrapped with cord, then partially smoothed (pl. 6, *c*). Some of the sherds are from the shoulder area, with the roughening extending to the neck. On these sherds the roughening is vertical. The twist of the cord is clearly distinguishable on three sherds. The twist on two sherds may be duplicated by holding two cords in the left hand and turning the ends to the right with the right hand; on the other sherd the cords were turned to the left with the right hand. The diameter of the cords ranged from 1.0 to 2.0 mm. The number of vessels bearing cord-roughened surfaces may have been greater than the 19 sherds would indicate, but the smoothing and obliteration of the cord marks render the original treatment indistinguishable. The paste of the sherds is the same as that of the Riggs Ware and the Fort Yates Ware and it is likely that they are from vessels of these wares. However, none of them are assignable to specific types.

Two sherds are check-stamped. Their exteriors are covered with small, depressed squares bordered by low, partially smoothed ridges (pl. 6, *d*). The stamps are 3 to 5 mm. on a side.

Biconical perforations in four body sherds may have served as holes for lacing cracked vessels together. Six loop handles and one strap handle are detached from the vessel rim and cannot be assigned to types. The strap handle is oval and the loop handles circular in cross section. They are all smooth and plain. The handles extend from the lip to the upper shoulder.

MISCELLANEOUS OBJECTS OF BAKED CLAY

Animal effigies
(5 specimens)

One of the specimens (fig. 6, *a*) represents a prairie chicken, or pinnated grouse (*Tymfanuchers americanus*). The general conformation of the body and the structure of the tail conform to this species, although there are some superficial structural similarities to the turkey. The turkey was not native to this region in early historic times. The head is lacking. The length is 35 mm. and the height 28 mm.

A specimen 32 mm. long has a circular body with two front legs (fig. 6, *b*). The hind part of the body rests on a tail. The modeling is too generalized to permit identification, but it may be a beaver or badger.

A third specimen may represent the head of a canid. In the illustration (fig. 6, *c*) the object is so oriented that it appears to have two long pointed ears and a sharp nose. These characteristics mark the swift or red fox, both of which were native to the locality in historic times.

An incomplete specimen suggests a round-bodied, but unidentifiable, animal. There are two short, stubby forelegs but the hind limbs are lacking. It is apparently a heavy-bodied animal (fig. 6, *d*).

The final specimen is an effigy handle from a vessel lip. The profile of the head (fig. 6, *e*), which extends 15 mm. from the lip, suggests that of a bear.

Bead
(1 specimen)

A perforated baked clay bead is oval in longitudinal section and pentagonal in cross section. It is 20 mm. long, with a maximum diameter of 18 mm. One intact end is concave. The hole appears to have been made by inserting a grass stem that burned away during the firing (fig. 6, *f*).

Shaped item
(1 specimen)

An irregular, bowllike object, probably modeled around the finger of a child, has a fingernail impression in the base of a shallow cavity. The base is flat, with a protrusion resulting from a downward pressure of the finger. The maximum diameter is at the midpoint. Height is 12 mm., and the diameter is 19 mm.

WORK IN STONE

Projectile points
(75 specimens)

Seventy-five artifacts are classed as projectile points, in that they are small, thin, bifacially worked, approximately symmetrical, and well made. Materials used for the points are: Knife River flint (chalcedony), 42; gray, brown, and black cherts, 28; white chalcedony, 4; and agate, 1. The 55 complete points are classed in 5 categories based on outline and other characteristics. The terms applied to the five projectile-point categories are descriptive (see Davis, 1956, pp. 64–69), but reference is also made to the point outline taxonomy published by Strong (1935, pp. 88–89).

Plain lanceolate, convex base (Strong NA b1).—A single specimen from the site has convex blade edges and a convex base. It measures 28×15×3 mm., and has a weight of 1.5 gm. (fig. 3, *a*). It is unnotched and is evenly and bifacially flaked.

a   b   c   d

e   f   g   h

0   5

cm.

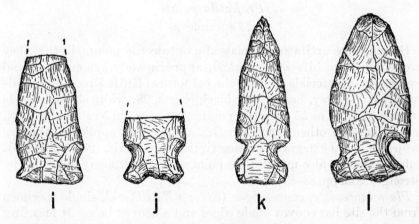

i   j   k   l

FIGURE 3.—Projectile points.

Plain lanceolate, straight base (Strong NBa).—The 18 examples in this category have gently convex edges and a straight base (fig. 3, *b–c*). This category is unnotched, with even bifacial flaking.

> *Length:* Mean 27.8 mm., range 23 to 42 mm.
> *Width:* Mean 15.6 mm., range 11 to 20 mm.
> *Thickness:* Mean 3.8 mm., range 2 to 5 mm.
> *Weight:* Mean 1.5 gm., range 0.9 to 3.0 gm.

Plain triangular, concave base (Strong NBb).—The two points in this category have gently convex edges and a concave base. The tips of both specimens are missing (fig. 3, *d*). The category is unnotched, and is evenly bifacially flaked. Dimensions (estimated when broken) are: $21 \times 15 \times 3$ mm. and $24 \times 12 \times 2$ mm. The former point weighs 1.1 gm., and the latter, 1.0 gm.

Plain lanceolate, straight base (Strong NBa1).—This is the largest single category, including 22 specimens. They have gently convex edges, a straight base, and two side notches (fig. 3, *e–f*). They are evenly bifacially flaked, and the blade edges usually have fine secondary flakes removed. Points are tapering and sharp.

> *Length:* Mean 30.2, range 19 to 56 mm.
> *Width:* Mean 14.1, range 11 to 21 mm.
> *Thickness:* Mean 3.8, range 2 to 7 mm.
> *Weight:* Mean 1.8 gm., range 0.6 to 6.4 gm.

Plain lanceolate, concave base (Strong NBb1).—The 12 specimens in this category have straight to gently concave edges, a convex base, and two side notches (fig. 3, *g–h, i–l*). They are evenly bifacially flaked but the flaking is less delicate on larger examples. Points are sharp and tapering to blunt.

> *Length:* Mean 33.4 mm., range 21 to 60 mm.
> *Width:* Mean 15.6 mm., range 12 to 24 mm.
> *Thickness:* Mean 4.4 mm., range 3 to 10 mm.
> *Weight:* Mean 1.8 gm., range 0.8 to 2.0 gm.

End Scrapers
(149 specimens)

The majority of these scrapers are made from Knife River flint. Other stone includes a gray chert, petrified wood, and agate. The outlines tend to be triangular to rectangular, although many are irregular. The working edges are steeply chipped on the end opposite the bulb of percussion, and the concave undersides are unmodified. Three groups are distinguished.

Group 1 (78 specimens).—Cross sections are triangular to shallowly U-shaped, with flaking over the entire upper surface, and usually with retouching along the sides. Lengths range from 20 to 58 mm., and

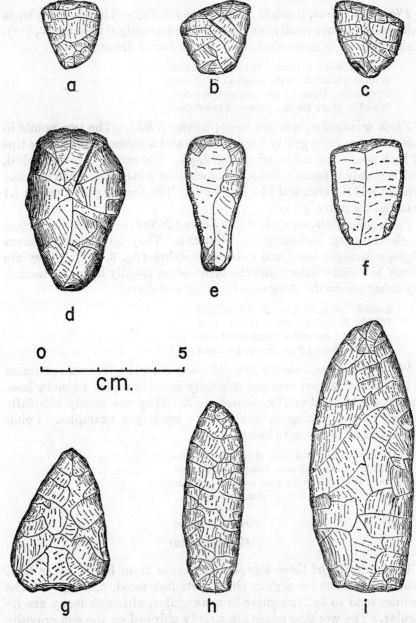

FIGURE 4.—End scrapers and knives.

widths from 15 to 28 mm. The working edge is rounded to straight in 43 specimens (fig. 4, a). In 19 specimens, it is skewed with respect to the long axis, sloping from the lower left up to upper right (fig. 4, b). In 16 specimens, the blade slopes down from upper left to lower right (fig. 4, c).

Group 2 (70 specimens).—Cross sections are triangular, shallowly U-shaped, or irregular, since many of the specimens are made from irregularly shaped flakes. There is little flaking on the upper surface and there is some retouching on the edges. Lengths range from 21 to 51 mm., and widths from 16 to 27 mm. In 47 specimens, the working edge is rounded to straight (fig. 4, *e*). In 19 specimens, it slopes from the lower left up to the upper right (fig. 4, *f*); in 4 specimens, the blade slopes down from the upper left to lower right.

Group 3 (1 specimen).—One large scraper, triangular in cross section, has a convex, flaked upper surface and an unmodified concave under surface. Larger than any scrapers in the preceding two groups, this implement measures 56 × 34 × 22 mm. (fig. 4, *d*).

Drills
(6 specimens)

Two slender shafts of Knife River flint and one of reddish-brown chert are 44 mm. long, with expanding bases. A fourth specimen is a base, with the drill shaft absent. They are bifacially flaked, with lenticular to diamond-shaped cross sections (fig. 5, *a*). One specimen consists of a narrow shaft of Knife River flint, 55 mm. long, with a round base. Near the tip it is bifacially flaked, but at the base only one side is worked. A final example is represented by a unifacially flaked drill shaft tip.

Broad Knives
(21 specimens)

All knives are bifacially flaked and are lenticular in transverse section and longitudinal section. Flaking is random, and the blade edges are retouched. The form outline used here follows that devised by Strong (1935, pp. 88–89).

Group 1, NAb1 (1 specimen).—The base is round, sides are convex, and the tip is blunt. Material is a gray chert; it measures 38 × 26 × 10 mm.

Group 2, NAb2 (4 specimens).—Bases are straight, sides are convex, and the tips are pointed but not sharp. Materials include gray chert and Knife River flint. Lengths range from 40 to 94 mm., widths from 23 to 35 mm., and thicknesses from 5 to 6 mm. (fig. 4, *i*).

Group 3, NAb2 (2 specimens).—These knives are similar to the Group 2 specimens but they are asymmetrical. The base is straight, but one side is nearly at right angles to the base, while the other side is at about 45 degrees to the base. The sides are gently convex, and the tips are blunt (fig. 4, *g*). Materials are gray and black chert. Lengths are 32 and 50 mm., widths 24 and 34 mm., and thickness 8 and 9 mm., respectively.

Group 4, NE (1 specimen).—Oval in outline, this specimen of Knife River flint is 44 mm. long, 28 mm. wide, and 12 mm. thick. The ends and sides are convex.

Group 5, base fragments (6 specimens).—These five specimens are convex base fragments from knives that had gently convex to straight sides. Materials include gray chert, Knife River flint, and petrified wood. These fragments are from knives that were originally more than 62 mm. long.

Group 6, blade tips (7 specimens).—These tips are from knives which had pointed but not sharp tips, and had convex sides. Lengths are in excess of 121 mm., and widths are from 22 to 35 mm. Materials are Knife River flint, gray chert, and Bijou Hills quartzite.

Narrow knives
(5 specimens)

Long slender knives, bifacially flaked, are made from Knife River flint. Two complete specimens are NAb2 in outline and one is NAa. Two are tips. The sides are gently convex and nearly parallel. Lengths are 66, 72, and 83 mm.; widths, 21, 14, and 18 mm.; thickness, 5, 5, and 6 mm., respectively (fig. 4, *h*).

Choppers
(34 specimens)

Group 1 (12 specimens).—These tools are oval to nearly circular, and are bifacially flaked, with large flake scars on both faces and retouching on the edges. Battering is evident on some of the ends. The material includes gray chert, quartzite, and quartz. They range in length from 70 to 172 mm.; in width, from 41 to 99 mm.; in thickness, from 18 to 28 mm.

Group 2 (10 specimens).—Roughly rectangular blocks of quartzite are bifacially flaked along one edge. The faces of the implements are unmodified. There is some use retouching along the blade edge, and the blades extend the length of the tool. Lengths are 90 to 205 mm.; widths, 50 to 90 mm.

Group 3 (12 specimens).—Irregular spalls of stone, including granite, quartzite, and gray chert have bifacially flaked edges along one edge of the stone and show some retouching. The specimens attain a maximum diameter of 130 mm.

Flake knives
(135 specimens)

Flakes of Knife River flint, petrified wood, gray chert or quartzite are classed as flake knives when they have a prepared edge on one or more edges.

Unmodified flakes
(203 specimens)

A sample of stone was saved from each excavated feature. Many of the pieces retained were unused, but some showed minute flaking along one or more edges, indicating that they had been used as cutting tools. Materials included Knife River flint, petrified wood, gray chert, agatized wood, quartzite, and quartz.

Grooved mauls
(5 specimens)

Each of three granite cobbles, from 87 to 107 mm. long, has a groove pecked around the small diameter of the stone. On two examples the groove encircles the stone; on a third, the groove encircles three-quarters of the stone. Two fragments of much larger mauls are not large enough to permit an estimation of the original extent of the groove. The mauls consist of oval cobbles shaped only by the addition of the pecked groove. Both ends are battered by use, but the stone is not otherwise modified.

Hammerstones
(49 specimens)

Cobbles and pebbles of granite, siltstone, quartz, and fine-grained sandstone are classed as hammerstones when one or more edges are battered.

Group 1 (45 specimens).—These hammers are made from oval stones. They are either battered on one or both ends or battered over the circumference of the stone. Lengths range from 39 to 221 mm.

Group 2 (4 specimens).—In a second group of hammerstones each is nearly circular in outline and has a rectangular cross section. The faces of this group are ground smooth and flat, and they are battered on all edges. One specimen has a small depression pecked into one face. Diameters are from 85 to 110 mm.

Ground stone spheres
(5 specimens)

Four of these objects are made of a buff siltstone and one is of a reddish-brown concretionary sandstone. The entire surface of the sandstone sphere and of one of the siltstone spheres is smoothed. The remaining specimens are partially smoothed and ground, and may be unfinished pieces. Diameters average 70 mm.

Shaft smoothers
(6 specimens)

These abraders consist of shaped blocks of a coarse, buff sandstone with either rounded or squared ends, convex sides, a flat grooved surface, and a flat or convex undersurface. The grooves are straight and are either V-shaped or U-shaped. One complete abrader is 161 mm. long. Another specimen, 64 mm. long, has a second grove on the undersurface. The illustration (fig. 5, *f*) depicts a fragment with a squared end.

Grooved abraders
(18 specimens)

These objects are composed of a buff or rust-colored, coarse-grained sandstone. There is considerable variation in size, ranging from specimens no more than 75 mm. in diameter to those 175 mm. in diameter. There is no consistent form; the pieces were not altered in form except for the V-shaped or U-shaped grooves worn into their surfaces. The grooves are of various lengths, depending upon the available surface. The grooves are commonly convex in longitudinal section.

Faceted abraders
(59 specimens)

Fifty-two pieces of scoria and seven pieces of sandstone, none of which exceeds 105 mm. in diameter, have been used as abraders. These objects consist of irregular pieces of stone that are faceted from rubbing or grinding. In some instances the entire stone is smoothed, and some such stones have a superficial resemblance in size and form to the bone abraders made from the cancellous tissue of bison humeri. Many of the stones also bear small, shallow V-shaped or U-shaped grooves.

Beads
(4 specimens)

A tubular piece of concretionary sandstone, 40 mm. long and 11 mm. wide, has a natural hole along its long axis. The ends of the hole are smoothed (fig. 5, *b*).

Two circular disks of scoria are biconically pierced. One of them is 8 mm. (fig. 5, *e*) and the other 12 mm. in diameter (fig. 5, *d*). The latter bead is not complete, since the perforation is not finished.

A scoria bead 16 mm. long and 15 mm. wide is split down the long axis, showing that the perforation was drilled from both ends. One end is ground flat (fig. 5, *c*).

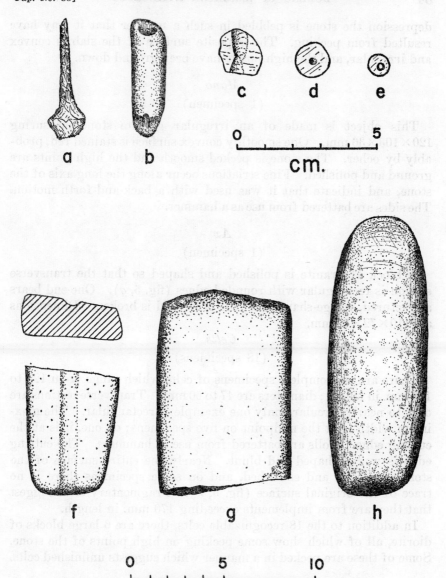

FIGURE 5.—Chipped and ground stone artifacts.

Mealing slab

(1 specimen)

A large rectangular block of fine-grained sandstone, 460 mm. in length, has one irregularly smoothed surface. Near one edge of this surface is a smoothed and polished depression. Near the edge of the depression the stone is pebbled in such a manner that it may have resulted from pecking. The opposite surface of the slab is convex and irregular, and the high points have been ground down.

Mano
(1 specimen)

This object is made of an irregular granite stone measuring $120 \times 103 \times 36$ mm. One smoothly convex surface is stained red, probably by ocher. The stone is pecked smooth and the high points are ground and polished. Fine striations occur along the long axis of the stone, and indicate that it was used with a back-and-forth motion. The sides are battered from use as a hammer.

Ax
(1 specimen)

A block of granite is polished and shaped so that the transverse section is rectangular with rounded edges (fig. 5, *g*). One end bears a fractured, wedge-shaped bit; the other end is broken. Dimensions are $110 \times 72 \times 32$ mm.

Celts
(18 specimens)

There are six complete specimens of celts which range from 122 to 170 mm. in length; diameters are 47 to 60 mm. Transverse sections are oval to nearly circular; only one example is rectangular. The maximum width is at the midpoint on five specimens; on one, it is at the cutting edge. Polls are battered from use as hammers. The cutting edge is wedge shaped and blunt. Nearly the entire surface of the stone is pecked and smoothed, and on some specimens there is no trace of the original surface (fig. 5, *h*). Fragmentary celts suggest that they are from implements exceeding 170 mm. in length.

In addition to the 18 recognizable celts, there are 6 large blocks of diorite, all of which show some pecking on high points of the stone. Some of these are pecked in a manner which suggests unfinished celts.

Unmodified calcite
(10 pieces)

These pieces of calcite, none of which exceed 117 mm. in length, are unmodified. One of them, 75 mm. long, has a form spuriously like that of an arrowpoint.

Unmodified pebbles
(5 specimens)

These oval pebbles are 24 to 58 mm. long. They show no signs of use, and the surfaces suggest that they were steam rounded.

Pigments
(15 pieces)

Fourteen small, irregular fragments of chalk were probably bases for pigment. The colors of these pigments given below approximate those of Maerz and Paul (1930). Three of the chalks are nearly white (10 A 1), and 11 are yellow, approaching in tone Pinard Yellow (9 K 2). Powdered hematite from one feature is Java Brown (8 L 10). The white chalk is fairly soft, approximating in hardness the consistency of softer grades of schoolroom chalk. The yellow chalk is more compact, and is about the hardness of talc.

WORK IN BONE

Scapula hoes
(109 specimens)

The scapulae of adult bison were used in the manufacture of this implement, although some smaller and more delicate specimens may have been from young bison or from elk. The supra scapular border is beveled on the side that bears the scapular fossae, and these fossae are hacked away so that the surface is nearly level. The edges of the implements are roughened by chopping at a distance of 100 to 150 mm. from the cutting edge, probably to provide a surface for binding a handle to the tool. The cutting edge may be rounded or straight, largely depending on the amount of wear. The articular end is retained without modification (fig. 6, g).

Notches occur on the side of nine implements near the articulating end. The notches may occur on either side (fig. 6, i). One hoe has a hole 12 mm. in diameter in the blade 115 mm. from the articulating end (fig. 6, h). Two hoes have deep, U-shaped indentations in the blade (see Hurt, 1953, fig. 19, 4-5). The edges of these indentations are smoothed, possibly from use as thong stretchers. The range in length of complete hoes is 250 to 410 mm., the shorter specimens showing much evidence of use.

Serrated fleshers
(2 specimens)

The one complete specimen, 310 mm. long, was made by cutting the shaft of a bison metatarsal diagonally to produce a chisel edge. The edge is serrated (fig. 7, h). The implement also includes several of the ankle bones, which were left in place to provide additional leverage. The shaft of the metatarsal is highly polished near the serrated end, but the rest of the metatarsal and the remaining bones have a natural finish, suggesting that the tool originally retained cartilage and hide over the ankle and heel bones. A fragment of a second serrated specimen was recovered.

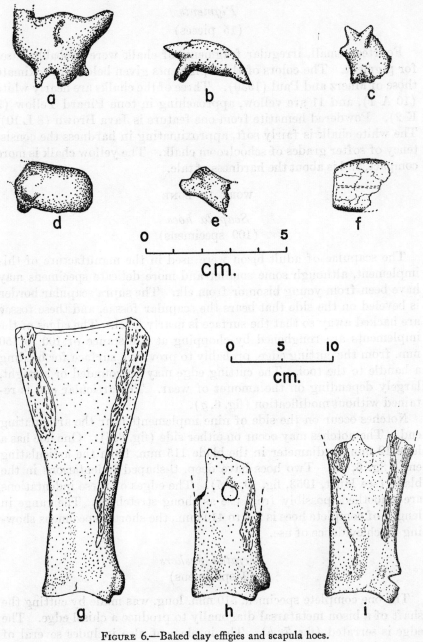

FIGURE 6.—Baked clay effigies and scapula hoes.

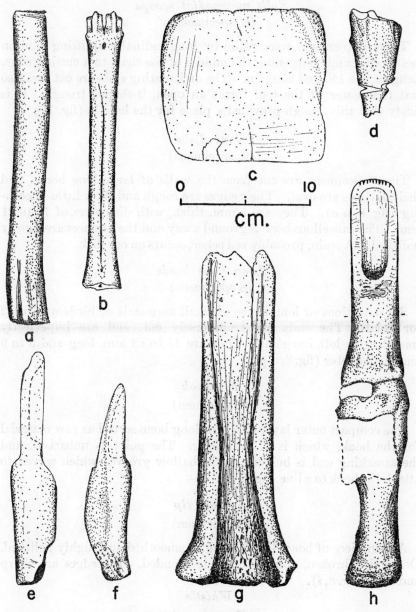

FIGURE 7.—worked bone.

Split metapodial scoops
(2 specimens)

These implements were made by longitudinally splitting a bison metapodial and sharpening the middle of the shaft to a cutting edge. Lengths are 140 and 250 mm. The articulating ends are cut away so that the center of the tool forms an open, U-shaped trough. It is likely that this trough provided a place for the handle (fig. 7, *g*).

Bone disks
(3 specimens)

These specimens are cut from the walls of large long bones, and their outlines are oval. Their edges are rough and show little smoothing (fig. 8, *a-c*). They are 5 mm. thick, with diameters of 12 to 21 mm. The cancellous bone is ground away and the surfaces are lightly polished. A stain, probably red ocher, occurs on one disk.

Long bone beads
(8 specimens)

Short sections of long bones of small mammals or birds were used for beads. The ends are transversely cut, and are imperfectly smoothed or left irregular. They are 14 to 29 mm. long and 5 to 9 mm. in diameter (fig. 8, *d-g*).

Fishhook
(1 specimen)

The compact outer layer of a bird long bone served as raw material for the hook, which is 27 mm. long. The point is unbarbed, and the attaching end is bulbous, with shallow grooves which served to attach the hook to a line (fig. 8, *h*).

Spatula tip
(1 specimen)

A thin piece of bone, 47 mm. long, is smoothed and highly polished. One end is broken, and the other is rounded. The edges are sharp and even (fig. 8, *i*).

Whistle
(1 specimen)

A section of the wing bone of a large bird is 110 mm. long. One end is transversely cut, polished, and smooth. On the other end is a V-shaped cut that served as the whistle opening. The instrument is highly polished, and the bone protuberances to which the quills were attached are reduced so that the surface is smooth (fig. 8, *j*).

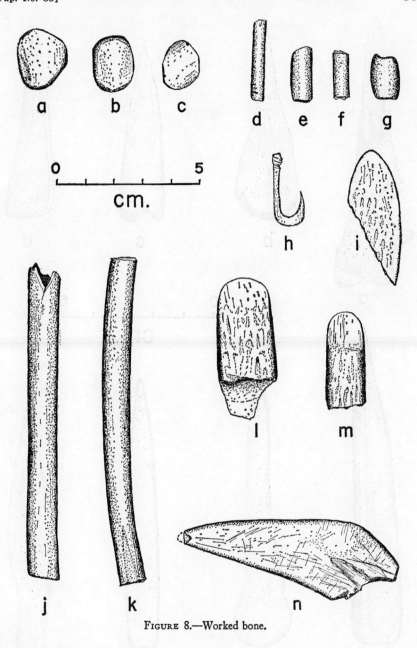

FIGURE 8.—Worked bone.

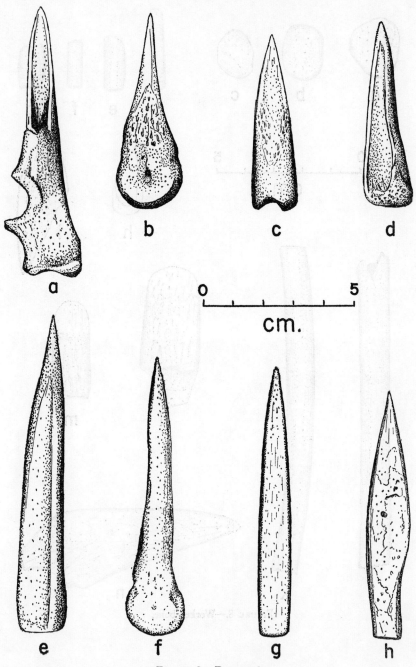

FIGURE 9.—Bone awls.

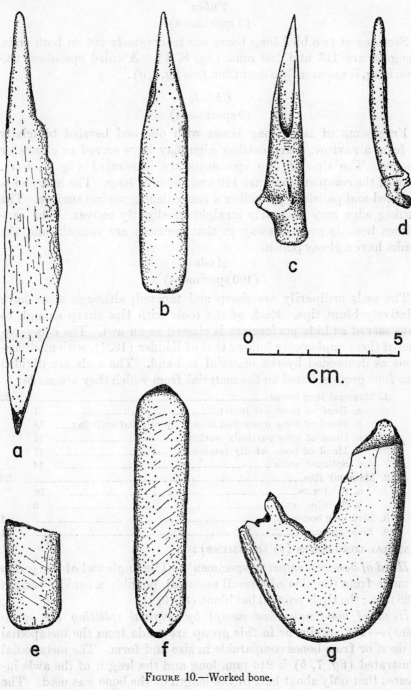

FIGURE 10.—Worked bone.

Tubes
(3 specimens)

Sections of two bird long bones are transversely cut on both ends. Lengths are 113 and 120 mm. (fig. 8, *k*). A third specimen, 235 mm. long, is apparently a deer tibia (see fig. 7, *a*).

Chisels
(9 specimens)

Fragments of large long bones with one end beveled bifacially to form a narrow, sharp cutting edge may have served as chisels or gouges. The tips of two specimens are illustrated (fig. 8, *l-m*). Two of the complete tools are 140 and 152 mm. long. The butt end is rounded and polished, providing a convenient grasping surface. The cutting edge may be nearly straight or slightly convex. The cancellous bone is ground away so that surfaces are smooth, and the blades have a glossy polish.

Awls
(100 specimens)

The awls ordinarily are sharp and tapered, although some have relatively blunt tips. Each of the tools with tips sharp enough to have served as hide perforators is classed as an awl. The classification of these implements follows that of Kidder (1932), with modifications as demanded by the material at hand. The awls are divided into four groups, based on the material from which they are made:

1. Mammal long bones_____ 62
    a. Head of bone left intact_____ 1
    b. Head of bone unworked except by original splitting____ 18
    c. Head of bone partially worked_____ 12
    d. Head of bone wholly removed_____ 17
    e. Splinter awls_____ 14
2. Mammal ribs_____ 33
    a. Split ribs_____ 28
    b. Splinter awls_____ 5
3. Bird long bones_____ 4
4. Fish spine_____ 1

MAMMAL LONG BONES (62 SPECIMENS):

Head of bone left intact (1 specimen).—The single awl of this group is made from the ulna of a small mammal, possibly a canid. Length is 88 mm.; the tip is pointed but blunt (fig. 9, *a*).

Head of bone unworked except by original splitting (18 specimens).—The specimens in this group are made from the metapodial of deer, or from bones comparable in size and form. The metapodial illustrated (fig. 7, *b*) is 210 mm. long and the length of the awls indicates that only about half of the length of the bone was used. The metapodials were split by longitudinal sawing in the U-shaped trough on one side of the bone and by wedging apart the proximal end, using the resulting half, third, or quarter of the ends as butts.

Two awls made from the proximal end of the bone are 63 mm. long (fig. 9, *b*). A third specimen is from an immature animal and the epiphysis is detached. Length is 55 mm. (fig. 9, *c*).

Fifteen awls made from the distal end of the bone are 50 to 121 mm. long. The longer ones are thin and evenly tapered, but shorter specimens are stubby (fig. 9, *d*).

Head of bone partially worked (12 specimens).—One specimen from the distal end of a deer metapodial is 186 mm. long, with a long, tapering shaft. The butt is smooth and rounded, all articulating facets and rough projections having been reduced, leaving a smooth swelling grip.

Eleven awls are made from the proximal end of deer metapodials, which are split lengthwise. The ends are smoothed and rounded, with little of the original surface remaining. Length is 60 to 177 mm. (fig. 9, *f*).

Head of bone wholly removed (17 specimens).—These tools have rounded and smoothed butts and short, tapering points. Each awl is split from a long bone. Most specimens have a groove down one side (fig. 9, *e*), a remnant of the central cavity of the parent bone, but some are completely smooth, with no evidence of the original surface (fig. 9, *g*). Lengths are 63 to 125 mm.

Splinter awls (14 specimens).—Fragments of long bones, the shape of which fitted them for use as awls after sharpening one end, are classed as splinter awls. There is no regularity of shape, and only the tip is worked. Lengths are 55 to 97 mm. (fig. 9, *h*).

MAMMAL RIBS (33 SPECIMENS):

Split ribs (28 specimens).—These awls are split from a large mammal rib, probably bison, and most of the surface is dressed. The cancellous bone is removed or nearly obliterated. Sides are nearly parallel and butts are squared (fig. 10, *b*). The awls are homogeneous in form but vary from 61 to 181 mm. in length.

Splinter awls (5 specimens).—These specimens are fragments of split ribs that served as awls after one of the sharp ends was ground to a point. Form is not consistent. Presumably the original splinter was chosen for convenience rather than form.

BIRD LONG BONES (4 SPECIMENS):

Each of these specimens is made from a whole bone, with one end sharpened to a stubby point. Two awls, made from an ulna (fig. 10, *c*) and a femur, are 74 mm. long. Two awls are made from wing bones, the longest of which is 175 mm. long.

FISH SPINE (1 SPECIMEN):

The spine of a catfish is sharpened to a blunt tip on the end opposite the articulating surfaces. The sharp ridges along one edge are ground away so that the shaft is smooth (fig. 10, *d*). These spines are sometimes erroneously identified as fish mandibles.

Knife handles
(3 specimens)

Handles, presumably for chipped stone knives, were made from the spines of bison dorsal vertebrae. The narrow stone knives, uniformly thin, usually are beveled on one side of the pointed end. The size and form of these knives suggest that they were made for insertion into these bone handles.

One handle is 176 mm. long, with a slotted groove in one end 60 mm. long, 10 mm. deep, and 4 mm. wide. The specimen is smooth and polished (fig. 7, *e*). A second handle is less elaborate but is similar in form (fig. 7, *f*). It is 147 mm. long, with a slot 55 mm. long, 14 mm. deep, and 7 mm. wide. A final specimen is 115 mm. long and has a slot in one side 40 mm. long, 8 mm. deep, and 3 mm. wide.

Knives
(10 specimens)

The proximal ends of scapulae, apparently bison, were used to make these knives. Complete specimens are rectangular in outline, with sharp cutting edges and smooth to polished surfaces (fig. 7, *c*). One knife has a perforation drilled from both sides in one end, 3 mm. in diameter. One edge of each knife has a smooth rounded edge.

Pottery modeling tools
(64 specimens)

This designation is applied to the class of artifacts described elsewhere as "quill flatteners" (Lehmer, 1954, p. 67; Wedel, 1955, pp. 125–126). Points favoring the use of these implements as pottery modeling tools were convincingly presented by Wheeler (1956, p. 18). These tools are the third most common class of bone artifacts at the site, ranking after scapula hoes and awls, and they must have functioned in an important industry. The tools are divided into two groups. Group 1 is worked over most of the surface, and Group 2 is worked only on one end.

Group 1 (37 specimens).—These are spatula-shaped objects made of split segments of heavy rib, with smoothed straight to irregular sides. Ends are polished and may be either flat (fig. 10, *e*) or rounded, or bluntly pointed (fig. 10, *f*). Length of complete specimens is from 74 to 235 mm. The cancellous bone on one side is smoothed and in some cases removed. A single implement, 118 mm. long, is serrated along both edges.

Group 2 (27 specimens).—These specimens, also made from heavy rib, have only one worked end. The opposing end is usually rough and unfinished, although sometimes it is slightly rounded or polished. A number of the specimens are not split, and the cancellous bone is rough and unfinished. The shafts of the implements are usually unfinished. Specimens are 85 to 235 mm. long. The round, worked end of two specimens is stained red, probably with ocher.

Rubbing tools
(13 specimens)

Fragments of large long bones and ribs often have one rounded and smoothed end. The high polish on these ends suggests that they were used for rubbing a soft, resilient material, possibly hide. Eight of them are made from large mammal ribs, four are of large mammal long bone fragments, and one is of deer ulna. Lengths are 91 to 285 mm.

Punches
(32 specimens)

Although these tools resemble awls in many particulars, the tips are too dull to have served as hide perforators. The points of some of them are scratched, and might have served as tools for flaking stone. A few are highly polished, and probably served as punches.

Fifteen of them are made from split ribs of large mammals. One end bears a blunt, rounded point; the other is usually rounded from use, and the surfaces and edges are smoothed. Three are made from fragments of the long bones of large mammals, and seven are made from the spinous processes of bison scapula (fig. 10, a). The latter specimens may be byproducts from the manufacture of scapula hoes, in which these processes are removed. Two tips, made from unidentified bones, were also recovered.

Slotted rib tip
(1 specimen)

A fragment of rib from a large mammal, probably bison, is 130 mm. long. There is a slot in one end made by removing part of the cancellous bone. The other end is broken.

Miscellaneous shaped objects
(2 specimens)

A piece of thin bone, probably from a scapula, is 75 mm. long and 3 mm. thick. The edges and flat surfaces are smooth and polished, showing minute striations from grinding on a relatively coarse-grained stone. One end is broken (fig. 8, n).

A J-shaped piece of bone cut from a bison scapula is polished on the outer edges and is rough on the inner edges. Both ends are broken, and the surface is smoothed. The length is 75 mm. (fig. 10, g).

WORK IN ANTLER AND TEETH

Bands
(6 specimens)

Some of these bands may represent bracelets, but others are too large for such an identification and may be pendants. One complete band is 220 mm. long, and is bent into an arc with a diameter of 140 mm. (fig. 11, *a*). Both ends are drilled from both sides and pierced. The transverse section is oval near the ends and circular in the middle. The convex surface is highly polished, and the concave surface is rough.

A broken band 116 mm. long has a perforation drilled from both sides in a square end, and a groove in the concave surface that extends for 60 mm. from the hole. The broken end is rounded and polished, and it may have been reworked (fig. 11, *i*). Four broken bands, none of which exceeds 80 mm. in length, have perforations in one end that are gouged from both sides. Surfaces are smooth but are not polished (fig. 11, *g*). One example is scored on both edges (fig. 11, *h*.) A final fragment, a midsection, is 70 mm. long. A longitudinal groove is cut into the convex face.

Tines
(4 specimens)

The tips of these deer tines are lightly polished, with occasional longitudinal scratches near the tip. The proximal ends are irregular, and the fractures indicate that the tines were hacked from the body of the antler with some blunt tool. The lengths are 51 to 180 mm.

Miscellaneous shaped objects
(3 specimens)

A rectangular piece of antler, measuring 41×17×5 mm., is cut transversely on both ends. The object was split longitudinally from the antler. The convex surface is scored lightly and smoothed; the under surface is rough (fig. 11, *d*).

A second object measures 51×17×15 mm. One large end is sawed transversely through the compact outer layer, and snapped off. The object tapers to a squared, polished end. Its form is spuriously similar to that of a modern pipe mouthpiece (fig. 11, *e*). The convex upper surface is smoothed on the high points, and the flat under side is longitudinally scored with deep gouges.

Another item is broken, but originally exceeded 200 mm. in length. It consists of a straight shaft of antler 10 to 11 mm. in diameter. One end is squared, and the other end tapers to a broken tip. The sides of the object are scored, and five incised lines occur on either side. Four notches are cut into the sides of the shaft at the square end (fig. 11, *f*).

Perforated elk teeth
(2 specimens)

Highly polished canines of adult elk have holes drilled from both sides in the roots. The holes are polished from a suspending cord or

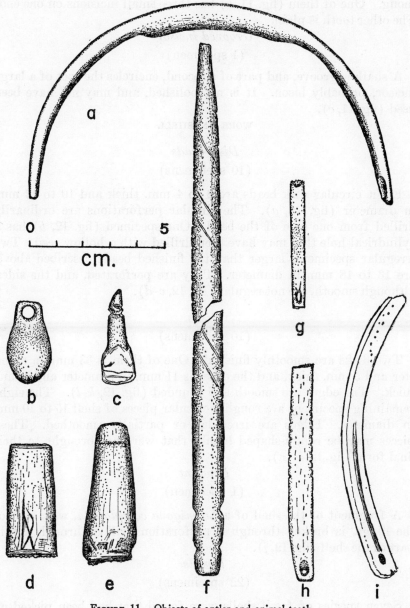

FIGURE 11.—Objects of antler and animal teeth.

thong.   One of them (fig. 11, *b*) has three small incisions on one end.
The other tooth is plain.

Grooved incisor
(1 specimen)

A shallow groove, and part of a second, encircles the root of a large
incisor, probably bison.   It is not polished, and may not have been
used (fig. 11, *c*).

WORK IN SHELL

Disk beads
(10 specimens)

Eight circular disk beads are 2 to 4 mm. thick and 10 to 12 mm.
in diameter (fig. 12, *a*).   The circular perforations are ordinarily
drilled from one side of the bead.   One specimen (fig. 12, *b*) has a
cylindrical hole that may have been drilled with a hollow reed.   Two
irregular specimens, larger than the finished beads described above,
are 13 to 18 mm. in diameter.   They are perforated, and the sides,
although smooth, are not regular (fig. 12, *c–d*).

Disks
(10 specimens)

Two disks are smoothly finished.   One of them is 33 mm. in diameter and 5 mm. thick, and the other is 11 mm. in diameter and 4 mm.
thick.   The edges are smooth and rounded (fig. 12, *k–l*).   The eight
remaining specimens are roughly circular pieces of shell 15 to 40 mm.
in diameter.   Edges are irregular or partially smoothed.   These
pieces may be rough-shaped blanks that were not brought to their
final form (fig. 12, *m, n*).

Pendant
(1 specimen)

A fragment of the shell of a *Lasmigona complanata*, with part of
the hinge, is broken through a perforation drilled through a thin
part of the shell (fig. 12, *j*).

Fossils
(22 specimens)

Seven species of fossil shells were found that had been picked up
elsewhere by the inhabitants and brought to the village.   Five of the
seven species are pierced or otherwise modified for suspension as beads
or pendants.

Three of the *L. nebrascensis* shells are beads (fig. 12, *e*).   The shell
wall is pierced by a longitudinal cut that is smooth and rounded.   A

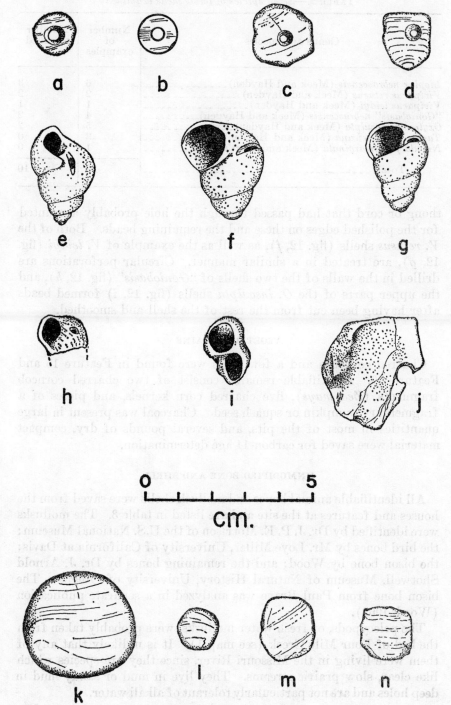

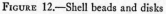

FIGURE 12.—Shell beads and disks

TABLE 2.—*Seven species of fossil shells examined*

Genus and species	Number of examples	Number modified
Lioplax nebrascensis (Meek and Hayden)_____	6	3
Viviparus retusus (Meek and Hayden)_____	2	2
Viviparus leidyi (Meek and Hayden)_____	1	1
"Goniobasis" nebrascensis (Meek and Hayden)_____	4	2
Oxytrema insculpta (Meek and Hayden)_____	5	2
Tancredia americana (Meek and Hayden)_____	3	0
Nucula planimarginata (Meek and Worthen)_____	1	0
Total_____	22	10

thong or cord that had passed through the hole probably accounted
for the polished edges on these and the remaining beads. Both of the
V. retusus shells (fig. 12, *f*), as well as the example of *V. leidyi* (fig.
12, *g*), are treated in a similar manner. Circular perforations are
drilled in the walls of the two shells of *"Goniobasis"* (fig. 12, *h*), and
the upper parts of the *O. insculpta* shells (fig. 12, *i*) formed beads
after having been cut from the rest of the shell and smoothed.

VEGETAL REMAINS

Charred corncobs and a few seeds were found in Feature 15 and
Feature 46. Identifiable remains consist of two charred corncob
fragments (*Zea mays*), five charred corn kernels, and pieces of a
fragmentary pumpkin or squash seed. Charcoal was present in large
quantities in most of the pits, and several pounds of dry, compact
material were saved for carbon-14 age determination.

UNMODIFIED BONE AND SHELL

All identifiable animal bones and mollusk shells were saved from the
houses and features at the site and are listed in table 3. The mollusks
were identified by Dr. J. P. E. Morrison of the U.S. National Museum;
the bird bones by Mr. Loye Miller, University of California at Davis;
the bison bone by Wood; and the remaining bones by Dr. J. Arnold
Shotwell, Museum of Natural History, University of Oregon. The
bison bone from Paul Brave was analyzed in a separate publication
(Wood, 1962).

The pelecypods, or fresh water mollusks, were probably taken from
the bed of Four Mile Creek (see map 1). It is unlikely that any of
them were living in the Missouri River, since they are species which
like clear, slow prairie streams. They live in mud or sandy mud in
deep holes and are not particularly tolerant of alkali water.

TABLE 3.—*Species identified at Paul Brave*

Class	Genus and species	Number of individuals
Mollusks:		
Gastropods	(Several fossil species; see table 2)	22
Pelecypods	*Anodonta grandis plana* Lea	1
	Lasmigona complanata (Barnes)	11
	Lampsilis siliquoidea (Barnes)	33
	Lampsilis cardium Rafinesque	1
Chordates:		
Fish	Catfish, probably *Ictalurus*	[1] x
Reptiles	Turtle (unidentified)	1
Birds of prey	Golden eagle (*Aquila chrysaetos*)	1
	Marsh hawk (*Circus cyaneus*)	5
	Hawk (*Buteo* sp.)	6
Wading and swimming birds	Whistling swan (*Cygnus columbianus*)	1
	Crane (*Grus canadensis*)	3
	Goose (*Branta canadensis*)	3
	Ducks (size of teal and gadwall)	4
Other birds	Heath hen (*Tympanuchus cupido*)	4
	Crow (*Corvus brachyrhynchos*)	2
Carnivores	Dog, wolf, or coyote (*Canis* sp.)	7
	Gray fox (*Urocyon cinereorgentus*)	1
Artiodactyls	Bison (*Bison bison*)	53
	Deer or antelope (*Odocoileus* or *Antilocapra* sp.)	7
	Elk (*Cervus canadensis*)	3
Rodents	Rabbit (*Lepus* and *Sylvilagus* sp.)	6
	Ground squirrel (*Citellus* sp.)	3
	Beaver (*Castor canadensis*)	2
	Muskrat (*Ondatra zibethicus*)	1
	Skunk (*Mephitis hudsonica*)	1

[1] Present but not counted.

DISCUSSION

STRUCTURES

The long rectangular houses at Paul Brave are not consistent in size, but they are similar in form. Lengths are 37.5 to 46.0 feet, and widths are 24 to 32.5 feet. The long walls of the houses are not parallel, and there is a variation in the end widths of 1.5 to 3.5 feet. This variation in width is present also at the Thomas Riggs site in houses 3 and 5 (Hurt, 1953, figs. 9, 11), and is reported in houses at the Huff site (32MO11) according to Will and Hecker (1944, pp. 19–20).

Houses 5 and 6 at the Thomas Riggs site (Hurt, 1953, pp. 7–8, figs. 11, 12) are similar in floor plan to House 2 at Paul Brave. There is a large post in the end of these houses opposite the entrance, and a large post centered on the house midline. These posts probably supported a ridge pole along the house midline. Houses 1 and 3 at Paul Brave (and apparently House 4 as well) have two intermediate rows of posts between the house midline and the walls. This feature is lacking at Thomas Riggs, but there seems to be evidence for a similar structural pattern in the Over Focus Swanson site (39BR16) (Hurt, 1951, figs. 12–13, 16).

In each of the houses at Thomas Riggs, a low bench of undisturbed native earth projects into the house floor between the two posts that mark the entrance. These ramps also occur at Paul Brave, but here they are small, not exceeding a foot in length, and might more appropriately be termed "steps."

Details of the house superstructure are rare. In House 3, timbers along one wall indicate that the wall posts were at least 5 feet high. There was no evidence of leaners on the bench of earth outside the house wall. These facts, together with the presence of small branches and twigs along the house walls, suggest that the walls were interlaced with branches. Some form of a wattle-and-daub wall may be represented in this architectural form rather than the earth-covered lodge of later, historic tribes. Each of the houses had a line of center posts which apparently supported a ridge pole. In House 2, the roof may have been A-shaped or gabled, but in houses 1 and 3 the roof form is complicated by the presence of the intermediate row of posts.

Bell-shaped pits predominate in the houses, but basin-shaped pits are also frequent. The bell-shaped pits in the house floors are not particularly large, nor are they deep. A maximum depth of about 2 feet prevails. Exterior cache pits are larger; some of them are 6 feet in diameter and attain a depth of 5 feet below the present surface. Originally they were probably no more than 4 feet deep. The additional depth is due to the soil accumulation over the site since it was abandoned. All the pits contained refuse, and even the bell-shaped pits were used for rubbish disposal after their primary function as food storage pits was fulfilled.

A long shallow trench in House 3, F70, may have an analogy in F67 in House 2, although this latter pit is irregularly shaped. These pits are similar to features in houses at Thomas Riggs (Hurt, 1953, p. 8, figs. 7–8, 10, 12). The pits at Thomas Riggs contained very little refuse, and some of them were lined with wooden slabs. Although the pits at Paul Brave contained no wood, their refuse content was low. These pits are also similar in form to a pit in the midline of the long rectangular house at 32ME59, the site of "Grandmother's Lodge," although here the pit contained small stones (Woolworth, 1956, pl. 2).

ARTIFACT COMPLEX

The Thomas Riggs site, in central South Dakota, is the only adequately excavated site that compares closely with Paul Brave, although limited comparisons are possible with "Grandmother's Lodge." The pottery and other artifacts from Paul Brave refer to the "Archaic Mandan" period, the earliest known village culture on the Missouri River in present-day North Dakota. Comparisons with other sites are possible, but are rather restricted because of a lack of data. Excavation in long rectangular house sites has been restricted primarily to testing in North Dakota, and space does not permit a detailed comparison of the artifacts from Paul Brave with the numerous but limited samples from sites listed by Will and Hecker (1944, pp. 118–121) as "Archaic Mandan." An inspection of the various collections in the

State Historical Society of North Dakota Museum indicates that Paul Brave resembles these sites in most particulars.

The pottery from Paul Brave is remarkably uniform with respect to paste, surface finish, and form. Briefly, the pottery was probably made by means of lump modeling, with the use of a grooved paddle and an anvil. The use of a cord-wrapped paddle was less common. Decomposed or calcined granite was added as temper, and the pottery was fired to a hardness of 3.0 to 3.5, with a resulting color that ranged from light buff through black. The upper parts of most vessels were horizontally smoothed. Although some shoulders were vertically simple-stamped, the marks are usually obliterated. Incised decorations were applied to a smoothed shoulder area. Both decorated and undecorated rims were smoothed. The bases of the vessels were simple-stamped in a random fashion. A few vessels were polished. Vessels were globular, with rounded bases, and wide, apparently round mouths. Loop handles and a few strap handles were attached to rims. There are two rim forms. One of these is straight and vertical, with many rims outflaring. Vessels bearing such rims are herein termed the "Riggs Ware." The other rim form is S-shaped, and the vessels with this character are herein termed "Fort Yates Ware." The general characteristics of the Paul Brave pottery already enumerated apply for the most part to that from Thomas Riggs. Differences in the pottery from the two sites are found only when more detailed comparisons are made.

The rim sherd samples from both sites are nearly the same: 863 rims at Thomas Riggs, and 886 rims at Paul Brave. The body sherd sample from Thomas Riggs is more than six times that from Paul Brave. The smaller sample from Paul Brave probably resulted from our practice of retaining only those sherds the size of a half-dollar or larger. Despite these quantitative differences, the percentages of types of body treatment at both sites are remarkably close. There is little more than a 5 percent difference between the two major groups of body sherds from the two sites. Cord-roughened body sherds are rare at both sites. The paste of the cord-roughened sherds at Paul Brave is identical with that of other body sherds, a circumstance that suggests that the sherds are indigenous. The rare check-stamped sherds at Paul Brave are not paralleled at Thomas Riggs, whereas the painted pottery at Thomas Riggs is absent at Paul Brave.

The percentage of decorated shoulder sherds from both sites is nearly the same. The range of designs on Paul Brave pottery is limited (figs. 1, 2), and most of them occur on pottery at Thomas Riggs (Hurt, 1953, figs. 27–28, 30–31). The most popular patterns are composed of alternating elements of nested chevrons and triangular "animal tracks." Most of the designs are incised or trailed, but one example (pl. 6, *e;* fig. 1, *b*) is composed of lines made by a stab-and-drag technique. The designs are almost exclusively composed of rectilinear elements. Curvilinear elements are present on only three vessels. The majority of shoulder designs are on the Riggs and Fort Yates Crosshatched rims; only 13 rims of Riggs Plain are decorated at Paul Brave.

Riggs Plain Rim comprises the bulk of the rims from both sites, averaging more than 85 percent of the total at Thomas Riggs[2] and nearly 70 percent at Paul Brave. Applique nodes are common on rims from both sites. On S-shaped rims, these nodes often serve as the apex for cord-impressed triangular elements (pl. 5, *f*). A unique example of applique work at Paul Brave is illustrated by Hewes (1949 b, pl. 6, right, *s*).

The S-shaped rims comprise a larger percentage of the total rims at Paul Brave than they do at Thomas Riggs, and there is more variation in the rim decorative elements. The presence at Thomas Riggs of the type Riggs Punctate, and an S-shaped rim with horizontally applied cord-impressed lines lacking triangular or curvilinear rainbow elements may be significant. Conversely, the lack of crosshatched rims at Thomas Riggs (except for a possible single trade sherd), the absence of Riggs Wavy Rim, and the lack of rims of Example A may have equal significance. These differences in the pottery from the two sites, however, do not appear to be as significant as the overall similarities. Some local specialization is expected (see table 4).

Site 32ME59, "Grandmother's Lodge," is a few miles downstream from the mouth of the Little Missouri River, in northwestern North Dakota. The pottery from this site may be classified as of types defined in this study. Example A is Fort Yates Cord Impressed Rim, and Example B is Riggs Plain Rim (Woolworth, 1956, pp. 90–91, pl. 5, *a–e*). Only in the presence of the grooved ax and the large chipped stone projectile point does the site differ from the inventory at Paul Brave.

The sample of 55 complete projectile points from Paul Brave is notably larger than the 18 from Thomas Riggs. There is no close correspondence in relative frequencies of projectile points, although most of the forms at one site occur also at the other. Most of the projectile points weigh 0.8 to 3.0 gm., are within the range of the small point tradition (Fenenga, 1953, p. 322), and may be interpreted as arrowpoints. Four points (fig. 3, *i–l*) that weigh more than 4.5 g. are in the range of the large point tradition and are probably knives or dart points.

The narrow knives from Paul Brave are similar to those from "Grandmother's Lodge" (Woolworth, 1956, pl. 6, *i–j*) and other sites

---

[2] The sherds of Riggs Straight Rim and Riggs Flared Rim from Thomas Riggs are herein classed together as Riggs Plain Rim.

TABLE 4.—*Pottery frequencies at Thomas Riggs and Paul Brave sites*

Pottery type	Thomas Riggs		Paul Brave	
	Number	*Percent*	*Number*	*Percent*
Riggs Plain [1]	749	86.8	619	69.9
Cross-Hatched	1	.2	54	6.1
Incised	32	3.7	6	.7
Pinched			26	2.9
Punctate	32	3.7		
Fort Yates Cord Impressed [2]	20	2.3	136	15.3
Fort Yates Cross-Hatched			30	3.4
Unnamed, cord impressed [3]	16	1.8		
Unclassified	3	.4		
Example A			10	1.1
Example B			1	.1
Example C			1	.1
Example D [4]	10	1.1	3	.3
	863	100.0	886	99.9
Twelve Mile Black on Gray	31	.33		
Smoothed	6,620	64.2	845	58.9
Simple-stamped	3,233	31.4	514	35.8
Cord-roughened	39	.4	19	1.3
Check-stamped			2	.1
Decorated	374	3.6	54	3.7
Unclassified	14	.1		
Total	10,311	100.03	1,434	99.8

[1] "Riggs Straight Rim" and "Riggs Flared Rim" from Thomas Riggs are grouped together here.
[2] At Thomas Riggs, these sherds are designated "Aldren Cord Impressed."
[3] At Thomas Riggs, these sherds are designated "Fort Yates Cord Impressed."
[4] Several rims of this example at Thomas Riggs are designated "Riggs Plain," but the small sample from either site does not seem to deserve type status.

along the Missouri River. The suggestion is made here that these knives were inserted into bone knife handles.

Siltstone spheres were found at Paul Brave, as well as one circular sandstone concretion. The latter object may have derived from the famed Cannonball formation, which outcrops some distance to the north at the Cannonball River. Specimens similar to the siltstone spheres are reported by Wedel from sites in the vicinity of the Grand River, in South Dakota (Wedel, 1955, pp. 113–114, pl. 58, *i–j*). A large block of sandstone was used as a mealing slab, and one mano, or handstone, may have been used on such a platform.

In many respects the objects of worked bone at Paul Brave parallel those at Thomas Riggs, although there are some differences. In some classes of artifacts, such as scapula hoes and awls, the number of specimens varies but the relative proportions remain much the same.

A point may be made concerning the serrated fleshing tools at Paul Brave. Tools of this nature occur in the Dodd and Phillips Ranch sites (39ST30 and 39ST14), in central South Dakota. Both of these sites contain trade goods (Lehmer, 1954, p. 110; figs. 33, *a–c*, and 49, *j–k*). They also occur in late Mandan sites (Will and Spinden, 1906, fig. 7 *a–d*). In the Central Plains, they are characteristic of early historic and historic complexes, and are rarely if ever found in prehistoric sites (Wedel, 1940, p. 316). Since Paul Brave lacks trade goods it seems that the usefulness of this tool as a late time marker is restricted to the Central Plains.

The three bone disks from Paul Brave are similar in size and form to incised disks in the collections of the State Historical Society of North Dakota from the Motsiff, Slant, and Double Ditch sites. The disks from these three sites are incised in much the same manner as the bone disks used in the Mandan woman's game of *Sha-we* (Libby, 1906, pp. 444–445). The specimens figured by Libby are cut from the walls of a heavy long bone and are carefully rounded. The identification of the bone as rib by Libby is erroneous.

A number of bone tools are classed as "pottery modeling tools," following the suggestion of Wheeler (1956, pp. 17–20). The bone tubes from the site may have been used as ornaments, but it is also possible that they were for medicinal use. In the collections of the State Historical Society are three bone tubes, two of which were collected by C. W. Hoffman on the Fort Berthold Reservation, N. Dak. They are said to have been used as emetics. These polished bird-bone tubes are 49 and 61 mm. long and 14 to 18 mm. in diameter. One of them has a hole in one side in the manner of a plume holder. A third bird-bone tube, collected by Frances Densmore prior to 1918 in northern Minnesota—probably among the Chippewa—is 64 mm. long and 12 mm. in diameter. This polished tube has two opposed holes in one end, and Densmore noted that it was swallowed "to be regurgitated."

The bone knife handles from Paul Brave are made from bison dorsal vertebrae spines, whereas most reported hafts are made from bison ribs. Specimens made of rib occur in many prehistoric and historic complexes in the Plains. They are known in Upper Republican (Kivett, 1949, p. 280; fig. 69, *b*), and in the Mitchell and Twelve Mile Creek sites of the Over Focus (Hurt, 1952). The use of these implements continued into historic times, occurring in Mandan sites (Strong, 1940, p. 365), in the Sheyenne-Cheyenne site (Strong, 1940, p. 375), and in Arikara sites in the vicinity of Mobridge (Wedel, 1955, pp. 122–123, plate 61, *f–h*). These specimens consist of a slotted rib with both ends cut square. The hafts from Paul Brave and from the Over Focus sites have a tonguelike projection on one end.

In addition to the bone knife handles are the bone knives (fig. 7, *c*), which were used by historic tribes as "squash knives." Most of these knives are rectangular in outline, but the form of one broken implement (fig. 8, *n*) suggests that it was part of a hook-bladed knife similar to examples from the Dodd site (Lehmer, 1954, p. 68, fig. 26, *m*).

Two perforated elk teeth from Paul Brave are identical with specimens found on costumes of historic Northern Plains Indians, as well as other groups to the west and south. The significance of these ornaments has been discussed in detail elsewhere (Wood, 1957, pp. 381–385), but it is relevant to state that they are prehistoric in the northern Middle Missouri area, but are lacking until the time of White contact in the Central Plains.

Several antler bands from Paul Brave are made from thin strips of antler. The steps in the manufacture of these ornaments have been fully described by Steinbrueck (1906, p. 456–459). These objects are known from the Double Ditch site (Will and Spinden, 1906, p. 172, pl. 36, *w–z*), where they are also made from antler. Similar specimens are in the collections of the State Historical Society of North Dakota from Slant Village, 32MO26.

Work in shell is relatively rare, the more common articles being disk beads and unperforated disks. The pierced snail shells from Paul Brave are made from local fossils, but otherwise are similar to specimens from Thomas Riggs. Shell disk beads also are shared by both sites. Circular disk beads are in the collections of the State Historical Society of North Dakota from the Badwater and North Cannonball sites. Circular disks, some of them probably game pieces, occur at Slant Village, Havens, Stanton Ferry, Hensler, and Demery. Pierced fossil snail shells at Boley, Motsiff, and Badwater include species identified at Paul Brave.

It may be relevant to mention the grooved sandstone slabs found at Havens, Gaines Ranch, Upper Sanger, and Motsiff, that are in the Historical Society collections. These sandstone slabs have U-shaped grooves as much as 12 mm. wide, and the grooves are frequently so smooth that they might be classed as lightly polished. The width of the grooves approximates the diameter of most of the perforated shell disk beads in the Historical Society collections, and it is possible that they may have functioned to smooth down rough-shaped shell beads. Such may not always have been the case, however, since disk beads occur at Paul Brave and grooved abraders of this character were not recovered.

OTHER SITES

Between Stanton, N. Dak., and Kenel, S. Dak., Will and Hecker (1944, pp. 118–121) list nearly fifty "Archaic Mandan" sites. Collections are available for a few of the sites in the vicinity of Paul Brave. In general, these collections are small, but those from the Robert Zahn and Havens sites are large enough for limited comparisons with Paul Brave.

ROBERT ZAHN SITE (32SI3)

(MAP 1)

Site 32SI3, in the E½ SE¼ sec. 9, T. 129 N., R. 79 W., covers about 10 acres on a level terrace and the adjoining slope of a low hill on the banks of a small stream. It is crossed by a gravel highway and much of it has been plowed. Will and Hecker (1944, p. 89) report that

TABLE 5.—*Comparison of traits at Paul Brave and Thomas Riggs sites*

Traits	Paul Brave	Thomas Riggs
I. Villages:		
Long-rectangular houses	X	X
Houses arranged in streets	X	X
Open village	X	X
Exterior cache pits	X	X
Central plaza		X
II. Houses:		
Built in shallow pit	X	X
Entrance to southwest	X	X
Offset fireplace	X	X
Center posts in house midline	X	X
Intermediate rows of posts	X	
Closely spaced wall posts	X	X
House ends open	X	X
Trench in house rear	X	X
Earth ramp at entrance	X	X
House walls not parallel	X	X
Braced posts	X	X
Interior, bell-shaped pits	X	X
III. Pottery (cf. table 4):		
Riggs Plain	X	X
Riggs Cross-Hatched	X	X
Riggs Incised	X	X
Riggs Pinched	X	
Riggs Punctate		X
Fort Yates Cord Impressed	X	X
Fort Yates Cross-Hatched		X
Unnamed, Cord Impressed		X
Unclassified		X
Example A	X	
Example B	X	
Example C	X	
Example D	X	
Twelve Mile Black on Gray		X
Smoothed or plain	X	X
Simple-stamped	X	X
Cord-roughened	X	X
Check-stamped	X	
Incised or trailed	X	X
Unclassified		X
IV. Miscellaneous objects of baked clay:		
Animal effigies	5	0
Bead	1	0
Shaped item	1	0
Pipes	0	2
V. Work in stone:		
Projectile points	55	18
NAb1	1	0
NAb2	0	2
NBa	18	4
NBa1	22	7
NBb	2	3
NBb1	12	1
SCb1	0	1
Drills	6	10
Expanding base	6	2
Straight-shafted	0	8
End scrapers	149	51
Flaked on upper surface	79	24
Upper surface not flaked	70	27
Broad knives	21	X
NAb1	1	X
NAb2	4	X
NAb2, asymmetrical	2	0
NE	1	X
Fragments	13	X
Narrow knives	5	0
NAa	1	0
NAb2	2	0
Fragments	2	0
Choppers	34	X
Flake knives	135	198
Grooved mauls	5	5
Full groove	2	2
Three-quarter groove	1	0
Sides grooved	0	2
Fragments	2	1
Axes	1	2
Celts	18	21
Manos, or handstones	1	19
Mealing slabs or metates	1	8
Hammerstones	49	14

TABLE 5.—*Comparison of traits at Paul Brave and Thomas Riggs sites*—Con.

Traits	Paul Brave	Thomas Riggs
V. Work in stone—Continued		
Stone spheres	5	0
Shaft smoothers	6	6
Grooved abraders	18	82
Faceted abraders	59	2
Beads	4	1
VI. Work in bone:		
Scapula hoes	66	42
Scapula hoes, notched glenoid	9	4
Scapula hoe, perforated blade	1	0
Scapula hoe fragments	31	53
Scapula "thong stretchers"	2	5
Serrated fleshers	2	0
Split metapodial scoops	2	13
Horn core and frontal scoops	0	2
Awls, mammal long bone	62	43
Head of bone intact	1	2
Head of bone split	18	20
Head of bone worked down	12	12
Head of bone removed	17	9
Splinter	14	0
Mammal rib awls	33	15
Split and worked	28	15
Splinter	5	0
Bison scapula splinter awl	0	1
Bird bone awls	4	4
Fish spine awls	1	3
Pottery modeling tools	64	6
Knives	10	9
Fishhooks	1	5
Knife handles	3	0
Punches	32	0
Chisels	9	0
Rubbing tools	13	0
Whistle	1	0
Slotted rib tip	1	0
Beads	8	0
Disks	3	0
Spatula tip	1	0
Needles	0	3
Shaft wrenches	0	2
Rib pendant	0	1
Tubes	3	4
Miscellaneous shaped objects	2	0
VII. Work in antler and teeth:		
Bands	6	0
Tines	4	7
Sections from main shaft	0	9
Miscellaneous shaped antler	3	0
Perforated elk teeth	2	0
Grooved bison incisor	1	0
VIII. Work in shell:		
Disk beads	10	16
Disks	10	1
Pendants	1	3
Fossil snail shell beads	10	0
Recent snail shell beads	0	2

house floors were once visible in the cut bank of the terrace and that the pottery was "Archaic Mandan." A test pit excavated south of the gravel road by the State Historical Society field party in 1955 recovered the artifacts described below from a shallow, irregular pit.

Three of the seven rim sherds are similar to the type herein described as Riggs Plain Rim; the lips of two sherds are indented. Two small rim sherds represent the type Fort Yates Cord Impressed. One rim, 30 mm. high, has a fillet on the mid-rim, the crest of which is 12 mm. below the lip. The rim profile resembles that of the type Riggs Punctate (Kleinsasser, 1953, p. 29, fig. 26, 2), but the fillet lacks the punctates that are characteristic of this type. A final rim is unclassified. Seven of the 18 body sherds are simple-stamped, and 7 are smoothed.

Work in stone includes two pieces of plate or vein chalcedony with bifacially prepared edges, two faceted scoria abraders, two end scrapers, and the bases of two arrowpoints of form NBb1 made from Knife River flint and white chert. A bone awl made from a split long bone and an antler tine tip complete the list of specimens.

There are similarities to Paul Brave apparent even in this small sample. Five of the seven rims are classified as of types described from Paul Brave, and the remaining artifacts are similar to examples from that site. The two variant rims, however, indicate that the Robert Zahn site has elements that are lacking at Paul Brave. Further testing and perhaps extensive excavations should be carried out here, since the site will be inundated by the Oahe Reservoir. The site may aid in determining the range of variation in the "Archaic Mandan" complex.

HAVENS SITE (32EM1)

(MAP 1)

This site, in the SW¼ NE¼ sec. 3, T129N, R79W, is situated on a low, rolling terrace and covers about 15 acres. It is on the east bank of the Missouri River across from the Paul Brave site. About 40 widely spaced house depressions are visible. The surface is in native sod, with about 8 or 10 inches of soil accumulation over the former village level. No refuse middens are apparent, and there is only a thin layer of village refuse. There is no indication of a ditch, and the oval house depressions suggest that the dwellings are long-rectangular houses (Will and Hecker, 1944, p. 76).

A large number of artifacts from the site are in the collections of the State Historical Society. Notes are not available for this sample, but it is likely that they were derived from the surface or from limited testing by Will and Hecker. The majority of the rim sherds may be classified as of types described from Paul Brave:

Riggs Plain	134
Riggs Cross-Hatched	3
Riggs Incised	2
Riggs Pinched	10
Fort Yates Cord Impressed	11
Fort Yates Cross-Hatched	1
Unclassified	1
Total	162

Body sherds are classed as follows:

Simple-stamped	10
Smoothed	49
Cord-roughened	1
Incised or trailed	13
Total	73

Stonework includes several flake knives, a number of end scrapers, and an arrowpoint of form NAb2, measuring 33 × 15 × 3 mm., made from Knife River flint.   Worked bone includes two long bone splinter awl fragments and part of a split rib pottery modeling tool.   An irregular shell disk is 15 mm. in diameter and 5 mm. thick.   A roughly circular piece of perforated shell, less than 1 mm. thick, averages 20 mm. in diameter.

This inventory is similar in most particulars to that of Paul Brave. Except for the single unclassified rim, all the sherds are of types occurring at Paul Brave, and the non-ceramic remains are also very similar.   This similarity in content suggests that the sites are closely related and may be nearly contemporaneous.   The site is not recommended for testing.   It is believed that the material in the site would duplicate the sample recovered from the Paul Brave site, and at this time it would be more relevant to excavate sites which will be flooded by the Oahe Reservoir but which differ from adequately sampled villages.

CONCLUSIONS

As early as 1919, George F. Will and Herbert J. Spinden recognized an archeological sequence within the Missouri River Valley in North Dakota that they regarded as a cultural sequence leading to the historic Mandan (Will, 1924, pp. 292, 342–344).   Subsequent to 1924, Will made further studies, and by 1944 had formulated with Thad. C. Hecker the postulate that Mandan history was divisible into four major periods: the Archaic Mandan, Middle Mandan, Later Heart River, and Decadent periods (Will and Hecker, 1944).   Paraphrasing their synthesis, it appears that the Archaic period was distinguished by small, unfortified villages of long-rectangular houses distributed along a large segment of the Missouri River.   The advent of the Middle period seems to be chiefly marked by the appearance of progressively developing fortifications, and by the concentration of these villages into large fortified sites of long-rectangular houses near the mouth of the Heart River.   The transition from the Middle period to the Later Heart River period is marked by three distinct changes.   The long-rectangular dwellings of the Middle period are replaced by circular earth lodges, the villages consist of houses tightly arranged within the fortification ditches, and the population concentrated in an even smaller area in the immediate vicinity of the mouth of the Heart River.   The Decadent period is associated with increasing contact with White traders after 1750.   In addition to these details of settlement patterning and domestic architecture, there is a progressive development of pottery types, culminating in the varieties which are found in historic Mandan and Hidatsa sites at the mouth of the Heart River (Will and Hecker, 1944, pp. 6–7, 10, 52–54, 117–118, passim).

In this formulation, they classed the Paul Brave site as "Archaic Mandan" (ibid., p. 89). The complex represented at Paul Brave is the earliest recognized village complex in the upper reaches of the Middle Missouri area, and to date it is represented at the following sites for which data are available:

Excavated:	Thomas Riggs, 39HU1 (Hurt, 1953)
	Grandmother's Lodge, 32ME59 (Woolworth, 1956)
	Paul Brave, 32SI4 (this study)
	Tony Glas, 32EM3 (Howard, 1962)
Tested:	Robert Zahn, 32SI3 (this study)
	Standing Soldier, 32SI8 (Scheans, MS.)
Surface collection:	Havens, 32EM1 (this study)

Most of these sites were termed "Archaic Mandan" by Will and Hecker. In a review of their work (Champe, 1948, pp. 261–262) it was pointed out that the utmost discretion is necessary in the application of terms such as "archaic" to relatively recent complexes. We fully endorse this sentiment, and submit that there is no reason to retain this loaded term. Another term for some of the same sites is the "Cannonball Focus" (Bowers, MS.), but the priority of naming and describing the material in usable form falls to Hurt in his description of the Thomas Riggs Focus (Hurt, 1953). Tables 4 and 5 in this study illustrate the degree of identity between the type site of this focus and Paul Brave, and Paul Brave is here identified as a component of that focus. It is urged that the designation of Paul Brave as a component of a "Fort Yates Focus" (ibid., p. 60), distinct from the Thomas Riggs Focus, be abandoned in view of their essential similarity.

Paul Brave is related to sites found throughout a considerable part of the Missouri River Valley in the Middle Missouri area. In 1951, the Missouri Basin Project of the Smithsonian Institution tested site 39LM55 in Lyman County, S. Dak., and in 1953 the University of Kansas made other tests in that same site. The site lies just a few miles north of the town of Chamberlain and just north of the mouth of the White River. Work at this site revealed tools and a long-rectangular house similar to those at the Thomas Riggs site (C. S. Smith, 1953, p. 198). Excavations at the site of Grandmother's Lodge (32ME59) (Woolworth, 1956) indicate that the Thomas Riggs Focus extends as far north and west along the Missouri River Valley as the mouth of the Little Missouri River in western North Dakota.

Site 39LM55 and Grandmother's Lodge are fully 300 airline miles apart; the river distance between them approaches 500 miles. Between these two extremes there are numerous small, isolated villages of the Thomas Riggs Focus. The near identity of the remains in these sites

along this immense tract of land is truly striking. If cultural similarity implies contemporaneity they cannot be widely separated in
time. The hypothesis that the downriver sites are the older is appeal-
ing, and it has the virtue of the support of the Mandan migration
traditions (Bowers, 1950, pp. 156–163) claiming a downstream origin
for that group. The village sites of this complex are confined, so far
as we are now aware, to the valley of the Missouri River. It is probable that surveys along major tributaries west of the Missouri would
reveal hunting campsites of these villages.

Until such time as radiocarbon, tree ring, or other dating methods
can be applied to material from Paul Brave, it is necessary to estimate
its age on the basis of comparative data. The tree-ring studies carried out by Will (1946, 1948), in conjunction with the analysis of
pottery traits, village patterns, and house forms (Will and Hecker,
1944) suggest a terminal date for the site. The lack of a fortifying
ditch suggests the site is earlier in time than the Huff site, for which
site the cutting dates of 11 timbers are A.D. 1458–1543 (Will, 1946, p.
16). A radiocarbon date of A.D. 1228± 200 has been released for the
Thomas Riggs site by the Missouri Basin Chronology Program
(Radiocarbon Laboratory, Michigan Memorial-Phoenix Project, University of Michigan, sample M–838). The similarity in the inventories of the Thomas Riggs and the Paul Brave sites implies approximate
contemporaneity. Sites in North Dakota here regarded as components
of the Thomas Riggs Focus have been variously estimated to date
about A.D. 1250–1300 (Howard, 1962), A.D. 1350–1450 (Hewes, 1949
a, p. 23), and A.D. 1200–1300 (Will, 1946, p. 17). If the radiocarbon
date for Thomas Riggs is accurate, and the postulated upstream
movement valid, it is our impression that Paul Brave and adjacent
sites date between about A.D. 1300 and 1400.

LITERATURE CITED

BOWERS, ALFRED W.
      ———— A history of the Mandan and Hidatsa. MS., Ph. D. dissertation,
            Univ. Chicago, 1948.
      1950. Mandan social and ceremonial organization. Univ. Chicago Press.
CHAMPE, JOHN L.
      1948. *Review:* The upper Missouri River Valley aboriginal culture in North
            Dakota, by George F. Will and Thad. C. Hecker. Amer. Antiq., vol.
            13, No. 3, pp. 261–262.
DAVIS, E. MOTT.
      1956. Archeological survey of the Big Sandy Reservoir area, southwestern
            Wyoming. Notebook No. 2, Lab. Anthrop., Univ. Nebraska.
FENENGA, FRANKLIN.
      1953. The weights of chipped stone points : a clue to their functions. South-
            west Jour. Anthrop., vol. 9, No. 3, pp. 309–323.

HEWES, GORDON W.
    1949 a. The 1947 summer field session in archeology, University of North
            Dakota. Proc. Fifth Plains Conf. for Archeol., Notebook No. 1,
            Lab. Anthrop., Univ. Nebraska, pp. 21–24.
    1949 b. Pottery from the sites excavated by the 1947 North Dakota field
            session. Proc. Fifth Plains Conf. for Archeol., Notebook No. 1,
            Lab. Anthrop., Univ. Nebraska, pp. 58–67.
HOWARD, JAMES H.
    1962. Report of the investigation of the Tony Glas site, 32EM3, Emmons
            County, North Dakota, Univ. North Dakota Anthrop. Pap., No. 1.
HURT, WESLEY R., JR.
    1951. Report of the investigations of the Swanson site, 39BR16, Brule
            County, South Dakota, 1950. South Dakota Archaeol. Comm.
            Archaeol. Studies, Circ. No. 3.
    1952. Hafted knives from South Dakota. Museum News, W. H. Over
            Museum, vol. 13, No. 8, pp. 1–2.
    1953. Report of the investigation of the Thomas Riggs Site, 39HU1, Hughes
            County, South Dakota, 1952. South Dakota Archaeol. Comm.
            Archaeol. Studies, Circ. No. 5.
KIDDER, A. V.
    1932. Artifacts of Pecos. Phillips Acad., Southwestern Exped. Pap. No. 6.
            New Haven.
KIVETT, MARVIN F.
    1949. Archaeological investigations in Medicine Creek Reservoir, Nebraska.
            Amer. Antiq., vol. 14, No. 4, pp. 278–284.
KLEINSASSER, GLENN.
    1953. Thomas Riggs pottery types. Appendix 4. *In* Report on the investi-
            gation of the Thomas Riggs site, 39HU1, Hughes County, South
            Dakota, by Wesley R. Hurt, Jr. South Dakota Archaeol. Comm.
            Archaeol. Studies, Circ. No. 5, pp. 22–31.
LEHMER, DONALD J.
    1954. Archeological investigations in the Oahe Dam area, South Dakota,
            1950–51. Bur. Amer. Ethnol. Bull. 158, Riv. Bas. Surv. Pap.,
            No. 7.
LIBBY, ORIN G.
    1906. A Mandan woman's game. State Hist. Soc. North Dakota, Coll., vol.
            1, pp. 444–445.
MAERZ, A., and PAUL, M. REA.
    1930. A dictionary of color.
MELEEN, ELMER E.
    1938. A preliminary report of the Mitchell Indian village site and burial
            mounds, on Firesteel Creek, Davison County South Dakota. Univ.
            South Dakota Museum, Archaeol. Studies, Circ. 2, pt. 1.
SCHEANS, DANIEL J.
    ———— The archeology of the Battle-Porcupine Creek area, Sioux County,
            North Dakota. MS. submitted to Nat. Park Serv., Region 2; on
            file at the State Hist. Soc. North Dakota, 1957. Bismarck.
SMITH, CARLYLE S.
    1953. Notes and news: Plains. Amer. Antiq., vol. 19, No. 2, pp. 197–198.
STEINBRUECK, EMIL R.
    1906. The manufacture of the horn ornaments of the Mandan. State Hist.
            Soc. North Dakota, Coll., vol. 1, pp. 456–459.

STRONG, WILLIAM D.
    1935. An introduction to Nebraska archeology. Smithsonian Misc. Coll.,
        vol. 93, No. 10.
    1940. From history to prehistory in the Northern Great Plains. Smith-
        sonian Misc. Coll., vol. 100, pp. 353–394.
WEDEL, WALDO R.
    1940. Culture sequence in the Central Great Plains. Smithsonian Misc.
        Coll., vol. 100, pp. 191–352.
    1955. Archeological materials from the vicinity of Mobridge, South Dakota.
        Bur. Amer. Ethnol. Bull. 157, Anthrop. Pap. No. 45, pp. 73–188.
WHEELER, RICHARD P.
    1954. Check list of Middle Missouri pottery wares, types, and subtypes.
        Plains Anthrop., No. 2, pp. 3–21.
    1955. Review: Report of the investigation of the Thomas Riggs Site, 39HU1,
        Hughes County, South Dakota, 1952, by Wesley R. Hurt, Jr. Amer.
        Antiq., vol. 20, No. 4, pt. 1, pp. 398–399.
    1956. "Quill flatteners" or pottery modeling tools? Plains Anthrop., No. 6,
        pp. 17–20.
WILL, GEORGE F.
    1924. Archaelogy of the Missouri valley. Anthrop. Pap., Amer. Mus. Nat.
        Hist., vol. 22, pt. 6, pp. 285–344.
    1946. Tree ring studies in North Dakota. North Dakota Agr. Coll. Exp.
        Station, Bull. 338.
    1948. Additional notes on dendro-chronology in the Dakotas. Plains Archeol.
        Conf. News Letter, vol. 1, No. 4, pp. 68–70 (reprint).
WILL, GEORGE F., and HECKER, THAD. C.
    1944. Upper Missouri River Valley aboriginal culture in North Dakota.
        North Dakota Hist. Quart., vol. 11, Nos. 1 and 2.
WILL, GEORGE F., and SPINDEN, H. J.
    1906. The Mandans, a study of their culture, archaeology, and language.
        Harvard Univ., Peabody Mus. Amer. Archaeol. and Ethnol. Pap.,
        vol. 3, No. 4.
WOOD, W. RAYMOND.
    1957. Perforated elk teeth: a functional and historical analysis. Amer.
        Antiq., vol. 22, No. 4, pt. 1, pp. 381–387.
    1962. Notes on the bison bone from the Paul Brave, Huff, and Demery sites
        (Oahe Reservoir). Plains Anthrop., vol. 7, No. 17, pp. 201–204.
WOOLWORTH, ALAN R.
    1956. Archeological investigations at site 32ME59 (Grandmother's Lodge).
        North Dakota Hist., vol. 23, No. 2, pp. 79–102.

PLATES

a, Aerial view of the Paul Brave site and environs.   *b*, House 2.

a, Feature 70 in House 3.   *b*, Burned timbers in House 3.

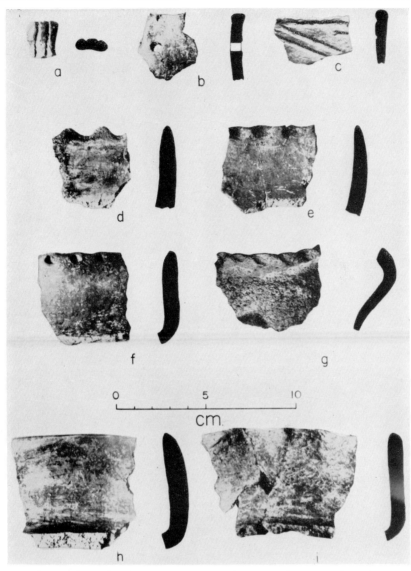

Pottery rim sherds. *a*, Fort Yates Cord Impressed strap handle; *b, d–h*, Riggs Plain Rim; *c*, Riggs Incised Rim; *i*, Riggs Pinched Rim.

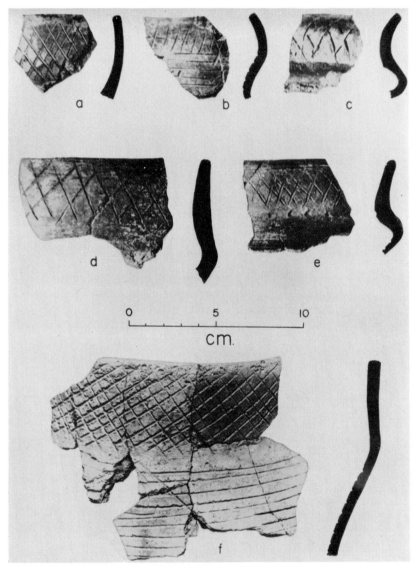

Cross-hatched rim sherds.   *a–b, f*, Riggs Cross-Hatched Rim; *c–e*, Fort Yates Cross-Hatched Rim.

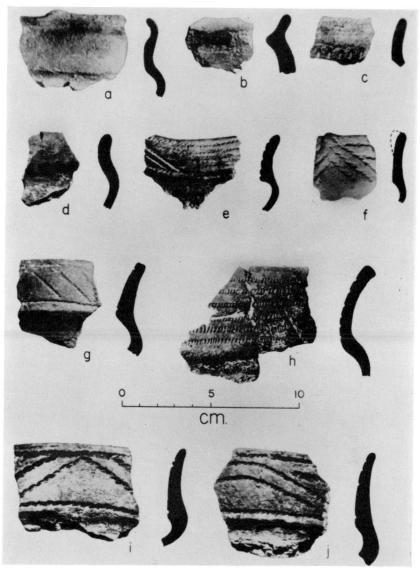

Pottery examples A–D, and cord-impressed rim sherds.   a, Example A; b, Example B;
c, Example C; d, Example D; e–j, Fort Yates Cord-Impressed Rim.

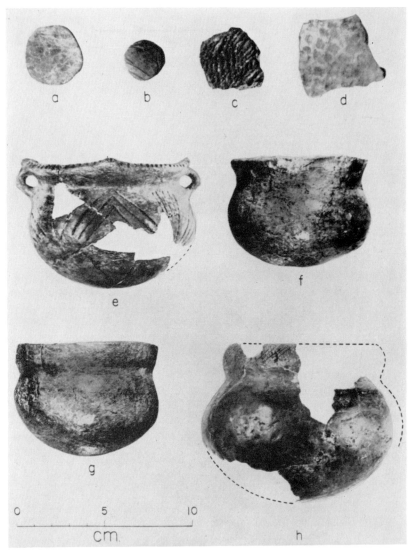

Pottery disks, body sherds, and vessels.   *a–b*, Pottery disks; *c*, cord-roughened body sherd; *d*, check-stamped body sherd; *e*, Riggs Plain Rim miniature vessel; *f–g*, plain miniature vessels; *h*, Fort Yates Cross-Hatched Rim vessel.

SMITHSONIAN INSTITUTION
Bureau of American Ethnology
Bulletin 189

River Basin Surveys Papers, No. 34

The Demery Site (39CO1), Oahe Reservoir Area, South Dakota

By ALAN R. WOOLWORTH and W. RAYMOND WOOD

661–932—64——6

CONTENTS

		PAGE
Introduction		71
Archeology of the site		73
Description		73
Excavations		75
Houses		78
Human remains		85
Features observed		86
Artifacts		88
Pottery		88
General characteristics		90
Body sherds		90
Descriptive categories and types		92
Chipped stone		105
Ground stone		113
Bone artifacts		116
Antler artifacts		123
Shell artifacts		124
Perishable remains		124
Faunal remains		126
Discussion		126
Structures		126
Pottery		128
Other artifacts		132
Conclusions		134
Literature cited		135

TABLES

1.	Features recorded during the excavation of Demery site, 39CO1	86
2.	Probable number of vessels represented by the rim sherd sample	105

ILLUSTRATIONS

PLATES

(All plates follow p. 138)

7. *a*, House 2. The view is southwest; excavation is beginning in House 3 in background. *b*, House 4. The view is southwest, toward the entrance.
8. *a*, The entrance passage of House 1; the view is southeast. *b*, Collapsed wall poles on the north wall of House 4.
9. Pottery rim sherds and handles.
10. Horizontally incised rim sherds. Note the stab-and-drag treatment to the left of the handle in *j*.
11. Cord-impressed rim sherds.
12. Incised and plain rim sherds.
13. Miscellaneous rim sherds.
14. Restored pottery vessels. *a*, Vessel 1, House 2. *b*, Vessel from Feature 93, House 4.

TEXT FIGURES

PAGE

13. Pottery rim profiles A–X_____ 91
14. Pottery rim and shoulder design elements_____ 93
15. Pottery rim and shoulder design elements_____ 94
16. Pottery shoulder design elements_____ 95
17. Projectile points_____ 107
18. Chipped stone knives_____ 108
19. Chipped and ground stone artifacts. *a–b*, Drills. *c–h*, End scrapers.
     i–j, Game pieces. *k*, Catlinite disk-bowl pipe_____ 109
20. Basketry, woodwork, and bone artifacts. *a*, Charred, twilled basketry
     fragment. *b*, Slotted bone knife handle. *c*, Charred, slotted wooden
     knife handle. *d–e*, Bison ulna tools. *f*, Bison radius pick. *g*, Bison
     scapula hoe_____ 111
21. Ground stone artifacts. *a, d*, Arrow shaft smoothers. *b*, Catlinite pipe
     bowl. *c*, Sandstone disk. *e*, Diorite celt. *f*, Grooved abrad-
     ing stone_____ 114
22. Artifacts of bone, antler, and shell. *a*, Scored bison rib. *b*, Serrated
     rib tip. *c*, Arrow shaft wrench. *d–e*, Shell scrapers. *f*, Antler
     cylinder. *g*, Scapula "cleaver." *h*, Bone knife_____ 117
23. Artifacts of antler and bone. *a–b*, Antler bracelets. *c*, Miniature
     bone awl. *d–e*, Fishhooks. *f*, Split rib awl. *g–h*, "Rib-edge" awls.
     i, Bone tube. *j*, Pottery modeling tool. *k*, Bird bone awl_____ 119
24. Artifacts of bone and shell. *a*, Pendant. *b*, Modified shell. *c*, Shell
     "face." *d*, Shell disk bead. *e*, Cancellous tissue abrader. *f–j*,
     Bone awls_____ 120

MAPS

6. Location of the Demery site and other sites discussed_____ 72
7. The Demery site (39CO1), showing excavations_____ 76
8. Excavations 5, 7, and 8_____ 77
9. Upper: Feature 1, excavation 2. Lower: House 5, excavation 5
     (facing) _____ 78
10. House 1, excavation 7_____ 79
11. House 2, excavation 5_____ 81
12. House 3, excavation 5_____ 83
13. House 4, excavation 5_____ 84

THE DEMERY SITE (39CO1), OAHE RESERVOIR AREA, SOUTH DAKOTA [1]

By Alan R. Woolworth and W. Raymond Wood

INTRODUCTION

In the summer of 1956 an archeological field party from the State Historical Society of North Dakota carried out excavations at the Demery site, in the upper part of the Oahe Reservoir, in Corson County, South Dakota. Funds for the project were provided under a cooperative agreement with the National Park Service, Department of the Interior, and through appropriations by the North Dakota State Legislature. The excavations were conducted between June 18 and August 31, 1956, under the supervision of Alan R. Woolworth and W. Raymond Wood, then staff archeologists with the State Historical Society, with Frederic Hadleigh-West serving as assistant archeologist.

The major reason for selecting Demery for excavation in 1956 was that the site is the northernmost manifestation of the "Category B" complex on the mainstem of the Missouri River. In 1949, Paul L. Cooper had described the Category B pottery complex from sites along the Missouri River in South Dakota (1949, pp. 303–306). The Category B rim design consists of a solid band of horizontally incised or trailed lines on rim exteriors. Cooper demonstrated the wide spatial distribution of this form of pottery rim decoration, and predicted that the delimitation of the temporal and spatial scope of this archeological complex would provide one of the more important chapters in Plains prehistory. The Demery site is only one of the many sites bearing pottery of this character in the Central Plains and Middle Missouri areas. Because of its extreme northern geographic setting, it was anticipated that Demery would provide data on a peripheral variant of the complex as it was known from work in sites in central and southeastern South Dakota. (See map 6.)

Much of the credit for the successful completion of the work at Demery is due Russell Reid, Superintendent of the State Historical

[1] Submitted February 1962.

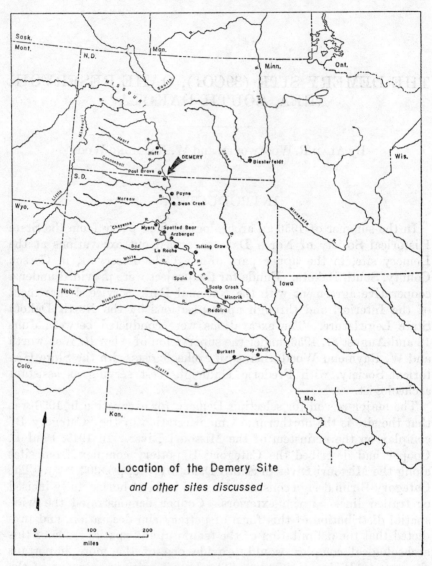

MAP 6.—Location of the Demery site and other sites discussed.

Society of North Dakota, for his unfailing assistance in every phase
of the work. The field party was established in the town of Fort
Yates, N. Dak. Mr. J. W. Wellington, then Superintendent of
the Standing Rock Indian Agency, in Fort Yates, did everything in
his power to make the summer a pleasant and successful one. The
Missouri Basin Project, Smithsonian Institution, loaned photographic
equipment and was, as always, helpful in many other matters. Bernard Weinreich, of Bismarck, N. Dak., prepared the photo-

graphic illustrations; their quality is a tribute to his skill. Frederic Hadleigh-West was in charge of mapping the site and the excavations, a task of no mean proportions considering the distances involved and the equipment available. Permission to excavate on tribal land was kindly granted by the Tribal Council of the Standing Rock Indian Reservation. Mr. J. Dan Howard, then Chairman of the Tribal Council, aided the field party in many ways. Crew members included Robert P. Barr and Stephen W. Robinson of Grand Forks, North Dakota; George E. Archambault and William C. Gipp of Fort Yates, N. Dak.; Mark F. Blum of Lincoln, Nebr.; and Craig Gannon of Bismarck, N. Dak. The assistance of each of these contributors is gratefully acknowledged. We are also grateful for the comments and constructive criticism of the manuscript provided by Robert L. Stephenson, Warren W. Caldwell, and Robert W. Neuman, of the Smithsonian Institution, Missouri Basin Project.

The laboratory analysis of the pottery was carried out by the junior author, who also prepared the final maps and the line drawings. The remaining artifacts were processed by the senior author, and both of us are jointly responsible for the discussion and conclusions. The field notes, maps, photographs, and artifacts from Demery are on file in the museum of the State Historical Society of North Dakota, in Bismarck, for preservation and further study.

ARCHEOLOGY OF THE SITE

DESCRIPTION

The Demery site, 39CO1, is in the SE1/4 of sec. 21, and in the SW1/4 of sec. 22, T. 23 N., R. 29 W., Corson County, S. Dak. It is on the west bank of the Missouri River about 16 miles downstream from the town of Fort Yates. The site lies on a large, flat terrace overlooking the floodplains of the Missouri River and John Grass Creek (map 7). A large gully separates the site area from the terrace to the south, and a low swale to the west leaves the site nearly surrounded by low land. To the west, the terrain is level for nearly half a mile, where the Missouri River bluffs rise gradually from the valley floor to the treeless plains. A small intermittent stream, locally known as Black Eagle Creek or as John Grass Creek, is just north of the site. The reputed cabin site of the Dakota chief, John Grass, is a few hundred feet upstream from the bridge spanning the creek bearing his name on the Kenel to Fort Yates road. The North Dakota-South Dakota boundary is just north of John Grass Creek. Fire Heart Butte, a high, flat-topped prominence, rises above the surrounding upland plains about 5 miles northwest of the site.

The 1,610-foot contour line roughly delimits the area containing cultural remains, but the majority of surface material and most of the excavations were carried out within an area covered by heavy vegetation (map 7). This area, consisting of about 2 acres, appears to have been the major village area. About 10 percent of the area was stripped of overburden by a bulldozer and a road patrol. Five houses were located by this method and subsequently excavated, and two other probable house sites were located. A speculative projection, based on the distribution of these houses, gives a total of about 30 dwellings in the village.

Demery appears to have been an open, unfortified site. A test trench dug from the east wall of House 4 in excavation 5 to the terrace edge revealed no evidence of fortification, and a close inspection of the terrain and of aerial photographs revealed nothing suggesting the presence of a fortifying ditch. In an effort to find burials, test pits were dug along the terrace edge south of excavation 7, but no positive evidence of either burials or occupational debris was found.

Most of the area bearing heavy vegetation had been cultivated, which obliterated indications of surface features. Only a few acres of grassland near the creek are still in undisturbed sod, and somewhere in this area Will and Hecker (1944, p. 87) reported a number of circular lodge ruins. Early in the field season a single circular depression was noted here, but excavation 2, which explored this feature, yielded the remains of an irregular pit, Feature 1, which was interpreted as a borrow area (map 9).

A few flint chips and body sherds were found near the bridge across John Grass Creek (designated by an "x" on map 7). Surface inspection of the terrace beyond the large gully south of the site, near the remains of the former Demery home, revealed no sherds or other evidence of aboriginal occupation, although there are a few sherds in the State Historical Society collections that are said to be from this vicinity. These sherds resemble those from the major occupation of the Demery site in all details, and they are probably the source for the statement by Will and Hecker (1944, p. 88) that there was a small site contemporaneous with Demery south of the gully.

A number of grassy surface irregularities, as well as many clumps of dense buckbrush, occurred throughout the site area. The excavations revealed no correlation between either these irregularities or the brush patches and the house sites. In fact, the houses appeared to have been on level, grassy areas. Toward the end of August, however, when a dense cover of sunflowers and weeds had overgrown the site, there were spots on level, grassy areas where this cover was exceedingly dense, and such areas we feel were house sites. Since the field season was over we did not have the opportunity to investigate them, although it would clearly have been desirable.

EXCAVATIONS

Six excavation units in different parts of the site were stripped to the approximate base of the plow zone by means of a bulldozer and a road patrol. At this depth the houses, pits, and other features became clearly visible as mixed earth in otherwise sterile soil. Features were marked by stakes while the soil was still moist and their outlines distinct, and later excavated by hand tools. Two other units, excavations 3 and 4, were excavated wholly by hand methods.

Houses appeared as large circular areas of mixed earth which sometimes contained charred timbers. Four of the houses found were fully excavated and a fifth house was cross sectioned. The presence of two additional houses, designated as Houses 6 and 7 on the site map (maps 7, 8), is postulated on the basis of charred timbers noted on the floor of the road patrol cuts, but time did not allow the investigation of these features. In view of the large areas stripped by the road patrol, houses were infrequent and widely separated. It is not probable that many houses were missed by the excavators, since soil disturbance was rather clearly defined in the dense, buff soil below the plow line.

The site maps were prepared by West with the use of a plane table and alidade, and distances were chained. The individual houses were mapped using a stake in the center of the primary fireplace as a datum.

Excavation 1 (map 7).—This unit, in the northwest part of the site, was originally a series of test pits laid out on a 5-foot grid. Features 40, 41, 42, and 43 were recorded here, respectively: an irregular trash-filled pit, two basin-shaped pits, and a bell-shaped pit. This area was later stripped with a bulldozer and subsequently smoothed by a road patrol. Numerous postholes and fireplaces were found, but no definite dwelling units were detected. The area apparently lay on the periphery of the village. The unit was 275 feet long and about 75 feet wide.

Excavation 2 (maps 7 and 9).—This excavation was designed to explore a circular depression in the northwest part of the site, which appeared from surface observations to be about 10 feet in diameter. It was heavily overgrown with weeds and buckbrush and superficially resembled an earth lodge depression. A test trench was dug from the north edge into the pit, and the bulldozer was then used to strip the overburden from an area 80 feet long and 55 feet wide. Feature 1, a large irregular pit nearly 20 feet in diameter, is interpreted as a borrow pit. The floor of the feature was littered with broken animal bones, pottery, and stone fragments. Features 48 and 49, both of them bell-shaped pits, were outside of this feature.

Excavation 3 (map 7).—This excavation was made in the north part of the village area, and consisted of a test trench 28 feet long and 5 feet wide. A single basin-shaped pit, Feature 50, was re-

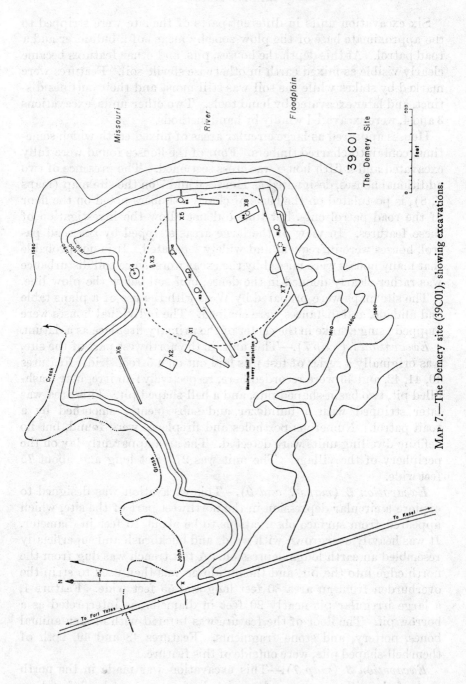

MAP 7.—The Demery site (39C01), showing excavations.

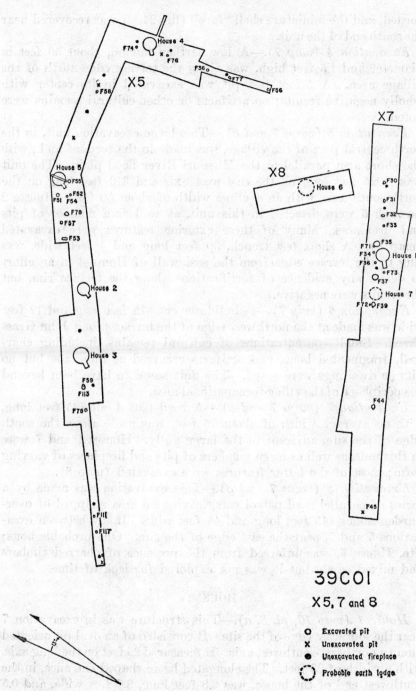

MAP 8.—Excavations 5, 7, and 8.

corded, and the miniature shell "face" (fig. 24, c) was recovered near the south end of the unit.

Excavation 4 (map 7).—A low earthen mound, about 50 feet in diameter and 1.5 feet high, was along the terrace edge north of the village area. A 5-foot test pit was excavated in its center with wholly negative results; no artifacts or other cultural remains were noted.

Excavation 5 (maps 7 and 8).—This large excavation unit, in the north central part of the village, was made in the form of an L, with the short arm parallel to the Missouri River flood plain. The unit was 1,025 feet long on the east-west axis and 310 feet long on the north-south axis, with an average width of about 50 feet. Houses 2 through 5 were detected in this unit, as well as a number of pits and fireplaces. Many of these exterior features were excavated (map 8). A short test trench, 30 feet long and 4 feet wide, was dug to the terrace edge from the east wall of House 4 in an effort to detect any evidence of fortifications along the terrace rim, but the results were negative.

Excavation 6 (map 7).—A bulldozer cut 315 feet long and 12 feet wide was made at the northwest edge of the terrace along John Grass Creek. Small concentrations of cultural remains, including charcoal, fragmented bone, and artifacts occurred at intervals, but no pits or dwellings were noted. The unit seems to have been beyond the periphery of the village occupational area.

Excavation 7 (maps 7 and 8).—A road patrol cut 725 feet long, with an average width of about 75 feet, was made along the south edge of the site, adjacent to the large gully. Houses 1 and 7 were in this unit, as well as large numbers of pits and fireplaces of varying form; most of the latter features were excavated (map 8).

Excavation 8 (maps 7 and 8).—This excavation was made by a series of parallel road patrol cuts, leaving an area stripped of overburden about 145 feet long and 45 feet wide. It lay between excavations 5 and 7, near the east edge of the site. One probable house site, House 6, was inferred from the presence of charred timbers and mixed earth, but it was not explored for lack of time.

HOUSES

House 1 (map 10, pl. 8, a).—This structure was in excavation 7 near the southeast edge of the site. It consisted of an oval pit oriented along a northeast-southwest axis. It measured 25 feet on the long axis, with a width of 23 feet. The elongated basin-shaped entrance, in the southwest end of the house, was 6.8 feet long, 2.7 feet wide, and 0.5 foot deep. A clearly defined row of posts occurred only along the southeast side, extending 10 feet out from the house shoulder.

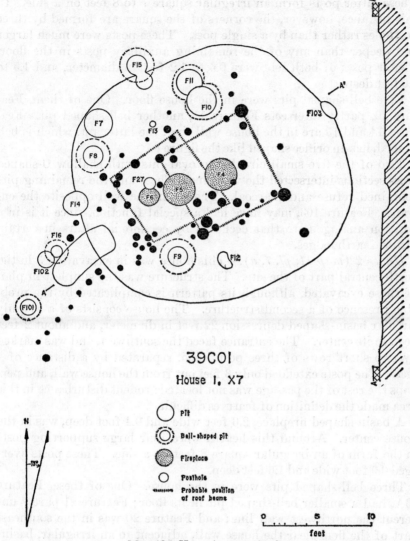

39C01

House 1, X7

○ Pit

◎ Bell-shaped pit

⦿ Fireplace

○ Posthole

⋯⋯ Probable position of roof beams

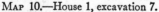

0   5   10

feet

MAP 10.—House 1, excavation 7.

There were three basin-shaped fireplaces in the shallow, dish-shaped house floor. Feature 4 was centrally located and was probably the hearth for the original lodge; it was 3 feet wide and 0.6 foot deep. Feature 5 was offset to the southwest from the midpoint of Feature 4, and was the same size as Feature 4. Feature 6 was a small auxiliary fireplace between Feature 5 and the entrance.

The four large center posts around Feature 4 form a square 8.5 feet on a side. Another set of postholes, around Feature 5, may be the result of rebuilding the house and setting the posts nearer the entrance.

These latter posts form an irregular square 7 to 8 feet on a side. In this instance, however, the corners of the square are formed by three postholes rather than by a single post. These posts were much larger and deeper than any of the remaining auxiliary posts in the floor. Center posts of both sets were 0.6 to 1.2 feet in diameter, and 1.5 to 2.0 feet deep.

Five bell-shaped pits were in the house floor. One of them, Feature 10, partly intersects Feature 11, another bell-shaped pit. Features 14 and 15 are in the house wall line; the latter pit, which is bell shaped, has an orifice shaped like the figure 8.

Two of the five small circular to oval pits with shallow U-shaped cross sections intersected the wall line. These and the remaining pits contained refuse and charcoal. The pit in the wall opposite the entrance, Feature 103, may have had a special function, since it is in a position analogous to that occupied by ceremonial altars in certain historic earth lodges.

House 2 (map 11, pl. 7, a).—This house was in excavation 5 in the north central part of the site. The structure was the simplest in plan of those excavated, although its pattern is complicated by the probable presence of a second structure. The house consists of a roughly circular basin-shaped depression 22 feet in diameter, and about 2 feet deep in its center. The entrance faced the southwest, and was marked by two short rows of three posts each, separated by a distance of 4 feet. The posts extended only 3 feet out from the house wall, and perhaps the rest of the passage was not located; rodent disturbance in this area made the definition of features difficult.

A basin-shaped fireplace, 2.6 feet wide and 0.4 foot deep, was in the house center. Around this hearth were four large supporting posts in the form of an irregular square 8 feet on a side. These posts averaged 0.9 foot wide and 1.6 feet deep.

Three bell-shaped pits were in the house. One of these, Feature 23A, had a smaller bell-shaped pit in its floor; Feature 21 partly undercut the northwest wall line; and Feature 20 was in the southeast part of the floor near the house wall, adjacent to an irregular, basin-shaped trash pit, Feature 112. Two circular, basin-shaped pits were in the house. One of them, Feature 24, was in the house wall opposite the entrance, in a position analogous to that of Feature 103 in House 1. The other pit, Feature 18, was between the two center posts facing the entrance; it contained several artifacts. Two shattered pottery vessels were near the north wall, opposite the entrance. Both of them were smashed flat, and must have been broken by the weight of the collapsed roof. One of them contained charred fragments of animal bone. Vessel 1 was restored (pl. 14, *a*).

Feature 22 was a fireplace in the southwest house wall line. It had a series of seven posts set about it, approximately in the form of a

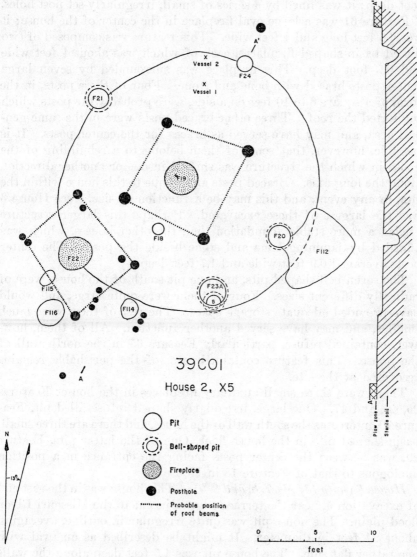

MAP 11.—House 2, excavation 5.

square, 6 to 8 feet on a side. It appears to be a second and smaller
structure overlapping with the floor of House 2, but whether it was
earlier or later could not be determined.

House 3 (*map 12*).—This structure was in excavation 5, in the
north central part of the site. The house was contained in an oval
depression 2 feet deep, 32 feet long, and 30 feet wide. The long axis
was in line with the orientation of the entrance. The shallow entrance
passage, facing the southwest, was 8 feet long, 4 feet wide, and 0.5

foot deep; it was lined by a series of small, irregularly-set post holes.

Feature 61 was a large oval fireplace in the center of the house; it was 6.6 feet long and 4 feet wide. This feature was composed of two linked basin-shaped fireplaces, each of which was about 4 feet wide and 0.8 foot deep. This fireplace was surrounded by seven large center posts braced with bone and stone. Four of these posts, in the form of a square 8 to 10 feet on a side, were probably the posts which supported the roof. Three other braced posts were in the same general area, and may have served as braces for the center posts. It is possible, however, that some of them belong to a rebuilding of the house in which the structure was shifted in one or another direction along the long axis. Braced posts are unique to this house within the site, in any event, and this may be a function of size, since House 3 was the largest of those excavated. Perhaps this larger structure needed a more stable foundation than the other houses, which was afforded by jamming bone and stone beside the posts. The center posts averaged 0.9 foot wide and 1.7 feet deep.

The seven bell-shaped pits, and one pit south of the house, were of radically different sizes. Four of them were quite large, and would have provided adequate storage space. The rest of them were much smaller, and may have served another function. All of them, however, contained refuse, particularly Feature 65 in the north wall of the house. This feature contained most of the perishable remains recovered at the site.

There were three small auxiliary fireplaces in the house: Features 25, 46, and 47. One large, irregularly shaped refuse-filled pit, Feature 79, intercepts the south wall of the house, and there are three small, basin-shaped pits in the house floor. One of the latter pits, Feature 29, was between the center posts facing the entrance in a position analogous to that of Feature 18 in House 2.

House 4 (*map 13; pls. 7, b, and 8, b*).—This house was in the east end of excavation 5, near the terrace edge adjacent to the Missouri River flood plain. The house pit was quite irregular in outline, averaging about 24 feet in diameter. It might be described as an oval with one rather flat side. The house pit was 1.5 feet deep along the walls and attained a maximum depth of 2.8 feet near the fireplace. An elongated, depressed entrance passage was in the southwestern perimeter of the house wall, measuring 6.5 feet long, 3.5 feet wide, and 0.4 foot deep.

Feature 91, the basin-shaped central fireplace, was 3.4 feet wide and 0.6 foot deep. It was an oval pit surrounded by and filled with white ash and burned earth. Another centrally located basin-shaped fireplace, Feature 104, joined Feature 91 on the northeast edge. The latter pit was oval in outline, measuring 1.8 by 2.1 feet, and was 0.4

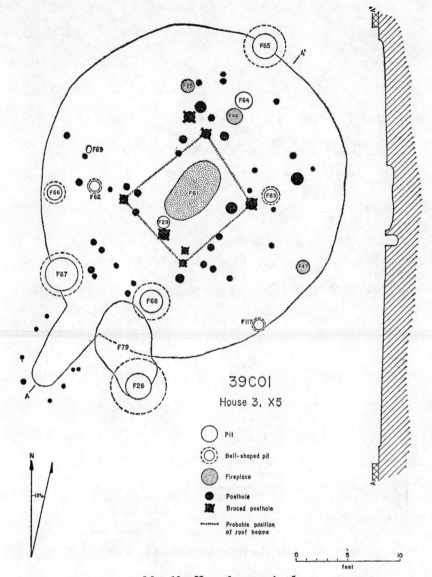

MAP 12.—House 3, excavation 5.

foot deep. It is possible that this fireplace belonged to a structure other than the one represented by Feature 91, the primary hearth.

This dwelling appears to have been rebuilt at least once and possibly twice. Hence, the center posts are a maze, but in general they form an irregular square 8 feet on a side around the hearth. These posts average about 0.7 foot in diameter and 2.0 feet in depth. In four instances, two or more of them were in small pits. These pits

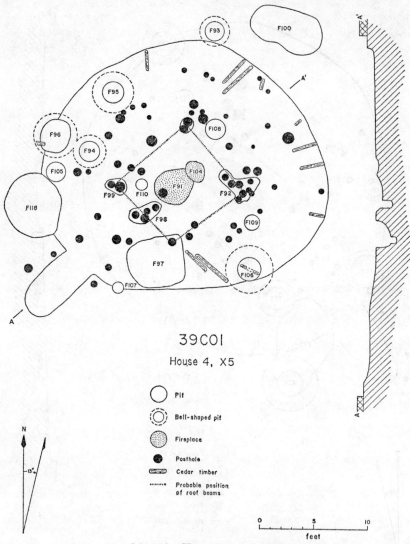

39C01

House 4, X5

○ Pit

◌ Bell-shaped pit

⬤ Fireplace

● Posthole

▭ Cedar timber

⋯⋯ Probable position
of roof beams

N

-13°-

0   5   10
feet

MAP 13.—House 4, excavation 5.

may have resulted from a reconstruction in which the old posts were
removed and new postholes dug beside the old ones.

Four bell-shaped pits were in the house floor and another was just
outside the house wall line. All of them were quite large, and two
of them, Features 94 and 96, intersected at their bases. Four small,
basin-shaped pits were in the house floor and another intersected the
wall line. One large irregular pit, Feature 97, was in the house floor;
this pit predates the house, since one of the center posts was intrusive
into it. This fact is relevant to the problem of cultural succession at

Demery, since sherds of Thomas Riggs Focus types were in it—pottery which predates the major occupation of the site. Another large pit, Feature 118, intersected the house wall north of the entrance.

The charred wall timbers along the walls inside the house pit are of special interest. They are discussed in more detail later in the text, but they are taken as evidence that the houses were covered by poles, the butts of which were set on the house shoulder outside the house with the tops leaning against the stringers connecting the center posts. These poles were covered by charred grass.

House 5 (map 9).—This structure was in excavation 5 in the northeast part of the site. Time did not permit its complete excavation, but a cross section revealed the basin-shaped central fireplace, two small bell-shaped pits, and three postholes. The entrance was not found. The house pit was 22 feet in diameter, with a central fireplace 2.5 feet in diameter and 0.5 foot deep. This feature was basin shaped, and somewhat more regular than those in the other houses. The house pit was about 1.5 feet deep.

HUMAN REMAINS

Three bones were found in widely separated parts of the site. A femur (and an incisor) were in Feature 32, an irregularly shaped pit in excavation 7; a sacrum was in Feature 77, an irregularly shaped pit in excavation 5; and a cranial fragment was in the backdirt of excavation 2. These bones, all of them from adults, were in refuse-filled pits outside of dwellings; none of them were stained with color or show any other special treatment.

The head was broken away from the femur at the neck, and the epicondyles and surrounding bone of the medial and lateral condyles are missing. The condyles are fused to the shaft, indicating that the individual was more than 17 or 18 years old. The third trochanter is 6 mm. high, and the middle of the shaft is oval, with a slight linea aspera. Measurements include:

	Millimeters
Maximum length (from surface of the lateral condyle to the upper extremity of the greater trochanter)	390
Subtrochanteric diameter, antero-posterior	20
Subtrochanteric diameter, lateral	32
Middle shaft diameter, antero-posterior	22
Middle shaft diameter, lateral	27

The crown of the incisor is worn down and the pulp exposed. The pulp cavity, however, had receded with the attrition of the tooth.

The fifth sacral vertebra of the sacrum and part of the fourth are lacking and, since the borders of the bone are broken, length and breadth are not obtainable. Since all the segments are fused, the individual was more than 25 or 30 years old. The cranial fragment appears to be part of the occipital bone; one edge shows part of a complex lamboidal suture.

FEATURES OBSERVED

The 118 features recorded during the excavation of Demery are tabulated below in table 1. While most of the feature numbers were assigned to pits in the houses and in the village area, a number of them were used to designate houses, entrance passages, and other structural details. These features are excluded from table 1 since they are described in detail in the preceding text. Maps 7–9 give a general picture of the major areas investigated at the site, and the location of all features not in or immediately contiguous to the houses.

TABLE 1.—*Features recorded during the excavation of the Demery site, 39CO1*

Feature No.	Excava- tion No.	Depth	Dimensions	Identification
			Feet	
1	2	2.0	Max. length, 21.0; width, 20.0.	Borrow pit.
4	7	.6	Diam., 3.0_____	Central fireplace, House 1.
5	7	.5	Diam., 3.0_____	Auxiliary central fire- place, House 1.
6	7	.4	Diam., 2.0_____	Auxiliary fireplace, House 1.
7	7	.5	Diam., 2.0_____	Basin-shaped pit, House 1.
8	7	2.0	Orifice, 1.8; base, 3.2__	Bell-shaped pit, House 1.
9	7	2.0	Orifice, 1.8; base, 3.5__	Bell-shaped pit, House 1.
10	7	2.1	Orifice, 2.8; base, 3.6__	Bell-shaped pit, House 1.
11	7	1.2	Orifice, 2.2; base, 2.8__	Bell-shaped pit, House 1.
12	7	1.1	Length, 1.7; width, 1.1_	Oval pit, House 1.
13	7	.6	Diam., 0.5_____	Basin-shaped pit, House 1.
14	7	1.0	Diam., 2.2_____	Basin-shaped pit, House 1.
15	7	3.5	Orifice, 2.0; base, 3.8__	Bell-shaped pit, House 1.
16	7	2.2	Orifice, 1.2; base, 2.2__	Bell-shaped pit, House 1.
18	5	1.3	Diam., 0.9_____	Circular pit, House 2.
19	5	.4	Diam., 2.6_____	Central fireplace, House 2.
20	5	1.9	Orifice, 2.0; base, 2.5__	Bell-shaped pit, House 2.
21	5	1.9	Orifice, 1.8; base, 2.4__	Bell-shaped pit, House 2.
22	5	.6	Diam., 1.7×2.6_____	Fireplace, House 2 (with secondary structure?).
23A	5	1.9	Orifice, 2.4; base, 2.7__	Bell-shaped pit, House 2.
23B	5	1.3	Orifice, 1.5; base, 2.6__	Bell-shaped pit, in base of Feature 23A.
24	5	1.1	Diam., 1.3_____	Basin-shaped pit, House 2.
25	5	.4	Diam., 1.2_____	Auxiliary fireplace, House 3.
26	5	4.6	Orifice, 2.4; base, 5.5__	Bell-shaped pit, House 3.
27	7	1.5	Diam., 1.2_____	Deep, circular pit, House 1.

TABLE 1.—*Features recorded during the excavation of the Demery site, 39CO1*—
Continued

Feature No.	Excavation No.	Depth	Dimensions	Identification
		Feet		
28	5	2. 7	Orifice, 2.6; base, 4.5__	Bell-shaped pit.
29	5	1. 2	Diam., 1.1_____	Deep, circular pit, House 3.
30	7	. 2	Diam., 5.0×6.3_____	Irregularly shaped pit.
31	7	. 3	Diam., 4.3×6.0_____	Irregularly shaped pit.
32	7	1. 2	Diam., 3.8×6.3_____	Irregularly shaped pit.
33	7	1. 2	Orifice, 1.3; base, 1.6__	Bell-shaped pit.
34	7	1. 0	Diam., 2.8_____	Circular pit with steep sides, House 1.
35	7	1. 0	Diam., 12.0×18.5_____	Irregularly shaped pit, House 1.
36	7	4. 9	Orifice, 2.3; vase, 4.7__	Bell-shaped pit, House 1.
37	7	. 5	Diam., 7.3_____	Basin-shaped pit, House 1.
39	7	1. 2	Diam., 12.0×15.0_____	Irregularly shaped pit.
40	1	Ca. 1. 0	Diam., ca. 3.0_____	Irregularly shaped pit.
41	1	1. 0	Diam., 2.8_____	Basin-shaped pit.
42	1	. 4	Diam., 3.0×4.0_____	Basin-shaped pit.
43	1	3. 1	Orifice, 2.4; base, 5.5__	Bell-shaped pit.
44	7	. 7	Diam., 12.0×14.6_____	Irregularly shaped pit.
46	5	. 1	Diam., 1.6_____	Auxiliary fireplace, House 3.
47	5	. 1	Diam., 1.2_____	Auxiliary fireplace, House 3.
48	2	3. 0	Orifice, 2.5; base, 4.5__	Bell-shaped pit.
49	2	2. 1	Orifice, 2.6; base, 3.7__	Bell-shaped pit.
50	3	. 5	Diam., 2.3×3.0_____	Basin-shaped pit.
51	5	1. 0	Diam., 15.0_____	Irregularly shaped pit, House 5.
52	5	2. 9	Orifice, 2.8; base, 3.8__	Bell-shaped pit, House 5.
53	5	. 9	Diam., 15.4×19.8_____	Irregularly shaped pit.
54	5	3. 0	Orifice, 2.7; base, 4.0__	Bell-shaped pit, House 5.
55	5	2. 5	Diam., 11.1×14.5_____	Irregularly shaped pit, House 5.
56	5	. 3	Diam., 6.0_____	Irregularly shaped pit.
57	5	1. 0	Diam., 6.3×9.0_____	Irregularly shaped pit.
58	5	. 2	Diam., 6.0×10.0_____	Irregularly shaped pit.
59	5	1. 0	Diam., 14.0×22.0_____	Irregularly shaped pit.
61	5	. 8	Diam., 4.0×6.6_____	Two linked fireplaces, House 3.
62	5	1. 2	Orifice, 1.0; base, 1.4__	Bell-shaped pit, House 3.
63	5	1. 2	Orifice, 1.2; base, 1.8__	Bell-shaped pit, House 3.
64	5	. 8	Diam., 1.6_____	Basin-shaped pit, House 3.
65	5	3. 8	Orifice, 2.4; base, 4.0__	Bell-shaped pit, House 3.
66	5	1. 6	Orifice, 1.4; base, 2.0__	Bell-shaped pit, House 3.
67	5	3. 0	Orifice, 3.2; base, 4.2__	Bell-shaped pit, House 3.
68	5	3. 0	Orifice, 2.2; base, 3.6__	Bell-shaped pit, House 3.
69	5	. 4	Diam., 0.6×1.0_____	Basin-shaped pit, House 3.
71	7	3. 8	Orifice, 1.9; base, 4.4__	Bell-shaped pit, House 1.
72	7	2. 5	Orifice, 2.8; base, 3.5__	Bell-shaped pit.
73	7	2. 4	Diam., 2.6×3.6_____	Oval pit, House 1.
74	5	. 8	Diam., 3.8×4.0_____	Irregularly shaped pit, House 4.
75	5	1. 6	Diam., 5.0×7.0_____	Irregularly shaped pit.
76	5	. 5	Diam., 2.4×2.9_____	Irregularly shaped pit, House 4.
77	5	. 9	Diam., 8.6×9.0_____	Irregularly shaped pit.
78	5	3. 3	Orifice, 3.7; base, 3.9__	Bell-shaped pit.

TABLE 1.—*Features recorded during the excavation of the Demery site, 39C01—*
Continued

Feature No.	Excava- tion No.	Depth	Dimensions	Identification
			Feet	
79	5	1. 5	Diam., 4.8×8.0_____	Irregularly shaped pit, House 3.
81	5	. 5	Diam., 2.5_____	Central fireplace, House 5.
82	5	1. 5	Orifice, 1.8; base, 2.4__	Bell-shaped pit, House 5.
83	5	1. 5	Orifice, 1.1; base, 1.8__	Bell-shaped pit, House 5.
91	5	. 6	Diam., 3.4_____	Central fireplace, House 4.
92	5	2. 0	Diam., 1.0×3.2_____	Irregular pit, House 4.
93	5	1. 6	Orifice, 1.8; base, 2.8__	Bell-shaped pit, House 4.
94	5	2. 7	Orifice, 1.6; base, 3.0__	Bell-shaped pit, House 4.
95	5	2. 5	Orifice, 2.2; base, 3.8__	Bell-shaped pit, House 4.
96	5	2. 6	Orifice, 2.8; base, 4.6__	Bell-shaped pit, House 4.
97	5	2. 3	Diam., 4.9×5.5_____	Irregularly-shaped pit, House 4.
98	5	2. 0	Diam., 1.5×3.0_____	Irregular pit, House 4.
99	5	2. 0	Diam., 1.5×2.0_____	Irregular pit, House 4.
100	5	1. 2	Diam., 4.0×7.0_____	Irregular pit, House 4.
101	7	1. 6	Orifice, 1.5; base, 2.5__	Bell-shaped pit, House 1.
102	7	0. 7	Diam., 1.6_____	Basin-shaped pit, House 1.
103	7	1. 0	Diam., 1.0×1.9_____	Basin-shaped pit, House 1.
104	5	. 4	Diam., 2.0_____	Auxiliary central fire- place, House 4.
105	5	. 8	Diam., 1.8_____	Basin-shaped pit, House 4.
106	5	3. 0	Orifice, 2.2; base, 4.4__	Bell-shaped pit, House 4.
107	5	. 8	Diam., 1.3_____	Basin-shaped pit, House 4.
108	5	. 4	Diam., 2.2_____	Basin-shaped pit, House 4.
109	5	. 3	Diam., 1.6_____	Basin-shaped pit, House 4.
110	5	. 4	Diam., 1.1_____	Basin-shaped pit, House 4.
111	5	Ca. 3. 0	Orifice, 2.2; base, 4.0__	Bell-shaped pit.
112	5	. 7	Diam., 5.5×7.0_____	Irregularly shaped pit, House 2.
113	5	2. 2	Orifice, 2.0; base, 4.4__	Bell-shaped pit, House 3.
114	5	. 6	Diam., 1.4×1.8_____	Basin-shaped pit, House 2.
115	5	1. 0	Diam., 1.2×1.6_____	Basin-shaped pit, House 2.
116	5	. 8	Diam., 2.2×2.5_____	Basin-shaped pit, House 2.
117	5	1. 3	Orifice, 1.0; base, 1.4__	Bell-shaped pit, House 3.
118	5	1. 2	Diam., 5.2×6.0_____	Irregularly shaped pit, House 4.

ARTIFACTS

POTTERY

The pottery from Demery is abundant and, despite an overall uniformity in paste and surface finish, is quite varied in the form of the
rim and the type of decoration applied to the outer rim. The heterogeneity of the rim forms and decorative elements suggested, prior to
excavation, the possibility that the site may have had more than one
occupation, and this possibility was one of the reasons the site was
chosen for excavation. During the fieldwork, however, and through
the laboratory analysis of the materials it became increasingly apparent that only one major occupation was present. A second and minor

occupation by a Thomas Riggs Focus group is suggested by a very few sherds.

The analysis of the pottery proceeded as follows. The rim and body sherds, sacked together from the same find-spot, were first matched for fits, and subsequently segregated. Body sherds were classed according to surface finish, these classes including: smoothed, simple-stamped, cord-roughened, check-stamped, and decorated (incised or trailed). Red-filmed sherds were also separated, but this filming occurred on three surfaces: smoothed, simple-stamped, and decorated. During the sorting, each sherd was individually inspected for temper. A single cord-roughened sherd which appears to contain crushed shell provides the only exception to the statement that all sherds are grit-tempered.

In the descriptions to follow, the unit of description is, insofar as possible, the whole vessel. Since the rim forms and the types of decoration are so varied, it is probable that the estimated number of vessels represented by each of the groups is reasonably accurate. In addition to the reasons cited by Krieger (Newell and Krieger, 1949, pp. 75–77) and by Spaulding (1956, pp. 130–131) for studying "vessel types" assembled from "sherd types," is the fact that there is often a discernible—and sometimes substantial—difference in the percentage of types represented in a count of rim sherds and a count of vessels from a site. In spite of efforts to describe vessel types here, the pottery described below should probably be regarded as rim types, since so few restorable vessels were recovered.

Only a few of the 17 pottery groups from the site are identified as previously named types. The unnamed groups might have been named as types by some workers, and perhaps tentative type names could have been given them here. The permanent nature of "temporary" type names, coupled with the fact that the complex at Demery is involved and geographically diffuse, suggests that type names would not be advantageous. At this time, when many sites closely related to Demery remain unexcavated and unreported—from the mouth of the Grand River in South Dakota to the mouth of the Niobrara River in Nebraska—it does not seem proper to attach type names to the ceramics from a single site, particularly when the range of variation in pottery at sites down the river is unknown, at least to the writers.

Except for the sherds attributed to the Thomas Riggs Focus occupation of Demery, the pottery is sufficiently similar in paste, surface finish, and form to permit a general description of these features that applies to all the ceramics from the major occupation of the site.

GENERAL CHARACTERISTICS

PASTE:

Method of manufacture: The vessels were probably lump modeled and finished with a paddle and anvil. The vessel walls are quite uniform in thickness from the lip to the bottom, but the pots do not appear to have been scraped, since traces of paddle impressions are visible over most of the vessel surface.

Temper: Grit, composed of calcined or decomposed granite, consisting of particles of quartz, mica, and feldspar, ranged in diameter from .5 to 2.0 mm. Temper is nearly always sparse, and many sherds—particularly those from the smaller vessels—appear to have contained no purposefully included grit.

Texture: Smooth to medium fine. The paste is compact and well worked, although many vessels have a tendency to split parallel to the vessel wall.

Hardness: 2.5 to 3.0, the majority about 3 (calcite).

Color: Light buff to black, ranging through several shades of brown and gray. Characteristically, the sherds are a mottled light buff or gray. Smoke clouding is common, and black, charred organic matter sometimes adheres to the interior or exterior surfaces.

SURFACE FINISH: The entire vessel seems to have been first paddled with a grooved or, more rarely, a cord-wrapped paddle. On the large restored vessel (pl. 14, *b*), simple stamps extend from the neck to the base; a number of vessels have vertical or oblique stamps on the outer rim. Shoulders are vertically stamped, and an incised or trailed pattern was sometimes applied to them over a partly smoothed surface. In nearly all cases the stamps are at least partly smoothed; in about 5 percent of the vessels they are unmodified. A few bases are lightly polished, but surfaces are generally dull, with little tendency to reflect light.

FORM:

Lip: Flat to rounded; a few are pointed and a small number are extruded (fig. 13).

Rim/neck: Characteristics of these areas vary with the individual groups and types (fig. 13).

Orifice: The vessel mouth is wide and round in all observable instances.

Shoulder: This area is rounded and steeply sloping, joining the body in a smooth curve. On a few small to medium-sized vessels the shoulders are sharply angular at the juncture with the body (pl. 10, *i*).

Appendages: The loop and strap handles are riveted to the upper shoulder and welded to the lip. Handles on large restored vessel segments are paired on opposite sides of the rim. A number of rim projections (castellations) and some applique nodes occur on some groups. Appendages of this character occur in fours, equally spaced around the rim.

BODY SHERDS

The majority of the sherds are either simple-stamped or smoothed. Most of them show some smoothing although few may be classed as even lightly polished. Every degree of transition from unmodified stamps through partly smoothed stamps to lightly polished surfaces was observed, sometimes on a single large sherd. All sherds that showed any evidence of stamping were classed as simple-stamped. Sherds were classed as smooth when the surface was so smooth that

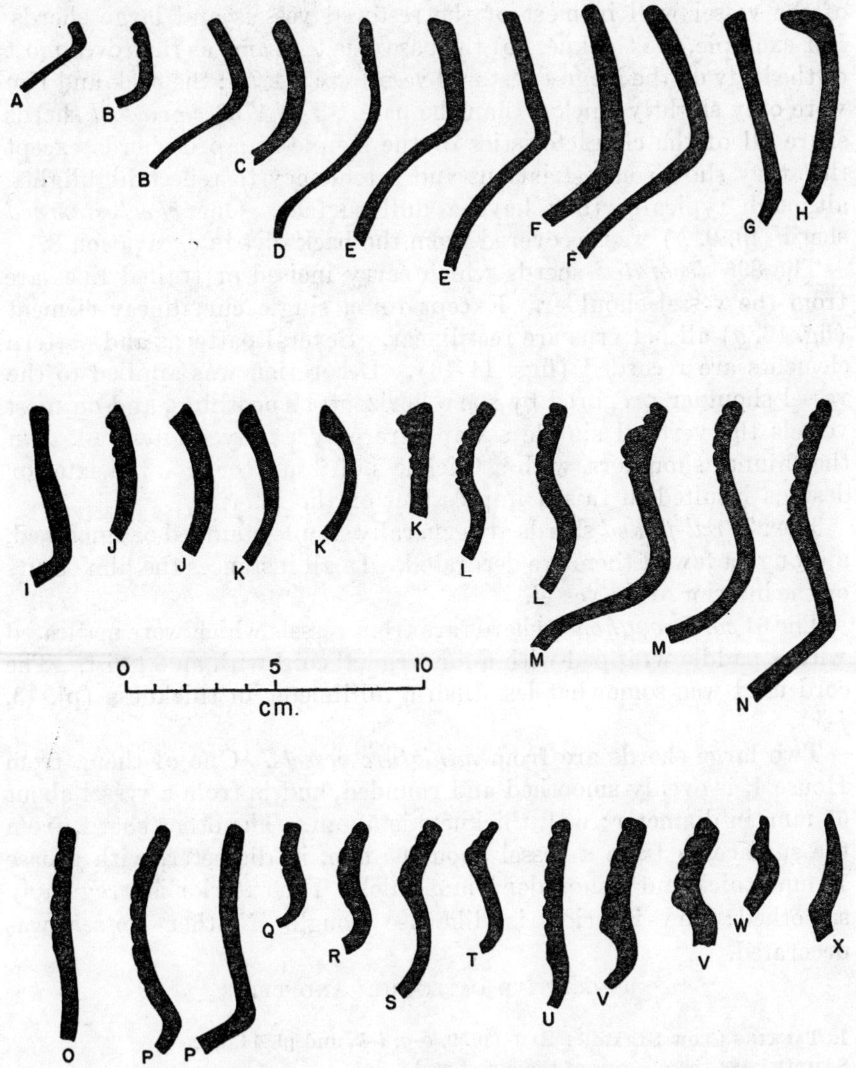

FIGURE 13.—Pottery rim profiles A–X.

irregularities were lacking. A third class was composed of sherds
with incised or trailed lines executed on simple-stamped or smoothed
sherds.

The 1498 sherds with distinguishable *simple stamps* show that the
stamps were applied vertically to the shoulders and rims, but near the
base they are random or oblique. These stamps are 5 to 8 mm. wide
and are of varying length, but in no instance do they exceed 30 mm.
Vessel walls are 1.5 to 6 mm. thick, averaging about 3 mm., although
rims are sometimes thicker. There is little variation in the thickness

of the vessel wall in most of the restored vessels and large sherds. For example, the thickness of the base was the same as that over most of the body on the largest restored vessel (pl. 14, *b*); the neck and rim were only slightly thicker than the base. The 1736 *smoothed* sherds share all of the characteristics of the simple-stamped sherds except that they show some striations and a tendency to reflect highlights, although typically they have a dull surface. One *check-stamped* sherd (pl. 9, *h*) was recovered from the back dirt in excavation 8.

The 896 *decorated* sherds which carry incised or trailed lines are from the vessel shoulder. Except for a single curvilinear element (fig. 16, *g*) all patterns are rectilinear. Several patterns and pattern elements are recorded (figs. 14–16). Decoration was applied to the vessel shoulder prepared by some horizontal smoothing, and on most vessels the vertical simple stamps are only partly obliterated. On the thinner shoulders, with a thickness of 2 mm. or less, the exterior designs resulted in raised impressions on the interior.

The 239 *red-filmed* sherds are generally simple-stamped or smoothed, although a few of them are decorated. In all instances the film occurs on the interior of the vessel.

The 61 *cord-roughened* sherds are from vessels which were malleated with a paddle wrapped with a fine vegetal cord with an S twist. The cord used was somewhat less than a millimeter in thickness (pl. 13, *j–k*).

Two large sherds are from *miniature vessels*. One of them, from House 4, is evenly smoothed and rounded, and is from a vessel about 55 mm. in diameter; wall thickness is 5 mm. The other sherd, from the surface, is from a vessel about 65 mm. in diameter, with a base 10 mm. thick and a shoulder 7 mm. thick. The exterior is irregularly smoothed; the interior is likewise rough. Neither vessel was decorated.

DESCRIPTIVE CATEGORIES AND TYPES

1. TALKING CROW STRAIGHT RIM (pl. 9, *e–g*, *i–k*, and pl. 14, *a*).

SAMPLE: 483 vessels, one of them restored.

SURFACE FINISH: The rims and shoulders are vertically simple-stamped and imperfectly smoothed, although a few shoulders, particularly near the neck, are wholly smoothed. Four rims are vertically brushed on the outer surface.

DECORATION:

Lip: The majority of lips are modified by tool impressions: 297 are obliquely impressed; 93 are transversely impressed; 66 are punctated; 2 are crosshatched; and 25 are plain. Tool impressions occur on the interiors of 79 rims (pl. 9, *i–j*); 57 are obliquely impressed and 22 are transversely impressed.

Rim: The rim exterior is plain.

Shoulder: This area is decorated with incised or trailed lines on 5 vessels. On 4 of them, decoration occurs on rims with oblique tool impressions on the rim interior. There are at least 2 occurrences of opposed diagonals

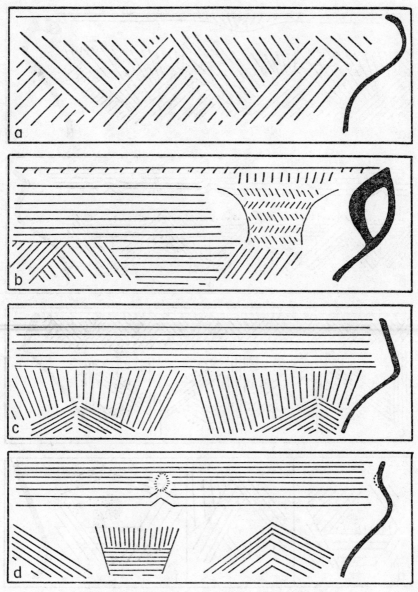

FIGURE 14.—Pottery rim and shoulder design elements.

(fig. 14, *a*) and one elaborate variant of the same pattern (fig. 15, *a*).
The latter pattern is on a vessel with 2 opposed, vertically pierced lugs.

FORM:

    Lip: Rounded to flat. On rims with deep or broad tool indentations there
    is some extrusion due to displaced clay.

    Rim: Characteristically straight to slightly outflaring, including rim forms
    A–B, D–G, and *I* (fig. 13). Height varies from 15 to more than 55 mm.,
    with a mean of about 35 mm.; thickness is from 4 to 8 mm., with a mean
    of 6 mm.

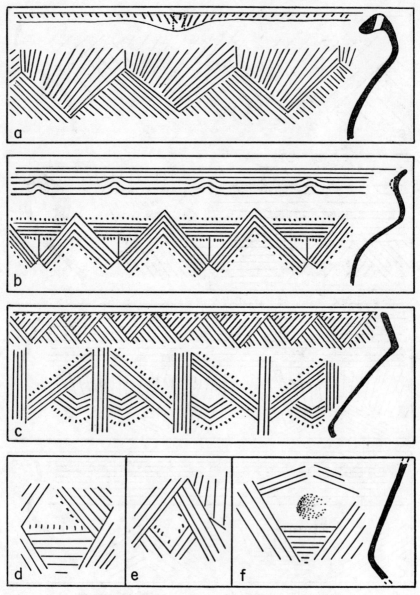

FIGURE 15.—Pottery rim and shoulder design elements.

Neck: Constricted on outflaring rims.

Shoulder: This area is usually about 45 degrees from the vertical, although some are more steeply sloping or more nearly horizontal.

Size: The projected arcs of 9 large rim sherds indicate vessel mouths of 46, 132, 158, 180, 190, 202, 210, 212, and 218 mm. diameter. Some vessel mouths may have been less than 40 mm. wide but probably only a few were more than 225 mm. wide.

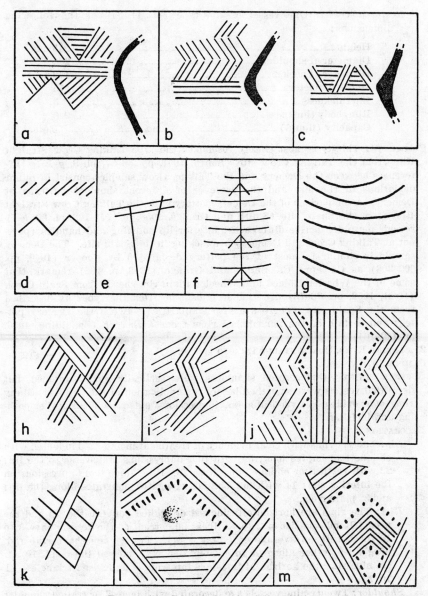

FIGURE 16.—Pottery shoulder design elements.

Appendages: A single plain loop handle was attached to the lip and shoulder of one rim, and there are 4 rim projections (pl. 13, *a*) and 49 lugs in this series. The lugs project out 5 to 8 mm. from the lip, generally at a 90-degree angle (pl. 9, *f-g*). Nine of the lugs are vertically or obliquely pierced (pl. 9). The rim projections, as well as the lugs, are commonly decorated by a continuation of the lip decoration.

Restored vessel: One vessel of this type (pl. 14, *a*) has the following dimensions:

Height	213 mm.
Diameter at shoulder	265
Diameter at neck	172
Mouth diameter	175
Lip thickness	5
Rim/body thickness	2–6
Capacity (liquid)	5 qts.

COMMENTS: This type most closely resembles the type Talking Crow Straight Rim from the Talking Crow site (Smith, 1951, pp. 36–37, pl. 8, *g–k*). Differences between the Demery and the Talking Crow samples consist of minor deviations in rim size and the presence of different shoulder patterns at Demery. A comparison of the Demery pottery with the Talking Crow Straight Rim from the Spain site (Smith and Grange, 1958, pp. 101–102, pl. 30, *h–j*) reveals more distinctive differences: interior lip notching and handles (present at Talking Crow and Demery) are lacking in the Spain site. The Demery sample is similar to most of the pottery designated by Cooper (1949, pp. 306–308) as Category C. Smith and Grange (1958, p. 102) remark that some of the Wheeler Ridged and Wheeler Plain rim sherds from Scalp Creek (Hurt, 1952, pp. 73–75) are "indistinguishable from the type" as described from the Spain site. There are also similarities between the Demery pottery and certain of the noncollared rims from Arzberger (Spaulding, 1956, pp. 149–164).

2. FLARING RIMS, HORIZONTALLY INCISED (pl. 10, *c–j*).

SAMPLE: 476 vessels.

SURFACE FINISH: Undecorated shoulders were vertically simple-stamped, but decorated vessels were smoothed before the application of the pattern. Many rims show evidence of vertical stamp impressions under the horizontal smoothing and incising.

DECORATION:

Lip: The 411 rims with clear evidence of treatment include 256 indented with oblique tool impressions; 59 with tool impressions transverse to the lip; 22 with vertical or oblique punctates; 28 with oblique tool impressions on the interior rim; 14 with low oblique, elongated punctates along the lip: and 32 plain rims.

Rim: The rims are horizontally incised or trailed between the lip and the neck. Bands consist of 2 to 13 lines; 90 percent of the vessels have 3 to 10 lines, with an average of 7 to a vessel. Twenty rims have stab-and-drag lines, either alone or in combination with incised lines (pl. 10, *j*). On nine rims the horizontal lines are interrupted by incised triangles (pl. 10, *h*).

Shoulder: Twenty-nine vessels are decorated with incised or trailed shoulder patterns. Three complete patterns observed include: Fig. 14, *a*, six examples; fig. 14, *b*, one example; and fig 14, *c*, one example. One large sherd from a small vessel is unique in having a continuous series of nodes at the angular break of the shoulder (pl. 10, *i*).

FORM:

Lip: Rounded to nearly flat. There are extrusions on a few rims due to coarse tool indentations.

Rim: Characteristically straight to slightly outflaring. Height varies from 8 mm. on small vessels to a maximum of 65 mm. on a large rim decorated with stab-and-drag lines; the average height is between 35 and 40 mm. Thickness is 4 to 8 mm., averaging between 5 and 6 mm. The thickness of the lip and the mid-rim is nearly the same, with the neck about 1 mm. thicker. Rim forms include *A–B, E–F,* and *H* (fig. 13).

Neck: Constricted on outflaring rims.

Shoulder: Most of the shoulders are about 45 degrees from the vertical, although some appear to have been more nearly horizontal.

Body: Several partly restorable rims indicate vessels with a globular body and wide, circular mouths.

Size: Three large rims have mouths of 118, 141, and 180 mm. diameter. A few sherds suggest that mouths may have attained widths of about 200 mm.

Appendages: The 18 handles include 14 loop handles and 4 strap handles; in each instance they appear to have been paired on the rim. They were riveted to the mid-rim or upper shoulder and welded to the lip. Loop handles are invariably decorated with horizontal lines, in effect a continuation of the rim design (pl. 10, *j*) but strap handles are often decorated with herringbones or other incised designs (pl. 10, *g*). Thirty-seven strap handles, detached from the rims, are arbitrarily assigned to this group since handles are lacking on most of the remaining groups; many of them are horizontally incised. There is much variation in the size and form of the strap handles, with widths varying from 12 to 65 mm.

Three rim projections are decorated by a continuation of the lip decorations; they extend vertically from the lip to a height of 5 mm. Twenty-four lugs, extending out at right angles from the rim (pl. 10, *h*) are decorated on the upper surface by the same impressions occurring on the lip, but here the impressions are larger and deeper. One lug is centrally incised (pl. 10, *e*).

COMMENTS: This pottery very closely approximates the type Grey Cloud Horizontal-Incised from the Spain site (Smith and Grange, 1958, pp. 102–103). It differs from this type in having a larger number of horizontally incised lines, in lacking the shoulder patterns common to Grey Cloud vessels, and in the presence of appendages. Grey Cloud Horizontal-Incised grades into Iona Horizontal-Incised at Spain, the latter type having protruded T- or L-shaped lips, lacking at Demery. The Demery sample is similar to most of the pottery designated by Cooper (1949, pp. 303–306) as Category B. This rim category is also related to the type Wheeler Horizontal-Incised from the Scalp Creek and La Roche sites (Hurt, 1952, p. 76); to certain of the horizontally incised noncollared rims at Arzberger (Spaulding, 1956, pp. 153–157); and to the type Evans Incised, from sites of the Redbird Focus in north central Nebraska (Wood, 1956).

3. FLARING RIMS, OBLIQUELY INCISED (pl. 13, *b*, *g*).

SAMPLE: 15 vessels.

SURFACE FINISH: The finish is not discernable on most sherds due to horizontal smoothing on the rim, and to the fact that most rims are broken from the body at the neck. On one partly restorable vessel (fig. 15, *c*) the entire body below the neck is cord-roughened. Above the angular shoulder the cord impressions are vertical, but below the shoulder they are random. The cord used was less than a millimeter in diameter; it was made from two twisted fibers, but smoothing has obscured the direction of the twist.

DECORATION:

Lip: Oblique tool indentations occur on 11 rims; on 1 rim the lip is punctated, and the other 2 are plain.

Rim: Opposed oblique incised lines form a continuous band around the rim of 11 specimens (fig. 15, *c*) ; vertical lines occur on 2 rims together with oblique lines ; and 1 rim is lightly incised with chevrons (pl. 13, *b*).

Shoulder: One of the two incised shoulders is decorated (fig. 15, *c*) over a cord-roughened surface. The other and fragmentary decoration was imposed over a surface of indeterminate nature.

FORM:

Lip: Flat to somewhat rounded.

Rim: Straight to somewhat outflaring, including rim forms *B* and *F* (fig. 13). Height ranges from 14 to 52 mm., averaging about 30 mm., and thickness from 4 to 8 mm., averaging about 6 mm.

Shoulder: The shoulder is flat and steeply sloping, with an angular break at the lower border on the cord-roughened vessel.

Size: Several measurements of the cord-roughened vessel include:

Height	ca. 130 mm.
Diameter at shoulder	ca. 150
Orifice diameter	ca. 100
Lip/rim thickness	7
Rim height	21
Body wall thickness	3

Appendages: One rim has a pierced lug extending out at a right angle 17 mm. from the rim, with a vertical perforation 9 mm. in diameter. It is on a lip decorated with punctates, although the top of the lug is decorated with transverse tool impressions.

COMMENTS : These rims are related to the recurved rims from Demery (Group 9) bearing obliquely incised lines, although they lack the pinched border below the incised rim design on the latter specimens. This group of rims clearly resembles some of those of the type Iona Diagonal-Incised from the Spain site (Smith and Grange, 1958, p. 100, pl. 30, *e–g*), but the Demery specimens lack the rim protrusion typical of Iona Ware.

4. FLARING RIMS, BEVELED OR BRACED (pl. 13, *c–f*, and pl. 14, *b*).

SAMPLE : 105 vessels, one of which is restored.

SURFACE FINISH : The interior and exterior rims are horizontally smoothed. This is the case with the restored vessel (pl. 14, *b*), where the entire surface of the vessel is smoothed, nearly obliterating the simple-stamping, which extends from the neck to the base. The stamps occur in a somewhat spiral fashion around the vessel body.

DECORATION :

Lip: On four vessels the lip interior is indented by oblique or transverse tool impressions.

Rim: Oblique to transverse tool impressions occur on the uppermost part of the exterior rim; some rims are decorated with oval or circular punctates.

FORM:

Lip: Usually pointed, although some are rounded.

Rim: The straight to outflaring rims are beveled at the lip, the lower edge of the bevel sometimes being extruded by decorative impressions. Rim form *J* is typical, but on three rims, paste extruded by the pressure applied during the decoration is pushed down, resulting in rim form *K* (fig. 13).

Shoulder: The rims join the body in a smooth curve. On the restored vessel (pl. 14, *b*) the shoulders are rounded and steeply sloping, and the body is globular with a round base.

Size: Measurements of the restored vessel include:

Height _____ 313 mm.
Diameter at shoulder _____ 355
Orifice diameter _____ 255
Lip thickness _____ 8
Rim height _____ 45
Rim/body thickness _____ 3–5
Capacity (liquid) _____ 18 qts.

Appendages: Lugs on three vessels project out from the lower limits of the lip bevel. They are decorated by a continuation of the rim design.

COMMENTS: Some of the attributes of this group are shared by pottery from Biesterfeldt, a Cheyenne site on the Sheyenne River in southeastern North Dakota (Strong, 1940, pp. 370–376; Wood, 1955, pp. 3–8). At the Biesterfeldt site the rim is characteristically beveled or "wedge-shaped" in cross section; this rim form occurs on a few of the Demery rims. A few of the rims from the Huff site of the type Huff Plain and Huff Braced Rim (Wood, MS. a) recall this rim form at Demery.

5. FLARING RIMS, CORD-ROUGHENED (pl. 13, *j–k*).

SAMPLE: Six vessels.

PASTE: Generally similar to that described under the heading "General Characteristics," except that the grit is somewhat coarser and the clay is not as well worked. The edges crumble easily on the more coarsely tempered sherds. A single sherd from Feature 51 contains particles of what appear to be shell, which effervesce under the action of diluted hydrochloric acid. It is possible that the shell was originally in the clay, and some of it has been destroyed by chemical weathering, since some of the particles effervesced only slightly even when treated with undiluted acid.

SURFACE FINISH: The exterior rim is vertically cord-roughened, this treatment extending down over the shoulder. There is some horizontal smoothing on necks, although body sherds may or may not be smoothed. The cord used had an S-twist.

DECORATION:

Lip: One rim is marked with oblique tool impressions; another has oblique punctates applied at a low angle to the lip top by a pointed tool; the other four are plain.

Rim/shoulder: No decoration observed.

FORM:

Lip: Flat.

Rim: Slightly outflaring, most rims closely resembling rim form *J* (fig. 13). Rim thickness is 7 to 8 mm.; height is indeterminate, but in excess of 30 to 50 mm.

Body: One large sherd built up from fragments suggests that the shoulder is rounded, probably blending smoothly with the rim. The even thickness of all body sherds, about 4 mm., indicates that the vessel walls were of nearly constant thickness.

Appendages: None observed.

COMMENTS: The cord-roughened surfaces and certain characteristics of the paste set this group of rims apart from the rest of the Demery pottery. From what can be observed, however, vessel form does not appear to depart signifi-

cantly from that observed of the pottery relating to the major occupation of
the site by the Demery Component. Since most of the Woodland pottery from
North Dakota appears to be sand-tempered (Wood, 1962 a) there seems no
good reason to attribute this pottery to a Woodland occupation of the site.
Perhaps the nearer affiliations of this pottery may be found in the Campbell
Creek types, defined at the Talking Crow site (Smith, 1951, pp. 37–39). A
major distinction between the Demery pottery and the Campbell Creek types
is the presence of a clearly defined rim-shoulder juncture on most of the
Campbell Creek pottery, and the lack of such a juncture on the Demery vessels.

6. FORT RICE CORD-IMPRESSED (pl. 11, *d–h, j–l*).

SAMPLE: 79 vessels.

SURFACE FINISH: The shoulders are vertically simple-stamped and are smoothed
Lips, rims, necks, and interiors are horizontally smoothed.

DECORATION:

Lip: On 6 vessels the lip is obliquely tool-impressed; on one it is obliquely
cord-impressed; the remaining lips are plain.

Rim: Horizontally applied cord-impressed lines alternate with curvilinear
or triangular elements. From 2 to 8 horizontal lines occur, most vessels
having 5 or 6 lines. In the 16 examples of triangular elements, the
center of the triangle is plain. At the apex of each triangle is a raised
tab (pl. 11, *f–g*); a single exception in which the tab is absent occurred
on a curvilinear element, or "rainbow." Ten curvilinear designs were
applied over a small applique node on the mid-rim; if a wholly restored
vessel rim is typical (fig. 15, *b*), four nodes occurred on each vessel. A
horizontal series of punctates occurs on the lower rim of two vessels (pl.
11, *d*). Three vessels, decorated with cord-wrapped stick impressions, are
otherwise similar to the above specimens (pl. 11, *l*).

Shoulder: The shoulder of only one vessel is decorated. The pattern consists of a complex rectilinear design (fig. 15, *b*) bordered by oblique
punctates.

FORM:

Lip: Predominantly flat, with a few rounded examples.

Rim: Eight forms were observed, of which six are recurved, including rim
forms *L-Q* (fig. 13). Two rims, of forms *V* and *W*, are somewhat more
angular and might be termed collared. Rims range from 30 to 60 mm.
in height, and are 4 to 7 mm. thick.

Neck: Constricted to varying degrees and, except for rim form *N*, they
join the shoulder in a smooth curve.

Body: Apparently globular, with round bottoms.

Size: The orifice of the reconstructed rim (fig. 15, *b*) measures 152×156
mm. Since the rim was badly shattered, the difference between the two
measurements need not be interpreted that the vessel mouth was oval.
The projected arcs of three large rim sherds indicated mouths between 182
and 250 mm. in diameter.

Appendages: There are no handles; nodes are discussed above, under
decoration.

COMMENTS: These rims are similar to the type Fort Yates Cord-Impressed
from the Paul Brave site (Wood and Woolworth, 1964, pl. 5; Hewes,
1949, pp. 65–66), but they differ in the conformation of the rim, the presence of the appliqued nodes, and the smaller cords used to impress the
design. Fort Yates Cord-Impressed rims have a wedge-shaped cross section due to a thickening near the rim base; only two rims from Demery are
so thickened. The type Fort Rice Cord-Impressed, described from the Huff

site (Wood, MS. a) is more nearly like the Demery pottery. There are only minor differences between the Huff pottery and that from Demery, principally in such matters as the number of cord-impressed lines and the degree of rim curvature. This pottery group is, therefore, tentatively identified as Fort Rice Cord-Impressed.

7. FORT RICE TRAILED (pl. 12, *e–h, j–m*).

SAMPLE: 132 vessels.

SURFACE FINISH: Shoulders are vertically or obliquely simple-stamped and partly smoothed. Necks and rims are horizontally smoothed, although traces of vertical stamps are often visible under the rim designs.

DECORATION:

Lip: The 128 rims with clear evidence of design include 45 with oblique tool impressions; 10 with transverse tool impressions; and 3 with punctates. The other 70 lips are plain.

Rim: The rim is horizontally incised or trailed with 2 to 11 lines. Of the 72 rims carrying complete series, 57 have 4 to 7 lines. Nine rims have stab-and-drag lines (pl. 12, *h*) either alone or in combination with incised lines. Triangular elements interrupting the horizontal lines occur on 28 rims (pl. 12, *k–m*). On 22 of these rims the apex of the triangle is near a small applique node or a rim projection.

Shoulder: The shoulders of two vessels are embellished with incised patterns consisting of alternating chevrons and horizontal and vertical lines bordered by oblique lines (fig. 14, *d*).

FORM:

Lip: Predominantly flat, although a few plain rims are rounded.

Rim: Gently curving recurved rims of nearly constant thickness from the lip to the shoulder include rim forms *L–P*, and *R* (fig. 13). A few rims thicken toward the base of the design area, and are more aptly termed collared. The latter rims include forms *T–V* (fig. 13). Height ranges from 35 to 65 mm., averaging about 45 mm.; thickness, from 4 to 9 mm., averaging about 5 mm.

Neck: Constricted.

Shoulder: Most of the shoulders are at about a 45-degree angle from the vertical, although a few were more nearly horizontal.

Size: The projected arcs of several large rim sherds indicate vessel mouths of 227 and 253 mm.

Appendages: Applique nodes applied to the mid-rim were on 9 vessels, and applique or pinched-out lugs or rim projections occur on 28 vessels. A few of the applique nodes on the mid-rim bear central, vertical punctates.

COMMENTS: The group of rims is related to the flaring rims with horizontally incised lines (Group 2). The latter group, however, lacks nodes applied to the mid-rim. The nearer affiliation of this pottery is with the type Fort Rice Trailed from the Huff site (Wood, MS. a). The only difference between the Huff pottery and that from Demery is the lack of collared rims at Huff (they are rare in Demery) and the smaller number of horizontal lines in the rim design at Huff. This pottery group is accordingly tentatively identified as Fort Rice Trailed.

8. RECURVED RIMS, HORIZONTALLY INCISED AND PINCHED/PUNCTATED (pl. 10, *a–c*).

SAMPLE: 23 vessels.

SURFACE FINISH: The interior and the exterior rim and the neck are horizontally smoothed.

DECORATION:

Lip: On the 11 rims with lips, 8 are impressed with oblique tool impressions; 1 has oblique tool impressions on the interior lip; 1 has circular punctates; and 1 is plain.

Rim: On the 11 rims complete from neck to lip there are 2 to 7 horizontally incised lines, with more than half of them (6) bearing 5 lines. Below these lines are finger-pinched indentations on 13 vessels, and punctates on 10 vessels (pl. 10, a–b). One rim with two horizontally incised lines above a line of punctates is incised with six lines below them; and one atypical rim (pl. 10, c) lacks either pinching or punctates.

FORM:

Lip: Flat to somewhat rounded.

Rim: Three forms occur. Rim forms U–V (fig. 13) are classed as collared, and comprise six of the eight classifiable rims. One rim is of form M, and another is of form X.

Neck: Constricted.

Body/size: Sherds are generally small, but one large rim indicates an orifice of about 200 mm. in diameter.

Appendages: None observed.

COMMENTS: A number of characteristics of this pottery, including rim form and decorative elements, are shared with the type Arzberger Horizontal Incised (Spaulding, 1956, pp. 139–141, pl. 8), although none of the Demery vessels appear to have cord-roughened shoulders.

9. RECURVED RIMS, OBLIQUELY INCISED AND PINCHED/PUNCTATED (pl. 13, h).

SAMPLE: 12 vessels.

SURFACE FINISH: Originally vertically simple-stamped, then horizontally smoothed on rims and necks. Two rims bear nearly obliterated impressions that suggest they were malleated with a cord-roughened paddle, then smoothed.

DECORATION:

Lip: Oblique tool impressions occur on five lips, and two are plain. The lip is absent on the remaining rims.

Rim: Oblique incised lines occur on 11 of the 12 rims; on one rim a series of 3 oblique lines, forming a chevron, interrupt a series of 10 horizontally incised lines. On the eight sherds retaining the lower rim, three have a finger-pinched border and five are punctated.

Shoulder: One rim bears traces of an incised pattern.

FORM:

Lip: Flat to somewhat rounded.

Rim: The gently recurved rims are of nearly constant thickness from the lip to the neck, except where the finger-pinchings thicken the cross section. Rim forms are U–V (fig. 13). Rim heights range from 25 to 47 mm.; thickness, from 4 to 8 mm.

COMMENT: These rims are related to the flaring rims with obliquely incised lines (Group 3), although the latter rims lack the rim profile and the modified rim base occurring on this group.

10. RECURVED RIMS, PINCHED IN MID-RIM (pl. 13, i).

SAMPLE: 3 vessels.

SURFACE FINISH: The rims are horizontally smoothed on the interior and exterior.

DECORATION:

Lip: Oblique tool impressions.

Rim: A horizontal series of finger-pinched impressions occur on two rims at the mid-rim; the remaining rim is obliquely tool-impressed (pl. 13, i).

FORM:

> *Lip:* Flat.
>
> *Rim:* Gently recurved, with constant thickness from the lip to the neck, of form *L* (fig. 13).
>
> *Neck:* Constricted.
>
> *Body size:* No data.

COMMENTS: These sherds seem to be variants of the rims with obliquely or horizontally incised lines with finger-pinched or punctated rim bases (Groups 7–9), but these rims are less complex.

11. RECURVED RIMS, PLAIN (pl. 12, *a–b, i*).

SAMPLE: 18 vessels.

SURFACE FINISH: The rims and shoulders were first simple-stamped and then horizontally smoothed.

DECORATION:

> *Lip:* Oblique tool impressions occur on five lips; one has transverse tool impressions; one has oblique tool impressions on the inner rim; and the rest are plain.
>
> *Rim:* Plain.
>
> *Shoulder:* Incised chevrons and oblique incised lines occur on the shoulder of one vessel (fig. 15, *f*).

FORM:

> *Lip:* Round to somewhat flat.
>
> *Rim:* Gently recurving rims of nearly constant thickness from the lip to the neck include forms *L–M* and *P–Q* (fig. 13). Height varies from 25 to 60 mm., averaging about 40 mm.; thickness, from 4 to 8 mm., averaging about 6 mm.
>
> *Neck:* Constricted.
>
> *Shoulder:* On two vessels it is about 30 degrees from the vertical.
>
> *Appendages:* An applique lug occurs on the mid-rim of one rim, and a lug scar appears on another rim.

COMMENTS: There are close similarities between this group and Examples *D* from the Paul Brave site (Wood and Woolworth, 1964), and "Riggs Plain" from the Thomas Riggs site (Kleinsasser, 1953, p. 28). It also resembles Example *D* from the Huff site (Wood, MS. a).

12. CORD-IMPRESSED RIMS, EXAMPLE A (pl. 11, *a*).

SAMPLE: 1 vessel.

PASTE:

> *Temper:* Sparse, minute particles, including some sand.
>
> *Texture:* Well-worked clay with a laminated core.
>
> *Color:* Light brown.

SURFACE FINISH: Interior and exterior horizontally smoothed.

DECORATION:

> *Rim:* Four horizontally cord-impressed lines on exterior.

FORM:

> *Lip:* Pointed.
>
> *Rim:* Straight, with an added fillet below the lip, of form *K* (fig. 13).

COMMENTS: This rim does not closely resemble any other reported pottery.

13. CORD-IMPRESSED RIMS, EXAMPLE B (pl. 11, *b*).

SAMPLE: 1 vessel.

PASTE AND SURFACE FINISH: See Example A.

DECORATION:

> *Lip:* Oblique tool impressions.
>
> *Rim:* Three horizontally applied cord-impressed lines.

FORM:

Lip: Flat.

Rim: Straight, with the rim blending smoothly with the shoulder, of form B (fig. 13).

COMMENTS: This example may be a cord-impressed variety of the horizontally incised, flaring rim sherds (Group 2).

14. CORD-IMPRESSED RIM, EXAMPLE C (pl. 11, i).

SAMPLE: 1 vessel.

PASTE AND SURFACE FINISH: See Example A.

DECORATION:

Lip: Chevrons, composed of shallow, oblique tool impressions on the interior and exterior.

Rim: Seven horizontally applied cord-impressed lines.

Shoulder: Herringbone pattern, the only occurrence of this design in the site sample.

FORM:

Lip: Pointed.

Rim: Straight to slightly recurved, of form D (fig. 13).

Shoulder: Flat and sloping, with an angular break at the juncture with the body.

Size: The orifice measures 95 mm. in diameter.

COMMENTS: This example may be another cord-impressed variety of the horizontally incised vessels with flared rims (Group 2).

15. CORD-IMPRESSED RIM, EXAMPLE D (pl. 11, c).

SAMPLE: 1 vessel.

PASTE:

Temper: Coarse grit.

Texture: Rather crumbly, with loosely compacted clay.

SURFACE FINISH: Horizontally smoothed on interior and exterior.

DECORATION:

Lip: Crosshatched.

Rim: Five horizontally applied cord-impressed lines.

FORM:

Lip: Beveled down and out.

Rim: Straight, of form J (fig. 13).

COMMENTS: This rim does not closely resemble any previously described pottery.

16. RIGGS CROSS-HATCHED RIMS (pl. 12, d).

The sample consists of five sherds from four vessels. The lip of one vessel is carefully crosshatched, but the same design on the outer rim is irregularly applied. The paste is coarse and the grit is large-grained. This single sherd is from House 4, while the rest of them are from the surface.

The other sherds are more carefully crosshatched, with oblique tool impressions on the lips of two vessels, and a plain lip on the other vessel. The paste and temper of these sherds is less coarse than that of the vessel from House 4. Each of the sherds of this type is identical to examples as decribed from the Paul Brave site (Wood and Woolworth, 1964), a component of the Thomas Riggs Focus a few miles north on the Missouri River.

17. RIGGS STRAIGHT RIM (pl. 13, l).

The 12 rims from the 9 vessels of this type are distinguishable from the other sherds from the site in having (a) a coarse temper and a crumbly, granular texture, (b) cross sections 8 to 14 mm. thick, as opposed to cross sections 4 to 8 mm. thick in the majority of rims, and (c) contorted cores, in contrast to the more commonly laminated cores. Vertical rim projections occur on two rims.

Four rim sherds are from the surface, and one each is from Feature 51 and Feature 55, irregularly shaped pits near House 5; sherds from 3 vessels were in House 4. A number of fragments of one large vessel were in Feature 97, a large irregular pit in the south side of House 4, and a decorated body sherd (fig. 16, *f*) was in the same pit. This sherd may be duplicated among those from Paul Brave (Wood and Woolworth, 1964, fig. 1). One of the center posts of House 4 was intrusive into the fill of this pit, providing evidence that the pit was dug and filled before the house was built. This circumstance suggests an occupation of the site by a group predating the occupation represented by the majority of excavated remains. This occupation, attributed to the Thomas Riggs Focus, is presumed to predate the Demery Component.

TABLE 2.—*Probable number of vessels represented by the "rim" sherd sample*

	Number of vessels	Percent
Demery Component		
1. Talking Crow Straight Rim	483	35. 6
2. Flaring rims, horizontally incised	476	35. 1
3. Flaring rims, obliquely incised	15	1. 1
4. Flaring rims, beveled or braced	105	7. 7
5. Flaring rims, cord-roughened	6	. 4
6. Fort Rice Cord-Impressed	79	5. 8
7. Fort Rice Trailed	132	9. 7
8. Recurved rims, horizontally incised and pinched/ punctated	23	1. 7
9. Recurved rims, obliquely incised and pinched/ punctated	12	. 9
10. Recurved rims, pinched in mid-rim	3	. 2
11. Recurved rims, plain	18	1. 3
12. Cord-impressed rim, Example A	1	. 07
13. Cord-impressed rim, Example B	1	. 07
14. Cord-impressed rim, Example C	1	. 07
15. Cord-impressed rim, Example D	1	. 07
Total	1, 356	99. 78
Thomas Riggs Focus Component		
16. Riggs Cross-Hatched Rim	4	30. 8
17. Riggs Straight Rim	9	69. 2
Total	13	100. 0

CHIPPED STONE

Projectile points (130 specimens):

The points in this sample are all essentially triangular in outline, with straight to somewhat convex edges. They were made by the careful removal of small pressure flakes from both faces, with a final product having evenly flaked sides and a lenticular or biconvex cross section. Three groups are distinguished on the basis of the shape of the base and the presence or absence of side notches. Seventy-nine of them are made from a light-gray chert, and twenty-two are made from Knife River flint (chalcedony). The remaining 29 specimens are made from quartzite (7), variously colored cherts (14), Badlands chalcedony (6), and agate and petrified wood (2).

Triangular blade, straight base, unnotched (75 specimens).—These points have straight to somewhat irregular bases, with gently convex blade edges. They range in length from 20 to 58 mm., although 80 percent of them are less than 40 mm. long. Width is 12 to 26 mm., with a mean of about 19 mm. Thickness ranges between 3 and 6 mm. The smallest point has a weight of 0.4 gram, and the largest weighs 16 grams, but only 5 points exceed 2 grams in weight (fig. 17, *a–d*).

Triangular blade, straight base, two side notches (27 specimens).— These points have fairly straight, regular bases, with straight to gently convex blade edges. They range in length from 20 to 41 mm., although 80 percent of them are less than 31 mm. long. Width is 10 to 18 mm., with a mean of about 14 mm. Thickness is from 2 to 6 mm. The smallest point has a weight of 0.6 gram, and the largest of them weighs 2.3 grams, most of them averaging about 1 gram (fig. 17, *e–h*).

Triangular blade, concave base, two side notches (15 specimens).— These points have even, concave bases, with straight to gently convex blade edges. Length ranges from 21 to 44 mm., although 80 percent of them are less than 33 mm. long. Width is from 12 to 18 mm., with a mean of about 14 mm. They are 3 to 7 mm. thick. The smallest point has a weight of 0.7 gram; the largest weighs 3.0 grams, but only one of them exceeds 1.6 grams in weight (fig. 17, *i–l*).

Point fragments (13 specimens).—These fragmentary points consist of the tips of points which have been broken through side notches; the form of the base is indeterminate.

End scrapers (226 specimens) :

The outlines of these specimens tend to be triangular to rectangular, although many of them are irregular in form. The working edge, on the end opposite the bulb of percussion, is generally steeply flaked. Most of them bear large flake scars on the convex upper surfaces (fig. 19, *d–g*), but a few of them are flaked on the upper surface (fig. 19, *c, h*). The smallest scraper measures $18 \times 19 \times 6$ mm., with the largest of them measuring $76 \times 46 \times 15$ mm.; the average is about $40 \times 24 \times 10$ mm. (fig. 19, *c–h*).

Expanding base drills (4 specimens) :

One complete specimen, made of petrified wood, has a short, triangular point on one side of a leaf-shaped flake. The specimen is unifacially flaked; it is 32 mm. wide and 29 mm. long (fig. 19, *a*). The other three specimens have nearly parallel-sided shafts which are broken off a few millimeters from the base (fig. 19, *b*). Bases are 18 to 32 mm. wide, and the shafts suggest lengths originally in excess of

a   b   c   d

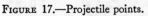

0   5

cm.

e   f   g   h

i   j   k   l

FIGURE 17.—Projectile points.

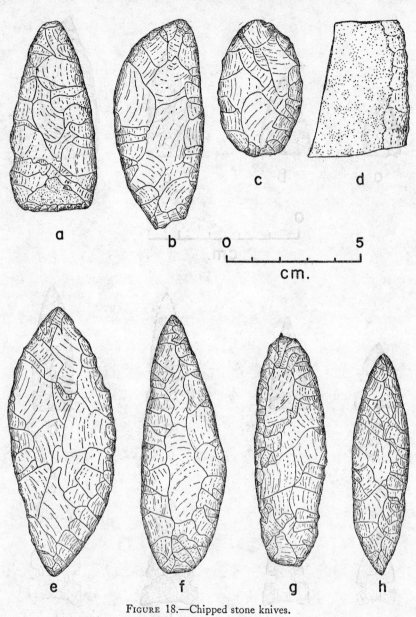

FIGURE 18.—Chipped stone knives.

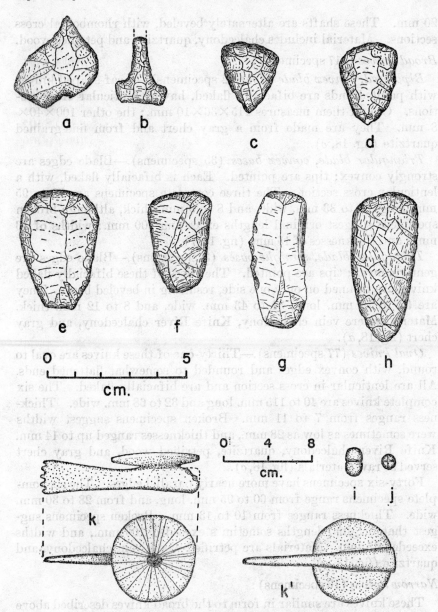

FIGURE 19.—Chipped and ground stone artifacts. *a–b*, Drills. *c–h*, End scrapers. *i–j*, Game pieces. *k*, Catlinite disk-bowl pipe.

20 mm. These shafts are alternately beveled, with rhomboidal cross sections. Material includes chalcedony, quartzite, and petrified wood.

Broad knives (117 specimens):

Bipointed, convex blade edges (2 specimens).—Leaf-shaped knives with pointed ends are bifacially flaked, having lenticular cross sections. One of them measures 115×36×10 mm.; the other 100×40× 8 mm. They are made from a gray chert and from fine-grained quartzite (fig. 18, *e*).

Triangular blade, convex bases (35 specimens).—Blade edges are strongly convex; tips are pointed. Each is bifacially flaked, with a lenticular cross section. The three complete specimens are 78 to 95 mm. long, 31 to 33 mm. wide, and 8 to 9 mm. thick, although broken specimens suggest original lengths exceeding 100 mm.; widths of 46 mm.; and thicknesses of 15 mm. (fig. 18, *f*).

Triangular blade, straight bases (3 specimens).—Blade edges are gently convex; tips are pointed. The bases of these bifacially flaked knives are thinned on only one side, resulting in beveled bases. They are 57 to 70 mm. long, 31 to 43 mm. wide, and 8 to 12 mm. thick. Materials were vein chalcedony, Knife River chalcedony, and gray chert (fig. 18, *a*).

Oval knives (77 specimens).—Thirty-one of these knives are oval to round, with convex edges and rounded to somewhat flattened ends. All are lenticular in cross section and are bifacially flaked. The six complete knives are 40 to 115 mm. long and 32 to 68 mm. wide. Thickness ranges from 7 to 11 mm. Broken specimens suggest widths were sometimes as low as 28 mm., and thicknesses ranged up to 14 mm. Knife River chalcedony, quartzite, petrified wood, and gray chert served as raw materials (fig. 18, *c*).

Forty-six specimens have more nearly parallel edges. The six complete specimens range from 60 to 95 mm. long, and from 28 to 30 mm. wide. Thickness ranges from 10 to 13 mm. Broken specimens suggest that original lengths sometimes exceeded 100 mm., and widths exceeded 45 mm. Materials are petrified wood, vein chalcedony, and quartzite (fig. 18, *g*).

Narrow knives (13 specimens):

These knives are similar in form to the broad knives described above as bipointed, with convex blade edges, but they are narrower and better made than the broad group. These differences may have resulted from their use in a special context. Their size and form is well adapted for insertion in the slotted bone or wood knife handles from the site (fig. 20, *b–c*). The five complete specimens are 62 to 83 mm. long, 15 to 24 mm. wide, and 6 to 10 mm. thick. One broken knife may originally have been 150 to 170 mm. long. Knife River chalcedony, quartzite, and variously colored cherts were used as raw materials (fig. 18, *h*).

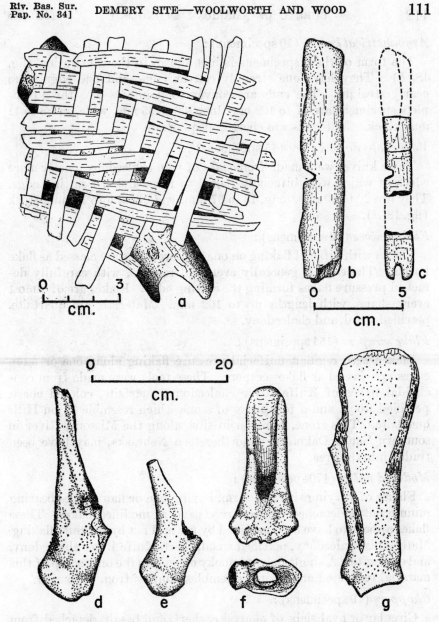

FIGURE 20.—Basketry, woodwork, and bone artifacts. *a*, Charred, twilled basketry fragment. *b*, Slotted bone knife handle. *c*, Charred, slotted wooden knife handle. *d-e*, Bison ulna tools. *f*, Bison radius pick. *g*, Bison scapula hoe.

Asymmetrical knives (10 specimens) :

The form of these specimens is best shown in the illustration (fig. 18, *b*). They have one strongly convex edge, and one edge more nearly straight. The ends are convex to pointed. The three complete specimens are 77 to 102 mm. long, 36 to 55 mm. wide, and 8 to 11 mm. thick. Materials are chert and quartzite.

Vein chalcedony knives (45 specimens) :

These knives were made from slabs of vein chalcedony, one or more edges of which were bifacially flaked to form a sharp cutting edge. They are 20 to 80 mm. long, 15 to 67 mm. wide, and 5 to 10 mm. thick (fig. 18, *d*).

Flake knives (39 specimens) :

Flakes with bifacial flaking on one or more edges are classed as flake knives. The edge is generally even and regular, with carefully detached pressure flakes forming the cutting edge. Flakes are of almost every shape, with lengths up to 102 mm. Materials are quartzite, petrified wood, and chalcedony.

Flake scrapers (154 specimens) :

Flakes with regular, unifacial pressure flaking along one or more edges are classed as flake scrapers. These tools were made from conchoidal flakes of Knife River chalcedony, quartzite, colored chert, petrified wood, and a few pieces of stone which resemble Bijou Hills quartzite. This stone, common in sites along the Missouri River in southern South Dakota and northeastern Nebraska, may have been traded into the area.

Modified flakes (170 specimens) :

Flakes of varying size and form, having one or more edges bearing minute flakes detached by use, are classed as modified flakes. These flakes appear to have been modified by use and not by pressure flaking. Material is chalcedony, petrified wood, chert, Knife River chalcedony, and quartzite. A single flake of smoky obsidian (the only scrap of this material recovered at the site) resembles samples from Wyoming.

Choppers (19 specimens) :

Circular or oval slabs of quartzite, chert, and basalt, detached from the parent material by percussion, may have been used as choppers. Most of them have convex to straight edges modified by coarse, unifacial percussion flaking, although some of them are bifacially flaked. These implements are large, measuring 90 to 260 mm. long and 55 to 30 mm. wide. One of them has shallow notches flaked into the edges and could have been hafted for use as an ax.

GROUND STONE

Grooved mauls (19 specimens):

Eighteen of these tools were made from oval granite pebbles, with one specimen of fossiliferous stone composed of calcified organic matter. Basically, they are oval stream pebbles modified only by the pecked groove that encircles them. These grooves are centered on 13 mauls, but on 6 of them they are offset toward one end. Only one of them has a polished groove. The ends are usually heavily battered. They range in size from 60×55 mm. to 135×180 mm.; weight ranges from ½ to 9¼ pounds, with a mean weight of 4 pounds.

Diorite celts (4 specimens):

Three of these tools are subrectangular in outline and in cross section, having been fully shaped by pecking and grinding (fig. 21, *e*). Lengths range from 115 to 145 mm.; widths, from 55 to 56 mm.; thickness, from 31 to 40 mm. The cutting edges are about the same width as the maximum width, and are blunted from use; polls are battered from use as hammers. A large piece of diorite, pecked over most of its surface, may be a celt in an early stage of manufacture.

Pebble hammerstones (46 specimens):

These implements were made from granite and quartzite pebbles, and occur in three forms. Five of them, about the size of baseballs, were made from pebbles which have been battered on all surfaces. Another group of six circular hammers are also battered on all surfaces, but they are consistently smaller and are evenly shaped. These latter implements are 50 to 65 mm. in diameter.

The remaining 35 hammers are irregularly shaped river pebbles, tending to be oval in shape. Most of them were battered on one or more faces, and usually on the ends, but none of them were purposefully shaped. They range from 30 to 100 mm. in diameter.

Discoidal hammerstones (8 specimens):

These tools are disk-shaped sandstone and quartzite stones; sides are flat and cross sections are oval. A shallow pit was pecked into each of the flat surfaces, possibly for finger holds, and the entire circumference of each stone is battered.

Abraders (61 specimens):

Irregular pieces of fine-grained sandstone, scoria, shale, diorite, and granite either have shallow, cup-shaped depressions or flat, smoothed areas on one or more surfaces that suggest they were used as abraders.

Grooved abraders (67 specimens):

These objects are composed of scoria and medium- to fine-grained sandstone. The irregular width and form of the grooves precludes

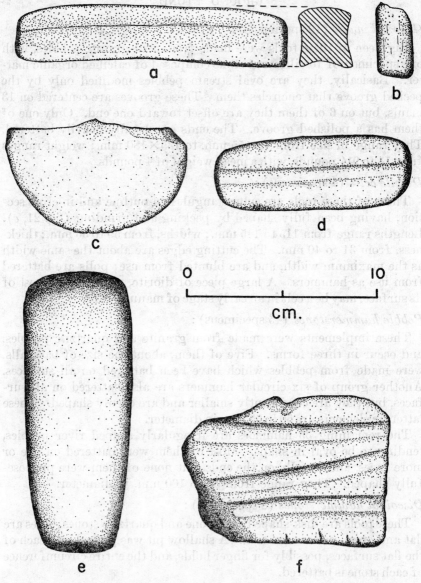

FIGURE 21.—Ground stone artifacts. *a, d,* Arrow shaft smoothers. *b,* Catlinite pipe bowl.
c, Sandstone disk. *e,* Diorite celt. *f,* Grooved abrading stone.

the possibility that they were used as shaft smoothers; it is more likely
that they were used to sharpen awls or other tools. Many of them
are small, with shallow V-shaped grooves which suggest that they
were used for delicate abrading. They are 30 to 70 mm. long, and
average slightly less in width. Other pieces of irregular sandstone
have larger, more prominent U-shaped grooves. They vary greatly

in size, ranging from 40 to 170 mm. long and 25 to 110 mm. wide (fig. 21, *f*).

Shaft smoothers (21 specimens):

Although most of these are fragmentary, they are generally elongated, boat-shaped pieces of coarse- to fine-grained sandstone with convex ends. All specimens have a U-shaped groove of varying depth along one flat side. One complete example is 100 mm. long and 40 mm. wide (fig. 21, *d*).

Catlinite pipes (2 specimens):

One complete disk-bowl pipe is 140 mm. long and 33 mm. high. The prow projects 60 mm. beyond the forward edge of the platform. The forward end of the prow is serrated, and the platform has 14 paired, incised lines radiating out from the orifice in the platform center. The bowl was drilled with a tapered drill (fig. 19, *k*). A second pipe is a tubular fragment of a cylindrical bowl. The piece is 40 mm. long and 16 mm. in diameter (fig. 21, *b*).

Sandstone disk (1 specimen):

One-half of a disk of fine-grained sandstone, 97 mm. in diameter and 10 mm. thick, has a lenticular cross section. The surfaces are smooth and even, and there is a shallow depression in the center of one face. The edges are scored by small notches, and one face is smudged with red ocher (fig. 21, *c*).

Game pieces (2 specimens):

One of these objects is a smooth, oval stone 24 mm. long and 15 mm. wide, with an encircling groove at its midpoint (fig. 19, *i*). The second stone resembles a smooth, fossil fruit stone; it is 8 mm. long and 7 mm. wide, with a raised ridge along the edges. One surface bears a deeply incised × (fig. 19, *j*).

Mealing slab (1 specimen):

A large slab of granite with one smooth, depressed surface measures 421 mm. in length, 254 mm. in width, and 127 mm. in thickness. The depressed surface was ground smooth; it was probably used after the manner of a mealing slab, although no manos or mullers were recovered.

Pigments (6 pieces):

Six pieces of sandstone and chalk may have been sources of paint. Four of them are of very fine-grained sandstone, impregnated with hematite; three of them are brick red in color and the other is light buff. Two small pieces of light yellow chalk have smooth, rounded surfaces.

Unworked stone (2 pieces) :

These items consist of a piece of unmodified calcite 65 mm. long, 22 mm. wide, and 12 mm. thick; and a piece of sheet mica 75 mm. square, with rounded corners. These two items may have been picked up and carried to the site as oddities.

BONE ARTIFACTS

Scapula hoes (100 specimens) :

The scapulae of adult bison were used in the manufacture of these implements, although some smaller specimens may be from young bison or from elk. The supra-scapular border was beveled on the side bearing the scapular fossae, and these fossae are hacked away so that the surface of the bone is nearly flat. In a few instances there are suggestions that the edges were roughened by chopping at points about 100 to 150 mm. from the cutting edge, probably to provide a rough surface for binding a handle to the tool. The cutting edge may either be rounded or straight; the more heavily worn tools are rounded, whereas the others are more nearly square. The articulating end is retained without modification (fig. 20, *g*).

Sixty-four hoes are made from the right scapula, and 36 are from the left scapula. The range in length of the 46 complete hoes is 270 to 480 mm. The shortest hoe, however, was about 40 mm. shorter than any other in the series, and the longest was about 40 mm. longer; excluding these two atypical specimens, the range in length is 310 to 440 mm.

Scapula knives (19 specimens) :

These specimens were made from various parts of bison scapulae. Two groups are identified in the series. The first group consists of 10 specimens made from parts of the scapula on which the spinous processes were hacked down, retaining part of the thin flat bone in the scapula center as a blade. In general, they are paddle shaped, with roughly parallel or convex edges. Parts of the medial or lateral border often project beyond the blade and may have served as handles. Some of them may have been made from broken scapula hoes, since they often have a beveled edge on one end, on the side bearing the scapular processes; this bevel is characteristic of hoe blades. The edge of the scapula opposite the scapular process is sharpened on each of them. The blades are either convex or concave, the latter specimens resembling a scythe blade in some respects. Lengths of complete specimens range from 220 to 390 mm. (fig. 22, *g*).

The other nine specimens classed as knives are oval, triangular, or rectangular scapula fragments sharpened on one or more edges. They resemble the familiar bone tools generally called "squash knives," and are 120 to 165 mm. long (fig. 22, *h*).

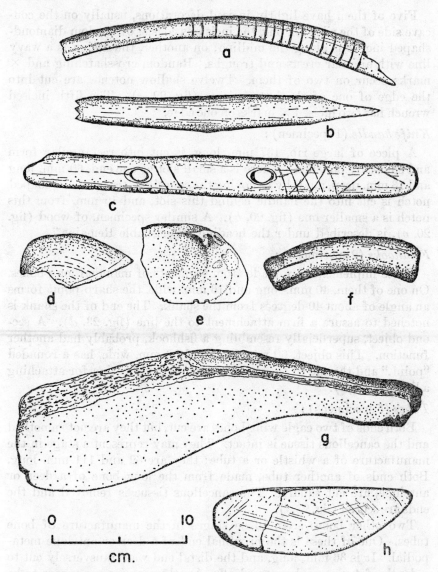

FIGURE 22.—Artifacts of bone, antler, and shell. *a*, Scored bison rib. *b*, Serrated rib tip.
c, Arrow shaft wrench. *d–e*, Shell scrapers. *f*, Antler cylinder. *g*, Scapula "cleaver."
h, Bone knife.

Shaft wrenches (13 specimens) :

These tools were made by drilling one or two roughly circular holes
through a large rib, and rounding the rib ends. The three complete
specimens are 240 and 295 mm. long; one of these has two oval holes
spaced 75 mm. apart (fig. 22, *c*). The other two wrenches have a
single, centrally located hole. All holes are oval, and all except one
have beveled or rounded edges; diameters range from 11 to 16 mm.

Five of them have lightly incised decorations, usually on the concave side of the rib. On one, the incisions consist of random diamond-shaped incisions along the midline; on another, the design is a wavy line with angular crests and troughs. Random crosshatching and ✕ marks occur on two of them. Twelve shallow notches are cut into the edge of one of the latter pieces (fig. 22, *c*). The fifth incised wrench has two incised ✕ marks on one edge.

Knife handle (1 specimen):

A piece of large rib, 137 mm. long, is cut into rectangular form and smoothly polished. There is a small slot at one end, 60 mm. long and 13 mm. deep, made by removing the cancellous tissue. A V-shaped notch is cut into the handle behind this slot, and 15 mm. from this notch is a smaller one (fig. 20, *b*). A similar specimen, of wood (fig. 20, *c*), is described under the heading, "Perishable Remains."

Fishhooks (2 specimens):

These implements are made from segments of mammal long bones. On one of them, 40 mm. long and 16 mm. wide, the sharp point forms an angle of about 40 degrees from the shank. The end of the shank is notched to assure a firm attachment to the line (fig. 23, *d*). A second object, superficially resembling a fishhook, probably had another function. This object, 60 mm. long and 20 mm. wide, has a rounded "point," and the end of the shank shows no modification for attaching a line (fig. 23, *e*).

Tubes (5 specimens):

Both ends of two eagle wing bones are cut, but they are not smoothed and the cancellous tissue is intact. They may represent a stage in the manufacture of a whistle or a tube; they are 62 and 111 mm. long. Both ends of another tube, made from the long bone of a deer or antelope, are cut square. The cancellous tissue is removed and the ends are scored (fig. 23, *i*).

Two other bones seem to be stages in the manufacture of bone tubes. One of these is the proximal end of a deer or antelope metapodial. It is 36 mm. long, and the distal end was transversely cut to a depth of 4 mm. and snapped off. Another specimen appears to be the proximal end of an eagle humerus. At a point below the humeral head, where the bone is oval, it was transversely cut and the end snapped off. Neither of these latter two bones was otherwise modified.

Cancellous tissue abraders (3 specimens):

These oval pieces of cancellous bone have rounded surfaces which suggest they were used as abraders. They do not seem to be "paint brushes" since they retain no paint in the interstices. Each seems to be made from a femoral head; they are 35 to 40 mm. in diameter (fig. 24, *e*).

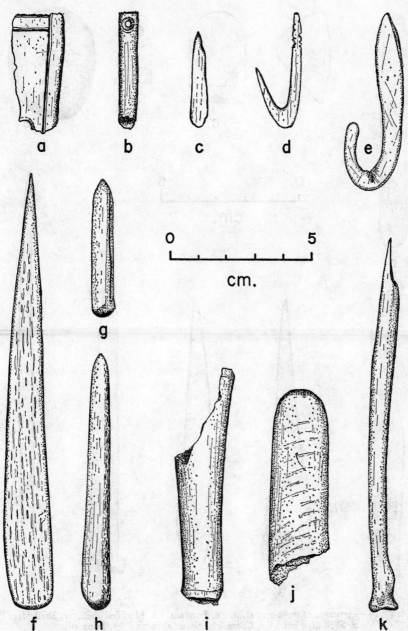

FIGURE 23.—Artifacts of antler and bone. *a–b*, Antler bracelets. *c*, Miniature bone awl.
d–e, Fishhooks. *f*, Split rib awl. *g–h*, "Rib-edge" awls. *i*, Bone tube. *j*, Pottery
modeling tool. *k*, Bird bone awl.

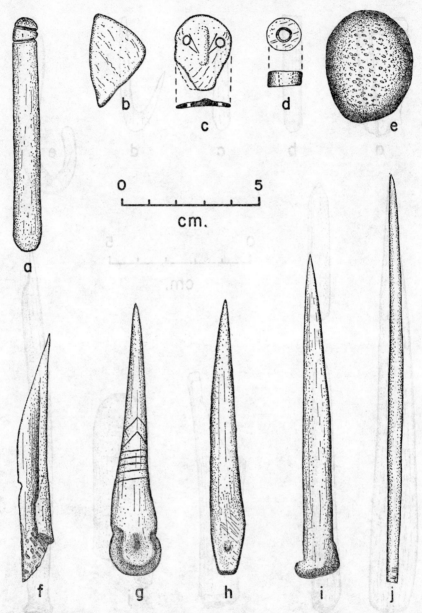

FIGURE 24.—Artifacts of bone and shell. a, Pendant. b, Modified shell. c, Shell "face."
d, Shell disk bead. e, Cancellous tissue abrader. f–j, Bone awls.

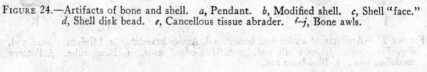

Scored ribs (4 specimens) :

These objects were made by cutting 8 to 16 transverse notches, 3 to 10 mm. apart, across the convex surface of large ribs. All of these objects seem to be broken, since both ends are fragmentary. They range from 95 to 253 mm. in length (fig. 22, *a*).

Awls (79 specimens) :

The awls from Demery generally have sharp, tapering points, although some of them are rather blunt. Each of the tools with points sharp enough to have served as hide perforators is classed as an awl. The classification of these implements follows that of Kidder (1932), with a few necessary modifications as required by the sample. The awls are divided into six groups, based on the material from which they are derived. The amount of work done to bring them to their final form is the basis for the following classification.

Mammal long bones	29
Head of bone left intact except for splitting (24).	
Distal ends of metapodials (18).	
Proximal ends of metapodials (6).	
Head of bone partially worked down (2).	
Circular, tapered awls (2).	
Splinter awl (1).	
Split mammal ribs	5
Neural spine awls ("rib edge")	39
Scapula splinters	2
Bird long bone	1
Miniature awls (source uncertain)	3
Total awls	79

Long bone: head of bone left intact except for splitting (24 specimens).—All of the specimens in this class were made from the metapodials of deer or antelope. They were split by longitudinally sawing the posterior side of the bone and by wedging apart the diastema in the proximal end, and using the resulting splinters, with the ends as butts. A complete metapodial was 237 mm. long, and the longest complete awl is 156 mm. long, revealing that the longest awls were about two-thirds the length of the bone. The butts were rounded and polished by use.

Eighteen awls were made from the distal end of the metapodial (fig. 24, *i*). An unfinished awl is 190 mm. long, but finished specimens are 66 to 156 mm. long. The longer awls are slender and evenly tapered; the shorter ones, thick and stubby, probably from repeated sharpening. Six awls are from the proximal end of the bone. The longest of these is 97 mm. long; the shortest, 69 mm. long; they were highly polished. One of them is incised (fig. 24, *g*).

Long bone: head of bone partially worked down (2 specimens).—

The two specimens of this class, made from the proximal end of metapodials, are of similar size and proportions. They are 98 and 101 mm. long, with long tapering shafts. The butts are smooth and rounded, having been worked so that articulating facets and projecting bone were removed, leaving a smooth, swelling grip (fig. 24, *h*).

Long bone: circular, tapered awls (2 specimens).—These two awls, made from sections of long bones, are 145 and 225 mm. long. There are faint traces of cancellous tissue along one side of the larger awl. The butt of the shorter awl is broken (fig. 24, *j*); the butt of the other is rounded.

Long bone: splinter awl (1 specimen).—The single awl of this class consists of a splinter of long bone which was sharpened on one pointed end. It is smoothed on all surfaces except the butt. Length, 88 mm. (fig. 24, *f*).

Split mammal rib awls (5 specimens).—The five complete specimens in this class were made from split bison ribs, and are 80 to 173 mm. long. They have sharp, tapering points; most of their surfaces are smoothed, although only one of them has a smooth, rounded butt (fig. 23, *f*).

Neural spine awls (39 specimens).—Specimens of this class, usually called "rib edge" awls, were almost certainly made from sections cut from the neural spine of bison thoracic vertebrae (see Wedel, 1955, pp. 119–120). In some cases, the edge is ground down so that the cancellous tissue is nearly gone; in others, part of it remains. They are usually triangular in section and the butts are rounded or faceted. A few of them are long and slender, tapering evenly to form a slender shaft (fig. 23, *h*), but more often they are short and stubby (fig. 23, *g*).

Scapula splinter awls (2 specimens).—Fragments of bison scapula spines, as much as 40 mm. long, are fashioned into awls by grinding one end smooth to serve as the butt, and the other into a sharp point.

Bird long bone awl (1 specimen).—The single awl of this class is made from what appears to be a radius, with one end brought to a sharp, stubby point. Length, 129 mm. (fig. 23, *k*).

Miniature awls (3 specimens).—These awls are made from unidentifiable, thin-walled bones. Two of them are slender and tapered, with sharp points. The third awl has nearly parallel edges and a blunt, stubby point (fig. 23, *c*). They are 32 to 62 mm. long, and 5 mm. wide.

Serrated rib tip (1 specimen):

One end of a large rib, 230 mm. long, is serrated; the bone adjacent to the serrations is polished and beveled from wear (fig. 22, *b*).

Pottery modeling tools (5 specimens):

These five incomplete items were probably made from bison ribs. Four of them have one convex and one broken end; the fifth one is fragmentary. Surfaces are smooth but they are not polished. The original lengths of these tools exceeded 68 to 160 mm. (fig. 23, *j*).

Ulna chisel (1 specimen):

The proximal end of a bison ulna and part of the shaft were used for this tool, which is 195 mm. long. The humeral articulating facet is lacking. The proximal end has a chisel-shaped edge which is turned at about a 45-degree angle from the flat surface of the bone (fig. 20, *e*).

Ulna picks (6 specimens):

The proximal ends of right bison ulnae have rounded and smoothed tips, perhaps indicating use as digging tools. Three of them are cut or hacked on the posterior surfaces below the distal ends. One of the latter tools has a smooth anterior surface below the distal end; the other two show signs of hacking. This modification probably had a function in hafting these tools (fig. 20, *d*).

Bison radius picks (4 specimens):

These tools were made by cutting away part of the shaft of a bison radius and sharpening the midsection to a chisellike edge. Three of the four specimens have oval holes 25 to 40 mm. in diameter extending longitudinally through the articulating surfaces into the marrow cavity. They range from 247 to 180 mm. in length (fig. 20, *f*).

Digging tools (6 specimens):

This residual category includes tools with polished, blunted points that are not readily identifiable as to function. The blunted to pointed, polished tips suggest that they may have been used as digging tools. Portions of spinous processes from bison scapula were used for three of them, which are 120 to 310 mm. long. One of them is from the medial edge of a left bison scapula; it is 170 mm. long. One tool is part of a bison rib, 134 mm. long, and a final specimen is part of a heavy long bone, 180 mm. long.

Pendant (1 specimen):

The rib of a small mammal has been cut into a segment 85 mm. long; it tapers from 9 mm. in width at one end to 8 mm. at the other. Both ends are convex; the smaller end has two grooves, by means of which it may have been suspended (fig. 24, *a*).

ANTLER ARTIFACTS

Cylinders (11 specimens):

These objects, sometimes called "tapping tools," were made from the proximal ends of mule deer antlers by cutting around the antler to a depth of 4 to 6 mm. and snapping the section off, about 40 mm. below the lowest tine. The attaching burrs are rounded and reduced;

the cut, distal ends are rounded and smoothed. Lengths range from 110 to 150 mm., with diameters from 20 to 40 mm. Only one of them is smooth and polished (fig. 22, f).

Tine flakers (15 specimens):

These tines were cut or broken from the racks of deer, and range in length from 25 to 120 mm. Seven of them consist simply of tips broken from a tine. Thirteen tips have beveled ends or the ends are striated in such a manner that they may have served as a flaking or knapping tool.

Bracelets (3 specimens):

A small piece of incised and pierced plate antler is probably part of a bracelet or some similar ornament (fig. 23, a). Two pieces of long, thin, pierced antler may also be bracelets. They were made from thin strips of the compact outer layer of antler; the ends were perforated by a tapered drill (fig. 23, b).

SHELL ARTIFACTS

Miniature shell "face" (1 specimen):

This object was made from a thin piece of mollusk shell, and is similar in some respects to large gorgets found in North Dakota mounds (Howard, 1953) and elsewhere; differences seem to be largely a function of the much smaller scale of this object. It is 20 mm. wide and 26 mm. high (fig. 24, c).

Disk beads (2 specimens):

One disk bead is 12 mm. wide and 5 mm. thick, with a conical hole drilled from one side (fig. 24, d). A roughly circular piece of mollusk shell, 18 mm. wide and 1 mm. thick, may be an unfinished bead.

Scrapers (23 specimens):

These tools are mollusk shells of a size and form that suggest they were used as scrapers, with the lip of the shell acting as the scraping edge. The shell edges are rounded or beveled, some of them having been worn into a straight edge. Five of them were purposefully shaped into triangular forms (fig. 22, d), and three of these are so worn that the hinges are now lacking.

Two small, roughly triangular pieces of shell, 30×40 mm. and 20×32 mm., have smoothly worn edges (fig. 24, b), and one shell, retaining the hinge, has a nearly flat scraping edge bearing two shallow serrations (fig. 22, e).

PERISHABLE REMAINS

The charred remains of several food plants were in the bell-shaped pits in Houses 3 and 4. The most common of these was corn: kernels,

pieces of cobs, roots, stalks, husks, and leaves were especially plentiful
in Feature 65 in House 3. A fragment of braided cornhusk from
Feature 65 suggests the treatment of ripened corn in which the ears
were husked and braided into long strings. The kernels from Feature
67 in House 3 resemble ethnological specimens which were picked
green, roasted on the cob, shelled and dried; those from Feature 65
seem to have been brought to maturity. The size and the internal
structure of a bean from Feature 67 resembles red beans of the variety
collected by Oscar H. Will on the Fort Berthold Reservation in North
Dakota (descendants of which are in the collections of the State Historical Society). The charred, peeled roots of Pomme blanche, or
Tipsina (*Psoralea esculenta* Marsh) were in Feature 65 in House 3,
and in Feature 94 of House 4. Gilmore (1919, p. 92) states that these
roots were dug in June or in early July.

A few items of material culture were also preserved by charring.
Perhaps the most significant and interesting of these is a piece of
basketry (fig. 20, *a*). The elements are woven under-three-over-
three, creating a diagonal pattern known as twilled plaiting. Gilmore, in discussing Arikara baskets made from the inner bark of black
willow and boxelder, illustrates two baskets which were apparently
woven in the same manner as the Demery fragment (1925, pp. 89–95,
figs. 41–42). A piece of peeled wood underlying the basketry may be
part of a post foundation; if this is the case, the original basket was
about the size of the *sátwa*, a large Arikara work basket that stood
knee high (Gilmore, 1925, p. 94). The elements in the Demery specimen are similar in size and form to those in Arikara workbaskets in
the State Historical Society collections.

A piece of wood, rectangular in cross section, is cut and slotted in
the same manner as a bone knife handle, and is probably correctly
identified as a wooden knife handle. A second piece of wood, rounded
on one end and bearing a deep notch, is from the same pit. The
growth rings are identical in both cross sections, and the pieces
obviously belong together: the object is tentatively restored (fig.
20, *c*).

A final perishable specimen is a fragmentary buckskin bag from
Feature 65. It was originally 150 mm. or more long and 100 mm. or
more deep. It was made by folding a rectangular piece of hide back
upon itself, piercing the edges, and lacing it together. Since the top
is now gone there is no way to determine how it was closed; since it
was found lying flat, it was probably closed by a flap rather than by
a drawstring. It was empty when found save for a few ounces of
sterile earth, and the surface of the bag indicated that it carried no
decoration that involved piercing the hide.

FAUNAL REMAINS

The following species have been identified among the artifacts and the food refuse at Demery:

Animal:	Number of individuals
Artiodactyls:	
Bison	95
Deer and antelope	5
Elk	1
Carnivores:	
Canids	12
Badger	1
Rodents:	
Rabbit	1
Ground squirrel	2
Fish and reptiles:	
Catfish	x
Turtles	4
Birds:	
White pelican	1
Marsh hawk	1
American rough-leg hawk	1
Ferruginous rough-leg hawk	1
Crane	1
Crow	1

The avian bones were identified by Mr. Loye Miller, Department of Zoology, University of California at Davis; the bison, fish, and turtles, by Wood; and the remaining animals by Dr. J. Arnold Shotwell, Museum of Natural History, University of Oregon.

Comments on the bison bone from Demery, Paul Brave, and Huff have appeared elsewhere (Wood, 1962 b). The remains of other species were too small for an analysis of butchering technique.

DISCUSSION

STRUCTURES

The houses at Demery stand in rather sharp contrast with those of other circular earth lodge village complexes in the Middle Missouri area. The lack of vertical wall posts along the house shoulder implies a style of roofing the dwellings that differs from the technique most commonly illustrated in the historic Mandan, Hidatsa, and Arikara earth lodges in this same general area.

The Demery lodges are small, ranging from about 20 to 30 feet in diameter. They are circular to oval, with the long axis of the house in line with the orientation of the entrance. The entrances, facing the southwest, overlooked the broad expanse of river terrace to the southwest, rather than the Missouri River or John Grass Creek. The houses were built in pits dug about a foot and a half into the ground, with shallow, dish-shaped floors. A central, unlined basin-shaped fireplace is in the house center, around which are four roof supports set in the form of a square with the posts oriented to the four cardinal directions. There are no postholes on the edge of the house floor; the walls and roof were probably composed of poles set along the edge of the house pit and leaned in against stringers resting on the center posts. Supporting evidence for this inference was observed in the charred timbers in House 4, which extend up to the shoulder of the house pit, where they were removed by the road patrol (pl. 8, *b*). House 2 presents the simplest floor plan; the other three houses fully excavated were rebuilt one or more times, and the posthole patterns are therefore more complex. All of the houses were destroyed by fire, since there were charred beams on the floors, with a film of ash covering the last floor level.

The entrances were usually elongated basin-shaped depressions 4 to 7 feet long, 2.5 to 4 feet wide, and 0.2 to 0.5 foot deep. Both sides of these depressions were lined with small postholes that formed the passage walls; in several of the houses these posts continue into, or originate in, the house floor. Bell-shaped pits were most common along the house walls; in six instances, they undercut the house shoulder, and their mouths were bisected by the house wall. A variety of irregular and basin-shaped pits were also in the house floor, as well as a few auxiliary fireplaces.

From the foregoing description, we may infer that the houses were nearly conical in form, with a covered entryway projecting from the southwest side of the structure. Evidence from House 4 suggests that the roof poles were covered with grass over twigs, and the mottled and disturbed nature of the soil overlying the floor seems indicative of an earth cover over the grass. The house fill, that is, resembles that of structures known to have been earth covered at Like-a-Fishhook Village.

The type of house just described is clearly analogous to the "eagle-trapping lodge" of the historic Mandan, as reported by Bowers (1950, p. 232, fig. 25). The same sort of structure has also been described for the Hidatsa by Wilson (1934, pp. 405–409, 411–415, fig. 40). Such dwellings conform in all major details with the type of house inferred from the floor plans of the Demery houses, although the structures at Demery are larger than those described by Bowers and Wilson, since they served as the principal dwelling type, rather than as an adjunct to it. The lack of wall postholes was also noted in houses at the Spotted Bear site in central South Dakota (Hurt, 1954, pp. 4–8, figs. 6–10).

The house walls at Demery were distinctly visible as a line separating the mixed earth of the house fill from the undisturbed native soil outside the house. The irregular nature of the house walls as mapped is a reflection of the actual situation at the site; the oval shape of the house floor area in Houses 1 and 3 may have resulted from rebuilding, but the flattened arc on the southeast side of House 4 may have some other explanation. The house with the simplest floor plan, House 2, was not rebuilt nor unduly complicated, and here the floor was roughly circular. The source for the innovation of building houses without vertical wall posts at Demery is unknown. These houses stand, therefore, as an interesting variation from a more nearly universal mode of construction.

POTTERY

The ceramics from Demery are varied and complex. Fifteen groups of rim sherds are described that probably relate to a single, major occupation termed the Demery Component. Two pottery types, Riggs Straight Rim and Riggs Cross-Hatched Rim, relate to an earlier occupation by a group which left the remains designated as the Thomas Riggs Focus Component.

The pottery of the major occupation is characteristically very thin and quite hard, and vessels are of excellent quality. The largest restored vessel (pl. 14, *b*) seems to be typical in form and execution. The malleating, shaping, and firing of this vessel required extremely fine control of the techniques of pottery making. This vessel weighs 7½ pounds, and even larger vessels are represented among the sherds. In contrast, the extremely thick sherds of Riggs Straight Rim (pl. 13, *l*), with their contorted cores and less compact paste scarcely approach the pottery of the Demery Component in skill of manufacture. The thinness of the Demery pottery is a characteristic feature of the ceramics, a feature shared by sites of the La Roche Focus and related foci farther south along the Missouri River.

The Demery Component pottery was probably made by building up the vessel by lump modeling, and shaping the walls by malleating it with a grooved paddle or, more rarely, by a cord-wrapped paddle. The six vessels represented by the Group 5 pottery are uniformly and conspicuously cord-roughened from the lip to the base. One vessel of Group 3 and two rims of Group 9 carry nearly obliterated markings that suggest they were originally cord-roughened. Only one-half of 1 percent of the Demery pottery was so treated; the remainder was simple-stamped, or so smoothed that the original surface finish is indistinguishable.

There are 1,356 vessels attributed to the occupation by the Demery Component. The range of variation in rim form, illustrated in fig.

13, includes both flaring rims and recurved ("S-shaped" and "collared") rims, as well as a few residual, unclassified examples. Eighty percent of the rims are flared or straight, with recurved rims of all varieties comprising the remaining 20 percent. There is more variation in design on the recurved rims than on the flaring rims, largely because the cord-impressed designs occur nearly exclusively on the recurved rims: cord impressions occur on flared rims only on the four rims described as Examples A–D. Decoration frequencies are as follows: horizontal incising, 44.8 percent; oblique incising, 3.7 percent; cord-impressing, 6.1 percent; and plain or indented 45.4 percent.

The affiliations of pottery groups 1 to 15 are not susceptible to ready generalizations. Typological considerations intimated, even before excavation, that the site was heterogeneous, and that it contained a mixture of ceramic traits typical of two geographically separated and culturally distinct groups. While superposition did establish the fact that 2 pottery types of the Thomas Riggs Focus—Riggs Cross-Hatched and Riggs Straight Rim—predate the major occupation of the site, the remaining 15 groups still convey an impression of heterogeneity, yet they appear to be characteristic of the major occupation by the Demery Component.

Three of these fifteen groups are tentatively identified as types described from other sites. Group 1 resembles the type Talking Crow Straight Rim, as described from sites in central South Dakota (Smith, 1951; Smith and Grange, 1958). Groups 6 and 7 are tentatively identified as the types Fort Rice Cord-Impressed and Fort Rice Trailed, as described from the Huff site (Wood, MS. a) of the Huff Focus. Many of the other types from Demery, including Groups 2–3 and 8, seem to be related to pottery from central South Dakota, including that of the La Roche and Shannon Foci, and the Arzberger site. Ceramically Demery is "transitional" between sites of the Chouteau Aspect and those of the Huff Focus. This is not to say that Demery is simply a fusion of these two complexes, but it seems obvious that its predecessors drew heavily upon sources both to the north (Huff Focus) and to the south (Chouteau Aspect) for its roster of material culture.

The Demery site is on the west bank of the Missouri River immediately south of the North and South Dakota boundary. Village sites are plentiful along both banks of the Missouri River to the north and south, but collections from nearby sites yield no pottery that suggests they are closely related to Demery. The material from the site cannot be correlated with any known site within the limits of North Dakota. Demery may be regarded as a site-unit intrusion (Willey, 1956, pp. 9–11) into the area, since it appears as a distinct complex in an area previously dominated by the Thomas Riggs and Huff Foci (Wood, MS. b) and is not closely related to either of these complexes.

There are no cultural predecessors for Demery to the north, but there are no complexes yet described to the south which provide sources for most of the traits that set Demery apart from the Thomas Riggs and Huff Foci. The flared-rimmed pottery at Demery carrying horizontally incised lines (Group 2) is related to pottery in sites downstream along the Missouri River in South Dakota and Nebraska. In 1949, Paul Cooper described a pottery complex along the Missouri River in South Dakota which he called Category B (1949, pp. 303–306), and demonstrated the wide geographic and temporal distribution of the rim design occurring on this pottery. The importance and the complexity of Category B are being revealed as the excavation and analysis of the many sites in the Fort Randall and Oahe Reservoirs in South Dakota have proceeded. A number of sites and foci have been described that are related to this complex and to Demery, including the Arzberger site (Spaulding, 1956); the La Roche and Scalp Creek sites, assigned to the La Roche Focus by Hurt (1952; see also Meleen, 1948); the Myers site (Hoard, 1949); the Shannon Focus, as represented at the Spain site (Smith and Grange, 1958); the Akaska Focus, as represented at the Swan Creek and the Payne sites (Hurt, 1957; Wilmeth, 1958); and sites of the Redbird Focus, north central Nebraska (Wood, MS., 1956). This brief review of related sites makes it evident that the primary orientation of Demery is to the south (see map 6); only a few traits at Demery indicate relationships to the north.

Arzberger appears to predate sites of the La Roche Focus and probably is at least in part ancestral to that complex. The pottery from Arzberger is complex and heterogeneous, but his analysis of the pottery modes at the site led Spaulding (1956, pp. 111–168) to the conclusion that there is only one occupation represented in the remains. The situation at Demery is comparable in that there are a great many varieties of pottery, but the majority of excavated material is attributed to a single occupation. The pottery at Arzberger was simple-stamped, cord-roughened, or check-stamped. All of these techniques occur at Demery, but only simple-stamping was of any importance: only one-half of 1 percent of the pottery was cord-roughened, and there was a single check-stamped body sherd.

The Arzberger pottery was divided into two groups, the Arzberger Group (collared rims) and the Hughes Group (straight or outflaring rims). Certain collared rims of the type Arzberger Horizontal Incised are similar to the horizontally incised rims from Demery with recurved rims and a pinched or punctated lower border (Group 8), and the collared Arzberger Opposed Diagonal rims are similar to the recurved rims from Demery decorated with opposed diagonals and finger pinchings or punctates (Group 9). There are even greater correspondences between certain of the Demery pottery and the Hughes Group, as the horizontally incised and plain rims of this group are closely analogous to the Group 1, or Talking Crow Straight Rims, and the Group 2 rims from Demery. In brief, there are enough similarities in rim form and decorative elements in these sites to indicate participation in a common tradition, if not contact or contemporaneity.

Since the cord-roughened pottery comprises such a small percentage of the Demery sample, and since cord-roughening seems to be an early trait, we may infer that Demery is later in time than Arzberger. The large number of rims decorated with cord-impressed lines at Demery clearly sets the site apart from Arzberger, since the five cord-impressed rims from Arzberger appear to be trade sherds from a "Middle Mandan" source. The angular and curvilinear "rainbows" on the cord-impressed and incised Demery rims may be duplicated in both the Thomas Riggs and Huff Foci, but it is more likely that Demery acquired these designs from the latter source: the recurved rims carrying these designs at Demery more closely resemble the S-shaped Huff rims than they do the collared Thomas Riggs rims. In sum, Demery appears to postdate Arzberger, for which there are two carbon-14 dates: A.D. 1461 and 1529 (samples M–1126 and M–1126a, run by the Radiocarbon Laboratory, University of Michigan, from samples provided by the University of Nebraska as part of the Missouri Basin Project Chronology Program).

The pottery complex at Demery is most closely related to sites of the Chouteau Aspect (Stephenson, 1954). Among the foci assigned to this aspect are the La Roche (Hurt, 1952), the Shannon (Smith and Grange, 1958), and the Akaska (Hurt, 1957). The outstanding ceramic trait of this aspect is the horizontally incised design applied to straight to outflaring rims. The Group 2 rims from Demery, which comprise 35.1 percent of the site sample, carry this rim design in its most characteristic form. The Demery pottery most closely resembles the type Grey Cloud Horizontal-Incised at the Spain site, which has protruded T- or L-shaped lips that are lacking in Demery. The type Wheeler Horizontal-Incised from La Roche Focus sites (Hurt, 1952, p. 76) similarly differs from the Demery pottery in having protruded lips. The type Nordvold Horizontal-Incised, from the Akaska Focus Swan Creek and Payne sites (Hurt, 1957, pp. 44–45; Wilmeth, 1958, p. 5) has brushed necks, a trait wholly lacking in the Demery sample. The Group 1 sherds at Demery are tentatively identified as Talking Crow Straight Rim, a common type in sites of the Chouteau Aspect (Smith and Grange, 1958). At Demery, this type comprises 35.6

percent of the rims; together with Group 2, these groups make up 70.7 percent of the site sample.

A number of the minority types at Demery, included in the remaining 29.3 percent of the rim groups, are comparable to minority types in Chouteau Aspect sites. The Demery Group 3 rims, for example, resemble the type Iona Diagonal-Incised Rim from the Spain site, although the Demery specimens lack the rim protrusion typical of Iona Ware. Again, the Group 5 rims resemble in a general way some of the Campbell Creek types as defined at the Talking Crow site (Smith, 1951, pp. 37–39). Groups 8 and 9 resemble some of the pottery from Arzberger (Spaulding, 1956, pp. 139–141), and the types Wheeler Horizontal-Incised and Wheeler Incised-Triangle from the Scalp Creek site (Hurt, 1952, pp. 75–76). In none of these instances do the groups from Demery and the types from the other sites approach identity. These correspondences, together with the presence of the type Talking Crow Straight Rim, are, however, indicative of the cultural affiliation of Demery with certain of the South Dakota sites and foci.

OTHER ARTIFACTS

The bone artifacts at Demery are abundant and of good quality. Scapula hoes are common, and except for the removal of the spine and the posterior border, the implements were modified only by the preparation of the broad end for use as a hoe. Other scapula tools include knives made from the thin bone from the scapula center and which resemble the historic "squash knives." A cleaverlike implement is more distinctive, although its function is unknown: it may have been used as a knife. This latter tool is also known from Arzberger (Spaulding, 1956, p. 49, pl. 4, 0). The bison radius picks from Demery resemble those from the Dodd site (Lehmer, 1954, p. 65, fig. 30, g) in having a hole through the articulating surface. They differ from those at the Paul Brave site (Wood and Woolworth, 1964, p. 38) and the Thomas Riggs site (Hurt, 1953, p. 34) since the picks from the latter two sites are longitudinally split.

The 79 bone awls from Demery are, for the most part, forms which are common to most sites in the Middle Missouri area. The principal exception is the class commonly termed "rib-edge" awls, but which appear to be made from the neural spine of bison vertebrae (Wedel, 1955, pp. 119–120), rather than from rib edges, as originally suggested by Kidder (1932). These implements, sometimes also called pins or flakers, are lacking at Paul Brave, Thomas Riggs, and Huff, and as far as present evidence is concerned they appear to be lacking also in historic Mandan and Hidatsa sites. Wedel, however, reports them from sites of probable Arikara origin in the vicinity of Mobridge, S. Dak. (1955, pp. 119–120), and Lehmer illustrates them from the Dodd and Phillips Ranch sites, in the vicinity of Pierre, S. Dak. (1954, pp. 65, 110, fig. 31, *j–n*). Similar specimens occur in the La Roche site (Meleen, 1948, pl. 3, 8–11), the Spain site (Smith and Grange, 1958, p. 111, pl. 34, *m*), in sites of the Redbird Focus in north central Nebraska (Wood, 1956), and in the Lower Loup Focus in central Nebraska (Dunlevy, 1936, p. 197, pl. 13, *b–d*). In central South Dakota, the La Roche Focus probably predates A.D. 1600, but the Redbird Focus is estimated to date somewhat later, from about A.D. 1600 to 1700. The known Lower Loup sites contain trade goods and probably date after 1700, although Wedel (1947, p. 155) has suggested that the complex was in existence by about A.D. 1550. On an earlier time level, Spaulding (1956, pp. 56–57, pl. 4, *b–e*) found them at Arzberger. Wedel (1955, p. 119) has suggested that these tools may be a late time marker in the Central Plains, but in the Middle Missouri area they are present in prehistoric times. They do not occur, however, in sites suspected of affiliation with the historic Mandan or Hidatsa.

The serrated fleshing tools made from bison or elk metapodials were lacking at Demery, but there appears to be a substitute in the form of a serrated rib tip. The wear on the working end of this tool is the same as that on the blade of metapodial fleshers.

Two antler artifacts are worthy of comment: these are the antler cylinders, or "tapping tools," and the pierced strip bracelets. The antler cylinders from Demery are identical to those from sites in the Central Plains. Moving from the Demery site to the south, the first instance of these tools appearing is at the Payne site (Wilmeth, 1958, p. 10, fig. 22), and they occur also at the Spotted Bear site (Hurt, 1954, p. 18, fig. 22, VIII), and at the Scalp Creek site (Hurt, 1952, p. 42, fig. 25, *9*). "Tapping tools" also occur in sites of the Redbird Focus (Wood, MS., 1956), in the Leary Oneota site (Hill and Wedel, 1936, pl. 10, *a*), and in sites of the Oneota, Nebraska, and Upper Republican aspects in the Central Plains. Short antler cylinders, usually only slightly longer than their maximum diameter, are in the Historical Society collections from the Biesterfeldt Cheyenne site and the On-a-Slant Mandan village, as well as at the Huff site (Wood, MS. a), but they are not known to be present in Thomas Riggs Focus sites. The affiliations of the "tapping tool" are felt to be with Central Plains complexes and with the later sites in the Middle Missouri area.

The two pieces of long, thin, pierced antler may be from bracelets. Similar specimens from Paul Brave (Wood and Woolworth, 1964, pp. 45–46, fig. 11, *a–i*), Double Ditch (Will and Spinden, 1906, pl. 36, *w–z*), and Slant Village are of essentially the same form. We find no record of them south of the vicinity of Mobridge (Baerreis and Dallman, 1961, pp. 316–327, figs. 88–90), and it is possible that the affiliation of this particular artifact class is with complexes that shared in the development of the Mandan or were in contact with the Mandans. As far as we can determine, these items are uniformly made from antler, although they are often erroneously identified as of bone.

About half of the mollusk shells from Demery show wear on one or more edges opposite the hinge, and are probably scrapers. A similar use of mollusk shell is reported from the La Roche site (Meleen, 1948, p. 18, pl. 4, *1–6*), and from the Arzberger site (Spaulding, 1956, p. 59, pl. 5, *r–t*). Shell scrapers also appear in the Huff site (Wood, MS. a), and there are 51 specimens from the Biesterfeldt site.

A carved shell "face" is similar in many respects to large gorgets recovered in mounds in North Dakota and elsewhere (Howard, 1953). Differences seem to be largely a function of the small scale of the Demery specimen. This is the only Demery artifact which appears to show a "Southern Cult" motif; the oblique incised lines between the raised nose and the eyes seem to be a simplified rendition of the "weeping eye" motif executed on Southern Cult items.

In contrast to the majority of local sites, perishables were relatively abundant at Demery. Among the charred food remains are corn, beans, and Tipsina root. Of special interest is the fact that evidence for braided corn was apparently present, and some corn kernels seemed to have been cut green, roasted on the cob, and shelled, giving insight into methods of food preparation and preservation. Other perishable objects included a fragment of twilled basketry, possibly from a large work basket, and a slotted knife handle. Leather work is represented by the remains of a small, rectangular buckskin bag.

CONCLUSIONS

The excavation of the Demery site provides a statement for the northernmost known manifestation of the Chouteau Aspect. The peripheral position of Demery to other sites of this aspect is a factor which in part accounts for the presence of traits that set it apart from other sites of the aspect. The proximity of Demery to another and distinct cultural entity, the Huff Focus, is advanced as an explanation for some of these traits.

Demery is not closely related to sites in its immediate geographic locality, neither those inferred to be earlier in time nor those that postdate it. Despite its proximity to sites which participated in the cultural stream that culminated in the historic Mandan, there are only a few ties with the prehistoric sites relating to that group. The closer relationships of Demery are to the south, downstream along the Missouri River, although there are details of the architectural pattern, the ceramic complex, and some other traits that set the site apart from the most closely related sites. For this reason the major occupation at the site is designated the Demery Component of an unnamed focus.

The village was built and occupied by a group of people who apparently moved north along the Missouri River from some point south of the mouth of the Grand River. These people lived at Demery for some years, probably peacefully, to judge from the lack of fortifications, and seem to have acquired some artifacts from the nearby and culturally distinct Huff Focus. A lengthy occupation is indicated by the fact that some of the houses were rebuilt by the occupants. In brief, Demery appears to be a site-unit intrusion into Huff Focus territory by a group of people from central South Dakota, who retired to the south after an extended occupation of this peripheral position. The time of this occupation and subsequent dislocation is inferred to have been between about A.D. 1550 and 1650.

The presence of a few sherds identified as types found in Thomas Riggs Focus communities indicates an occupation of the Demery site by this focus, previous to the time of the major occupation by the Demery Component.

LITERATURE CITED

BAERREIS, DAVID A., AND DALLMAN, JOHN E.
    1961.   Archaeological investigations near Mobridge, South Dakota. Soc. Amer. Archaeol., Archives of Archaeol., No. 14. Univ. Wisconsin.
BOWERS, ALFRED W.
    1950.   Mandan social and ceremonial organization. Univ. Chicago.
COOPER, PAUL L.
    1949.   Recent investigations in Fort Randall and Oahe Reservoirs, South Dakota. Amer. Antiq., vol. 14, No. 4, pt. 1, pp. 300–310.
DUNLEVY, MARION L.
    1936.   A comparison of the cultural manifestations of the Burkett and Gray-Wolfe sites. Chap. Nebr. Archaeol., vol. 1, No. 2, pp. 147–247. Lincoln.
GILMORE, MELVIN R.
    1919.   Uses of plants by the Indians of the Missouri River region. 33d Ann. Rep. Bur. Amer. Ethnol. for 1911–12, pp. 43–154.
    1925.   Arikara basketry. Mus. Amer. Ind., Heye Found., Indian Notes, vol. 2, No. 2. New York.
HEWES, GORDON W.
    1949.   Pottery from the sites excavated by the 1947 North Dakota field session. Proc. Fifth Plains Conf. Archeol., Notebook No. 1, Lab. Anthrop., Univ. Nebraska, pp. 58–67.
HILL, A. T., AND WEDEL, WALDO R.
    1936.   Excavations at the Leary Indian village and burial site, Richardson County, Nebraska. Nebraska Hist. Mag., vol. 17, No. 1, pp. 3–73.
HOARD, LYON J.
    1949.   Report of the investigation of the Meyer site, Stanley County, South Dakota. South Dakota Archaeol. Comm., Archaeol. Stud., Circ. No. 2.

HOWARD, JAMES H.
1953.   The Southern Cult in the Northern Plains. Amer. Antiq., vol. 19,
No. 2, pp. 130–138.
HURT, WESLEY R., JR.
1952.   Report of the investigation of the Scalp Creek site, 39GR1, and the
Ellis Creek site, 39GR2, Gregory County, South Dakota, 1941, 1951.
South Dakota Archaeol. Comm., Archaeol. Stud., Circ. No. 4.
1953.   Report of the investigation of the Thomas Riggs site, 39HU1, Hughes
County, South Dakota, 1952. South Dakota Archaeol. Comm.,
Archaeol. Stud., Circ. No. 5.
1954.   Report of the investigation of the Spotted Bear site, 39HU26, and
the Cottonwood site, 39HU43, Hughes County, South Dakota, 1953.
South Dakota Archaeol. Comm., Archaeol. Stud., Circ. No. 6.
1957.   Report of the investigation of the Swan Creek site, 39WW7, Wal-
worth County, South Dakota, 1954–1956. South Dakota Archaeol.
Comm., Archaeol. Stud., Circ. No. 7.
KIDDER, A. V.
1932.   Artifacts of Pecos. Phillips Acad., Southwestern Exped. Pap., No. 6.
New Haven.
KLEINSASSER, GLENN.
1953.   Thomas Riggs pottery types. In Hurt, South Dakota Archaeol.
Comm., Archaeol. Stud., Circ. No. 5, pp. 22–31.
LEHMER, DONALD J.
1954.   Archeological investigations in the Oahe Dam area, South Dakota,
1950–51. Bur. Amer. Ethnol. Bull. 158, Riv. Bas. Surv. Pap.,
No. 7.
MELEEN, ELMER E.
1948.   A report on the investigation of the La Roche site, Stanley County,
South Dakota. Univ. South Dakota Mus., Archaeol. Stud., Circ.
No. 5.
NEWELL, H. PERRY, AND KRIEGER, ALEX D.
1949.   The George C. Davis site, Cherokee County, Texas. Soc. Amer.
Archaeol. Mem., No. 16.
SMITH, CARLYLE S.
1951.   Pottery types from the Talking Crow site, Fort Randall Reservoir,
South Dakota. Plains Archeol. Conf. News Letter, vol. 4, No. 3,
pp. 32–41.
SMITH, CARLYLE S., AND GRANGE, ROBERT T., JR.
1958.   The Spain site (39LM301), a winter village in Fort Randall Reser-
voir, South Dakota. Bur. Amer. Ethnol. Bull. 169, Riv. Bas. Surv.
Pap., No. 11, pp. 79–128.
SPAULDING, ALBERT C.
1956.   The Arzberger site, Hughes County, South Dakota. Univ. Michigan,
Mus. Anthrop. Occas. Contr. No. 16.
STEPHENSON, ROBERT L.
1954.   Taxonomy and chronology in the Central Plains-Middle Missouri
area. Plains Anthrop., No. 1, pp. 15–21.
STRONG, WILLIAM D.
1940.   From history to prehistory in the Northern Great Plains. Smithsonian Misc. Coll., vol. 93, No. 10.
WEDEL, WALDO R.
1947.   Culture chronology in the Central Great Plains. Amer. Antiq., vol.
12, No. 3, pp. 148–156.

WEDEL, WALDO R—Continued
    1955. Archeological materials from the vicinity of Mobridge, South Da-
        kota. Bur. Amer. Ethnol. Bull. 157, Anthrop. Pap., No. 45, pp.
        73–188.
WILL, GEORGE F., and HECKER, THAD. C.
    1944. The Upper Missouri River valley aboriginal culture in North Dakota.
        North Dakota Hist. Quart., vol. 11, Nos. 1–2.
WILL, GEORGE F., and SPINDEN, HERBERT J.
    1906. The Mandans; a study of their culture, archaeology, and language.
        Pap., Peabody Mus. Amer. Archaeol. and Ethnol., Harvard Univ.,
        vol. 3, No. 4.
WILLEY, GORDON R.
    1956. An archeological classification of culture contact situations. *In:*
        Robert Wauchope, ed., Seminars in archaeology: 1955. Soc. Amer.
        Archaeol. Mem., No. 11, pp. 1–30.
WILMETH, ROSCOE.
    1958. Report of the investigation of the Payne site, 39WW302, Walworth
        County, South Dakota. South Dakota Archaeol. Comm., Archaeol.
        Stud. Archaeol., Circ. No. 8.
WILSON, GILBERT L.
    1934. The Hidatsa earthlodge. Arr. and ed. by Bella Weitzner. Amer.
        Mus. Nat. Hist., Anthrop. Pap., vol. 33, pt. 5, pp. 341–420.
WOOD, W. RAYMOND.
    1955. Pottery types from the Biesterfeldt site, North Dakota. Plains
        Anthrop., No. 3, pp. 3–12.
    ——— The Redbird Focus. MS., M.A. thesis, Dept. Anthrop., Univ. Nebraska,
        1956.
    MS. a. The Huff site, 32M0211, Oahe Reservoir, North Dakota. MS. a sub-
        mitted to Nat. Park Serv., Reg. 2, on file at the State Hist. Soc.
        North Dakota, 1961. Bismarck.
    MS. b. An interpretation of Mandan culture history. Ph. D. dissertation,
        Dept. Anthrop., Univ. Oregon, 1961. Eugene.
    1962 a. Cord-roughened pottery in north central North America. Plains
        Anthrop., vol. 7, No. 18, pp. 232–236.
    1962 b. Notes on the bison bone from the Paul Brave, Huff, and Demery
        sites (Oahe Reservoir). Plains Anthrop., vol. 7, No. 17, pp.
        201–204.
WOOD, W. RAYMOND, and WOOLWORTH, ALAN R.
    1964. The Paul Brave site, 32SI4, Oahe Reservoir area, North Dakota.
        Bur. Amer. Ethnol. Bull. 189, Riv. Bas. Surv. Pap. No. 33.

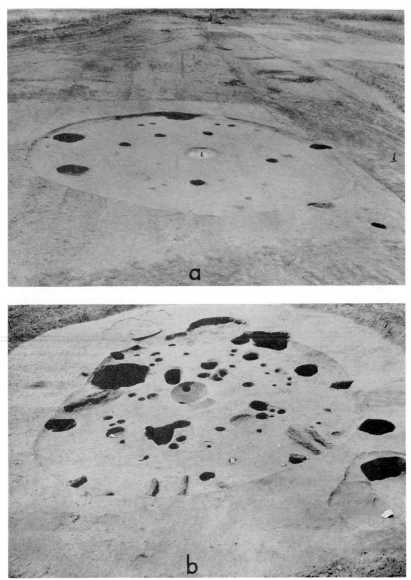

a, House 2. The view is southwest; excavation is beginning in House 3 in background.
b, House 4. The view is southwest, toward the entrance.

a, The entrance passage of House 1; the view is southeast. *b*, Collapsed wall poles on the north wall of House 4.

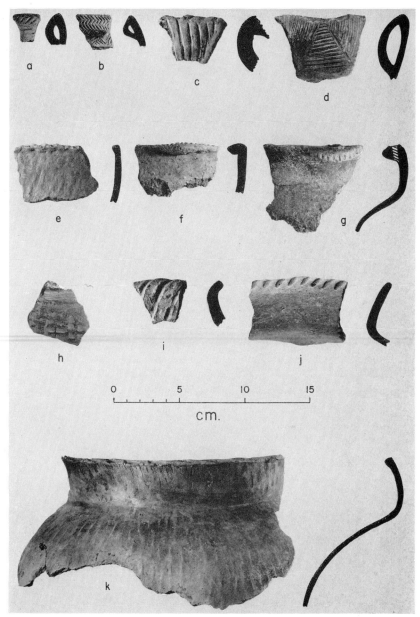

Pottery rim sherds and handles.   *e–g, i–j*, Talking Crow Straight Rim; *i–j*, interior of sherd.

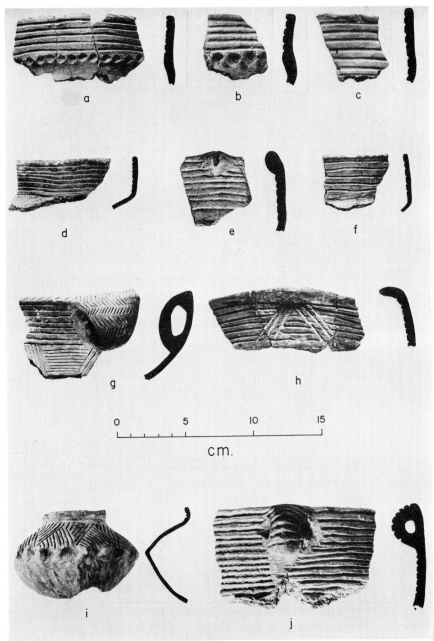

Horizontally incised rim sherds. Note the stab-and-drag treatment to the left of the handle in *j*.

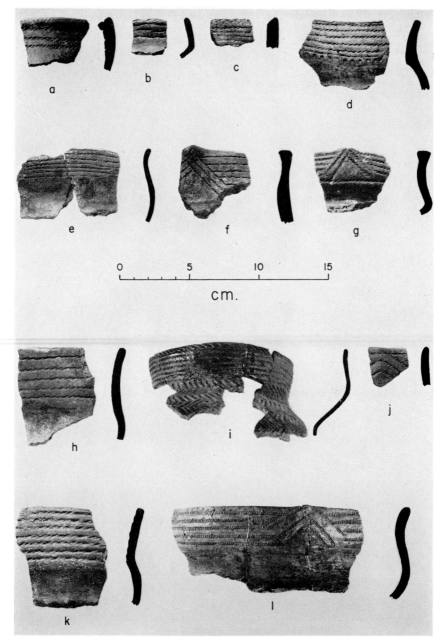

Cord-impressed rim sherds.

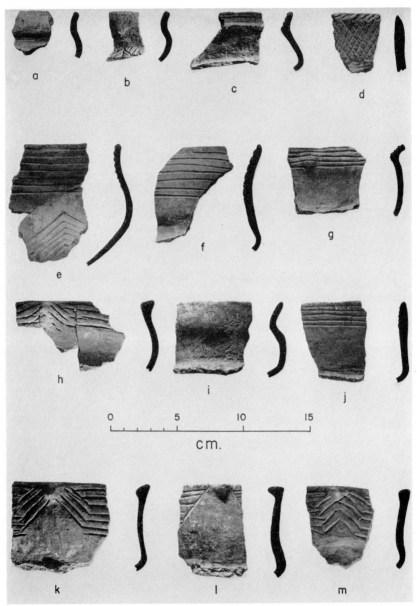

Incised and plain rim sherds.

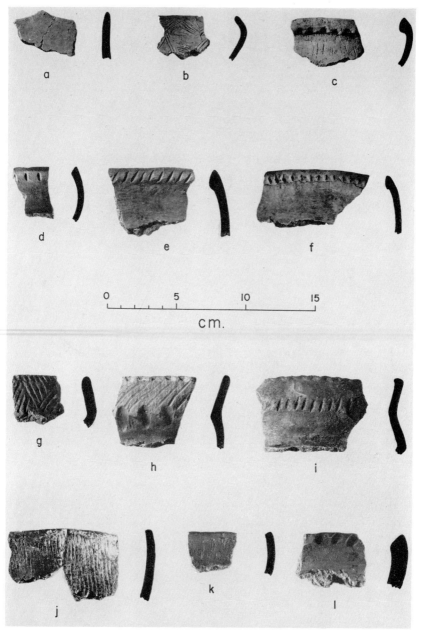

Miscellaneous rim sherds.

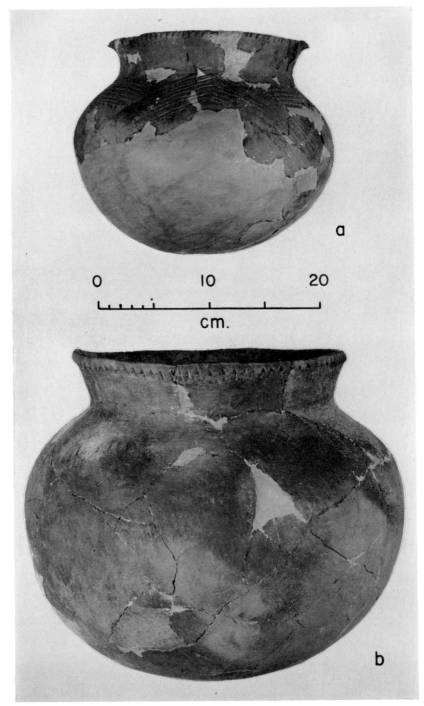

Restored pottery vessels. *a*, Vessel 1, House 2. *b*, Vessel from Feature 93, House 4.

SMITHSONIAN INSTITUTION
Bureau of American Ethnology
Bulletin 189

River Basin Surveys Papers, No. 35
Archeological Investigations at the Hosterman Site (39PO7),
Oahe Reservoir Area, Potter County, South Dakota, 1956

By CARL F. MILLER

139

CONTENTS

	PAGE
Introduction	145
Excavations	146
Fortification ditch	148
Palisade	150
Houses	151
Feature 22	154
Feature 34	154
Feature 32	155
Cache pits	156
Slaughtering or butchering areas	157
Midden pits	159
Artifact material	160
Pottery	160
Classification of body sherds as to exterior treatment	162
Common traits of wares	163
Detailed study of body sherds	165
Lip treatment	167
Rim forms and their treatment	171
Shoulder treatment	182
Handles	183
Vessel shapes	186
Painted pottery	188
Miniature vessels	189
Exotic vessel of possible Caddoan extraction	190
Clay dawdles	191
General statement	192
Artifacts other than pottery	193
Chipped-stone artifacts	193
Projectile points	193
Microblades	194
Scrapers	195
Ovoid bifaces	203
Biface choppers	203
Knives	203
Burinlike implements	205
Stone perforators or gravers	206
Lamellar flake tools	207
Ground and pecked stone tools	208
Hematite and other paint substances	211
Bone artifacts	212
Fetish or trophy skull	220
Scored bird sternum	220
Worked teeth	220
Shell	221
Copper	222
Summary and conclusions	222

PAGE

Trait list_____ 226
Appendix 1. Vegetal remains_____ 231
Appendix 2. Faunal remains_____ 233
Appendix 3. Insect remains_____ 238
Appendix 4. Tables of measurements_____ 239
Literature cited_____ 257
Appendix 5. Human skeletal material from the vicinity of the Hosterman
    site (39PO7), Oahe Reservoir, South Dakota, by William M. Bass____ 259

ILLUSTRATIONS

PLATES

(All plates follow page 266)

15. Vertical and S-shaped rim types, Hosterman site.
16. Rim types, showing typical forms and treatments.
17. Typical rims with and without handles.
18. Rim types, Hosterman site.
19. Cord-impressed rim treatments, Hosterman site.
20. Incised rim sherds, Hosterman site.
21. Double spouted miniature vessel, unusual to the Plains.
22. Group 1 and Group 2 projectile types, Hosterman site.
23. Group 3, Group 4, and notched projectile types.
24. Microblades and lamellar flake knives.
25. Scraper types, Hosterman site.
26. Scraper types, Hosterman site.
27. End and side scraper types.
28. Side scrapers and burin form, Hosterman site.
29. Knife forms and biface ovates.
30. Flake knives and side scrapers; grooved ax and maul.
31. Graver forms, Hosterman site.
32. Lamellar flake tools.
33. Cut bone sections, worked antler, bone tubes, and scapula hoes.
34. Scapula tools; fleshers and sickles.
35. Scapula knives and fleshing tools.
36. Scapula cleaver, pentagonal-shaped tool, hafted knives, and antler tools.
37. Bone awl types and miscellaneous worked-bone objects.
38. Fetish or trophy skull of *Vulpes velox*.

TEXT FIGURES

PAGE

25. The Hosterman site, 39PO7_____ (facing) 147
26. Feature 22, Hosterman site_____ 148
27. Cross section of the fortification ditch, Hosterman site_____ 149
28. Detail of stockade post arrangement, Hosterman site_____ 150
29. Feature 34, Hosterman site_____ 155
30. Feature 32, Hosterman site_____ 155
31. Origin of various shaped pits, Hosterman site_____ 157
32. Landmarks on pottery vessel, Hosterman site_____ 162
33. Pottery trend within Hosterman site_____ 164
34. Horizontal parallel incised rim sherd_____ 166

		PAGE
35.	Vertical rim profiles, Hosterman site	168
36.	S-shaped rim profiles, Hosterman site	169
37.	S-shaped rim decorations	172
38.	Barrel-shaped rim, simple-stamped rim sherd	173
39.	Line-block zonal decorations	176
40.	Rim treatment and decorative zones	180
41.	Restoration of vertical rimmed, simple-stamped vessel	183
42.	Shoulder decoration on large jar sherd, Hosterman site	184
43.	Rim and shoulder area of S-shaped rimmed vessel	185
44.	Line-block design on shoulder area, Hosterman site	186
45.	Line-block design on shoulder area, Hosterman site	187
46.	Line diamond design on shoulder area, Hosterman site	188
47.	Handle types showing points of origin	188
48.	Various miniature vessel types, Hosterman site	190
49.	Two-spouted vessel, Hosterman site, showing decorative design	191
50.	Keeled scraper types	197
51.	Burin with arrows indicating position and direction of flaking	205
52.	Craniostat drawings of adult male (Individual No. 6) from the Hosterman site, Potter County, South Dakota	262

ARCHEOLOGICAL INVESTIGATIONS AT THE HOSTERMAN SITE (39PO7) IN THE OAHE RESERVOIR AREA, POTTER COUNTY, SOUTH DAKOTA, 1956 [1]

By CARL F. MILLER

INTRODUCTION

The Hosterman site, named for John B. Hosterman, owner of the property, is located in sec. 36, T. 119 N., R. 79 W., Potter County, S. Dak., on a high bluff on the east bank overlooking the Missouri River about 2½ miles north of Whitlocks Crossing. It is on the western margins of the Coteau du Missouri, "that part of the Missouri Plateau section of the Great Plains province which lies east of the Missouri River." [2] The name of the Coteau dates back to the days of the French fur traders. The bluff slopes gently toward the Missouri River, then pitches steeply into the river valley about a mile from the present stream. The former stockaded village overlooked the gently sloping plain with a broad view of the valley and the high tableland extending to the east, north, and south. The elevation of the site, 50 or more feet above the flood plain, was advantageous in the defense of the village from attack from the west because of the sharp rise of the bluff on that side.

The village site was first surveyed by Dorothy E. Fraser on August 7, 1949. She described it as

residing on a high bench 75 feet above river bottom on the north side of a small creek and now a half mile or more from the present stream bed. It is a beautiful specimen of what appears to be a really old site. River probably swept in at the foot of bluff at time of occupation. Owner extremely interested and cooperative. It was he who directed attention to this site, hitherto unknown. [3]

Paul L. Cooper revisited the site in September 1949, and he noted that there were

12–15 depressions within (the) ditch which extends from river terrace border to tributary gully at south of site. Area within ditch ca. 320' by 290' (paced).

---

[1] Submitted February 1960.

[2] An excellent study of the Pleistocene geology of eastern South Dakota, including data on the physiographic environment, climate, soils, and biogeography, was issued by the U.S. Geological Survey in 1955. (See Flint, 1955.)

[3] Field notes in files of Missouri Basin Project.

145

House pits occur outside of the ditch to the east and northeast. Depressions rather shallow and poorly defined. Ditch is also relatively shallow throughout most of its length; varies from ca. 0.5′ to ca. 2.5′ in depth. [4]

Early in October 1951, Richard P. Wheeler revisited the site and put down a series of test holes within the palisaded area. He noted:

The total area (inside and outside the ditch) measures about 500′ north-south and 400′ east-west, and cover a little over 4½ acres. Elevation, 1,570′ to 1,580′. Test pits produced evidence similar to that reported by Dorothy Fraser in 1949; a blanket of sterile silt underlain by two strata of occupation debris separated by a layer of sterile sand . . . . Windblown silt has all but obscured the house depressions and defense ditch (on the east side of the site): artifact material does not appear on the surface. A small amount of pothunting has occurred and the specimens found in an anthill in 1953 were discarded by relic hunters.[4]

I began a partial investigation of the site on June 23, 1956, at which time my crew consisted of: John Anderson, Lincoln, Nebr.; Norman Barka, Chicago, Ill.; Tyler Bastian, Stockton, Wis.; Gordon Dentry, Baltimore, Md.; Edwin Floyd, Canyon City, Colo.; Hugh Carl Jones, Provo, Utah; and Dale Osterholt, Platte, S. Dak. Mrs. Ruth Miller, my wife, acted as housekeeper and cook for the crew.

EXCAVATIONS

Prior to the beginning of the 1956 work, the major part of the site was covered with a heavy sod that had sealed in almost all of the cultural debris deposited by the former occupants, and the area to the north and east of the stockade trench was planted to watermelons. The area under cultivation showed islands of heavy cultural debris and shell material presumably marking refuse dump areas outside of dwellings. Shell deposits were heavier outside the stockaded area than inside. The surface inside of the stockade ditch was marked with a series of depressions of various shapes and sizes. The most prominent depressions were circular in outline and of various sizes, ranging from 20 to 40 feet across; the others were irregular in outline and of various depths, but none were very distinct or deep. Surrounding the main portion of the village were the remains of a stockade ditch in the form of a crescent, the open ends being to the west and southwest and terminating at the edge of the western bluff.

During excavation, it was found that the normal stratigraphy within the site consisted of a relatively distinct sod layer with its attendant root zone that extended to a depth of 0.5 foot. This zone was culturally sterile, and below it for another 1.0 to 2.0 feet was a zone of sterile windblown loess of silt and fine sand. Below the latter was the uppermost layer of cultural debris accumulated during

---

4 Field notes in files of Missouri Basin Project.

the occupation of the site. This layer was of uneven thickness and varied from 0.5 foot to 2.5 feet in thickness, depending upon the contour of the former surface and the presence of shallow pits, and below this were patches of a former humus zone that was not entirely destroyed by the former occupants of the site. Below this zone was another thin layer of cultural material that was rather spotty in deposition.

The area within the protective moat measured 269 feet from the inside, or eastern side, of the stockade trench to the brink of the bluff on the west, and 340 feet north and south.

Before starting the excavation a north-south line, y coordinate, was established 9 degrees east of north, and an east-west line, x coordinate, was run at right angles to it, bisecting the north-south line at the 160-foot stake dividing the site into four quarters of almost equal size. The site was then staked off in 10-foot squares. Square designation was determined by the number of the stake in the upper right-hand corner of each square. Thus, square 170 is determined by having this number in the upper right-hand corner of the square.

The coordinate position of each archeological feature was obtained by scaling x and y coordinates of the approximate center of the site. Each feature was then plotted to scale on a coordinate base chart according to the square in which it appeared.

An exploratory trench, 10 feet wide, was started at square 170 and extended for a distance of 100 feet so as to intercept four of the depressed areas in order to test their validity as house sites. At the same time other men were placed in squares 180 and 190 (fig. 25).

Along the east faces of squares 170, 180, and 190, we found the first indication of cultural material at a depth of 1.0 foot below the root system of the present sterile windblown grass-covered loess. Progressing westward this layer slowly decreased and the overburden of sterile material became noticeably greater. The upper portion of this cultural debris consisted mainly of small fragments of bone. Sherds were derived from the top 0.2 foot of this deposit whereas the number and size of the bone fragments increased as the distance downward was increased. Entire bones were found at the base of this level. Artifacts were few. A small unnotched isosceles triangular projectile point and a badly decayed bear's jaw were recovered from this bone layer.

The main purpose of cutting this exploratory trench across the area was to test the four depressions that were thought to be the remains of dwellings. None of them proved to be such. They were either cattle or bison wallows. The house structures uncovered were not manifested in any way by surface indications. Other areas tested where depressions occurred proved this contention.

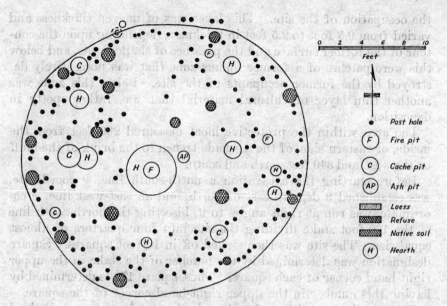

FIGURE 26.—Feature 22, Hosterman site.

Near the west end of the exploratory trench we located and completely uncovered the remains of a circular structure, Feature 22 (fig. 26). Once the house pit was outlined, all of the fill was passed through screens down to within 0.5 foot of the floor. This portion was carefully removed by trowels; the material was screened and placed in separate containers. Even with all this care we recovered very few artifacts from the zone.

After the floor had been cleared, the various features, such as postholes, cache pits, and firepits, were cleaned of their contents. Anything found within any of these features was kept separate from that found on the floor. Later the surrounding area was explored in order to locate the entranceway or any other feature that might have been associated with the structure. We not only failed to find any evidence of a passageway, but we found nothing that we could positively associate with the house structure.

Cache pits within the house floor ranged from small shallow depressions to fairly large bell-shaped pits of a size sufficient for an average-sized man to squeeze into easily. Most pits contained loose soil; some had an occasional artifact and the larger bell-shaped pit was completely filled with disarticulated bones and very little soil.

FORTIFICATION DITCH

The fortification ditch began to the northwest of the site and proceeded eastward along the north side, gently curving to the south. Along the east side it continued around to the south to a place where it gradually blended into the steep sides of a gully, thus surrounding the major portion of the occupation area.   On the surface it appeared as a shallow trench almost 20 feet wide and of various depths.   The greater depths were found in the northern section; the eastern section displayed the shallowest.

Selecting a place where the ditch was the deepest, we cut a 10-foot trench not only to cross-section the ditch but to determine if any remains of a stockade still persisted.   Six-inch levels were maintained at all times.   The trench walls exposed four distinct humus zones; the uppermost averaged 0.4 foot in thickness and incorporated the grass roots of the present ground cover.   Underlying this was a layer of sterile loess 1.2 feet in thickness.   Beneath this was a second humus layer 0.5 foot in thickness.   This in turn rested upon 1.6 feet of sterile loess, and beneath this was the third humus zone, which averaged 0.3 foot in thickness.   Underneath was a very thin zone, 0.2 foot in thickness, of very fine silt, which rested upon a deposit of midden 0.4 foot in thickness.   Beneath the midden layer was the earliest humus zone, which measured 0.3 foot in thickness.   This humus rested upon a 0.3 foot zone of sterile loess, which in turn covered 1.2 feet of laminated silts deposited in the original bottom of the ditch as constructed by the inhabitants of the site (fig. 27).

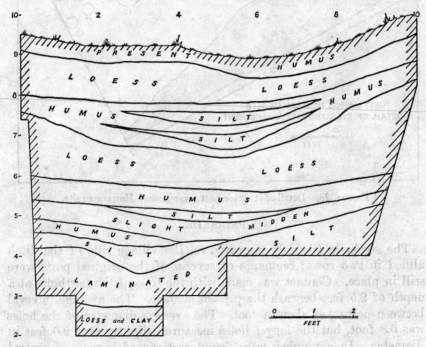

Figure 27.—Cross section of the fortification ditch, Hosterman site.

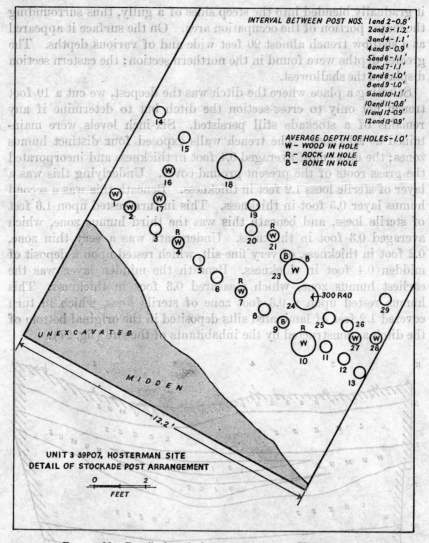

FIGURE 28.—Detail of stockade post arrangement, Hosterman site.

PALISADE

The stockade (fig. 28) appeared on the village side of the ditch
alined in two rows; remnants of several of the original posts were
still in place. Contact was made with the tops of the postholes at a
depth of 2.5 feet beneath the present surface. The average interval
between posts was about a foot. The average diameter of the holes
was 0.8 foot, but the larger holes measured slightly over 2.0 feet in
diameter. In a number were found sections of bones and several
stones that were used to wedge the post firmly in place. Whether the

double stockade was erected at the same time or represented an interval of time could not be determined, for both lines of posts
originated on the same level. It is suspected that the two structures were contemporaneous, since the site appeared to have been
occupied for only a short time.

HOUSES

Houses were of two general shapes: round or circular and rectangular. Apparently the rectangular house, which was partially uncovered, was of an earlier period than the circular houses. One circular
house was completely excavated, and only a part of another was
exposed.

Circular structures, Features 22 and 34, are characterized by a circular pit that was excavated at various depths, depending upon the
inclination of the builder, into the sterile native soil. We found no
signs of any plaster being used on the walls of the pit, and the floor
was firmed by trampling. There were four centrally placed roof supports set in a rough square surrounding the centrally placed firepit.
Such pits were basin shaped. When these were uncovered we found
them completely and firmly packed with a whitish ash that could have
resulted from the burning of cottonwood or buffalo chips. Cottonwood, which does not burn with a high heat, was likely used, since
not only the basin itself but the area around the basin was burned a
brick red. Scattered over the floor between the central four supports
and the edge of the floor were a number of smaller postholes and a
number of pits, some of which were used as cache areas and others
for midden disposal. Placement of the wall posts showed some variation, which also must have been true for the superstructure.

In Feature 22 there were 10 large peripheral posts incorporated
within the wall that were more or less evenly spaced around the circumference of the structure. The intervals between these were filled
with fairly evenly spaced smaller posts. Precedent indicates that the
round houses of the Plains were entered by way of a roofed and walled
entranceway constructed at right angles to the line of the two primary roof supports. Such a structure was not found connected with
this house.

Postholes appeared as either soft spots or darkened circular areas
in the house floor. Their diameters varied from 0.25 foot to 2.1 feet
and in depth from 0.3 foot to 3.5 feet. In most cases the holes were
filled in with a light, fluffy soil, and sometimes the butt end of the
former posts still rested therein. In several of the larger postholes
were sections of bison bones and ribs or waterworn cobbles that were
inserted as wedges to stabilize the posts. Field examination of the
wooden fragments indicated that most of the posts were of cotton-

wood; only an occasional piece of juniper was used. Probably the use of cottonwood was due to the fact that it grew readily at hand in the nearby bottom lands, whereas juniper had to be transported from a greater distance. The general practice probably was to choose the material closer at hand.

Within the floor area we found the same variation as to the placement of pits. In Feature 22 there were a number of pits. Some were undercut and bell shaped; others were straight sided, and still others were what we have called pocket caches, for they were small and shallow. All appeared to have been dug while the house was occupied, for they all originated at floor level. In Feature 34, which was only partially exposed, we found no floor pits outside the centrally placed firepit.

Lehmer (1954, p. 31) suggests that

other holes in the floor may have contained wooden mortars after the fashion of the historic Arikara and Mandan. These holes were cylindrical, somewhat larger than the largest postholes, and were always located more or less on a line between the firepit and the entrance. They were generally slightly offset toward the entrance from a line connecting the eastern pair of primary roof posts.

Of all the structures investigated, none was burned. It would appear that they were abandoned and allowed to decay gradually, leaving no tangible evidence as to the arrangement of the elements of their superstructure.

On the other hand, Feature 32 was characterized by a rectangular pit of considerable size with rounded corners and outlined with small individual posts more or less uniformly spaced. The west wall was completely excavated, and also parts of the north and south walls. Again, there was no evidence of the use of plaster on the walls of the pit. The floor of native material was firmly packed. Entrance into the structure was gained by a walled and roofed passageway from the west-northwest, overlooking the river and the bottom land. There was no evidence of any antechamber. Several hearth areas were uncovered within the area of the structure. No arrangement of central roof supports could be found. Whether all of these hearths were coeval with the structure could not be determined, for there was some indication that the whole area had been worked rather intensively by the Indians after all traces of the structure had disappeared. There were several large deep refuse and cache pits present in the area.

The wall posts, when first found, appeared as small soft circular spots along the periphery of the house floor. When cleaned of their contents they were found to be cylindrical with a rounded base averaging 0.3 foot in diameter and 0.9 foot in depth. A number of them did contain some midden material.

The arrangement of the posts inside the house and the entranceway would suggest that some sort of baffle or screen must have been put up to shield the occupants from the chilly north winds of winter. While working at the site we noticed that the prevailing winds were out of the north and south rather than from either the east or west. Whether there is a change during the winter months is not known, but there must be some correlation between the wind direction and the placement of the entranceways. Then, too, the Missouri River is to the west of the site. Perhaps these two factors may have determined the placement of entranceways.

Circular houses were characterized by being more or less round in outline and sunk into pits that now occur from 1.8 feet to 2.8 feet below the present ground level. There was no sign of plastering on any of the walls, and the floors were firmed simply by trampling the bottom of the pit. In cross-sectioning the floors we found that no surfacing material was brought in to cover the floors. Despite extensive search we failed to find the entranceways into the circular houses, especially in Feature 22. Houses in comparable sites normally have definite passageways leading into them. They were constructed at right angles to the line of wall posts and were walled and roofed with the posts set into well-defined holes. Entrance floors usually rose somewhat at the end away from the house.

There was some variation in the number of central roof supports. One of the circular houses had four, which appears to be the conventional number in the Plains, and another had five. There was also considerable variation in the construction of the superstructure of the individual house. The number and size of the poles that went into the superstructure could vary considerably in their placement.

The main firepits were always located at the center of the house floor and were basin shaped. The floor area around these fire basins nearly always was burned as much as the walls of the firepit. From this condition it would appear that no one ever took the time to clean out the pit once a fire was started. Ashes were allowed to accumulate, becoming firmly packed as time went on. As the basin became filled and fires kept burning over it, the heat of the fire spread over the floor area surrounding the pit, changing the physical structure of the clay floor. Such evidence throws insight into the character of the Indian housewife. She was either too busy with her other chores to take the time to carry out the ashes or it was customary to leave them.

Small hearth areas were found scattered around the perimeter of the floor, probably representing individual cooking fires that were built to supplement the heat given off by the central firepit. It would appear that each house furnished shelter for more than one family.

Floor pits were not excessively numerous. Some were bell-shaped, others were cylindrical, while the smaller examples were shallow basin-shaped pits probably dug to hide certain objects. All appear to have been constructed during the life of the house. Some were definite cache pits and others were midden disposal areas.

FEATURE 22

Shape: Circular in outline.

Dimensions: Diameter, 26.0 feet east-west; 27.0 feet north-south. Depth of pit from present surface, 3.0 feet.

Pit walls: Vertical unfaced midden and native soils.

Floor: Trampled bottom of the pit.

Roof supports: Five primary central posts arranged around the central fire basin. Other large posts were spaced at irregular intervals around the perimeter of the house floor and interspaced with a ring of smaller posts, some of which may have supported a sort of bench or platform as well as afforded storage racks.

Entranceway: No such feature could be determined. It was probably thought to have joined the structure from the west or northwest if such a feature ever existed.

Firepits: Large centrally located basin filled with compact whitish ash. Slightly to the east-northeast was a smaller firepit containing firmly packed whitish ash.

Hearths: Several were scattered around the perimeter of the floor.

Floor pits: Five such pits occupied positions within the floor of the structure. Three were bell shaped and filled with some ash, midden material, and a few artifacts. One such pit was filled completely with the disarticulated bones of an antelope. The smaller cache pits contained a few projectile points or scrapers.

FEATURE 34

Shape: Circular in outline.

Dimensions: Diameter, ca. 40.0 feet east-west; 30.0 feet north-south. Depth of pit from present surface, 3.5 feet.

Pit walls: Unfaced refuse and native soil.

Floor: Trampled bottom of pit.

Roof supports: Four primary posts and a row of posts outlining the floor area. Some of the smaller floor posts may have served as supports for benches or platforms as well as storage racks.

Entrance passageway: Opening to the west. There were some well-defined postholes on each side of the entranceway and this sloped slightly upward.

Floor pits: One vertical-sided pit just to the north of the entranceway that might have contained a wooden mortar. To the north of this was a small cache pit slightly bell shaped in cross section. To the east of the mortar pit was a small basin-shaped pit containing a few sherds.

Firepit: Centrally located basin filled with compact whitish ash that was superimposed upon an earlier hearth area.

Associations: None.

Comments: This structure was found to the east of a surface depression and showed no relationship to the depression.

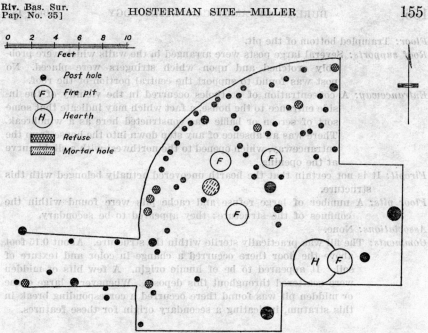

FIGURE 29.—Feature 34, Hosterman site.

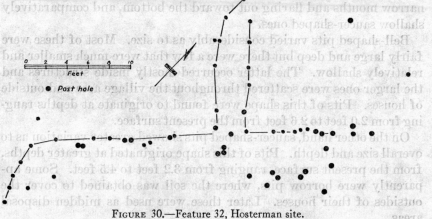

FIGURE 30.—Feature 32, Hosterman site.

FEATURE 32

Shape: Rectangular with rounded corners.

Dimensions: 32.0 feet by ? feet. Depth of pit from present surface, 2.0 feet to 2.3 feet.

Pit walls: Unfaced refuse and native soil.

Postholes: Holes indicate wall posts were rather small, averaging between 0.25 foot to 0.3 foot in diameter. These were very definite in outline but rather shallow, which would seem to indicate that posts leaned against some sort of support and were not firmly planted into the ground.

Floor: Trampled bottom of the pit.

Roof supports: Several large posts were arranged in the walls which were probably crotched and upon which stringers were placed. No post was found to support the central portion of the roof.

Entranceway: A concentration of postholes occurred in the vicinity of the inside entrance to the house, a fact which may indicate that some sort of screen or baffle was constructed here as a windbreak. There was an absence of any step down into the house from the entranceway, which opened to the northwest with a slight curve at the opening.

Firepit: It is not certain that the hearth uncovered actually belonged with this structure.

Floor pits: A number of large refuse and cache pits were found within the confines of the structure; they appeared to be secondary.

Associations: None.

Comments: The fill was practically sterile within the structure. About 0.15 foot above the floor there occurred a change in color and texture of soil. It appeared to be of humic origin. A few bits of midden were scattered throughout this deposit. Whenever a large cache or midden pit was found there occurred a corresponding break in this stratum, indicating a secondary origin for these features.

CACHE PITS

In general, cache pits were of two general shapes: bell shaped with narrow mouths and flaring out toward the bottom, and comparatively shallow saucer-shaped ones.

Bell-shaped pits varied considerably as to size. Most of these were fairly large and deep but there were a few that were much smaller and relatively shallow. The latter occurred mostly inside structures and the larger ones were scattered throughout the village area and outside of houses. Pits of this shape were found to originate at depths ranging from 2.0 feet to 2.6 feet from the present surface.

On the other hand, saucer-shaped pits showed greater variation as to overall size and depth. Pits of this shape originated at greater depths, from the present surface, ranging from 3.2 feet to 4.5 feet. Some apparently were borrow pits, where the soil was obtained to cover the outsides of their houses. Later these were used as midden disposal areas.

Whether these points of origin designated their relative age within the site is suspected as an index but when the contents of both types were compared there was practically very little difference in the general overall contents. The bell-shaped pits were always richer in cultural remains, whereas the saucer-shaped pits were more or less on the lean side. From all appearances the earlier ceramic forms would seem to be confined to the saucer-shaped pits.

Plotting the depths of the origins of both types of pits on a chart shows, more clearly, the placement and separation of the types as to depths (fig. 31).

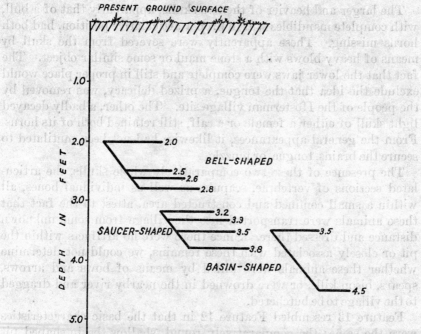

FIGURE 31.—Origin of various shaped pits, Hosterman site.

SLAUGHTERING OR BUTCHERING AREAS

Four unique features, 12, 13, 14, and 19, distinctive for the Hosterman site, were uncovered. These consisted of large basin-shaped pits with parts of articulated bison remains resting within. Not all portions were articulated. The appearance of the remains would suggest either slaughtering or butchering areas; possibly both functions were represented.

Being basin shaped, the top of Feature 12 was first picked up at a depth of 3.5 feet from the present surface. Three-tenths of a foot deeper the outline of the pit was distinct. At this depth it measured 8.0 feet in maximum length and 7.0 feet in maximum width. Later the base of the pit was found to be comparatively flat and at a depth of 6.7 feet from the present surface. Inside were not only the articulated sections of vertebrae, and individual bones, but the skulls of two bisons. From the arrangement of the bones, it was surmised that this was a slaughtering or butchering area inside the village proper and that animals were brought in, butchered, and the unwanted sections discarded.

The larger and heavier of the two skulls, apparently that of a bull, with complete mandibles still in proper articulative position, had both horns missing. These apparently were severed from the skull by means of heavy blows with a stone maul or some similar object. The fact that the lower jaws were complete and still in proper place would exclude the idea that the tongue, a prized delicacy, was removed by the people of the Hosterman village site. The other, a badly decayed light skull of either a female or a calf, still retained both of its horns. From the general appearances, it likewise had not been mutilated to secure the brains, tongue, or muzzle.

The presence of these two comparatively whole skulls, the articulated sections of vertebrae, scapula, as well as individual bones, all within a small confined and constructed area, attest to the fact that these animals were transported into the village from some unknown distance and dressed there. Since there were no artifacts within the pit or closely associated with these remains, we could not determine whether these animals were killed by means of bows and arrows, spears, bison kills, or were drowned in the nearby river and dragged to the village to be butchered.

Feature 13 resembled Feature 12 in that the basic characteristics were the same: the comparatively round, shallow, basin-shaped pit that contained not only individual bones but whole sections of animals still in articulative condition. This specially constructed pit originated at a depth of 4.5 feet from the present surface, measured 7.8 feet in maximum length, 6.4 feet in maximum width, with a depth of 2.9 feet. Resting therein were the articulative hindquarters of a single bison together with its caudal vertebrae. The impression was that the flesh of this particular animal was mostly wasted, for most choice cuts are derived from this part of the animal. There is no telling whether the Hostermanites cut away the heavy flesh from the bones, took the kidneys and kidney fat, and left the undisturbed bones to be covered over with clean wind-blown material as we found them.

Feature 14 has been labeled as "slaughtering area number 3," in that it, too, conformed to the generalized pattern established by both Features 12 and 13. Like the others, the pit was found at a depth of 4.5 feet from the present surface; it was saucer shaped; it measured 6.8 feet in maximum length, 4.8 feet in maximum width, and had a vertical depth of 1.2 feet. Resting therein were sections of vertebral columns, all articulated, and portions of leg bones. Like the former areas this feature was barren of any midden material. Clean, windblown sand surrounded the bones. This was the smallest of the slaughtering areas.

Feature 19, the largest of the slaughtering areas, had its origin 4.5 feet below the present ground surface. It measured 10.6 feet in maximum length, 10.0 feet in maximum width, and had a vertical depth of 2.5 feet. This pit, like Feature 12, contained the skulls of two adult animals, together with individual bones, articulated sections of vertebral columns, and other portions all in proper alinement. Horn cores were intact and the muzzle portions were not complete, a fact which may indicate that portions of the nasal cartilages and upper lips were removed. White (1954, p. 167) surmised that these portions were probably considered a delicacy similar to those of the moose, which the northern Indians converted into a rich stew. From the appearance of the skulls these portions were removed while in the butchering area.

Caudal vertebrae of one individual were in place, indicating that the tail was not always removed along with the hide.

Superimposed above this feature were a number of random post molds. A sterile layer of loess and sand, 1.3 feet in thickness, separated the two features. None of the postholes were deep enough to penetrate into the mouth of the slaughtering area. There is a definite time differential between the two.

All four of the butchering areas had their origin at a greater depth than any of the other features located. This would indicate that they represented the primary occupancy of the site. Whether this was the nucleus out of which the village was established or was just a hunting campsite could not be determined, since only a very small portion of the site was investigated through excavation. I lean toward the theory that these were probably the remains of an early hunting camp near a place that bison frequented, since there were no cultural remains found in direct association with these features.

MIDDEN PITS

After a time lapse and at a higher level in the site, we found that the midden pits, which were probably early borrow pits, tended to be saucer shaped and fairly shallow, with the exception of Features 10 and 20. Feature 10 had a vertical depth of 4.1 feet; Feature 20 had a vertical depth of 5.3 feet. Other saucer-shaped pits were: Features 2, 3, 15, 16, 23, 24, 27, 33, and 35. Feature 35 was the shallowest of the series, being only 0.3 foot in depth, and Feature 16 was the deepest, being 2.2 feet in depth. Some were circular in outline, another was quasi-rectangular with rounded base, and one had an irregular outline with walls sloping in toward the center. All contained some midden mixed with loess. Depths from the present surface ranged from 3.2 feet to 3.8 feet (see chart of depths for the various types of pits (fig. 31)).

Deviating from the norm were Features 10 and 12. Instead, their contents appeared to have been richly mixed with humus and very loosely inserted into the pits. In other features the pit fill leaned toward the compact and had to be troweled out. In Features 10 and 12 the fill could be lifted out by the unaided hand.

The rest of the pits originated between 2.0 feet and 2.8 feet. These were bell shaped and probably were initially intended for storage purposes. When no longer needed or used for storage, they were converted into midden disposal areas. Their overall sizes varied. Some contained more midden material than others, but in general they followed a pattern. (See table 1.)

TABLE 1.—*Pit measurements (feet) and general shapes*

Feature No.	Depth from surface	Maximum length of base	Minimum length of base	Depth of feature	General shape
11	2.0	4.0	4.0	2.5	Bell shape.
18	2.0	7.6	7.1	.9	Saucer shape.
21	2.0	8.0	7.6	5.3	Bell shape.
26	2.4	3.0	2.4	.7	Vertical wall.
25	2.5	7.5	7.3	4.8	Bell shape.
9	2.6	9.4	9.1	5.3	Do.
6	2.8	5.2	4.3	3.7	Do.
23	3.2	5.8	5.5	1.3	Saucer shape.
24	3.2	4.6	3.6	.9	Do.
27	3.2	3.2	2.2	.85	Do.
33	3.2	6.9	5.0	1.1	Do.
35	3.2	3.4	2.8	.3	Do.
16	3.3	3.6	3.0	2.2	Do.
10	3.3	8.2	7.1	4.1	Bell shape.
2	3.5	12.3	9.0	1.3	Saucer shape.
15	3.5	3.0	2.6	.6	Do.
20	3.5	7.0	6.8	5.3	Do.
3	3.8	8.8	5.4	2.0	Do.
12	3.5	8.0	7.0	2.9	Basin shape.
13	4.5	7.8	6.4	2.9	Do.
14	4.5	6.8	4.8	1.2	Do.
19	4.5	10.6	10.0	2.5	Do.

ARTIFACT MATERIAL

POTTERY

During the course of the excavations at the Hosterman site numerous fragments of pottery, of various sizes, were found. They occurred most abundantly in cache pits, in some quantity in the shallow pits under house floors, in postholes, and in small isolated midden heaps. Only a few were recovered while we were sectioning the fortification ditch that surrounded the site proper. Pottery was practically absent from the surface, since the cultural deposit was rather deeply buried. Occasionally, small bits were found around a few of the gopher holes or where some pot hunter had dug in the past.

Practically all of the pottery remains were those from vessels. They exhibited a paste made by mixing the natural local clays with a tempering material of crushed igneous rock; the resulting paste is quite uniform insofar as hardness, color, and firing practices are concerned. Color ranges from buffs and tans through browns to various shades of grays to soot black. Fire clouds are fairly common. Texture is medium to coarse, and there is a common tendency to develop internal cleavage planes parallel to the vessel walls that is mainly due to the method of manufacture. All vessels were either modeled or made by using the paddle and anvil method. Insofar as we can determine, all of the vessels were basically jar shaped, globular in outline with vertical or S-shaped necks, and medium to large in size. Vertical necks are medium to high; some with slightly everted rims. There are various modifications in the S-shaped variety. Vertical types predominated over the S-shaped variety. A few miniature and unusual forms are present but they constitute only a fractional part of the ceramic complex. Handles, although of various shapes, are not numerous.

Most of the sherds—since this is a study based solely on sherds rather than on whole vessels—have smoothed exterior surfaces, but there is strong evidence that a grooved or thong-wrapped paddle was used during the last stages of manufacture and later this exterior surface treatment was partially or entirely smoothed over. The paddle striations covering the major part of the exterior surface are vertical or nearly so. Once the exterior surface has been smoothed it may be given a number of different treatments. Necks may be vertically brushed and the upper parts incised; the shoulders may be incised, covered with the original simple stamp, brushed, or even smoothed over and left plain. Lips, upper rims, and shoulders were the favorite portions of vessels to be treated. They may be incised, punctated, impressed, pinched, or left plain.

As in other archeological areas of the United States, entirely too much stress has been placed on the ceramics in the Plains. In truth, this trait was only one of the many that made up the economy of these people; however, there are many other traits, though of less permanence, that were of greater importance to the makers and users of these forms. Only because of its permanence and durability does pottery overshadow, in quantity, the rest of the cultural remains. Then, too, it does reflect considerable responsiveness to cultural changes, through time and space, in the kinds of decoration used, the shapes of the vessels themselves, methods of manufacture, and other features.

Wheeler's (1954, pp. 3–4) definitions for morphological parts of the vessel have been standardized as follows: "The lip is the juncture of the exterior and interior surfaces of the rim; the rim is the section between the orifice and the neck; the neck is the point of maximum constriction, or the point of marked change in trend or direction of the vessel; the shoulder area is the space between the neck and the point of maximum diameter of the vessel." (See fig. 32.)

Before going into the morphological details of the pottery remains, I must say that I am in close agreement with Lehmer (1951) and

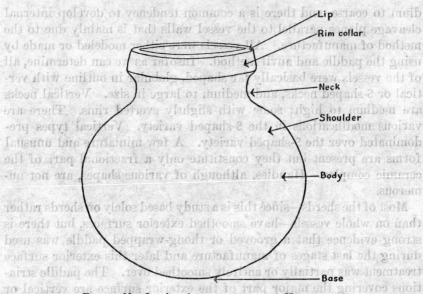

FIGURE 32.—Landmarks on pottery vessel, Hosterman site.

Smith (1951) in regard to the methodology used in typing Plains pottery, so ideas similar to theirs need not be repeated here. Like Smith, I, too, was confronted with the problem of associating not only the exterior surface treatment with rim decoration but with lip decoration and treatment as well.

The Hosterman site pottery description is based on a total of 75,814 body sherds, 3,155 rim sherds, and 5 possibly restorable vessels that were never restored.

The pottery was first washed in the field laboratory at Lincoln, Nebr., and the rim sherds were sorted and cataloged. The body sherds were not cataloged individually, as were the rim sherds, but were grouped according to the square, depth, and feature from which they were derived. In making the ceramic analysis, the body sherds were first studied en masse in order to acquire a reasonable working knowledge of the exterior surface treatments so as to avoid making certain snap judgments based upon misconceptions as to what should be found. Once the body sherds were studied and analyzed they were resacked according to the lot bags.

CLASSIFICATION OF BODY SHERDS AS TO EXTERIOR TREATMENT

All of the body sherds were classified, according to the exterior surface treatment, into eight main categories: *plain*, 42.16 percent; *simple-stamped*, 40.09 percent; *incised*, 13.96 percent; *brushed*, 2.19 percent; *curvilinear-stamped*, 0.84 percent; *cord-impressed*, 0.22 percent; *mat-impressed*, 0.18 percent; *fabric-impressed*, 0.12 percent.

The minor types were: *painted*, 0.06 percent; *punctated*, 0.05 percent; *pinched ridged*, 0.01 percent; *fingernail pinched*, 0.01 percent; and *corncob-impressed*, 0.01 percent.

Out of the various types present there are four main wares: *plain, simple-stamped, incised,* and *brushed.* Percentages of these were plotted, according to our arbitrary levels within the site, on a common graph to determine their trends. This superimposition of wares reveals that the *plain, simple-stamped,* and *incised* follow almost identical advancements and declines throughout their existence, but *brushed* described a different curve for the first five levels within the site. On the next to the top level (sixth from the bottom) all were in fair agreement, proceeding along similar curves up to the time that the site was abandoned. *Brushed* had advanced steadily, even though it had a late start, and had gained prominence over the other three, percentagewise, before the sixth level was reached. All of this is shown on the graph (fig. 33).

TABLE 2.—*Composite data on body sherds, Hosterman site (39PO7)*

Exterior treatment	Body sherds at indicated level (feet)								
	0.0–1.0	1.0–1.5	1.5–2.0	2.0–2.5	2.5–3.0	3.0–3.5	3.5–4.0	4.0–4.5	Total
Incised	113	506	229	408	261	51	3	8	--------
Plain	293	1,987	871	1,110	378	201	--------	--------	--------
Brushed	14	104	46	27	36	--------	--------	--------	--------
Simple stamped	166	1,033	829	1,225	387	59	10	16	--------
Number	586	3,630	1,975	2,770	1,062	311	13	24	10,351
Percent	5.6	35.0	19.0	26.8	10.3	3.0	0.1	0.2	100
Plain:									
Number	293	1,987	871	1,110	378	201			4,840
Percent	6.1	41.1	18.0	22.9	7.8	4.1			100
Brushed:									
Number	14	104	46	27	36				227
Percent	6.1	48.8	20.3	11.9	15.9				100
Incised:									
Number	113	506	229	408	261	51	3	8	1,649
Percent	6.9	30.8	18.1	24.7	15.8	3.0	0.2	0.5	100
Simple stamped:									
Number	166	1,033	829	1,225	387	59	10	16	3,725
Percent	4.7	27.7	22.3	32.9	10.3	1.5	0.2	0.4	100

While examining and studying the body sherds, it was determined that manufacture was by modeling rather than by using the coil system. A microscopical examination of the paste was made at the same time but we could not differentiate the physical characteristics. Once these were determined and described, we felt that there would be no need to repeat them for each of the wares.

COMMON TRAITS OF WARES

PASTE:

Method of manufacture: Probably made by lump modeling using a paddle and anvil instead of coiling.

Temper: Grit tempered, ranging from particles that are barely visible up to those around 3 mm. in diameter; probably crushed granite. Sometimes

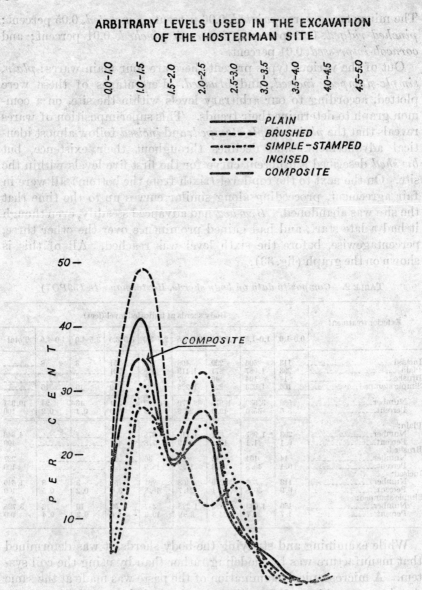

FIGURE 33.—Pottery trend within Hosterman site.

the larger particles protrude on the surface; this occurs mostly on the interior surfaces where the vessels have been roughly smoothed or brushed. Freshly broken edges have a granular appearance, depending somewhat on the quantity and the aplastic coarseness.

Texture: Medium to coarse and at times flaky.

Cohesive tendency: There is a tendency for the walls to split into unequal sections owing to the method of manufacture.

Structure: Tendency toward lamination. Easily splits parallel to the surface, and edges are crumbly.

Color: Color varies from a light tan, buff, and gray, and often a sooty
   black. Fire clouds are common on the lighter colored sherds. Cross
   section may be the same as the surface or it may have a darker center.
SURFACE FINISH : In most cases the paddle was used on the exterior surface during
   manufacture. It was wrapped with some sort of vegetal fiber or gut or was
   roughly carved. The overall design of parallel grooves was repeated, the
   application of the paddle imparting grooves and lands. Grooves measure
   roughly 3 mm. in width by 15 or more mm. in length. The lands are round
   to round pointed and the grooves are U-shaped in cross section and somewhat
   rounded in general shape. Usually the stamping is vertical to the lip but
   there are rare cases when the stamping occurs on a slight diagonal to the
   lip. The initial stamped design apparently covered the complete exterior
   surface of the vessel but this was either completely eradicated through subsequent smoothing or partially obliterated by brushing. Interior surfaces
   may be roughly smoothed or brushed. Occasionally one appears to have been
   semiburnished by having been rubbed with a pebble or some other hard substance. When brushing occurred interiorly it was always applied horizontally
   to the main axis of the vessel and parallel to the lip. Decoration varies with
   the component types. Decoration of lips is frequent. Decoration on shoulders
   consists of series of parallel lines arranged in opposition to each other, in
   contiguous plats forming a broad continuous band around the vessel. Bases
   were untreated except for the initial surface treatment.

DETAILED STUDY OF BODY SHERDS

During the process of manufacture some sort of paddle was applied
to the outside of the vessel. It was either carved with a series of shallow parallel ridges or wrapped with narrow strips of leather, the
results of which show up as a series of shallow parallel lands and
troughs that cover practically the entire outside of the vessel. Usually
these impressions run vertically, but over the base of the vessel they
may overlap and crisscross. Such treatment has been described as
"simple-stamping." Wares impressed with a carved paddle had more
regular impressions and show a uniformity of depth, whereas the
leather wrappings were not as regularly placed and there was some
variation in the overall depth and width of the impressions.

Plain wares are those whose exterior surfaces were smoothed over
completely so as to eradicate any previous surface treatment. Some
were subsequently rubbed, sometimes with a small stone, or a similar
object, to impart a pseudopolish or burnish. Vessels treated in this
way were much smoother than those that were simply smoothed by
hand.

Decorations of incised elements were confined to various portions
of the vessel: the lip, rim, or shoulder area. They were confined to
zones around these areas. Decorations that had repetitious elements
within the zone have been called "line block" in this report. There is
wide variation as to the method of rendition, the width of the elements themselves, and the placement of the designs. Some decorations

FIGURE 34.—Horizontal parallel incised rim sherd.

show that a very sharply pointed instrument was used, resulting in a very narrow line of moderate depth. Others, of a trailing nature, were made by using a wide blunt-bladed implement, resulting in a wide, coarse, shallow, troughlike line showing a poor sense of symmetry and touch. The design was not only carelessly drawn but it was not always complete (fig. 34). This kind has been called *Nordvold Horizontal Incised*. These are the extremes; there are some that range in between.

Brushing was confined mostly to the exterior neck and upper shoulder areas. It was also associated with various other exterior surface treatments. Some brushing, in which parallel strokes were used, occurred in the upper portion of throat areas, but this was not a prevalent practice. The areas that were brushed carried a series of sharply defined parallel vertical or horizontal scratches either at right angle to the lip or parallel to the lip and appeared to be the result of using a bundle of coarse grass or small twigs.

Several sherds were noticed bearing red pigment mostly on the interior. These showed that some sort of slurry made of powdered ocher was applied. None of the vessels appeared to have been fired after this application of the pigment, which, at the present time, could easily be brushed off onto the finger as it was rubbed across the surface. This color can truly be called a "fugitive red" even though some of the pigment had worked its way into the natural pores of the vessel walls and in so doing had given the surface a faint pinkish or reddish hue. This trait was checked under a microscope a number of times and it was seen that the porosity of the vessel walls was just a "natural" for absorbing this material.

Whenever cord impressions occurred, they were confined to the rim, the lip, or to the upper portions of the shoulder area. Cord impressions on the lip were rare, but they were numerous enough so that various types of treatment could be determined. They occurred either as a series of parallel impressions running straight across the lip, or at a diagonal, or as a series of parallel impressions covering most of the lip as they encircled the vessel. Practically all of the cord was

of the right-hand twist.   Diameters varied somewhat, even on the same
vessel; but on the average it measured around 1 mm.

In the group of body sherds there were several whose exterior surfaces were extra rough.   When a positive impression was made of this
treatment, with the aid of plastic clay, it was found that some sort of
coarse fabric had been used.   This fabric was not applied flat but was
apparently wadded up and then applied, hence the term "fabric-
impressed."   On a few sherds we found that a coarse mat impression
covered very limited portions of the exterior surface.   These sherds
were small and we could not determine how extensively this technique
had been used.

We noted that in several instances corncobs had been used to
roughen the exterior surfaces of vessels.   This practice was apparently
not common, for we found only a limited number of sherds treated in
this fashion.

Among the rare forms were a small number of plain sherds that were
from scattered positions within the site.   They were of a curious green
color, more of a bile green, on the exterior, which seemed to go through
the entire thickness of the wall.   They were made of a hard and
homogeneous paste, and their exteriors were very carefully smoothed.
The thickness of each is uniform, ranging from 1.5 mm. to 3.0 mm.
We could not determine their source or where they would fit into the
general picture.

LIP TREATMENT

Lips were of many forms: they were *simple-rounded*, *flattened*,
rounded and flattened, *inward beveled*, *outward beveled*, *reinforced
and beveled*, *reinforced and rounded*, and even *folded* (see lip profiles,
figs. 35 and 36).

Lips had been given several types of treatments.   They were
smoothed or left plain; ticked or "tooled" in various ways with different size sticks or other tools or ticked by having sections of cords
impressed across them; incised by having herringbone designs
drawn across them; punctated in various manners; indented by
pinching the unfired clay into undulations or indentations; impressed
with a number of twisted cord elements running parallel with the lip;
given a wavy effect by pressure of the finger on either side of the lip;
or given the stab-and-drag treatment with a rounded, pointed, or
squared pointed implement resulting in a line of shallow punctations.

Lips that were punctated, in some instances in the literature were
referred to as "tool impressed," impressed with a rounded, squared, or
pyramidal pointed stick; the size and the shape of the impression
depending on the actual outline of the tool and the amount of pressure
used to bring about this effect.   Some impressions were narrow, others

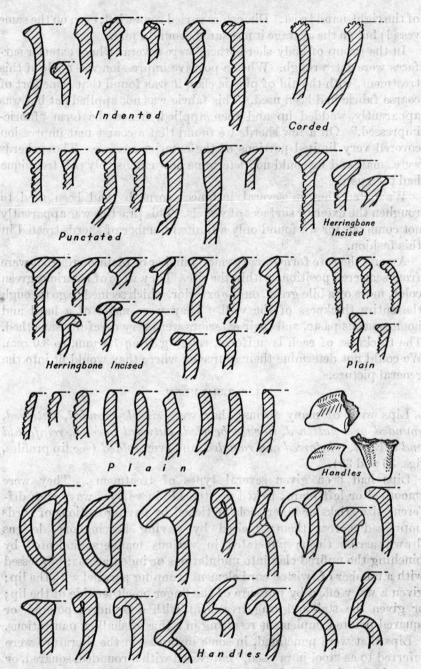

FIGURE 35.—Vertical rim profiles, Hosterman site.

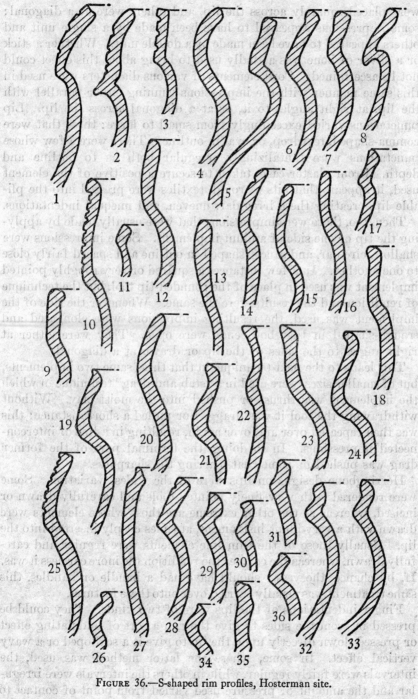

FIGURE 36.—S-shaped rim profiles, Hosterman site.

were placed squarely across the lip, and others were at a diagonal; some impressions appeared to have been made by a single unit and others appeared to have been made by a double unit. Whether a stick or a sliver of bone was actually used to bring about this effect could not be ascertained. Cord elements of various diameters were used in this same manner with the impressions running either parallel with the lip, at right angles to it, or at a diagonal across the lip. Lip punctations varied exceedingly from small to large: those that were comma-shaped, teardrop, or oval in outline. There were a few whose punctations were tantalizingly irregular both as to outline and depth. From plaster casts taken to secure a positive of the element used, it appears that bits of rough textiles were pressed into the pliable lip, creating these irregular, uneven, and unequal indentations.

Then, too, there were impressions that were usually made by applying the tip or one side of a blunt implement. Some impressions were shallow, circular, and saucer shaped in outline and spaced fairly close to one another. In a few instances a squared or very roughly pointed implement was used in place of the rounded-tip tool, but the technique of rendition and the results were the same. Whenever the side of the implement was used, the resulting impressions were elongated and trough-shaped in that both ends were open. They were either at right angles to the sides of the lip or drawn at a diagonal.

This leads to the next technique in that these same two implements, but of smaller sizes, were used in a "stab-and-drag" technique in which the implement was thrust or pushed into the moist clay. Without withdrawing the tool it was dragged or pulled a short distance; this was then repeated over and over again, resulting in a line of interconnected impressions. In so doing, the terminal part of the former drag was pushed in, somewhat marring the sharpness.

Herringbone designs on lips were of the widest variation. Some were rendered with very finely pointed tools and carefully drawn or incised, whereas at the other extreme are those whose elements were drawn with a very blunt instrument, at times deeply inserted into the lip. Usually those of the thin line elements were regular and carefully drawn, whereas the coarser the rendition the more careless it was. If, by chance, the vessel should have had a handle or handles, this same treatment was usually carried over onto these features.

Finger indentations of the lips were of two kinds. They could be pressed in from the sides to give the rim a sort of undulating effect or pressed down directly upon the lip to give it a scalloped or a wavy vertical effect. In some, where the latter method was used, the intervals were fairly regular, while in others the intervals were irregular and the amount of pressure used varied from point of contact to point of contact; in other words, the "trough" varied in depth and was not at all consistent.   This same scalloped effect was brought about by pressing some rodlike tool onto the plastic lip.   The intervals between pressure points were never uniform.   Whenever pressure was brought to bear vertically upon the lip it caused a certain amount of thickening to that feature.   Whenever pressure was applied at right angles to the lip the areas affected were thinned so that the intervening portion of the lip was thicker than the area worked on (fig. 40, *a–d*).

TYPE NAME: "Le Beau Finger Indented" (pl. 19, *A, h*).
TYPE MATERIAL: 142 sherds.

   Form:

      Rims: Vertical to gently flaring.

      Lips: Lips were rounded in preparation to being treated with the finger. After this the lips were broadened in the area by the downward pressure, bringing about a certain amount of thickening.   Whenever finger pressure was applied alternately to the interior and exterior a wavy effect was created and the thickness of the walls was reduced.

      Thickness: Vessel walls varied from 3 to 5 mm. in thickness.

      Vessel form: Probably globular in shape, rounded shoulders, and straight to slightly flaring neck.

   Decoration:

      Variant A: Like the type description of Hurt's (1957 a, p. 39) these rims were indented by applying the finger from the interior and exterior in an alternating pattern giving a wavy effect.

      Variant B: In this case the pressure was brought directly downward from the top of the lip giving a scalloped effect.   The difference between pressure points may vary.   Some may be a continuous group; others were spaced with an alternate plain area.   In every case the lips were rounded.

STRATIGRAPHIC POSITION: Hurt has found that this type of pottery was associated with the Le Beau Focus at the Swan Creek site (39WW7) and that percentagewise there was a tendency to increase with time.

Ticked lines across the lips, frequently referred to in the Plains literature as "tool impressed," have the widest variation as to width, length, and the amount of pressure used to bring about this effect.   On some of the specimens the lines were very thin, short, and exceedingly shallow.   On others the lines were long enough to reach completely across the lip and were both wide and deep.   Still others were made at an angle.

Inside measurements of the orifices of jars showed that there was not a great variation.   Openings ranged from 10.3 cm. to 21.7 cm. (See Appendix 4.)

RIM FORMS AND THEIR TREATMENT

Rims of the *plain, incised, brushed,* and *cord-marked* wares were separated.   It was found that all shared common basic characteristics in temper, method of manufacture, texture, hardness, color, surface finish, and general vessel form.   All types are primarily groups of similar rim forms decorated in more or less the same general way.

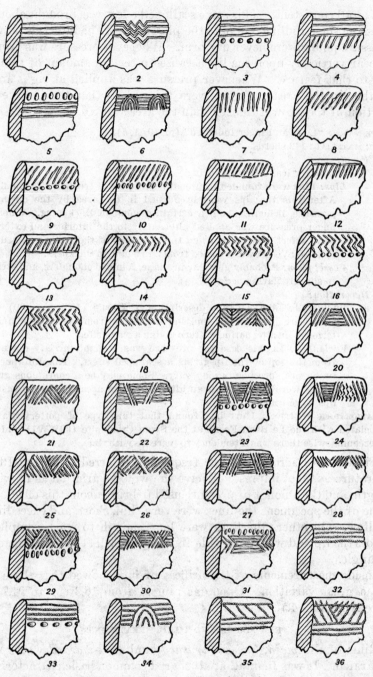

FIGURE 37.—S-shaped rim decorations.

Rims are of two main shapes, depending upon the configuration of the neck: vertical and S-shaped. Vertical rims ranged from short to tall and a few had the tendency to flare slightly at the top. There are several minor rim types present, but these are of limited number. After the rims were separated according to the two rim forms, they were next separated according to lip treatment, for I found this combination to be most diagnostic and one that was fairly sensitive.

Each rim type was further subdivided according to the final exterior surface treatment of the rim. These include such treatments as: incised with a series of *horizontal parallel lines; plain* after smoothing; incised with a series of either short *vertical and/or diagonal lines; herringbone incised;* a zone of either conjoining parallel lines or chevrons arranged as a band around the tip of the neck or rim, called *line block; cord-impressed; simple-stamped;* and *brushed.* In separating the rim sherds into the various types it was necessary to take into consideration three main factors: (1) the general configuration of the rim, (2) the treatment of the lip area, and (3) the final exterior surface treatment of the rim or neck area.

After all separation and counts had been made and tallied, it was found that 1,592 were vertical rims, 1,039 were S-shaped, and 524 were too fragmentary or incomplete to make positive classification possible.

There are four types of vertical necks: (1) those that are almost vertical with just the slightest degree of outward flaring near the top (pl. 15, *A, a*) ; (2) those that are almost vertical with the exception of being slightly barrel shaped (pl. 19, *B, e*, fig. 38) ; (3) those that have vertical necks surmounted with a certain amount of rim thickening (pl. 15, *B, a*) ; and (4) those that were short and flared outwardly at the top (pl. 16, *B, a*).

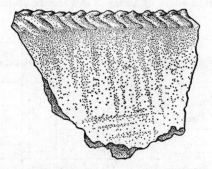

FIGURE 38.—Barrel-shaped rim, simple stamped rim sherd.

S-shaped rims were curved, flattened, or short with an acute angle. In either type the zone of decoration was confined mostly to the upper portion of the figure "S" (pls. 17 and 18; fig. 36).

TYPE NAME: Hosterman S-shaped rims (resembling typical Le Beau series).

TYPE MATERIAL: 1,039 rims or 32.9 percent of all rims.

   Exterior surface treatments:
       (1) Horizontal parallel line incised—372 rims, 35.8 percent (pl. 17, *B*; fig. 37, 1–6).
       (2) Line block—277 rims, 26.7 percent (fig. 37, *19–31*).
       (3) Plain—138 rims, 13.8 percent.
       (4) Herringbone incised—124 rims, 11.9 percent (pl. 15, *B*, *a*; fig. 37, *14–18*).
       (5) Vertical and/or diagonal line incised—66 rims, 6.4 percent (fig. 37, *7–13*).
       (6) Cord-impressed—62 rims, 5.9 percent (pl. 20, *A*, *a–d*; fig. 37, *32–36*).

PASTE:
   All, with the exception of a very few, showed the general traits listed and described for the Hosterman pottery.

FORMS
   Rims: There was quite a variation in the S-shaped and so-called collared rims.
   Lips: Since this was one of the variables, considerable variation was noted:
       (1) Ticked or tooled lips—546 lips, 52.6 percent of all lips.
       (2) Plain—309 lips, 28.8 percent.
       (3) Herringbone incised—138 lips, 13.3 percent.
       (4) Punctated—45 lips, 4.3 percent.
       (5) Finger indented—1 lip.
   Vessel form: Globular bodies with constricted necks with rather high rims. In some the curve is pronounced; in others the upper portion of the curve tends to be flattened somewhat.

STRATIGRAPHIC POSITION: S-shaped rims were found in all levels of occupation at the Hosterman site and fragments of these same vessels were widely scattered.

TABLE 3.—*Types and numbers of S-shaped rim sherds, Hosterman site (39PO7)*

S-shaped rims	Lip treatment					Total	
	Plain	Ticked	Herring-bone incised	Punc-tated	Finger indented	Number in group	Percent-age
Exterior surface treatment:							
Parallel-horizontal line incised	80	252	33	7	----------	372	35.8
Plain	27	32	57	21	1	138	13.3
Vertical and/or diagonal line incised	52	7	----------	7	----------	66	6.4
Herringbone incised	30	58	31	5	----------	124	11.9
Line block	77	180	16	4	----------	277	26.7
Cord-impressed	43	17	1	1	----------	62	5.9
Total	309	546	138	45	1	1,039	100.0

INCISED S-SHAPED RIMS: 839 rims or 80.8 percent of rims.

FORM:
   Rims: Varied in height and in curvature. Some were rounded, others were flattened, still others had a distinct ridge or collared effect (fig. 35).

Lips: Several lip treatments were represented in this group:

1. Plain and rounded—239 lips, 28.5 percent of lips.
2. Ticked or tooled—497 lips, 59.2 percent of lips.
3. Herringbone incised—80 lips, 9.5 percent of lips.
4. Punctated—23 lips, 2.8 percent of lips.

DECORATION: A zone of incised decoration was confined to the upper portion of the S-shaped rims, excluding lip treatment. Design techniques consisted of incising, including broad trailing, sometimes combined with punctations (fig. 39, *a*, *b*, *c*). There is a wide latitude in the design form from the simplest, which is a series of horizontal parallel lines crudely drawn across the upper portion of the neck. In certain vessels these lines were interspersed with an equal number of herringbone elements, or were bordered either at the top or bottom with punctations, or short diagonal lines. Then, there were rows of vertical or diagonal incised lines with their combinations; herringbone designs; opposed diagonals; lineated bands framed by diagonals; broad incised diagonals; broad-trailed diagonals; and curvilinear "rainbows" on a lineate field.

PLAIN S-SHAPED RIMS: 138 rims; 13.2 percent of rims.

FORM:

Rims: Same as for incised.

Lips: Same as for incised with the addition of finger indented—1.

DECORATION: Surface has been smoothed after being paddled. No decoration applied.

CORD-IMPRESSED S-SHAPED RIMS: 62 rims, 6.0 percent of rims.

FORM:

Rims: Same as for incised.

Lips: The four basic lip treatments still apply with the exception that four additional sherds were present whose lips were crossed with cord impressions.

DECORATION: *Type A* (Le Beau Horizontal Cord Impressed) has a series of horizontal cord impressions running parallel in the series starting just below the outer edge of the lip and continued down over the major part of the upper curve of the S-shaped rim. *Type B* (Rygh Rainbow Corded) has its series of horizontal parallel impressions interrupted by the insertion of a rainbow element made by impressing short segments of cords in this fashion to create this effect.

CORD-IMPRESSED S-SHAPED RIMS: 62 rims, 6.0 percent of rims. These resemble the Le Beau Horizontal Corded of Hurt's (1957 b, p. 41, fig. 21, 5) type description and a few are identical with the Rygh Rainbow Corded (ibid., p. 42, fig. 21, *1*). Both of these types are well described and illustrated by Hurt so there will be no need to repeat these here.

Rim decoration (fig. 37, *7–12*), on vertical necked vessels with rounded lips, resembles the "unnamed" ware of Hewes (1949, pp. 59–60, pl. VI, *a*, *b*) of the Heart Butte Campsite, 32GT1, North Dakota. As indicated by Hewes this ware resembles one from the Burgois or Double Ditch site on the Missouri River, North Dakota (Will and Spinden, 1906, fig. 40, *a*) and from sites in the Upper Missouri Valley, North Dakota (Will and Hecker, 1944, pl. 6) all of which date in the late 17th and early 18th centuries.

Rim decoration (fig. 37, *32* and *33*), which is cord impressed on S-shaped rims with rounded lips, resembles part of the "unnamed" ware

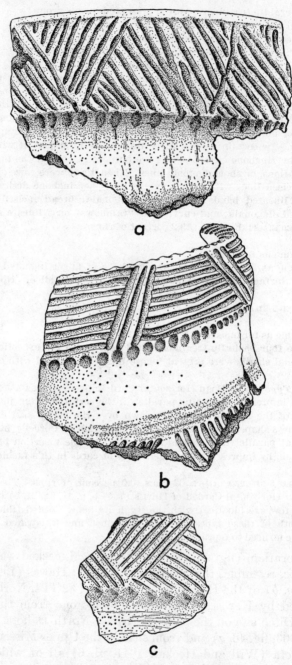

FIGURE 39.—Line-block zonal decorations.

of Hewes (1949, p. 60, pl. VI, *c*) from the Heart Butte Campsite, North Dakota, 32GT1, which is similar to "pottery in many Upper Missouri River village sites of the Mandan-Hidatsa culture, specifically Sperry, Larson, Fort Lincoln, 32SI4 near Fort Yates, Hagen site (Mulloy, 1942). Pottery of this general type covers a wide area in the North Plains and probably several centuries of time." (Ibid., pp. 59–61.)

Rim decoration (fig. 37, *35* and *36*) on S-shaped rims resembles a ware illustrated by Hewes (1949, pl. VI, *d*, *q*) with the exception that the pottery from the Heart Butte Rockshelter, 32GT5, North Dakota, is cord-impressed and the sherds from the Hosterman site, 39PO7, are for the most part incised (fig. 40, *h*, *i*). There is a certain amount of this same cord-impressed ware at the Hosterman site, but it is not abundant (pl. 20).

Rim decoration (fig. 37, *34*) resembles Hurt's (1957 b, fig. 25, *2a*, *2b*) Le Beau Cord-wrapped rod designs as well as Rygh Rainbow corded. The difference between the Le Beau Cord-wrapped rod and the Hosterman cord-impressed is only in the element used. Those from Le Beau used cord-wrapped rods, and those from the Hosterman used sections of cords (fig. 40, *k*). The placement of the elements on S-shaped rims of the Hosterman site and Rygh Rainbow Corded is identical. Whether there is a time differential is not known at the present time, but it is suspected that the treatment of the Hosterman group precedes that of the Le Beau and the Rygh forms.

TYPE NAME: Hosterman Vertical rims (fig. 35).
TYPE MATERIAL: 1,592 rims; 50.5 percent of rims.

Exterior surface treatments:
1. Plain—579 rims, 36.4 percent of rims.
2. Horizontal parallel incised lines—397 rims, 24.9 percent of rims.
3. Brushed—245 rims, 15.4 percent of rims.
4. Simple-stamped—232 rims, 14.6 percent of rims.
5. Line block incised—53 rims, 3.3 percent of rims.
6. Herringbone incised—42 rims, 2.6 percent of rims.
7. Cord-impressed—27 rims, 1.7 percent of rims.
8. Vertical and/or diagonal lined incised—17 rims, 1.1 percent of rims.

PASTE: All showed the general traits described for the Hosterman pottery.
FORM:
  Rims: There was some variation in the overall height and some that had a slight tendency to be everted at the very top, but on the whole they are fairly uniform.
  Lips: Since this is one of the variables in determining types we found that there is quite a range in lip treatment, thus:
1. Herringbone incised—494 lips, 31.0 percent of lips.
2. Ticked or tooled—462 lips, 29.0 percent of lips.
3. Punctated—394 lips, 24.8 percent of lips.
4. Finger indented—142 lips, 8.9 percent of lips.
5. Plain—96 lips, 6.0 percent of lips.
6. Cord-impressed—4 lips, 0.3 percent of lips.
  Vessel form: Globular-bodied vessels with vertical necks.

STRATIGRAPHIC POSITION: Vertical-necked vessels were found in all levels of occupation within the areas explored at the Hosterman site, and often fragments of the same vessel would appear widely scattered.

TABLE 4.—*Types and numbers of vertical rim sherds* (*Hosterman site, 39PO7*)

Vertical rims	Lip treatment					
	Plain	Ticked	Herring-bone incised	Punc-tated	Finger indented	Cord-impressed
Exterior surface treatment:						
Parallel-horizontal line incised	17	79	255	45		
Plain	27	165	150	162	75	1
Vertical and/or diagonal line incised	3	13		1		
Herringbone incised	6	21	15			
Line block	8	39	2	4		
Cord impressed	14		9	3		1
Simple stamped	6	66	43	93	24	
Brushed	15	79	20	86	43	2
Total	96	462	494	394	142	4

If we group all the recognizable rim sherds on the basis of exterior surface treatment, irrespective of whether they are vertical or S-shaped in form, as apparently has been the practice in the past, we get the following:

> Horizontal parallel incised lines—769 rims, 29.2 percent.
> Plain—717 rims, 27.3 percent.
> Incised line block of triangles, etc.—330 rims, 12.5 percent.
> Brushed—245 rims, 9.3 percent.
> Simple-stamped—232 rims, 8.8 percent.
> Herringbone incised—166 rims, 6.3 percent.
> Cord-impressed—89 rims, 3.4 percent.
> Vertical and/or diagonal line incised—83 rims, 3.2 percent.

This grouping at best reduces the bulk to eight wares. It is not only misleading but is all too inclusive. For example, if we choose to place all cord-impressed into a single category we have lumped two distinct wares—the Le Beau Horizontal Corded and the Rygh Rainbow Corded—as a single ware.

As to the exterior surface treatment of the rims themselves, some retained the marks of the paddle used during the formative stage of manufacture, better known as simple stamping. These marks formed a permanent exterior surface and as such can be considered a form of decoration. In others the simple-stamped effect was either completely dissipated or partially obliterated, resulting in a smoothed plain surface. The process did not stop there, for this plain surface acted as the background upon which various linear geometric designs were incised and—in a few instances—impressed. The simplest form of incised design consisted of a series of encircling horizontal parallel lines starting just below the juncture of the neck and exterior margin of the lip and extending downward sometimes for a short distance and sometimes covering the major part of the neck of the vessel (fig. 40, *e*).

Similar treatment occurred on Wheeler Horizontal Incised from the Scalp Creek site and the La Roche site (Hurt, 1952, p. 13; fig. 14, *1–3*), and Nordvold Horizontal Incised (Wilmeth, 1958, fig. 17).

A variation of this design was brought about by breaking the lines and filling in the gaps with interconnecting herringbone designs, thus:

The intervals between the lines varied considerably on some specimens and on others were very carefully drawn. Those that were carelessly drawn had the lines wandering either upward or downward or even inserted small segments that started anywhere and ended nowhere.

Other variations of the horizontal parallel line patterns consist of the series of parallel lines delimited by a row of short diagonal dashes, delimited by a row of punctates, surmounted by a row of punctates, or separated by concentric rainbow designs.

Next in simplicity are those vessels decorated by drawing a row of diagonal or vertical lines starting just below the juncture of the rim and the outer edge of the lip and carrying them down a short distance on the rim (fig. 40, *l–n*). Variations of this motif consist of an encircling incised line above the series of lines, an encircling incised line below the series of lines, a row of punctates delimiting the lines at their base, or a series of horizontal dashes just below the base of the lines.

Those incised with herringbone designs may have one or more lines of this design used as the decorative motif. Variations consist of a single horizontal incised line drawn above the herringbone design and separating it from the top of the rim area; delimited by a row of vertical punctates at the base, or delimited by a row of round or oval punctates at the base.

The most complex are those decorated with linear geometric designs. These consist of a series of interlocking triangles filled with horizontal lines, diagonal lines, and herringbone designs. These interlocking triangles may be separated from one another by one to six parallel lines. Then, too, a row of punctates can appear at the top or the bottom of the zone of interlocking triangles. In this paper whenever any reference is made to this type of decoration the term "line block" will be used.

Vertical brushing covers not only the rim and neck sections of a great many vessels but is also found on the upper portions of the shoulder area. Some of the Talking Crow Brushed types described

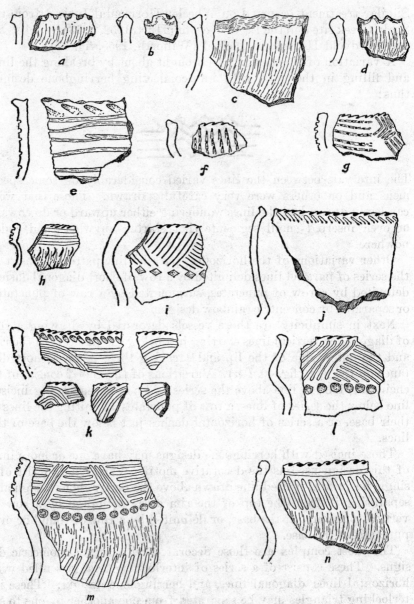

FIGURE 40.—Rim treatment and decorative zones.

by Carlyle S. Smith (Smith, 1951, pp. 34–37) are almost identical with some of those found at the Hosterman site. The majority do not fit into this category.

TICKED LINE, INCISED—Type "A":

This type consists of a series of horizontal parallel lines which start just below the lip and cover the entire neck area. Necks are vertical to slightly flaring or excurvate. Lines are not carefully drawn or joined and many are just short segments; some join while others start and stop without any unity with the rest of the group (fig. 40, *e*). On the whole it portrays a lack of fineness of design and a distinct indication of a lackadaisical inclination toward the satisfaction of creating something that has been carefully done. Lines are drawn either with sharply pointed tools, a form of incising, or with dull, flat-bladed tools, a form of trailing. Some of the lines are drawn as close together as 2 mm.; others as far apart as 6 mm.

On the whole, the surface of the neck was smoothed before the lines were incised upon it, but there are any number that show that the surface was first brushed and then the incised or trailed lines were drawn upon this rough surface. Several appear with wavy lines because the surface was poorly prepared rather than because of the shakiness of the potter herself.

Perhaps this group can be divided into two subgroups: A_1 and A_2.

A₁ has a row of diagonal incisions directly beneath the lip and above the series of horizontally drawn lines.

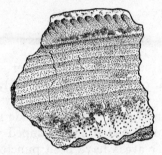

A₂ has a row of punctations below the series of horizontal parallel lines to set the lines apart from the shoulder area.

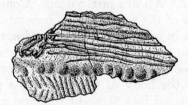

Wall thickness varies from slightly under 4 mm. to 8 mm. Color variation still persists. Soot incrustations are still present. Interiors are smoothed without any evidence of brushing.

TICKED LINE, INCISED—Type "B":

The same holds true for type "B" with the exception that there are no subtypes.

Color, soot incrustation, brushing on exterior, wavy lines, the way the lines were incised or trailed, distance apart, type of tool used, and general appearances are all alike.

TICKED LINE, INCISED—Type "C":

The same holds true for type "C."

Plain lip, vertical neck that is covered with a series of horizontal parallel lines. All the characteristics as described for the *ticked lip group* apply here. There is one exception. Two specimens have their lines drawn rather deeply penetrating about half the thickness of the wall itself.

Punctated.—All of the characteristics common to the others are present here. The only difference is in the treatment of the lip itself. In this case the lip is punctated. Punctations appear to have been made by:

    (1) Fabric impressions
    (2) Round blunt tipped tool
    (3) Comma-shaped tool
    (4) Teardrop-shaped tool
    (5) Small grass stem
    (6) Pyramidal-tipped tool

SHOULDER TREATMENT

Shoulders of the various vessels were either simple-stamped (figs. 41–43) plain-smoothed, or incised (figs. 44, 45), and from the presence of a few black-on-gray painted sherds, it would appear that the shoulders were occasionally painted with crude geometric designs.

Parts of three medium-sized simple-stamped vessels are unique in that all of the shoulder areas have been punctated with a series of large punctates, ca. 12 mm. in diameter. The punctates on two of the vessels are spaced about equally apart and appear on the upper part of the shoulder. All are fairly deep. Consequently, nodes appear on the interiors of the vessels. The punctates on the third vessel have been arranged in groups of vertical series, two rows to a series and four or more punctates to a row. The punctates start just at the base of the neck constriction or the top of the shoulder and run downward midway onto the body of the vessel (see pl. 20, *B, b*). The punctates are not placed in a straight line and appear to have been made by tapping the vessel quite firmly, while it was still plastic, with the tip of the finger or some implement of comparable size.

Shoulder incising appears to be quite popular at the Hosterman site. It consists of various combinations of line-filled triangles (fig. 46), triangles filled with zigzags, or crude herringbone designs. None can be said to be very carefully drawn. Apparently, the potters were not after carefully executed work but rather the effect of the design

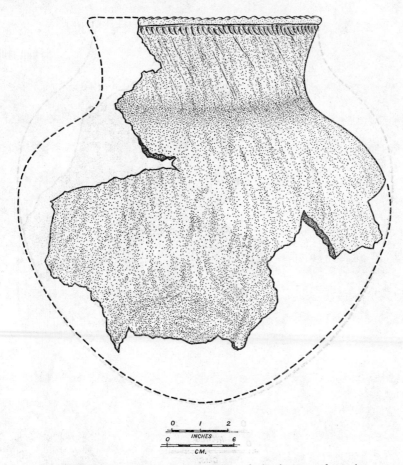

FIGURE 41.—Restoration of vertical rimmed, simple-stamped vessel.

itself, otherwise, it seems, they would have been more careful in drawing the lines of the design (figs. 45 and 46).

HANDLES

Handles on Hosterman vessels are not common (pls. 16, A, a; 17, B; 18, A; 19, A, a). In the main they are of two varieties: strap (19 specimens) and horizontal lug (16 specimens). Strap handles, as a rule, are either welded at the lip or are tonguelike elongations of the lip that curve downward a short distance to be welded or riveted to the body of the vessel. On the other hand, there are rare instances when the strap handle may originate just a short distance below the lip, on the upper portion of the rim, and follow the same pattern as the others in their basal attachment to the walls of the vessel. Most of the strap handles project horizontally before curving downward to make their

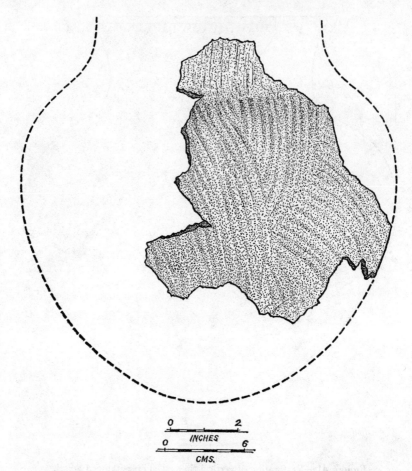

FIGURE 42.—Shoulder decoration on large jar sherd, Hosterman site.

juncture. Usually the upper section of all strap handles is much wider at the top than at the bottom, giving the handles a triangular appearance. In cross section most are oval near the base, others are flat, while a few are concavo-convex. Handles of this type may appear as pairs, opposite each other on opposite sides of the vessel, or they may be separated by small lugs appearing in the opposite quadrants.

The same design used on the adjoining lip decorates most strap handles, being simply carried over onto the handle. The design may be herringbone incised (16 specimens), horizontal cord impressed (1 specimen), horizontal line incised (1 specimen), or horizontal stab and drag (1 specimen) (fig. 47). None were left undecorated.

Lug handles are somewhat variable as to shape, size, and placement. Practically all are tonguelike projections off the lip or side of the vessel. Others may appear lower down on the neck or at the

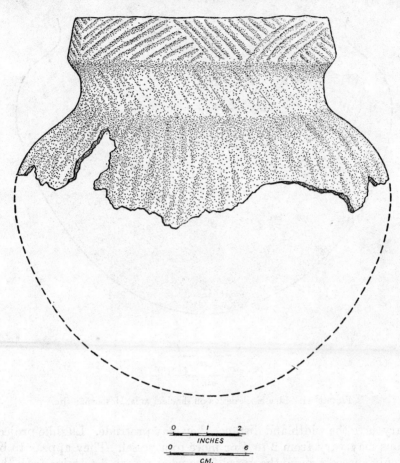

FIGURE 43.—Rim and shoulder area of S-shaped rimmed vessel.

bottom of S-shaped rims. Mostly they are just paired horizontal projections extending a short distance out from the exterior surface of the vessel. Almost all appear to have been fashioned at the same time the vessel was finished off; only a very few appear to have been welded onto the vessel afterward. They are roughly triangular in shape. One rare case is that of an S-shaped rim upon which are five luglike projections on the upper part of the "S" that are but slight downward elongations. Each projection is separated by an equal number of cord-impressed rainbow designs that also appear on the lugs (pl. 19, B, a). These are spaced equidistant around the rim of the vessel. These projections vary in the distance they protrude and whether they droop, sag, or extend straight out from the sides of the vessel. As on the strap handles the incised herringbone design is carried over onto the tops of most of them. Width and length may

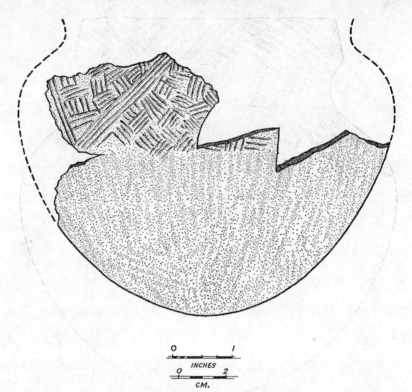

INCHES

CM.

FIGURE 44.—Line-block design on shoulder area, Hosterman site.

vary as to the width and distance they may protrude. Luglike projections may vary from 2 to 4 or more to a vessel. They appear to be evenly spaced around the vessel from what we can determine from the sherds.

One lug handle, on specimen No. 3372/16, is unique in that it became limp shortly after it was fashioned onto the vessel and dropped down onto the neck of the vessel forming a very tenuous joint with it. It appears to have been unintentional but whether it was or not it would appear to function as an evolutionary trend in explaining the formation of a type of strap handle from the lug type.

VESSEL SHAPES

Vessel shapes appear to lean to globular with vertical and slightly everted necks, rounded shoulders and bases, with the shoulders decorated with incised motifs and the necks covered with a series of incised horizontal parallel lines. This type of vessel shape is rather widespread for it also occurs at the Swan Creek site (39WW7), Steamboat Creek site (39PO1), and the Four Bears site (39DW1),

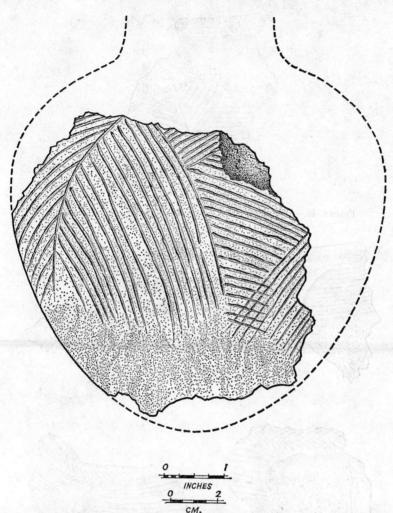

FIGURE 45.—Line-block design on shoulder area, Hosterman site.

all of which are neighboring villages. This does not in any way suggest a contemporaneity but only an indication of the relative occurrence of similar vessel shapes with similar exterior surface treatments within a temporal and spatial relationship of a very small area.

A large number of vessels had a heavy incrustation of soot which had adhered to the outside of them, filling in all depressions made by the various design elements, blotting out all indications that the vessel was decorated in any manner. This heavy soot incrustation may be and could be due to the tendency of the potters of the Plains, as pointed out by Will (1906), and others, to coat the outside of vessels heavily with grease prior to firing. The intense heat used

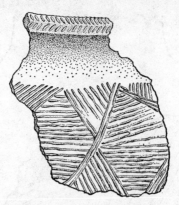

FIGURE 46.—Line diamond design on shoulder area, Hosterman site.

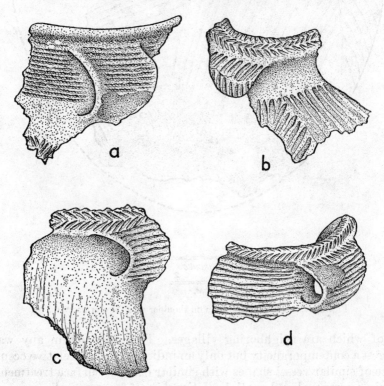

FIGURE 47.—Handle types showing points of origin.

would change the hydrocarbon into pure carbon consolidating it into a firm mass surrounding the exterior of the vessel.

PAINTED POTTERY

Three small potsherds found in the large mass of body sherds had fragmentary designs in black painted on their exteriors. Since none of these sherds were very large, it was impossible to determine the complete design of the original. The basic surface finish of each differed somewhat. Two of them had their exteriors smoothed before the paint was applied and the third one still retained the initial simple-stamped treatment over which the paint was applied. The very presence of even this small number of painted sherds would render this site unique since painted designs on the exteriors of vessels are rare rather than commonplace.

The use of a red pigment on the interiors and some exteriors has been reported from other sites. This trait appears to be common enough in the Plains. Even so, it is not too prevalent here at the Hosterman site; so this, too, can be classed as a rarity.

MINIATURE VESSELS

Several fragmentary vessels in the form of jars were found in various areas in the site. Four basic forms are represented. All have two traits in common: rounded bases and globular bodies.

The smallest of the six miniature vessels, field cat. No. 3428, has the following measurements based on possible reconstruction: diameter of the mouth, 35 mm.; diameter of the neck, 30 mm; diameter of the body, 43 mm.; and height, 45 mm. The neck is slightly constricted and above the constriction is a small rim section (see outline drawings of these vessels, fig. 48).

The second vessel, field cat. No. 742, is slightly larger, and resembles the first with the exception that it is squattier. It has the following measurements: diameter of mouth, 36 mm.; diameter of neck, 32 mm.; diameter of body, 61 mm.; and height, 50 mm.

The next vessel, which also has a constricted neck, is larger and the constriction is not as abrupt; field cat. No. 290/60. It has the following measurements: diameter of mouth, 46 mm.; diameter of neck, 40 mm.; diameter of body, 59 mm.; and height, 50 mm.

The next larger vessel, field cat. No. 290/56, has a unique shape in that the constriction is about midway down from the lip and nearly separates the vessels into two equal parts. Whether the base is sub-conoidal as represented or more rounded appears to be questionable. Its measurements are as follows: diameter of mouth, 63 mm.; diameter of neck constriction, 57 mm.; diameter of body, 68 mm.; and estimated height, 63 mm.

Next to the largest vessel is a globular vessel, field cat. No. 3206/1, with a slightly constricted short neck. It measures 61 mm. across the mouth, 61 mm. just above the shoulders, 84 mm. in body diameter, and 84 mm. in height.

The last and largest of the series, field cat. No. 290/116, is a variation in shape of the vessel just described. The mouth of the vessel

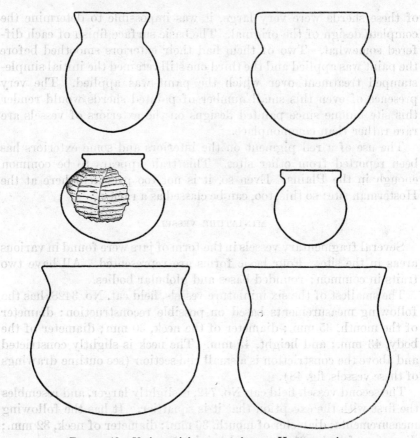

FIGURE 48.—Various miniature vessel types, Hosterman site.

measures 85 mm. in diameter, 83 mm. across the slightly constricted neck, 97 mm. in body diameter, and 95 mm. in height.

Four of the vessels have smoothed exteriors. Specimen No. 742 has a series of radiating lines starting at the top of the shoulder and running down almost to the base. Between these radiating lines are series of horizontal parallel lines spaced so as to fill in the intervals. Specimen No. 290/116 has the rim and the upper portions of the neck covered over with corncorb impressions that are quite distinct. Apparently the entire exterior of the vessel was treated with a corncob and later most of the impressions were obliterated. Small patches retain these impressions. The interior of the vessel has a smoothed surface but is rather uneven as to thickness. The vessel tends to be lopsided. Table 5 gives the measurements of all the miniature vessels.

EXOTIC VESSEL OF POSSIBLE CADDOAN EXTRACTION

One very noticeable miniature vessel, field cat. No. 1347, possesses two mouths or spouts (pl. 21). It was found in a cache pit, Feature 9,

TABLE 5.—*Measurements of miniature vessels*

Field specimen No.	Diameter of mouth	Diameter of neck	Diameter of body	Height
	mm.	mm.	mm.	mm.
3428	35	30	43	45
742	36	32	61	50
290/60	46	40	59	71
290/56	63	57	68	63
3206/1	61	61	84	84
290/116	85	83	97	95

at a depth of 5.8 feet from the present surface. This is a most unusual find because its form is one seldom found in the Upper Plains. Its surface color is mottled in that it runs from a tan to gray and black with fire clouds very much in evidence. When the vessel was complete it was oval in outline and rather squatty in height. The spouts, or mouths, are atop two short vertical necks that are not decorated. Between the spouts and covering on the shoulders a crude herringbone design was cut only moderately deep into the clay. Over the rest of the body appears a series of vertical and diagonal incised parallel lines, some of which crisscross. The lips of the two spouts are crudely punctated. Walls at the top are rather thin, 3.0 mm., and the basal portion is fairly thick, 8.0 mm. (fig. 49).

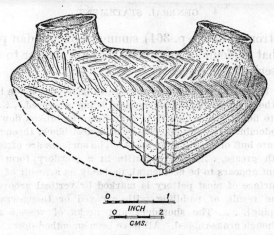

FIGURE 49.—Two-spouted vessel, Hosterman site, showing decorative design.

CLAY DAWDLES

Throughout the site and in some of the midden pits were several objects of clay that appear to have been leisurely and probably unintentionally fashioned into vaguely recognizable or unrecognizable objects. Some resemble miniature clay vessels or toys; others are in the form of spheres or marbles, known during my early years as "Dough babies"; still others are nondescript in form. All have been fired to insure permanency. It is probable that such objects were made while members of the community were seated around campfires on some cold winter night and, to pass the time away, took up clumps of moist clay that were handy and unconsciously molded these objects into shape. When the interest in the object no longer existed it was cast into the open fire and soon forgotten by the maker. Later, when the fire area was cleared away, these objects were tossed into a midden pit along with the ashes or scattered onto midden piles within the confines of the village area.

Furthermore, a lump of compacted ashy clay was found in Feature 2 at a depth of between 1.0 foot and 2.0 feet. It is roughly triangular in outline and has a maximum length of 4.7 cm., a breadth of 3.8 cm., and a maximum thickness of 2.4 cm. Near the apex of the piece there is a truncated conical hole that is widest at its point of entry (1.9 cm.) and tapers down to a diameter of 1.0 cm., continuing through the clay object. Under microscopic examination there are no vertical striations inside the bore, a fact indicating that the object was never used as a form of abrader. The physical composition of the object is rather soft; a fine powder comes off on the finger when rubbed across the surface. The purpose and use of these objects is problematical.

GENERAL STATEMENT

I found Strong's (1940, p. 364) summary of Mandan pottery noteworthy in that he found many traits that are similar to those of the Hosterman series. He stated:

The pottery is rather granular and appears to have been made by the paddle-and-anvil method, no evidences of coiling being observed. . . . is tempered with medium to fine grit obtained from granitic rocks broken down in the fires. Colors are predominantly dark but run from almost black, through browns and gray, to very rare buff or even orange tones. The surfaces are often superficially blackened with grease. . . . Red hematite in a powdery form occurs inside some sherds but appears to be accidental, probably as a result of use in mixing paint. The surface of most pottery is marked by vertical grooves and ridges, apparently the result of paddling with grooved or thong-wrapped paddles [simple stamping]. . . . The shoulders and necks of vessels show vertical scratches as though grass-rubbed. All have been smoothed down, and the small vessels often have a plain surface. . . . Rims and necks that are S-shaped are most common [which is not true of the Hosterman site, as shown earlier], flaring profiles with lips somewhat thickened next [which are a minority form at the Hosterman site], and intermediate forms [7 percent]. Castellations, lugs, spouts, and strap handles are rare. . . . The S-shaped rims are usually decorated with horizontal or diagonal twisted single-cord impressions, closely spaced. A curvilinear design suggesting a rainbow is very common. . . . Incised designs are common on the shoulders of vessels, usually consisting of opposed diagonals. About one-fourth of the rims are plain, and finger-pinched rims are common.

On the other hand, Cooper (1949, p. 303) noted that the pottery remains from a number of sites between Pierre and the mouth of the

Cheyenne River were apparently identifiable with Arikara ceramics as described by Strong (1940, pp. 368–369, 381). The Hosterman site, situated about 40 miles upstream from the mouth of the Cheyenne River, could fall well within the sphere of the Arikara settlement pattern and hence one would expect to find to a certain extent comparable pottery forms and types of this group at the site. There is close resemblance between the two.

ARTIFACTS OTHER THAN POTTERY

CHIPPED-STONE ARTIFACTS

PROJECTILE POINTS

Six hundred fifty-nine projectile points, either whole or fragmentary, were recovered. Several varieties of stones were used in their manufacture: quartzite, chalcedony, and chert. Two specimens were made of obsidian. Nearly all are thin, and a number show a primary scar on one face, whereas most were made by secondary chipping of a small detached flake. The final shaping of the edges was accomplished by flaking from both sides. Two hundred sixty-nine were sufficiently complete to allow for classification. Flaking is neat and rather delicate in most specimens, and since it proceeded from both sides the resulting point is very symmetrical and slightly lenticular in cross section.

Most of the stone used in the manufacture of projectile points occurs in the vicinity of the Hosterman site, in the riverbed or on the terraces around the site. Some, like obsidian, had to be brought into the area from other vicinities.

The arrow points of the Hosterman site are small, light, and pressure flaked. Four basic styles are represented as well as the inevitable scattering of deviants.

GROUP 1 (pl. 22, *A*) ; 62 specimens.—Triangular in shape with straight or slightly convex edges; sides are slightly longer than the base; straight bases as a rule, but there are some slightly concave or convex bases that occur rarely.

　Length: Mean of 14 mm., ranges from 13 mm. to 19 mm.

　Width: Mean of 13 mm., ranges from 9 mm. to 18 mm.

　Thickness: Mean of 3 mm., ranges from 2 mm. to 4 mm.

GROUP 2 (pl. 22, *B*) ; 112 specimens.—Isosceles triangular in shape with straight or slightly concave edges; straight or concave bases. Maximum width at base.

　Length: Mean of 25 mm., ranges from 20 mm. to 29 mm.

　Width: Mean of 14 mm., ranges from 11 mm. to 17 mm.

　Thickness: Mean of 3 mm., ranges from 2 mm. to 6 mm.

GROUP 3 (pl. 23 *A*) ; 21 specimens.—Triangular with straight or convex edges, straight or convex bases. Maximum width at base.

　Length: Mean of 34 mm., ranges from 24 mm. to 43 mm.

　Width: Mean of 24 mm., ranges from 19 mm. to 29 mm.

　Thickness: Mean of 7 mm., ranges from 5 mm. to 9 mm.

GROUP 4 (pl. 23, *B*); 66 specimens.—Side-notched, straight-sided triangular, maximum width at base, straight base, slightly concave or convex bases occur rarely. The notches are at right angles to the long axis and are often very narrow or shallow.

Length: Mean of 38 mm., ranges from 18 mm. to 58 mm.

Width: Mean of 17 mm., ranges from 12 mm. to 22 mm.

Thickness: Mean of 4 mm., ranges from 2 mm. to 6 mm.

MISCELLANEOUS (pl. 23, *B*); 8 specimens.—These eight specimens were complete and none of them fit into the four basic groups. One small point is stemmed; another is corner notched; several have expanded bases; and the remainder are side-notched but of a different pattern than those of group 4.

MICROBLADES

Microblades (pl. 24) are made of small thin flakes of chalcedony, quartzite, chert, jasper, and obsidian. Unlike the microblades from the areas to the Far North, the blades from the Hosterman site were not struck from specially prepared cores, for not one really good core was found throughout our excavations. Out of the aggregate we separated two groups. Group I are much longer, ranging in length from 25 mm. to 57 mm. Group II are much finer and shorter and range in length from 18 mm. to 38 mm. Both groups are very finely retouched along the edges. Evidently, such small blades must have been inserted into handles of wood, for we found no bone handles that would fit such small flake blades. They were probably used as knives or sickles.

Two of the lots are bifaced in that they were retouched on both faces. Whether these are a form of drill, punch, or perforator of some type cannot be determined.

Others are forms of side scrapers or knives since one or both edges have been very carefully retouched and the very small thin flaking scars indicate that work was performed on these small thin flakes to convert them into workable tools. The initial flakes were not struck from specially prepared cores, for none were found within the area investigated. Apparently, the workmen were skillful chippers, for they were capable of striking off thin flakes from any one core without too much trouble. Not only were they capable of securing thin flakes but they were qualified in casting off flakes of sufficient lengths that could be converted into workable functional tools. If the bulbar end, or the dorsal or underside surface, is placed downward and toward the workers and the worked edge is noted, it will be found that only 30 percent of these small tools were retouched in the left edge.

Many of the flakes, both large and small, show signs of use about one or more edges as though they had been picked up from the scrap heap and used temporarily for scraping or cutting. Once the job was completed or they were too dull to be of further use they were thrown away.

SCRAPERS

Scrapers, since they occur over long periods of time, are much too ubiquitous to be considered as good horizon markers as they first appear in Early Man sites, continuing through the Archaic and into pottery-making horizons. They have become so well adapted that they have continued to be manufactured over long periods of time; thus, their usefulness as "index fossils" has been destroyed.

Scrapers are flake tools. They vary both as to size and form. They are characterized by a plane or slightly curved undersurface (ventral face) surmounted by a dorsal keel or flatness displaying one or more abruptly retouched edges. The working edge is somewhat convex, except in the case of a very thin variety. The convexity is clearly the essential feature. Maximum thickness is not confined to any particular portion of the scraper. They are unifaced and ovate, elliptical, lunate, triangular, subtriangular, trapeziform, circular, or irregular in outline.

The very presence of scrapers portends certain technical knowledge of the preparation of pelts into leather goods for the manufacture of clothing, etc.

I believe Stewart's (1946, p. 45) definition of a scraper is an excellent one. He describes it as:

A primitive thing called a scraper is crude and not at all eloquent until you realize that it points to much else. It means not only a scraper, but a thing to be scraped, most likely a hide; therefore it means a growing ability to kill, to take the hide and cure it. That is just the beginning, for a scraper also shows a knowledge of how to scrape, and a desire for scraping, and enough leisure (beyond the struggle to get food) to allow time for scraping. All this means self restraint and thought for the future, and it implies a certain confidence in the ways of life, because no one would be liable to go to all the trouble of scraping if he did not have the reasonable hope of enjoying the results of his work.

Scrapers can roughly be divided into two classes: end and side scrapers. End scrapers have the working edge or edges on the ends of flakes and are roughly convex, and where there is a central keel it frequently rises up fanwise to meet it. Sometimes much fluting occurs along the side of the flake to trim it into the desired form. End scrapers can be subdivided into: *keeled, circular, large and small teardrop, small planoconvex, large and small flake, flat thumbnail, beveled, triangular, subtriangular, peaked planoconvex,* and *scraper-graver combination.* Side scrapers are subdivided into: *large flake single edged, large flake triple edged, large planoconvex triple edged, double edged, prismatic flake, thin pointed double edged,* and *combination side scraper—spokeshave.*

Practically all of the scrapers have been neatly made. The majority of the end scrapers occur on especially prepared flakes. The bulb of percussion of the ventral surface indicates that flakes were utilized and purposefully struck off in the manufacture of scrapers. The scraper end, opposite the bulb end, is neatly trimmed and one or more sides are retouched forming a tool with either a rounded, straight, or ogival double working surface. As a rule, retouching occurs on all edges, but it can occur on only one edge. Scrapers are characterized by retouching along one or more edges of the dorsal surface, and the ventral surface is unworked and is either flat or concave as the result of the initial flaking in which the piece was cast off from a core.

MacNeish (1954, p. 246), while observing Slave practices, found that end scrapers were used primarily in fleshing and scraping the skins of the animals they killed. On the other hand, side scrapers could also function equally as well as skinning knives and were used in separating the skin from the animal and in the preliminary removal of muscle tissue from the skin. Both functions appear plausible from the form of the many scrapers recovered from the Hosterman site.

The total collection of scrapers from the Hosterman site includes 777 specimens. Materials used in the manufacture of scrapers appear to represent the entire range of silicious minerals present at the site or in the immediate vicinity of it. They are described as chalcedonies, quartzites, jaspers, cherts, and flints. By far the more common are the chalcedonies.

As described many times, the basic scraper form is the result of striking a core a blow aimed slightly inward so as to produce a short flake. In a number of instances it breaks with a hinged fracture. The flake when viewed from the side is usually considerably thicker at the end opposite to the striking platform and the bulb of percussion. In some there is a pronounced downward curve near the thicker end. When viewed from the top, many are trapezoidal or pointed oval in outline with the greatest breadth at or near the thickened end.

"As is true at so many of the later Plains sites, end scrapers made on flakes are a common type of chipped stone artifact. . . . The only retouching considered to be indispensable was that on the broader end, that produced a more or less straight or smoothly curved working edge and a steep face that intersects the flake scar at an angle approaching 90 degrees. Retouching on the sides was presumably intended to produce the proper shape only; it may be absent if the flake already had a suitable form, or it may be present on only one side. Very thick flakes sometimes show a steep and bold retouch with flake scars from both sides meeting in or near the center to form a longitudinal keel.

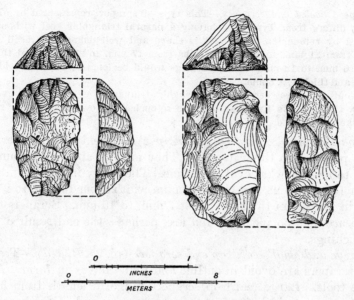

FIGURE 50.—Keeled scraper types.

In others the back was simply left in its original form, often showing longitudinal facets where previous flakes had been struck off the core. It would appear that the makers were not overly concerned with the method by which the result was obtained so long as a serviceable implement resulted" (Spaulding, 1956, pp. 43–44). Nor were they concerned as to the final shape taken by the implement whether it was trianguloid, rhomboidal, or rectangular. There is quite a range in size as to length, width, and thickness.

Lehmer (1954, pp. 57–58), in studying the Dodd site, separated the end scrapers into five distinct groups depending somewhat upon their outline and method of chipping to determine the shape. These same forms, as well as others, occur at the Hosterman site in quantity.

Keeled end scrapers (fig. 50).—Scrapers of this class were made from flakes having flat to concave ventral surfaces and a single ridged dorsal surface. The working edge has been rounded and steeply retouched. Sides taper somewhat to a blunt squared end. Scrapers of this type have been subdivided into type 1 and type 2 (pl. 25).

Type 1 keeled end scrapers.—This type of scraper, represented by 75 specimens, has all sides retouched with the small fluted scars meeting at a central ridge or keel. Overall length varies from 20 mm. to 37 mm.; overall width from 15 mm. to 27 mm.; and overall thickness from 7 mm. to 12 mm. Mean readings would be lengths, 25 mm.; widths, 22 mm.; and thickness, 9 mm.

The retouching along the sides rises up fanwise to a single rounded keel on the dorsal surface varying the thickness of the specimen so that no two are exactly of a uniform thickness. The presence of this type of chipping indicates that the person creating such an artifact was most capable in his ability to cast off these long thin chips uniformly and regularly.

Type 2 keeled end scrapers.—This type of scraper, represented by 57 specimens, differs from Type 1 by having a natural triangular keel without being
shaped by retouching. The keel is sharp and well defined. Overall lengths
vary from 21 mm. to 40 mm.; widths from 17 mm. to 27 mm.; and thickness
from 6 mm. to 12 mm. Mean readings would be lengths, 29 mm.; widths, 21
mm.; and thickness, 8 mm.

In outline, these scrapers are roughly triangular with slightly excurvate
edges. Type 1 has its dorsal surface retouched all over rising to a rounded
keellike prominence.

Small round scrapers (pl. 25, *A, p–z*).—Twenty-one scrapers have
been placed into this category. They are not absolutely round, but
tend to be somewhat oval in outline. They vary in maximum length
from 19 mm. to 28 mm., in maximum width from 18 mm. to 25 mm.,
and in maximum thickness from 7 mm. to 10 mm. Scrapers of this
form are not too plentiful and are, perhaps, the end result of many
retouchings.

Large and small teardrop end scrapers (pl. 25, *B, a–d*).—Teardrop
end scrapers are ovoid in outline and planoconvex in form. All are
flake tools. Large teardrop scrapers range in length from 37 mm.
to 51 mm., in width from 21 mm. to 30 mm., and in thickness from
6 mm. to 11 mm. Small teardrop scrapers range in length from 23
mm. to 33 mm., in width from 16 mm. to 19 mm., and in thickness
from 5 mm. to 8 mm. The ventral sides are always concave while
the dorsal surfaces have the edges retouched gradually sloping to
a flat keel. The lateral edges are slightly excurvate in outline. Each
of these forms is represented by 6 specimens or 12 in all.

Small planoconvex end scrapers (pl. 25, *B, e–m*).—End scrapers of
this type do not conform to any special group but are established
solely upon form. Seven specimens have been assigned to this type.
In length they vary from 23 mm. to 32 mm., in width from 16 mm. to
22 mm., and in thickness from 7 mm. to 10 mm. One scraper (field
cat. No. 1387) has a distinct graver tip near the butt end of the tool.

Large flake end scrapers (pl. 25, *B, n*).—There are 20 specimens in
this group. Flake end scrapers are mostly irregular fragments of
flint with a flat ventral surface and retouching on one end. The rest of
the artifact was never retouched. Their lengths range from 27 mm.
to 56 mm., widths from 14 mm. to 29 mm., thickness from 2 mm. to
11 mm. One specimen (field cat. No. 3049) has a wide notch worked
out near the base. The specimen measures 17 mm. across. Apparently
this was used to smooth down wooden tools, such as arrow shafts, etc.

Small flake end scrapers (pl. 25, *B, o–u*).—There are 43 specimens
in this group. These are much smaller flakes and, like the larger, are
worked on only one end. The difference between the two is a matter
of length. These scrapers vary in length from 17 mm. to 29 mm.,

in width from 13 mm. to 23 mm., and in thickness from 3 mm. to
10 mm. One specimen (field cat. No. 2407) has a burinlike base.

Flat end scrapers (pl. 26, *A*, *a–f*).—Thirty-three specimens are in
this group. All were made of comparatively thin flakes. Measurements show that they vary in length from 15 mm. to 38 mm., in widths
from 16 mm. to 30 mm., and in thickness from 4 mm. to 9 mm. The
retouched surface may be straight or curved.

Thumbnail end scrapers (pl. 26, *A*, *g–z*).—Twenty-two specimens
are in this group. Most are very small and very well made. They vary
in outline from trianguloid to rectanguloid. In length they range
from 14 mm. to 23 mm., in width from 12 mm. to 19 mm., and in
thickness from 3 mm. to 7 mm. The average length runs from 17
mm. to 19 mm. The average widths can range between 14 mm. and
17 mm.; and the average thickness is about 5 mm.

Beveled retouched edge end scrapers (pl. 26, *B*, *a–i*).—There are
two types of these scrapers: those that slope upward to the right
and those that slope to the left. Nine specimens have retouched edges
that slope to the left whereas only six slope to the right. Whether
these are valid types can only be verified by examination of other
nearby collections. Most of the ventral surfaces are flat, but there
is an occasional one that is planoconvex in outline.

Those scrapers that slope upward to the right come very near to
being uniform in length. Three are 25 mm. long; two are 24 mm.
long; and only one is 21 mm. in length. Widths run about the same:
three are 17 mm. in width; two are 18 mm. in width; and the third
is 20 mm. in width. Thickness ranges from 4 mm. to 8 mm. Five are
excurvate trianguloid in outline and the other is roughly rectangular.

The scrapers that slope upward and to the left are not quite as
uniform as to size. They range in length from 23 mm. to 29 mm., in
width from 15 mm. to 21 mm., and in thickness from 6 mm. to 9 mm.

Triangular end scrapers (pl. 26, *B*, *j–r*).—Nine specimens. These
are excurvate edged triangles and are made from comparatively thin
flakes. They range in length from 22 mm. to 29 mm., in width from
18 mm. to 25 mm., and in thickness from 4 mm. to 8 mm. Ventral surfaces are uniformly flat and the dorsal surfaces have retouching on all
three sides rising to a rounded keellike prominence.

Slightly modified nodular end scrapers (pl. 27, *A*, *a–l*).—End
scrapers of this type were made from pieces of jasper that still retained part of the natural unmodified outer surface of the rock. The
shape of these flakes seemed immaterial to the one manufacturing end
scrapers of this type. Some of the flakes are roughly rectangular in
outline, others are triangular, and the rest are somewhat irregular
in shape. From the table of measurements in Appendix 4 one will
note that most of the flakes are about 6 mm. thick, but the range is from

4 mm. to 10 mm. Lengths of the flakes are very consistent, and the greatest variation occurs in the widths. Cutting ends have been sharply retouched either in a slight arc or straight across.

Trapezoidal end scrapers (pl. 27, *A*, *m*, *o*).—Scrapers of this type, 15 specimens, are roughly four sided; two of which are parallel. Of the total number, 9 have all four edges retouched while the remaining 6 have retouching only along three sides. Cutting edges can range in shape from a pronounced arc to almost a straight line. Size is fairly uniform.

End scrapers with left carinate (*type 3*).—These 37 specimens are a form of keeled scraper in which the keel appears as a distinct flake scar ridge on the left side of the dorsal surface, creating the thickest part of the tool. All are medium sized and several of them have had the positive bulb of percussion chipped away to bring about a flatter ventral surface.

Contrariwise there are 32 other specimens, type 4, that possess a distinct ridge along the right side of each scraper. Whether these are distinct and purposeful tools cannot be determined, but there are far too many of them to be accounted as just accidental objects, or end scrapers.

What was once a type 3 end scraper ended up by being an eccentric scraper; not only were the edges retouched but the working edges were retouched on the ventral surface, creating a very pronounced bevel. The cutting edge now resembles similar edges found on gouges or chisels. Whether this particular tool was intended to function as a gouge cannot be determined, but it is well suited for just this purpose (field specimen No. 1008).

End scraper-graver combination (pl. 27, *A*, *p–v*).—A few end scrapers had short graver tips at one or both sides of the working face. These were made by carefully chipping a small, fine, sharp point along one edge of the tool. The ventral face is flat, as was that of the scraper itself, and the edges are beveled and brought to a point. At the present time these points are not as sharp as they once were but have been rendered dull through apparent use. Evidently this trait is a carryover from an earlier cultural manifestation and was in its terminal phase at the Hosterman site, as represented by the small number of specimens.

Modified end scrapers—(two specimens).—These are slightly triangular in outline with a pronounced groove down the dorsal surface, creating a moderately high ridge on the left-hand side of the scraper and one less pronounced on the right-hand side. The two side edges have been carefully retouched, terminating in a rounded butt, and the scraping edge was given additional retouching to give the ventral surface a beveled inward curve while the dorsal surface was carefully

beveled to create a chisellike cutting edge. Perhaps artifacts of this
type were used as a form of gouge.

Twenty-three fragments of end scrapers are too indefinite to be
classified into the various types found at this site.

Side scrapers.—Side scrapers are flake tools. It appears that their
essential characteristic is the presence of a scraping edge formed along
one or more sides of a suitable flake as the result of secondary working
or retouching. The ventral surface, or under face, is unworked as a
rule. The scraping edge is produced by secondary flaking from the
ventral surface upon one or more edges. They vary greatly in size and
shape depending primarily upon the type of flake chosen to be converted into a side scraper.

It would seem that any suitable flake, regardless of size or shape,
could have had its edges or edge trimmed for use as a scraper. The
working edge is somewhat convex in outline. Several of these flakes
are very thin, long, with parallel sides. Most of the Hosterman site
side scrapers are made from some sort of chalcedony, quartzite, chert,
or jasper. The trimmed edge, in most cases, was formed by pressure
chipping in which small fine chips were cast off. On the other hand, a
minority was just the opposite in that large rough flakes or chips
were cast off with no care taken as to placement of the chips, resulting
in large, thick, uneven edged flakes converted into side scrapers. Usually the larger scrapers were made of quartzite.

Side scrapers from the Hosterman site have been subdivided into
the following types: *Small flake side scrapers*, 111 specimens; *medium-
sized flake side scrapers*, 15 specimens; *large flake side scrapers*, 3
specimens; *lunate side scrapers*, 30 specimens; *triple-edged side scrapers*, 6 specimens; *prismatic side scrapers*, 12 specimens; *double-edged
side scrapers*, 13 specimens; and *combination side scraper-spokeshave*,
15 specimens.

Small flake side scrapers.—These were made from the small ubiquitous flakes found scattered at knapping stations within the site or
on various dump heaps. The side edge was, as a rule, very carefully
chipped with very fine retouching, but there is an occasional specimen
whose scraper edge was made by casting off much larger and heavier
chips. Measuring along the scraper edge, the greatest and smallest
lengths are 36 mm. and 16 mm., greatest widths of the flakes utilized
ranged from 31 mm. to 15 mm., and the thickness varies from 2 mm.
to 11 mm.

Large flake side scrapers (pl. 27, *B*, *a–c*).—Three have the following measurements:

Length	Width	Thickness
107 mm.	50 mm.	9 mm.
63	53	17
122	66	22

These measurements would indicate that any flake over 60 mm. in length converted into a side scraper would immediately be placed in the large-flake category.

Double-edged side scrapers (pl. 28, *A*, *a*).—Scrapers of this type have opposing sides retouched to scraper surfaces. Measurements show considerable variations: in length, 22 mm. to 67 mm.; in width, 14 mm. to 41 mm.; and in thickness, 4 mm. to 10 mm. Five of the specimens have a carinated dorsal surface, and the remainder have a fluted dorsal surface.

Triple-edged side scrapers (pl. 28, *A*, *b*).—Scrapers of this type have two sides and the adjoining end of a flake converted into scraping surfaces. The adjoining end can be convex or straight in outline. At the Hosterman site we have two subtypes depending solely upon size. Type 1 scrapers range in length from 67 mm. to 130 mm., in width from 30 mm. to 65 mm., and in thickness from 13 mm. to 16 mm. Type 2 scrapers range in length from 20 mm. to 28 mm., in width from 18 mm. to 29 mm., and in thickness from 4 mm. to 6 mm.

Prismatic flake end scrapers (pl. 28, *A*, *d*).—These tend to be triangular in cross section and have only one of the edges converted into scraping surfaces. They range in length from 22 mm. to 49 mm., in width from 10 mm. to 19 mm., and in thickness from 5 mm. to 11 mm.

Lunate side scrapers.—Lunate side scrapers have one convex edge that was retouched to a scraping edge. Most of the flakes when cast off had an edge roughly convex in outline and were converted into this type of scraper. Only the retouched edge was worked; the rest of the surface of the artifact was untouched. The size of the flake varies in length from 21 mm. to 61 mm., in width from 10 mm. to 44 mm., and in thickness from 4 mm. to 14 mm.

Side and concave scrapers (pl. 28, *A*, *c*).—Scrapers of this type are combinations of a side scraper and a spokeshave or a concave scraping surface. Most of these have only one concave surface, but one of these scrapers has two concave surfaces. These are carefully retouched so that they are not the result of a false blow or breakage. The flake may range in length from 27 mm. to 78 mm., in width from 18 mm. to 42 mm., and in thickness from 5 mm. to 14 mm.

Another form of side scraper is that which has two sides that join to form a dull point. Both of the sides are scraper surfaces. These have been called *pointed side scrapers* in that the two sides may vary in outline from straight to slightly convex. If the two sides are projected to a point, the angle formed may range from 13 degrees to 87 degrees. This diversity indicates that there is wide variance at which the two sides may join to form the blunt point. There is quite a latitude in the size of the flake utilized both as to length and thickness. The juncture of the two scraping surfaces may vary from a blunt tip to one that is somewhat squared (pl. 28, *A*, *e–h*).

Modified side scrapers (1 specimen).—This is a small chalcedony
flake that had one of its edges carefully retouched. The opposing
edge was not only chipped but rubbed to form a backing to the cutting
surface (pl. 32, *A*, *b*). This is an unusual treatment and one not often
encountered at this site.

OVOID BIFACES

Several small bifacially chipped stone implements (?) were separated out of the assemblage of stone artifacts. These are roughly oval
shaped and resemble in a very general way the shape of a human
patella or knee cap. In some instances the chipping has been carefully performed and on others the object has been shaped by means
of percussion chipping. Materials were either chalcedony or quartzite (pl. 29 *B*).

> *Length:* Mean of 34 mm., ranges from 23 mm. to 41 mm.
> *Width:* Mean of 25 mm., ranges from 15 mm. to 35 mm.
> *Thickness:* Mean of 9 mm., ranges from 6 mm. to 13 mm.

They are not numerous and occurred at various levels within the
site. MacNeish (1958, p. 117) reports that "ovoid bifaces occur in
all cultural phases," and, "They occur in all horizons so far found in
eastern Manitoba and were very numerous at the Larter site."

BIFACE CHOPPERS

Choppers are not numerous. Two are roughly circular in outline;
one is ovoid; and two are ovoid but notched as for hafting. All bear
bifacial chipping and are shaped by means of percussion chipping.
Several have some retouching and appeared to be battered, a condition
that may have resulted from use.

> *Length:* Mean of 98 mm., ranges from 72 mm. to 123 mm.
> *Width:* Mean of 77 mm., ranges from 63 mm. to 90 mm.
> *Thickness:* Mean of 29 mm., ranges from 21 mm. to 37 mm.

These occur in all levels from 1.0 foot to 6.0 feet and are by no
means diagnostic of the cultures represented.

KNIVES

Stylized knives are characterized by the presence of a double-
beveled working edge. Other artifacts have been classified as being
knives or having served temporarily as knives. Ribbon flakes with or
without retouched edges have also been classed as knives in accordance
with traditional usage and probable function.

Nearly all of the knives from this site can be separated into five
categories: (1) large four-edged roughly rectangular (pl. 29, *A*, *b*),
(2) four-edged slim and with parallel sides and rounded ends (pl. 29,
A, *a*), made from elongated vein chalcedony, (3) four-edged diamond
shaped specimens (pl. 29, *A*, *d*, *g*, *h*), (4) bifaced blades of several

forms mostly leaf-shaped (pl. 29, A, f), and (5) ribbon flakes (pl. 32, A).

The four-edged roughly rectangular knives are made from elongated fragments of vein chalcedony. Most are fragmentary. One outstanding specimen (pl. 29, A, c) has a curved blade that is not rare but does occur less regularly than the straight-edged forms. The finished form was undoubtedly influenced by the peculiar nature of the material, for this vein chalcedony occurs as flat, thin slabs. A serviceable knife could easily be manufactured by simply selecting a fragment of the proper size and retouching the desired edges to form a cutting edge. Some knives have only one cutting edge along the long side of the artifact. Others not only have this one cutting edge but the opposing edge sharpened, while others have all four edges chipped to a double bevel. Those with only a single cutting edge may have been hafted, or, when large enough, held in the unaided hand and used without a handle.

Also present were several thin-bladed forms in which the chalcedony was chipped so that the original cortex no longer remained (pl. 29, A, e). Cutting edges are fairly sharp. Such artifacts when tapped with a slight blow emit a ring almost metallic in sound. Knives like this are much too thin and delicate to have been held in the unaided hand. They must have been hafted when originally used.

The four-edged diamond-shaped variety is present but in no great number. Not only are the cutting edges worked but so are the faces. A form of quartzite and some chalcedony were used in the manufacture of such knives. In cross section they are lenticular.

Bifaced forms are of several shapes but most of them are leaf-shaped.

Ribbon flake knives are well represented in the collection (pl. 32, A). Many show that they must have been struck from cores primarily as temporary knives. Not a great deal of work was ever expended on them. When they became too dull through use to function properly they were soon abandoned. The dulled edge or edges bear small nicks with very fine chips that were not the result of intentional chipping but were brought about by using the flake as a cutting edge.

Some of the ribbon flake knives were pressure chipped on only one edge; others were chipped on both of the long sides from both faces, resulting in a double beveled effect. Those with only a single chipped edge are hard to distinguish from side scrapers, for both were fashioned by pressure chipping. Ribbon flake knives were made from chalcedony, quartzite, jasper, and chert. Some of the smaller knives are in the range of microblades and probably were hafted so that several were used in a common artifact.

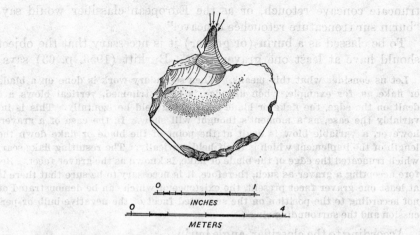

FIGURE 51.—Burin with arrows indicating position and direction of flaking.

BURINLIKE IMPLEMENTS

Burinlike implements have not been recognized as part of the usual cultural assemblage of the Plains. This does not exclude the fact that such implements were manufactured and used by the occupants of the Plains, for, in the past, they were mostly overlooked and very little attention has been given to other than well recognized artifacts of established categories.

More and more attention is being given to spalls and to the so-called broken artifact as well as to the castoff material resulting from the manufacture of stone artifacts. In this mass of material there have been found many heretofore unrecognized artifacts that have enriched the cultural picture of the Plains. True, the source of the various types of stone cannot always be traced since the Plains have been subjected to glacial action; neither can it be told just how far the material used in the manufacture of stone material was carried. Unless there are undisturbed deposits nearby or within reasonable distance of the sites under investigation, we cannot be certain that it is of local origin. Therefore, artifacts must be classified according to the type of stone from which they were made without any reference as to source.

This is true of an unusual chalcedony artifact recovered from Feature 3, a cache pit, at a depth of between 2.0 feet and 2.5 feet from the present surface. This is a combination tool, scraper—burin [5] (pl. 28, B, and fig. 51). One end has been shaped into a well-made end scraper and the opposite end has been altered into what has been classified as resembling a type of burin known as an angle burin with a

[5] Both Drs. H. R. Collins and R. Solecki have examined this artifact and have classified it as a true burin.

truncate concave retouch, or as the European classifier would say, "burin sur troncature retouchée concave."

To be classed as a burin (or graver) it is necessary that the object should have at least one graver facet. Burkitt (1956, p. 63) says:

Let us consider what this means. When secondary work is done on a blade or flake as, for example, when an edge is to be trimmed, vertical blows are dealt on the edge, the flake or blade itself being held horizontally. This is invariably the case, as a moment's thought will show. In the case of a graver, however, a variable blow is dealt at the point of the blade or flake down the length of the implement which is itself held vertically. The resulting flake scar, which truncated the edge of the blade or flake, is known as the graver facet. Before accepting a graver as such, therefore, it is necessary to be sure that there is at least one graver facet present, the existence of which can be demonstrated or not according to the position on the suspected facet of the negative bulb or percussion and the surrounding rings.

According to the classifier, angle burins

. . . have trimming on the other side of the working edge to the graver facet. When the trimmed edge is at right angles or nearly so to the longer axis of the blade or flake, the term "transverse" is given. There its direction is inclined at an angle to this longer axis and the term "oblique" is applied. The trimmed edge itself in both cases may be straight or concave, and in the oblique variety also convex, but not of course in the transverse variety, as no working edge would result. If the student will draw for himself a transverse convex angle burin, he will at once see the truth of this statement. [Ibid, p. 65.]

STONE PERFORATORS OR GRAVERS

Perforators or gravers (pl. 31) were made by pressure chipping a flake on one end into (1) short needlelike tips by beveling the sides so that they met on the dorsal, or top, surface leaving the ventral, or undersurface untouched, i. e., they were retouched from one plane face only, and (2) larger and heavier tips were made by using this same pressure chipping method on larger and slightly heavier flakes. All graver tips are triangular in cross section. The smaller artifacts with graver tips varied in length from 18 mm. to 31 mm., in breadth from 15 mm. to 22 mm., in thickness from 3 mm. to 8 mm., and the tips themselves from 1 mm. to 4 mm. in length. The larger specimens varied in length from 26 mm. to 48 mm., in breadth from 13 mm. to 24 mm., and in thickness from 4 mm. to 15 mm. Both types are within the limits of those reported by Roberts (1935, pl. 13) from the Lindenmeier site in northern Colorado.

Most of the flakes were modified along the sides and some on the dorsal surface but the ventral surfaces were never intentionally altered or modified.

Small perforators or graver tips also occurred on other tools. All were formed by this same type of retouch from one plane face. One of the lamellar flake side scrapers had a well-preserved graver tip worked at one corner of the blade (pl. 32, *A*, *n*). Several end scrapers show working corners, and all were definite graver tips. Others had this same feature, but on a slightly reduced measure. Whether the size was intentional or the result of prolonged use could not be determined. It appeared to be intentional, but we could not be sure of this. If it was intentional, then it could possibly represent a graver variant. These tips were all worked at the ends of the broadest beveled face of the scraper and their shaping was an integral part of the shaping of the scraper edge and was not a later modification or an unintentional feature. Most of these show, under magnification, that they had received considerable usage and were worn somewhat at the tip.

LAMELLAR FLAKE TOOLS

A class of tools utilizing thin lamellar flakes of chalcedony or chert was found at the Hosterman site. These were either small knives or side scrapers (pl. 32, *A*). Knives are represented by *b*, *c*, *d*, *e*, *k*, *l*, *n*, *o*, and *q*. Specimen *b* is unique in that it was pressure-chipped along three edges from both sides with the exception of the wider bottom or basal edge. Later the S-shaped edge was abraded so as to partially obliterate the scarified edge, enabling the artifact to be either hafted into some sort of slotlike aperture in a bone or wooden handle or to facilitate its use without the use of a handle.

Specimen *c* received a double beveled edge along three of its edges. Chipping was very carefully controlled and is very uniform in size.

Specimen *n* is a combination tool, a knife, scraper, and graver. All edges have been worked. At one corner is a small graver tip which under magnification displays much finer chipping, attesting to the fact that it was functional.

The best of the lamellar flake tools is represented by specimen *d*. This was struck from a core of quartzite and is roughly rectangular in outline. All edges have been carefully chipped creating a bevel-edged implement. Earlier flake scars are shown on the dorsal surface of the implement.

Specimen *b* (pl. 32, *B*) is the larger of these tool types and is probably a part of a much larger tool. The sides are roughly parallel and the long sides have been given a bevel sloping upward to the top or dorsal surface. The beveled edges are more prominent on this artifact than on others in the collection.

With the exception of specimen *a* they fall within a range whose lengths vary from 28 mm. to 49 mm., breadths from 13 mm. to 22 mm., and thicknesses from 2 mm. to 6 mm. Specimen *a* measures 56 mm. in length, 22 mm. in breadth, and 4 mm. in thickness.

Gravers, as a rule, consist of chance flakes modified in that the needlelike tips were formed on one side or an end. Any flake was suitable provided it appealed to the worker. These could be chosen from the flaker's discard pile or at random from the surface of the site. The small tips did not occur just by chance but were purposefully made so that the under side is always flat and the two upper sides are beveled so as to bring the tip to a very fine point. Gravers can be distinguished from drills in that gravers are retouched on only two sides and drills have all sides retouched. On top of this a graver can have one or more such tips.

GROUND AND PECKED STONE TOOLS

Tools in this category were formed by grinding their surfaces or by pecking. The pecked stone tools include pebble hammerstones, full-grooved mauls, anvil stones, and paint grinders. Ground stone tools include slabs of stone with grooves worn into them, anvil stones, and some rubbing stones, besides a grooved ax.

Anvil stones.—These are irregular nodules of granite, quartzite, or other tough crystalline rock. Many of them have been subjected to much abrasion. They were found scattered throughout the site.

It has been suggested that anvil stones were used to pulverize dried meat, seeds, and berries by pounding rather than grinding and in so doing the anvil stone was "probably set in a sort of rawhide 'pannier' and the food substance placed on it to be crushed with a stone-headed pounder. This was the method followed by the Dakota, who in some instances at least used anvils almost identical to those of the Pawnee" (Wedel, 1936, p. 75). Since this site is neither Dakota nor Pawnee, it has been attributed to a pre-Arikara—Arikara group in whose cultural assemblage there is comparable agreement.

Rubbing stones.—These are usually flat, round stones, and range in size from small pebbles to those easily handled in the fist. They were used as a rule without any retouching and were probably used in rubbing down hides as several have acquired a rather high polish and are very soft and smooth to the touch. Several show very shallow parallel scratches resulting from use.

Pecking stones.—These are small pebbles of granite, quartzite, diorite, or some such hard stone. Usually, these are unaltered pebbles; some are round, others are natural elongated forms. Both forms show much battering or abrading. Similarly, others that are small, flat, and circular are worn about the edges.

Paint stones.—These paint stones are usually highly granular stones that were chosen because of this trait. Several show that they had been used to reduce lumps of hematite into powder by grinding. Specks of hematite have worked themselves well into the surface of these stones and cannot easily be rubbed off. Paint stones are not plentiful and are widely scattered in the site.

Grooved mauls.—These mauls are represented by two specimens. They are made of granite boulders, roughly shaped, smoothed, and grooved about the center for hafting. The smaller and squattier specimen is oval in cross section while the larger is somewhat tringuloid in cross section. In actual weight there is a very little difference. The smaller specimen weighs exactly 4 pounds 6 ounces and the larger one weighs 4 pounds 12 ounces. Neither is badly battered. Both show that they had received considerable usage, probably in the crushing of dried meat, nuts, or berries. Exterior surfaces are finely dimpled (pl. 30, *B*).

Grooved stone ax (pl. 30, *B*).—Only one stone ax was recovered and this is not a complete specimen, for the butt end is missing. Apparently this is an unusual type in that it has a groove completely encircling the implement separating the blade from the butt. During the life of the implement the butt section had been completely broken away and another groove was being pecked ahead of the older groove which was never finished, for the blade became broken and the tool discarded. The tool was well fashioned and finished. The blade is still fairly sharp. This particular ax was made of a greenish-colored diorite, a stone which does not occur locally. It must have been traded into this region from the general Southwest for it resembles those occurring in that region. In its present form it weighs 2 pounds 4 ounces. Both fragments were found in Feature 9, a cache pit, at a depth of between 7.0 and 7.5 feet.

Pumice abraders.—Pieces of waterworn pumice or naturally burned lignite of various shapes and sizes, some less than an inch across up to pieces as large as grapefruit or larger, were utilized as abraders. Several have faceted sides, others have narrow shallow grooves, and still others have wide and deep grooves. The shallower grooves were probably made from sharpening pointed bone and wooden implements while the wider and deeper grooves were probably used and made as arrowshaft straighteners and smoothers.

Sandstone abraders.—Bits of sandstone, of various degrees of coarseness, show one or more surface grooves resulting from the rubbing of honed implements across them. Some are irregular bits of sandstone and others appear to have been shaped into rough rectangular blocks and used as hones or specialized whetstones for sharpening bone awls or smoothing arrowshafts.

Arrowshaft straighteners.—Implements for this purpose were made of sandstone and display one or more grooves running the length of the implement. Usually they are rectangular in shape, but some are triangular in cross section. Whether these constitute distinct types or just individual likes as to shape must be taken into consideration. Some may have liked the rectangular form, others preferred the triangular, while still others were not too discriminating and used whatever shape of sandstone came to hand. Probably too much stress has been brought to bear upon implement shape by both the professional archeologist and the amateur. They both fail to take into consideration that they are not only dealing with inanimate objects but with human personalities as well and it is the latter that are the real determining factor. Personal likes and dislikes play a distinct role in the implement form and use according to the type of material to be utilized.

Handstones.—Several roundish stones were recovered not only from cache pits but from the general site. These have been classified as handstones because they display a certain amount of wear. Five of these are outstanding in that they were pecked and then smoothed. They are roughly circular in shape and resemble, to a certain extent, stone balls. None of the edges have been battered even though they show considerable wear, which would appear to indicate that such pieces were never used as hammerstones but were probably used for pounding a resilient substance such as softening a dried up animal hide, dried beef during the manufacture of pemmican, or even soft berries. One specimen, in particular (field specimen No. 2014), appears to have had a fatty substance driven into the cortex of the stone giving it a distinct color and feel. Maximum lengths of these handstones range from 55 mm. to 81 mm. Minimum lengths range from 51 mm. to 75 mm. Maximum thickness varies from 34 mm. to 57 mm.

Another form of handstone is represented by a single specimen. It is disk shaped and almost circular in outline with opposing faces. One of its faces is almost flat and the other is a flattish dome with a shallow central pit sunk into it. The pitted face shows no evidence of having ever been used as a grinding tool. The pit probably served as a finger hold. Maximum and minimum lengths are 52 mm. and 50 mm. Maximum thickness is 34 mm.

Utilized pebbles.—Small river hardheads were among the stones present within the site. Most of them are oval in outline and somewhat flattish. In many cases the ends of the long axis had been pecked or show that they were utilized as either light hammerstones or used to peck away irregularities on the faces of other stones to be utilized as tools.

Then too, there are those that have one of their flat faces rubbed very smooth and somewhat polished. Such tools were probably used in the manufacture of pottery since they could have easily functioned as an anvil opposite the paddle used in shaping clay into vessels.

Others are egg shaped with a tendency towards flatness. Both of the flat faces bear a number of parallel scars at right angles to the main axis and cover an area roughly 27 mm. in diameter. These surfaces

were smoothed prior to scarification. Their purpose and function are
not known.

Practically all of the rock, of any size, found within the site was put
to some use at one time. Not all are recognizable tools. Some of the
larger fractured pieces may have served as a form of chopper; others
are hammerstones, etc.

HEMATITE AND OTHER PAINT SUBSTANCES

During the partial exploration of the Hosterman site, several
worked nodules of hematite were found with faceted faces. These
must have been rubbed to reduce them to a powdered form to be used
as a paint. Then, too, a couple of lumps of a whitish material were
found along with a lump of a creamy whitish material and a lump of
powdered red ocher. These substances were found mostly in midden
pits, Features 9 and 22, as well as in small cache pits within the
circular house pattern of Feature 22.

Since no paint brushes were found during this period it raises
some doubt as to how this paint was applied. Various sherds had
paint stains on their interior surfaces. That this red paint was put
into these sherds as a container or as a crude sort of palette seems
very likely but it cannot be proved that such was ever the case.
Several of the bone implements bore reddish stains as though they
had come in contact, at one time or another, with red paint.

Catlinite.—Four fragments of catlinite pipes were recovered from
Features 10, 16, and 22. The largest of these four pieces is about half
of a bulbous pipe bowl. The bowl rim has been brought to a sharp
edge rounding somewhat as the wall proceeded downward. The basal
section of this fragment is covered with numerous vertical parallel
thin scratches and the major part of the exterior has been smoothed
and polished. The smaller fragment of a pipe bowl appears to be
tubular in form. It, too, is covered on the exterior with a number of
scratches that form a rough hatchure. One of the broken edges had
been reworked, and four shallow grooves partially cross the thickness
of the wall. The lip of this particular pipe is flat and bevels slightly
outward. The other smaller fragments are terminal sections of pipe
stems. Some work was started to reshape the larger portion but this
was never completed and the section was discarded.

A large section of rough catlinite was recovered that has one cut
surface. Shallow scratches cover the surface of this piece. A number
of its edges have been rubbed but still the piece does not conform to
any known object. It is just one of those partially worked pieces
which appear to clutter up the site without indicating their purpose.

A small well-rubbed piece of catlinite, 21 mm. in length, 9 mm. in
width, and 8 mm. in thickness, was found at a depth of between 2.5

feet and 3.0 feet in the village midden. Whether catlinite was ever reduced to a powder and this product used as a body or facial paint or dust is not known to the writer but this piece resembles similar pieces of rubbed stone which were put to this use.

One other small flat nondescript piece of catlinite completes the collection.

Belemnite.—Sections of belemnite, a conical fossil shell of an extinct cephalopod, were recovered from two of the cache pits, Features 9 and 13, and from various isolated midden areas within the site. The blunt spicule ends of two specimens were encircled as though some sort of attachment was added so that they could be suspended. Whether these were worn on the person or attached to some sort of garment could not be determined. Three other sections were unworked.

BONE ARTIFACTS

Several types of bone tools were found in considerable quantity at the Hosterman site. They were particularly abundant in cache pits, midden areas, and to some extent in house fills. Preservation was exceptionally good even though many were broken by the aborigines themselves during the period of occupation.

Normally, bones from bison, deer, and pronghorn were converted into major types of tools but the bones from other types of animals were converted into other types of tools whenever the need arose.

Cut animal bones.—Several of the articulative ends of deer, pronghorn, turkey, and other bird bones were found that were severed from their shafts. A V-shaped cut was made almost into the medullary canal, and with slight effort this section was separated from the shaft. These ends are the waste from the manufacture of tubes and beads (pl. 33, *A*).

The most outstanding bone tools are those manufactured from the scapulae of bison. In this group are scapula hoes, digging tools, knives, scrapers, hide scrapers, thong stretchers, and even sickles.

Scapula hoes.—This ubiquitous Plains implement was quite prevalent at the Hosterman site. Scapulae of bison were not greatly modified in the process of manufacturing these implements (pl. 33, *B*). The articulative ends remained unaltered, and there was no evidence that any hafting was ever attempted. The making of a hoe necessitated only the removal of the spine and the posterior border (postscapular process and acromian), from the exterior surface to about the level of the fossae, thus creating a more or less flat implement. Before the scapula could be put into use as a hoe the working edge (suprascapular border) must be trimmed and sharpened. On some the areas from which the postscapular process and acromian had been removed were left relatively rough. On others this was smoothed down. Subsequent usage would eradicate any evidence of working on the suprascapular border, for it would quickly take on new character and the area would be given a high polish by soil abrasion, the blade would become beveled and in a number of instances deeply scored. From the evidence at hand, one might say that scapula hoes continued to be used until they became exhausted and quite short; they were then discarded as no longer serviceable.

The mortality rate was rather high among scapula hoes. When this occurred the thinner interior sections, as well as other sections of unworked scapulae, were converted into many other types of tools. Knives, hide scrapers, and possibly thong stretchers are among some that can be listed.

Scapula spines.—The spines were removed from the shoulder blade when the blade was converted into hoes, and the spines themselves converted into digging tools. The sharp picklike distal end readily lent itself to this purpose. Wear was never excessive on any of the Hosterman specimens and apparently they were only expedient tools and were quickly discarded (pl. 34, *B, b*).

Metcalf (1956, p. 306) considers implements such as these to be a "type of awl that has not been previously recorded from the Plains." The Dodd site gave up a number of tools made from these scapula spines. Those being reported from the Hosterman site were recovered from the diggings by pot hunters in a midden area prior to our work there.

Scapula knives.—Knives of various shapes and sizes were made from thin sections of bison scapula (pl. 35, *A*). Some are roughly oval in outline with one or more edges sharpened; others are rectanguloid shaped; still others are roughly diamond shaped. Practically all have acquired a very high polish even though there is considerable variation in the overall lengths. The shortest specimen measured 12.5 cm. in length; the longest measured 19.6 cm. in length. Most knives were made from the flat section between the acromian and postscapular process; others were derived from the postscapular section of the bones having one exposed edge of cancellous material opposite the working edge. Constricted sections may have served as handles. Their period of usefulness was evidently short, for many fragmentary knives were recovered from the site.

Scapula cleavers.—Several knifelike cleavers are in the collection (pl. 36, *A*). These were fashioned from bison scapulae by cutting lengthwise through the postscapular fossa so that a long comparatively thin blade was created. The back edge of the cleaver is considerably thicker and a portion of the acromian or postscapular process was left intentionally for the purpose of strengthening the implement. Like the knives, the tapered end served as a handle.

Among the fragmentary forms were those that were spatulate in outline and comparatively thin. These were made from the post-scapular fossae sections with the sides ground to a thin beveled cutting edge and the ends neatly rounded.

Scapula scrapers.—These were made from fragments of the post-scapula fossae sections. Most were worked from fragments into rectanguloid shapes. Those that were made from sections of the post-scapular process and acromian were much thicker and required much more work to complete. Others were cut so that only a fractional part of the scapula spine formed one edge (pl. 35, *B*).

Scapula hide scrapers.—Like other scapula scrapers, these were cut from sections of bison scapulae. Most of them are either from the posterior border and display scars where the ridge was left intact or partially obliterated or were cut so that only a fractional part of the scapula spine formed one edge. Basically, these tools are rectanguloid in shape with a constricted section forming a ready handle. The working portion of the blade has parallel sides and the cutting surface was given a pronounced bevel over the entire edge. They roughly resemble the blade in a modern carpenter's woodworking plane in shape (pl. 35, *B*). On the backs there appear series of shallow parallel scratches which have been acquired during the life of the implement. The specimen shown in plate 35, *B*, is 13.0 cm. in length, 6.4 cm. in width, and is the best of the type found at the Hosterman site.

Thong stretchers.—A single thong stretcher was found. This was made from a small thin section of a bison scapula (pl. 34, *B*, *b*), whose working edge was given a pronounced U-shaped notch. The edges and sides of the notch acquired a very high polish and the sides were well smoothed. The specimen shown here is 7.5 cm. in overall length and 4.1 cm. in greatest width. The notch itself measures 3.2 cm. across the opening, 0.7 cm. near the base, and is 1.2 cm. in depth.

Scapula sickle.—What appears to be a fragmentary scapula sickle was recovered from Feature 25, a midden pit. Metcalf (1956, fig. 103, *b*), features a complete sickle derived from the floor of a rectangular house at site 39LM3, Lyman County, S. Dak. This fragment appears to be a section of the handle with its adjoining notch where the blade joins the handle. From the base of the handle up through the notch this object displays considerable wear, accompanied by a high polish. It is 25.0 cm. long. Another formative sickle is illustrated in plate 34, *B*, *a*.

Flakers.—Four flakers were made from bison rib bones. The heads of the tools were rounded and the tips were brought to an abrupt dull point. These are distinctly triangular in cross section and one side appears to have been smoothed, for it has a smoother feel than does the opposite side. The cancellous tissue is still in evidence. Lengths of these four flakers are 72 mm., 64 mm., 50 mm., and 32 mm.

Needlelike tool.—A very thin sliver of bone was converted into what appears to have been a needle. It is incomplete in that the butt, or eye, portion is missing. This object is 75.5 mm. in length and at the broken base it measures less than 2 mm. in diameter. Needles of this sort have not been described from sites in the Plains of South Dakota. Whether this is an intrusive tool from North Dakota or out of Minnesota cannot be determined.

Shaft wrenches.—Shaft wrenches of various lengths were made from sections of bison rib bones. Most of them have but a single hole, and these tend to be oval in shape with the sides beveled from use. Apparently the wrench was held at a slight angle to the shaft in the straightening process. In one the hole is beveled in three directions. This is not the rule but an exception. Some of the rib bones are highly polished. Very few were complete, for most of them had been broken and apparently discarded by their owners. This fracture tendency is at right angles across the hole dividing it in half.

An incomplete wrench was attempted. On one flat surface of a rib fragment there appears a conical pit 3 mm. in depth and 8 mm. across the top that had penetrated the cortical bone and started into the cancellous portion of the core. Drilling was attempted only on one side. There was no evidence that any attempt was made to drill from the opposite side to meet this section of the perforation.

Knife handles.—Knife handles were made from segments of bison ribs. These were grooved along one edge sufficiently deep to allow for the insertion of a stone knife blade. A complete knife was recovered from a shallow cache pit beneath the floor of Feature 22, a circular house (pl. 36, *B*). Other handles and blades were found unjoined.

Hide grainers.—Sections of bison humeri and femurs were sectioned so that a wide expanse of cancellous tissue was exposed. Four specimens were recovered from the Hosterman site. These were used during the process of dressing down hides into usable pelts.

Notched ribs.—Two fragmentary ribs have opposing notches at the ends at right angles to the long axis. These were meant to receive either string or gut attachments. Not having heard that any of the Plains Indians ever made use of a bullroarer, it is suggested that these two objects could easily have functioned along this line. This could have been some boy's toy.

Cut ribs.—Numerous sections of ribs were recovered that were undoubtedly either unfinished and broken artifacts or rejects. Some had acquired a high polish.

Punches.—In Lehmer's definition (1954, p. 66) he describes his Group 1 type as: "Irregular plates split from bison or elk ribs, cancellous tissues of split surface sometimes ground down, sometimes unmodified; edges unmodified; butts rounded; tips worked down to a blunt point."

Two similar specimens were found at the Hosterman site. Both of them follow a common configuration, but one has its edges smoothed and polished and the other has untreated edges; one has a tip that was brought to a modified point, and the other has a spatulate point. The complete specimen, except the extreme tip, measures 168 mm. in length, and 25 mm. in width across the base, and has an average thickness of 6 mm.

Scapula hoes with deep U-shaped notch.—This notch which was worn or cut into the bit end may have functioned, under certain conditions, as a type of thong stretcher. The inner edge of the longer spur has been beveled while the edge bordering the shorter spur is not quite as sharp (pl. 33, *B, a*).

Worked pronghorn metapodial bones.—One complete and one fragmentary pronghorn metapodial bone showed signs of having been used. The complete specimen was from a young individual, as shown by the incomplete joining of the epiphyses (ankylosis) to the shaft of the bone. The distal end was drilled. The shaft is lightly scarified by a series of parallel scratches running at a diagonal to the main axis of the shaft. Just above the basal articulative surface, on the shaft, is another series of shallow cuts. These cuts are at right angles to the axis of the shaft. The purpose and use of these scratches are unknown.

Fishhooks.—Four fragmentary and one unfinished bone fishhook were recovered during the process of uncovering remains at the Hosterman site. All were made of a very composite bone. With the exception of the unfinished hook, the others were round in cross section. All are of the unbarbed type and display excellent workmanship. The unbarbed arms are pointed and scored with a series of shallow parallel incisions at right angles to the main axis of the arm. The shank arms also are scored near the ends, probably to prevent whatever tie was used from slipping off.

The unfinished hook is from a section of bison long bone, demonstrating the method by which this sort of implement was made.

Worked animal scapula.—A small section of what appears to be the scapula of *Canis* sp. has two small holes just 9 mm. below the posterior border that were punched through the thin section of the blade. The two holes are 10 mm. apart and are not clean cut. None of the edges of this bone object were smoothed or worked. There is some question as to whether this particular bone object was perforated for suspension as an ornament or for some other purpose (pl. 37, *B*).

Pentagonal-shaped bone tool.—A large pentagonal-shaped bone

tool (pl. 36, *A*), prepared from a bison's scapula, shows considerable
wear in that the surfaces as well as the bordering edges were polished.
It measures 9.8 cm. across the base; the lateral sides are 16.4 cm. long,
and the tapering sides average around 11.1 cm. in length. Both
the tapering sides as well as the lateral edges show that they have
received considerable wear. On both faces, bordering the sharp
working edge, are series of thin shallow scratches running almost the
entire length of the implement. Superimposed over these, on one
face, is a roughly ovoid area that is highly polished, a gloss resulting
from long-continued use. This ovoid area measures roughly 6.5 cm.
in length and 4.0 cm. in width, and is located 3.3 cm. from the base
of the implement; it was probably the position of the thumb while
the tool was in use. It is definite that this was never used to dig
into the soil, for the edges of this thin object could not have with-
stood such use. Its actual use cannot be determined. Similar objects have not been reported from this section of South Dakota.

Bone tubes.—Twenty-eight bone tubes of various lengths were
recovered from the Hosterman site. Out of this number only one was
fragmentary. Fourteen were made from cylindrical sections of bird
bones. Most of them had their cut edges polished and smoothed,
but few of them were completely polished. They ranged in length
from 28 mm. to 119 mm. (pl. 33, *A*). The other 14 were from sections
of mammal bones, and practically all of them had their cut surfaces
smoothed and had developed a good polish. None of the bone tubes
were decorated in any way. The lengths ranged from 56 mm. to
128 mm.

On the basis of lengths, the bone tubes were separated into three
groups:

Group 1, 5 specimens:
   Lengths: Range from 28 mm. to 49 mm., mean of 38 mm.
Group 2, 15 specimens:
   Lengths: Range from 53 mm. to 94 mm., mean of 73 mm.
Group 3, 7 specimens:
   Lengths: Range from 102 mm. to 128 mm., mean of 115 mm.

Bone awls.—Various types of bone awls are present at the Hosterman site (pl. 37, *A*). One of the prevalent types comprises those made
from *split deer* or *pronghorn metapodial* bones with split distal ends
forming the butt. The spit surfaces on most of the specimens were
ground and smoothed and the cancellous material removed, leaving
a U-shaped shaft to the tool. Both the shaft portion and the articulative surface had acquired a high polish through heavy use. Lengths
varied from 58 mm. to 100 mm. This group easily falls within the
limits of similar awls reported from the Dodd site, and Swan Creek
site, and is ubiquitous in the Plains. Nineteen specimens are represented.

Rough splinter awls.—Seven specimens. Awls of this group are comparatively few in number. They were made from rough, irregular splinter sections of bison ribs and long bones as well as some of the long bird bones. They are unworked with the exception of the tip, which is ground to a smooth point. Lengths varied from 31 mm. to 118 mm.

A combination tool, made from a splinter of a long bone of bison, consists of an awl and a spokeshave. This tool, 19.6 cm. in length, was brought to a sharp point at one end; the other was broken off squarely. Forty-six mm. from the base there is a wide notch that functioned as a spokeshave. On either side of the notch the tool was well smoothed. Under magnification there is a series of parallel grooves within the notch at right angles to the axis of the bone, indicating that this was a working surface.

Other splinter awls were made from sections of shaft of long bones, mostly deer or antelope. These were well worked over most of the surface. In cross section some are round, others are on the flat side, and still others are shallow U-shaped. One of the specimens has a V-shaped cut on three of its sides near the base as though its owner intended to reduce the overall size of the implement and rid it of its irregular rough butt, but the task was never completed. Lengths range from 55 mm. to 131 mm.

Specimens from another group were made from the edges of bison ribs cut so that a portion of the cancellous tissue was still included. The cut sides were carefully smoothed and the butt ends were finished off either by working into a rounded, squared finish or bringing them to an abrupt, dull point. In some, the tips were brought to a gradual point; in others the tips tend to be more abrupt. In cross section the awls of this group tend to be triangular. Lengths range from 57 mm. to 144 mm., the majority being around 90 mm. in length.

In the next group, represented by seven specimens, the awls were made from edges of bison ribs with portions of the cancellous tissue included. As in the group immediately preceding, the awls received about the same treatment to convert the raw material into workable tools. Instead of being triangular in cross section, these tend to be more circular with tips brought to a more abrupt point.

Cancellous bone balls.—Three small ovoid-shaped cancellous bone balls were recovered. Two of them were found in Feature 9, a cache pit. One was found at a depth of between 6.5 feet and 7.0 feet; the second came from a depth of between 7.0 feet and 7.5 feet. The third ball came from one of the small isolated midden areas at a depth of between 2.0 feet and 3.0 feet from the present surface. Whether these were the remnant portions of bone abraders, or were actual abraders intended for some much finer work, or were a form of toy could not be determined from the evidence at hand.

Bone picks.—A form of pick was made from the shaft of a bison radius by splitting it lengthwise, leaving a part of the proximal articulative end intact and sharpening the other end. The one specimen that was recovered is badly battered. At the present time it measures 17.1 cm. in length, which is far from its original length. One edge has been smoothed to within 8 cm. of the articulative end. This smoothing was probably not intentional but acquired through use.

Split pronghorn metapodial bones.—Pronghorn metapodial bones were split lengthwise and the halves were used as beamers. The bone was sawed lengthwise in order to split it into two equal parts. The distal end displays additional saw marks that were not carried to completion. Awl blanks were similarly constructed from the splitting of metapodial bones.

Perforated rib sections.—Sections of small ribs were perforated at both ends. These were probably used as ornaments of dress since they were attached to objects, or they may have been worn as pendants. In the collection there is one complete specimen and fragments of five others (pl. 37, *B*).

Punches.—Punches were made from the cutoff or broken ends of deer or elk antler. The tip ends of these show definite signs of having been sharpened. Several acquired a fairly high polish.

Antler sections.—Sections of antlers with their prong tips missing definitely show the tips were severed from the main portion. To do this the prongs were sawed or cut almost through and then broken away from the stem. In one instance the prong was sharpened before it was severed from the stem for it must have been easier to do it this way than to do it afterward (pl. 36, *B*).

Split antler section.—A small section of deer's antler was cut and broken off and the ends left unworked. Later it was split down the center and most of the cancellous tissue removed. The long edges were then smoothed and evened up, leaving a sharp outer edge. From the looks of this artifact it would appear that it was intended to be used as some sort of scraper-smoother.

Mineralized bone.—A small fragment of mineralized bone was found in Feature 22, a cache pit. It apparently was never used by the occupants of the Hosterman site. It was probably either picked up from the surface outside of the village and brought in as a sort of curiosity, and lost or discarded afterward; or, it could have appeared naturally on the surface of the site and later gathered up along with the rest of the trash and dumped into the midden pit.

Cut antler fragments.—Two large basal segments of deer antlers were made into percussion instruments or hammers by having one end slightly rounded and the other roughened. One was 17.0 cm. long with a diameter of 3.7 cm., the other was 19.4 cm. long with a diameter of 4.6 cm.

FETISH OR TROPHY SKULL

The skull of one of the Plains kit foxes (*Vulpes velox*) was found in the midden of Feature 2 at a depth of 1.8 feet. This fragmentary skull (pl. 38) is peculiar in that there are, at the present time, four small round perforations with beveled edges occurring in the occiputal region penetrating the brain cavity. The diameter of these openings is 4 mm. on the outside, tapering somewhat until they entered the interior of the brain case. They were spaced so that they covered this area rather well. The central perforation just touches to the right of the sagital suture, two others are equidistant on either side of this suture about 1.25 cm. distant, and the fourth opening is just above the right auditory meatus. Whether there ever was a comparable opening above the left auditory meatus is not known, since that portion of the skull is missing, but it would seem plausible that such was the case.

As we do not know exactly why this particular skull was treated in this manner, we have assumed that there must have been some religious ritual significance attached to it. We do know that the Mandans and other Plains Indian groups utilized the skulls of bisons and humans during certain ceremonies. Then, too, each man had his own medicine bundle usually wrapped in some animal pelt. Whether the skull of this particular fox was especially valued would appear likely since so much work was performed on it.

SCORED BIRD STERNUM

A fragmentary sternum of *Aquila chrysoelus canadensis* (golden eagle) was found in Feature 3, a cache pit, at a depth of 3.0 feet from the present surface (pl. 37, *B*). Across the right keel and along the posterior margins are numerous sharp and shallow incisions. There is no definite pattern these scars take. It would appear that they were the result of cutting away the heavy fleshy parts during the term of a meal. Whether eagles were obtained just for their tail feathers and the flesh eaten afterward is not known; but it would seem very probable that the fleshy parts of the bird were consumed.

WORKED TEETH

The front half of the post-lingual surface of a split beaver's incisor, recovered from the floor of the circular house, Feature 22, shows cutting marks on the concave surface, the beveled cutting surface, and a shallow cut at the base of the tooth. Similarly prepared beaver incisor teeth were reported from the Dodd site in South Dakota, from

various sites in Minnesota, Ohio, and North Dakota, and they appear
to be common throughout the Northeastern United States as well as
in some of the Southeastern sites. This is a specific trait of the Point
Peninsula Focus (Ritchie, 1944, p. 117), which appears to relate somewhat to the cultural horizon represented at the Hosterman site.

A heavily eroded wapiti's tooth (*Cervus canadensis*) was found
in Feature 34. It had been perforated for suspension and was probably used as a pendant worn around the neck of some individual.
It is the only specimen of this sort found at the site.

Human remains are represented by 5 incisors and 1 canine tooth.
The five incisors were found in a small pit along with other debris,
but no human bones were present. The single canine tooth was found
in a nearby midden pit. All of the six teeth were greatly worn,
having been reduced to about the gum line. All were flat across
the top. Adhering to the sides of the roots of the five incisors was
an osseous growth, known as cementosis. The amount of this growth
or deposit was not constant; some teeth have more of it than others.
This is an apparent indication of age, for all five teeth appear to
have belonged to a single individual.

SHELL

Shells were not numerous at the Hosterman site. Several large
mussel shells were found thinly scattered throughout the midden,
some appeared in midden-cache pits, and a few came from house areas.
Dr. J. E. P. Morrison, Department of Zoology, U.S. National Museum, identified four species of shells from this site. They are: *Lasmigona complanata* (Barnes); *Anodonta grandis plana* (Lea); *Olivella biplicata* (Sowerby) that was introduced from California; and
Succinea grosvenori (Lea). Usually these shells are unworked. Sections of *Lasmigona complanata* were cut into triangular, rectangular,
and other simple geometric forms, though none were perforated.
Other *Lasmigona complanata* were converted into spoons or scrapers
whereas portions of others were shaped to disk pendants that were
perforated for suspension. A small section of a serrated shell fragment was found within the midden area at a depth of 2.5 feet to
3.0 feet. The margins on either side of the serrations have been
rubbed smooth, while the basal section holds the fractured break.
Apparently this was some form of pendant.

TABLE 6.—*Shell identified*

Species	Number	Artifact	Source
Anodonta grandis plana (Lea)	5	Unworked	Local.
Lasmigona complanata (Barnes)	20	do	Do.
Do	14	Worked	Do.
Olivella biplicata (Sowerby)	1	Bead	California.
Succinea grosvenori (Lea)	2	Unworked	Local.

A shell disk, 34 mm. in diameter, is incomplete. Near the outer margin is a small perforation for suspension. Presumably the pendant was made from a section of *Lasmigona* sp., for this type of shell was more numerous than any other and the texture fits this sort of shell.

COPPER

A single small copper bead, 16 mm. in length and 3 mm. in diameter, was found near the mouth of Feature 16. It is the only metal found during the period of excavation. The bead was made by rolling a small sheet of copper around a twig or some similar object. At the present time its surface is completely covered with a verdigris. From its location in the site, it is presumed that it was intrusive there either after the site was abandoned or at the terminal phase of occupancy.

SUMMARY AND CONCLUSIONS

The existence of rectangular house pits suggests that a group of the Upper Republican culture had established at least one permanent residence here at the Hosterman site. True to their nature they spaced and scattered their houses widely apart and without pattern.

Their economy consisted of limited agriculture with greater stress being placed on hunting and seasonal gathering. The presence of limited amounts of charred corn and a few beans and squash seeds attests that they had enriched food habits. Pits of wild plums and choke-cherries show that these fruits were then in use. There is evidence that they were supplemented, in season, with the wild berries of the nearby area as well as with seeds from the many wild grasses growing there. Communities were located on bluffs or terraces and, in this case, the main stem of the Missouri River.

During this period, house pits were rectangular in form and were sunk to various depths, depending upon the inclination of the builders. This variation in depth probably accounts for the unevenness of the aeolian deposits that accumulated over the remains after the site was finally abandoned. Inside the pit was constructed a house with individual posts fairly closely spaced, surrounding four centrally located roof supports that in turn surrounded a centrally placed firepit. The walls served as studding to support the wall plates. Rafters were closely spaced, running from the wall to the center of the structure. Over this basic framework were piled layers of brush, grass, and finally a heavy dirt cover. The finished house resembled a low dome-shaped earthen mound which was entered by means of a long, narrow, covered passageway. Smoke escaped from a centrally placed opening in the roof.

Hunting played a paramount role in their economy. With limited farming and plenty of meat these people were assured of an abundance of food. There must have been surpluses that required storage. To meet this problem they dug storage or cache pits that were bell-shaped, narrow at the top and widest at the base. Most of these pits were placed outside of the houses, but smaller examples were found beneath the floors of some houses. The large pits were rather deep and were capable of holding vast quantities of supplies.

From the bison, and to some extent, the lesser animals, they obtained the bone material out of which they fashioned awls, flakers, bodkins, fishhooks, hoes, knives, scrapers, arrow-shaft wrenches, sickles, cleavers, and many other forms. The essential forms of many of the artifacts had carried over from an earlier Archaic horizon.

Flint tools were still common. Snub-nosed scrapers were very much in evidence, and though projectile points varied little in form and size they were never plentiful. They made use of the local stones, which furnished sandstone shaft polishers, hones, and smoothers of pumice. Hammerstones were many and were usually natural round boulders that were small enough to fit comfortably into the hand. Some were fashioned deliberately by pecking them into the desired shape; others were used as they were found. Some were employed until they shattered through use. The scattered fragments were found in midden piles and in midden pits.

Grooved axes were present, but they were few in number. They were not replaced at the Hosterman site by the broad, flat chisel or gougelike implement called a celt.

After these people abandoned the site, another group, presumably from farther north, moved in and built circular houses around four centrally placed poles surrounding a firepit. The floors were sunk to various depths. Attached were covered entranceways. Smoke escaped from centrally placed openings in the roofs.

Subsistence apparently was equally divided between limited agriculture, hunting, and gathering, with fishing playing only a minor role. Charred corn, beans, and squash seeds demonstrate their limited capabilities. Seeds of wild fruits, charred and uncharred, indicate that gathering during the proper season was still of prime importance economically, while the greatest stress was placed on the plentiful supply of wild animals and the hunt.

Byproducts of the hunt consisted of the hides, bones, and sinew out of which were fashioned not only the tools used to sew the tanned or prepared hides into articles of clothing but those for other major purposes as well. The scapulae of the plentiful bison were fashioned into hoes which were used in the cultivation of crops in the rich bottom land below their village and for grubbing for roots and tubers that grew wild in the immediate vicinity. Other bones were made into awls, punches, knives, hide scrapers, and grainers.

For some reason projectile points of stone were not plentiful. Those that were used were small, triangular forms. Earlier a side-notched variety was introduced. They all ranged from small to medium in size.

The crude grooved stone mauls, similar in form to those found at the Payne and Swan Creek sites, apparently were used in the preparation of pemmican, for none were badly battered.

Both hafted and unhafted flint knives were adequate for the skinning of animals or for cutting purposes.

The manufacture of pottery was among the chief industries at the Hosterman site, as is demonstrated by the quantity of sherds recovered from the limited exploration. Due to the fragile nature of the pottery, its attrition rate must have been great. Pottery was first modeled and finished by the paddle-anvil method. The paddle was usually carved with simple shallow grooves that imprinted a simple decoration of ridges and sunken lands of the simple stamped variety. It was tempered with a fine to medium-sized grit of decomposed granite and fired to a tan, gray, or black color, depending upon the use of a covering of bison fat on the exterior. The use of fat was demonstrated by the heavy encrustation of soot on the exteriors of vessels. Their chief form of decoration was by crudely incising geometric patterns over portions of the lip, rim, upper neck, and shoulder areas. Cord-impressed and brushed designs occurred infrequently.

There is considerable range in both size and shape from miniature vessels to those capable of holding 3 to 5 gallons or more. No two pots are exactly alike. This same holds true as to decoration, for it seems that little if any attempt was made to establish a definite style. Bases, as a rule, are rounded, while most mouths are wide. Ornamentation is either incised or cord-impressed. Incised designs are neither precise nor carefully applied. Designs of both types appear on rims, necks, and shoulders.

Incised designs are linear geometric elements consisting chiefly of series of parallel lines, chevrons, triangles, or herringbones. They appear to have avoided the use of the curved line in their incised designs. When it does occur, which is a rare event, the sherd fragment does not give any indication as to the design element. Punctations, while limited, are used either at the top or bottom of the designs or as a unit. On the whole, incised designs were rather carelessly applied and never developed to any great extent.

Contrariwise, the cord-impressed designs show greater fineness, neatness, and precision in that they were carefully applied either as a band of horizontal impressions around the rim, as short diagonal lines

bounded by encircling lines, or as interspersed "rainbow" elements between series of horizontal parallel lines comparable to types illustrated
by Will and Spinden (1906, pl. XL, *g*, *i*, and *o*). No two patterns are
exactly alike. The size of the cords may vary—some are rather small
and others are coarse; some have the horizontal elements closely spaced
and others are spaced farther apart and not quite so carefully placed;
and still others show greater neatness in covering up the ends of the
diagonal lines by the horizontal lines.

The cultural pattern, as represented at the Hosterman site, does
not seem reasonable. While the main portion of the settlement was
surrounded by a palisade and ditch, which would indicate that it
was built for defense against external marauding parties, other houses
together with their trash areas occurred to the east and north of the
palisaded area unsurrounded by any protective device. Why it should
be necessary for one portion of the site to be protected by a palisade
and ditch while another section of the same village did not require
such features poses a problem. Whether the palisade was maintained
throughout the short history of the site or only for a brief period,
could not be determined. However, since there was such a feature
the inhabitants must have felt the need for it; otherwise they would
never have expended the time and effort to secure the necessary material and to erect such a structure. Furthermore, only a comparatively few projectile points were recovered. These were of insufficient
number to arm the inhabitants against any agressive exterior action,
to say nothing about the number that the hunters would require to
secure sufficient game to feed the hungry. There must be some logical
explanation to the situation, but it is not apparent. It may be that
other materials were used on projectiles, such as hardened wooden
tips, which were not preserved in the site.

Contrariwise, stone scrapers far exceeded in number the stone projectile points. This appears to indicate that the need for scraping
far exceeded that of a killing nature and that the materials were at
hand upon which these tools were used. The scrapers have been used
to fashion wooden containers and tools but such would seem highly
unlikely. With the great mass of animal bones present, attesting to
success in the hunt, hides must have been plentiful and they would
have had to be prepared for use. Hence the large number of scrapers.

Cultural refuse was nowhere thick on the site except in midden pits.
Within the village it was sparse. Even house floors, while firmly
packed, were not only barren of refuse but were not as firmly packed
as they should have been if the house had been occupied over a long
period of time. These two characteristics apparently would indicate
a limited occupancy of the site, one of very short duration.

No traces of any European trade goods or contact were found.

On the basis of the correlation of pottery traits, dwelling forms, and village plan with others in the immediate vicinity, it would appear that the Hosterman site, while having certain characteristics commonly attributed to the pre-Arikara, is more closely associated with those of the pre-Mandan of North Dakota and possibly Minnesota.

TRAIT LIST

The following list of traits for the Hosterman site (39 PO7) has been prepared from the present excavation. An attempt has been made to arrange these in a functional order (Fairbanks, 1942, pp. 228–229).

SUBSISTENCE ACTIVITY:
    Collecting Complex:
        Collecting of shellfish (*Anodonta grandis* (Say))
        Collecting of wild plant seeds (*Chenopodium acuminatum*)
        Collecting of wild fruits (*Cleome capparius*)
        Collecting of wild fruits (*Prunes virginiana*)
        Collecting of wild fruits (*Celtis* sp.)
        Collecting of wild fruits (*Rebes* sp.)
        Collecting of wild fruits (*Prunus americana*)
    Agricultural Comlpex:
        Limited growing of maize (*Zea mays*)
        Limited growing of beans (*Phaseolus vulgaris*)
        Limited growing of squash (*Cucurbita pepo*)
        Limited growing of squash (*Cucurbita mixta*)
    Hunting and fishing Complex:
        Bison, deer, pronghorn, fox, rabbit, turkey, waterfowl, beaver, badger, coyote, red fox, gray fox, skunk, black bear, otter, prairie dog, ground squirrel, meadow vole, muskrat, pocket gopher and various kinds of fish. Use of hook and line. Domestic dog.
    Use of bow and arrow inferential from the presence of small isosceles triangular projectile points.
COMMUNITY PLAN ACTIVITY:
    Village location and plan Complex:
        Village located in close proximity to stream
        Houses clustered without plan
        Palisaded village with accompanying ditch
        Village without benefit of palisade or ditch
        Midden pits numerous and outside of houses
        Cache pits numerous and outside of houses
        Cache pits, small, and inside of houses
        Hearth areas (fired areas) with broken stones
        Fire-cracked stones in debris
        Hearths outside of structures irregular in outline
    Architectural Complex:
        Circular house structures
        Rectangular house structure
        Bell-shaped midden and cache pits
        Midden and cache pits beneath floors of houses
        Centrally located hearths in structures
        Four central roof poles

TECHNOLOGICAL AND ARTISTIC ACTIVITY:

  Pottery Complex:

Modeling or molding of clay vessels
Use of paddle and anvil in manufacture of clay vessels
Pulverized granite tempered
Jar shapes only
Rims vertical
Rims S-shaped
Plain
Simple stamped
Incised
Brushed
Curvilinear stamped
Cord impressed
Mat impressed
Fabric impressed
Painted
Punctated
Corncob impressed
Horizontal line punctates
Random punctates
Incising, narrow line
Incising, broad line
Herringbone
Horizontal incised lines
Horizontal bands of incised lines
Horizontal cord impressions
Curvilinear cord impressions
Clay dawdles

  Rough-stone Complex:

Hammerstones, natural hardheads
Hammerstones, rough discoidals
Hammerstones, pitted

  Chipped-stone Complex:

  Projectile points:

Triangular with straight or convex edges, sides slightly longer than base, straight base as rule, some slightly concave or convex
Isosceles triangular with straight or slightly concave bases
Triangular with straight or convex edges, straight or convex base. Maximum width at base.
Side-notched, straight-sided triangular, maximum width at base, straight bases, slightly concave or convex bases occur rarely. Notches are at right angles to long axis and are often narrow or shallow.

  Microblades.

  Scrapers:

End scrapers:
  Keeled end scrapers
    Type 1
    Type 2
  Small round scrapers
  Large and small teardrop end scrapers

TECHNOLOGICAL AND ARTISTIC ACTIVITY—Continued
   Chipped-stone Complex—Continued
      Scrapers—Continued
         End scrapers—Continued
            Small planoconvex end scrapers
            Large flake end scrapers
            Small flake end scrapers
            Flat end scrapers
            Thumbnail end scrapers
            Beveled retouched edge end scrapers
               Type 1
               Type 2
            Triangular end scrapers
            Slightly modified nodular end scrapers
            Trapezoidal end scrapers
            End scrapers with left carinate, type 3
            End scrapers with right carinate, type 4
            End scraper-graver combinations
            Modified end scrapers
         Side scrapers:
            Small flake side scrapers
            Medium flake side scrapers
            Large flake side scrapers
            Double edged side scrapers
            Triple edged side scrapers
            Prismatic flake side scrapers
            Lunate side scrapers
            Side and concave side scrapers
            Pointed side scrapers
            Modified side scrapers
     Ovoid bifaces
     Biface choppers
     Knives
     Burinlike implements
     Burin
     Perforators or gravers
     Lamellar flake tools
   Ground and pecked stone tools Complex:
      Anvil stones
      Rubbing stones
      Paint stones
      Grooved mauls
      Catlinite
      Belemnite
      Pumice abraders
      Sandstone abraders
      Arrowshaft straighteners
      Grooved ax
      Handstones
      Utilized pebbles
      Hematite and other paint substances

TECHNOLOGICAL AND ARTISTIC ACTIVITY—Continued
  Bone artifacts:
        Cut animal bones
        Scapula hoes
        Scapula spines
        Scapula knives
        Scapula cleavers
        Scapula hide scrapers
        Scapula thong stretchers
        Scapula sickle
        Flakers
        Needlelike tool
        Shaft wrenches
        Knife handles
        Hide grainers
        Notched ribs
        Cut ribs
        Punches
        Worked pronghorn metapodial bones
        Fishhooks
        Worked animal scapula
        Problematical bone tool
        Bone tubes
        Awls:
              Rough splinter awls
                    Type 1 (group 1)
                    Type 2 (group 2)
                          group 3
                          group 4
        Cancellous bone balls
        Bone picks
        Split pronghorn metapodial bones
        Perforated rib fragments
        Punches
        Worked antler fragments
        Mineralized bone
        Antler hammers
        Worked teeth:
              Beaver incisor chisels
              Wapiti's tooth pendant
              Human teeth
        Fetish or trophy skull
  Shell:
        Disk
        Unworked
  Metal: copper tubular bead

TECHNOLOGICAL AND ARTIFACT ACTIVITY—Continued
Bone artifacts:
Cut animal bones
Scapula tools
Scapula spines
Scapula knives
Scapula choppers
Scapula hide scrapers
Scapula tissue streichers
Scapula skelis
Flakers
Needlelike tool
Shaft wrenches
Knife handles
Ribs scrapers
Notched rib
Cut ribs
Tubes
Worked growth in metapodial bones
Fishhooks
Worked animal scapula
Problematical bone tool
Bone tube
Awls:
Bone splinter awls
Type 1 (group 1)
Type 2 (group 2)
Group 3
Group 4
Cancellous bone balls
Bone picks
Split metapodial metapodial bones
Perforated rib fragments
Tubules
Worked antler fragments
Mineralized bone
Antler hammers
Worked teeth
Beaver incisor chisels
Wapiti's tooth pendant
Human teeth
British crotopic skull
Shell:
Disk
Unworked
Metal: copper tubulators

APPENDIX 1

VEGETAL REMAINS

A number of plant remains were recovered at the Hosterman site (39PO7). These were identified for the Smithsonian Institution by Hugh Carter, aided by Leonard Blake, John Bower, and Winton Meyer, of the Missouri Botanical Gardens, St. Louis.

They state:

All of the carbonized cultivated plant remains are of varieties similar to those grown in historic times by the Mandans and Omaha. The corn of this site has few rows, usually 8 but occasionally 10 or 12, and belonged to the race called Northern Flint (Brown and Anderson, 1947). The cupules are not as wide, the kernels thicker and the shanks more slender than in the eastern forms of this race. This difference may have been the result of mixture with corn from the south and west or with the race of corn which was grown at this site in earlier times. In the middle Mississippi Valley the Northern Flint race of corn came later than a race with more rows of grains, smaller grains, and smaller but deeper cupules. Corn similar to this earlier race is found in pre-1000 A.D. Among the cobs from 39PO7 it was possible to distinguish quite readily a few which were very much like the eastern form of Northern Flint. The fact that these were quite distinct makes it likely that they were grown as a special variety. The Mandans grew several kinds of corn and kept their varieties quite distinct.

The corn is almost identical to that described by Nickerson and Hou (1954). More collections of corn from dated sites over a wide area must be studied before a reasonable explanation for the distribution of the various kinds of corn can be prepared. The median measurements of the corn follows:

	Median for all 39PO7	Median for extreme variety	Median for all Northern Flints	Eastern extreme of Northern Flints	Dodd site 39ST30	Phillips Ranch site 39ST14
Row number	8	8	8	8	8	8
Kernal thickness	4. 0	4. 6	4. 2	4. 0	4. 0	3. 4
Shank diameter	12. 0	--------	17. 0	22. 0	(18. 0?)	11. 4
Cupule width	9. 0	12. 0	10. 0	12. 0	9. 5	8. 0
Cupule depth	--------	. 5	. 5	. 75	. 25	--------
Number of rows of grain	8	10	12	14	16	--------
Corncobs measured	87	21	4	--------	1	--------

Several kinds of *Cucurbita pepo*, the common pumpkin and squash, were grown. Most abundant, nearly 700 seeds, was a very small-seeded (9 × 5.5 mm.) variety, probably like the one called "Mandan," with small green-striped fruit which sug-

231

gests in many respects, including flavor and texture, some of the wild species of *Cucurbita*. Most of the other seeds were small (12 × 7 mm.) or medium (15 × 7 mm.) in size and probably came from fruits like the small sugar pumpkin grown in the Plains area. There were very few large (18 × 8.5 mm.) seeds and two of these were so thick that they resembled some of the less extreme forms of *Cucurbita mixta*, especially the Green-striped Cushaw variety, but this species had not been collected in sites this far east. The only peduncles were of *C. pepo*.

Although small fragments of a *Cucurbita* (probably *C. pepo*) rind were found, there were no fragments of the bottle gourd (*Lagenaria*).

A single seed (10.5 × 6 × 5 mm.) and some charred pods of the common (or kidney) bean (*Phaseolus vulgaris*) were not in good enough condition to determine the variety.

Wild materials found included, in order of abundance:

    Wild plum seeds, *Prunus americana*, and ?

    Chokecherry seeds, *Prunus virginiana*

    Hackberry seeds, *Celtis occidentalis*

    Grass stem fragment,

    Seeds, *Chenopodium* ?, goosefoot.

APPENDIX 2

FAUNAL REMAINS

Animal remains within the deposits of the Hosterman site (39PO7), were very abundant. All identifiable whole and fragmentary bones were preserved and later identified by Dr. Theodore White and H. W. Setzer, as follows:

Class: Amphibia:
    Rana sp.
Class: Aves; order undetermined:
    *Aquila chrysoelus canadensis*_____ golden eagle.
Class: Mammalia:
    Order Artiodactyla, family undetermined
        Antilocarpa americana (Ord)_____ pronghorn.
        Bison bison (Linnaeus)_____ bison.
        Odocoileus, referred_____ deer
    Order Carnivora:
        *Canis familiaris*_____ dog.
        *Canis latrans*_____ coyote.
        *Canis lupus*_____ red fox.
        *Urocyon cinereoargentheus*_____ gray fox.
        Mephitis sp._____ skunk.
        *Euarctos americanus*_____ black bear.
        *Lutra canadensis*_____ otter.
        *Taxidea taxus*_____ badger.
    Order Lagomorpha:
        *Lepus townsendii*_____ jack rabbit (white
                                          tailed).
        *Sylvilagus floridanus*_____ cottontail.
    Order Rodentia:
        *Cynomys ludovicianus*_____ prairie dog.
        Citellus sp._____ ground squirrel.
        Microtus sp._____ meadow mole.
        *Ondatra zibethicus*_____ muskrat.
        *Castor canadensis*_____ beaver.
        *Geomys bursarius*_____ pocket gopher.
Class: Pisces; order undetermined.

As White (1954, p. 161) has indicated:

The numerical count of the elements found in a site is subject to the accidents of preservation, the length of occupation, and the size of the excavation, but the ratio of various elements to each other and to the greatest number of individuals represented, from an excavation which satisfies the archeological requirements, should provide an adequate sample for this type of study. . . .

Throughout this study the "number of individuals" means the greatest number represented by any single element, i.e., in this site, as shown

233

TABLE 7.—*Frequency distribution of the various animal elements in the Hosterman site*

Element	Canis familiaris (dog)	Vulpes velox (swift fox)	Antilocapra americana (antelope)	Bison bison (bison)	Sylvilagus floridanus (cottontail rabbit)	Canis latrans (coyote)	Odocoileus sp. (deer)	Citellus sp. (ground squirrel)	Lepus townsendii (W. T. jackrabbit)	Cynomys ludovicianus (prairie dog)	Taxidea taxus (badger)	Castor canadensis (beaver)	Mephitis sp. (skunk)
		Distribution of skeletal elements of indicated number of individuals represented											
Skull, occiput	12	4	22	7	10	----	4	----	1	4	----	1	1
Skull, frontals	----	----	5	4	----	----	----	----	----	----	----	----	----
Skull, horn cores	----	----	15	25	----	----	----	----	----	----	----	----	----
Skull, maxilla	3	11	48	29	6	9	11	2	4	1	----	----	----
Mandible	29	38	55	91	27	5	11	11	4	10	3	1	4
Hyoid	----	----	7	24	8	----	----	----	----	----	----	----	----
Vertebra, atlas	15	6	19	5	6	2	3	1	----	----	----	----	1
Vertebra, axis	8	8	21	5	5	5	7	----	----	1	2	1	1
Vertebra, cervical	31	14	100	15	27	11	14	----	----	1	4	3	1
Vertebra, dorsal	51	31	183	64	35	26	16	3	1	2	2	----	----
Vertebra, lumbar	38	24	172	17	116	13	42	----	9	2	3	12	----
Vertebra, sacral	1	1	9	10	2	----	1	----	----	----	----	----	----
Vertepra, caudal	2	18	8	144	----	----	----	----	----	----	----	----	----
Scapula	11	12	51	27	27	3	18	----	9	4	1	1	3
Humerus, proximal	10	20	26	8	56	1	2	8	5	9	4	2	----
Humerus, distal	17	14	63	33	----	----	9	----	----	----	----	----	----
Radius, proximal	9	19	48	37	32.	3	10	----	4	2	2	1	2
Radius, distal	3	4	40	23	----	----	5	----	----	----	----	----	----
Ulna	25	19	39	20	42	7	11	----	4	6	2	2	2
Metacarpal	2	----	58	39	----	----	10	----	----	----	----	----	----
Pelvis	18	17	56	13	50	2	7	6	13	4	3	3	1
Femur, head	----	----	2	5	----	----	----	----	----	----	4	----	----
Femur, proximal	5	18	26	12	29	5	6	16	4	10	----	1	1
Femur, distal	9	6	26	15	----	----	3	----	----	----	----	----	----
Tibia, proximal	5	21	37	14	26	2	----	5	12	6	----	4	----
Tibia, distal	6	7	22	20	----	----	10	----	----	----	4	----	----
Astragalus	7	9	27	32	----	4	14	----	1	1	----	2	----
Sacrum	----	3	7	3	4	----	1	----	2	----	----	----	----
Metatarsal	122	67	45	34	104	21	12	----	12	1	----	3	----

by the dorsal vertebrae of the antelope. This is not too highly indicative, since the animal was small enough to be easily transported from the point of killing to the village without too much discomfort on the part of the hunter. On the other hand, there are 91 whole mandibles of bison represented in the collection. Of this number 46 are right and 45 are left, indicating, at least, that there are more than 45 individual bison represented in the lot. Fragmentary mandibles were not saved due to the large mass of bone encountered. This is true also of the rest of the bone material. Only recognizable whole bone and some with identifiable articulative surfaces were salvaged for identification purposes.

An examination of table 7 discloses that certain elements are consistent (horn cores, maxillae, hyoids, scapulae, humerus distals, radius proximals, radius distals, ulnae, and tibia distals), which may indicate the maximum number of individuals represented in the bison grouping. Other elements (occiputs, frontals, atlas vertebrae, axis vertebrae, and sacra) are conspicious by their scarcity. This can be partially explained in that animals that were killed at a distance from the village were dressed in the field and only the most desired portions were transported back to the village. In dressing, the head, along with the atlas and axis, was severed from the vertebral column, probably with a blow of the ax. As has been pointed out numerous times, the head, as a whole, is a heavy unwieldly part of the animal and is covered at the most with a minimum amount of usable meat; hence it was not usually transported from the kill to the village. On the other hand, if the brains and tongue were desired they could just as easily be removed at the time of the kill.

White (1954, p. 164) seemed to think that the mandibles at the Dodd site are close to the greatest number of individuals represented and that none were ever used for anything and were probably brought into the village along with the tongue of the animal. He states: "Certainly the easiest way to remove the tongue would be to smash the ascending ramus of the jaw and remove jaws and tongue as a unit for further cutting at a more convenient time." If the percentage were low, then he suggests that most hunting was performed at considerable distance from the village and the tongue eaten at the hunting camp and the mandibles discarded there.

Practically all of the mandibles in the Hosterman site were complete with the ascending rami entire. This fact would indicate that they were part of the skull when introduced into the village and that we did not find the entire assemblage.

On the other hand, we recovered 24 hyoid bones, which is a small bone attached to the tongue. This number approximates the number of maxillae, a fact that may be significant.

Vertebrae.—Very few animals are represented by the vertebrae, for their distribution covers the entire column. However, the interesting thing is the large number of caudal vertebrae, which signify that the entire tail was left intact with the pelt as it was removed from the animal and brought back to the village to be processed. This fact indicates that the tail was an important ornamental feature, since it was left attached to the hide after skinning.

Fish.—The remains of several fish were found in various of the midden pits. Fishbones were mixed with the midden in Features 1, 2, and 3. In Feature 9 they were found at various levels: between 3.0 feet and 3.5 feet, between 4.0 feet and 4.5 feet, and between 5.5 feet and 8.0 feet. Many were just miscellaneous bones, but the complete articulated skeletons would appear to indicate that the complete fish was discarded because it was not considered to be palatable by the Indian. Fish remains were also found in Features 10, 18, 21, 22, 24, and 25. Individual fishbones appeared in many of the small isolated midden heaps.

Dr. William Taylor, Division of Fishes, U.S. National Museum, rapidly examined the fish remains and has identified not only the families to which they belong but also certain skeletal elements. He states:

The fish material from site 39PO7 consists of remains of two families of fishes, Cyprinidae and Ictaluridae. The Cyprinidae remains are all pharyngeal arches, probably of *Hybopsis* (*Platygobio*) *gracilis* (Richardson). This cyprinid inhabits large streams and rivers in the Plains. The Ictaluridae or catfish remains consist chiefly of spines, pectoral girdles, and vertebrae, with relatively few of the heavy skull elements present, suggesting that the skull parts were often disposed of before reaching the midden. The bullheads, which probably live in the region, are not represented. All material seems referable to the channel catfish, *Ictalurus punctatus* (Rafinesque) and the blue catfish *I. furcatus* (Le-Sueur). Since these two species are superficially very similar, I do not wish to rest heavily on definite identifications of either species for any of the bones. Where identifications are made to species, they should be regarded as probable and not positive, for that species.

A brief list follows of elements from site 39PO7.

Catalog No.

2481____ Cleithra (3) of *Ictalurus punctatus* and 2 vertebrae of catfish.
1248____ Pectoral spines (2) and dorsal spine (1) plus parts, 2 cleithra of *I. punctatus*; also miscellaneous vertebrae and skull elements of catfish.
1117____ Spine and parts of cleithrum of *I. punctatus*.
1535____ Vertebrae, opercle, cleithrum, and spine of *I. punctatus*.
1403____ Miscellaneous bones, vertebrae, etc., of at least 2 individuals of *I. punctatus*.
1427____ Vertebrae, spine, cleithrum, etc., of *I. punctatus*.
3465____ Spine of *I. punctatus* and 2 catfish vertebrae.
1668____ Several bones of catfish, chiefly *I. punctatus*.
252____ Spine of catfish, probably *I. punctatus*.
234____ 2 spines of *Ictalurus*, probably *I. punctatus*.
3323____ Vertebrae and vertebral complex of catfish.
1302____ Vertebrae, opercle, vertebral complex, etc., of catfish; cleithrum of *I. punctatus*.
3983____ Spines of *I. punctatus* (2).
421____ Spine and cleithrum of *I. punctatus*.
1182____ Miscellaneous catfish bones, including spine and cleithrum of *I. punctatus*.
1344____ Miscellaneous bone of catfish.
1469____ Spines and cleithra of *I. punctatus*.
1864____ Miscellaneous bones and spines of *I. punctatus*.
1962____ Lower jaw of catfish.
2357____ Miscellaneous catfish bones.
1609____ Many vertebrae and miscellaneous bones of catfish.
4186____ Spine and cleithra of *I. punctatus*; other catfish bones.
976____ Pectoral spine of *I. punctatus*.
1173____ 4 catfish vertebrae.
1497____ Catfish vertebrae and bones.
2477____ 2 catfish bones.
1483____ Miscellaneous catfish bones, some identifiable as *I. punctatus*.

1270____ Catfish bones including supraoccipital of *I. punctatus*.

1103____ Spine of *I. punctatus*; other catfish bones.

1608____ Spines of *I. punctatus* and 1 vertebra.

4074____ Many catfish bones, including parts of 5 skulls and ribs, vertebrae, cleithra, spines, etc., of *I. punctatus*.

1518____ Cleithra of *I. punctatus*.

1249____ Pharyngeal arch of cyprinid fish, probably *Hybopsis* (*Platygobio*).

3463____ Catfish bones and pharyngeal of cyprinid, probably *Hybopsis* (*Platygobio*).

1428____ 2 pharyngeals of cyprinid, probably genus *Hybopsis* (*Platygobio*).

1917____ Catfish bones.

1343____ Part of lower jaw of catfish.

3979____ Cyprinid pharyngeal with 1 to 4 teeth.

1862____ Fish rib and part of 2 catfish spines.

2480____ Cyprinid pharyngeal arch.

1271____ Cyprinid pharyngeal arch.

4102____ Catfish spine, *I. punctatus*.

1363____ Supraoccipital of catfish, *I. punctatus*.

3536____ Hyoid apparatus, catfish.

4185____ Pharyngeal of cyprinid, probably *Hybopsis* (*Platygobio*).

3749____ Pharyngeal of cyprinid, probably *Hybopsis* (*Platygobio*).

 684____ Pharyngeal of cyprinid, probably *Hybopsis* (*Platygobio*) both arches.

2476____ Pharyngeal of cyprinid, probably *Hybopsis* (*Platygobio*) one arch.

 420____ Pharyngeal of cyprinid, probably *Hybopsis* (*Platygobio*).

 350____ 2 spines of *I. punctatus*.

1433____ Bones of rather large catfish, genus *Ictalurus*, part of supraoccipital possibly *I. furcatus*.

1585____ Miscellaneous bones, spines, etc., of catfish, including some identifiable as *I. punctatus;* some upper skull elements, possibly of *I. furcatus*.

1282____ Catfish bones, mostly skull, some axial; spines recognizable as *I. punctatus*.

1515____ Miscellaneous bones, some skull of catfish including *I. punctatus*.

2457____ 2 pharyngeal arches of cyprinid: *Hybopsis* (*Platygobio*).

1918____ Bones of catfish, mostly identifiable as *I. punctatus*.

Birds.—Outside of the golden eagle sternum, identified by Dr. Herbert Friedmann, Department of Zoology, U.S. National Museum, none of the other bird bones have been identified. Bird bones were not scarce in the village fill and today there is still no scarcity of birds in the region. Today there are many large waterfowl that frequent the area during certain seasons of the year, and small birds number over 150 species according to Over and Thomas (1921).

APPENDIX 3

INSECT REMAINS

The chitinous remains of several insects were recovered while Feature 3, a cache pit, was being cleaned out. These have been identified by members of the U.S. National Museum staff and the U.S. Department of Agriculture as belonging to Carabidae *Pasimachus* sp. and Calliphoridae sp.

In most instances, remains of this sort are not saved, but since these were found in undisturbed deposits within the cache pit, the lowest stratum—between 5.0 feet and 5.5 feet—and the highest—between 1.5 feet and 2.0 feet—it was deemed wise to get determinations in case anyone should be interested in this phase of life at the Hosterman site.

APPENDIX 4

TABLES OF MEASUREMENTS

Projectile Points

Catalog No.	Maximum length	Maximum width	Maximum thickness	Shape	Material
	Mm.	*Mm.*	*Mm.*		
194	21	14	2	Isosceles triangular	Quartzite.
331	28	15	3	Small side notches triangular, concave base.	Chalcedony.
332	21	14	3	Isosceles triangular	Quartzite.
359	20	13	3	Small side notches triangular, concave base.	Do.
360	21	17	3	Medium side notches triangular, concave base.	Chalcedony.
361	15	11	3	Isosceles triangular	Quartzite.
362	20	13	3	____do	Chalcedony.
363	23	16	3	____do	Quartzite.
364	18	14	3	____do	Chalcedony.
365	17	13	3	____do	Quartzite.
366	20	11	3	____do	Do.
367	18	11	2	____do	Jasper.
433	15	12	2	Isosceles triangular, with slight side notches.	Quartzite.
446	27	15	3	Isosceles triangular square side notches, square base.	Chalcedony.
447	17	12	3	Isosceles triangular	Quartzite.
457	18	13	3.5	____do	Do.
458	24	16	4	____do	Do.
459	28	16	5	Isosceles triangular, concave base	Do.
520	29	18	3	Isosceles triangular	Chalcedony.
521	21	16	3	____do	Do.
522	21	19	2.5	____do	Quartzite.
524	28	17	4	Isosceles triangular side notches, concave base.	Do.
575	22	16	3	Isosceles triangular	Do.
617	29	15	3	____do	Do.
618	18	14	3	Isosceles triangular, side notched	Do.
619	17	13	4	Isosceles triangular	Do.
625	43	29	7	____do	Chalcedony.
654	17	15	3	____do	Quartzite.
704	26	17	6	____do	Do.
705	27	8	5	____do	White flint.
706	32	20	6	____do	Chalcedony.
743	24	14	3	Isosceles triangular, side notched	Quartzite.
744	41	23	4	Isosceles triangular, side notched, concave base.	Chalcedony.
745	48	16	4	____do	Do.
746	20	9	3	Isosceles triangular, slightly concave base	Do.
747	24	15	3	Isosceles triangular	Do.
753	34	19	3	Presumably isosceles, concave base	Obsidian.
783	32	14	4	Isosceles triangular, side notched	Quartzite.
784	26	19	3	Isosceles triangular, slightly concave base.	Do.
785	23	13	3	Isosceles triangular	Do.
786	21	17	3	____do	Do.
788	20	16	3	____do	Chalcedony.
888	23	19	4.5	Isosceles triangular, concave base	Quartzite.
895	29	15	3	Isosceles triangular	Do.
915	24	18	4	Isosceles triangular, side notched	Chalcedony.
940	____	15	4	____do	Do.
988	25	16	3	Isosceles triangular, slightly concave	Quartzite.
989	21	14	2.5	Isosceles triangular, side notched	Do.
1038	24	14	4	Isosceles triangular, slightly triangular base.	Do.
1058	24	14	3	Isosceles triangular, slightly side notched concave base.	Do.
1078	18	9	3	Isosceles triangular	Do.
1084	17	14	2	____do	Do.
1088	38	23	5	____do	Do.
1095	19	15	3	Isosceles triangular, deep concave base	Chalcedony.
1163	23	14	3	____do	Do.
1164	25	15	2	____do	Quartzite.
1195	30	20	6	____do	Chalcedony.

239

TABLES OF MEASUREMENTS—Continued

Projectile Points—Continued

Catalog No.	Maximum length	Maximum width	Maximum thickness	Shape	Material
	Mm.	*Mm.*	*Mm.*		
1274	48	22	5	Isosceles triangular, deep concave base__	Quartzite.
1285	37	21	7	_____do_____	Chalcedony.
1297	18	13	2	Isosceles triangular, side notched_____	Do.
1305	16	15	3	Isosceles triangular, concave base_____	Do.
1306	24	12	2	Isosceles triangular, slightly concave base.	Quartzite.
1307	25	15	3	_____do_____	Do.
1308	24	16	3	_____do_____	Do.
1309	26	15	5	Isosceles triangular_____	Chalcedony.
1351	22	17	4	Isosceles triangular, slightly concave base	Do.
1367	18	14	3	Isosceles triangular, side notched_____	Quartzite.
1369	22	13	3	Isosceles triangular, slighty concave base.	Do.
1412	16	13	3	_____do_____	Chalcedony.
1413	16	11	2.5	Isosceles triangular_____	Quartzite.
1414	22	15	4	_____do_____	Do.
1415	21	13	4	_____do_____	Do.
1451	25	17	5	Side notched_____	Chert?
1452	21	14	3	Isosceles triangular, concave base_____	Quartzite.
1453	25	15	_____	_____do_____	Chalcedony.
1459	20	18	5	Equal sided triangular sides, slightly concave.	Do.
1505	23	18	4	Isosceles triangular, slightly concave base.	Quartzite.
1521	28	14	5	Side notched_____	Chalcedony.
1522	24	20	5	Isosceles triangular_____	Do.
1523	17	17	3	_____do_____	Do.
1546	20	13	3	Side notched_____	Do.
1547	21	18	3	Isosceles triangular_____	Do.
1612	19	13	3	_____do_____	Quartzite.
1615	23	13	3	Side notched_____	Do.
1620	42	17	4	Isosceles triangular, side notched_____	Chalcedony.
1651	22	15	3	Isosceles triangular, slightly concave base.	Jasper.
1710	23	14	4	Isosceles triangular_____	Quartzite.
1733	28	15	3	_____do_____	Do.
1745	20	14	3	Isosceles triangular, slightly concave base.	Chalcedony.
1746	20	14	3	_____do_____	Quartzite.
1747	25	18	5	_____do_____	Do.
1764	21	14	3	_____do_____	Do.
1772	19	14	3	_____do_____	Do.
1792	30	15	4	Isosceles triangular, slightly concave base.	Chalcedony.
1793	24	15	3	Isosceles triangular, side notched_____	Quartzite.
1795	20	14	3	_____do_____	Do.
1835	24	15	2.5	_____do_____	Do.
1836	20	15	3.5	Convex-sided triangular, concave base___	Do.
1837	46	20	5	Isosceles triangular, side notched_____	Chalcedony.
1886	21	18	3	Stemmed_____	Do.
1887	26	14	4	Isosceles triangular_____	Quartzite.
1898	19	14	3	Isosceles triangular, slightly concave base.	Do.
1935	21	14	4	Isosceles triangular_____	Chalcedony.
1964	29	17	4	Isosceles triangular, slightly concave base.	Quartzite.
1979	17	11	3	_____do_____	Chalcedony.
2052	28	19	4	Convex sided triangular, concave base__	Quartzite.
2071	23	13	4	Isosceles triangular, slightly concave base.	Chalcedony.
2074	27	18	4	Convex sided triangular, straight base__	Do.
2090	23	16	3	Isosceles triangular, side notched_____	Quartzite.
2091	19	13	3	Isosceles triangular, slightly concave base.	Chalcedony.
2092	27	16	4	Isosceles triangular_____	Jasper.
2093	31	13	4	_____do_____	Quartzite.
2149	23	14	2	Isosceles triangular, slightly side notched_	Do.
2150	22	13	3	_____do_____	Do.
2151	22	12	3	_____do_____	Do.
2152	17	12	2	Isosceles triangular_____	Chalcedony.
2153	17	15	3	_____do_____	Quartzite.
2154	20	15	3	_____do_____	Chalcedony.
2155	17	14	4	Isosceles triangular, slightly concave base.	Quartzite.
2156	22	16	4	Isosceles triangular_____	Chalcedony.
2157	27	16	6	Isosceles triangular, slightly side notched_	Quartzite.
2158	26	13	3	Isosceles triangular_____	Do.
2159	24	21	5	_____do_____	Do.
2161	23	18	4	Isosceles triangular, side notched_____	Do.
2171	23	16	4	_____do_____	Do.
2172	_____	_____	_____	Fragmentary side notched_____	Do.
2178	29	14	3	Isosceles triangular, slightly side notched_	Do.
2180	30	21	8	Isosceles triangular, unfinished_____	Chalcedony.
2238	21	13	4	Isosceles triangular, side notched_____	Quartzite.
2239	_____	_____	_____	Fragmentary side notched_____	Do.
2253	_____	_____	_____	Very crude point?	Do.
2276	18	16	3	Convex sided triangular concave base___	Do.

TABLES OF MEASUREMENTS—Continued

Projectile Points—Continued

Catalog No.	Maximum length	Maximum width	Maximum thickness	Shape	Material
	Mm.	*Mm.*	*Mm.*		
2277	31	26	3	Side notched_____	Quartzite.
2278	------	------	------	Isosceles triangular_____	Jasper.
2326	25	16	3	Isosceles triangular, side notched_____	Obsidian.
2327	19	14	3	Isosceles triangular, slightly side notched_	Chalcedony.
2328	29	14	3	Isosceles triangular_____	Quartzite.
2330	25	13	3	Isosceles triangular, slightly concave base_	Chalcedony.
2335	22	17	3	_____do_____	Do.
2346	35	14	4	Isosceles triangular_____	Quartzite.
2388	24	14	3	_____do_____	Do.
2390	22	16	3	_____do_____	Do.
2391	24	17	3	_____do_____	Do.
2394	19	13	4	Isosceles triangular, slightly side notched_	Do.
2464	19	12	3	Isosceles triangular_____	Do.
2469	25	14	3	Isosceles triangular, slightly concave base_	Do.
2470	21	10	3	_____do_____	Do.
2484	20	11	3	_____do_____	Do.
2537	16	15	3	Triangular_____	Do.
2539	35	21	5	Isosceles triangular_____	Do.
2680	18	18	2	_____do_____	Do.
2681	21	15	3	Isosceles triangular, slightly concave base_	Do.
2720	21	14	3	_____do_____	Do.
2741	17	13	4	Convex sided triangular, convex base__	Do.
2742	22	12	3	_____do_____	Do.
2765	21	12	3	Concave base_____	Do.
2766	13	12	2	Triangular_____	Do.
2767	23	14	4	Isosceles triangular_____	Do.
2768	17	15	3	Triangular, side notched fragmentary__	Do.
2769	------	------	------	Fragmentary, side notched_____	Do.
2770	20	16	3	Isosceles triangular, slightly concave base_	Do.
2831	15	12	2	Triangular_____	Chalcedony.
2864	15	13	3	_____do_____	Quartzite.
2865	25	17	5	Isosceles triangular_____	Do.
2866	27	12	3	Crude side notched_____	Chert ?
2867	18	13	3	Isosceles triangular_____	Quartzite.
2882	------	------	------	Fragmentary side notched_____	Chalcedony.
2888	20	16	4	Side notched_____	Quartzite.
2889	32	22	5	Isosceles triangular_____	Do.
2901	15	14	3	Side notched_____	Do.
2903	22	16	3	Isosceles triangular_____	Do.
2904	25	16	4	_____do_____	Do.
2907	19	14	3	Side notched_____	Chalcedony.
2963	21	13	3	_____do_____	Quartzite.
2964	24	20	4	Convex sided triangular_____	Do.
2994	31	21	6	Isosceles triangular_____	Chalcedony.
3058	27	12	4	Isosceles triangular, slightly concave base_	Quartzite.
3059	27	14	3	_____do_____	Do.
3060	------	------	4	Fragmentary side notched_____	Do.
3090	16	12	3	Isosceles triangular_____	Chalcedony.
3107	16	12	3	_____do_____	Chert.
3130	24	14	4	Isosceles triangular, side notched_____	Do.
3153	14	13	2	_____do_____	Chalcedony.
3208	20	12	3	_____do_____	Do.
3306	16	13	3	Side notched straight base, abrupt tip_	Quartzite.
3308	22	17	3	Isosceles triangular, slightly concave base_	Chalcedony.
3334	25	15	3	Side notched_____	Quartzite.
3335	28	14	4	Isosceles triangular_____	Do.
3378	22	15	5	_____do_____	Do.
3389	15	13	2	_____do_____	Do.
3397	15	12	3	_____do_____	Do.
3430	22	15	4	_____do_____	Do.
3431	17	11	2	Isosceles triangular, slightly concave base.	Do.
3471	16	11	3	_____do_____	Do.
3472	20	10	3	_____do_____	Do.
3473	16	13	3	Convex sided triangular, concave base__	Do.
3489	25	16	4	Corner notched_____	Chalcedony.
3490	15	14	3	Isosceles triangular_____	Quartzite.
3491	21	13	3	Isosceles triangular, slightly concave base_	Chalcedony.
3500	18	13	4	Stemmed slightly_____	Quartzite.
3515	18	14	4	Isosceles triangular_____	Chalcedony.
3521	21	15	3	_____do_____	Do.
3522	28	14	3	Isosceles triangular, side notched_____	Do.
3539	17	14	4	Isosceles triangular, slightly concave base.	Quartzite.
3540	24	15	4	_____do_____	Do.
3541	23	13	3	_____do_____	Chalcedony.
3546	21	14	3	_____do_____	Quartzite.
3601	32	19	6	_____do_____	Do.
3615	58	22	6	Isosceles triangular, side notched slightly concave base.	Chalcedony.

TABLES OF MEASUREMENTS—Continued

Projectile Points—Continued

Catalog No.	Maximum length	Maximum width	Maximum thickness	Shape	Material
	Mm.	*Mm.*	*Mm.*		
3616	29	14	4	Isosceles triangular_____	Quartzite.
3617	19	12	3	Isosceles triangular, slightly concave base.	Do.
3633	18	14	3	Isosceles triangular, medium concave base.	Chalcedony.
3634	17	13	3	_____do_____	Quartzite.
3647	18	15	3	Isosceles triangular, slightly concave base.	Do.
3649	26	14	4	_____do_____.	Do.
3661	24	15	5	_____do_____	Do.
3663	18	14	4	_____do_____	Do.
3694	24	16	4	_____do_____	Chalcedony.
3714	19	14	3	Side notched, short and stubby_____	Quartzite.
3715	20	13	3	Isosceles triangular, slightly concave base.	Chalcedony.
3721	20	13	4	_____do_____	Quartzite.
3752	20	14	4	_____do_____	Chalcedony.
3760	24	15	3	Isosceles triangular, chipped one side___	Quartzite.
3872	30	14	3	Side notched, chipped one side only, slightly concave base.	Chalcedony.
3873	25	14	3	Isosceles triangular, concave base_____	Quartzite.
3874	21	13	4	_____do_____	Chalcedony.
3876	21	14	4	_____do_____	Quartzite.
3877	26	15	4	Isosceles triangular, convex sided, concave base.	Chalcedony.
3878	21	13	3	Isosceles triangular_____	Do.
3879	20	14	3	_____do_____	Quartzite.
3948	19	15	3	_____do_____	Do.
3987	20	12	3	_____do_____	Do.
3988	33	16	4	Isosceles triangular, side notched_____	Do.
3989	18	13	3	_____do_____	Do.
3990	32	14	3	_____do_____	Chalcedony.
4029	19	16	4	_____do_____	Quartzite.
4050	21	14	4	Isosceles triangular, medium concave base.	Chalcedony.
4106	32	12	3	Side notched_____	Quartzite.
4134	28	20	5	Isosceles triangular, slightly concave base.	Do.
4165	22	15	4	_____do_____	Do.
4197	19	13	2	Isosceles triangular, side notched_____	Do.
4201	28	15	3	Side notched, tip missing_____	Chalcedony.
4202	25	14	3	Side notched, one ear missing_____	Do.

TABLES OF MEASUREMENTS—Continued

Microblades: Group 1

Catalog No.	Length	Width	Thickness
	Mm.	Mm.	Mm.
4009	31	13	[1] 3
1244	32	18	4
541	34	13	3. 5
2746	35	12	5
3068	35	14	2
1929	35	16	2
1631	36	16	3
4236	37	13	2
1358	37	15	4
2784	38	22	4
2281	38	17	4
1928	39	14	8
3116	40	16	4
763	40	18	4
1007	40	20	4
950	45	15	5
2210	47	16	6
2056	47	13	2. 5
2212	49	16	5. 5
1491	57	23	4

[1] With attached graver tip. Longest, 57 mm.; shortest, 31 mm.

Microblades: Group 2

Catalog No.	Length	Width	Thickness
	Mm.	Mm.	Mm.
3655	18	12	2
2485	19	12	3
185	20	19	2. 5
875	20	15	2
2730	20	16	3
1511	22	13	4
2486	22	21	4
452	23	16	6
2058	23	16	5
3072	24	12	3
951	25	17	3
2370	25	17	5
3901	25	17	5
1601	25	14	3
3667	25	15	3
2006	25	14	4
3010	26	17	3
2414	36	11	4
3495	26	16	5
305	26	13	3
3934	36	17	5
1568	27	14	2
2982	27	15	5
3363	27	15	3
1945	28	14	3
3154	29	17	3. 5
1382	29	19	2
2571	30	17	3

TABLES OF MEASUREMENTS—Continued

Pointed Side Scrapers

Catalog No.	Degree of angle	Maximum length	Maximum width	Maximum thickness
		Mm.	*Mm.*	*Mm.*
184	62	31	31	11
403	50	30	20	4
407	65	28	23	5
508	81	35	22	9
594	32	39	28	11
640	26	35	25	6
813	26	26	21	3
818	43	50	27	13
822	32	34	25	8
901	45	26	20	4
1109	13	25	23	6
1216	74	42	41	9
1336	28	44	29	9
1393	69	44	43	6
1630	59	43	40	5
2102	18	32	26	9
2206	30	26	21	7
2314	87	31	22	7
2419	31	42	33	5
2421	30	22	24	4
2594	84	33	30	7
3012	71	17	31	8
3181	78	39	34	5
3384	58	34	27	5
3445	67	25	22	5
3606	69	19	32	10
3899	57	22	20	6

Keeled End Scrapers, type 1

Field catalog No.	Maximum length	Maximum width	Maximum thickness
	Mm.	*Mm.*	*Mm.*
280	21	17	9
299	24	18	9
339	28	22	9
390	25	21	7
397	27	22	11
401	32	22	11
475	34	26	11
517	37	22	7
538	32	24	10
588	30	23	11
641	22	20	8
642	30	21	6
643	27	19	8
646	26	17	7
647	25	18	7
648	30	19	9
758	28	22	7
759	31	22	11
797	24	22	9
807	25	22	10

TABLES OF MEASUREMENTS—Continued

Keeled End Scrapers, type 1—Continued

Field catalog No.	Maximum length	Maximum width	Maximum thickness
	Mm.	Mm.	Mm.
922	21	18	9
923	23	20	6
924	31	17	[1] 5
926	14	17	6
955		22	11
961	40	25	[1] 12
1213	34	23	[1] 8
1330	34	20	9
1334	25	23	9
1388	39	16	8
1390	35	21	9
1462	24	20	[1] 7
1463	26	21	10
1508	24	23	9
1557	23	21	6
1719	26	22	9
1858	24	21	5
1904	28	23	8
1905	25	19	8
1940	28	22	7
2055	39	21	8
2081	24	17	8
2124	24	19	8
2126	31	21	8
2196	27	18	7
2201	39	27	[1] 14
2217	23	19	10
2312	35	24	9
2403	29	18	10
2408	33	16	5
2488	25	16	7
3046	28	21	12
3095	23	19	8
3215	20	17	9
3342	30	18	9
3381	33	22	9
3409	22	17	8
3410	29	19	8
3439	28	20	7
3440	28	20	[1] 9
3528	32	27	12
3555	23	19	9
3622	26	21	7
3798	33	17	8
3846	25	19	7
3863		25	12
3896	26	26	9
3952	28	17	[1] 7
4025	24	18	7
4033	37	21	11
4113	25	20	9
4138	16	20	7
4139	34	15	11
4173	32	19	[1] 10

[1] Slightly planoconvex.

TABLES OF MEASUREMENTS—Continued

Keeled End Scrapers, type 2

Field catalog No.	Maximum length	Maximum width	Maximum thickness
	Mm.	Mm.	Mm.
300	35	24	10
437	28	18	8
649	48	24	[1] 10
672	32	20	11
803	28	21	7
1004	27	17	[1] 7
1024	33	24	10
1165	29	21	8
1212	31	18	9
1214	35	24	[1] 8
1242	30	22	8
1331	28	26	6
1333	31	23	11
1392		25	[1] 12
1461	21	18	10
1563	33	19	9
1565	23	16	[1] 6
1785	36	24	[1] 11
1871	27	24	9
1878	27	19	9
1906	28	23	11
1926	40	27	10
1941	24	21	8
1966	23	18	7
2054	29	21	12
2187	26	21	11
2190		18	8
2198	30	20	[1] 11
2199	30	22	7
2200	30	25	9
2248	44	27	16
2404	30	24	9
2485	24	17	6
2546	47	26	12
2583	25	21	6
2756	29	20	10
2780	26	18	7
2781	41	23	8
2919	29	25	12
2920	29	16	7
3009	32	19	[1] 6
3156	29	19	8
3437	29	22	7
3443	38	23	9
3444	29	19	11
3556	22	19	8
3665	26	17	[1] 6
3745	24	20	8
3815	23	13	5
3817	24	20	7
3821		26	11
3847	34	20	12
3898	31	22	12
3911	33	21	9
3951	30	19	10
4004		22	7
4032	28	23	9

[1] Slightly planoconvex.

TABLES OF MEASUREMENTS—Continued

Carinated End Scrapers, type 1 (cutting edge advancing to the right)

Field catalog No.	Maximum length	Maximum width	Maximum thickness
	Mm.	*Mm.*	*Mm.*
614	23	20	[1] 7
804	29	19	6
2194	25	19	7
2745	23	19	9
3155	25	21	7
3526	28	20	6
3893	29	18	[1] 6
3904	25	15	[1] 6
4135	25	15	8

[1] Slightly planoconvex.

Carinated End Scrapers, type 2 (cutting edge advancing to the left)

Field catalog No.	Maximum length	Maximum width	Maximum thickness
	Mm.	*Mm.*	*Mm.*
392	25	17	8
396	25	18	7
954	24	18	6
2984	24	17	[1] 4
4001	21	17	6
4137	25	20	8

[1] Slightly planoconvex; rest are trianguloid

TABLES OF MEASUREMENTS—Continued

End Scrapers with Left Carinate—type 3

Field catalog No.	Maximum length	Maximum width	Maximum thickness
	Mm.	*Mm.*	*Mm.*
319	25	22	8
536	29	16	6
644	23	18	5
645	31	22	7
650		28	10
760	25	19	7
856	43	30	12
1006		21	6
1209	25	19	7
1211		22	5
1275	26	22	10
1391	26	31	10
1464	32	20	9
1510	26	20	5
1558	24	23	8
1627	28	25	6
1717	22	20	8
1775	23	18	10
1816	27	22	5
1924	25	19	7
2079	24	19	6
2193	24	23	5
2202	39	20	11
2416	31	21	5
2422	29	22	[1] 4
2423	28	20	5
2663	31	21	7
2921	21	19	5
2968	21	18	7
3411	25	23	6
3441	27	22	7
3506	26	22	6
3581	24	21	7
3790	25	16	6
3999	29	21	7
4098	39	26	7
4224		30	11

[1] Planoconvex ventral surface.

TABLES OF MEASUREMENTS—Continued

End Scrapers with Right Carinate, type 4

Field catalog No.	Maximum length	Maximum width	Maximum thickness
	Mm.	*Mm.*	*Mm.*
212	25	21	[1] 7
342	34	21	[1] 6
391	24	19	5
438	24	18	6
540	23	20	6
591	24	22	6
652	25	19	6
798	22	22	4
799	32	22	7
1089	24	19	[1] 6
1203	26	21	5
1241	28	17	5
1385	23	18	7
1509	22	22	[1] 4
1624	26	19	5
1625	29	19	[1] 6
1628	35	28	11
2080	26	20	5
2082	30	19	4
2197	28	17	[1] 7
2240	22	23	[1] 7
2661	27	20	6
3096	33	19	[1] 9
3212	22	17	[1] 6
3438	25	19	6
3909	30	26	9
3953	24	18	7
4002	25	24	6
4034	28	28	5
4068	18	18	6
4136	22	17	6
4239	26	20	[1] 6

[1] Slightly planoconvex.

Slightly Modified Nodular End Scrapers

Field catalog No.	Maximum length	Maximum width	Maximum thickness
	Mm.	*Mm.*	*Mm.*
219	26	22	6
398	23	19	6
437	28	18	7
958	24	19	[1] 7
1328	23	16	4
1968	26	24	[1] 7
2037	26	20	8
2077	23	18	[1] 6
2662	26	20	[1] 6
2313	30	23	[1] 10
3908	22	21	8
4003	24	15	6
4056	23	19	8

[1] Slightly planoconvex.

TABLES OF MEASUREMENTS—Continued

Scraper-graver End Scrapers

Field catalog No.	Maximum length	Maximum width	Maximum thickness	Side
	Mm.	Mm.	Mm.	
227	27	21	5	Left.
800	27	22	9	Right.
1289	23	20	7	Do.
1879	30	26	7	Left.
1909	30	26	10	Do.
2313	32	25	9	Do.
2926	25	23	7	Both.

Small Rounded Scrapers

Field catalog No.	Maximum length	Maximum width	Maximum thickness
	Mm.	Mm.	Mm.
317	26	20	10
338	28	26	9
715	22	22	9
716	22	22	6
717	28	25	9
761	25	20	8
1329	24	19	7
1529	22	22	8
1556	22	20	8
1859	24	24	9
1972	43	39	11
2189	25	20	8
2316	16	16	9
2490	21	19	7
2778	23	20	8
2871	19	17	4
3158	19	18	8
3159	19	19	6
3214	23	21	6
4007	20	20	10
4019	28	23	11

Large Teardrop End Scrapers

Field catalog No.	Maximum length	Maximum width	Maximum thickness
	Mm.	Mm.	Mm.
929	40	22	7
1243	51	25	9
1420	46	30	9
2127	38	26	11
2339	37	21	[1] 9
2380	40	23	6

[1] Positive bulb of percussion on ventral surface eradicated by chipping.

TABLES OF MEASUREMENTS—Continued

Small Teardrop End Scrapers

Field catalog No.	Maximum length	Maximum width	Maximum thickness
	Mm.	*Mm.*	*Mm.*
1064	31	19	7
1356	25	16	5
1672	23	19	8
1716	30	19	8
2125	33	18	6
2755	31	18	8

Large Flake End Scrapers

Field catalog No.	Maximum length	Maximum width	Maximum thickness
	Mm.	*Mm.*	*Mm.*
389	34	15	2
474	28	24	8
476	37	20	9
1389	35	17	7
1908	32	22	6
1925	32	18	8
1993	45	14	7
2019	38	25	6
2078	33	17	7
2195	32	19	5
2783	30	28	6
2923	27	22	9
3047		29	9
3049	39	29	6
3479	31	16	6
3527	56	25	11
3557	36	20	4
3602	30	23	8
3717	33	24	9
3820	29	29	9

Small Planoconvex End Scrapers

Field catalog No.	Maximum length	Maximum width	Maximum thickness
	Mm.	*Mm.*	*Mm.*
1332	32	20	9
1387	23	16	[1] 8
1827	26	18	6
1943	29	20	7
2499	29	20	10
3774	27	22	9
3785	29	18	7

[1] Has a graver tip attached to side of scraper edge.

TABLES OF MEASUREMENTS—Continued

Small Flake End Scrapers

Field catalog No.	Maximum length	Maximum width	Maximum thickness
	Mm.	Mm.	Mm.
172	27	18	6
182	21	17	3
302	25	20	7
318	28	17	6
320	24	21	5
321	20	21	7
388	22	20	5
394	17	23	9
428	26	23	8
537	29	16	10
590	25	19	7
802	26	14	6
803	26	17	6
927	26	19	7
1003	21	15	6
1205	24	17	6
1206	24	17	10
1210	28	21	6
1289	23	20	[1] 7
1290	23	17	9
1507	17	20	6
1598	18	20	6
1626	26	13	7
1660	27	16	7
1690	25	18	7
1752	22	16	5
1939	27	17	6
1944	25	15	5
2100	24	16	5
2209	27	15	8
2405	27	16	5
2407	25	19	[2] 5
2560	23	17	7
2724	29	18	7
2925	24	21	6
3066	22	21	7
3084	22	20	8
3180	15	19	6
3442	29	19	6
3574	29	21	9
3818	25	18	8
3895	28	19	9
4114	22	16	4
4115	26	17	6

[1] Possible graver tip.
[2] Burinlike tool at base.

TABLES OF MEASUREMENTS—Continued

Thin Flat End Scrapers

Field catalog No.	Maximum length	Maximum width	Maximum thickness
	Mm.	*Mm.*	*Mm.*
263	18	26	5
281	18	18	4
399	38	23	9
400	28	22	8
650	24	19	5
815	22	19	5
956	26	18	5
1204	23	23	5
1208	18	19	4
1559	----	20	5
1661	26	20	8
1662	27	20	4
1718	23	16	6
1720	17	17	6
1877	19	18	5
1967	23	22	4
2142	24	23	7
2144	27	21	7
2420	20	22	5
2518	21	19	8
2664	25	25	7
2723	17	18	6
2969	23	23	6
3115	24	23	6
2194	----	19	3
3242	28	24	7
3296	----	20	7
3391	15	18	4
3848	34	30	5
3892	24	21	9
4006	20	20	5
4112	24	16	5
4204	28	18	7

TABLES OF MEASUREMENTS—Continued

Thumbnail End Scrapers

Field catalog No.	Maximum length	Maximum width	Maximum thickness
	Mm.	*Mm.*	*Mm.*
426	21	17	[1] 5
812	17	17	6
904	21	16	[1] 4
921	19	15	5
953	18	17	5
1555	18	14	4
1562	18	14	6
1691	17	17	5
1842	14	12	5
1903	16	19	5
2572	22	18	[1] 7
2744	15	16	5
2924	19	18	7
2947	19	14	3
3383	14	14	6
3554	21	15	[1] 4
3603	17	17	5
3819	16	17	6
3903	18	14	3
3905	23	13	[1] 6
3906	19	14	5
3950	20	15	[1] 6

[1] Borderline specimens. Probably should have been placed in type 1 keeled end scrapers.

Triangular End Scrapers

Field catalog No.	Maximum length	Maximum width	Maximum thickness
	Mm.	*Mm.*	*Mm.*
472	22	18	4
615	24	22	6
925	25	18	4
952	23	22	[1] 4
1739	27	20	6
1751	23	25	[1] 8
1992	29	20	7
3114	23	24	5
3436	27	21	7

[1] Planoconvex.

TABLES OF MEASUREMENTS—Continued

Trapezoidal End Scrapers

Field catalog No.	Maximum length	Maximum width	Maximum thickness
	Mm.	Mm.	Mm.
473_____	28	22	7
806_____	26	22	1 6
928_____	29	23	6
1560_____	26	18	5
1857_____	23	19	7
1942_____	23	22	7
2031_____	19	23	1 7
2188_____	22	17	4
2191_____	30	22	7
2192_____	24	18	6
3211_____	26	21	6
3673_____	23	22	7
3816_____	24	20	6
3894_____	24	19	5
3904_____	27	20	6

1 Slightly planoconvex.

Lamellar Flake Tools

Field catalog No.	Length	Breadth	Thickness	Tool type
	Mm.	Mm.	Mm.	
950_____	45	15	5	Possibly hafted knife.
1358_____	37	14	4	Scraper.
2784_____	38	22	4	Do.
4009_____	31	13	3	Knife-scraper-graver.
541_____	34	13	4	Knife.
4236_____	37	14	3	Scraper.
1945_____	28	14	3	Do.
1631_____	36	16	3	Do.
2056_____	42	13	3	Do.
3068_____	35	14	2	Do.
3116_____	40	16	4	Do.
1491_____	56	22	4	Do.
2210_____	48	16	6	Do.
763_____	40	18	4	Do.
2212_____	49	16	5. 5	Do.
1007_____	40	19	4	Do.

TABLES OF MEASUREMENTS—Continued

Large Gravers

Catalog No.	Length	Breadth	Thickness
	Mm.	Mm.	Mm.
2931	48	21	15
3261	43	24	12
276	42	19	6
535	31	19	6
3811	36	13	8
4018	26	17	7
4055	29	13	6
3912	26	16	5
477	31	24	5
957	27	16	7
3407	34	18	4

Comparable gravers from Lindenmeier site (after Roberts, 1935, pl. 13)

h	33	30	
i	37	24	
j	39	16	
k	39	30	
l	43	24	
m	39	23	

Small Gravers

Catalog No.	Length	Breadth	Thickness
	Mm.	Mm.	Mm.
809	24	21	7
2220	24	17	4
3722	19	18	4
905	18	15	4
3910	21	18	7
2315	24	17	5
341	22	20	3
3311	20	17	3
808	25	17	3
808	25	18	[1]7
2104	31	18	3
2777	22	19	6
197	27	22	8

[1] Scraper-graver. Lengths of tips range from 1 mm. to 4 mm.

LITERATURE CITED

BROWN, W. L., and ANDERSON, EDGAR.
    1947. The northern flint corns. Ann. Missouri Bot. Garden, vol. 34, pp. 1–28.
BURKITT, MILES CRAWFORD.
    1956. The old Stone Age: A study of Paleolithic times. 3d ed. New York.
COOPER, PAUL L.
    1949. Recent investigations in Fort Randall and Oahe Reservoirs, South
        Dakota. Amer. Antiq., vol. 14, No. 4, pp. 300–310.
FAIRBANKS, CHARLES H.
    1942. The taxonomic position of Stalling's Island, Georgia. Amer. Antiq.,
        vol. 7, No. 3, pp. 223–231.
FLINT, RICHARD FOSTER.
    1955. Pleistocene geology of Eastern South Dakota. U.S. Dept. Interior,
        Geol. Surv. Prof. Pap. No. 262.
HEWES, GORDON W.
    1949. The 1947 summer field session in archeology, University of North
        Dakota. Proc. Fifth Plains Conf. for Archeol., Notebook 1, Lab.
        Anthrop., Univ. Nebraska, pp. 21–24.
HURT, WESLEY R., Jr.
    1952. Report of the investigation of the Scalp Creek site, 39GR1, and the
        Ellis Creek site, 39GR2, South Dakota, 1941, 1951. South Dakota
        Archaeol. Comm. Archaeol. Studies, Circ. No. 4.
    1957 a. The Rosa archeological project. Museum News, W. H. Over Mu-
        seum, vol. 19, No 6.
    1957 b. Report of the investigation of the Swan Creek site, 39WW7, Wal-
        worth County, South Dakota, 1954–1956. South Dakota Archaeol.
        Comm., Archaeol. Studies, Circ. No. 7.
LEHMER, DONALD J.
    1951. Pottery types from the Dodd site, Oahe Reservoir, South Dakota.
        Plains Archeol. Conf. News Letter, vol. 4, No. 2, pp. 3–15.
    1954. Archeological investigations in the Oahe Dam area, 1950–1951. Bur.
        Amer. Ethnol. Bull. 158, Riv. Bas. Surv. Pap. No. 7.
MACNEISH, RICHARD S.
    1954. The Pointed Mountain site near Fort Liard, Northwest Territories,
        Canada. Amer. Antiq., vol. 19, No. 3, pp. 234–253.
    1958. An introduction to the archeology of southeast Manitoba. Nat. Mus.
        Canada Bull. 157, Anthrop. Ser. No. 44. Department of Northern
        Affairs and National Resources, Ottawa.
METCALF, GEORGE.
    1956. Additional data from the Dodd and Phillips Ranch sites, South Dakota.
        Amer. Antiq., vol. 21, No. 3, pp. 305–309.
NICKERSON, N. H., and HOU DING.
    1954. Maize from the Dodd and Phillips Ranch sites. Bur. Amer. Ethnol.,
        Bull. 158, Riv. Bas. Surv. Pap. No. 7, Appen. 6, pp. 180–181.
OVER, W. H., and THOMAS, C. S.
    1921. Birds of South Dakota. South Dakota Geol. and Nat. Hist. Surv.
        Bull. No. 9.
RITCHIE, WILLIAM A.
    1944. The pre-Iroquoian occupation of New York State. Mem. Rochester
        Museum of Arts and Science.
ROBERTS, FRANK H. H., JR.
    1935. A Folsom Complex. Smithsonian Misc. Coll., vol. 94, No. 4.

SHANTZ, HOMER L., and ZON, RAPHAEL.
    1924. The natural vegetation of the United States. Atlas of American Agri-
        culture, U.S. Dept. Agric., Washington.
SMITH, CARLYLE S.
    1951. Pottery types from the Talking Crow site, Fort Randall Reservoir,
        South Dakota. Plains Archeol. Conf. News Letter, vol. 4, No. 3,
        pp. 32–41.
SPAULDING, ALBERT C.
    1956. The Arzberger site, Hughes County, South Dakota. Univ. Michigan,
        Mus. Anthrop., Occ. Contr. No. 16.
STEWART, GEORGE R.
    1946. Man : an autobiography. New York.
STRONG, WILLIAM D.
    1940. From history to prehistory in the northern Great Plains. Smithsonian
        Misc. Coll., vol. 100, pp. 353–394.
WEDEL, WALDO R.
    1936. An introduction to Pawnee archeology. Bur. Amer. Ethnol. Bull. 112.
WHEELER, RICHARD P.
    1954. Check list of Middle Missouri pottery wares, types, and subtypes.
        Plains Anthrop. No. 2, pp. 3–21.
WHITE, THEODORE.
    1953. Observations on the butchering technique of some aboriginal people,
        No. 2. Amer. Antiq., vol. 19, No. 2, pp. 160–164.
    1954. Observations on the butchering techniques of some aboriginal people.
        Amer. Antiq., vol. 19, No. 3, pp. 254–264.
WILL, GEORGE F., and HECKER, THAD C.
    1944. The Upper Missouri River Valley aboriginal culture in North Dakota.
        North Dakota Hist. Quart., vol. 11, Nos. 1 and 2.
WILL, GEORGE F., and SPINDEN, HERBERT J.
    1906. The Mandans; a study of their culture, archeology and language.
        Pap. Peabody Mus. Amer. Archeol. and Ethnol., Harvard Univ., vol.
        3, No. 4.
WILMETH, ROSCOE.
    1958. Report of the investigation of the Payne site, 39WW302, Walworth
        County, South Dakota, 1956. Archeol. Stud., Cir. No. 8.

APPENDIX 5

HUMAN SKELETAL MATERIAL FROM THE VICINITY OF THE HOSTERMAN SITE (39PO7), OAHE RESERVOIR, SOUTH DAKOTA

By William M. Bass

Department of Sociology and Anthropology, University of Kansas

INTRODUCTION

The preceding article by Carl F. Miller describes the archeological investigation of the Hosterman site (39PO7) in Potter County, S. Dak. No human skeletal material was recovered during his excavations. In September of 1962, while boating on the Oahe Reservoir, Richard Weeks of Pierre, S. Dak., discovered the partial remains of six human burials eroding out of the east bank of the Missouri River and sent the bones to me for identification. Mr. Weeks is an amateur collector who, in the past few years, has checked the changing banks caused by the rising waters of the Reservoir. I accompanied Mr. Weeks on two such boat trips in the summer of 1962 and at that time encouraged him to collect carefully all human skeletal material for study. Charles L. Keeler, a student in anthropology, assisted in the preparation of the material herein described.

The skeletal material was found just north of Whitlocks Crossing on the east side of the Reservoir at an elevation of 1,565–1,570 feet. The location of the find corresponds to that of the Hosterman site, and the burials therefore may have been associated with that earth-lodge village.

In his letter of transmittal, Mr. Weeks states that the skeletons were found in three different concentrations. The first was found in 1 foot of water; the ribs, vertebrae, and mandible were in the original burial position in the mud with the rest of the bones scattered nearby in the water. A few more scattered bones were found on the bank approximately 30 feet south. A complete burial was found in the bank about 10 feet from the first group. The skeleton "was on its back, head toward the west, legs flexed to the right, arms down to the sides with hands on pelvis" (Weeks, 1962, personal communication).

In no case were there any associated artifacts, covering, or anything else which might suggest cultural affiliation.

DESCRIPTION OF BURIALS

The bones were submitted in groups corresponding to the three areas of concentration in which they were found. We have retained these area designations and have assigned individual numbers to the remains of the six individuals present. Many of the bones were broken and scattered due to wave action and slumping of the loess. Whenever possible the bones were reconstructed to obtain anthropometric measurements.

GROUP 1

Group one (those found in the water) consists of portions of two skeletons. These have been numbered Individuals 1 and 2.

Individual 1.—Male, 35–45 years old; the skeleton material of this individual was fairly complete though fragmentary, but the skull was broken beyond repair. Age at death is based on changes in the pubic symphysis after McKern and Stewart (1957, p. 85). Although not a good criterion for aging, cranial suture closure substantiates the assessed age according to Krogman (1962, pp. 76–91). There is complete endocranial closure but ectocranially all of the sutures are visible except for a small area of the sagittal suture between the apex and obelion. The determination of sex is based on pelvis, cranial, and long bone morphology. Stature estimations are based on measurements of the left humerus using Trotter and Gleser's (1958, p. 120) formula for Mongoloids. The three parts of the sternum (manubrium, body, and xiphoid process) have fused completely. Slight arthritic lipping is present on all of the vertebrae with fusion of the second and third cervicals.

Stature range:		
Low	167. 02 cm.	(5′ 5⅝″)
Mean	171. 18 cm.	(5′ 7½″)
High	175. 34 cm.	(5′ 9″)

Individual 2.—Child, approximately 6 years old, represented only by a right humerus. Age, based on a maximum diaphyseal length of 162 mm., is estimated from mean measurements given by Johnston (1962, p. 251), whose measurements of sub-adult Indian Knoll skeletons go only through 5.5 years with a mean humeral length of 154.67 mm. for the age group 4.5 to 5.5.

GROUP 2

The analysis revealed the partial remains of at least three individuals based upon the occurrence of three right femora.

Individual 3.—Male, 35–50 years old; represented by a right femur and possibly a right and left humerus, a fragmentary right scapula and a mandible. The femoral head has a maximum diameter of 46 mm.

which places it in the male range for this measurement (Krogman 1962, p. 144). The mandible, two humeri, and scapula were assigned to this individual on the basis of coloring of the bones and general morphological characteristics. The mandible has a square chin indicative of the male sex. The humeri are rugged and neither contains a septal aperture. Age is based on wear of the teeth. The enamel of the masticating surfaces of the eight remaining teeth are worn off completely and correspond to Hrdlička's (1952, p. 53) third stage of wear. Age for this stage is suggested as 35–50. Only eight teeth (four incisors, right canine, left first premolar and the right and left first molars) are present. The remaining six teeth were lost after death. The third molars have not erupted. The missing right first premolar was abscessed and may have been lost just prior to death since little or no resorption had taken place. There is a cavity in the first left molar below the gum line and all of the teeth present contain tarter.

Stature range:

Low	162. 51 cm.	(5' 4'')
Mean	166. 31 cm.	(5' 5½'')
High	170. 11 cm.	(5' 7'')

Individual 4.—Adult female (?) represented by a fragmentary and weathered right femur shaft only. Sex, which is questionable, is based on the smallness and gracility of the shaft.

Individual 5.—Child, approximately 7 years old, represented by a right femur shaft only. Age is based on maximum diaphyseal length (222 mm.) which, when compared with the generalized postnatal growth curve of the femur given by Stewart (1954, pp. 407–450) suggests an age of around 7 years.

GROUP 3

Group 3 consists of the complete flexed burial of an adult interred with the head oriented toward the west. When first discovered only a small portion of the skull was exposed in the face of the bank. No artifacts or covering of the burial were found. Mr. Weeks states, however, that "the soil was very discolored, a yellowish green" (personal communication) and suggests that this may be due to a decayed hide covering.

Individual 6.—(fig. 52). Male, 30–40 years old. Age of this individual is based on changes in the pubic symphysis and corresponds to a mean age of 35.84 according to McKern and Stewart's (1957, p. 85) classification. Wear on the teeth compares with stage 3 in Hrdlička's (1952, p. 53) system. Cranial sutures are beginning to close endocranially and are visible ectocranially. Arthritic lipping is present in the fourth and fifth lumbar vertebrae only. Sex is based on

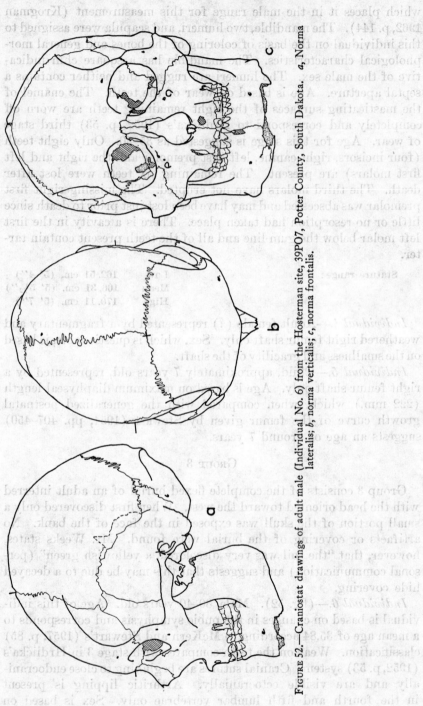

FIGURE 52.—Craniostat drawings of adult male (Individual No. 6) from the Hosterman site, 39PO7, Potter County, South Dakota. 4, Norma lateralis; b, norma verticalis; c, norma frontalis.

pelvic, cranial, and long bone morphology. All are consistent in exhibiting characteristics considered to be those of the male sex. Stature was calculated using the formula for Mongoloids on measurements for the femur plus the tibia given by Trotter and Gleser (1958, p. 120).

Stature range: Low   168.51 cm. (5′ 6 6/8″)
               Mean 171.74 cm. (5′ 7 5/8″)
               High 174.98 cm. (5′ 8 7/8″)

ANALYSIS

Table 1 gives the cranial measurements and indices for Individuals 1 and 6 and for the mandible of Individual 3. All are males and represent the only measurable cranial material.

Stature calculations could be made on three individuals, all males. It is interesting to note that the mean estimated stature does not vary more than 5.43 cm. (2⅛ inches) among the three. Individual 1 has a calculated mean stature of 171.18 cm. (5 feet, 7½ inches); Individual 3, 166.31 cm. (5 feet, 5½ inches); and Individual 6, 171.74 cm. (5 feet, 7⅝ inches) for a sample mean stature of 169.74 cm. or 5 feet, 6⅝ inches.

TABLE 1.—*Measurements and indices of 39PO7 male crania* [1]

	No. 1	No. 3	No. 6	Mean
	Mm.	*Mm.*	*Mm.*	*Mm.*
Maximum length			177	
Maximum breadth			137	
Basion-bregma height			(132)	
Basion-porion height			(20)	
Cranial module			(148.66)	
Bizygomatic breadth			143	
Minimum frontal breadth			92	
Endobasion-nasion			102	
Nasal height	53		57	55
Nasal breadth	26		26	26
Orbital height:				
Right	35			
Left			37	
Orbital breadth:				
Right	47			
Left			42	
Length-height			(74.58)	
Breadth-height			(96.35)	
Indices:				
Cranial [2]			77.40	
Mean height			(84.08)	
Fronto-parietal			67.15	
Orbital:				
No. 1	74.47			
No. 6			88.10	81.28
Nasal	49.06		45.61	47.34
Flatness of cranial base			(15.15)	
Mandible:				
Bigonial breadth	113	102	(106)	(107)
Symphysis height	(36)	38		(37)
Bicondylar diameter		132		
Ascending Ramus height		72	76	74
Corpal length (Gonion-Gnathion)	88	93		90.5

[1] In all tables figures in parentheses represent estimated measurements.
[2] Indices of the cranium are based on measurements indicated here.

DISCUSSION

Because there were no cultural artifacts associated with the burials, no positive cultural identification can be assigned. However, a comparison of the morphological characteristics of the crania may give some indication of possible cultural affiliation. Table 2 compares selected cranial measurements and indices for two adult males from 39PO7 with samples of Arikara, Mandan, Pawnee, and Central Plains Phase associated skeletons. The Arikara and Mandan were inhabitants of the region around the Hosterman site. Recently, summaries of anthropometric measurements of skeletal material for protohistoric Arikara (Bass, 1961) and Mandan (Bass and Birkby, 1962) have been published.

One of the major areas of cranial difference between the Arikara and Mandan is in the index. The Mandan are dolichocranic, whereas the Arikara are mesocranic. The only individual from 39PO7 upon which a cranial index could be calculated gave an index of 77.40 or mesocranic. On the basis of both the length-height and mean height indices, the single male from the Hosterman site falls closer to the Arikara means. Although cultural associations based on cranial measurements of only one individual are quite speculative, Individual 6 seems to be related most closely morphologically to the Arikara.

TABLE 2.—*A comparison of selected mean measurements and indices*

	39PO7 No. 1	39PO7 No. 6	Arikara [1] N 116 [3]	Mandan [2] N 12	Pawnee [1] N 29 [4]	Central [1] Plains N 37 [5]
	Mm.	Mm.	Mm.	Mm.	Mm.	Mm.
Glabella-occipital length		177	174.7	184.50	175.8	174.7
Maximum breadth		137	140.7	136.17	139.6	143.0
Basion-bregma height		(132)	132.9	131.75	128.7	137.7
Indices:						
Cranial		77.40	78.6	73.90	79.3	82.5
Length-height		(74.58)	74.5	71.49	73.2	79.5
Mean height		(84.08)	83.59	82.31	81.55	86.35
Upper facial		52.45	53.40		51.80	51.50
Nasal	49.06	45.61	49.27		49.03	51.96
Orbital:						
Right	74.47					
Left	8	88.10	82.31		85.66	78.65

[1] Bass, 1961.
[2] Bass and Birkby, 1962.
[3] The sample size varies with the individual measurement but in no case are there less than 49.
[4] In no case is the sample size less than 17.
[5] In no case is the sample size less than 14.

REFERENCES CITED

BASS, WILLIAM M.

———— The variation in physical types of the prehistoric Plains Indians. Ph. D. dissertation. University of Pennsylvania, Philadelphia, 1961.

BASS, WILLIAM M., AND BIRKBY, WALTER H.

1962. The first human skeletal material from the Huff site, 32MO11, and a summary of putative Mandan skeletal material. Plains Authrop., vol. 7, No. 17, pp. 164–177.

HRDLIČKA, ALEŠ.
   1952. Practical anthropometry. T. D. Stewart, ed. The Wistar Institute
         of Anatomy and Biology. Philadelphia.

JOHNSTON, FRANCIS E.
   1962. Growth of the long bones of infants and children at Indian Knoll.
         Amer. Journ. Phys. Anthrop., n.s., vol. 20, No. 3, pp. 249–254.

KROGMAN, W. M.
   1962. The human skeleton in forensic medicine. Charles Thomas. Spring-
         field.

MCKERN, THOMAS W., and STEWART, T. D.
   1957. Skeletal age changes in young American males. Headquarters Quarter-
         master Research and Development Command. Tech. Rep. No. EP–
         45. Natick, Mass.

STEWART, T. D.
   1954. Evaluation of the evidence from the skeleton. *In* Legal Medicine.
         Mosby, St. Louis.

TROTTER, MILDRED, AND GLESER, GOLDINE C.
   1958. A re-evaluation of estimation of stature based on measurements of
         stature taken during life and of long bones after death. Amer.
         Journ. Phys. Anthrop., n.s., vol. 16, No. 1, pp. 79–123.

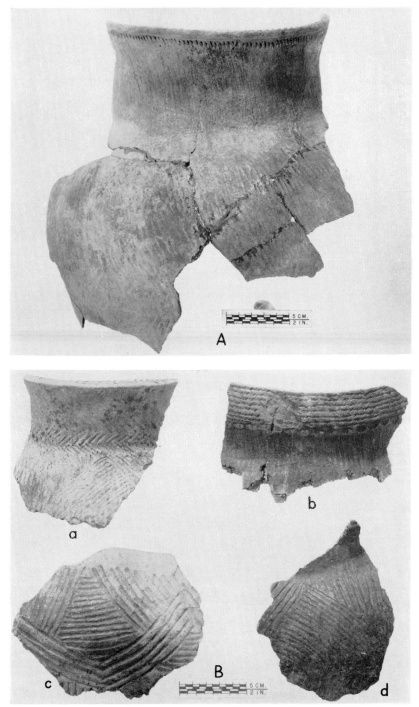

A, B, Vertical and S-shaped rim types, Hosterman site.

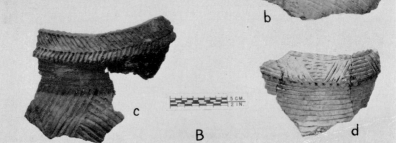

A, B, Rim types, showing typical forms and treatments.

A, B, Typical rims with and without handles.

A, B, Rim types, Hosterman site.

A, B, Cord-impressed rim treatments, Hosterman site.

A, B, Incised rim sherds, Hosterman site.

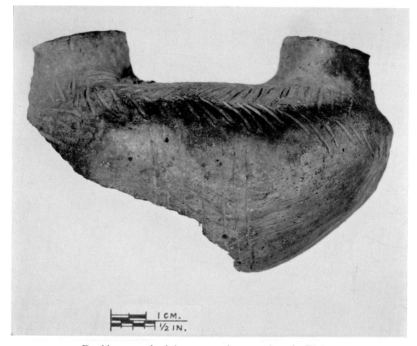

Double spouted miniature vessel, unusual to the Plains.

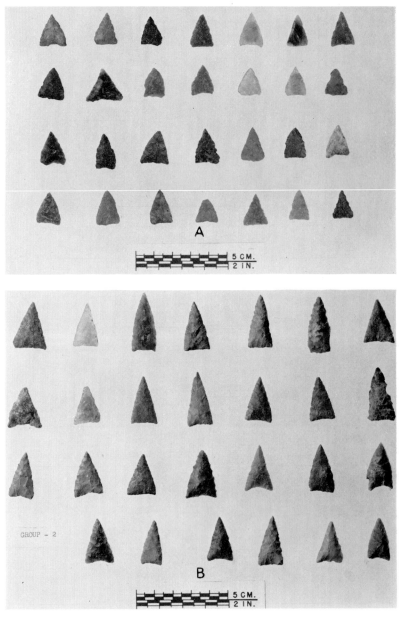

A, *B*, Group 1 and Group 2 projectile types, Hosterman site.

A, B, Group 3, Group 4, and notched projectile types.

A, B, Microblades and lamellar flake knives.

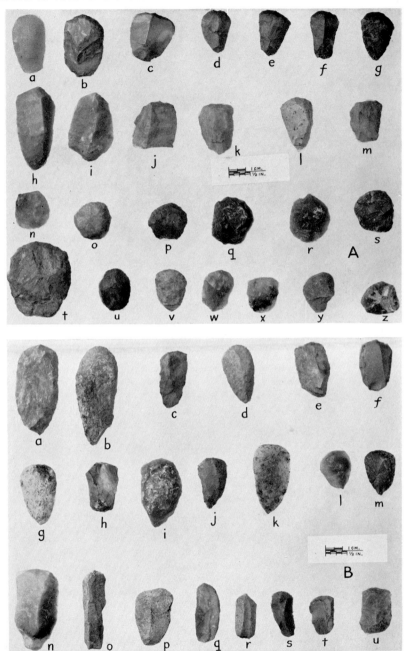

A, B, Scraper types, Hosterman site.

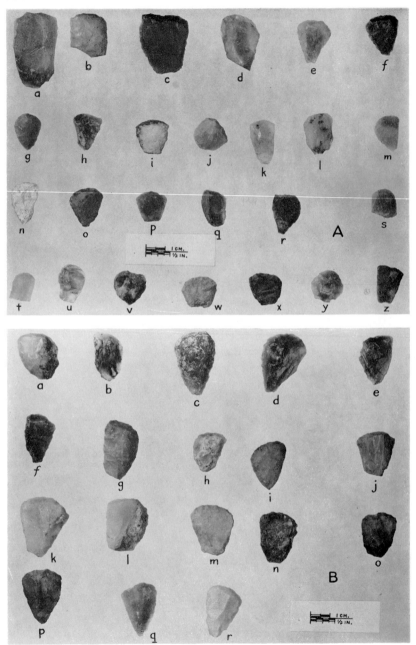

A, *B*, Scraper types, Hosterman site.

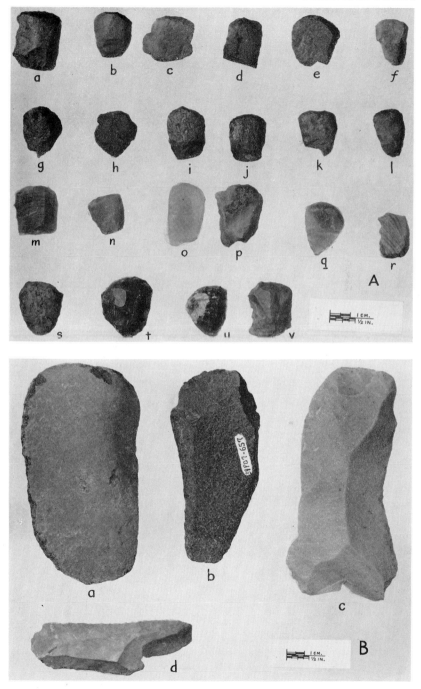

A, B, End and side scraper types.

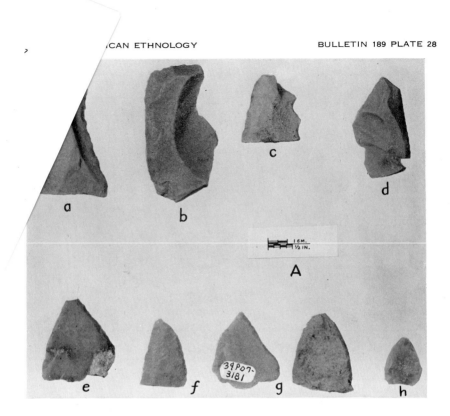

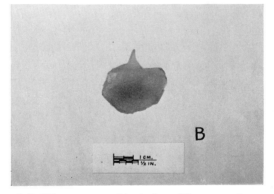

A, B, Side scrapers and burin form, Hosterman site.

A, B, Knife forms and biface ovates.

A, B, Flake knives and side scrapers; grooved ax and maul.

Graver forms, Hosterman site.

A, B, Lamellar flake tools.

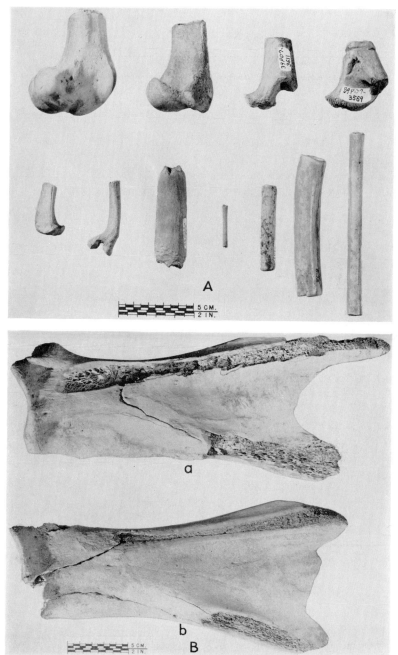

A, B, Cut bone sections, worked antler, bone tubes, and scapula hoes.

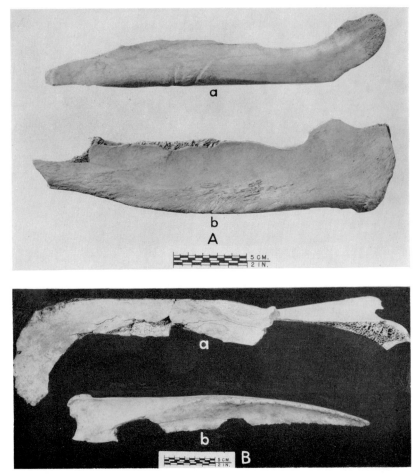

A, B, Scapula tools; fleshers and sickles.

A, *B*, Scapula knives and fleshing tools.

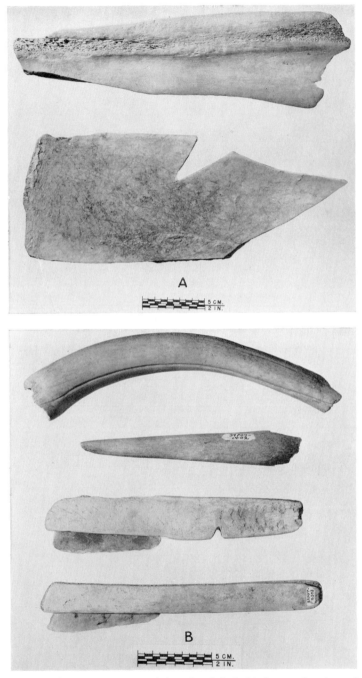

A, B, Scapula cleaver, pentagonal-shaped tool, hafted knives, and antler tools.

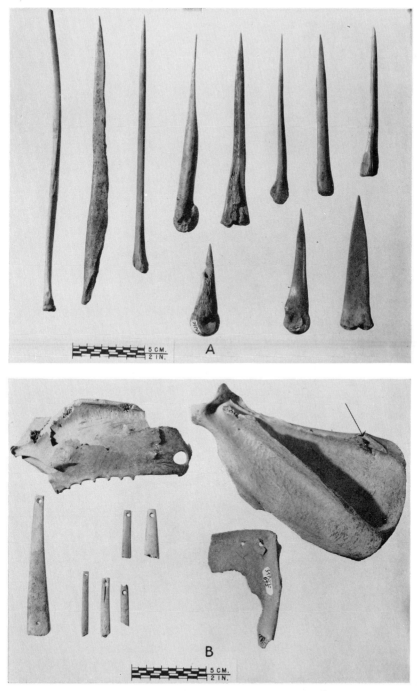

A, B, Bone awl types and miscellaneous worked-bone objects.

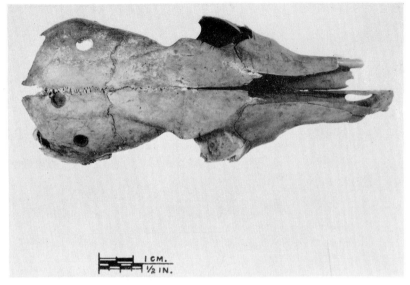

Fetish or trophy skull of *Vulpes velox*.

SMITHSONIAN INSTITUTION
Bureau of American Ethnology
Bulletin 189

River Basin Surveys Papers, No. 36
Archeological Investigations at the Hickey Brothers Site (39LM4),
Big Bend Reservoir, Lyman County, South Dakota

By WARREN W. CALDWELL, LEE G. MADISON, and BERNARD GOLDEN

267

CONTENTS

	PAGE
Introduction	271
The Hickey Brothers site (39LM4)	272
Excavation procedure	273
Stratigraphy	274
Features	275
Fortifications	276
Habitation areas	279
Artifacts	284
Pottery	284
Lithic materials	285
Bone materials	286
Conclusions	287
Literature cited	289

ILLUSTRATIONS

(All plates follow page 290)

PLATES

39. *a*, The Hickey Brothers site, looking across the northwestern bastion, Missouri River flood plain in middle distance; 39LM4–3. *b*, Feature 4, the southeastern bastion, prior to excavation; 39LM4–16.
40. *a*, Feature 4 cleared of sod and staked in 10-foot squares; 39LM4–19. *b*, Surface contour of ditch in the vicinity of Feature 5, prior to excavation; 39LM4–22.
41. *a*, The stockade line of Feature 4, excavation completed; 39LM–46. *b*, Feature 18, postholes of the stockade along the inner edge of the defensive ditch, fire area about 5.0 feet to the east; 39LM4–48.
42. *a*, Profile of west wall, Feature 5. The dark fill outlines the aboriginal ditch excavation; 39LM4–30. *b*, Profile of east wall, Feature 6, showing rodent disturbance and possible postholes; 39LM4–24.
43. *a*, Feature 10, excavation completed, 1958; 39LM4–40; *b*, Feature 25, a burned area with a concentration of sherds, possibly roof fill of a house; 39LM4–42.
44. *a*, Feature 39, a house of indeterminate form, postholes, firepit on pedestals; 39LM4–51. *b*, Celt. *c*, *d*, Shaft smoothers. *e*, Chopper. *f*, *g*, Fleshers. *h*, Scapula hoe. *i*, Quill flattener. *j*, Shaft wrench.
45. *a–d*, Projectile points. *e*, *g*, *h*, *j*, *m*, *n*, Knives. *f*, *i*, *k*, Scrapers. *l*, *o*, Pipe fragments.
46. *a*, *d*, *g*, Riggs Punctate. *b*, *c*, *e*, *h*, Riggs Flared Rim. *f*, *i*, Anderson Low Rim. *j*, Cord-roughened body sherd. *k*, Simple stamped body sherd.

269

TEXT FIGURES

PAGE

53. The Hickey Brothers Site, plan_____ (facing) 273
54. Plan of bastion, Feature 4_____ (facing) 277
55. Profiles, plan, Features 5 and 7_____ 278
56. Profiles, plan, Features 3 and 6_____ 280
57. Feature 39, plan_____ 282

THE HICKEY BROTHERS SITE (39LM4), BIG BEND RESERVOIR, LYMAN COUNTY, SOUTH DAKOTA [1]

By Warren W. Caldwell, Lee G. Madison, and Bernard Golden

INTRODUCTION

The Hickey Brothers site (39LM4) was excavated during the summer of 1958 as part of the investigations of the Missouri Basin Project, Smithsonian Institution, within the projected Big Bend Reservoir of central South Dakota. The site was approached with every expectation of adding materially to the corpus of data bearing upon the "middle period" of village occupation along the Missouri main stem. The Hickey Brothers site appeared to be particularly important because it was fortified in a distinctive manner and the fortification system was so well preserved. Unfortunately, the site remains an enigma. The results of the intensive excavations of 1958 were disappointing, even shocking. An insignificant number of artifacts was found, and beyond a detailed coverage of bastion construction, there was little evidence of architectural features.

Since problems had been created rather than solved by the 1958 season, a brief period was devoted to further work at the site in 1959. Feature 10, a putative house depression tested the previous summer, was reexcavated and a portion of the original trench widened and extended. A corner of a poorly preserved rectangular structure was uncovered, but because of time limitations the work could be carried no further. Beyond a few very small potsherds, there was no addition to the artifact inventory.

The excavations of the 1958 season and the initial analysis of site features and artifacts were carried out by Bernard Golden, then attached temporarily to the staff of the Missouri Basin Project. The brief investigations of 1959 were under the direction of Warren W. Caldwell, archeologist, Missouri Basin Project. The final statement presented here is the joint effort of Lee G. Madison, museum aide, Missouri Basin Project, and Warren W. Caldwell. Madison is responsible for the description and analysis of artifacts and site features, while Caldwell functioned largely in an editorial capacity.

[1] Submitted December 1959.

271

THE HICKEY BROTHERS SITE (39LM4)

The Hickey Brothers site is a large village area enclosed by an elaborate fortification ditch. The site is situated in Lyman County, S. Dak., on the right or west bank of the Missouri River, approximately 7 miles north of the modern reservation town of Lower Brule and 35 road miles northwest of Chamberlain. This is one of a large group of important sites concentrated in the constricted neck of the great loop that forms the downstream margin of the Big Bend of the Missouri.

This site lies on the eastern or riverward edge of MT–1 (Coogan and Irving, 1959), the second terrace above the river. MT–0, the current flood plain, is poorly developed here. It forms a narrow bench just below the site, widening to the south but pinching out abruptly a short distance upstream from the village. Fresh-water springs emerge from the face of MT–1 in the immediate vicinity of the site. Although the springs are scarcely usable today, there is evidence that they have produced a much larger flow in the past.

To the west of the site, MT–1 rises gently toward an irregular remnant of MT–2, the highest terrace, which forms a jagged backbone within the loop of the bend. Immediately to the north is a deep ravine system, and to the south the village is bounded by site 39LM215, a late village occupation probably related to the Fort Thompson Focus.

In the immediate vicinity of the village, the terrace surface is level and sparsely grassed (pl. 39, a). Tree cover is restricted to MT–0. Such surface irregularities as are evident consist of archeological features or result from recent ranch activities. The Hickey Ranch buildings formerly stood on the site, and much of the area within the village was used for stock pens and corrals. The foundations of the ranchhouse are still visible near the east-central border of the village.

The principal feature of the site is a fortification system consisting of a well-conceived and carefully executed ditch or moat with seven projecting bastions (fig. 53). The fortified perimeter is about 2,000 feet in total length, enclosing an area of slightly less than 2 acres. The ditch is present only on three sides of the village. The eastern boundary, fronting on the river, is formed by the terrace edge. Since it is quite steep, the scarp itself would have served as an excellent defense, particularly if it were backed by a palisade or curtain wall.

The area enclosed by the ditch is best described as "coffin-shaped." It measures 1,150 feet along the north-south axis and 700 feet in an east-west direction. The long axis is oriented toward magnetic north. The southern arm of the ditch forms a straight line on azimuth 90° to 270°. At its western end, it angles abruptly north, expanding in a gentle arc to the widest point of the village enclosure (about ⅘ of the distance from the southern end), where it swings to the northeast in a wide curve back toward the terrace edge.

The seven bastions are all similar in form and size. Each is roughly semicircular, averaging 40 feet wide and projecting outward about 40 feet from the moat line. Bastions were built at the corners of the village enclosure and in the intervals between. The distances separating bastions, proceeding in a clockwise direction from the southeast corner, are as follows:

Feet

No. 1 to No. 2—310
No. 2 to No. 3—310
No. 3 to No. 4—310
No. 4 to No. 5—250
No. 5 to No. 6—240
No. 6 to No. 7—230

The distance between adjacent bastions decreases along the curved portion of the ditch that forms the northern edge of the village. This fact suggests that the location of each defensive feature was carefully planned in relation to the whole. Reducing the distance between the bastions on a curved section of wall was a necessity if the enfilade was not to be lost. Otherwise there would be blind areas along the wall which could not be reached by the defenders' fire. It is worth noting that the bastions at the Black Partizan site (39LM 218), a short distance to the south of the Hickey Brothers site, average only 150 feet apart. Here the ditch forms a great oval, thus demanding a shorter bastion interval. The fortifications at the Hickey Brothers site, from a functional point of view, were efficient and well thought out.

Within the area enclosed by the defensive ditch are a number of shallow, circular depressions of various sizes. The largest are about 50 feet in diameter and seldom deeper than 0.5 foot at the center. Such depressions are scattered widely over the site but with no apparent pattern of arrangement. Since they appeared to be house depressions, a number were tested, both by area excavation and trench or pit tests. In only three cases was there firm evidence of aboriginal occupation (see below).

EXCAVATION PROCEDURE

A grid system was utilized in conjunction with a detailed map of the site made by a Missouri Basin Project reconnaissance party in 1956. A north-south base line, paralleling the long axis of the site, was established from a primary datum located at the southwest corner of the ranchhouse foundation mentioned above (fig. 53). An east-west line, perpendicular to the initial base line was extended from the primary datum to a point beyond the western edge of the ditch.

The datum stake was arbitrarily designated as N1000, E1000, thus confining the entire site to the northeast quadrant of the grid, with the zero point 1,000 feet south and 1,000 feet west of the primary datum. All points on the grid are given as coordinates, first north from the east-west zero line, then east from the north-south line, i.e., N700, E800.

Stakes were set at convenient intervals for the purpose of laying out excavation units. The only such unit not planned in this way was Feature 3, since work on it had begun before the grid was established. Several excavation units consisted of 5.0-foot and 10.0-foot squares. These were designated by the position of the grid point in the southeast corner of the square.

For vertical recording, the top of the primary datum stake was arbitrarily assigned an elevation of 100.0 feet and all other elevations were related to this point. Elevations were systematically recorded at the top of each grid stake and at the ground surface next to it via stadia rod and transit. The provenience of artifacts and other material of special significance was recorded by means of two horizontal coordinates on the grid and a vertical measurement taken from the ground level nearest the find or from a datum line based on a grid stake. All obviously recent materials from at or near the surface, unidentifiable fragments of unworked bone, stones, and small undecorated sherds, were discarded. In each case, however, a note was made of the quantity and level in which they appeared.

After the sod was removed from an area to be excavated, the underlying fill was skimmed with shovels so that architectural or other features might be seen as soon as they appeared. Trowels were used to scrape a clean floor at the end of each level and also to profile the trench and pit walls. In a few instances, where little or no cultural material was apparent, 0.5-foot increments were removed by spading. Except Feature 3, which was dug by natural levels, all excavation units were divided into 0.5-foot vertical intervals. Profiles in all excavation units were scraped clean and the stratigraphy noted.

Earth pillars were left to support the grid stakes, and in Feature 4, the southeastern bastion, north-south and east-west balks remained after excavation. In most cases, the trenches and pits were excavated to a depth of 4.0 feet below surface, well into the gray silt or loess that underlies the site (see below).

STRATIGRAPHY

A uniform stratigraphic sequence was found throughout the site. Three distinctive units were present:

Zone 1—surface to 0.4–0.8 foot is composed of dark brown, moist humus containing many small rootlets. Aboriginal material occurred in this deposit, together with an abundance of modern refuse.

Zone 2—0.4–0.8 foot to 1.0–1.4 feet below surface is limited to a dark-brown
   humus horizon. It is lacking in some portions of the site so that locally,
   zone 1 may be in direct contact with zone 3. Artifacts were present in
   this layer together with small quantities of recent material.

Zone 3—1.0–1.4 feet to limit of excavation is a dry, compact, silty deposit (loess),
   light gray in color. Aboriginal material was found in the upper part
   of this layer.

As noted above, the majority of excavation units reached a depth
of only 4.0 feet below surface; however, the central pit in Feature 8
was carried to 12.0 feet. Here there was a gradual transition (3.5–5.0
feet) from the matrix of zone 3 to a layer of silt and sand. The sandy
texture increased from 5.0 to 6.6 feet. From 6.6 to 7.5 feet the deposit
consisted of brown clay with areas of dark carbon staining. The pit
terminated in gravel at 10.0 to 12.0 feet.

In the section of the defensive ditch excavated adjacent to Feature
4, the southeast bastion, there was a black midden deposit slightly
below the present ground surface. It undoubtedly accumulated as
refuse thrown in the ditch (see p. 276).

FEATURES

The term "Feature" was applied to anything at the site which
required description or discussion. After designating the site as
Feature 1, and the defensive system as Feature 2, numbers were assigned consecutively to cultural phenomena and to each excavation
unit (i.e., trench or test pit) (see fig. 53). Actually, only a small
proportion of the features represent the former; the majority designate excavation units.

In the course of the 1958 season, a number of the surface depressions
were examined and a large portion of the site was investigated by
means of test pits. In addition, one bastion was excavated, a section
of the palisade wall was exposed, and two transverse trenches were
cut across the defensive ditch.

Test trenches.—Four trenches were excavated; three of them (Features 8, 10, and 11) were intended to test well-marked depressions
within the village enclosure. Feature 9 was excavated beyond the
southern limits of the defensive ditch in order to test for cultural
material outside of the fortified area. The test trenches were 5.0
feet wide and ranged from 35.0 to 50.0 feet long. Each was dug to a
depth of 2.0 feet below surface, then a 5.0 by 5.0 foot section in the
center of the trench was continued downward to ascertain if cultural
material lay at a greater depth.

In Features 8 and 9, the fill was entirely sterile. Metal, brick,
crockery, and other objects of recent origin were present on the sur-

face of Features 10 and 11, occurring to a depth of 0.5 foot in the former. The reexcavation of Feature 10 during the 1959 season produced some evidence of a rectangular structure; this will be described in greater detail below.

Test pits.—Since the initial trenches proved to be largely unproductive, a number of smaller test pits were excavated in an attempt to locate more intensely occupied areas. A total of 25 pits (5.0 by 5.0 feet, 4.0 feet deep) were dug, 19 of which failed to produce positive results, although bone fragments and unworked stones appeared in some. In Feature 20, a projectile point, an animal bone, and a quantity of charcoal were excavated from zone 1. Feature 26, located within a shallow, circular depression, about 35.0 feet in diameter, contained a dark matrix which included stone and mammal bone in the 0.5- to 1.0-foot interval. No structural evidences were found in either of these pits. Four additional tests, however, produced enough evidence to warrant expansion of the excavation units. These Features (12, 14, 22, 23) will be described below in the discussion of Features 25, 39, and 40.

FORTIFICATIONS

Feature 4, the bastion situated near the southeast corner of the site, was semicircular in shape, with a diameter of slightly more than 40 feet (fig. 53). Prior to excavation, the surrounding ditch averaged about 10 feet in width and 2 feet in depth, measured from the adjacent soil surface (pl. 39, *b*).

The bastion and adjoining ditch areas were excavated in 0.5 foot levels following the surface contour (pl. 40, *a*, *b*). The excavation was carried to a depth of approximately 1 foot over the entire area and a foot or so lower in the northern part in an effort to locate postholes. In addition, a 5.0-foot test pit was dug into the center of the feature to a depth of 4.0 feet. The stratigraphy here did not differ from that found elsewhere in the site, except for a narrow band of burned material (about 2 inches thick) at the bottom of zone 1. In addition, flecks of charcoal were scattered throughout the deposits in the pit.

At about 4.0 feet below the surface, in the deepest part of the defensive ditch, was a soft, very dark matrix that contained two concentrations of disarticulated animal bone. Although the quantity of midden material is not large, it does suggest that the ditch was used for refuse disposal during the life of the village.

A small number of artifacts was found in the course of the bastion excavation. Included were projectile points, pipe fragments, a trapezoidal blade, a ground celt, and part of what might be an arrowshaft wrench. These will be described in greater detail in a subsequent section. In addition, there were potsherds, plain and cord roughened, other worked stones, stone chips, shell and bone fragments and, on the surface, metal objects of recent manufacture.

A total of 77 post molds was located on the bastion. Most appeared between 1.0 and 2.0 feet below surface (fig. 54; pl. 41, *a*). Not all were clearly defined and, since several did not seem to fit into the stockade pattern, they may be the remains of random or intrusive posts. The depths of the excavated postholes varied from 0.35 to 2.5 feet; some of the deepest contained fragments of wood. Diameters ranged from 0.2 to 0.5 foot and the holes were spaced evenly, varying only from 1.0 to 1.5 feet. About one-third of the postholes slope in toward the center of the bastion or toward the village in the case of those along the ditch.

The palisade structure forming the bastion wall approximates the shape of a keyhole, with a narrow passage (6.0 feet wide) extending 11.5 feet south of the curtain wall, then expanding to form a circular enclosure with a maximum width of 12.5 feet. The palisaded strong-point projects 32.0 feet from the village wall. The post line of the latter was traced on the west side of the bastion passage, but it was not found to the east.

Two trenches, Features 5 and 7, were cut through the ditch, the former just east and the latter just west of the bastion (figs. 53–54; pl. 42, *a*). Each trench was 25.0 feet long, 5.0 feet wide, and 3.5 feet deep. The stratigraphy in both sections was quite complex (fig. 55). In the profiles, the original ditch contour was visible as an area of very dark fill, roughly U-shaped but with gently sloping walls. The ditch was 2.0 feet wide at base and 3.5 feet deep, measured from the present surface level. In Feature 7, the dark fill rests directly on the gray silt of zone 1, but in Feature 5, a 0.5-foot layer of light-brown fill intervenes.

The cultural material from Features 5 and 7 included sherds, animal bone, and stone fragments. Although the trenches were carried back beyond the edges of the ditch, no certain evidence of palisade posts was found. Four post molds and one recent post appeared in Feature 5. Two of these, found at about 1.0 foot below surface at the north end of the trench, are possibly palisade posts, since they correspond in size and relative position with others at the end of the bastion.

Additional evidence of the palisade was found in Feature 18, on the western side of the village adjacent to bastion No. 4 (pl. 41, *b*). A row of 11 post molds, spaced at 2.0-foot intervals, extended along a slight rise just inside of the ditch line. The post molds were encountered at depths ranging from 1.0 to 3.0 feet below surface and ranged from 0.35 to 0.5 foot in diameter. Depths varied from 0.34 to 1.43 feet. Eight of the molds contained traces of wood.

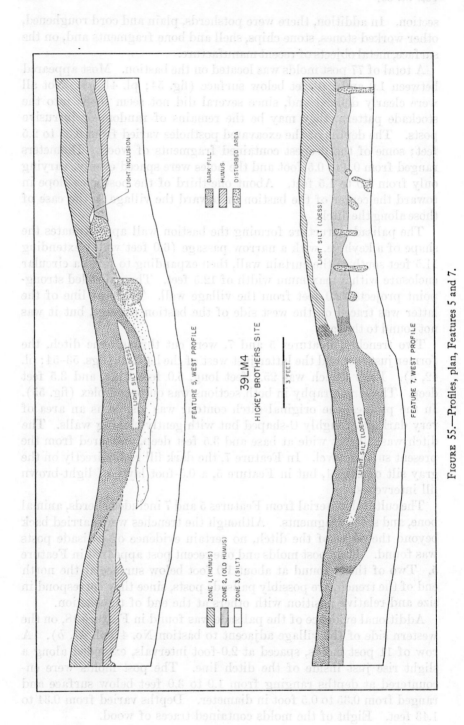

FIGURE 55.—Profiles, plan, Features 5 and 7.

Five feet east of the stockade line and at a depth of 1 foot was a saucer-shaped area (1.3 feet in diameter, 0.3 foot thick) filled with soft white ash surrounded by reddish, burned earth. Sherds (Riggs Flared Rim in zone 1, plain body sherd in zone 2), stone artifacts, and fragments of animal bone were in association.

HABITATION AREAS

Evidence of domestic occupation or related phenomena was found in five areas. The following features are involved:

> Features 3 and 6
> Feature 10
> Features 25 and 14
> Features 39 and 12
> Features 40, 22, 23, and 41

Features 3 and 6.—Feature 3 was a pronounced circular depression about 30 feet in diameter, situated in the south-central portion of the village enclosure. An area 30 by 35 feet was carefully skimmed to a depth of about 1.0 foot, following natural stratigraphic levels. Since little cultural evidence was appearing, work was concentrated in the southern one-half of the excavation, skimming the floor to 2.0 feet below surface. Two small tests were carried to a slightly greater depth. No structural features were noted, but the profile of Feature 6 (fig. 56, pl. 42, *b*), a 5.0 by 5.0 foot pit excavated to a depth of 5.7 feet, suggests that a nebulous house floor may have been present. Some of the depressions originally labeled as rodent burrows are strikingly like postholes in profile. Again, the southeast profile of Feature 3 (fig. 56) indicates at least one, and perhaps two, cache pits deriving from the same level.

The few artifacts from this feature were found above the 2.0 foot depth, mostly in the upper 0.6 foot of zone 3. Five rim sherds of the type Riggs Flared Rim and two of Anderson Low Rim were recovered from the 0.0 to 1.4 foot level. From 1.4 to 2.0 feet, the upper portion of zone 3, only Anderson Low Rim sherds were reported. This level is coincident with the putative house floor suggested in the previous paragraph. Other occupational debris included stones, unidentifiable bone fragments, and stone chipping detritus.

Feature 10.—Feature 10 was a circular depression, approximately 50.0 feet in diameter, situated 340 feet south of the primary datum. An east-west trench (pl. 43, *a*), 45.0 feet long and 5.0 feet wide (between N660–N665 and E940–E985) was excavated in 0.5-foot levels to a depth of 2.0 feet, following the surface contour. A central pit, 5.0 by 5.0 feet, was dug to a depth of 4.0 feet below surface.

The stubs of five fenceposts and numerous items of recent manufacture were found in the 0.0- to 0.5-foot depth interval. These were in-

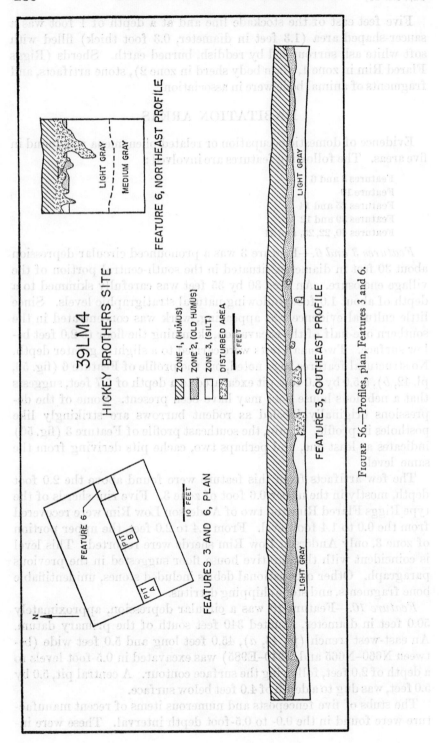

FIGURE 56.—Profiles, plan, Features 3 and 6.

cluded within the zone 1 layer. Zone 2 began at about 0.6 foot and persisted to a depth of 1.3 feet. From 1.3 to 3.3 feet, in the central pit, was a brown fill, overlying the matrix of zone 3. The surface of the brown fill was broken by several small pits that resemble postholes in profile.

In 1959, the central pit and a portion of the trench were reexcavated and, in addition, an irregular area 7.5 feet (east-west) by 18.0 feet (north-south) was opened at the western end of the feature (fig. 53). At a depth of 1.0 foot below surface, a distinct "wall line" was found. The fill was then skimmed to a "floor" at 1.5 feet below surface. Several posts were found in the process, but they could not be definitely related to either floor or wall line. The resulting pattern suggests a fragment of a rectangular structure with a rounded corner. The floor level at 1.5 feet is approximately the same depth as the putative posthole level observed in the central portion of the trench. Unfortunately, no additional structural details were observed, and artifacts were limited to several small, plain body sherds.

Features 25 and 14.—Test pit 14 was situated in the north-central part of the village enclosure. When a patch of carbon staining was found at 0.5 foot below surface, the excavation was expanded to include an area of approximately 13.0 by 15.0 feet and labeled as Feature 25 (pl. 43, *b*). Additional irregularly shaped, dark, mottled areas, together with areas of fire-reddened earth, were found just beneath the sod line. One of these contained the remains of a charred log. Four large unworked stones were found in the center of the area, but they had no apparent arrangement. An unidentifiable bone fragment, a piece of glass, and some sherds were the only specimens recovered. All came from near the surface of zone 1. The only rim found falls into the Riggs Punctate category.

No structural elements, such as post molds, were observed, and the area had obviously been disturbed by ranch activity, but Madison and Caldwell do not discount the possibility that the fill represents roof dirt, overlying a more deeply buried earth-lodge floor.

Features 39 and 12.—Test pit 12 was intended to sample a shallow depression located near the east edge of the site. The initial test was enlarged to an area 27.0 by 30.0 feet (Feature 39) following the discovery of three post molds and fragments of animal bone. The entire excavation unit was stripped to an average depth of 0.8 foot (pl. 44, *a*). Twenty-one additional post molds and postholes were found, occurring from just below surface to a depth of 1.0 foot (fig. 56). They ranged in depth from 0.10 to 2.5 feet and in diameter from 0.13 to 0.72 foot. More than one-half contained wood or charcoal. In one instance a fragment of milled timber was found; several other posts may also be of a recent date.

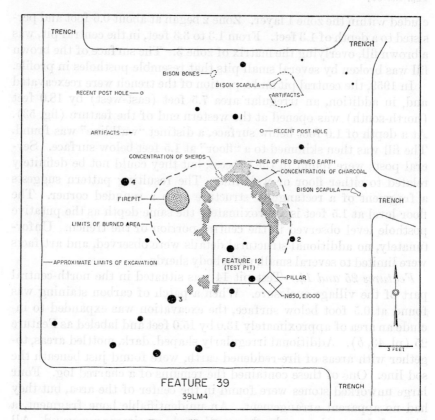

FIGURE 57.—Feature 39, plan.

A circular firepit filled with compact white ash was found slightly below the surface. Just to the east was an irregular area of reddish earth, mottled with carbon stains and charcoal fragments. The outlines of charred maize cobs were also visible.

Artifacts were found to the north and west of the firepit. Eight rim sherds of the type Riggs Punctate were present in the 0.0 to 1.0 foot interval (zone 2). In addition, a knife of Bijou Hills Quartzite, an end scraper, irregular flake scrapers, four shaft smoothers, a split metapodial flesher, a quill flattener, and a possible scapula hoe were found in this zone in association with glass and other recent objects.

Despite the obvious disturbance of Feature 39, it is possible that the true floor level was not reached. The concentration of charcoal and burned areas suggests roof fall or above-floor fill. Similarly, the excavation may not have been enlarged enough to uncover the entire post pattern. Posthole Nos. 1, 2, 3, and 4, oriented about the firepit, suggest the four central roof supports of a circular earth lodge (fig. 57). On the other hand, post molds can be selected to form the corner of a rectangular house. The case remains unproven, but considered with the associated rim sherds, the latter house type would appear to be the best possibility.

Features 22, 23, 41, and 40.—Test pits 22 and 23 were excavated adjacent to the terrace edge. Since a number of artifacts were found, the two test pits were connected by a trench 95.0 feet long and 5.0 feet wide (Feature 40). Near the center of the trench, the stratigraphic sequence varied from the usual. Intervening between the uppermost humus (zone 1) and the old humus deposit (zone 2), was a brown deposit (0.7 to 0.8 foot thick) divisible into a darker upper half and a lighter basal portion. Zone 1 extended to depth 0.4 foot, zone 2 from 1.1 to 1.4 feet, and zone 3 below 1.4 feet.

Two aboriginal pits were found within the limits of the trench. Near the center, originating at depth 0.4 foot (the surface of the brown matrix) and extending to 2.0 feet, was an excavation of indeterminate shape. It was filled with a sterile "whitish" fill, probably ash. About 3 feet to the north was a globular cache pit with a constricted neck. The pit apparently originated at or somewhat below the surface of zone 3. The mouth was approximately 1.6 feet in diameter, widening to 2.2 feet maximum width of body. The convex bottom extended to 2.2 feet below the upper margin of zone 3. The fill contained flecks of charcoal and ash, a few plain body sherds, and rodent bones.

About 25 feet north of the cache pit was a burned area consisting of reddened earth and flecks of charcoal. At the south end of the trench, near Feature 23, another firepit (Feature 41) was discovered at a depth of 0.9 foot below surface (brown stratum). The fire basin was a shallow (0.5 foot) saucer-shaped depression 2.3 feet in diameter, containing a mass of white ash. A few sherds were present adjacent to the fire area. The Riggs Punctate examples with fingernail impressions were concentrated here.

Three post molds were found close to the surface near the north end of the trench. Two contained wood fragments. Diameters ranged from 0.35 to 0.55 foot, depths from 1.0 to 2.0 feet. The posts were spaced about 15.0 feet apart on a north-south alinement, suggesting that they are the remains of a recent fence line.

With one exception, a plate chalcedony knife from zone 3, all artifacts were restricted to zone 1 and the underlying brown stratum. Six rim sherds of the type Riggs Punctate and two of Riggs Flared Rim were excavated in association with leaf-shaped knives of Bijou Hills Quartzite, one plate chalcedony knife, a single end scraper, a single irregular spall with worked edges, and a large metapodial flesher.

ARTIFACTS

The number of artifacts excavated from the Hickey Brothers site is inordinately small, totaling only 479 specimens, of which 435 are potsherds. Artifacts of bone, stone, and shell are largely undistinguished and are not of great help in suggesting areal or temporal relationships. The most that may be said is that the bone and lithic sample is not out of character with the pottery.

POTTERY

A. RIM SHERDS: The rim sherds fall within two well-recognized pottery series, Thomas Riggs (Hurt, 1953) and Anderson (Lehmer, 1954).

Riggs Punctate: 15 sherds, portions of 5 vessels (pl. 46, *a, d, g*).

  Temper: Moderately abundant sand and grit, probably crushed or decomposed granite, diameters to 2.0 mm.

  Texture: Medium, some specimens well smoothed.

  Color: Tan to dark gray (interior, exterior, and core).

  Hardness: 3.0 (Moh).

  Surface treatment: Plain.

  Decoration: Limited to fillet applied below lip. Motifs include deep hemispherical punctations (pl. 46, *g*), hemiconical notches (pl. 46, *a*), wide gouges, and oblique fingernail incisions (pl. 46, *d*).

  Rim profile: Straight to slightly flaring.

   Rim height: 35.0–45.4 mm.

   Rim thickness: 4.1–7.0 mm.

  Lip: Rounded to slightly beveled, thickened into exterior flange in a few cases.

   Thickness: 5.0–7.0 mm.

   Rim modification: None.

  Remarks: No additional indication of vessel form. The Hickey Brothers sample lacks the lip decoration reported for the collection excavated from the Thomas Riggs Site (Kleinsasser, in Hurt, 1953). The oblique fingernail incision does not seem to have been reported previously.

Riggs Flared Rim: 9 sherds, portions of 4 vessels (pl. 46, *b, c, e, h*).

  Temper: Moderately abundant sand or decomposed granite; diameter of inclusions is particularly large, ranging to 3.0 mm.

  Texture: Medium to fine, one specimen (39LM4–108) has a slight luster.

  Color: Tan to dark gray, core gray.

  Hardness: 3.5 (Moh).

  Surface treatment: Plain.

  Decoration: Restricted to lip. Motifs include deep punctation and notching (39LM4–108).

  Rim profile: Flared.

   Rim height: 50 mm.

   Rim thickness: 7.0–9.0 mm.

  Lip: Rounded and flattened, often distorted through application of decoration.

   Thickness: 6.0–9.0 mm.

   Rim modification: None.

Remarks: No additional indication of vessel form.

Anderson Low Rim: 7 sherds, portions of 2 vessels (pl. 46, *f*, *i*).

   Temper: Sand and grit, with inclusions to 3.0 mm. diameter.

   Texture: Medium.

   Color: Tan to gray, exterior, interior, and core.

   Hardness: 4.0 (Moh).

   Surface treatment: Smoothed; smoothing over cord roughening is apparent on two sherds. Cord roughening appears on lower rim and shoulder in one instance (39LM4–4/2).

   Decoration: Oblique punctates or incisions on lip bevel and lip-rim juncture (pl. 46, *f*), hachure on lip (pl. 46, *i*).

   Rim profile: Flared.

   Rim height: 19.0–30.0 mm.

   Rim thickness: 2.5–5.9 mm.

   Lip: Everted or beveled.

Remarks: No rim modification, vessel form unknown.

B. BODY SHERDS:

   Plain: 276 sherds; temper, color and hardness are similar to the rims described. In addition, there is a group of 60 sherds with slightly burnished surfaces.

   Cord roughened: 36 sherds (pl. 46, *j*).

   Temper: Similar to described rims.

   Color: Tan to dark-gray exterior, interior, and core.

   Hardness: 3.5–4.0 (Moh).

   Simple stamped: 30 sherds (pl. 46, *k*), temper, color, and hardness are similar to the rims described.

   Brushed: 1 sherd.

LITHIC MATERIALS

A. PROJECTILE POINTS (4 specimens).

   1. Small, triangular, straight edges, flat to slightly concave bases, with medium-to-wide side notches (3 specimens) (pl. 45, *b-d*). Two additional body fragments probably belong with this group.

      Length: 21.0–22.9 mm.

      Width: 4.6 mm.

      Thickness: 2.0–2.7 mm.

   2. Small, triangular, straight edges and slightly concave base (39LM4–64) (pl. 45, *a*).

      Length: 18.0 mm.

      Width: 3.9 mm.

      Thickness: 4.0 mm.

B. KNIVES:

   1. Large leaf-shaped blades (fragmentary) of Bijou Hills Quartzite, bifacially flaked, retouched edges, cross section biconvex (5 specimens) (pl. 45, *h*, *n*).

      Length: —.

      Width: 26.0–58.0 mm.

      Thickness: 9.0–11.0 mm.

      Angular intersection: 30°–50°.

   2. Fragments of plate chalcedony with retouched edge (4 specimens) (pl. 45, *g*, *j*, *m*). 39LM4–30 may also have been used as a drill or reamer.

3. Trapezoidal blade, bulb of percussion intact, minute retouches along one edge, longitudinal flake scars with hinge fractures (39LM4–58) (pl. 45, e).

> Length: 54.0 mm.
> Width: 29.0 mm.
> Thickness: 8.0 mm.

C. SCRAPERS:

1. Large end scrapers, thick, heavy flakes, retouched from one surface to form a thick body with a low keel (5 specimens) (pl. 45, i).

> Length: 29.0–58.0 mm.
> Width: 25.0–42.0 mm.
> Thickness: 10.0–15.0 mm.

2. Irregular spalls with purposefully retouched or use-retouched edges (10 specimens) (pl. 45, k, f).

D. MISCELLANEOUS STONE OBJECTS:

1. Biface chopper or large blade formed from a massive flake, convex triangular body, irregular convex bit (39LM4–22) (pl. 44, e).

> Length: 90. 0 mm.
> Width: 37.0 mm.
> Thickness: 23.0 mm.

2. Uniface chopper formed from a quartzite cobble spall, chopping edge formed by removing large flakes from cortical surface (39LM4–61).

> Length: 109.0 mm.
> Width: 76.0 mm.
> Thickness: 37.0 mm.

3. Polished celt (diorite), wide asymmetric bit tapering to a flattened poll, bit edge crushed (39LM4–53) (pl. 44, b).

> Length: 120.0 mm.
> Width: 47.0 mm.
> Thickness: 31.0 mm.

4. Ovoid hammerstone of granite, deeply pecked over most of surface (39LM4–132).

> Length: 72.0 mm.
> Diameter: 61.0 mm.

5. Arrowshaft smoothers of sandstone, elongate ovoid body, one flat surface with deep longitudinal groove, body cross section irregularly convex (4 specimens, 2 fragmentary) (pl. 44, c, d).

> Length: 40.0–78.0 mm.
> Width: 30.0–40.0 mm.
> Thickness: 18.0–26.0 mm.

6. Fragmentary pipe bowl, material unknown, subrectangular bowl, thick rectangular flange projecting around orifice (39LM4–41, 45) (pl. 45, l, o).

7. Tubular concretion (?) (39LM4–98).

III. BONE MATERIALS

A. Bison metapodial flesher (fragmentary), cancellous tissue removed, proximal end of bone forms butt, body beveled abruptly to form a thin, serrated bit (39LM4–168) (pl. 44, g).

> Length: 180.0 mm.
> Width: 32.0 mm.
> Thickness: 13.9 mm.

B. Bison metapodial flesher, split segment of shaft, distal portion beveled to a broad, thin bit (39LM4–190) (pl. 44, *f*).

> *Length:* 154.0 mm.
> *Width:* 30.0 mm.
> *Thickness:* 38.3 mm.

C. Pottery tool or quill flattener (fragmentary), split section of bison rib with rounded end, cancellous tissue partially smoothed (39LM4–155, 156) (pl. 44, *i*).

> *Length:* 65.0 mm.
> *Width:* 14.0 mm.
> *Thickness:* 5.0 mm.

D. Arrowshaft wrench, segment of bison rib perforated with gouged hole (39LM4–78) (pl. 44, *j*).

E. Proximal fragments of bison scapula; 39LM4–170 has the suprascapular spine removed (3 specimens) (pl. 44, *h*).

CONCLUSIONS

It is obvious that the occupation of the Hickey Brothers site was not intensive, yet despite the relative scarcity of artifacts and architectural data, it is altogether probable that two components are present. Pottery forms the most distinctive unit of the artifact inventory. Of the total group of rim sherds, 72 percent (23) resemble the typical pottery from the Thomas Riggs site. The remaining nine rims are plainly Anderson Flared Rim Ware. The small quantity of cord-roughened body sherds (about 1 percent) is somewhat less than one might expect, yet it does provide a basis for the inference that a considerable proportion of the Anderson pottery had smoothed bodies.

Pottery of the Riggs grouping occurs only in the upper portions of the cultural deposit, particularly in zone 1. Anderson Flared Rim ware is restricted to zone 3, particularly to the surface and uppermost part of that zone, and to the lower part of zone 2. The stratigraphic occurrence of nonceramic artifacts is preponderantly in the upper zones in association with the Riggs pottery. The assemblage contains nothing not reasonably "at home" in the Thomas Riggs context (see Hurt, 1953). Plate chalcedony knives, end scrapers of the type described above, and split metapodial fleshers apparently are not characteristic of earlier horizons.

Recognizing the disabilities imposed by the small number of artifacts, still it is not unreasonable to postulate the presence of two components, the early represented by the few Anderson sherds, the late by the Riggs-like occupation. While the architectural data is even less adequate, it is a fair inference that long-rectangular houses were present, too. The limited information from Feature 10 offers good support for such an assertion. Evidence from other features is inconclusive, although one might contend that Feature 39 is a house representative of the Thomas Riggs occupation. Stratigraphically, it falls within the Riggs pottery zone.

Unfortunately, there is no direct data linking the fortification system with either occupation. A few cord-roughened body sherds, present in Feature 4, might suggest an Anderson tie, but the fortification itself is more characteristic of a later time, in fact it resembles the Huff site in south-central North Dakota, in most significant respects. The Hickey Brothers bastion is longer and narrower in proportion than the excavated example at the Huff site (Howard, 1959, personal communication) and the "tower room" or strongpoint features at the Huff site are lacking at Hickey Brothers. It is worth noting that the situation at the Hickey Brothers site suggests that the village defenses were completed prior to the large-scale building of houses.

Tentative as the foregoing observations are, they cannot be construed to offer any explanation for the negligible occupation found at the Hickey Brothers site. The insignificant artifact return and the diffuse architectural remains are difficult to rationalize with the large-scale, well-engineered project represented by the village fortifications. A number of possible explanations come to mind, but there is no real support in fact for any of them.

One of the more enticing suggestions is based in the possibility of a local ecological shift following the beginning of village construction. A season of severe drought, or even a large prairie fire, might have made the area temporarily uninhabitable, or might have destroyed usable building material. Today there is virtually no bottom land adjacent to the site. An ice jam or a shift in riverflow by some other agency could well have reduced the bottoms to such a degree that the tillable land available to the village could not support the expanding settlement.

The explanation might even be more simple. A mere change in leadership, the heavy toll of an epidemic, or pressure from enemies might have made a shift of locale necessary before the village was really well established. A sudden attack could have ended the incipient village at a single blow. The concentration of charcoal in house areas, particularly Features 25 and 39, offers some support for this view.

The sum of these speculations (and postulations) amounts to an enigma. The data will support no firm statements. In extirpation of the insecure position that we have been forced to assume, we do not feel too self-conscious in restating the useful cliche—more work needs to be done to solve the case of the unfinished village.

LITERATURE CITED

COOGAN, ALAN H., and IRVING, WILLIAM N.
   1959. Late Pleistocene and recent Missouri River terraces in the Big Bend
       Reservoir, South Dakota.   Journ. Iowa Acad. Sci., vol. 66.
HURT, WESLEY R., JR.
   1953. Report of the investigations of the Thomas Riggs site, 39HU1, Hughes
       County, South Dakota, 1952. South Dakota Archaeol. Comm.,
       Archaeol. Studies, Circ. No. 5.
LEHMER, DONALD J.
   1954. Archeological investigations in the Oahe Dam area, South Dakota,
       1950–51.   Bur. Amer. Ethnol., Bull. 158, Riv. Bas. Surv. Pap. No. 7.

a, The Hickey Brothers site, looking across the northwestern bastion, Missouri River flood plain in middle distance; 39LM4–3. *b*, Feature 4, the southeastern bastion, prior to excavation; 39LM4–16.

a, Feature 4 cleared of sod and staked in 10-foot squares; 39LM4–19. *b,* Surface contour of ditch in the vicinity of Feature 5, prior to excavation; 39LM4–22.

a, The stockade line of Feature 4, excavation completed; 39LM4–46. *b*, Feature 18, post-holes of the stockade along the inner edge of the defensive ditch, fire area about 5 feet to the east; 39LM4–48.

a, Profile of west wall, Feature 5; the dark fill outlines the aboriginal ditch excavation; 39LM4–30.   *b*, Profile of east wall, Feature 6, showing rodent disturbance and possible postholes; 39LM4–24.

a, Feature 10, excavation completed, 1958; 39LM4–40.   *b*, Feature 25, a burned area with a concentration of sherds, possibly roof fill of a house; 39LM4–42.

a, Feature 39, a house of indeterminate form, postholes, firepit on pedestals; 39LM4–51. *b*, Celt; *c*, *d*, shaft smoothers; *e*, chopper; *f*, *g*, fleshers; *h*, scapula hoe; *i*, quill flattener; *j*, shaft wrench.

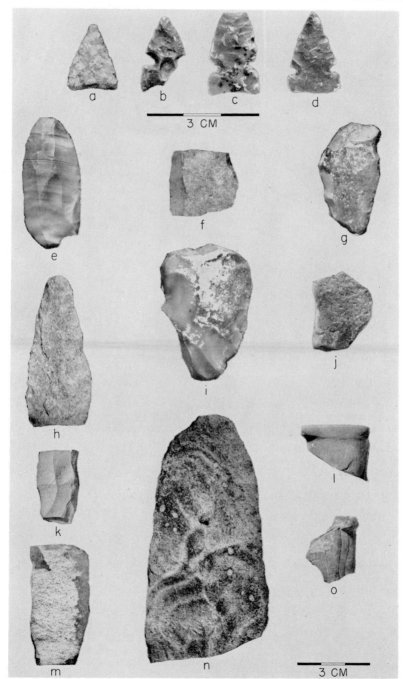

a–d, Projectile points; *e, g, h, j, m, n,* knives; *f, i, k,* scrapers; *l, o,* pipe fragments.

Ceramic remains from Hickey Brothers site.   *a, d, g,* Riggs Punctate; *b, c, e, h,* Riggs Flared Rim; *f, i,* Anderson Low Rim; *j,* cord-roughened body sherd; *k,* simple-stamped body sherd.

SMITHSONIAN INSTITUTION
Bureau of American Ethnology
Bulletin 189

River Basin Surveys Papers, No. 37
The Good Soldier Site (39LM238), Big Bend Reservoir, Lyman County, South Dakota

By ROBERT W. NEUMAN

661–932—64——21

CONTENTS

	PAGE
Introduction	295
Acknowledgments	295
Location and description	296
Excavations	296
Good Soldier Component (39LM238)	297
Features	297
Artifacts	299
Pottery	299
Iona Indented	300
Grey Cloud Horizontal-Incised	300
Talking Crow Straight Rim	301
Cadotte Collared	301
Stanley Tool Impressed	302
Miscellaneous	302
Stone	303
Projectile points	303
End scrapers	303
Knives	304
Drill	304
Miscellaneous chipped stone	304
Ground stone artifacts	304
Shaft smoothers	304
Abraders	305
Bone artifacts	305
Good Soldier Component and related sites	305
Badger Component (39LM238)	308
Features	308
Pottery	308
Group A	308
Group B	310
Group C	310
Stone	311
Projectile points	311
End scrapers	312
Knives	313
Worked flakes	314
Problematical object	314
Discussion of the Badger Component	314
Conclusions	315
Appendix	316
Literature cited	317

ILLUSTRATIONS

PLATES

(All plates follow p. 318)

47. *a.*, View east-northeast of Good Soldier site and surrounding vicinity. Missouri River flows eastward in the upper left. *b*, View north of trench cross-sectioning the long axis of the natural mounds. Broken rocks are adjacent to the large pit (Feature 4).
48. Pottery specimens from the Good Soldier Component: *a, b,* Iona Indented; *c, d,* Grey Cloud Horizontal-Incised; *e, f,* Talking Crow Straight Rim; *g,* Cadotte Collared; *h,* Stanley Tool Impressed; *i–k,* miscellaneous.
49. Stone and bone specimens from the Good Soldier Component.
50. Pottery and stone specimens from the Badger Component.

TEXT FIGURE

PAGE

58. Plan and cross section drawings of excavations at the Good Soldier site_____ 298

THE GOOD SOLDIER SITE (39LM238), BIG BEND RESERVOIR, LYMAN COUNTY, SOUTH DAKOTA

By Robert W. Neuman

INTRODUCTION

In July of 1958 a field party of the Missouri Basin Project, Smithsonian Institution, spent 14 days conducting archeological excavations at the Good Soldier site (39LM238), a prehistoric Indian camp site in the Big Bend Reservoir area, South Dakota. The site was first recorded and tested in 1956 by a survey team of the Missouri Basin Project under the direction of Harold A. Huscher (Huscher and McNutt, 1958). The 1958 investigations were supervised by the writer; James J. Stanek acted as field assistant.[1] Excavations at this prehistoric site were made possible through Federal funds provided for the Inter-Agency Archeological Salvage Program of the Smithsonian Institution, the National Park Service and cooperating Federal, State, and local institutions.

ACKNOWLEDGMENTS

A number of people from the Missouri Basin Project assisted in the compilation of this report, and to the following I am sincerely grateful: Warren W. Caldwell, G. Hubert Smith, and Robert L. Stephenson, who read the original manuscript and offered helpful suggestions; Evelyn B. Stewart, who proofread and handled the illustrations; Ione Wilson, who did the final typing; Jerry Livingston, who did the drafting; and Wayne Nelson, who did the photographic work for the plates.

Special thanks are due Hobart Eagle, Superintendent of Maintenance, Bureau of Indian Affairs, at the Crow Creek Indian Reservation. It was through his cooperation that I was loaned a boat, motor, and other water equipment for our daily crossings of the Missouri River from Fort Thompson to the Good Soldier site. To the crew of the 1958 field party I am also deeply indebted, because no task or suggestion was beyond their endurance.

---

[1] Members of the 1958 field party were as follows: Lee Azure, Joseph Benthall, Eugene Brother-of-All, Adolph Burns Day, Michael Forth, Donald Howe, Milo Kearney, Frederick Middle Tent, Horace Slow, and Junior Yellow Back.

LOCATION AND DESCRIPTION

The Good Soldier site (39LM238) lies on a low, flat terrace (Missouri River Terrace 1, Coogan, 1960) in a narrow valley formed by Good Soldier Creek (formerly Badger Creek) just south and west of the confluence of this tributary and the Missouri River in Lyman County, central South Dakota. The valley is bounded on the east and west by steep, thoroughly dissected breaks that rise abruptly to heights of 30 to 90 feet above the valley floor. The occupational debris at the site was concentrated on a low hummock located about 400 feet south of the right bank of the Missouri River and 150 feet west of the left bank of Good Soldier Creek (the approximate intersection of latitude 44°02'30'' N. and longitude 99°27' W.) at an elevation of 1,372 feet m.s.l. (Missouri River Map (1:24,000) Omaha District, Corps of Engineers, Sheet No. 52, 1949). The hummock measured 130 feet north-south and 65 feet east-west and had a maximum apical height of 5 feet (pl. 47, a).

EXCAVATIONS

During the 1956 reconnaissance a test pit was dug at the southern end of the rise to a depth of 1.0 foot below the surface. Artifacts recovered from this test include pottery sherds from a single vessel and several hematite-coated bison rib fragments. The restorable portion of the vessel was reconstructed in the laboratory and is identified as of the type Iona Indented (Smith and Grange, 1958, pp. 98–100).

At the time of the 1958 investigations a grid of 5-foot squares oriented with the cardinal directions was superimposed over the natural rise and the peripheral area. Each square was given a letter and number designation noting its location in the grid. The squares were scraped horizontally with shovels, and artifacts were placed in bags labeled according to their vertical and horizontal provenience within the grid. All excavations, except eight widely scattered 5- by 5-foot test pits, were conducted within the northwest quadrant of the grid. Depth measurements were made from the top of the present soil surface downward.

Excavations were initiated by digging a trench 5 feet wide and 130 feet long across the north-south axis of the mound (pl. 47, b). As work progressed it became apparent that the mound was a natural structure of stream-deposited gravel capped with five distinct soil strata. The stratigraphic sequence in the trench profiles read as follows from top to bottom: Stratum 1, the top soil zone, consisted of a layer of undisturbed sod and humus about 0.3 foot thick. Only rarely were artifacts present in this zone. The underlying soil zone, stratum 2, was composed of a brownish silt. This deposit ranged from 0.3 to 0.5 foot in thickness and became increasingly thicker along the east and west slopes of the mound. Stratum 2 contained the artifactual material belonging to the latest component at the site. The third deposit, stratum 3, was a zone of yellowish, loess-like material generally 0.3 foot thick. This zone was sterile of cultural material except for the intrusion of postholes from stratum 2. The next soil layer, stratum 4, was composed of a fine, grayish silt, ranging from 1.2 to 1.4 feet in thickness. Stratum 4 contained the archeological specimens belonging to the earliest component found at the site. The deepest soil deposit was stratum 5; it was composed of a thin, yellowish layer identical in appearance to stratum 3. This deepest deposit was about 0.2 foot thick and was present only in the central area of the mound (fig. 58).

Soon after beginning excavations at the Good Soldier site it became evident that two distinct archeological deposits were involved. The deposits were separated by the yellow band of silt designated as stratum 3. A closer examination, in the laboratory, of the artifact proveniences and other archeological data left no doubt that at least two human occupations were represented. In this report the top, and last, occupation is called the Good Soldier Component; the deepest occupation is referred to as the Badger Component.

GOOD SOLDIER COMPONENT (39LM238)

All of the archeological material belonging to this component was recovered from the two top soil zones, stratum 1 and stratum 2. The most characteristic trait is sherds from globular vessels that have straight to flaring rims and are simple-stamped on their exterior surface. Another trait, somewhat less diagnostic, was the occurrence of numerous posthole remains; 29 post molds were randomly distributed over the central portion of the mound. Of the 29, 13 contained only soft, dark earthfill. Bison bone wedges or supports were found in 14 of the postholes; 2 of these contained small rock fragments, 2 others contained portions of the original posts, and in another a stone projectile point was found. Two postholes contained the remains of unwedged wooden posts. The diameters of the postholes ranged from 0.3 foot to 1.1 feet, the majority being between 0.4 and 1.1 feet. The depths of the postholes ranged from 0.2 to 1.9 feet. Whether or not these postholes are the remains of an earth lodge or lodges cannot be determined from the available data.

FEATURES

In the field certain peculiarities, such as soil discolorations that marked the locations of pits or concentrations of archeological re-

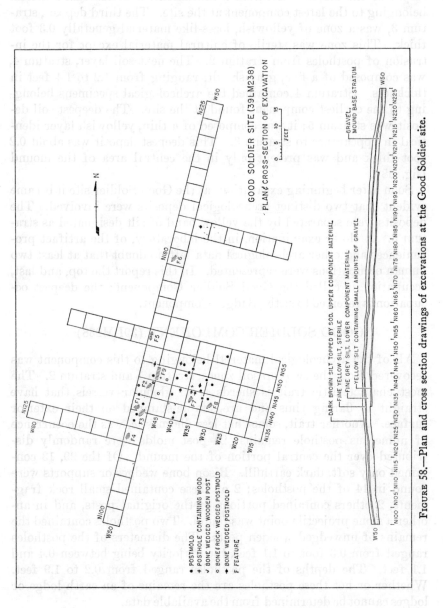

FIGURE 58.—Plan and cross section drawings of excavations at the Good Soldier site.

mains, were designated as features. Each feature was numbered, carefully described on special "Feature Forms," and photographed in the order of its discovery regardless of the component with which it was associated. Therefore, the feature numbers assigned to the various components are not in consecutive order. Features 2, 7, 8, and 9 were associated with the Good Soldier Component and are described in detail below.

Feature 2.—One posthole and three articulated bison vertebrae. The bone was 2.0 feet north of the posthole. After being cored, the posthole was found to contain a portion of coyote skull. No artifacts were located in direct association with these remains. The top of this feature was in square N140W50 at 0.6 foot below the surface.

Feature 7.—A concentration of pottery, a fragment of worked bison scapula and several catfish bones. The pottery fragments, 3 rims and 14 body sherds, all belong to a single vessel. This section of the vessel was restored in the laboratory and is identified as the type Iona Indented (Smith and Grange, 1958). Feature 7 was located in square N140W35 at 0.8 foot below the surface.

Feature 8.—Consists of five articulated and two separate bison vertebrae. The remains were located in situ at square N140W30 between 0.3 and 0.5 foot below the surface.

Feature 9.—A line of stones 5 feet in length, two postholes, and a basin-shaped pit. The stone line, oriented almost exactly north-south, consisted of 17 hand-sized cobblestones. The two postholes were located symmetrically on opposite sides and about 1 foot from the stones. A line joining the centers of the postholes would be perpendicular to the line of stones and would intersect it at a point 2.0 feet from the south end. The easterly posthole had bison bone wedges while the western one contained the remains of a cedar post. The basin-shaped pit was located less than 1 foot east of the eastern posthole. Fill from the pit was composed of hematite-stained soil and a small amount of burned earth. The pit measured 2.3 feet north-south, 2.0 feet east-west, and had a maximum depth of 0.5 foot. This feature was located in square N145W45 at 1.5 feet below the surface.

ARTIFACTS

POTTERY

The ceramic collection associated with the Good Soldier Component at 39LM238 includes the following pottery types: Iona Indented, Grey Cloud Horizontal-Incised, Talking Crow Straight Rim, Cadotte Collared, Stanley Tool Impressed, and a few miscellaneous rims.

A total of 241 body sherds was recovered; 83 of these were simple stamped and 158 were plain surfaced. In addition, there were 51 decorated sherds, almost all of which are from the shoulder area of vessels; 39 of these sherds bear parallel incised lines, 2 have parallel trailed lines, 8 are incised with opposed diagonals, 1 has trailed, opposed diagonals, and 1 bears an incised herringbone motif. These decorative designs are common to all of the above-named pottery types, and I have not attempted to correlate any of the decorated sherds with particular rim-sherd types.

This pottery has been described in detail and assigned as a component type of Iona Ware by Smith and Grange in the Spain site (39LM301) report (Smith and Grange, 1958). There are no significant differences between the Iona Indented pottery from the Spain and Good Soldier sites.

SAMPLE: Two partially restored vessels (pl. 48, a and b) and four separate rim sherds.

METHOD OF MANUFACTURE: Probably built up from lumped clay by the paddle and anvil technique. There is no evidence of coiling.

PASTE:

> Temper: Moderate amounts of tiny grit particles composed of quartz, mica, and feldspar.
>
> Texture: Medium coarse to smooth.
>
> Color: Buff, grading into gray. Many areas on the interior and exterior surfaces are blackened from use.

FORM:

> Lip: Thickened, T-shaped or resembling an inverted L. Flattened or rounded on top. Lip thickness ranges from 9 mm. to 11 mm. At the Spain site most lips were from 9 mm. to 16 mm. thick.
>
> Rim: Slightly flaring to straight. Heights range from 36 mm. to 46 mm. Most rims at the Spain site were from 26 mm. to 47 mm. in height.
>
> Shoulder: Quite rounded. The rims extend out from the vertical at an angle of about 25 degrees. The angle between the exteriors of the rim and the shoulder ranges from 85 degrees to 110 degrees on the two measurable specimens.
>
> Base: Presumably rounded.
>
> Appendages: None recovered at the Good Soldier site; however, four strap handles and one lug are reported for the Spain site.

SURFACE FINISH:

> Interior: Smoothed, otherwise unmodified.
>
> Exterior: Simple-stamped, large areas have been smoothed to the extent of almost obliterating the simple-stamped impressions.
>
> Decoration: Limited to lip and shoulder areas. Two rims have a continuous series of opposed diagonals on the lip. Four other rims are decorated with a series of diagonal lines interrupted at equal intervals by single, opposing lines. The shoulder of one vessel bears incised opposed diagonal lines.

Pottery of this type has been described in detail and assigned the above name by Smith and Grange (1958, pp. 102–103) in the Spain site report. Only three Grey Cloud Horizontal-Incised rims were recovered at the Good Soldier site.

The first rim is grit tempered, buff shading into gray and black on the exterior and light buff on the interior surface; the core is gray. The rim is slightly flaring and has a flat lip. Decoration consists of a se-

ries of diagonal punctates on the lip and four horizontally trailed lines
on the rim exterior (pl. 48, *d*). The rim measures 27 mm. in height
and the lip is 6 mm. thick. This specimen most closely resembles the
type Grey Cloud Horizontal-Incised, Variety A.

The second rim is incomplete, it resembles the first rim in all respects
except that it is decorated on the lip with a series of tool identations.
I have also classified this specimen as Grey Cloud Horizontal-Incised, Variety A (Smith and Grange, 1958, p. 103).

The third rim is grit tempered, buff colored on the exterior and gray
on the interior surface; the core is also gray. The rim is slightly
flaring and the lip is somewhat rounded and beveled toward the exterior. Decoration consists of four horizontally trailed lines on the
rim exterior and a series of vertically oriented tool indentations on the
lip interior (pl. 48, *c*). This sherd falls within the Grey Cloud Horizontal-Incised, Variety C category as described by Smith and Grange.
This type is also represented by a small number of sherds from the
Talking Crow site (39BF3).

TALKING CROW STRAIGHT RIM

Talking Crow Straight Rim is a component type of Talking Crow
ware (Smith, 1951, pp. 36–37; Smith and Grange, 1958, pp. 101–102).
Charles H. McNutt, in a subsequent classification of certain Plains
pottery (McNutt, 1959), prefers to assign similar sherds to the Russell
Plain Rim type, a component of Russell ware. I have grouped five of
the rim sherds from the Good Soldier Component into the Talking
Crow Straight Rim category (pl. 48, *e*, *f*).

The rims are grit tempered. The exterior surfaces are buff, grading
into gray, and one sherd is black and orange. Interior surfaces are
buff to gray on four of the specimens and black on the fifth. Cores
are generally lighter than the darkest side-surfaces. In form the rims
are straight and the lips are flat to slightly rounded. Decoration is
confined to the lips and consists of a series of diagonal tool indentations on three of the specimens and punctations on the remaining two.
Three of the rims are complete enough to measure; they range from
31 mm. to 41 mm. in height. Lips range from 5 mm. to 7 mm. in
thickness.

CADOTTE COLLARED

Pottery of this type has been described in a manuscript prepared by
Carlyle Smith. The ceramic classification is based upon specimens
excavated at the Two Teeth site (39BF204). Smith (personal communication) also includes four collared rims, listed under the Miscellaneous category in the Spain site report, as Cadotte Collared (Smith
and Grange, 1958, p. 104, pl. 31, *b*). Only one rim sherd from the
Good Soldier Component can be classified within this grouping (pl.
48, *g*).

The rim is grit tempered; gray shading into black on the exterior and buff shading into black on the interior surface. Only a small portion of the shoulder area remains; however, the collared area and the lip are complete. The collar is straight in form and measures 39 mm. in height. The lip is slightly rounded and beveled toward the exterior; it is 6 mm. thick. Decoration consists of a series of vertically oriented tool indentations on the lip interior and four rows of punctations on the exterior of the collared area. The only difference between this sherd and Cadotte Collared, Variety D, is that the type description of Variety D makes no mention of lip decoration.

STANLEY TOOL IMPRESSED

This pottery type was established by Donald J. Lehmer (1954, p. 45) as a component type of Stanley Braced Rim ware. Only one rim fragment from the Good Soldier Component is classified under this category (pl. 48, h).

The rim is grit tempered, buff to gray on the exterior and gray on the interior surface. The rim is slightly flaring and has a braced fillet extending down onto the rim exterior. The lip is flattened. Decoration is limited to the braced area and the lip and consists of a series of opposed diagonal impressions.

MISCELLANEOUS

Included in this category are three rim sherds, one appendage, and one incised body sherd.

The first specimen is a grit-tempered rim sherd; it is gray on the exterior and interior surfaces. The rim is straight and the lip is rounded. Decoration consists of two diagonal tool impressions on the lip exterior and three horizontally incised lines on the rim exterior (pl. 48, i).

The second specimen is also a grit-tempered rim sherd. It is buff to gray on the exterior and interior surfaces. The rim is flaring and has a rounded lip. Decoration is limited to the rim interior at the lip in the form of vertical tool indentations. Incised lines, which undoubtedly decorated the shoulder area, extend up to the lower extremity of the rim (pl. 48, j). The specimen measures 18 mm. in rim height and the lip is 5 mm. thick. This rim resembles pottery classified by W. Raymond Wood as Evans Indented, a component type of Evans ware reported from late prehistoric sites in Holt and Knox Counties, northeast Nebraska (Wood, MS.)

The third rim is grit tempered, buff on the exterior and gray on the interior surface. The rim is straight in form and the lip is rounded. An appendage has been broken from the upper portion of the rim. The remaining portion of the projecting appendage is round and suggestive of a loop handle or lug. There are two parallel incised lines extending longitudinally on the lip. To one side of the appendage, on the rim exterior, there are two horizontally trailed lines (pl. 48, *k*).

The fourth specimen appears to be a loop handle. It is gray and lacks decoration. The appendage measures 15 mm. in height and is 6 mm. thick.

The fifth specimen is a body sherd with an incised motif on the exterior surface. The sherd is grit tempered, buff on the exterior and black on the interior, and measures 6 mm. in thickness. It is quite jagged around the edges and unsymmetrical. Portions of the design have been broken off; however, the remaining portion consists of a circle and two diagonal lines that intersect each other in the approximate center of the circle.

STONE

PROJECTILE POINTS
(5 specimens)

Triangular, straight base (one specimen).—It is a planoconvex in cross section and displays jagged percussion flake scars on both faces and along all side edges. The point is made from a reddish-brown quartz. It measures 30 mm. long, 22 mm. wide, 7 mm. thick and weighs 4.8 gm. (pl. 49, *a*).

Triangular, concave base (one specimen).—The point displays fine, bifacial pressure flaking. It is made from a brown jasper and measures 20 mm. long, 11 mm. wide, 3 mm. thick and weighs 0.8 gm. (pl. 49, *b*).

Triangular, basal notched.—This point lacks a portion of the tip. There is some doubt as to whether or not the very shallow basal notch was intentionally made. The specimen is made from a yellowish-brown quartzite. It measures 34 mm. long (estimated), 20 mm. wide, and 6 mm. thick (pl. 49, *c*).

Triangular straight base, side notched (two specimens).—The largest point is made from a gray chert. It measures 19 mm. long, 14 mm. wide, 3 mm. thick, and weighs 0.8 gm. (pl. 49, *d*). The smaller point is made from a whitish chalcedony. It measures 14 mm. long, 12 mm. wide, 3 mm. thick, and weighs 0.5 gm. (pl 49, *e*).

END SCRAPERS
(2 specimens)

The first specimen is triangular in outline and planoconvex in cross section. The "keel" has been removed from the convex face, and secondary chipping on that face is limited to the working end and one side edge. A single percussion flake scar extends down the total length of the long axis on the convex face. The scraper is made of Knife River flint and measures 40 mm. long, 28 mm. wide, and 8 mm. thick (pl. 49, *f*). The second specimen is rectangular in outline and concavoconvex in cross section. The convex face has been retouched along the working end and the two side edges. The planer surface is flat near the working end, but it has a pronounced concavity at the opposite end. The specimen is made of a clear, banded quartz. It measures 27 mm. long, 21 mm. wide, and 5 mm. thick (pl. 49, *g*).

KNIVES
(2 specimens)

Specimens in this category are bifacially flaked along one or more edges. Each piece is but a fragment of the original tool.

The first fragment is rectangular in outline and has two flat faces. Chipping is limited to one end and one side edge. The chipping along the side edge has resulted in a steep bevel from one face. This specimen is made from plate chalcedony; it measures 49 mm. long, 30 mm. wide, and 7 mm. thick.

The second specimen appears to be the main portion of an elliptical knife. One end and a side have been chipped from only one face. The other side edge has been bifacially chipped, but it has a definite bevel from one face. The knife is made of Bijou Hills quartzite; it measures 63 mm. long, 43 mm. wide, and 8 mm. thick.

DRILL
(1 specimen)

This piece appears to be the butt end of an expanded base drill. The sides and the base are quite straight. Both faces have been flaked along the edges, and in cross section the drill resembles a flattened oval. The specimen is made from tan quartz; it measures 32 mm. long (estimated), 12 mm. wide, and 5 mm. thick (pl. 49, *h*)

MISCELLANEOUS CHIPPED STONE

Four specimens, generally ovoid in outline, bear a small amount of retouching along one or more edges. These may have been modified intentionally for immediate use and then discarded. Two of the flakes are made of quartz, one of quartzite, and the other of gypsum. They range from 21 mm. to 41 mm. long, 19 mm. to 27 mm. wide, and 6 mm. to 15 mm. thick.

GROUND STONE ARTIFACTS
SHAFT SMOOTHERS
(1 specimen)

This piece consists of a fragment of scoria. It is slightly triangular in outline and planoconvex in cross section. There is a shallow U-shaped groove extending longitudinally down the entire length of the planer surface. Toward one end, the groove becomes quite shallow and narrow.

(3 specimens)

The first specimen somewhat resembles a discoidal. One of the faces has been smoothed from use, the opposite face is rough and unaltered. It is made from a piece of scoria and measures 26 mm. thick and 56 mm. in diameter.

The second specimen is shaped like a parallelogram. The two faces are flat and have rounded side edges. The sides vary from wedge shaped to rounded to flat. The specimen is made of gypsum. The top and bottom measure 50 mm. and 48 mm. long respectively; it is 29 mm. in width and 15 mm. thick.

The third specimen is a rectangular piece of sandstone that appears to have been artificially shaped. Both faces and one long side are quite smooth. One face has a shallow, ovoid concavity and the side surface of one end bears pecking scars. The tool measures 98 mm. long, 57 mm. wide, and 27 mm. thick.

BONE ARTIFACTS
(4 specimens)

Scapula fragments (three specimens).—Each is a fragment of bison scapulae. The first fragment is from a right scapula which has had the spine removed. The proximal and distal portions are lacking, as is the posterior border. The remaining distal portion of the anterior border has been smoothed from wear. The specimen measures 231 mm. in length.

The second specimen is also a fragment of a right scapula. It is a rectangular piece lacking the proximal and distal portions and the posterior border. The proximal end of the fragment, as well as the lateral surface and the anterior border, has been smoothed from wear. This specimen is 174 mm. long (pl. 49, *i*).

The third fragment is a thin, elongated piece of scapula that converges to a rounded point at one end; the opposite end is fractured. Both side edges along the pointed half of the bone are sharp and smooth from wear. Each face of the bone is marked with numerous longitudinal scratches, most of which are concentrated toward the pointed end. The specimen is 182 mm. long (pl. 49, *j*).

Cut bone (one specimen).—A portion of the proximal end of a bison or elk right metacarpal. The bone has been cut diagonally down from the articular facets to a point along the vascular groove. No other area on the bone appears to be artificially altered. The specimen is 39 mm. long.

GOOD SOLDIER COMPONENT AND RELATED SITES

In the following discussion I have attempted to describe the Good Soldier Component more fully by relating its remains to similar material from other sites. This method, I hope, will afford the reader a meaningful understanding of the people represented by these archeological data.

The excavated remains that have been assigned to the Good Soldier Component at site 39LM238 were recovered from the two top strata of a natural mound. Features, of which there were four, consisted of concentrations of worked and/or unworked mammal bone, stone artifacts, and pottery fragments. One rather interesting feature was a line of cobblestones associated with postholes and a firepit. The inventory of pottery, stone, and bone was indeed meager; of these specimens, only pottery and specifically vessel rims, are diagnostic enough to show relationships between the Good Soldier Component and certain other sites.

The ceramic collection from the Good Soldier Component includes vessel rims assigned to five pottery types. Each of these types is characterized by globular vessels having constricted necks. The rims are straight, slightly flaring or collared. The trait of simple-stamping the exterior surface of the vessels is common to each of the types. This trait is generally associated with the "farming-hunting villages" of the late prehistoric and historic peoples who lived on the northern and central Great Plains. The earliest date on a simple-stamped pottery occupation in these regions is from the Thomas Riggs site (39HU1), a rectagular house village in Hughes County, S. Dak. A charcoal specimen from this site provided a carbon-14 date of A.D. 1228±200 years (Missouri Basin Chronology Program, Statement No. 2, Missouri Basin Project, June 15, 1959, Lincoln).

A site bearing close artifactual relationships to the Good Soldier Component is the Spain site (39LM301). This small, compact village is located about 1 mile upstream from the mouth of Bull Creek in Lyman County, S. Dak. The creek flows eastward into the Missouri River about 33 miles downstream from the Good Soldier site. Excavations at the Spain site were conducted in 1953 by a field party of the University of Kansas under the direction of Carlyle S. Smith.

The principal occupation at the Spain site has been designated Component A and is characterized by a small, prehistoric village situated in the tree-sheltered bottoms of a minor stream course (Smith and Grange, 1958). The remains of two and probably four earth lodges were located on low hummocks or rises. The ecological situation closely duplicates what was found at the Good Soldier site, where the occupational remains were concentrated on a low, natural rise in a narrow stream valley.

The one completely excavated house at Spain had a basin-shaped floor 29 feet in diameter and an extended entryway 7 feet long and 4 feet wide. The entryway faced southeastward toward Bull Creek. Features within the house included a central hearth, a secondary firepit, and two small pocket caches. A bell-shaped cache pit and a midden deposit were located along the outer edge of the house. Abundant remains of charred beams indicated that the structure had been destroyed by fire.

TABLE 1.—*Collection of identifiable rim sherds from Spain site (Component A)*

Pottery type	Total	Percent
Iona Indented	328	26. 5
Iona Horizontal-Incised	311	25. 2
Iona Diagonal-Incised	82	6. 6
Iona S-Rim, Variety A	77	6. 2
Iona S-Rim, Variety B	50	4. 1
Iona S-Rim, Variety C	14	1. 1
Iona S-Rim, Variety D	8	. 7
Talking Crow Straight Rim	311	25. 2
Grey Cloud Horizontal-Incised	54	4. 4

There are also 320 rims, representing 20.5 percent of the total collection, that are listed under the heading of Miscellaneous. As mentioned previously, four of these were later classified as Cadotte Collared. It is apparent that the ceramic inventories and their proportional representation, at the Spain site (Component A) and the Good Soldier Component at 39LM238, are very similar, indicating a close archeological relationship. The presence of one Stanley Tool Impressed rim at Good Soldier and the absence of such a type at Spain may be reason to suspect that the former site was occupied at a slightly later date. Component A at the Spain site has been assigned to the Shannon Focus of the Chouteau Aspect; a postulated date for the component lies between A.D. 1550 and 1650. (Smith and Grange, 1958).

Another component of the Shannon Focus is the Two Teeth site; excavated in 1955 by a crew of the University of Kansas under the supervision of Carlyle S. Smith. This village is located across the Missouri River and about 4 miles upstream from the Good Soldier site. Excavations here were conducted into the remains of two circular earth lodges and several midden deposits. Smith (1959) states that the same pottery types found at Spain plus "Cadotte Collared, a small amount of Stanley Braced Rim Ware, and one stray Campbell Creek Cord Marked sherd" were present at Two Teeth. It would seem that the pottery inventories from Two Teeth and Good Soldier are almost identical and that each of the components may be contemporaneous occupations. On this basis the Good Soldier Component fits into the Shannon Focus of the Chouteau Aspect and dates no later than A.D. 1600.

BADGER COMPONENT (39LM238)

FEATURES

On the basis of their location within stratum 4, Features 1, 3, 4, 5, and 6 were assigned to the Badger Component of the Good Soldier site. The features and their associations are described below.

Feature 1.—A small pile of 31 unworked stone chips, some of which fit together. The concentration, 0.3 foot by 0.4 foot, measured 0.3 foot from top to bottom. The chips range from 38 mm. to 53 mm. long, 26 mm. to 35 mm. wide, and 3 mm. to 14 mm. thick. The cache was located at a depth of 1.2 feet in square N125W50.

Feature 3.—A small, basin-shaped firepit containing charred and uncharred bone fragments and a small quantity of charcoal. The pit was 2.6 feet in diameter and had a maximum depth of 0.4 foot. The top of the pit was defined at 2.2 feet below the present ground surface in square N130W50.

Feature 4.—A large, basin-shaped firepit containing charred and uncharred bone fragments, charcoal, and 225 fire-cracked, handsized, granitic rocks. Most of the rocks were in the bottom two-thirds of the pit. The feature measured 3.3 feet by 4.6 feet and had a maximum depth of 1.4 feet. A definite outline of the pit was apparent at 2.0 feet below the surface; however, indications of the pit were noticeable at a depth of 1.5 feet in square N125W50. A charcoal specimen from Feature 4 was submitted to the University of Michigan carbon–14 laboratory; it was cataloged M–1090a and dated 419 ± 150 years B.C.

Feature 5.—Two shallow, basin-shaped firepits. The fill in the northernmost pit was stained red with hematite. It measured 1.9 feet in diameter and had a maximum depth of 0.19 foot. The second pit, located about 0.3 foot south of the first, measured 0.9 foot in diameter and 0.4 foot in depth. Fill from this pit contained charcoal, flint chips, and fragments of bone. The pits became apparent at 1.2 feet below the present ground surface in square N155W50.

Feature 6.—A shallow, basin-shaped firepit containing burned earth, small flecks of hematite, and fragments of bone, stone, and shell. The pit, 1.3 feet in diameter and 0.4 foot in maximum depth, was located at 1.6 feet below the surface in square N180W50.

POTTERY

The pottery collections from stratum 4 at the Good Soldier site consist of sherds, most of which have been cord-paddled on their exterior surfaces. At least two vessel shapes are represented, one being globular with a constricted neck and a straight, everted rim. The other is an almost shoulderless vessel with a conoidal base. The shapes and decorations on the rims are such that they may be sorted into three groups.

GROUP A

This category consists of two undecorated rims, apparently from the same vessel (pl. 50, *b* and *c*). They measure 24 mm. in height and are 7 mm. thick, becoming slightly thinner in the area immediately below the lip. The flattened lip slopes slighty downward toward the vessel exterior and is 8 mm. wide. The interior suface is smooth, almost polished in appearance, and dark gray to black. The exterior, tan to dark brown, has faint, vertical, cord-paddled impressions extending a short distance up the rim. Both specimens are abundantly tempered with fine to medium-sized grit particles. The largest rim was located at a depth of 1.6 feet in square N145W15. The other rim came from a depth of 2.1 feet in square N145W20. These fit the descriptions of the plain Great Oasis pottery reported by Lloyd A. Wilford (1945 pp. 35–36; 1955 p. 138). Elden Johnson, of the University of Minnesota, examined the sherds and stated "The flat-lipped rims . . . are identical to Wilford's Great Oasis undecorated rims" (Personal communication March 24, 1961). Other Great Oasis sherds have been collected from at least four sites in South Dakota; the Oldham site (39CH7) in Charles Mix County (Cooper, 1955, p. 60), and the Gavins Point site (39YK203) in Yankton County (Hall, 1961). In November 1960, this writer was allowed to examine the private collection of Mr. Francis Deuder of Ree Heights, Hand County. The collection included a number of decorated Great Oasis rims from the Ree Heights Buffalo Kill site (39HD3). Finally, sherds bearing some resemblance to Great Oasis pottery are mentioned in the Swanson report (Hurt, 1951, p. 38). The comparison is made with the type Chamberlain Incised Triangle; Hurt notes that ". . . none of the Chamberlain Incised Triangle found at the Swanson site has a cord-marked body like Great Oasis pottery." This should make little difference in the comparison, since a fair percentage of Great Oasis wares do not have cord-paddled exterior surfaces (Wilford, 1945, p. 36). It is worth mentioning here that a wooden post, excavated from a rectangular house at the Swanson site was analyzed at the University of Michigan carbon-14 laboratory; it was cataloged M–839 and dated A.D. 858±250 years.

In a 1949 publication Wilford refers to a vessel and some sherds ". . . which are clearly of the Great Oasis type" and speculates that they may represent prehistoric Omaha pottery because they are from the Ryan site (25DK2) which is thought to be a burial place for the Omaha "Large Village." The vessel and its resemblance to Great Oasis is mentioned again in Wilford's 1955 report. John L. Champe, of the Laboratory of Anthropology, University of Nebraska, permitted an examination of this vessel and another from the same excavation. The specimens excavated in 1939 are from a natural mound designated 25DK2A near the town of Homer in Dakota County, Nebr. Stanley Bartos, Jr., supervised the excavations and his notes, on file at the University of Nebraska, state that the mound measured 125 feet north-south, 20 to 50 feet east-west, and had a height of 2.5 feet (also see Champe, 1946, pp. 117–118). It contained prehistoric secondary burials, and at a later date primary interments ascribed to the Omaha, were intruded into it.

GROUP B

These are five undecorated rim sherds, four of which fit together. All five apparently belong to a single vessel (pl. 50, *d*). The rim section is about 9 mm. thick and has a rounded lip. The interior surface is black and smooth. The exterior, ranging from tan to dark gray, is covered with large (3 per centimeter), parallel, cord-paddled impressions extending diagonally downward from the lip. The sherds are tempered with minute particles of calcite and occasional large and small grit inclusions. They were recovered from the 2.0–2.5 foot level in square N135W40. The specimens bear a general resemblance to several varieties of Plains Woodland vessels that are almost shoulderless and have conoidal bases. Calcite tempering is a characteristic of Harlan Cord-Roughened, the diagnostic pottery of the Keith Focus (Kivett, 1953). Two sites within this focus have been dated by radiocarbon methods. The Woodruff Ossuary in north-central Kansas (Kivett, 1953) was dated at A.D. 611±240 years (Wedel and Kivett, 1956), and site 25FT18 in south-central Nebraska was dated at A.D. 828±200 years (Crane and Griffin, 1960, p. 40). The Valley Cord-Roughened is characteristic of the Valley Focus (Hill and Kivett, 1941), the type site being 25VY1 in central Nebraska (Kivett, 1949). A dendrochronological estimate of A.D. 1000 to 1150 was assigned to a Valley Focus occupation at Ash Hollow Cave in southwest Nebraska (Champe, 1946, p. 86). The trait that allies the Group B specimens from the Good Soldier site to Valley Cord-Roughened is the diagonal orientation of the cord impressions on the vessel exterior.

GROUP C

Only one large rim and shoulder section of a vessel is represented here (pl. 50, *a*). The rim is vertical with a very faint outward bulge between the neck and the lip. A very weak shoulder is evident below the neck. The lip is flat and slants downward toward the vessel exterior. Rim height, measured between the neck and lip top, is 34 mm. and the thickness is 6 mm. The specimen is abundantly tempered with grit particles ranging up to 2.0 mm. in size. The interior surface is a brownish-orange and smooth. The exterior is the same color, but it is covered with extremely fine, parallel, cord-paddled impressions that extend vertically down from the lip. The rim is decorated with parallel, notched-stick indentations that extend from the lip top diagonally downward onto the rim exterior. The indentations are about 13 mm. in length and V-shaped in cross section. The notches run perpendicular to, and average about six per indentation. The rim was recovered at a depth of 2.0 feet in square N145W50. Although this rim does not resemble any of the reported pottery types on the northern and central Plains, I was able to find two similar specimens that belong to a single vessel. They are from site 39BR11, located on the opposite side of the Missouri River and about 21 miles downstream from the Good Soldier site. Field parties of the Smithsonian Institution located and made tests at the site in 1947, 1953, and 1954. Paul L. Cooper's notes (on file at the Lincoln office of the Smithsonian Institution) show that an occupation area at 39BR11 was overlain by two distinct strata. The uppermost was the plow zone or present surface, under which was a sterile zone of fine, yellowish silt. Beneath the silt was a "dark brown" layer of soil containing small, basin-shaped firepits and artifacts. One of the rims (cat. No. 39BR11–18) was recovered from this stratum at "Profile 6 . . . 2.6' to 3.3'" below the surface; the other rim (cat. No. 39BR11–37) came from dirt that had sloped down onto the riverbank.

There are also certain artifactual similarities between the Badger Component and the Clear Lake site, which is located along the Illinois River in Tazewell and Mason Counties, Ill. (Fowler, 1952). I believe the rim from Group C (Badger Component) resembles those from the conoidal vessels of Weaver ware, the predominant pottery type at Clear Lake. The projectile points from Group 2 (Badger Component) also bear a resemblance to those of Group A that are illustrated on page 155 of the Clear Lake Report. Melvin L. Fowler kindly examined specimens from the Badger Component and his statements, regarding the Group C rim and the Group 2 points, are as follows: ". . . I would not compare it closely with Weaver. The general resemblances are there in the rather tightly twisted parallel cords and general vessel shape. The paste is different and not as compact as Weaver. . . . In general, if such a sherd were found in Illinois, it would be classified as Late Woodland on a general Weaver Horizon. . . ." (Fowler, personal communication February 2, 1960).

"The projectile points are not Weaver but are similar to those associated with the so-called Maples Mills and Dillenger cultures in Illinois. . . ." Weaver ware is generally assigned to the Woodland period in the Illinois Valley and the ware has been dated by carbon-14 from the Irving Village at A.D. 770±250 years, and from the Rutherford Mound at A.D. 425±200 years (Griffin, 1958, pp. 12–13 and 15).

STONE

PROJECTILE POINTS
(6 specimens)

Group 1. Triangular, straight base (two specimens).—Each has slightly convex sides and shows haphazard bifacial flake scars. The largest specimen lacks the tip and is made from a grayish-brown quartzite (pl. 50, *f*). It measures 20 mm. long (estimated), 18 mm. wide, and 5 mm. thick. The other point (pl. 50, *e*), made from a crystal clear quartz, is 15 mm. long, 17 mm. wide, 4 mm. thick and weighs 1.8 gm. Both points were recovered from the 1.0–1.5 foot level in square N145W45.

Group 2. Triangular, corner-notched (four specimens).—None are complete, but all show straight to slightly convex sides. Evenly placed, bifacial flake scars extend outward at right angles from the longitudinal axis to the side edges. One point, broken almost its entire length down the long axis, has a slightly convex base (pl. 50, *g*). It is made from a brown chalcedony, but one face is completely coated with a white patination. The specimen measures 38 mm. long, 27 mm. wide (estimated), and 5 mm. thick; it was located at a depth of 1.3 feet in square N125W70. The next piece also has a convex base, but lacks the tip portion (pl. 50, *h*). It was made from a very fine-grained, light-brown quartzite and measures 32 mm. long (estimated), 24 mm. wide and 4 mm. thick. The specimen was recovered 2.2 feet below the surface in square N175W50; it is similar to a point (Catalogue No. 43) found at site 39BR11, Brule County, S. Dak. The third specimen, made of basalt, lacks the base, and the tangs were accidentally broken off in the laboratory (pl. 50, *i*). It was located at a depth of 2.3 feet in square N190W40. The fourth piece, made from a fine-grained, olive-drab quartzite, consists only of a point section (pl. 50, *j*). It was recovered from a depth of 1.8 feet in square N150W35.

END SCRAPERS

(10 specimens)

Group 1 (four specimens).—All are planoconvex in cross section, ovoid in outline, show little or no secondary flaking on the convex surface, and have been retouched at one end and both side edges. The first specimen (pl. 50, *k*), made from a gray chalcedony, is 40 mm. long, 28 mm. wide and 7 mm. thick. It was located at a depth of 2.3 feet in square N155W15. The second scraper (pl. 50, *l*), made from a brown chalcedony, is patinated on the convex surface. It measures 35 mm. long, 29 mm. wide, 10 mm. thick and was recovered from the 1.5–2.0 foot level in square N155W25. The third piece (pl. 50, *m*), also made from a brown chalcedony, is patinated on the base and along the side edges. It measures 26 mm. long, 12 mm. wide, 7 mm. thick and was found in the 1.0–1.5 foot level at square N135W50. The fourth specimen has been fractured opposite the working end; it was made from a brown chalcedony and is heavily patinated on the convex surface (pl. 50, *n*). The fragment measures 22 mm. wide, 9 mm. thick and was located in the 1.0–1.5 foot level at square N145W40.

Group 2 (*three specimens*).—All are planoconvex in cross section, rectangular in outline and have a keel toward one side of the convex surface extending down the long axis for almost the entire length of the scraper. The first specimen, made from a brown chalcedony and patinated on one side, has a small semicircular notch chipped into one side edge (pl. 50, *o*). The piece measures 18 mm. long, 18 mm. wide, and 7 mm. thick. It was recovered from the 2.0–2.5 foot level at square N150W40. The next specimen, made from a mottled gray flint, is patinated along portions of one end and a side edge and has secondary chipping along the opposite side edge (pl. 50, *p*). It is 20 mm. long, 18 mm. wide, 5 mm. thick and was located in the 2.0–2.5 foot level at square N145W35. The third specimen is incomplete; it is made from a brown chalcedony and shows retouching only at the working end (pl. 50, *q*). The fragment was recovered from the 1.5–2.0 foot level in square N160W50.

Group 3 (*three specimens*).—These pieces are planoconvex in cross section, triangular in outline and have been retouched over the entire convex surface. The largest scraper, made from a brown chalcedony (pl. 50, *r*), is 30 mm. long, 23 mm. wide, and 6 mm. thick. It was located in the 1.0–1.5 foot level at square N135W35. The second scraper, also a brown chalcedony (pl. 50, *s*), is 19 mm. long, 21 mm. wide, and 6 mm. thick. It was located in the 1.0–1.5 foot level at square N135W35. The last specimen, made from a yellowish-brown jasper (pl. 50, *t*) is 20 mm. long, 19 mm. wide, 6 mm. thick and was recovered from the 1.5–2.0 foot level at square N140W50.

KNIVES
(7 specimens)

Group 1 (*three specimens*).—Ovoid in outline, each of these pieces displays large, bifacial, percussion flake scars. The largest knife has been finely retouched on one face almost entirely around the outer edge. It is made from a brown chalcedony and has a thin, whitish patination on one face (pl. 50, *u*). The knife is 87 mm. long, 65 mm. wide, 13 mm. thick and was recovered from 1.8 feet below the surface at square N150W30. The second specimen is incomplete, but the recovered portion lacks any secondary flaking (pl. 50, *v*). It is made from a fine-grained, mottled brown and tan quartzite and measures 46 mm. long (estimated), 35 mm. wide, and 10 mm. thick. The piece was located in the 1.0–1.5 foot level at square N155W55. The third specimen, also incomplete, is made from a fine-grained, yellowish quartzite (pl. 50, *w*). It measures 47 mm. wide, 9 mm. thick and was recovered from the 1.5–2.0 foot level at square N140W50.

Group 2 (*two specimens*).—Triangular in outline, each shows haphazard, bifacial chipping along the two side edges. The first piece, made from a fine-grained, purple quartzite, measures 32 mm. long,

28 mm. wide, and 12 mm. thick (pl. 50, *x*). It was found in the 1.0–1.5 foot level at square N145W45. The second specimen is a knife fragment. It consists of a fine grained, grayish quartzite that is patinated along portions of one face and a side edge (pl. 50, *y*). The piece is 20 mm. long, 34 mm. wide, and 6 mm. thick. It was located at a depth of 1.3 feet in square N150W50.

Group 3 (two specimens).—Both pieces are steeply beveled along the side edges, rectangular in outline, and are made of Bijou Hills quartzite. The larger specimen is incomplete and appears to be the upper portion of a knife, or possibly a drill with opposite faces alternately beveled. It was located in the 1.0–1.5 foot level at square N145W30. The smaller piece is the midsection of a bifacially flaked blade that has been steeply beveled along one side edge from both faces. It was located in the 1.0–1.5 foot level at square N145W45.

WORKED FLAKES
(14 specimens)

These pieces consist of asymmetrical flakes showing unifacial retouch along one or more side edges. A few are no doubt fragments broken from side and/or end scrapers. One specimen has a semi-circular notch chipped into each of its two side edges. It has been suggested that this type of tool may have been used for cutting arrow shafts (Cosner, 1956). All of these flakes were recovered from within 1.0 to 2.5 feet depths.

PROBLEMATICAL OBJECT
(1 specimen)

This specimen is tubular and broken at one end. It may be a section of a bead, or simply a limestone concretion (pl. 50, *z*). The piece measures 22 mm. long, has an outside diameter of 14 mm. and an inside diameter of 6 mm. It was located in the 1.5–2.0 foot level at square N190W50.

DISCUSSION OF THE BADGER COMPONENT

In describing the pottery and certain projectile point specimens from this component I have referred to other sites from which similar artifacts were collected. It is evident that the remains of at least three types of pottery vessels are represented in the relatively thin soil zone of stratum 4; evidence as to whether or not the makers of these vessels occupied the site contemporaneously or at different times is inconclusive. A comparable archeological situation involving the kinds of specimens assigned to the Badger Component has not been reported. Nevertheless, in light of the carbon-14 dates related to pottery specimens similar to those in Groups A, B, and C,

I do not think that the possibility of a simultaneous occupation for the component should be ruled out.

Two discrepancies remain to be discussed. The first concerns the question of whether or not Great Oasis pottery is prehistoric Omaha in origin. Statements alluding to the possibility of this origin have appeared in print at least twice (Champe, 1946, p. 48; Wilford, 1949, p. 36), and each reference concerns the vessel or vessels recovered from the excavations at 25DK2A mentioned earlier in this report. I have examined the field notes and sketches from the site and am of the opinion that the vessels, both of which are good Great Oasis specimens, belong to the prehistoric burial remains rather than to the intrusive Omaha interments that were accompanied by European trade goods. I am not aware of any Great Oasis ceramics found in undisturbed, direct association with White trade material. The trait of cord-paddling that appears on the exterior surface of some Great Oasis vessels is not a late prehistoric technique in the central Plains or Middle Missouri region, nor is this pottery type very similar to others that are diagnostic of the protohistoric or historic periods in those areas. Great Oasis sherds have been more aptly compared to pottery from the Middle Ceramic Period (Champe, 1946), and tracing this pottery type up through time to Omaha occupations has yet to be validly demonstrated.

The second problem is in connection with the carbon-14 date obtained from charcoal at Feature 4. This date, 419 B.C.±150 years, is certainly not compatible with the artifactual material of the component; however, it may be a perfectly acceptable date for the basin-shaped pit in Feature 4. As other sites are dug, in locales where stratigraphy is not so subject to stream erosion and deposition, artifacts may be found that show significant relationships to *some* of those in the Badger Component, thus validating an earlier occupation not recognized now.

In conclusion, the Badger Component represents an early occupation site, the artifacts of which are most closely comparable to those from other sites assigned to the Plains Woodland Period, and a date no later than A.D. 1200 is suggested for the occupation of this component.

CONCLUSIONS

The Good Soldier site (39LM238), located along the Missouri River in central South Dakota, consists of two stratigraphically separated occupations. The latest has been named the Good Soldier Component. It comprises remains closely resembling those from two other sites in the vicinity and has been assigned, together with those sites, to the Shannon Focus of the Chouteau Aspect. The early occupation at

39LM238 is designated the Badger Component. Its artifactual resemblances to certain other sites in Minnesota, Nebraska, and South Dakota indicate that it falls within the Plains Woodland Phase. The possibility of a still earlier occupation at the Good Soldier site is suggested.

APPENDIX

BONE AND VEGETAL IDENTIFICATION FROM THE GOOD SOLDIER SITE [2]

BONE

The small quantity of bone from the Good Soldier site was more or less evenly distributed throughout the arbitrary half-foot levels of the excavations. Buffalo (*Bison bison*) remains were by far the most common, while the whitetailed deer (*Odocoileus speleus*), coyote (*Canis latrans*), kit fox (*Vulpes velox*), prairie dog (*Cynomys ludovicianus*), and the cottontail rabbit (*Syvilagus floridanus*) are also present. Included in the inventory are a few fish bones; however, there was no evidence of fowl in the excavations.

I have assigned all of the osseous remains recovered from the surface, down to 1 foot in depth to the Good Soldier Component and all below that depth to the Badger Component. The results are shown in table 2.

TABLE 2.—*Osseous remains from Good Soldier and Badger Components*

GOOD SOLDIER COMPONENT

Bison	Number	White-tailed deer	Number	Coyote	Number	Kit fox	Number	Catfish	Number
Lower jaw___	1	Upper tooth_	3	Muzzle_____	1	Humerus__	1	Dorsal vertebra__	1
Occiput_____	2	Lower jaw___	1	Lower jaw___	1			Pectoral girdle_____	1
Scapula_____	1	Meta- carpal_____	1	Atlas_____	1			Fin parts___	4
Humerus_____	1	Phalanges___	1	Axis_____	1				
Radius_____	3	Cuboid_____	1	Humerus____	1				
Tibia_____	3			Calcaneum__	1				
Metacarpal__	2								
Metatarsal___	1								
Phalanges____	11								

BADGER COMPONENT

Bison	Number	Prairie dog	Number	Cottontail	Number
Lower jaw___	2	Lower jaw___	1	Humerus____	1
Teeth_____	4				
Ulna_____	1				
Radius_____	1				
Metacarpal__	3				
Femur_____	1				
Astragalus___	3				
Cuboid_____	1				
Phalanges____	14				

[2] The fish bone was identified by David H. Dunkle, United States National Museum. All other bone was analyzed by Theodore E. White, Dinosaur National Monument. Norton H. Nickerson, Washington University, identified the vegetal specimen.

The lists show buffalo, deer, coyote, kit fox, and fish associated with the Good Soldier Component, and buffalo, prairie dog, and rabbit with the Badger Component.   Interestingly, almost all of the buffalo remains are from the limbs of the animals; previous writers have suggested that this phenomena indicates that the kills and the butchering took place some distance from the main camp or village (Lehmer, 1952; White, 1952 a, 1952 b, 1954).

VEGETAL

Only one vegetal specimen, a pit of the *Prunus americana*, was recovered.   It came from square N140W40 in the 1.0–1.5 foot level.

LITERATURE CITED

BARTOS, STANLEY, JR.
————— Field notes.   Manuscript on file at the Laboratory of Anthropology
     Univ. Nebraska, 1939, Lincoln.
CHAMPE, JOHN L.
     1946. Ash Hollow Cave.   Univ. Nebraska Stud., n.s. No. 1.   Lincoln.
COOGAN, ALAN H.
     1960. Geological age of Soldier Creek, Buffalo County, South Dakota.   Proc.
          Iowa Acad. Sci., vol. 67, pp. 314–325.
COOPER, PAUL L.
     1955. The archeological and paleontological salvage program in the Mis-
          souri Basin, 1950–1951.   Smithsonian Misc. Coll., vol. 126, No. 2.
          99 pp.
COSNER, AARON J.
     1956. The "Stone Scraper" and Arrow "Wrench."   Amer. Antiq., vol. 21,
          No. 3, pp.. 300–301.
CRANE, H. R., and GRIFFIN, JAMES B.
     1960. University of Michigan radiocarbon dates V.   Amer. Journ. Sci., Radio-
          carbon Suppl., vol. 2, p. 40.   New Haven.
FOWLER, MELVIN L.
     1952. The Clear Lake site: Hopewellian occupation.   Hopewellian Com-
          munities in Illinois, edited by Thorne Deuel.   Illinois State Mus.,
          Sci. Pap., vol. 5, No. 4.   Springfield.
GRIFFIN, JAMES B.
     1958. The chronological position of the Hopewell Culture in the Eastern
          United States.   Univ. Michigan, Anthrop. Pap., No. 12.
HALL, ROBERT L.
     1961. An archaeological investigation in the Gavin's Point area, Yankton
          County, South Dakota.   Museum News, W. H. Over Museum, vol.
          22, No. 7.
HILL, A. T., and KIVETT, MARVIN F.
     1941. Woodland-like manifestations in Nebraska.   Nebraska Hist., vol. 21,
          No. 3.
HURT, WESLEY R., JR.
     1951. Report of the investigation of the Swanson site 39BR16, Brule County,
          South Dakota, 1950.   South Dakota Archaeol. Comm., Archaeol.
          Stud., Circ. No. 3.

HUSCHER, HAROLD A., and MCNUTT, CHARLES H.
      1958. Appraisal of the archeological resources of the Big Bend Reservoir,
            South Dakota. Mimeographed report prepared by the Missouri
            Basin Project, Smithsonian Institution. Lincoln.
KIVETT, MARVIN F.
      1949. A Woodland pottery type from Nebraska. Proc. Fifth Plains Conf.
            Archeol. Note Book No. 1, Lab. Anthrop., Univ. Nebraska, pp. 67–69.
      1953. The Woodruff Ossuary, a prehistoric burial site in Phillips County,
            Kans. Bur. Amer. Ethnol., Bul 154, Riv. Bas. Surv. Pap., No. 3,
            pp. 103–142.
LEHMER, DONALD J.
      1952. Animal bone and Plains archeology. Plains Archeol. Conf. News Let-
            ter, vol. 4, No. 4.
      1954. Archeological investigations in the Oahe Dam area, South Dakota,
            1950–51. Bur. Amer. Ethnol., Bull. 158, Riv. Bas. Surv. Pap., No. 7.
MCNUTT, CHARLES H.
      1959. Comments on two Northern Plains pottery wares. Abst., Proc. Sixty-
            Ninth Ann. Meet. Nebraska Acad. Sci.
SMITH, CARLYLE S.
      1951. Pottery types from the Talking Crow site, Fort Randall Reservoir,
            South Dakota. Plains Archeol. Conf. News Letter, vol. 4, No. 3,
            pp. 32–41.
      1959. The temporal relationships of coalescent village sites in Fort Randall
            Reservoir, South Dakota. Actas del XXXIII. Congreso Internacional
            de Americanistas, tomo II, pp. 11–123. San Jose, Costa Rica.
SMITH, CARLYLE S., and GRANGE, ROGER T., JR.
      1958. The Spain site (39LM301), a winter village in Fort Randall Reser-
            voir, South Dakota. Bur. Amer. Ethnol., Bull. 169, Riv. Bas. Surv.
            Pap., No. 11.
WEDEL, WALDO R., and KIVETT, MARVIN F.
      1956. Additional data on the Woodruff Ossuary, Kansas. Amer. Antiq.,
            vol. 21, No. 4, pp. 414–416.
WHITE, THEODORE E.
      1952 a. Observations on the butchering technique of some aboriginal peoples :
            I. Amer. Antiq., vol. 17, No. 4, pp. 337–338.
      1952 b. Suggestions on the butchering technique of the inhabitants at the
            Dodd and Phillips Ranch sites in the Oahe Reservoir Area. Plains
            Archeol. Conf. News Letter, vol. 5, No. 2.
      1954. Butchering techniques at the Dodd and Phillips Ranch sites. Bur.
            Amer. Ethnol., Bull. 158, Riv. Bas. Surv. Pap. No. 7, Appen. 4, pp.
            165–172.
WILFORD, LLOYD A.
      1945. Three villages of the Mississippi pattern in Minnesota. Amer. Antiq.,
            vol. 11, No. 1, pp. 32–40.
      1949. Archeological field work in Minnesota. Proc. Fifth Plains Conf.
            Archeol., Note Book No. 1, Lab. Anthrop., Univ. Nebraska, pp. 34–36.
      1955. A revised classification of the prehistoric cultures of Minnesota.
            Amer. Antiq., vol. 21, No. 2, pp. 130–142.
WOOD, W. RAYMOND.
      ——— The Redbird Focus. MS., MA thesis, on file at the Lab. Anthrop.,
            Univ. Nebraska, 1956.

a, View east-northeast of Good Soldier site and surrounding vicinity. Missouri River flows eastward (upper left).   *b*, View north of trench cross-sectioning the long axis of the natural mound.   Broken rocks are adjacent to the large pit (Feature 4).

Pottery specimens from the Good Soldier Component: *a, b*, Iona Indented; *c, d*, Grey Cloud Horizontal-Incised; *e, f*, Talking Crow Straight Rim; *g*, Cadotte Collared; *h*, Stanley Tool Impressed; *i–k*, miscellaneous.

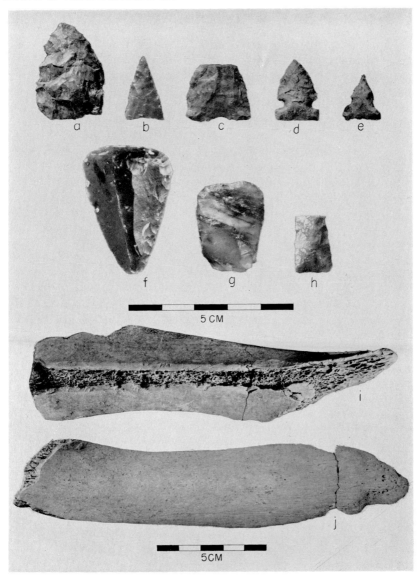

Stone and bone specimens from the Good Soldier Component.

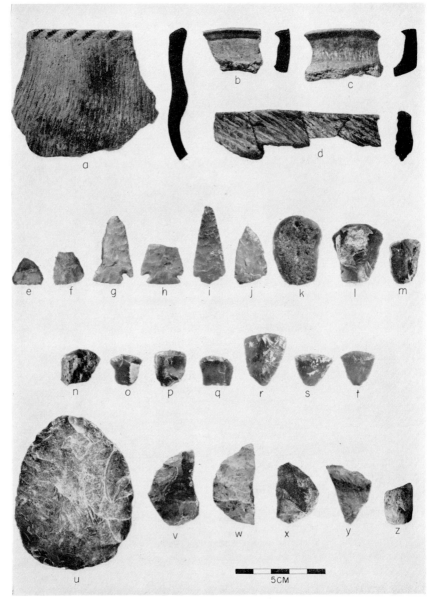

Pottery and stone specimens from the Badger Component.

SMITHSONIAN INSTITUTION
Bureau of American Ethnology
Bulletin 189

———

River Basin Surveys Papers, No. 38
Archeological Investigations in the Toronto Reservoir
Area, Kansas

By JAMES H. HOWARD

CONTENTS

PAGE

Introduction _____ 323
The sites _____ 327
   Site 14WO203 _____ 328
      Excavations _____ 328
      Specimen descriptions _____ 329
      Cultural affiliation _____ 332
   Site 14WO209 _____ 332
      Excavations _____ 332
      Specimen descriptions _____ 334
      Cultural affiliation _____ 337
   Site 14WO215 _____ 337
      Excavations _____ 337
      Specimen descriptions _____ 338
      Cultural affiliations _____ 341
   The Walleye Rockshelter (14WO222) _____ 341
      Excavations _____ 342
      Petroglyphs _____ 342
      Specimen descriptions _____ 344
      Cultural affiliations _____ 346
   Dry Creek Rockshelter (14WO224) _____ 347
      Excavations _____ 348
      Petroglyphs _____ 348
      Specimen descriptions _____ 350
      Cultural affiliations _____ 353
   The Outlaw Rockshelter (14WO225) _____ 353
   Little-Water-Man petroglyph (14WO226) _____ 353
   The Possum Point site (14WO228) _____ 354
      Excavations _____ 354
      Specimen descriptions _____ 354
      Cultural affiliations _____ 357
   Site 14GR210 _____ 357
      Excavations _____ 357
      Specimen descriptions _____ 358
      Cultural affiliation _____ 360
   Site 14GR216 _____ 360
      Excavations _____ 361
      Features _____ 361
      Specimen descriptions _____ 361
      Cultural affiliations _____ 366
Summary and conclusions _____ 366
Appendix. Tabulation of Toronto Reservoir sites _____ 368
Literature cited _____ 369

ILLUSTRATIONS

PLATES

(All plates follow page 370)

51. *a-l*, Artifacts from site 14WO203. *m-k'*, Artifacts from site 14WO209.
52. *a-d'*, Artifacts from site 14WO215. *e'-p'*, Artifacts from Walleye Rockshelter (14WO222).
53. Petroglyphs from Walleye Rockshelter (14WO222).
54. *a*, Excavation of Dry Creek Rockshelter (14WO224). *b-t*, Artifacts from Dry Creek Rockshelter (14WO224).
55. *a*, *b*, Petroglyphs from Dry Creek Rockshelter (14WO224). *c*, Petroglyph at the Outlaw Rockshelter (14WO225). *d*, *e*, Petroglyph from site 14WO226.
56. *a*, Excavation at Possum Point site (14WO228). *b-k*, Artifacts from Possum Point site (14WO228).
57. *a*, View of site 15GR210. *b-m*, Artifacts from site 14GR210.
58. *a*, Portion of excavated area in site 14GR216. *b-w*, Artifacts from site 14GR-216.

TEXT FIGURES

	PAGE
59. Site map of the Toronto Reservoir area _____ (facing)	327
60. Plan of site 14WO203, showing excavations _____	329
61. Plan of site 14WO209, showing excavations _____	333
62. Plan of site 14WO222, showing excavations _____	343
63. Plan of site 14WO224, showing excavations _____	349
64. Plan of site 14WO228, showing excavations _____	355
65. Plan of site 14GR210, showing excavations _____	359
66. Plan of site 14GR216, showing excavations _____	362

ARCHEOLOGICAL INVESTIGATIONS IN THE TORONTO RESERVOIR AREA, KANSAS [1]

By JAMES H. HOWARD

INTRODUCTION

The Toronto Dam and Reservoir, a flood-control and conservation project of the U.S. Army, Corps of Engineers, Tulsa District, is located on the Verdigris River in Greenwood and Woodson Counties, southeastern Kansas (see fig. 59). The dam is a rolled, earthfill structure, 4,712 feet in length and 90 feet in height, above the river channel. It is 3½ miles south of the town of Toronto in Woodson County, Kans., 55 miles north of the Oklahoma border, and 75 miles west of the Missouri border. It forms a reservoir some 11½ miles long, with a maximum width of approximately 1½ miles at full-pool level of 931 feet (m.s.l.). This reservoir extends up the Verdigris River and its tributaries in the eastern portion of Woodson County and the western portion of Greenwood County to cover a total area of approximately 10,000 acres. Dam construction was begun in November 1954 and was essentially completed in December 1959. Flooding of the reservoir began in the spring of 1959 with maximum pool level to be reached intermittently after completion.

In this area the Verdigris River flows in a generally southeasterly direction, forming a wide flood plain between bluffs of Pennsylvanian sandstone and limestone. Numerous bends and meanders indicate that the drainage system is old. A heavy growth of trees, principally scrub oak, elm, cottonwood, and hackberry, clothes the valley and the sides of the bluffs. Above the valley proper, the bluffs slope gradually upward to rolling, grass-covered plains. This upland country is used mainly for grazing, since numerous sandstone and limestone outcrops hinder the use of the plow for breaking the land.

In early historic times, two Thegiha-speaking Siouan tribes, the Osage and the Kansa, are known to have lived in this area along the Verdigris River (McDermott, 1940). However, no sites that could definitely be attributed to either of these tribes were located during the archeological investigation.

[1] Submitted September 1959.

Archeological sites here are characteristically located on slight rises close to a river or stream. Numerous sandstone fragments lie on or near the surface of the sites, and other than these stones, all surface archeological features have been obliterated by intensive cultivation. The principal stone used in the manufacture of chipped-stone artifacts is a chert from the Flint Hills region, some 50 miles to the northwest, in Marion, Chase, and Morris Counties, Kans. A popular source of material for ground-stone tools is a coquina-like Permian limestone of the Cottonwood formation, which outcrops in Greenwood County.

The Inter-Agency Archeological Salvage Program has conducted three seasons of archeological investigations within the area of the Toronto Dam and Reservoir (see report of the Committee for the Recovery of Archaeological Remains, 1958). The first season of investigations consisted of a brief, initial survey of a portion of the area in May 1953 by Edward H. Moorman, working out of the Region 3 Office of the National Park Service. The short time available for this survey limited the results to the locating, visiting, and recording of but three archeological sites in Greenwood County (14GR1-3) and two sites in Woodson County (14WO1-2). No testing or excavation was possible, but the survey was sufficient to indicate that considerable archeological potential existed in several sections of the flood area. Additional survey and investigation was recommended within the framework of the Salvage Program.

The second season of salvage in the Toronto Reservoir was undertaken in September and October 1956, by Alfred E. Johnson and two assistants, working out of the Lincoln, Nebr., office of the River Basin Surveys, Smithsonian Institution. Johnson, then a student at the University of Kansas and a temporary staff member of the River Basin Surveys, and his party worked intermittently for 6 weeks in the area, revisited the sites located by Moorman, made additional surface collections from them, and excavated three 5-foot test squares in one of the most promising of them (14WO1). In addition, this party located, visited, and recorded 18 more sites in Greenwood County (14GR201-218) and 13 more sites in Woodson County (14 WO201-213), to bring the total of sites in the Toronto Reservoir area to 36. Johnson also dug three 5-foot test squares in site 14WO203 and excavated three hearths in site 14GR209 that had been partially exposed by heavy equipment in road-construction activities. Surface collections of artifacts were made from nearly all sites located, petroglyphs were recorded in one site, and data regarding terrain, geology, and general archeological considerations were recorded. Johnson (1957) prepared a report of these sites, analyzing the materials recovered, recommending certain sites for more intensive investigation, and suggesting that some portions of the reservoir area still might provide additional sites.

On the basis of surface collections and the three brief, subsurface tests, Johnson was able to identify tentatively the cultural assemblages of nine of the sites as follows:

14RG2	Upper Republican
14GR202	Kansas City Hopewell and Keith Focus
14GR205	Upper Republican
14GR212	Kansas City Hopewell
14GR216	Upper Republican, Keith Focus, and Archaic
14GR217	Keith Focus
14WO1	Woodland
14WO203	Kansas City Hopewell
14WO209	Upper Republican

The remaining 27 sites did not provide sufficient material upon which a cultural identification could be based, though many of them appeared to be simple, nonceramic (Archaic?) camps. The nature of most of these sites was such that no significant results would appear likely from further investigations, and none were recommended. However, there were seven sites (14GR2, 14GR202, 14GR210, 14GR 212, 14GR216, 14WO203, and 14WO209) where further work appeared likely to produce clarifying information. These sites were, therefore, recommended for additional investigation.

Johnson then drew the following conclusions regarding the cultural manifestations in the area:

Preceramic remains are rare. Only one component of a three-component site (14GR216) can definitely be assigned to an Archaic complex. Some of the sites presented under the heading "Nonceramic Sites," may also be associated with an Archaic complex, but the remains are so scanty that no positive statement can be made in that respect.

Woodland remains are fairly common. There are four sites or components of sites affiliated with this pattern. Of these, three have artifacts which allow them to be placed within a subdivision of the pattern, the Keith Focus. The remaining site contains traits which do not permit its placement in one of the previously defined foci, but this may be because of the insufficient quantity of material collected. The fact that Keith Focus remains are present in the reservoir extends the distribution of this complex further to the east and south than previously realized.

The Hopewell complex has a known distribution through central Kansas as far as Ellsworth. The presence of three sites in the Toronto Reservoir, having an affiliation with this complex, extends its distribution farther to the south and indicates that the complex may have a much wider distribution throughout the eastern section of the state than was previously realized.

The presence of sites of an Upper Republican affiliation, situated within the boundaries of the Toronto Reservoir, extends the limits of this cultural complex considerably farther to the south. The nearest site with an Upper Republican affiliation which could be found in a perusal of the literature is located in the Kanapolis Reservoir, on the Smoky Hill River to the north and west (Smith, 1949, p. 295).

Using a recently published date as a starting point, we find that the area to be inundated by the waters of the Toronto Reservoir was occupied, at least, from A.D. 611 (plus or minus 240 years) on. This date is from the Woodruff Ossuary, situated just south of the Nebraska line in Phillips County, Kansas, which has been assigned to the Keith Focus of the Woodland Pattern (Wedel and Kivett, 1956, p. 414). This beginning date would probably be extended considerably into the past if the material from the Archaic component at 14GR216 were sufficient to allow its identification with other sites from that complex. [Johnson, 1957, pp. 58-59.]

The third and final season of archeological salvage in the Toronto Reservoir area was accomplished during a continuous 6-week period from May 15 to June 30, 1957, by Dr. James H. Howard and four assistants, working out of the Lincoln, Nebr., office of the River Basin Surveys, Smithsonian Institution. Howard, then a temporary staff member of the River Basin Surveys, and his party revisited many of the sites located by Moorman in 1953, and by Johnson in 1956, made additional surface collections from them, and conducted excavations in four of the sites that had been recommended by Johnson for further work. All four were open, occupation areas. One of these was site 14GR210, where four 5-foot test squares were excavated, and to which Johnson's data did not permit assignment of a cultural affiliation. A second was site 14GR216, where a trench 65 feet long and 5 feet wide was excavated and later widened by excavation of three 5-foot squares on each side of the base trench. Johnson had assigned the three components of this site to the Upper Republican Aspect, the Keith Focus, and the Archaic, respectively. A third was site 14WO203, one of those briefly tested by Johnson with three 5-foot test squares. The Howard party dug three additional 5-foot test squares. Johnson's identification of this site was Kansas City Hopewell. The fourth was site 14WO209, to which Johnson had assigned a cultural designation of Upper Republican, and within which Howard excavated two 5-foot squares. The other three sites recommended by Johnson for further work (14GR2, 14GR202, and 14GR212) were revisited in 1957, and additional surface materials were collected, but the sites were not considered of sufficient potential, at that time, to warrant excavation.

In addition to revisiting these previously recorded sites, the 1957 party located, visited, and recorded 3 more sites in Greenwood County (14GR219-221) and 18 more sites in Woodson County (14WO214-231) to bring the final total of recorded sites in the Toronto Reservoir area to 57. Only four of these new sites were of sufficient archeological significance to warrant excavation or assignment of cultural affiliation, though petroglyphs were recorded in two others (14WO225 and 14WO226). The four significant sites included 14WO215, in which Howard excavated two 5-foot test squares; the Walleye Rockshelter (14WO224), in which nearly the entire surface area (eleven 5-foot squares) was excavated; and the Possum Point site (14WO228), in which he excavated six 5-foot squares. The present report will detail the work done by Howard's party in the eight excavated sites and the two petroglyph sites mentioned above.

The work of Edward H. Moorman in the 1953 season was done under the supervision of Dr. Erik K. Reed and Charlie R. Steen of the Region 3 office of the National Park Service, Santa Fe, N. Mex., under whose jurisdiction the southern Kansas area was administered at that time. The work of Alfred E. Johnson and his party in 1956, and that of Dr. James H. Howard and his party in 1957, was done under the administrative supervision of Dr. Frank H. H. Roberts, Jr., Director of the River Basin Surveys, and Dr. Robert L. Stephenson, Chief of the Missouri Basin Project. The Toronto Reservoir is situated outside the Missouri Drainage Basin, and funds for the work were transferred by the National Park Service from the appropriations for work outside the Basin. For purposes of convenience and economy, the work was administered through the Missouri Basin Project office of the River Basin Surveys, Smithsonian Institution, in Lincoln, Nebr.

Assisting Johnson in the field were Wayne O. Wallace and Gaylord S. Tefft. Tefft and Richard Fischer assisted Johnson in his laboratory analyses, and Sidney Anderson identified the animal bones. All five were students at the University of Kansas, where Dr. Carlyle S. Smith kindly made laboratory facilities available to Johnson. Assisting Dr. Howard in the field were Edward A. Danaczko, D. William Chatfield, August Love, and Joseph Marshno, employed by the Smithsonian Institution for the project. The regular staff of the Missouri Basin Project in Lincoln assisted Howard in his laboratory analyses and preparation of this report. Others who assisted in a number of ways in the archeological salvage in the Toronto Reservoir area include George Fritz, Mark Sample, George Phillips, Albert Webb, George Webb, Frank J. Adenauer, J. E. Sower, H. W. Pashe, and Fred Jamison, all of Toronto, Kans.; Richard Phillips and Lester Harding of Yates Center, Kans., and Mr. and Mrs. Kenneth Landes and Mrs. James H. Howard of Kansas City, Mo. Mr. Lloyd Tanner of the University of Nebraska State Museum in Lincoln identified the bone materials from the 1957 excavations. Sincere thanks are expressed to all of these people for their generous assistance, without which the work would have been much less pleasant and rewarding.

THE SITES

The 57 archeological sites recorded in the Toronto Reservoir are located on the reservoir map (fig. 59) and tabulated in the Appendix. Johnson (1957) has described and identified some of these sites, and others are so insignificant as to warrant but little comment. These latter produced so few artifacts and so little archeological data that no more may be said than that they are probably places where aboriginal peoples of unknown affiliation have camped at some unknown time. A third group of these sites did, though, provide sufficient information, when excavated, to support cultural identification and thus warrant rather full descriptions here.

The following analyses of sites include only those in the third group, the sites that were partially or fully excavated in the 1957 season. As 6 of these 10 sites have more than 1 component, they will be described in the order in which they were investigated, rather than in the order of cultural sequence. The Woodson County sites are described first, followed by the Greenwood County sites.

Five culture complexes have been identified in the Toronto Reservoir area. These are: Archaic (5000 to 200 B.C.); Kansas City Hopewell (200 B.C. to A.D. 500); Plains Woodland (A.D. 500 to 900); Aksarben (A.D. 1100 to 1500); and Great Bend (A.D. 1500 to 1700). The dates given in parentheses are provisional and subject to any revisions which new information may suggest.

SITE 14WO203

This site is located on a slight rise on the northwest side of the Verdigris River (fig. 59). It is bounded on the northeast by an abandoned railroad grade, on the southeast by the Verdigris River, and on the southwest and northwest by an oxbow lake. An area of refuse concentration approximately 150 feet in length by 140 feet in width lay near the center of the site. The entire site has an overall length of 900 feet. Long utilization of the site for agricultural purposes has obliterated any traces of surface features, if they were ever present (fig. 60).

EXCAVATIONS

Johnson and his party tested this site by means of three 5-foot-square test pits. Two of these were carried to a depth of 1.5 feet, and a third to a depth of 2.0 feet. Arbitrary levels of 0.5 foot were maintained during the excavation. As agricultural operations had obliterated all traces of these test pits by the time the site was mapped in 1957, the locations of these pits do not appear on the site plan.

In the summer of 1957, Howard and his party further tested the site by means of three more 5-foot-square test pits, placed in areas of greatest surface concentration and artifacts. Two of these were carried to a depth of 4.0 feet, and one to a depth of 2.0 feet. In the first of these, no artifacts were recovered below the surface until a

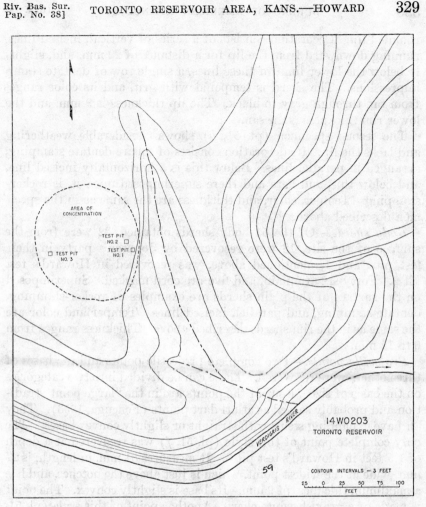

FIGURE 60.—Plan of site 14WO203, showing excavations.

depth of 1.0 foot was reached. Here the broken end of a drill or projectile point and a fragmentary scraper were recovered. Nothing was found below this depth.

In the second pit, the only artifact, a large body sherd, was recovered at a depth of 0.5 foot. The third pit also yielded but a single artifact. This was a large, expanding-stem point, which appeared at a depth of 1.5 feet.

SPECIMEN DESCRIPTIONS
(pl. 51, a–l)

Rim sherds.—Two rim sherds were recovered, one from the surface of the site and one from a test pit dug by Johnson's party. The specimen from the surface (pl. 51, *a*) is slightly flaring and has a rounded lip. Decoration consists of a series of vertical, incised lines, running downward from the lip for a distance of 22 mm. and, slightly below the lower limit of these lines, a single row of dentate stamp impressions. The sherd is tempered with grit, and its color ranges from tan through gray to black. The lip thickness is 9 mm. and the lower rim thickness is the same.

The second specimen (pl. 51, *b*) shows considerable weathering and lacks the lip. Its decoration consists of square dentate stamping, arranged in parallel lines. Below this is a horizontally incised line, and below this, and here and there superimposed upon it, is rocker-stamping. Temper, color, and thickness are the same as in the specimen described above.

Body sherds.—Of the 51 body sherds obtained, 32 were from the surface of the site, 18 were recovered by Johnson's party in their test pits, and 1, mentioned above, was recovered in Howard's test pit 2. Forty-six are plain, and five are cord marked. Superimposed on the surface of the plain sherds are examples of rocker-stamping, dentate-stamping, and parallel, incised lines. Temper and color are the same as in the rim sherds described above. Thickness ranges from 6 to 12 mm.

Projectile points.—Two complete projectile points and the bases of three others were recovered. These can be divided into two categories on the basis of size. Four of the points are in the "large point" tradition and probably served as atlatl dart points (Fenenga, 1953). They all have expanding stems with straight or slightly convex bases. The only complete point of this style (pl. 51, *f*) was recovered at a depth of 1.5 feet in Howard's test pit 3. It measures 84 mm. in length, is 27 mm. wide at the widest point, which is just above the notches, and has a maximum thickness of 9 mm. Its base is slightly convex. The point is made of a grayish-white chert. Another point of this style (pl. 51, *e*), consisting of only the basal portion, is made of a gray chert with white inclusions. It has a maximum width of 40 mm. and a maximum thickness of 7 mm. Its base is straight. The third point of this style, also a fragment, has a slightly convex base (pl 51, *d*). It has a maximum width of 40 mm. and a maximum thickness of 8 mm. It is made of gray Flint Hills chert. The fourth large point, very fragmentary, is of dark gray chert. Its maximum thickness is 5 mm.

The remaining point is in the "small point" tradition (pl. 51, *c*) and probably served as an arrowhead (Fenenga, 1953). It is triangular in outline and unnotched, made of gray Flint Hills chert. Its length is 11 mm., its maximum width 9 mm., and its maximum thickness 2 mm. Points of this type are generally considered to be "late horizon" markers, i.e., characteristic of late prehistoric and historic cultures.

Drill.—One possible drill point, fashioned from gray chert, was obtained. This specimen was found in Howard's test pit 1 at a depth of 1 foot. The point of the drill is 2 mm. wide. It has a maximum thickness of 6 mm., measured at the point where this portion was broken off, and a maximum width of 15 mm., measured at the same place.

Graver.—One graver, suitable for incising wood or bone, was obtained by Johnson in his testing. It has been fashioned from an irregularly shaped flake of gray Flint Hills chert. The only modification of the flake is in the point itself, which is extremely narrow. The width of the point is 2 mm.; the width of the base 20 mm.; and the length of the tool 33 mm. Its maximum thickness is 3 mm.

Blades.—The bases of three blades were recovered, two from the surface of the site and one from one of Johnson's test pits. The largest blade fragment is of gray Flint Hills chert (pl. 51, *g*). It is rounded, indicating that the complete blade may have been pyriform in shape. It is 47 mm. in width and has a maximum thickness of 11 mm. A second rounded base, also of gray Flint Hills chert, measures 28 mm. in width and has a maximum thickness of 6 mm. The third basal fragment has a contracting stem with a rounded base. This piece is of pink chert. Its dimensions are: maximum width, 29 mm., maximum width of stem, 22 mm., maximum thickness, 5 mm.

End scrapers.—Five objects of this sort were collected. Three are of gray Flint Hills chert, two are of pink chert. In all examples the working end is thicker and has been sharpened by the removal of flakes almost at right angles to the plane of the artifact. Two of the scrapers are pyriform in outline, one is trianguloid, and the remaining two, fragments, appear to have been rectanguloid when complete. Lengths of the pyriform specimens are 51 and 72 mm., maximum widths are 30 and 42 mm., and maximum thicknesses are 10 and 14 mm., respectively (pl. 51, *h*, *i*). The trianguloid specimen, which appears to be the reworked tip of a projectile point, measures 24 mm. in length by 17 mm. in width, with a maximum thickness of 4 mm. (pl. 51, *j*). The maximum widths of the rectanguloid specimens are 40 and 20 mm., their maximum thicknesses 7 and 6 mm. (pl. 51, *k*, *l*).

Flake scraper.—One fragmentary artifact bearing traces of secondary chipping along two edges was recovered. It is made of gray Flint Hills chert, is quite irregular in form, and has a planoconvex cross section. It is 43 mm. long, 33 mm. wide, and has a maximum thickness of 14 mm.

Chopper.—One fragmentary chopper, made from a fine-grained green quartzite, was found on the surface of the site. The flaking is entirely of the percussion type, and is restricted to the edges of the specimen. The edges show evidence of repeated pounding, indicating a possible secondary use as a hammerstone. Dimensions: width at point of breakage, 48 mm., maximum thickness, 18 mm.

Miscellaneous chipped stone fragments.—In addition to the above specimens, which can be placed in artifact categories, 31 specimens were collected that are too fragmentary to be classified. These consist of 6 projectile-point tips, 5 projectile-point or blade fragments from the area between the base and the point, 2 probable end-scraper fragments, and 18 fragments which show secondary chipping along only one edge. The predominant material is gray Flint Hills chert. One unfinished projectile point was also recovered.

Unidentified artifact.—One piece of highly siliceous, worked hematite with a hardness of 6.5 (vesuvianite in the modified Mohs hardness scale) was recovered. It shows definite signs of rubbing and scratching on two surfaces. Were it not for its hardness, one might suspect that it had served as a source of pigment. The piece measures 54 mm. in length, 34 mm. in width, and averages 7 mm. in thickness.

Paint.—Three limonite fragments and four burned limestone fragments were collected. All are probably of local origin, and probably served as sources of yellow and white paint.

Unworked stone.—There were 327 irregularly shaped flakes of chert, lacking any traces of secondary chipping, recovered at the site. Gray Flint Hills chert is the predominant material, although tan and white cherts are also represented.

CULTURAL AFFILIATION

Potsherds with dentate- and rocker-stamping and large, expanding-stem projectile points indicate an identification with Kansas City Hopewell as defined by Wedel (1943). Since no cultural stratification could be discovered and the artifacts appear to be culturally homogeneous, it is assumed that the site has but one component. Therefore, specimens from the surface were grouped with those from the excavations for descriptive purposes.

SITE 14WO209

This site is located on a slight rise on the northeast side of the Verdigris River (fig. 59). It covers an area approximately 1,100 feet in length (NW–SE) by 300 feet in width (NE–SW). A slightly heavier concentration of material is found at the southeast end of the site in an area 200 feet by 130 feet. Any surface features that may once have been present have been destroyed by cultivation (fig. 61).

EXCAVATIONS

Two 5-foot-square test pits were laid out in the area of greatest surface concentration. The first of these was excavated to a depth of 1.0 foot, the second to a depth of 0.7 foot, at which point work was

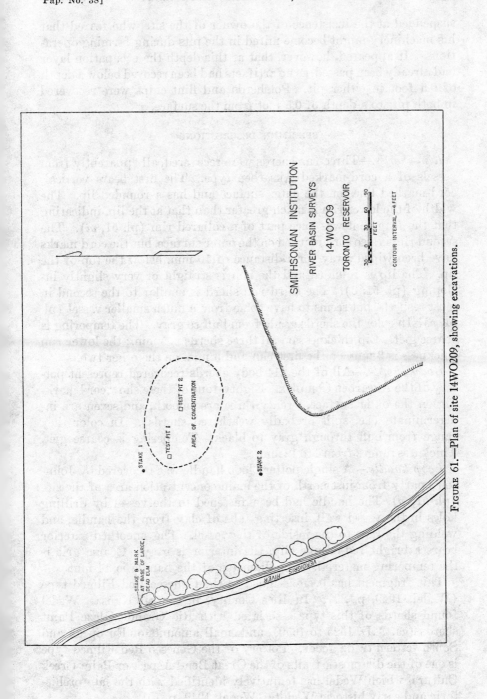

FIGURE 61.—Plan of site 14WO209, showing excavations.

suspended at the insistence of the owner of the site, who feared that his machinery might become mired in the pits during farming operations. It appeared, however, that at this depth the occupation layer had already been passed, as no artifacts had been recoved below a depth of 0.5 foot in either pit. Potsherds and flint chips were recovered in both pits to a depth of 0.5 foot from the surface.

SPECIMEN DESCRIPTIONS

Rim sherds.—Three rim sherds were recovered, all apparently from vessels of a cord-marked Aksarben type. The first bears vertical, cord-marked lines on the outer surface and has a rounded lip. The width of the lower rim is much greater than that at the lip, indicating that the fragment was once part of a collared rim (pl. 51, *m*). The second rim is also cord marked on the outer surface, but the cord marks have been wiped away for a distance of 10 mm. below the top of the lip. The lip is rounded and the rim is straight or very slightly insloping (pl. 51, *o*). The third rim sherd is similar to the second in most respects, but seems to have come from a much smaller vessel (pl. 51, *n*). In color the sherds grade from buff to gray. The tempering is coarse grit. Lip thickness on all three sherds is 5 mm.; the lower rim thickness is 9 mm. on the first rim and 5 mm. on the other two.

Body sherds.—All of the 114 body sherds recovered represent pottery of the Aksarben Complex. Eighty-four of these show cord marking on the outer surface, twenty-three are smooth, and seven are indeterminate (i.e, split or badly weathered sherds). In color they range from buff through gray to black. Tempering is coarse grit. Thickness ranges from 4 to 12 mm.

Loop handle.—A single pottery loop handle was recovered by Johnson's party from just north of the main concentration area of the site (pl. 51, *p*). The handle had been fastened to the vessel by drilling holes in the vessel wall, inserting tabs of clay from the handle, and welding the tabs to the inside of the vessel. The smoothed exterior bears a bright red-orange slip, the interior is gray. Coarse grit is the tempering material. The diameter of the handle is 14 mm.

This fragment has been assigned to the Geneseo Red Filmed type (Wedel, 1949, p. 89). In Rice County, in central Kansas, Wedel found sherds of this type associated with Rio Grande Glaze Paint sherds (ca. A.D. 1525 to 1650), and small amounts of European and Southwestern trade goods. Pottery of the Geneseo Red Filmed type is one of the diagnostic traits of the Great Bend Aspect or Paint Creek Culture, which Wedel has tentatively identified with the late prehistoric and early historic Wichita (Wedel, 1942, p. 10).

Projectile points.—Twenty projectile points that were sufficiently complete for classification were recovered. These have been grouped into six different styles. The first, represented by one incomplete specimen, is large and thick, and has in-sloping shoulders and a slightly expanding stem with a straight base. It is made of red chert and measures 45 mm. in length by 21 mm. maximum width by 10 mm. maximum thickness. Typologically, it would seem to belong to the Archaic Culture (pl. 51, *q*).

The second style, also Archaic typologically, is represented by two complete points. Both are large and thick, with in-sloping shoulders and contracting stems. The first measures 49 mm. in length, 21 mm. in maximum width, and 11 mm. in maximum thickness. It is made of tan chert (pl. 51, *r*). The second is 56 mm. in length, 22 mm. in maximum width, and has a maximum thickness of 11 mm. It is made of gray Flint Hills chert (pl. 51, *s*).

The third style is represented by five incomplete specimens. These points are large, with expanding stems and straight or slightly convex bases. The first measures 25 mm. in width and has a maximum thickness of 8 mm. (pl. 51, *t*). The second is 27 mm. wide and has a maximum thickness of 11 mm. (pl. 51, *u*). Both are of gray Flint Hills chert. The third specimen, of gray Flint Hills chert, has a maximum width of 28 mm. and a maximum thickness of 7 mm. The fourth is 21 mm. wide, with a maximum thickness of 5 mm. It is of gray Flint Hills chert that has white banding. The fifth is 27 mm. in maximum width and 5 mm. in maximum thickness, made of gray Flint Hills chert.

The fourth style is represented by one complete point, one reworked point, and three fragmentary specimens. Points of this type are distinguished by their large size and their contracting stems. The complete specimen measures 70 mm. in length, is 23 mm. wide, and has a maximum thickness of 10 mm. (pl. 51, *w*). Other points of this type are wider, the widest being 33 mm. in maximum width. Three are of tan chert, the other two of gray Flint Hills material (pl. 51, *v, x, y*).

All of the above are in the "large point" tradition. The two remaining styles are "small point" forms. The fifth style is made up of small, triangular, "late horizon" points. Two specimens are unnotched. They measure 24 and 20 mm. in length, 13 and 14 mm. in width at their bases, and 3 and 5 mm. in maximum thickness, respectively. Materials are white and gray Flint Hills cherts (pl. 51, *z, a'*). The remaining points are notched. Two of the points have double side notches, one has single side notches, and one (perhaps accidentally) has one side notch and a basal notch. Two are of gray Flint Hills chert, the others are of a pinkish chert. They average 20 mm. in length by 15 mm. maximum width, with a thickness of 3 mm. (pl. 51, *b', c', d'*).

A sixth style, possibly a drill rather than a projectile point, is represented by a single broken specimen. It is slender, with shallow side notches, and is slightly curved when viewed from the side. It was probably about 33 mm. in length when complete, has a maximum width of 10 mm., and a maximum thickness of 3 mm. It is made of gray Flint Hills chert (pl. 51, e').

Blades.—Four pyriform blades, two nearly complete and two fragmentary, were recovered. All are of gray Flint Hills chert. They vary in width from 22 to 40 mm., and in thickness from 9 to 13 mm. The two nearly complete specimens measure 53 and 59 mm. in length (pl. 51, f').

End scrapers.—Two complete planoconvex end scrapers were recovered. Both are manufactured of gray Flint Hills chert. The first measures 35 by 30 mm. and has a maximum thickness of 7 mm. (pl. 51, h'). The second measures 45 by 30 mm. and has a maximum thickness of 10 mm. (pl. 51, g').

Flake scrapers.—Two artifacts of this description were recovered. The first is made of pink chert and measures 26 x 20 mm. with a maximum thickness of 4 mm. The second, of tan chert, is 72 mm. long, 27 mm. in width, and 11 mm. thick (pl. 51, j'). Both are ovate in form, flat on one side, worked on the other.

Chopper.—The basal portion of a heavy stone chopper was recovered at the site. It is 70 mm. in width at the point of breakage and has a maximum thickness of 25 mm.

Celts.—Three small celts, similar to each other in shape, but of varied materials, were found at the site. The first and smallest has been chipped from a fragment of dark gray micaceous schist. Its cutting edge is polished from use. It measures 80 mm. in length, 43 mm. in width, and has a maximum thickness of 13 mm. (pl. 51, i'). The second is made of the Cottonwood formation limestone so common in artifacts from this area. It has apparently been cut into shape by an implement of some harder stone. This celt is 100 mm. long, has a maximum width of 46 mm., and a maximum thickness of 27 mm. It seems rather odd to find a celt made of this soft, rather porous stone (hardness 3.5, celestite), yet collections from this area contain celts, boatstones, and even grooved axes fashioned of this material.

The third celt has been chipped from a light tan chert. It is 123 mm. long, has a maximum width of 60 mm., and a maximum thickness of 27 mm. (pl. 51, k').

Manos.—Eight manos, and mano fragments, were recovered. Seven of these are of sandstone, and the smallest specimen is made of micaceous schist. All are subrectangular, with smooth grinding surfaces on the top and bottom and partially smoothed edges and corners. The largest specimen is 153 mm. long, 96 mm. wide, and 40 mm. thick. Six of the others are but slightly smaller than this. The eighth specimen is but 55 mm. long, 50 mm. wide, and 23 mm. thick, and appears to have been used as a grinding tool for small materials such as medicines or perfumes.

Three of the larger manos appear to have been used also as cup-stones or anvils, as they have paired depressions on the two opposite, flat surfaces. The only complete specimen of this sort measures 117 mm. in length, 55 mm. in width, and is 56 mm. thick. The pecked depressions are 23 mm. in diameter and 4 mm. thick.

Hammerstones.—Three hammerstones were recovered. All are unworked river pebbles of a size to fit conveniently in the hand of the user, and all show signs of battering on one or more surfaces.

Core.—A pyriform core of gray Flint Hills chert was found at the site and probably represents a piece of material roughly shaped at the quarry for transportation to the site, where it could be made into points, scrapers, etc. It is 102 mm. long, 72 mm. wide, and has a maximum thickness of 35 mm.

Miscellaneous stone artifacts.—In addition to the artifacts described above, there were 28 chipped-stone specimens too fragmentary to classify. One of these seems to represent the end of a small end scraper. Three seem to be portions of flake scrapers, and the remainder may be portions of projectile points or blades. The predominant materials are gray Flint Hills chert, tan chert, and pink chert.

CULTURAL AFFILIATIONS

Although no cultural stratification could be discovered, the artifacts from this site indicate that at least two components are present: Archaic (as defined by Spaulding, 1955, pp. 15–19) and Aksarben.[2] A single loop-handle fragment may represent the third and most recent component at the site, Great Bend.

SITE 14WO215

This is a small site, limited to a low knoll and an adjacent level area near the Verdigris River (fig. 59). The area has been under cultivation for some time and has also been subjected to continual flooding during periods of high water. Nevertheless, it is still quite rich in surface materials.

EXCAVATIONS

The site was tested by means of two 5-foot-square test pits, excavated in the area of greatest surface concentration. The first pit was excavated to a depth of 2.5 feet, the second to a depth of 2.0 feet. The fill was clay loam at the surface, grading into hard clay at a depth of 1.0 foot. Numerous sandstone blocks were encountered at the top

---

[2] The term "Aksarben" is used for the archeological remains which make up the Upper Republican and Nebraska cultures.

of this hard clay. Plow disturbance was evident to a depth of 0.5 foot. The only artifact recovered in the first pit was a cupstone, which appeared at a depth of 1.1 feet in the northwest corner of the square. In the second pit an occupation level was reached at a depth of 1.0 foot and continued to a depth of 1.5 feet. It contained a flake scraper and numerous small chips.

SPECIMEN DESCRIPTIONS

Rim sherd.—Only one rim sherd was recovered from this site (pl. 52, *b'*). It is, however, a rather unusual specimen, since it seems to have come from a bowl-shaped vessel. The sherd is cord marked on the outer surface, smooth on the inner. It is grit tempered, with a light-gray interior and buff exterior. It is 7 mm. in thickness. The upper surface of the lip and the outer rim, for a distance of 12 mm. below the lip, are decorated with diagonal cord marking. Below this, the cord marking is vertical. At a distance of 18 mm. below the lip edge, there is a very pronounced shoulder. Although rather atypical, this sherd seems to be identifiable as of Aksarben origin.

Body sherds.—Seven cord-marked body sherds and five smoothed body sherds were recovered. The cord-marked body sherds are all of Aksarben types. They range in color from dark gray to orange-buff, with gray interiors. Thickness ranges from 6 to 8 mm. (pl. 52, *c'*).

The smoothed sherds are also grit tempered, but the particles of grit are much larger than in the cord-marked sherds. They vary in surface color from reddish-gray to buff, and interiors are uniformly gray. Thicknesses vary from 5 to 9 mm. One of the sherds bears a decoration of two fine, incised, parallel lines on its outer surface (pl. 52, *d'*).

The smooth, undecorated sherds have been tentatively assigned to the Geneseo Plain type (Wedel, 1949, p. 88). The incised sherd fits no described type known to the writer, although, like the Geneseo sherds, it probably represents a late time period. The incised lines on this sherd are reminiscent of those on sherds of the Oneota Aspect (ca. A.D. 1600–1800).

Projectile points.—A total of 34 projectile points, sufficiently complete to be classified, were recovered. These have been grouped into six categories for descriptive purposes.

The first style is represented by two incomplete specimens. These are rather large, thick, leaf-shaped points, with only a slight indication of a shoulder. The first is made of a brown chert with white inclusions. It measures 22 mm. in width, has a maximum thickness of 11 mm., and when complete was probably 64 mm. long (pl. 52, *b*). The other point of this type, made of gray Flint Hills chert, has a maximum width of 20 mm., is 8 mm. thick, and when complete measured approximately 62 mm. in length (pl. 52, *a*).

The second style, represented by two complete points and four fragments, is of the contracting-stem type generally identified with the Archaic or Early Woodland cultures. The longer of the two specimens is made of tan chert. Its dimensions are: length, 62 mm.; maximum width, 23 mm.; and maximum thickness, 8 mm. (pl. 52, *c*). The other, apparently a reworked point, is 53 mm. long, with a maximum width of 30 mm. and a maximum thickness of 8 mm. (pl. 52, *d*). Maximum widths of the other four specimens are 37, 33, 25, and 24 mm.

The third and most numerous style is large, with barbed shoulders and an expanding stem, either straight or convex at the base. Four nearly complete specimens range in length from 56 to 42 mm., while a clearly reworked point is only 30 mm. long. Widths vary between 36 and 22 mm., and maximum thicknesses between 6 and 10 mm. Seven incomplete specimens of this type were also recovered. Materials are tan and gray Flint Hills cherts (pl. 52, *e–i*).

A fourth style is represented by four nearly complete specimens and one fragment. Here the stems are straight, and the barbed shoulders characteristic of the previous style are absent. Lengths of the four nearly complete specimens are 59, 51, 48, and 38 mm. Widths are 24, 22, 24, and 24 mm. The average maximum thickness is 8 mm. Materials are gray Flint Hills chert, tan chert, and pink chert (pl. 52, *k, l*).

The fifth style is represented by one complete projectile point and three fragments. These are small, expanding-stem points with barbed shoulders, and resemble those recovered in Plains Woodland sites in Nebraska and Kansas (Kivett, 1952, pl. IX A, Nos. 6, 9, and 10; pl. XVI A, No. 4; 1953, pl. 23 *a*, bottom row, 3d, 4th, and 5th specimens). Materials are gray and pink cherts. The only complete specimen is 37 mm. long. Widths of the points are 17, 16, 16, and 12 mm. Maximum thicknesses are 4, 4, 4, and 3 mm. (pl. 52, *j, m–o*).

The sixth style is represented by five complete specimens. This is the familiar "late horizon" triangular style. All lack side notches, but one has a basal notch. Lengths of the specimens vary from 30 to 19 mm.; widths, measured at the base, between 15 and 11 mm. The points average 3.5 mm. in maximum thickness. Materials are gray and cream-colored cherts (pl. 52, *p–t*).

In addition to these specimens, 30 fragments of projectile points, all in the "large point" tradition, were recovered. Materials employed are gray Flint Hills chert, tan chert, and cream-colored chert.

Knives and blades.—Twenty-seven fragments of knives or blades were recovered at the site. Twenty-three of these were apparently pyriform in shape when complete. The other four were undoubtedly of the style known as the "Harahey knife." Typically, these Harahey knives are lozenge shaped, with alternate beveling on the upper right and lower left edges, as one views the object from either face (pl. 52, z). Such artifacts are frequently found at Aksarben sites, but are by no means limited to those sites.

One of the pyriform blade fragments is of white chert, five are of tan chert, two are of pink chert, two are of gray-green chert, and eight are of gray Flint Hills chert (pl. 52 x, y). Four fragments, apparently representing the bases of blades, are of a reddish-gray jasper, while another is of banded tan chert. The four Harahey knife fragments are of tan chert.

Drill.—One slender, chipped piece apparently represents a section of a drill stem. It is lozenge shaped in cross section, with a width of 10 mm. and a maximum thickness of 7 mm.

Shaft scrapers.—Five artifacts, each distinguished by a semilunar notch on one edge, have been referred to as shaft scrapers. Three of these have small, deep notches, and would have been ideal for shaping arrowshafts with a diameter of 7 or 8 mm. (pl. 52, a'). Two others, with shallower notches, may have served as bowshaft scrapers. Both deep- and shallow-notched specimens are small, ranging in length from 25 to 40 mm. Three are made of light-gray chert, one is of tan chert, and one is of gray Flint Hills chert that has white inclusions.

End scrapers.—A total of 45 end scrapers were recovered, 27 of which are complete and 18 of which are recognizable fragments. The complete specimens range in length from 30 to 72 mm., in maximum width from 20 to 36 mm., and in maximum thickness from 7 to 13 mm. Light gray, tan, and gray Flint Hills cherts are the usual materials (pl. 52, u–w).

Flake scrapers.—Ninety-one flakes with one or more edges bearing secondary chipping were recovered. These vary greatly in size and shape. The materials are tan, white, and gray Flint Hills cherts.

Choppers.—Two choppers, both of gray Flint Hills chert, were recovered. They are ovoid in outline, and show percussion flaking on both faces. They measure 92 and 90 mm. in length, 69 and 68 mm. in maximum width, and 17 and 22 mm. in maximum thickness, respectively. These tools are so alike in material and workmanship that it seems very likely that they were made by the same person.

Miscellaneous worked fragments.—Five small fragments which cannot be assigned to any particular category were recovered. These may be portions of projectile points, knives, blades, or scrapers. All show some evidence of secondary chipping. Materials are tan, brown, white, and gray Flint Hills cherts.

Cores.—Four cores were recovered. These are the irregularly shaped pieces remaining after numerous flakes have been removed from a large quarry blank. Three are of tan chert and one is of gray Flint Hills material.

Manos.—Four complete manos and one fragmentary specimen were recovered. They are subrectangular, with the upper and lower surfaces worn smooth. Three of the complete specimens are of sandstone, as is the fragment, while the remaining artifact is of limestone.

The three sandstone manos have the following dimensions: lengths, 140, 125, and 72 mm.; widths, 94, 90, and 60 mm.; thicknesses, 55, 41, and 30 mm., respectively. The limestone specimen is 117 mm. long, 94 mm. wide, and 55 mm. thick. All of the specimens show plow scars.

Hoe.—A single hoe or hoe-like implement was found. It is made of a quartzite river pebble, roughly triangular in outline, which has been sharpened at the broad end by percussion flaking. It is 108 mm. in length, has a maximum width of 66 mm., measured at the broad end, and a maximum thickness of 32 mm., measured at the narrow end.

Celt.—A single celt was recovered. It is made of Cottonwood limestone, a rather poor material for a cutting tool, one would think, because of its softness. The celt is typical in shape of those pecked from harder material. It is 83 mm. long, has a maximum width of 51 mm., measured at the blade end, and a maximum thickness of 23 mm., measured at the poll.

Unidentified stone objects.—Two pieces of worked siliceous hematite were recovered. Both appear to be too hard to have served as sources of paint, although it is difficult to conceive any other use for them. Perhaps they were rubbed on some abrasive surface to secure the desired pigment. One measures 27 mm. in length, 23 mm. in width, and 9 mm. in thickness. The other is 22 mm. long, 10 mm. wide, and 4 mm. thick.

Unworked stone.—A small piece of micaceous schist found at the site was probably brought there by an individual who was attracted by its sparkle and texture. It is 43 mm. long, 31 mm. wide, and 8 mm. thick.

CULTURAL AFFILIATIONS

No cultural stratification could be distinguished at the site, since all of the diagnostic artifacts were surface finds. On the basis of typology, three components may be distinguished: Archaic, Aksarben, and Great Bend.

THE WALLEYE ROCKSHELTER (14WO222)

This site is a small rockshelter overlooking Finger Creek, which enters the Verdigris from the north (fig. 59). Several rather striking petroglyphs are present on a fallen slab in front of the shelter (pl. 53). A narrow occupation area about 10 feet in width and 40 feet in length is located immediately below the bluff overhang. The fill of the occupation area is a rich humus mixed with fallen sandstone fragments from the bluff. The area has been disturbed by rodent activity, picnickers, and the activities of local enthusiasts who believe that the petroglyphs are a treasure map. For this reason, no cultural stratification could be distinguished.

EXCAVATIONS

The entire area beneath the bluff overhang was laid out in 5-foot squares (fig. 62). Each of these squares was carried down to bedrock, maintaining arbitrary 0.5-foot levels during the excavation. A total of 13 squares was excavated.

The 0-foot to 0.5-foot level yielded the following artifacts: Two small triangular points; a large expanding-stem point; the tip of another point or blade; a slender drill; portions of three end scrapers; two flake scrapers; three cord-marked, grit-tempered potsherds of Aksarben affiliation; one thick, plain, grit-tempered sherd; one sandstone shaft smoother; one cupstone; one stone hoe; one hammerstone; one core; and one plum seed.

The 0.5-foot to 1.0-foot level yielded the following: One large expanding-stem point; two blade or point fragments; one Aksarben sherd; one shell-tempered sherd; and one fragmentary limestone celt or hoe.

The 1.0-foot to 1.5-foot level yielded the base of a large, expanding-stem point; the tip of a large blade; a large, smooth, shell-tempered sherd; and a piece of charred vegetal material.

The 1.5-foot to 2.0-foot level yielded the tip of a large point or blade and a complete point of the small, triangular, "late horizon" type.

The 2.0-foot to 2.5-foot level, present in only three of the squares, yielded only one artifact, a modified flake. Charred wood also appeared in this level.

Unworked flakes, animal bone, and other refuse were apparent at all levels.

PETROGLYPHS

Several petroglyphs, both incised and pecked, were found on a large sandstone slab which once formed a part of the overhang of the shelter. From the orientation of the petroglyphs it seems evident that they were made at a time before this slab had broken loose from the bluff face. If the slab were restored to its original position, the majority of the figures would be upright and on the outer face of the overhang, while one of the figures (pl. 53, a, b), a warrior with a bow and arrow, would be on the undersurface.

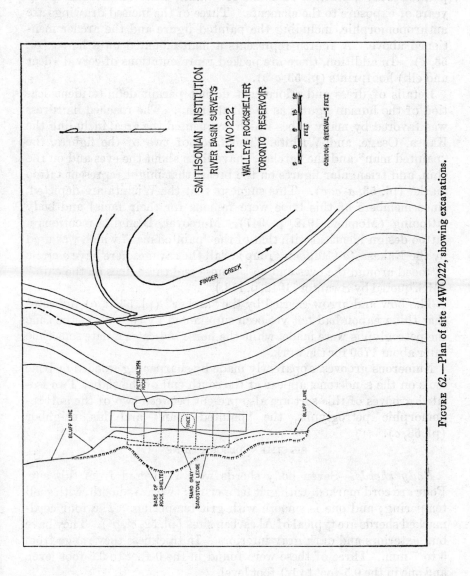

FIGURE 62.—Plan of site 14WO222, showing excavations.

Although the figures are highly conventionalized, the work is skillfully executed, and seems to conform to a definite aboriginal art style. One of the figures (pl. 53, c, extreme left, and f) has been painted with a weather-resistant red paint, still visible after many years of exposure to the elements. Three of the incised drawings are anthropomorphic, including the painted figure and the archer mentioned above. A fourth represents a man mounted on a horse (pl. 53, e). In addition, there are pecked representations of cervid (deer and elk) hoofprints (pl. 53, c–e).

Details of dress and adornment do not permit definite identification of the human figures as to tribal group. The roached hairdress was favored by many tribes which frequented the area, including the Kansa, Osage, and Wichita. The faces of two of the figures, the "painted man" and the "archer," have lines about the eyes and on the chin, and triangular figures on the breast that might represent tattoo marks (pl. 53, a–c, e). This suggests that the Wichita are depicted, since members of this tribe were famous for their facial and body tattooing (Mooney, 1912, p. 947). Moreover, Bienville mentions a tattoo design identical with that of the "painted man" which was used by the Nakasa (a Caddoan group): "all the savages here have a circle tattooed around the eyes and on the nose and three lines on the chin." (MS. quoted by Swanton, 1942, p. 143.)

The bow and arrow carried by the "archer" (pl. 53, a, b) indicates that this weapon had not yet been supplanted by the rifle at the time the petroglyphs were made, while the horse indicates a date sometime after about 1750 for the work.

Numerous grooves, apparently made by sharpening wooden or bone tools on the sandstone, appear at the south end of the slab. Two isolated grooves of this sort are also present between two of the anthropomorphic petroglyphs, the "painted man" and his neighbor (pl. 53, c).

SPECIMEN DESCRIPTIONS

Body sherds.—Seven body sherds were recovered from this site. Four are cord marked, with grit tempering; two are smooth, with shell tempering; and one is smooth with grit tempering. The four cord-marked sherds are typical of Aksarben sites (pl. 52, e', g'). They have buff exteriors and dark gray interiors. In thickness they range from 5 to 7 mm. Three of these were found in the 0-foot to 0.5-foot level, and one in the 0.5-foot to 1.0-foot level.

The two shell-tempered sherds (pl. 52, f') vary in thickness from 5 to 8 mm. They are buff on the exterior surfaces, with interiors of dark gray to buff, flecked with white from the tempering material. In some places the tempering has leached away, leaving a pitted surface. One of these sherds was found in the 0.5-foot to 1.0-foot level, the other in the 1.0-foot to 1.5-foot level. These sherds have been tentatively identified with the Cowley Plain type (Wedel, 1949, p. 87).

The single smooth, grit-tempered sherd is light buff on its exterior surface, gray on the interior. Its thickness is 8.5 mm. The outer surface of this sherd seems to have been wiped with a bunch of grass when the vessel was in a "leather" state. It was recovered in the 0-foot to 0.5-foot level of the site. It has been tentatively identified with the Geneseo Plain type (Wedel, 1949, p. 88).

Projectile points.—Five complete projectile points and three fragments were recovered at the shelter. These are readily divisible into two groups on the basis of size. Two of the complete points and the three fragments are "large point" styles, while the remaining specimens are "small point" forms. All are manufactured of gray Flint Hills chert.

The largest of the projectile points (pl. 52, *m'*) has an expanding stem with a convex base. It is 50 mm. in length, has a maximum width of 36 mm., and a maximum thickness of 9 mm. This projectile point was found in the 0-foot to 0.5-foot level. The second large projectile point (pl. 52, *h'*) also has an expanding stem, but the base is concave. The shoulders, in the form of barbs, are carried back from the notches to the level of the base of the stem. This point style seems to be quite rare in this section of the country, judging from local collections. It is 39 mm. in length, has a maximum width of 30 mm., and a maximum thickness of 7 mm. It was recovered in the 0.5-foot to 1.0-foot level.

One of the small points is of the plain, triangular, unnotched variety. It is 20 mm. in length, has a maximum width of 13 mm., and a maximum thickness of 3 mm. (pl. 52, *i'*). Another is shouldered and has a straight stem with a convex base. It is 17 mm. in length, has a maximum width of 12 mm., and a maximum thickness of 3 mm. (pl. 52, *k'*). Both of these were recovered in the 0-foot to 0.5-foot level. A third small projectile point, recovered in the 1.5-foot to 2.0-foot level, has side notches and a basal notch. It is 20 mm. long and has a maximum width of 12 mm., with a maximum thickness of 3.5 mm. (pl. 52, *j'*).

Drill.—A beautifully chipped drill of pink and tan chert was recovered in the 0-foot to 0.5-foot level. It is 61 mm. in length, has a maximum width of 13 mm., and a maximum thickness of 8 mm. (pl. 52, *l'*).

End scrapers.—Fragments of three end scrapers were recovered, all in the 0-foot to 0.5-foot level. An almost complete specimen measures 40 mm. in length, has a maximum width of 20 mm., and a maximum thickness of 6 mm. This specimen is made of pink chert, the other two are of light-gray chert (pl. 52, n').

Flake scrapers.—Two artifacts of this type were recovered, both in the uppermost level. The first has three edges that show secondary chipping. It measures 60 mm. by 30 mm., with a maximum thickness of 8 mm. The second also has three working edges. It measures 57 mm. in length by 35 mm. maximum width, with a maximum thickness of 7 mm. Both are made of gray Flint Hills chert.

Sharpening tool.—A sandstone sharpening tool, probably employed to sharpen and smooth wooden, bone, and antler implements, was found in the uppermost level of the site. It has smoothed faces on opposite sides, and a narrow groove toward one end. It is 74 mm. long, has a maximum width of 40 mm., and a maximum thickness of 11 mm.

Cupstone.—A single cupstone, made of reddish sandstone, was found in the 0-foot to 0.5-foot level. It is irregular in shape, measuring 85 mm. by 85 mm., with a maximum thickness of 30 mm. On one face there is a circular, pecked depression, 26 mm. in diameter and 5 mm. in maximum depth (pl. 52, o').

Hoes.—One complete hoe and a fragment that apparently represents the blade of another were recovered. The complete hoe is made of a grayish-green indurated sandstone. The broad edge of the tool has been sharpened by the removal of several large percussion flakes. The pointed end could have been hafted to a wooden handle. This object measures 160 mm. in length, 63 mm. in width at the widest part, and is 19 mm. thick. It was recovered in the 0-foot to 0.5-foot level (pl. 52, p').

The fragment is made of Cottonwood limestone. It is 56 mm. wide at the point of breakage and has a maximum thickness of 15 mm. It was recovered in the 0.5-foot to 1.0-foot level.

Hammerstone.—A single hammerstone, consisting of a river pebble with signs of battering on several faces, was recovered in the 0-foot to 0.5-foot level. It is 50 mm. in length and 35 mm. in diameter at the center.

Core.—A gray chert core was recovered in the 0-foot to 0.5-foot level. It is 40 mm. in length, 32 mm. in width, and has a maximum thickness of 37 mm.

CULTURAL AFFILIATIONS

At least three, and perhaps four, components are present at this site. The petroglyphs represent the latest, and can be attributed to some historic tribe, since one of them depicts a man mounted on a horse. Smooth shell and grit-tempered sherds identify a component of the Great Bend Aspect. These sherds may well be associated with the petroglyphs, as Great Bend materials often occur with European trade goods. Thin, cord-marked pottery identifies the next-oldest component, Aksarben. Large, expanding-stem projectile points may indicate a still earlier Woodland or Archaic occupation.

DRY CREEK ROCKSHELTER (14WO224)

This is a fairly large rockshelter in the valley of Dry Creek (fig. 59). This site, as well as site 14WO226, is outside the reservoir area proper, but due to potential destruction by picnickers, was considered as a part of the salvage project at the time of the 1957 excavations in the Toronto Reservoir area. Low hills with grass cover and some scrub pine and blackjack oak surround it. The area of occupation consists of the entire floor of the shelter. Several petroglyphs are to be seen on a slab of rock toward the front of the shelter (pl. 55, a). The site is quite disturbed, as it has been a favorite picnic spot for local people since at least 1880. Apparently, many petroglyphs once present in the shelter have been completely obliterated by initials, dates, and other personal memorials left by visitors.

Andreas' "History of the State of Kansas," published in 1883, mentions the shelter and some of the petroglyphs visible at that time. Under the heading "A Prehistoric Cave," appears the following description:

This cave is situated about twelve miles north of Toronto, on Section 13, Township 24, Range 14. Its mouth is about fifty feet wide and ten feet high, and the cave extends back about twenty feet. In the mouth of the cave lies a rock about nine feet long by six feet wide, the surface of which is nearly horizontal, the rock having evidently fallen from the roof of the cavern. On the surface of this rock are cut numerous figures of various sizes and shapes, some of which are indescribable. No system of regularity was observed by the inscribers, but the different figures and groups of incisions are scattered promiscuously, often overlapping and interlacing each other, as if done more for pastime than for the purpose of leaving any record of events then occurring, to be read by future generations. Some of the figures represent the human body, others parts of the body, as the head, with a small hat on, and marks down the chin, which may have been meant to represent the beard. One may have been designed to represent a little idol, another a bird's foot, another looks like a capital A, etc.

Great interest is manifested in them by the people of Woodson County which is doubtless altogether owing to the fact of their mysteriousness. The same interest will probably always attach to them. There is but little reason to hope that they will be so deciphered as to throw any light on the history of the past.

These tracings, or figures, or hieroglyphics, as some call them, were discovered about May 15, 1858, by Esquire Robert Daly, while out on a private hunting expedition. At the time of discovery, they were covered over with dirt and debris, and partially overgrown with moss. Mr. Daly, who was one of the first settlers in this part of the county, has resided in the vicinity ever since, and now lives about one and a half miles south of this prehistoric cave. (Andreas, 1883, p. 1190.)

EXCAVATIONS

Eleven 5-foot-square test pits were excavated in the floor of the cave (fig. 63). Each of these was carried down to bedrock. Arbitrary 0.5-foot levels were maintained throughout the work (pl. 54, a). It was found that the floor fill had been badly disturbed to a depth of from 0.7 foot to 1.1 feet. Since no diagnostic artifacts were recovered below this level, no cultural stratification could be obtained at the site.

The fill is not more than 4.5 feet at the maximum. It consists of organic material combined with roof fall. A section from the deepest part of the fill, which is toward the front of the shelter and in the center, revealed five layers. The top stratum, which had an average thickness of 0.3 foot, consisted of a dark clay-humus. Underlying this was a layer of light-yellow sandy soil with an average thickness of 0.6 foot. This layer was underlain by a very thin stratum of light-brown sandy soil, 0.2 foot thick. The fourth layer consisted of orange-red sand with thin, angular fragments of sandstone. It was 0.6 foot thick. The fifth layer was gray clay, containing large fragments of slightly decomposed sandstone and small lenses of organic humus with a clay admixture. At a depth of 1.3 feet the color of the clay changed to a deep gray-blue shade.

PETROGLYPHS

Of the several petroglyphs mentioned in the Andreas account, only two major examples remain intact. The first of these occurs on the upper surface of a large slab, undoubtedly the same one described in the Andreas account. It is incised in the rock and is apparently intended to represent a horse, since the tail is quite long (pl. 55, a). Below the head of the creature, which is square rather than elongated, there is a line through the neck. A bilobed arrow is incised above the horse's back. The treatment of this horse reminds one of the representations of the mythical Underwater Panther in Plains and Woodland Indian song pictographs. Here such a line through the neck indicates that the creature is emerging from beneath the earth (James, 1956, pp. 345–346).

The second petroglyph occurs on the side of a large boulder a few feet south of that bearing the horse design. It seems to be a representation of some growing plant, such as corn, or grass (pl. 55, b). Because this petroglyph is so different in style from the others and from those at other sites in the area, it may well be spurious. On the other hand, it is scarcely the sort of thing a White picnicker might dash off on a Sunday afternoon. No tracing was made of this petroglyph because of the roughness of the stone on which it is inscribed.

Of those petroglyphs described in the Andreas account that have since been destroyed, one seems to merit special mention. This is the

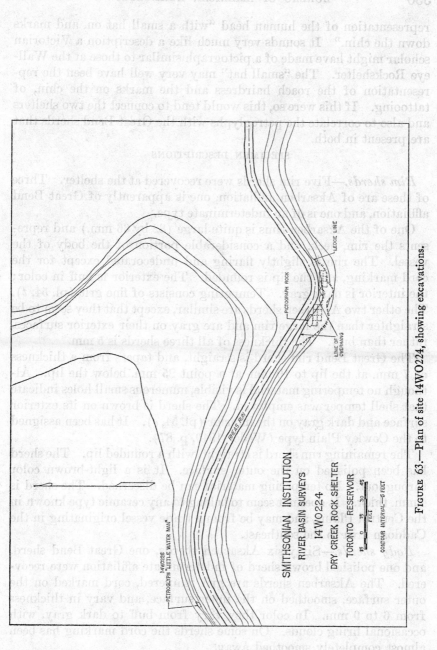

SMITHSONIAN INSTITUTION
RIVER BASIN SURVEYS
14WO224
DRY CREEK ROCK SHELTER
TORONTO RESERVOIR

CONTOUR INTERVAL—5 FEET

LEDGE LINE

PICTOGRAPH ROCK

LINE OF OVERHANG

RILEAS RUN

14WO226
PETROGLYPH "LITTLE WATER MAN"

PETROGLYPH "LITTLE MAN"

FIGURE 63.—Plan of site 14WO224, showing excavations.

representation of the human head "with a small hat on, and marks down the chin." It sounds very much like a description a Victorian scholar might have made of a pictograph similar to those at the Walleye Rockshelter. The "small hat" may very well have been the representation of the roach hairdress and the marks on the chin, of tattooing. If this were so, this would tend to connect the two shelters and also to correlate the petroglyphs with the Great Bend sherds that are present in both.

SPECIMEN DESCRIPTIONS

Rim sherds.—Five rim sherds were recovered at the shelter. Three of these are of Aksarben affiliation, one is apparently of Great Bend affiliation, and one is of an indeterminate type.

One of the Aksarben rims is quite large (82 by 66 mm.) and represents the rim, neck, and a considerable portion of the body of the vessel. The rim is slightly flaring and undecorated except for the cord marking, and the lip is rounded. The exterior is buff in color; the interior is dark gray. Tempering consists of fine grit (pl. 54, *t*). The other two Aksarben sherds are similar, except that they seem to be straighter than the large rim and are gray on their exterior surfaces, rather than buff. The thickness of all three sherds is 5 mm.

The Great Bend rim sherd is straight, and tapers from a thickness of 7 mm. at the lip to 10 mm. at a point 25 mm. below the lip. Although no tempering material is visible, numerous small holes indicate that shell temper was employed. The sherd is brown on its exterior surface and dark gray on the interior (pl. 54, *s*). It has been assigned to the Cowley Plain type (Wedel, 1949, p. 87).

The remaining rim sherd is straight, with a rounded lip. The sherd has been polished on the outer surface. It is a light-brown color throughout. No tempering material can be discerned. The sherd is 4 mm. thick. It does not seem to belong to any ceramic type known in the Central Plains, and may be from a trade vessel originating in the Caddoan area to the southeast.

Body sherds.—Sixty-six Aksarben sherds, one Great Bend sherd, and one polished brown sherd of indeterminate affiliation were recovered. The Aksarben sherds are grit tempered, cord marked on the outer surface, smoothed on the inner surface, and vary in thickness from 6 to 9 mm. In color they vary from buff to dark gray, with occasional firing clouds. On some sherds the cord marking has been almost completely smoothed away.

The Great Bend sherd is shell tempered and smoothed, but not polished, on both the inner and outer surfaces. It is brownish gray in color and is 6 mm. thick. It has been assigned to the Cowley Plain type (Wedel, 1949, p. 87).

The polished sherd is brown in color throughout. The nature of the tempering material, if any, cannot be ascertained. It is polished on the outer surface and smooth, but unpolished, on the inner surface. Its thickness is 5 mm.

Projectile points.—The 13 projectile points from the shelter fall into three distinct groups. The first, represented by two fragments, is in the "large point" tradition (pl. 54, *g, h*). These points have expanding stems. One has a convex base; the base of the other is straight. Maximum widths of the two points are 31 and 30 mm.; maximum thicknesses are 9 and 7 mm., respectively. The second point shows evidence of attempted rechipping before abandonment. Both points are made of gray Flint Hills chert that has white inclusions.

The second style is represented by two specimens. These points are small, and resemble those recovered in Plains Woodland sites in Nebraska and Kansas. Points of this style were also recovered at sites 14WO215, 14GR210, and 14GR216. The first, nearly complete, has an expanding stem with a concave base. It measures 30 mm. in length by 12 mm. in width, and is 3 mm. thick (pl. 54, *e*). The other has an expanding stem with a straight base. Its edges are serrated. It is 13 mm. in width and 3 mm. thick (pl. 54, *f*). The first is made of gray Flint Hills chert, the second of tan chert.

The remaining group is made up of nine points, two of which are complete. They are in the small, triangular, "late horizon" style (pl. 54, *c, d*). All are unnotched. The two complete specimens measure 19 and 24 mm. in length by 11 and 15 mm. in maximum width, with maximum thicknesses of 2 and 3 mm., respectively. Four of the points are of gray Flint Hills chert, three of cream-colored chert, one of pink chert, and one of brown jasper.

In addition to the above specimens, eight additional projectile point fragments, not complete enough for meaningful description, were recovered. Four of these seem to have been in the "large point" tradition, the remainder of the "small point" type. The materials are tan and gray Flint Hills cherts.

Blades.—One complete and one fragmentary blade were recovered. The complete blade is small, triangular in shape, and only 45 mm. long. It has a maximum width of 23 mm. and a maximum thickness of 7 mm. (pl. 54, *l*). The large blade appears to have been slightly wider in the midsection than at the base. The maximum width of the fragment, measured at the point of breakage, is 47 mm. Width at the base is 34 mm., and the maximum thickness is 5 mm. (pl. 54, *o*).

Knives.—Fragments of two lozenge-shaped, alternately beveled, Harahey knives were recovered at the shelter. The more complete specimen is made of light-gray chert, the other from a dark reddish-gray chert (pl. 54, *b*).

Flake knives.—Two of these artifacts, which seem to represent a rather rare type in this area, were found. Both have been made from long lamellar flakes, rectanguloid in outline, and with a prominent dorsal ridge (pl. 54, *k*). One has been retouched with secondary chipping along one cutting edge, the other has been sharpened along both sides. The first specimen, of gray chert, measures 60 mm. in length by 17 mm. maximum width. It has a maximum thickness of 4 mm. The other is made of tan chert. It is 61 mm. long, has a maximum width of 17 mm. and a maximum thickness of 8 mm.

Drill.—A single fragmentary drill was found at the shelter. It is of the expanding-base type, and made of gray Flint Hills chert. The base is 20 mm. wide and the blade is 6 mm. wide at the point of breakage. Maximum thickness of the base is 3.5 mm. and maximum thickness of the blade is 2.5 mm. (pl. 54, *m*).

End scrapers.—Fifteen artifacts of this type were found, representing ten complete scrapers and five fragments. Workmanship varies from fine to exceedingly crude. All of the scrapers are subtriangular in shape. The complete specimens range in length from 46 mm. to 25 mm., and in maximum width from 27 to 15 mm. The maximum thickness of the largest is 14 mm., that of the smallest is 5 mm. Materials employed are tan jasper, a translucent brown chalcedony, and white, pink, and gray Flint Hills cherts (pl. 54, *i, j, n*).

Flake scrapers.—Thirty-eight flake scrapers were recovered. They exhibit no uniformity in size or shape and are distinguished merely by one or more edges that show secondary chipping. Materials are cream-colored, tan, pink, and light and dark gray cherts.

Choppers.—Four choppers were recovered at the site. These are large, heavy pieces of gray Flint Hills chert worked to an edge by percussion flaking on both faces. Though quite irregular, they tend to be ovoid in shape. The largest specimen is 92 mm. long and has a maximum thickness of 22 mm. The smallest is 49 mm. long and has a maximum thickness of 14 mm.

Shaft smoother.—The only shaft smoother recovered is made of sandstone (pl. 54, *g*). It bears a single straight groove along one face that was very likely employed to smooth arrowshafts. It measures 77 mm. in length by 38 mm. in width and is 27 mm. thick. The groove would accommodate a shaft 7 mm. in diameter.

Sharpening stone.—This specimen is similar to that just described, but has semiconical grooves on three faces that seem to have been used to sharpen wooden, bone, or antler tools. It is of sandstone and measures 57 mm. in length by 20 mm. in width and has a maximum thickness of 18 mm.

Bone needles.—Two bone needles were recovered in the shelter. The first represents the tip and a portion of the shank. It has been worked from a section of mammal long bone. It is 43 mm. in length and 3.5 mm. in diameter (pl. 54, *p*). The second fragment represents a part of the shank of a much larger object, with a diameter of 7 mm. It has also been worked from a section of mammal, probably deer, leg bone.

Bone awls.—Three bone awls were recovered. All are made from mammal long bones. These objects differ from the needles just described in that their shanks are much wider than their points. Lengths of the three objects are 55 mm., 52 mm., and 33 mm. Maximum widths are 14 mm., 13 mm., and 10 mm.

Bone bead.—A tubular, bone bead is made from a section of the long bone of some small bird or mammal. It is 41 mm. in length and 8 mm. in diameter.

Miscellaneous worked bone.—Three pieces of bone, bearing recognizable tool marks, were recovered. They have no recognizable form and are probably scraps left after the manufacture of other objects.

Metal objects.—Two metal objects were recovered in the shelter fill. One is a fragment of a small iron kettle (pl. 54, *r*). It has a rather elaborate design on its outer surface and on the inner surface a raised numeral "2". The second piece seems to be part of the handle of a brass spoon. Both objects may be assigned to either the historic Indian occupation of the site or to subsequent use of the shelter by White picnickers.

CULTURAL AFFILIATIONS

At least two, and perhaps three, components are represented at the site: Aksarben, Great Bend, and historic Indian. The first two are identified by ceramic materials. The last, which may prove to be identical with Great Bend, is identified by the petroglyph of a horse.

THE OUTLAW ROCKSHELTER (14WO225)

This site is a very small rockshelter with a petroglyph on the rear wall. The name derives from a local tradition that this shelter was used by one of the Dalton gang or Jesse James as a hideout. The shelter is very shallow, low-ceilinged, and damp.

The petroglyph is possibly a representation of an Indian dwelling covered with grass thatching, pieces of bark, or hides. According to local tradition, the initials "N.C." were added by a man named Norman Curtis, about 30 years ago, "to fool people" (pl. 55, *c*).

LITTLE-WATER-MAN PETROGLYPH (14WO226)

This site consists of a single anthropomorphic petroglyph deeply incised in the rocky outcrop along Dry Creek about 300 feet upstream from the Dry Creek Rockshelter (14WO224).

The name of the petroglyph was given by Mr. D. Wm. Chatfield, a member of the 1957 Smithsonian party, who discovered and reported it. According to Chatfield, who is an Ojibwa Indian of Cass Lake, Minn., the pictograph closely resembles Ojibwa drawings of a supernatural being called the "Little-water-man." The figure holds an object, perhaps a banner, in his left hand (pl. 55, *d*, *e*).

THE POSSUM POINT SITE (14WO228)

This is a small occupation site which was apparently used for only a short time. It is located on a series of small, low knolls, bounded on the northeast and west by Finger Creek and by scrub growth and sandstone outcrops on the south (fig. 59). The area of occupation is approximately 1 acre in extent, and there seems to be a slightly greater concentration of material at the west end of the site (fig. 64). The site area has apparently been under cultivation for some time, and no surface features were visible.

The topsoil layer, a dark, sandy loam, is from 0.3 to 0.4 foot in depth (pl. 56, *a*). Beneath this is a lighter-colored soil, perhaps an old erosion surface, of light-brown to yellow soil, probably derived from sandstone, which is from 1.5 to 2.0 feet in depth. A hard clay is found below this, with sandstone blocks at the top. There is evidence of plow disturbance to a depth of 0.3 foot.

EXCAVATIONS

A test trench was laid out in the area of greatest surface concentration. This trench was 20 feet long and 5 feet wide, divided into four 5-foot squares. Later, following out the area of surface concentration, two additional squares were excavated to the east of this trench and adjoining it.

Heavy orange-buff potsherds, projectile points, and chips were recovered from the surface to a depth of 0.5 foot, where they thinned out and disappeared. No cultural stratification was found at the site.

SPECIMEN DESCRIPTIONS

Rim sherds.—Seven rim sherds were recovered at the site. They represent at least four different vessels. All have been assigned to the Geneseo Plain type, although they differ slightly in color and seem to be, on the average, slightly thicker than those described by Wedel. Tempering material consists of large sand particles, ranging from 1 to 3 mm. in diameter. Hardness varies between 3.5 (celestite) and 4 (fluorite). The core color is buff to slate-gray, the exteriors orange buff to light gray or brown. There are occasional firing clouds. Sur-

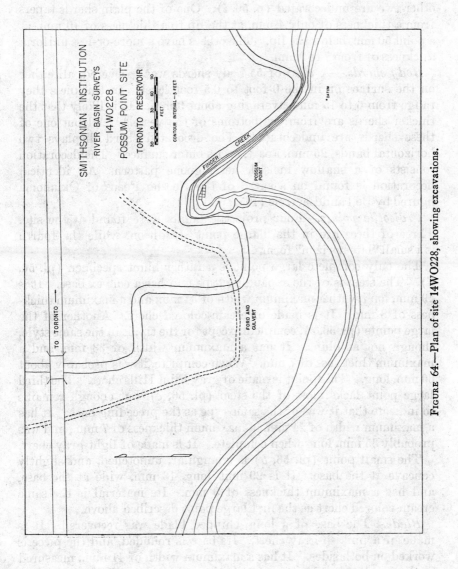

FIGURE 64.—Plan of site 14WO228, showing excavations.

faces are generally smooth. A few sherds show evidence of having been wiped with grass before firing.

Rims are straight or slightly flaring. The lip is usually rounded, but in one example is flattened. Shallow, vertical indentations are present on the outer lip of five of the sherds (pl. 56, *g, h, j, k*) ; the other two are undecorated (p. 56, *i*). One of the plain sherds tapers from a thickness of only 4 mm. at the lip to a thickness of 10 mm. at a point 50 mm. below the lip. The others have a more-or-less uniform thickness of from 7 to 9 mm.

Body sherds.—A total of 55 body sherds was recovered, all either on the surface or in the 0-foot to 0.5-foot level. In thickness they range from 6 to 15 mm., averaging about 9 mm. It is likely that the thicker sherds are from the bottoms of the vessels. All but one of these sherds are undecorated. The decorated sherd displays two horizontal bands, 25 mm. apart, on its outer surface. The decoration consists of a shallow incised, herringbone pattern. An identical decoration is found on a sherd of the Neosho Focus of Oklahoma figured by Bell and Baerreis (1951, pl. 13, 1).

Projectile points.—Four projectile points were found at the site. Three of these are in the "large point" tradition, while the fourth is a small "late horizon" form.

The only complete large point is a rather blunt specimen (pl. 56, *d*). The stem is of the expanding type and has a convex base. It is 49 mm. long, with a maximum width of 34 mm. and a maximum thickness of 8 mm. It is made of cream-colored chert. Another of the large points (pl. 56, *e*), complete except for the tip, is in the same style, though not as blunt. It has a maximum width of 33 mm. and a maximum thickness of 7 mm. When complete, it was probably about 60 mm. long. This point is made of gray Flint Hills chert. The third large point lacks most of the stem (pl. 56, *c*), but enough remains to indicate that it was of the same type as the preceding ones. It has a maximum width of 24 mm., a maximum thickness of 7 mm., and was probably 35 mm. long when complete. It is made of light-gray chert.

The small point (pl. 56, *b*) is triangular, unnotched, and slightly concave at the base. It is 29 mm. long, 13 mm. wide at the base, and has a maximum thickness of 3 mm. Its material is the same cream-colored chert as the first large point described above.

Blade.—The base of a long, chipped blade was recovered. It is made of a pinkish-gray chert. Its base is rounded, and the piece is worked on both sides. It has a maximum width of 41 mm., measured at the point of breakage, and a maximum thickness of 10 mm.

Abrader.—A fragment of a sandstone abrader was found on the surface of the site. Both ends are missing. It is rectangular in cross section and measures 35 mm. by 30 mm.

Cupstone.—A single cupstone, with pits on opposite faces, was found at the site. The material is a reddish sandstone. It is 104 mm. in length, with a maximum width of 63 mm. and an average thickness of 33 mm. The two pits measured 31 and 20 mm. in diameter and are pecked to depths of 8 and 4 mm., respectively (pl. 56, *f*).

Hoe.—A rather crude hoe, made of Cottonwood limestone, was recovered. It is flat on one surface, rounded on the other, and has been sharpened at one end. It is 154 mm. in length, 70 mm. in width, and has a maximum thickness of 24 mm.

Flake.—A very large gray chert flake was found on the surface of the site. One edge shows some secondary chipping, and perhaps the piece served as a scraper. It is 94 mm. long, has a maximum width of 77 mm., and a maximum thickness of 23 mm.

CULTURAL AFFILIATIONS

Heavy orange-buff potsherds and small triangular projectile points identify this site with the Great Bend Aspect, previously designated the Paint Creek Culture, and hitherto known only from central Kansas (Wedel, 1940, pp. 332–334; 1942, p. 10; 1949, pp. 86–90; Smith, 1949, pp. 292–300). As noted earlier in this paper, this may represent the late prehistoric and early historic Wichita tribe. Apparently very closely related is the Neosho Focus of northeastern Oklahoma (Bell and Baerreis, 1951, pp. 71–75). Possibly a second and much earlier Woodland or Archaic Component is represented by the large expanding-stem projectile points found at the site.

SITE 14GR210

This site is located on a slight rise on the south side of Walnut Creek, one of the main tributaries of the Verdigris in this area (fig. 59). The area of occupation is quite extensive, measuring approximately 1,000 feet in length (NW–SE) by 300 feet in width (NE–SW). The site was under cultivation in 1957 and has been for a number of years (pl. 57, *a*).

EXCAVATIONS

The site was tested by means of four 5-foot-square test pits, which were placed in areas of greatest surface concentration (fig. 65). The first two of these were excavated to a depth of 3.0 feet, the other two to a depth of 2.5 feet. Results were disappointing. The only artifact recovered from any of these pits was a fragmentary projectile point in the 0-foot to 0.5-foot level of test pit 2. The fill was a thin layer of clay-loam topsoil which graded into a heavy clay at depths varying from 0.3 to 0.7 foot.

SPECIMEN DESCRIPTIONS

Projectile points.—A total of 13 projectile points sufficiently complete to permit classification and fragments of 18 others were recovered. The more complete specimens fall into three styles, two of the "large point" tradition and one of the "small point" tradition.

The first style is represented by two points, one of which is complete (pl. 57, c, h). These points have contracting stems and are quite thick. The complete specimen is 61 mm. in length. Maximum widths of the points are 25 and 27 mm., and their maximum thicknesses 12 and 9 mm. Both are made of gray Flint Hills chert.

The second style is represented by nine fragmentary specimens (pl. 57, d, g). These points have expanding stems and pronounced, sometimes barbed, shoulders. Three of the points have convex bases, two have straight bases, and two have concave bases. The bases are missing from the remaining examples. Lengths of the two nearly complete specimens are 40 and 30 mm., widths 28 and 24 mm., and maximum thicknesses 7 and 4 mm., respectively. One of the fragments represents a point much larger than the rest, perhaps a knife or spearpoint rather than a projectile point (pl. 57, i). It is 43 mm. in width and probably measured at least 95 mm. in length when complete. Materials are white, tan, pink, and gray cherts. The large point is of gray Flint Hills chert.

The third point style is represented by only two specimens (pl. 57, e, f). Both have expanding stems with serrated edges. The complete specimen measures 23 mm. in length, and is 12 mm. wide at the base, with a maximum thickness of 4 mm. It is made of tan chert. The second specimen, a fragment, is 2 mm. thick. It is of gray Flint Hills chert. As noted elsewhere in this paper, points of this style have been recovered in Plains Woodland sites in Nebraska and Kansas.

Blades.—Fragments of eight blades were recovered. Although none is sufficiently complete to indicate the style, it is possible that they may have been pyriform in shape. White, cream-colored, tan, and gray Flint Hills cherts are the materials.

Knife.—One nearly complete beveled knife was recovered (pl. 57, b). It is straight along one edge, shouldered on the other. The straight edge has been chipped from one side of the piece, the shouldered edge from the other. The stem may have been utilized for hafting. The knife measures 54 mm. in length, has a maximum width of 17 mm., and a maximum thickness of 6 mm.

End scrapers.—Seven end scrapers were found. They are all of the familiar planoconvex type, with a rather abruptly chipped edge at the thick end. Three are of cream-colored chert and four are of gray Flint Hills chert. Lengths vary from 40 to 68 mm., widths from 28 to 48 mm., and maximum thicknesses from 11 to 16 mm.

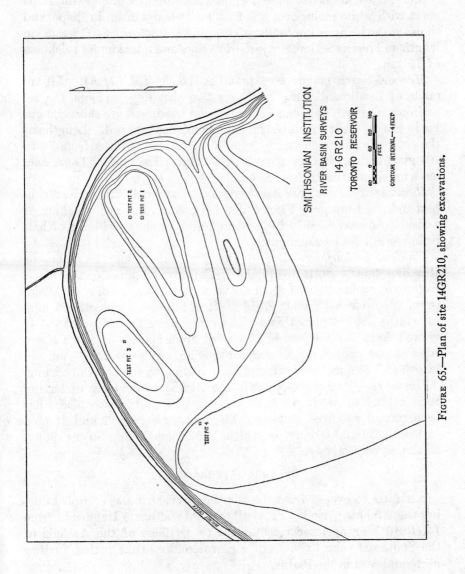

FIGURE 65.—Plan of site 14GR210, showing excavations.

Flake scrapers.—There were 18 objects of this sort found, all with one or more edges showing secondary chipping. They exhibit no uniformity in either size or shape. Materials are tan and gray Flint Hills cherts (pl. 57, *j–l*).

Chopper.—One heavy chopper, manufactured of gray Flint Hills chert with white inclusions, was found. It is pyriform in shape, and shows no evidence of secondary chipping. It measures 118 mm. in length and has a maximum width of 65 mm. and a maximum thickness of 35 mm.

Manos.—Seven manos were found at the site (pl. 57, *m*). All are made of local sandstone. Six have two abrading surfaces, the remaining specimen only one. The bifacial specimens are subrectangular in shape, while the unifacial specimen is loaf shaped. Lengths of the complete specimens vary from 15 to 83 mm., widths from 76 to 104 mm., and thicknesses from 39 to 50 mm. The unifacial specimen has a maximum thickness of 83 mm.

Hammerstones.—Three hammerstones, two made from river pebbles and one from gray Flint Hills chert, were recovered. All are of a size to fit conveniently in the hand, and all show evidence of battering on at least two surfaces.

Unidentified objects.—Two unidentified objects may be manos or abrading tools. Both are made of Cottonwood limestone. One is rectangular when viewed from above, with the outline of a parallelogram when viewed from the side. It is 148 mm. in length, 75 mm. in width, and 23 mm. thick. The other piece is wedge shaped if viewed from the side, ovoid if viewed from above. It has a sharp edge at one end, perhaps used for cutting. It measures 87 mm. in length and 73 mm. in width, and has a maximum thickness of 22 mm.

Hematite.—Two pieces of soft hematite show evidence of having been rubbed to produce paint. The smaller of the two pieces has been rubbed on three surfaces. The pieces measure 62 and 31 mm. in length, 52 and 30 mm. in width, and 29 and 9 mm. in maximum thickness, respectively.

CULTURAL AFFILIATION

Artifacts recovered from the site suggest that it was occupied during the Archaic period. Projectile points and blade fragments from 14GR210 bear a closer resemblance to artifacts of the Archaic of the Southeast than to those of a corresponding time period further north and west in the Plains.

SITE 14GR216

This is a rather extensive site located on a slight rise on the west side of the Verdigris River (fig. 59). Brazell Creek flows into the

Verdigris River just north of the site on the opposite side of the
river. The area of occupation is approximately 1,000 feet in length
(NW–SE) by 350 feet in width (NE–SW). There seems to be a
greater concentration of artifacts at the northwest end of the site
(fig. 66). Although the site has been plowed for some time, it is
nevertheless quite rich in surface materials.

EXCAVATIONS

A trench 65 feet in length and 5 feet in width was run through the
area of greatest surface concentration at the north end of the site.
This was marked off into thirteen 5-foot squares. Near the center of
this trench, part of a circular hearth was uncovered at a depth of 0.5
foot (pl. 58, *a*). The trench was then widened to 15 feet in this area
in order to expose the remainder of the hearth and to locate possible
post molds or other features. Although this widened section, 15 feet
square, was shaved down to a depth of 2.5 feet, no additional features
were discovered. The remainder of the trench was excavated to a
depth of 1.5 feet. Since no cultural stratification could be found,
material from the surface of the site has been grouped with that from
the excavations for purposes of description.

FEATURES

Hearth.—At a depth of 0.5 foot from the surface, a circular hearth
was discovered. It measured 2.0 feet in diameter and had a maximum
depth of 0.3 foot at the center. The fill was white ash with occasional
lumps of charcoal. Beneath the hearth was a lens of burned earth
approximately 0.5 foot in thickness at the center and tapering to
0.2 or 0.3 foot at the outer perimeters. The hearth was lined with
limestone slabs, some of which were set on edge, while others were
laid flat.

Although flecks of charcoal and bits of burned earth appeared
throughout the test trench at approximately the same level as the
hearth, no additional features appeared. If this hearth was the
central fireplace of a dwelling, the structure must have been of a
rather temporary sort.

Associated with this hearth were three artifacts: a bone awl, a section of antler (possibly a flint-working tool), and a small bone bead.
All of these objects seem to have been preserved by the ash of the
hearth, and were the only objects of bone or antler secured at the site.

SPECIMEN DESCRIPTIONS

Rim sherds.—The three rim sherds recovered were apparently from
vessels of Aksarben affiliation. They are tempered with fine grit.

Verdigris River just north of the site on the opposite side of the river. The area of occupation is approximately 1,000 feet in length (NW-SE) by 350 feet in width (NE-SW). There seems to be a greater concentration of artifacts at the northwest end of the site (fig. 66). Although the site has been plowed for some time, it is nevertheless quite rich in surface materials.

EXCAVATIONS

A trench 64 feet in length and 5 feet in width was run through the area of concentration at the north end of the site. Near the center of this trench, portion of a circular ash pit was encountered.

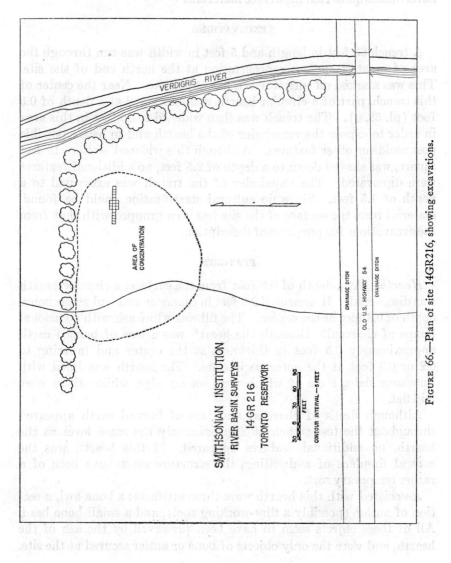

FIGURE 66.—Plan of site 14GR216, showing excavations.

The first is large enough to indicate that it came from a vessel with a constricted neck (pl. 58, *o*). The rim is straight, with a flat lip. The outer surface bears vertical cord impressions, the inner surface is smooth. The color is dark brown throughout. Thickness is 5 mm. at the lip and 8 mm. at the point of breakage. The second sherd is also straight, with a rounded lip (pl. 58, *n*). Decoration consists of a series of parallel, horizontal, incised lines and notching on the outside of the lip. The color is dark brown throughout. The lip thickness is 3 mm. and the lower rim thickness, at the point of breakage, is 4 mm. The third rim is too fragmentary to be described meaningfully. It is orange buff in color on its exterior surface, dark brown on the interior.

Body sherds.—A total of 15 body sherds was recovered. Five of these are much thicker than the rest and have coarser cord marking. They have been assigned to the Plains Woodland component of the site. The remainder are of the Aksarben Complex.

The five Woodland sherds are grit tempered, cord marked on the outer surface, and smooth on the inner surface. They have buff exteriors, with blue-gray interiors flecked with white specks. These specks are probably the remains of small fossils present in the clay at the time it was secured, although at first glance they might be taken for tempering material. Thicknesses of the sherds vary between 8 and 9 mm. (pl. 58, *r, s*).

The Aksarben sherds are also grit tempered. In color they vary from buff to black. They are cord marked on the outer surface, smooth on the inner. Thicknesses range from 4 to 7 mm. (pl. 58, *p, q*).

Projectile points.—Twenty-two projectile points sufficiently complete for classification were recovered at the site, as well as twenty-five unclassifiable fragments, such as tips or the section between the tip and the shoulders. Those points that are classifiable fall into five distinct styles.

The first style, represented by six specimens, is a large, thick form that has been assigned to the Archaic component of the site (pl. 58, *b–d*). Shoulders are not pronounced and stems are contracting, straight, or slightly convex at the base. The only complete specimen is of tan chert. It is 50 mm. long, with a maximum width of 23 mm. and a maximum thickness of 8 mm. Maximum widths of the other points are 19, 18, 21, 30, and 29 mm., and maximum thicknesses range between 7 and 9 mm. Materials are dark gray chert and tan chert.

Points of the second style, represented by 10 specimens, have straight stems and definite shoulders, sometimes terminating in barbs (pl. 58, *e, f*). The three complete specimens measure 58, 55, and 43 mm. in length. Maximum widths vary between 20 and 32 mm., and maximum thicknesses between 3 and 8 mm. Materials are white, tan, and gray cherts, and quartzite.

The third style is represented by a single complete specimen (pl. 58, *g*). This point has an expanding stem with a convex base. It is 47 mm. long, has a maximum width of 22 mm., and a maximum thickness of 7 mm. The material is tan chert.

The fourth style is represented by two specimens, one of which is incomplete (pl. 58, *h*, *i*). These points are small, with expanding stems and either straight or convex bases. The incomplete specimen has a serrated blade. Length of the complete point is 20 mm., and its maximum width 11 mm. The serrated point is 9 mm. wide. Both points have maximum thicknesses of 3 mm. Materials are gray Flint Hills chert and tan chert. These two points may, with some assurance, be assigned to the Plains Woodland component of the site, and suggest an identity with the Keith Focus (Marvin F. Kivett, personal communication, 1957).

The fifth style, represented by three specimens, is the "late horizon" triangular form (pl. 58, *j–l*). Two of the points are unnotched, while a third, probably a reworked specimen, has four side notches, two to a side, plus a basal notch. Length of the only complete unnotched point is 16 mm., and its maximum width is 9 mm. It is 2 mm. thick. The incomplete unnotched point is 15 mm. wide at the base and 4 mm. thick. The notched specimen is 14 mm. long, 16 mm. wide at the base, and 2 mm. thick. Materials of these points are tan and gray cherts.

Spatulate object.—This small object, which may be a knife, is manufactured of gray Flint Hills chert. The base is rounded, but the exact shape of the complete specimen is not known, since a large portion of the tip is missing. It is very neatly flaked, has a maximum width of 17 mm. and a maximum thickness of 3 mm.

Blades.—Portions of 14 blades were recovered. Judging from the larger fragments, they were pyriform in shape. Maximum widths range between 26 and 37 mm., thicknesses between 9 and 15 mm. Materials are cream-colored, tan, and gray Flint Hills cherts (pl. 58, *v*).

Turtleback scrapers.—Four objects of this sort were recovered. Two are flat on one side and rounded by chipping on the upper surface. The other two have been chipped on both faces, but are much flatter on one face than on the other. The first specimen measures 54 mm. in length, has a maximum width of 30 mm., and a maximum thickness of 12 mm. The second (pl. 58, *u*), a fragment from one end of a scraper, has a maximum width of 18 mm. and a maximum thickness of 7 mm. They are of tan and cream-colored cherts, respectively. The larger of the bifacial specimens is 50 mm. in length, 41 mm. in width, and has a maximum thickness of 20 mm. It is manufactured of gray-brown chert. The smaller specimen is 68 mm. in length, 26 mm. in width, and has a maximum thickness of 16 mm. It is of tan chert.

Flake scrapers.—Fourteen artifacts of this description were found at the site. They are distinguished by one or more edges that show secondary chipping. There seems to be no uniformity in size or shape. Materials employed are tan and gray chert and, in one instance, red jasper.

Choppers.—Eight specimens assigned to this category were recovered at the site. Six are of tan chert and two of gray Flint Hills material. They tend to be ovoid in shape and are worked to a cutting edge by percussion flaking on two faces. The largest specimen is 83 mm. in length and 20 mm. in maximum thickness. The smallest is 50 mm. long and has a maximum thickness of 13 mm.

Celt.—One celt was recovered. It is made of Cottonwood limestone and measures 94 mm. in length, 52 mm. in width, and 17 mm. in thickness. The bit shows considerable wear.

Ax.—One chipped ax of Cottonwood limestone was recovered. It was apparently double-bitted originally, but one end has been broken off. The bit measures 97 mm. in width, the groove 74 mm. It has a maximum thickness of 31 mm. (pl. 58, *w*).

Pick.—The site yielded one pick, also made of Cottonwood limestone. The bit is slightly curved. The pick is 114 mm. in length, has a maximum width of 69 mm., and a maximum thickness of 35 mm.

Manos.—Seven manos were recovered, six of which were fragments. The fragments are all of sandstone. When complete, the sandstone manos were probably subrectangular in shape, with two smooth grinding surfaces. The only complete specimen is of Cottonwood limestone. It has the outline of a parallelogram when viewed from above. It is 133 mm. long, 59 mm. wide, and 23 mm. thick.

Cupstone.—A single cupstone was recovered (pl. 58, *t*). When complete it was apparently ovoid, with two smooth faces on opposite sides. In the center of each of these faces is a small depression. The piece measures 74 mm. in diameter and has an average thickness of 43 mm. The depressions are 22 and 27 mm. in diameter, and 3 and 4 mm. in depth.

Hammerstones.—Four battered hammerstones were recovered. Three are of tan jasper, one of reddish-brown jasper. They are of a size to fit conveniently in the hand and show no evidence of artificial shaping.

Core.—Only one core was recovered. It is made of a rather granular gray chert.

Paint.—The site yielded two paint stones. One is yellow limonite, the other reddish-brown hematite. Both have been rubbed and scratched to secure pigment. The limonite specimen is 32 mm. in length and the hematite specimen is 24 mm. in length.

Awl.—A single bone awl, worked from a deer metapodial, was recovered (pl. 58, *m*). It rested on the surface of the hearth, Feature 1. It is 74 mm. long and has a maximum width of 15 mm.

Flaking tool.—A section of antler, possibly a flaking tool, in a very poor state of preservation, was also found on top of the hearth. It measured 90 mm. in length and 15 mm. in diameter. The specimen crumbled when removal was attempted.

Bone bead.—A small tube of bird or small mammal bone was probably used as a bead. It is 15 mm. long and 3.5 mm. in diameter. This, too, was recovered in the hearth ash.

CULTURAL AFFILIATIONS

On the basis of typology, three components have been isolated at this site. In probable order of sequence, late to early, they are: Aksarben; Plains Woodland, perhaps the Keith Focus of the Orleans Aspect; and Archaic.

SUMMARY AND CONCLUSIONS

The archeological investigations at the 10 sites in the Toronto Reservoir area that have been reported in this paper reveal an aboriginal occupation of the locality beginning about 5000 B.C. and extending into the historic period. Although no Paleo-Indian material was recovered by the 1957 party, the presence of many Paleo-Indian points in local collections indicates that worthwhile sites of this period may be present somewhere in the vicinity.

The materials described are attributable to five cultural groupings, each on a slightly different time level, as follows:

(1) The *Archaic Culture* (ca. 5000 B.C. to 200 B.C.) is represented by site 14GR210 and by components at 14WO209, 14WO215, the Walleye Rockshelter (14WO222), the Dry Creek Rockshelter (14WO224), and 14GR216, with a possible representation at the Possum Point site (14WO228). At the multicomponent sites the Archaic components have been defined on admittedly shaky evidence, namely by the presence of large projectile points and by the absence of ceramic materials that would identify these points with the cultural complexes. At 14GR210, which appears to be predominantly Archaic, large unnotched and side-notched points are accompanied by large chipped blades, a beveled knife, end scrapers, flake scrapers, a chopper, and manos. The inventory suggests that these people were hunters and gatherers of

wild food. They lacked horticulture, as well as the bow and arrow and the ceramic arts.

(2) The *Kansas City Hopewell Culture* (ca. 200 B.C.–A.D. 500) is represented by one site, 14WO203. It is identified by smoothed, grit-tempered pottery, decorated with dentate- and rocker-stamping, together with large, expanding-stem projectile points, drills, gravers, pyriform blades, and scrapers, flake scrapers, choppers, and pieces of worked hematite. The Kansas City Hopewell people practiced maize horticulture and made pottery but were apparently not familiar with the bow and arrow. Settlements were larger and more permanent than in Archaic times.

(3) The *Plains Woodland Culture* (ca. A.D. 500–900) is represented at one multicomponent site, 14GR216, where it was identified by five thick, cord-marked, grit-tempered sherds. Small expanding-stem points, with or without serrated blades, are also assignable to this component of the site, and suggest specific identification with the Keith Focus of the Orleans Aspect. Since 14GR216 is an unstratified multicomponent site, it is not known which of the other artifacts recovered, such as scrapers, choppers, manos, etc., should be assigned to the Plains Woodland component.

The Plains Woodland people (representing the Middle Woodland time level) possessed a culture very similar to that of the Kansas City Hopewell groups, and the artifacts of the two cultures show a close relationship. Like the Hopewell people, the Plains Woodland groups practiced horticulture, supplementing the food secured in this manner with wild vegetal products and game. The presence of both large and small projectile points at Plains Woodland sites indicates that both the bow and arrow and the atlatl were in use.

(4) Components assignable to the *Aksarben Aspect* (ca. A.D. 1100–1500) were present at five sites, all of which had more than one component. These are: 14WO209, 14WO215, the Walleye Rockshelter (14WO222), the Dry Creek Rockshelter (14WO224), and 14GR216. The Aksarben components are identified by moderately thin, cord-marked, grit-tempered pottery with either plain flaring or incised collared rims. At site 14GR216 the small side-notched and unnotched projectile points can be assigned to this component, which is the latest occupation present there. The Aksarben people, like the Kansas City Hopewell and Plains Woodland folk, were dependent upon hunting, gathering, and maize horticulture. Villages tended to be larger and more numerous than in earlier periods. Apparently the bow and arrow had completely supplanted the atlatl.

(5) Four sites had components of the *Great Bend Aspect* (ca. AD. 1500–1700). These are: 14WO215; the Walleye Rockshelter (14WO 222); the Dry Creek Rockshelter (14WO224); and the Possum Point

site (14WO228), with a possible component at 14WO209. The Possum Point site seems to be predominantly Great Bend. Components of this aspect were identified by heavy, smooth, grit- or shell-tempered pottery, gray, buff, or orange-buff in color. The presence of this material in the Toronto Reservoir area extends the known distribution of this aspect, hitherto known only from sites in Central Kansas.

The Great Bend people continued the hunting, gathering, and maize horticulture subsistence pattern established and developed in the area by the earlier Kansas City Hopewell, Plains Woodland, and Aksarben people. Great Bend sites are apparently smaller than those of the Aksarben Aspect, a fact which may reflect the unstable conditions that seem to have characterized this area in early historic times.

APPENDIX

TABULATION OF TORONTO RESERVOIR SITES

Site	Type	Culture	Fieldwork
14GR1	Minor camp	?	Visited.
14GR2	Minor village	Upper Republican	Do.
14GR3	Minor camp	?	Do.
14GR201	do	?	Do.
14GR202	Village-camp	Kansas City Hopewell and Keith Focus.	Do.
14GR203	Minor camp	?	Do.
14GR204	do	?	Do.
14GR205	Village	Upper Republican	Do.
14GR206	Minor camp	?	Do.
14GR207	do	?	Do.
14GR208	do	?	Do.
14GR209	Village (?)	?	Tested in 1956.
14GR210	Major camp	Archaic Complex	Tested in 1957.
14GR211	Minor camp	?	Visited.
14GR212	Village (?)	Kansas City Hopewell	Do.
14GR213	Minor camp	?	Do.
14GR214	do	?	Do.
14GR215	do	?	Do.
14GR216	Village-camp	Aksarben, Keith Focus, and Archaic.	Excavated in 1957.
14GR217	Minor camp	Keith Focus	Visited.
14GR218	do	?	Do.
14GR219	Minor village	Woodland and a later component.	Do.
14GR220	Minor camp	?	Do.
14GR221	do	Woodland	Do.
14WO1	do	do	Tested in 1956.
14WO2	do	?	Visited.
14WO201	do	?	Do.
14WO202	do	?	Do.

TABULATION OF TORONTO RESERVOIR SITES—Continued

Site	Type	Culture	Fieldwork
14WO203	Village_____	Kansas City Hopewell	Tested in 1956 and 1957.
14WO204	Rockshelter_____	?	Visited.
14WO205	Minor camp_____	?	Do.
14WO206	_____do_____	?	Do.
14WO207	_____do_____	?	Do.
14WO208	_____do_____	?	Do.
14WO209	Village-camp_____	Aksarben and Archaic_	Tested in 1957.
14WO210	Minor camp_____	?	Visited.
14WO211	_____do_____	?	Do.
14WO212	_____do_____	?	Do.
14WO213	_____do_____	Woodland_____	Do.
14WO214	_____do_____	?	Do.
14WO215	Village-camp_____	Great Bend, Aksarben, and Archaic.	Tested in 1957.
14WO216	Minor camp_____	?	Visited.
14WO217	Mound_____	?	Do.
14WO218	Minor camp_____	?	Do.
14WO219	Village_____	?	Do.
14WO220	Minor camp_____	?	Do.
14WO221	_____do_____	?	Do.
14WO222	Rockshelter_____	Historic, Great Bend, Aksarben, and Archaic.	Excavated in 1957.
14WO223	Village_____	?	Visited.
14WO224	Rockshelter_____	Historic, Great Bend, and Aksarben.	Excavated in 1957.
14WO225	_____do_____	?	Recorded in 1957.
14WO226	Petroglyph_____	?	Recorded in 1957.
14WO227	Village_____	Aksarben_____	Visited.
14WO228	_____do_____	Great Bend, Archaic___	Tested in 1957.
14WO229	Historic Fort_____	White (Fort Belmont) _	Visited.
14WO230	Minor camp_____	?	Do.
14WO231	_____do_____	?	Do.

LITERATURE CITED

ANDREAS, A. T.
    1883. A history of the state of Kansas. Western Historical Company,
        Chicago.
BELL, ROBERT E., and BAERREIS, DAVID A.
    1951. A survey of Oklahoma archaeology. Bull. Texas Archaeol. and
        Paleont. Soc., vol. 22, pp. 7–100.
COMMITTEE FOR THE RECOVERY OF ARCHAEOLOGICAL REMAINS.
    1958. The Inter-Agency Archeological Salvage Program after twelve years.
        Univ. Missouri Press.
FENENGA, FRANKLIN.
    1953. The weights of chipped stone points; a clue to their functions.
        Southwestern Journ. Anthrop., vol. 9, No. 3, pp. 309–323.

JAMES, EDWIN, EDITOR.
  1956. A narrative of the captivity and adventures of John Tanner, during thirty years residence among the Indians in the interior of North America. (Original ed. New York, 1830.) Reprinted, Minneapolis.

JOHNSON, ALFRED E.
  1957. Appraisal of the archeological resources of the Toronto Reservoir, Greenwood and Woodson Counties, Kansas. Mimeographed report, Smithsonian Institution. Inter-Agency Archaeological Salvage Program. Lincoln.

KIVETT, MARVIN F.
  1952. Woodland sites in Nebraska. Nebraska State Hist. Soc. Publ. Anthrop., No. 1.
  1953. The Woodruff Ossuary, a prehistoric burial site in Phillips County, Kansas. Bur. Amer. Ethnol. Bull. 154, Riv. Bas. Surv. Pap. No. 3, pp. 103–142.

KREIGER, ALEX D.
  1946. Culture complexes and chronology in northern Texas. Univ. Texas Publ. No. 4640.

MCDERMOTT, JOHN FRANCIS, EDITOR.
  1940. Tixier's travels on the Osage Prairies. Univ. Oklahoma Press.

MOONEY, JAMES.
  1912. Wichita. Handbook of American Indians North of Mexico. Bur. Amer. Ethnol., Bull. 30, pt. 2, pp. 947–950.

SMITH, CARLYLE S.
  1949. Archeological investigations in Ellsworth and Rice Counties, Kansas. Amer. Antiq., vol. 14, No. 4, pt. 1, pp. 292–300.

SPAULDING, ALBERT C.
  1955. Prehistoric cultural development in the eastern United States. 75th Anniv. Vol. Anthrop. Soc. Washington.

STEPHENSON, ROBERT L.
  1954. Taxonomy and chronology in the Central Plains-Middle Missouri River area. Plains Anthrop., No. 1.

SUHM, DEE ANN, and KRIEGER, ALEX D.
  1954. An introductory handbook of Texas archeology. Bull. Texas Archaeol. and Paleont. Soc., vol. 25.

SWANTON, JOHN R.
  1942. Source material on the history and ethnology of the Caddo Indians. Bur. Amer. Ethnol. Bull. 132.

WEDEL, WALDO R.
  1940. Cultural sequence in the Central Great Plains. Essays in historical anthropology of North America. Smithsonian Misc. Coll., vol. 100, pp. 291–352.
  1942. Archeological remains in central Kansas and their possible bearing on the location of Quivira. Smithsonian Misc. Coll., vol. 101, No. 7.
  1943. Archeological investigations in Platte and Clay Counties, Missouri. U.S. Nat. Mus. Bull. 183.
  1949. Some Central Plains sherd types from Kansas. Proc. Fifth Plains Conference for Archeology, Note Book No. 1, Lab. Anthrop., Univ. Nebraska, pp. 86–90.

WEDEL, WALDO R., and KIVETT, MARVIN F.
  1956. Additional data on the Woodruff Ossuary, Kansas. Amer. Antiq., vol. 21, No. 4, pp. 414–416.

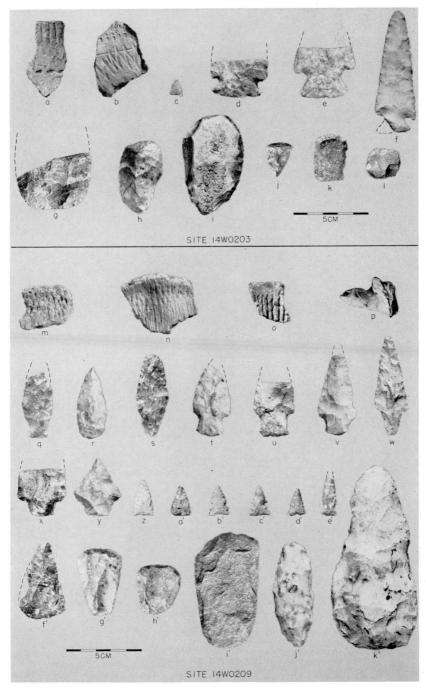

Artifacts from site 14WO203, Toronto Reservoir, Kansas. *a, b*, Dentate-stamped rim sherds; *c–f*, projectile points; *g*, basal fragment of large blade; *h–l*, end scrapers. Artifacts from site 14WO209, Toronto Reservoir, Kansas. *m–o*, Cord-marked rim sherds; *p*, pottery vessel loop handle; *q–e'*, projectile points; *f'*, small blade; *g', h', j'*, scrapers; *i', k'*, chipped stone celts.

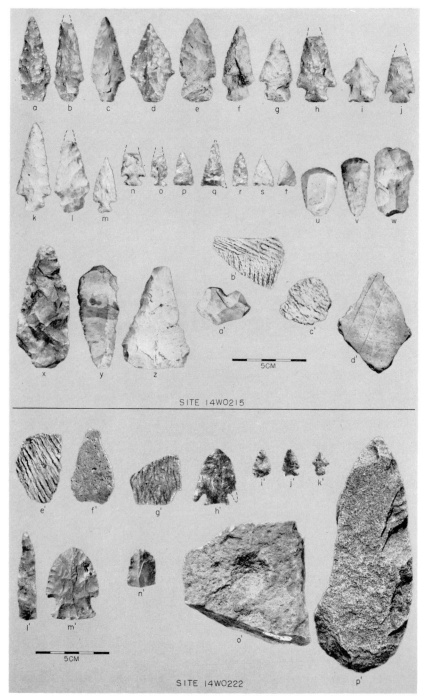

Artifacts from site 14WO215, Toronto Reservoir, Kansas.   *a–t*, projectile points; *u–w*, end scrapers; *x–z*, blades; *a'*, spokeshave; *b'–d'*; potsherds.   Artifacts from Walleye Rockshelter (14WO222), Toronto Reservoir, Kansas.   *e'–g'*, potsherds; *h'–k'*, projectile points; *l'*, drill; *m'*, projectile point; *n'*, end scraper; *o'*, cupstone or anvil; *p'*, hoe.

Petroglyphs from Walleye Rockshelter (14WO222), Toronto Reservoir, Kansas. *a, b,* Photograph and drawing of human figure; *c–f,* photograph and drawings of several petroglyphs of human figures. *f,* Like the others, this is incised and pecked into the stone, but it is also painted over in red.

Dry Creek Rockshelter, site 14WO224, Toronto Reservoir, Kansas. *Upper*, view of excavator at work in Rockshelter; *a*, "Harahey" blade. *Lower*, Artifacts from the Dry Creek Rockshelter. *b–h*, Projectile points; *i–j* and *n*, end scrapers; *k*, flake knife; *l*, *o*, blades; *m*, drill; *p*, bone needle; *q*, shaft smoother; *r*, iron kettle fragment; *s–t*, Aksarben rim sherds.

a, b, Photographs of petroglyphs on large roof rock at the Dry Creek Rockshelter (14WO224);
c, petroglyph at the Outlaw Rockshelter (14WO225); *d, e* photograph and drawing of
"Little-Water-Man" petroglyph at site 14WO226

Possum Point site (14WO228) Toronto Reservoir, Kansas.   *a*, Initial excavations underway; *b–e*, projectile points; *f*, cupstone; *g–k*, rim sherds.

Site 14GR210, Toronto Reservoir, Kansas.   *a*, View of site; *b*, knife; *c–i*, projectile points; *j–l*, flake scrapers; *m*, mano.

Site 14GR216, Toronto Reservoir, Kansas. *a*, View of a portion of the excavated area showing hearth in place in right center; *b–l*, projectile points; *m*, bone awl; *n–s*, potsherds; *t*, cupstones; *u*, scraper; *v*, blade; *w*, ax.

LIST OF REPORTS, ARTICLES, AND NOTES RELATING TO THE SALVAGE PROGRAMS PUBLISHED IN OTHER SERIES

(As of August 1, 1963)

ADAMS, WILLIAM RICHARD.
  1946. Archeological survey of Martin County. Indiana Hist. Bull., vol. 23, No. 6, pp. 195–224.
  1949. Archeological notes on Posey County, Indiana. Indiana Hist. Bur. Indianapolis.

ADAMS, WILLIAM Y., and NETTIE K.
  1959. An inventory of prehistoric sites on the Lower San Juan River, Utah. Mus. Northern Arizona Bull. 31, pp. 1–54.

ANDERSON, HARRY H.
  1956. A history of the Cheyenne River Indian Agency (South Dakota) and its military post, Fort Bennett, 1868–1891. South Dakota Hist. Coll., vol. 28, pp. 390–551.
  1961. The Fort Lookout Trading Post sites—A reexamination. Plains Anthrop., vol. 6, No. 14, pp. 221–229.
  1962. Additional descriptive material on Fort Pierre II, an historic site on the Oahe Dam area, South Dakota. Plains Anthrop., vol. 7, No. 17, pp. 193–196.

BABY, RAYMOND S.
  1946. Survey of Delaware Reservoir area. Mus. Echoes, vol. 19, No. 8, Ser. No. 208.
  1949. Cowan Creek Mound exploration. Mus. Echoes, vol. 22, No. 7, Ser. No. 243.
  1949. Stratton-Wallace site. Ann. Rep., Ohio State Archeol. and Hist. Soc., pp. 11–12.
  1951. Explorations of the Cordray and Goldsmith Mounds. Mus. Echoes, vol. 24, No. 12, Ser. No. 272.

BASS, WILLIAM M.
  1962. A preliminary analysis of burial data on 255 individuals from the Sully site, 39SL4, Sully County, South Dakota. Plains Anthrop., vol. 7, No. 16, pp. 77–78.

BASS, WILLIAM M., and BIRKBY, WALTER H.
  1962. The first human skeletal material from the Huff site, 32MO11, and a summary of putative Mandan skeletal material. Plains Anthrop., vol. 7, No. 17, pp. 164–177.

BELL, ROBERT E.
  1948. Recent archeological research in Oklahoma. Bull. Texas Archeol. and Paleont. Soc., vol. 19, pp. 148–154.
  1949. Recent archeological research in Oklahoma, 1946–1948. Chronicles of Oklahoma, vol. 27, No. 3, pp. 303–312.

BELL, ROBERT E.—Continued

1949. Archeological research in Oklahoma during 1947. Proc. Fifth Plains
Conf. Archeol., Note Book No. 1, Lab. Anthrop., Univ. Nebraska,
pp. 6–7.

1949. Archeological excavations at the Harlan site, Fort Gibson Reservoir,
Cherokee County, Oklahoma. Plains Archeol. Conf., Newsletter,
vol. 3, No. 1, pp. 3–15. Lincoln.

1950. Notes on work at the Harlan site. Archeol. Newsletter, vol. 1, No. 4,
pp. 1–2. Norman.

1951. Notes on work in Eufaula and Tenkiller Reservoirs. Archeol. Newsletter, vol. 2, No. 2, pp. 1–2. Norman.

1951. Notes on Tenkiller excavations. Archeol. Newsletter, vol. 2, No. 3,
pp. 1–2. Norman.

1951. Notes on work at the Vanderpool sites. Archeol. Newsletter, vol. 2,
No. 4, pp. 1–2. Norman.

1951. Notes on Tenkiller and Eufaula excavations. Archeol. Newsletter, vol.
2, No. 5, pp. 1–4. Norman.

1952. Notes on Keystone Reservoir survey. Oklahoma Anthrop. Soc. Newsletter, vol. 1, No. 1, p. 8.

1952. Prehistoric Oklahomans: or the Boomers came lately. Oklahoma
Quart., vol. 1, No. 3, pp. 33–35.

1952. Keystone archeological survey. Oklahoma Anthrop. Soc. Newsletter,
vol. 1, No. 2, p. 4.

1952. Archeological field work, Morris site. Oklahoma Anthrop. Soc. Newsletter, vol. 1, No. 3, pp. 1–3.

1953. Digging for Indian history. The Indian Sign, vol. 4, No. 2, pp. 9–12.

1953. The Scott site, Le Flore County, Oklahoma. Amer. Antiq., vol. 18, No.
4, pp. 314–331.

1954. Excavations at Lake Texoma, Marshall County, Oklahoma. Oklahoma Anthrop. Soc. Newsletter, vol. 3, No. 3, pp. 2–3.

1956. Radiocarbon date from the Harlan site, Cherokee County, Oklahoma.
Oklahoma Anthrop. Soc. Newsletter, vol. 5, No. 3, pp. 6–7.

1956. Radiocarbon dates from the Harlan site, Cherokee County, Oklahoma.
Oklahoma Anthrop. Soc. Newsletter, vol. 5, No. 6, p. 2.

1958. Notes and news—Harlan site excavations. Oklahoma Anthrop. Soc.
Newsletter, vol. 7, No. 3, pp. 1–2.

1958. Archeological investigations at the Boat Dock site, Ma–1, in the Lake
Texoma area, Marshall County, Oklahoma. Oklahoma Anthrop.
Soc. Bull. VI, pp. 37–48.

1958. Radiocarbon dates from Oklahoma. Oklahoma Anthrop. Soc. Newsletter, vol. 7, No. 3, pp. 3–4.

1959. Radiocarbon dates from Oklahoma sites. Oklahoma Anthrop. Soc.
Newsletter, vol. 8, No. 4, pp. 2–3.

BELL, ROBERT E., and BAERREIS, DAVID A.

1951. A survey of Oklahoma archeology. Bull. Texas Archeol. and Paleont.
Soc., vol. 22, pp. 7–100. (General study which contains information
obtained by salvage program.)

BELL, ROBERT E., and DALE, CHARLENE.

1953. The Morris site, Ck–39, Cherokee County, Oklahoma. Bull. Texas
Archeol. and Paleont. Soc., vol 24, pp. 69–140.

BELL, ROBERT E., and FRASER, RICHARD.
1952. Archeological discoveries at the Morris site, Cherokee County, Oklahoma. Chronicles of Oklahoma, vol. 30, No. 2, pp. 216–235.

BIRKBY, WALTER H.
1962. A preliminary report on the dentition of the skeletal population of the Sully site. Plains Anthrop., vol. 7, No. 16, p. 79.

BLISS, WESLEY L.
1949. Archeological reconnaissance in Wyoming and Montana, 1946–1947. Proc. Fifth Plains Conf. Archeol., Note Book No. 1, Lab. Anthrop., Univ. Nebraska, pp. 7–12.
1949. Early Man in the Northwestern Plains. Proc. Fifth Plains Conf. Archeol., Note Book No. 1, Lab. Anthrop., Univ. Nebraska, pp. 121–126.
1950. Birdshead Cave, a stratified site in the Wind River Basin, Wyoming. Amer. Antiq., vol. 15, No. 3, pp. 187–196.

BRAY, ROBERT T.
1956. Some outstanding finds from Table Rock Reservoir area. Missouri Archeol. Soc. Newsletter, No. 99, pp. 5–7.

BRETERNIRZ, DAVID A.
1957. Heltagito rock shelter (NA6380). Plateau, vol. 30, No. 1, pp. 1–16. Flagstaff.
1957. A brief archeological survey of the Lower Gila River. Kiva, vol. 22, Nos. 2–3. Tucson.

BREW, J. O. and OTHERS.
1947. Symposium on river valley archeology. Amer. Antiq., vol. 12, No. 4, pp. 209–225.

BRUES, ALICE M.
1959. Skeletal material from the Morris site, Ck–39. Bull. Oklahoma Anthrop. Soc., vol. 7, pp. 63–70.

BUCK, ARTHUR DEWEY, JR.
1959. The Custer Focus of the Southern Plains. Bull. Oklahoma Anthrop. Soc., vol. 7, pp. 1–32.

BULLEN, RIPLEY P.
1950. An archeological survey of the Chattahoochee River Valley in Florida. Journ. Washington Acad. Sci., vol. 40, No. 4, pp. 101–125.

BURGH, ROBERT F.
1949. Archeological field work of the University of Colorado Museum in 1947. Proc. Fifth Plains Conf. Archeol., Note Book No. 1, Lab. Anthrop., Univ. Nebraska, pp. 12–14.

BURROUGHS, JOHN.
1958. Last look at a forgotten civilization. Popular Mechanics, pp. 114–116. May.

BUTLER, B. ROBERT.
1955. The Wakemap Project—"Operation Last Chance." Mazama, vol. 37, No. 13, pp. 33–38.
1957. Dalles Reservoir prehistory: A preliminary analysis. Washington Archaeol., vol. 1, No. 8, pp. 4–7.
1958. Ash Cave (45 WW 61): A Preliminary Report. Washington Archaeol., vol. 2, No. pp. 3–10.

CALDWELL, JOSEPH R.

1948. Palachacolas Town, Hampton County, South Carolina, Journ. Washington Acad. Sci., vol. 38, No. 10, pp. 321–324.

1950. A preliminary report on excavations in the Allatoona Reservoir. Early Georgia, vol. 1, No. 1, pp. 5–22.

1955. Cherokee pottery from northern Georgia. Amer. Antiq., vol. 20, No. 3, pp. 277–280.

1958. Trend and tradition in the prehistory of the eastern United States. Mem. No. 88, Amer. Anthrop. Assoc. Sci. Pap., vol. 10; Amer. Anthrop., vol. 60, No. 6, pt. 2.

CALDWELL, JOSEPH R.; THOMPSON, CHARLES E.; and CALDWELL, SHEILA K.

1952. The Booger Bottom mound; A Forsyth Period site in Hall County, Georgia. Amer. Antiq., vol. 17, No. 4, pp. 319–328.

CALDWELL, SHEILA KELLY.

1950. Reconstruction of the Woodstock Fort. Early Georgia, vol. 1, No. 2, pp. 22–30.

CALDWELL, WARREN W.

1956. The archeology of Wakemap: A stratified site near The Dalles of the Columbia. Abs., microfilmed, Publ. No. 17, 119, University Microfilms, Ann Arbor.

1957. Cultural traditions in the Columbia Plateau and Southern Northwest Coast. Abs., Proc. Nebraska Acad. Sci., p. 4, April.

1957. Archeological salvage in the Missouri Basin. Progress, Missouri River Basin. Interior Missouri Basin Field Committee, October–December, pp. 47–55. Billings, Mont.

1958. Important archeological discoveries in the Arkansas Valley. Ozarks Mountaineer, vol. 6, No. 8, p. 7.

1960. The Black Partizan site (39LM218), Big Bend Reservoir, South Dakota: A preliminary report. Plains Anthrop., vol. 5, No. 10, pp. 53–57.

1960. Firearms and related materials from Ft. Pierre II (39ST17), Oahe Reservoir, South Dakota. Missouri Archaeol., vol. 22, December. Columbia.

1961. Excavations at certain La Roche and Thomas Riggs sites in the Big Bend and Oahe Reservoirs, 1960. Plains Anthrop., vol. 6, No. 12, pt. 1, p. 57.

CALDWELL, WARREN W.; McNUTT, CHARLES H.; and SMITH, G. HUBERT.

1960. Fort Randall Reservoir. Corps of Engineers, Omaha, Nebraska, Spec. Publ. December.

CASON, JOE F.

1952. Report on archeological salvage in Falcon Reservoir, season of 1952. Bull. Texas Archeol. and Paleont. Soc., vol. 23, pp. 218–259.

CHAMPE, JOHN L.

1949. White Cat Village. Amer. Antiq., vol. 14, No. 4, pt. 1, pp. 285–292.

CHAPMAN, CARL H.

1949. Archeological field work in Missouri, 1946–1947. Proc. Fifth Plains Conf. Archeol., Note Book No. 1, Lab. Anthrop., Univ. Nebraska, pp. 17–19.

1954. Preliminary salvage archeology in the Pomme de Terre Reservoir area, Missouri. Missouri Archaeol., vol. 16, Nos. 3–4. Columbia.

CHAPMAN, CARL H., and BRAY, ROBERT T.
   1956. Preliminary salvage archaeology in the Table Rock Reservoir area,
      Missouri. Missouri Archaeol., vol. 18, Nos. 1–2. Columbia.

CHAPMAN, CARL H., ET AL.
   1957. Table Rock salvage archeology. *In* A report of progress, archeological
      research by the University of Missouri, 1955–1956. Special Publ.
      Missouri Archeol. Soc., February, pp. 5–37. Columbia.

CHAPMAN, CARL H.; MAXWELL, THOMAS J., JR.; and KOZLOVICH, EUGENE.
   1951. A preliminary archeological survey of the Table Rock Reservoir area,
      Stone County, Missouri. Missouri Archeol., vol. 13, No. 2, pp. 8–38.
      Columbia.

COALE, GEORGE L.
   1956. Archeological survey of the Mt. Sheep and Pleasant Valley Reservoirs.
      Davidson Journ. Anthrop., vol. 2, No. 1, pp. 1–27.

COOGAN, ALAN H., and IRVING, WM. N.
   1959. Late Pleistocene and recent Missouri River terraces in the Big Bend
      Reservoir, South Dakota. Abs., Iowa Acad. Sci., vol. 66, pp. 317–327.

COOLEY, MAURICE E.
   1958. Physiography of the Glen-San Juan Canyon area, pt. 1. Mus. North-
      ern Arizona, Plateau, vol. 31, No. 2, pp. 21–33. Flagstaff.
   1958. Physiography of the Glen-San Juan Canyon area, pt. 2. Mus. Northern
      Arizona, Plateau, vol. 31, No. 3, pp. 49–60. Flagstaff.

COOPER, PAUL L.
   1949. Recent investigation in Fort Randall and Oahe Reservoirs, South
      Dakota. Amer. Antiq., vol. 14, No. 4, pt. 1, pp. 300–311.
   1949. An archeological survey of the Fort Randall Reservoir, South Dakota.
      Proc. Fifth Plains Conf. Archeol., Note Book No. 1, Lab Anthrop.,
      Univ. Nebraska, pp. 19–20.
   1955. The archeological and paleontological salvage program in the Mis-
      souri Basin, 1950–1951. Smithsonian Misc. Coll., vol. 126, No. 2.

CORBETT, JOHN M.
   1949. Salvage archeology in river basins. Planning and Civic Comment,
      Quart. Amer. Planning and Civic Assoc., July–Sept.
   1954. New dates from old data. Reclamation Era, vol. 40, No. 3, pp. 56–58.

CRAMPTON, C. GREGORY.
   1959. Outline history of the Glen Canyon region, 1776–1922. Univ. Utah,
      Anthrop Pap. No. 42.

CREER, LELAND HARGROVE.
   1958. Mormon towns in the region of the Colorado. Univ. Utah, Anthrop.
      Pap. No. 32.
   1958. The activities of Jacob Hamblin in the region of the Colorado. Univ.
      Utah, Anthrop. Pap. No. 33.

CRESSMAN, L. S.
   1960. Cultural sequences at The Dalles, Oregon. Trans. Amer. Philos. Soc.,
      vol. 50, pt. 10. December.

CRESSMAN, L. S.; COLE, DAVID L.; DAVIS, WILBUR A.; NEWMAN, THOMAS M.;
   and SCHEANS, DANIEL J.
   1959. Cultural sequences at The Dalles, Oregon. Univ. Oregon.

CUMMINGS, THOMAS S.
    1953. A preliminary report on the Blue Stone Focus, White Rock Aspect,
        Abs. Proc. Nebraska Acad. Sci., May.

DANSON, EDWARD B.
    1958. The Glen Canyon Project. Plateau, vol. 30, No. 3, pp. 75–78. Flag-
        staff.

DAUGHERTY, RICHARD D.
    1952. Archeological investigations in O'Sullivan Reservoir, Grant County,
        Washington. Amer. Antiq., vol. 17, No. 4, pp. 374–383.
    1956. Archeology of the Lind Coulee site, Washington. Proc. Amer. Philos.
        Soc., vol. 100, No. 3, pp. 224–278.
    1956. An archeological survey of Rocky Reach Reservoir. Northwest Arche-
        ology Number, Research Stud. State College of Washington, vol.
        24, No. 1, pp. 1–16.
    1959. Early Man in Washington (Archeology of Lind Coulee site). Div.
        Mines and Geol., Inf. Circ. No. 32.

DAVIS, E. MOTT.
    1950. The present status of the study of "Early Man" in Nebraska. Abs.
        Proc. Nebraska Acad. Sci., May.
    1951. "Early Man" sites in the Medicine Creek Reservoir area. Abs. Proc.
        Nebraska Acad. Sci., April.
    1953. Early human occupation of the Plains area. Abs. Proc. Nebraska Acad.
        Sci., May.
    1953. Recent data from two paleo-Indian sites on Medicine Creek, Nebraska.
        Amer. Antiq., vol. 18, No. 4, pp. 380–386.
    1954. The Bridger Basin, Wyoming : An area of archeological promise. Abs.
        Proc. Nebraska Acad. Sci., April.
    1956. Archeological survey of the Big Sandy Reservoir area, southwestern
        Wyoming. Notebook No. 2, Lab. Anthrop. Univ. Nebraska.
    1961. Archeological sequence at the Ferrell's Bridge Reservoir, northeastern
        Texas. Plains Anthrop., vol. 6, No. 12, pt. 1, p. 61.
    1962. Archeological salvage investigation of the Harling Mound in Fannin
        County, Texas. Year-Book of the Amer. Philos. Soc., pp. 487–489.
    1962. Archeology of the Lime Creek site in Southwestern Nebraska. Spec.
        Publ. Univ. Nebraska State Museum, No. 3, pp. 1–106.

DAVIS, E. MOTT, and SCHULTZ, C. BERTRAND.
    1952. The archeological and paleontological salvage program at the Medicine
        Creek Reservoir, Frontier County, Nebraska. Science, vol. 115, No.
        2985, pp. 288–290.

DAVIS, HESTER A.
    1961. 1960 fieldwork in Beaver Reservoir, Arkansas. Plains Anthrop., vol.
        6, No. 12, pt. 1, p. 72.

DAVIS, WILLIAM A., and DAVIS, E. MOTT.
    1960. The Jake Martin site : An Archaic site in the Ferrell's Bridge Reser-
        voir area, Northeastern Texas. Univ. Texas, Archeol. Ser., No. 3.

DE BAILLOU, CLEMENS.
    1962. Archeological salvage in the Morgan Falls Basin. Univ. Georgia
        Lab. Archeol. Ser., No. 4, pp. 1–18.

DEJARNETTE. DAVID L., and HANSEN, ASAEL T.
    1960. The archeology of the Childersburg site, Alabama. Florida State
        Univ. Notes Anthrop., No. 6.

DIBBLE, CHARLES E.
    1959. Ecological studies of the flora and fauna in Glen Canyon. Univ. Utah,
        Anthrop. Pap., No. 40.

DIBBLE, DAVID S., and DAY, KENT C.
    1962. A preliminary survey of the Fontenelle Reservoir, Wyoming. Univ.
        Utah. Anthrop Pap., No. 58. (Upper Colorado Ser., No. 7).

DI PESO, CHARLES C.
    1953. The Sobaipuri Indians of the Upper San Pedro River Valley, South-
        eastern Arizona. The Amerind Foundation, Inc., Dragoon, Ariz.,
        No. 6.

DITTERT, ALFRED E., JR.
    1957. The salvage archeology program is resumed at the Navajo Dam. El
        Palacio, vol. 64, Nos. 7–8, pp. 245–246. Santa Fe.
    1958. Salvage archeology and the Navajo Project: A progress report. El
        Palacio, vol. 65, No. 2, pp. 61–72. Santa Fe.
    1958. Recent developments in Navajo project archeology. El Palacio, vol.
        65, No. 6. pp. 201–211. Santa Fe.

DITTERT, ALFRED E., JR.; HESTER, JIM J.; and EDDY, FRANK W.
    1961. An archaeological survey of the Navajo Reservoir district North-
        western Mexico. School Amer. Res. and Mus. New Mexico, No. 23.
        Santa Fe.

DRAGOO, DON W.
    1951. Archeological survey of Shelby County, Indiana. Indiana Hist. Bur.,
        Indianapolis.

DUFFIELD, LATHEL F.
    1961. The Limerick site at Iron Bridge Reservoir, Rains County, Texas.
        Bull. Texas Archeol. Soc., vol. 30, pp. 51–116.
    1962. Archeology of the Sanford Reservoir in the Texas Panhandle. Plains
        Anthrop., vol. 7, No. 16, p. 79.

DUFFIELD, LATHEL F., and JELKS, EDWARD B.
    1961. The Pearson site: A historic Indian site at Iron Bridge Reservoir,
        Rains County, Texas. Univ. Texas, Archeol. Ser., No. 4.

EDDY, FRANK W.
    1961. Excavations at Los Pinos Phase sites in the Navajo Reservoir dis-
        trict. Mus. of New Mexico Pap. in Anthrop., No. 4, pp. 1–107. Santa
        Fe.

EVANS, OREN F.
    1958. Analysis of flint materials from the Lee and Lacy sites. Oklahoma
        Archeol. Soc. Newsletter, vol. 6, No. 7, pp. 2–3. Norman.

FAIRBANKS, CHARLES H.
    1954. 1953 excavations at Site 9HL64, Buford Reservoir, Georgia. Florida
        State Univ. Stud. Anthrop., No. 16, pp. 1–25.

FENENGA, FRANKLIN.
    1952. The archeology of the Slick Rock Village, Tulare County, California.
        Amer. Antiq., vol. 17, No. 4, pp. 339–347.
    1953. Rediscovering the past in the Missouri Basin. Progress, Missouri
        River Basin, Interior Missouri Basin Field Committee, June, pp.
        202–209. Billings, Mont.
    1953. The ice-glider game, an 18th-century innovation in Northern Plains
        culture. Abs. Proc. Nebraska Acad. Sci., May.

FENENGA, FRANKLIN—Continued
    1954. The interdependence of archeology and ethnology as illustrated by the
        ice-glider game of the Northern Plains. Plains Anthrop., No. 1, pp.
        31–38. May.

FLOWERS, SEVILLE, ET AL.
    1960. Ecological studies of the flora and fauna of Flaming Gorge Reservoir
        Basin, Utah and Wyoming. Univ. Utah, Anthrop. Pap., No. 48
        (Upper Colorado Series No. 3).

GAINES, XERPHA M.
    1957. Plants in Glen Canyon. Mus. Northern Arizona, Plateau, vol. 30, No.
        2, pp. 31–34. Flagstaff.

GANT, ROBERT.
    1962. The Big Bend burials, 39BF221, Buffalo County, South Dakota.
        Museum News, W. H. Over Museum, State Univ. South Dakota, vol.
        23, Nos. 4–5, pp. 3–7.

GARRETT, JOHN W.
    1952. Preliminary investigations of an aboriginal occupation site near Sanish,
        North Dakota. Montana State Univ. Anthrop. and Sociol. Pap.,
        No. 13.

GARTH, THOMAS R.
    1951. Historic sites in the Fort Randall Reservoir area. Abs. Proc. Nebraska
        Acad. Sci. April.

GILBERT, ELIZABETH X.
    1961. A pithouse village on the San Juan River, N. Mex. Southwestern Lore,
        vol. 27, No. 1, pp. 9–16.

GROVE, FRED.
    1949. Archeologists uncover real Sooners. Univ. Oklahoma News of the
        Month, vol. 2, No. 3, pp. 2–3.

GUNKEL, ALEXANDER.
    1961. The archeology of the Rocky Reach Reservoir. (A comparative cul-
        tural analysis of four archeological sites in the Rocky Reach Reser-
        voir region, Washington.) Washington State Univ., Dept. Sociol.
        and Anthrop.

GUNNERSON, JAMES H.
    1958. Archeological survey of the Kaiparowitz Plateau. A preliminary re-
        port. Utah Archeology Newsletter, vol. 4, No. 3, pp. 9–20. Salt
        Lake City.
    1959. 1957 excavations, Glen Canyon area. Univ. Utah, Anthrop. Pap., No.
        43.

HANDLEY, CHARLES O., JR.
    1953. A new South Dakota locality for the kangaroo rat, *dipodomys*. Journ.
        Mammalogy, vol. 34, No. 2, p. 264. May.

HARRIS, R. K.
    1951. Plainview point from site 18C7–3. The Record, Dallas Archeol. Soc.,
        vol. 10, No. 1, p. 2.

HASKELL, HORACE S.
    1958. Flowering plants in Glen Canyon—late summer aspect. Mus. Northern
        Arizona, Plateau, vol. 31, No. 1, pp. 1–3. Flagstaff.

HEDDEN, MARK.
    1958. Surface printing as a means of recording petroglyphs. Amer. Antiq.,
        vol. 23, No. 4, pt. 1, pp. 435–439. April.

HELDMAN, DONALD P.
    1961. Archaeological work within the proposed Joanna Reservoir. Plains
        Anthrop., vol. 6, No. 12, pt. 2, pp. 110–111.

HENNING, DALE R.
    1961. Archaeological research in the proposed Joanna Reservoir, Missouri.
        Missouri Archaeol., vol. 23, pp. 133–183.
    1962. The Joanna Reservoir. Plains Anthrop., vol. 7, No. 16, pp. 84–86.

HENSLEY, G. S.
    1952. Story of first midwest farmers unfolds in White River Valley. Missouri
        Farmer, pp. 6–9. September. Columbia.

HEWES, GORDON W.
    1949. The 1947 summer field session in archeology, University of North Da-
        kota. Proc. Fifth Plains Conf. Archeol., Note Book No. 1, Lab.
        Anthrop., Univ. Nebraska, pp. 21–24.
    1949. Pottery from the sites excavated by the 1947 North Dakota field ses-
        sion. Proc. Fifth Plains Conf. Archeol., Note Book No. 1, Lab.
        Anthrop., Univ. Nebraska. pp. 58–67.
    1949. Burial mounds in the Baldhill area, North Dakota. Amer. Antiq.,
        vol. 14, No. 4, pp. 322–328.
    1950. Sheyenne River, Proc. Sixth Plains Archeol. Conf. (1948), Univ. Utah,
        Anthrop. Pap. No. 11, p. 9.

HOCKMAN, STEVEN.
    1952. The history of Fort Sully (South Dakota). South Dakota Hist. Coll.,
        vol. 26, pp. 222–227.

HOLDER, PRESTON, and WIKE, JOYCE.
    1949. The frontier culture complex, a preliminary report on a prehistoric
        hunter's camp in southwestern Nebraska. Amer. Antiq., vol. 14,
        No. 4, pp. 260–266.
    1950. The Allen site (FT–50) : Archeological evidence of an early hunter's
        camp on Medicine Creek, Frontier County, Nebraska. Proc. Sixth
        Plains Archeol. Conf. (1948), Univ. Utah, Anthrop. Pap., No. 11,
        pp. 105–107.

HOWARD, JAMES H.
    1962. Report of the investigation of the Huff site, 32MO11, Morton County,
        North Dakota, 1959. Univ. North Dakota, Anthrop, Pap., No. 2.

HOWARD, LYNN E.
    1951. Archeological survey in the Bull Shoals region of Arkansas. Missouri
        Archaeol., vol. 13, No. 1, pp. 3–17. Columbia.

HUGHES, JACK T.
    1949. Investigations in western South Dakota and northeastern Wyoming.
        Amer. Antiq., vol. 14, No. 4, pp. 266–277.
    1950. An experiment in relative dating of archeological remains by stream
        terraces. Bull. Texas Archeol. and Paleont. Soc., vol. 21, pp. 97–104.

HURT, AMY PASSMORE.
    1958. The race for treasure. Denver Post, Sunday Empire Mag., Aug. 31,
        1958.

HURT, WESLEY R., JR.

1951. Report of the investigations of the Swanson site, 39BR16, Brule
County, South Dakota, 1950. South Dakota Archaeol. Comm., Archaeol. Stud., Circ. No. 6.

1952. Report of the investigation of the Scalp Creek site, 39GR1, and the
Ellis Creek site, 39GR2, South Dakota, 1941, 1951. South Dakota
Archaeol. Comm., Archaeol. Stud., Circ. No. 4.

1952. House types of the Over Focus, South Dakota. Plains Archeol. Conf.
News Letter, vol. 4, No. 4, pp. 51–52.

1953. Report of the investigation of the Thomas Riggs site, 39HU1, Hughes
County, South Dakota, 1952. South Dakota Archaeol. Comm., Archaeol. Stud., Circ. No. 5.

1954. Report of the investigations of the Spotted Bear site, 39HU26, and
the Cottonwood site, 39HU43, Hughes County, South Dakota, 1953.
South Dakota Archaeol. Comm., Archaeol. Stud., Circ. No. 6.

IRVING, WILLIAM N.

1958. The chronology of early remains at the Medicine Crow site, 39BF2,
South Dakota. Abs. Proc. Nebraska Acad. Sci., p. 3. April.

JELKS, EDWARD B.

1952. The River Basin Surveys archeological program in Texas. Texas
Journ. Sci., vol. 4, No. 2, pp. 131–138.

1953. Excavations at the Blum rockshelter. Bull. Texas Archeol. and Paleont. Soc., vol. 24, pp. 189–207.

1959. Archeologists add new data on Texas' past. Univ. Texas, Engineering
Science News, vol. 7, No. 1, pp. 1–4.

1962. The Kyle site, a stratified Central Texas Aspect site in Hill County,
Texas. Univ. Texas Archaeol. Ser., No. 5.

JELKS, EDWARD B., and TUNNELL, CURTIS D.

1959. The Harroun site: A Fulton Aspect Component of the Caddoan area,
Upshur County, Texas. Univ. Texas Archaeol. Ser., No. 2.

JENNINGS, JESSIE D.

1947. An atlas of archeological sites within the reservoirs located in the
Missouri River Basin. U.S. Dept. Interior, Reg. Two, Nat. Park
Serv. Missouri Basin Recreation Survey. Omaha.

1948. Plainsmen of the past, a review of the prehistory of the Plains. U.S.
Dept. Interior, Reg. Two, Nat. Park Serv., Missouri Basin Recreation Survey. Omaha.

1948. Saving a segment of history. Reclamation Era, vol. 34, No. 10, pp.
192–193. October.

1955. The archeology of the Plains: an assessment. U.S. Dept. Interior,
Reg. Two., Nat. Park Serv. and Univ. Utah, Dept. Anthrop. (Super-
sedes Jennings, 1948.)

1961. Salvage and scholarship. Northwestern Univ. Tri-Quart., vol. 3, No.
2, pp. 43–47. Winter.

1963. Administration of Contract Emergency Archaeological Programs.
Amer. Antiq., vol. 28, No. 3, pp. 282–285.

JOHNSON, FREDERICK.

1951. The Inter-Agency Archeological Salvage Program in the United States.
Archaeology, pp. 25–40. Spring.

JOHNSON, LEROY, JR.
1961. The Devils Mouth site: A river terrace midden, Diablo Reservoir, Texas. Bull. Texas Archeol. Soc., vol. 30, pp. 255–285.

JOHNSON, LEROY, JR., and JELKS, EDWARD B.
1958. The Tawakoni-Ysconi village, 1760: A study in archeological site identification. Texas Journ. Sci., vol. 10, No. 4. December.

JOHNSON, LEROY, JR., SUHM, DEE ANN, and TUNNELL, CURTIS D.
1962. Salvage Archeology of Canyon Reservoir: The Wunderlich, Footbridge, and Oblate sites. Bull. Texas Mem. Mus., No. 5, pp. 1–26.

KEEFE, JIM, and SAULTS, DAN.
1953. Out of the dust of yesterday. Missouri Conservationist, vol. 14, No. 1. January.

KELLAR, JAMES H., KELLY, A. R., and MCMICHAEL, EDWARD V.
1962. The Mandeville site in southwest Georgia. Amer. Antiq., vol. 27, No. 3, pp. 336–355.

KELLER, CHARLES M.
1961. Activities in the Kasinger Bluff Reservoir. Plains Anthrop., vol. 6, No. 12, pt. 1, p. 67.

KELLY, A. R., and NEITZEL, R. S.
1961. The Chauga site in Oconee County, South Carolina. Univ. Georgia Lab. Archaeol. Ser., Rep. No. 3.

KELLY, A. R., NONAS, RICHARD, ET AL.
1962. Survey of archaeological sites in Clay and Quitman Counties, Georgia. Univ. Georgia Lab. Archaeol. Ser., Rep. No. 5.

KIEHL, MARY.
1953. The Glen Elder and White Rock sites in north central Kansas. Abs. Proc. Nebraska Acad. Sci. May.

KIVETT, MARVIN F.
1948. Mechanized archeology. Plains Archeol. Conf. News Letter, vol. 1, No. 4, pp. 16–17.
1949. Archeological investigations in Medicine Creek Reservoir, Nebraska. Amer. Antiq., vol. 14, No. 4, pp. 278–284.
1949. An archeological survey of the Garrison and Baldhill Reservoirs. Proc. Fifth Plains Conf. Archeol., Note Book No. 1, Lab. Anthrop., Univ. Nebraska, pp. 24–25.
1950. An Archaic horizon? Plains Archeol. Conf. News Letter, vol. 3, No. 4, pp. 4–7.
1952. Woodland sites in Nebraska. Nebraska State Hist. Soc. Publ. in Anthrop., No. 1. (While some of the material in this report was obtained during earlier investigations, a considerable portion of the publication is based on the results of salvage projects.)
1954. Notes on the burial patterns of the Central Plains Indians. Abs. Proc. Nebraska Acad. Sci. April.
1962. Archaeological field report, 1961. Plains Anthrop., vol 7, No. 16, p. 77.

KIVETT, MARVIN F., and HILL, A. T.
1949. Archeological investigations along Medicine Creek. Proc. Fifth Plains Conf. Archeol., Note Book No. 1, Lab. Anthrop., Univ. Nebraska, pp. 25–26.

LEHMER, DONALD J.
    1951. Pottery types from the Dodd site, Oahe Reservoir, South Dakota.
        Plains Archeol. Conf. News Letter, vol. 4, No. 2, pp. 1–15.
    1952. The Turkey Bluff Focus of the Fulton Aspect. Amer. Antiq., vol.
        17, No. 4, pp. 313–318.
    1952. The Fort Pierre Branch, central South Dakota. Amer. Antiq., vol.
        17, No. 4, pp. 329–336.
    1952. Animal bone and Plains archeology. Plains Archeol. Conf. News Let-
        ter, vol. 4, No. 4, pp. 53–55.
    1954. The sedentary horizon of the northern Plains. Southwestern Journ.
        Anthrop., vol. 10, No. 2, pp. 139–159.
LINDSAY, ALEXANDER J., Jr.
    1961. The Beaver Creek agricultural community on the San Juan River,
        Utah. Amer. Antiq., vol. 27, No. 2, pp. 174–187. October.
LIPE, WILLIAM D.
    1960. 1958 excavations, Glen Canyon area. With appendices by Christy G.
        Turner II, Lyndon L. Hargrave. Univ. Utah, Anthrop. Pap., No.
        44. (Glen Canyon Ser., No. 11).
LIPE, WILLIAM, and FOWLER, DON.
    1958. Archeological excavations and survey in Glen Canyon: Preliminary
        reports of 1958 work. Utah Archeol., vol. 4, No. 4, pp. 4–16. Salt
        Lake City.
LIPE, WILLIAM D.; SHARROCK, FLOYD W.; DIBBLE, DAVID S.; and ANDERSON,
        KEITH M.
    1960. 1959 excavations, Glen Canyon area. With appendix by Christy G.
        Turner II, and addendum by Dee Ann Suhm. Univ. Utah, Anthrop.
        Pap., No. 49. (Glen Canyon Ser. No. 13.)
LISTER, ROBERT H.
    1957. Salvage archeology in the Southwest. Southwestern Lore, vol. 23,
        No. 3, pp. 34–35. Boulder.
    1957. The Glen Canyon survey in 1957. Univ. Utah, Anthrop. Pap., No. 30.
    1958. A preliminary note on excavations at the Coombs site, Boulder, Utah.
        Utah Archeol.: A Newsletter, vol. 4, No. 3, pp. 4–8. Salt Lake City.
    1959. The Coombs site, with a chapter, Pottery, by Florence C. Lister. Univ.
        Utah, Anthrop. Pap., No. 41.
    1962. Archaeological Survey of the Blue Mesa Reservoir, Colorado. South-
        western Lore, vol. 28, No. 3, pp. 41–60.
LISTER, ROBERT H.; AMBLER, J. RICHARD; and LISTER, FLORENCE L.
    1960. The Coombs site. Part II. Univ. Utah, Anthrop. Pap., No. 41.
LISTER, ROBERT H., and LISTER, FLORENCE C.
    1961. The Coombs site. Part III, summary and conclusions. Univ. Utah,
        Anthrop. Pap., No. 41, October.
MCDOUGALL, WALTER B.
    1959. Plants of the Glen Canyon area in the Herbarium at the Museum of
        Northern Arizona (mimeographed).
MCKUSICK, M. B., and WATSON, R. S.
    1959. Grinding implements from Vaquero Reservoir, San Luis Obispo and
        Santa Barbara Counties. Univ. California, Ann. Rep., Archeol.,
        Surv., Dept. Anthrop.-Sociol., pp. 13–14. Los Angeles.

McMICHAEL, EDWARD V., and KELLAR, JAMES H.
    1960. Archeological salvage in the Oliver Basin. Univ. Georgia Lab. Archeol.
        Ser., Rep. No. 2.

McNUTT, CHARLES H.
    1958. La Roche ware and relative chronology. Abs., Proc. Nebraska Acad.
        Sci., April, pp. 3–4.

McNUTT, CHARLES H., and WHEELER, RICHARD P.
    1959. Bibliography of primary sources for radiocarbon dates. Amer. Antiq.,
        vol. 24, No. 3, pp. 323–324.

MALOUF, CARLING.
    1950. The archeology of the Canyon Ferry region, Montana, 1950. Univ.
        Montana Anthrop. and Sociol. Pap. No. 11.
    1951. Archeological studies of aboriginal occupation sites in northwestern
        North Dakota. Montana State Univ. Anthrop. and Sociol. Pap.,
        No. 7.

MARSHALL, RICHARD.
    1962. Archaeological survey of Jasper County, Missouri. Plains Anthrop.,
        vol. 7, No. 16, pp. 82–84.

MATTES, MERRILL J.
    1947. Historic sites in Missouri Valley reservoir areas. Nebraska Hist., vol.
        28, No. 3, pp. 1–15.
    1949. Historic sites in the Fort Randall Reservoir area. South Dakota Hist.
        Coll., vol. 24.
    1952. Revival at old Fort Randall. Military Engineer, vol. 44, No. 298,
        pp. 88–93.
    1952. Salvaging Missouri Valley history. The Westerners Brand Book, vol.
        9, No. 3, pp. 17–19, 22–24.
    1954. Under the wide Missouri [historic sites in Missouri Basin reservoirs].
        North Dakota Hist., vol. 21, No. 4, pp. 146–167.

MATTISON, RAY H.
    1951. Old Fort Stevenson, a typical Missouri River military post. North
        Dakota Hist., vol. 18, Nos. 2–3, pp. 2–40.
    1954. The Army post on the northern Plains, 1865–1885. Nebraska Hist.,
        vol. 35, No. 1, pp. 1–27.
    1954. Report on historical aspects of the Oahe Reservoir area, Missouri
        River, South and North Dakota. South Dakota Hist. Coll. and Rep.,
        vol. 27.
    1955. The Indian reservation system on the upper Missouri, 1865–1890. Ne-
        braska Hist., vol. 36, No. 3, pp. 141–172.
    1955. Report on historic sites in the Garrison Reservoir area, Missouri River
        [North Dakota]. North Dakota Hist., vol. 22, Nos. 1–2, pp. 5–73.
    1956. The military frontier on the upper Missouri. Nebraska Hist., vol. 37,
        No. 3, pp. 159–182.
    1956. Report on historic sites adjacent to the Missouri River, between Big
        Sioux River and Fort Randall Dam, including those in the Gavins
        Point Reservoir area (South Dakota and Nebraska). South Dakota
        Hist. Coll., vol. 28, pp. 22–98.

MAYER-OAKES, WILLIAM J.

1953. An archeological survey of the proposed Shenango River Reservoir area in Ohio and Pennsylvania. Ann. Carnegie Mus., vol. 33, art. 3, pp. 115–124, Anthrop. Ser. No. 1.

1962. Archaeological work at Grand Rapids, Manitoba. Plains Anthrop., vol. 7, No. 16, p. 88.

MELEEN, E. E.

1949. A preliminary report on the Thomas Riggs village site. Amer. Antiq., vol. 14, No. 4, pt. 1, pp. 310–321. (This paper includes material from investigations in the Oahe Reservoir area prior to the salvage program but also reports on work done in 1947.)

METCALF, GEORGE.

1956. Additional data from the Dodd and Phillips Ranch sites, South Dakota. Amer. Antiq., vol. 21, No. 3, pp. 305–309.

MILLER, CARL F.

1948. Early cultural manifestations exposed by the archeological survey of the Buggs Island Reservoir in southern Virginia and northern North Carolina. Journ. Washington Acad. Sci., vol. 38, No. 12, pp. 397–399.

1949. The Lake Spring site, Columbia County, Georgia. Amer. Antiq., vol. 15, No. 1, pp. 38–51.

1949. Appraisal of the archeological resources of the Buggs Island Reservoir in southern Virginia and northern North Carolina. Quart. Bull., Archeol. Soc. Virginia, vol. 4, No. 1.

1949. Early cultural manifestations exposed by the archeological survey of the Buggs Island Reservoir in southern Virginia and northern North Carolina. Quart. Bull., Archeol. Soc. Virginia, vol. 4, No. 2.

1950. Early cultural horizons in the southeastern United States. Amer. Antiq., vol. 15, No. 4, pp. 273–288. (A general article but containing data collected during survey work.)

1950. An analysis and interpretation of the ceramic remains from site 38 Mc6 near Clarks Hill, South Carolina. Journ. Washington Acad. Sci., vol. 40, No. 11, pp. 350–354.

1956. Burin types from southern Virginia: A preliminary statement. Amer. Antiq., vol. 21, No. 3, p. 311.

1959. Physical structure of Rock Mound at 9ST3, Georgia. Southern Indian Stud., Archeol. Soc. North Carolina and Res. Lab. Anthrop., Univ. North Carolina, vol. 11, pp. 16–19.

MILLER, E. O., and JELKS, EDWARD B.

1952. Archeological excavations at the Belton Reservoir, Coryell County, Texas. Bull. Texas Archeol. and Paleont. Soc., vol. 23, pp. 168–217.

MILLER, LOYE H.

1957. Bird remains from an Oregon Indian midden. The Condor, vol. 59, No. 1, p. 59–63. January–February.

MILLER, WILLIAM C., and BRETERNITZ, DAVID A.

1958. 1957 Navajo Canyon survey, preliminary report. Plateau, vol. 30, No. 3, pp. 72–74. Flagstaff.

1959. 1958 Navajo Canyon survey, preliminary report. Plateau, vol. 31, No. 1, pp. 3–7. Flagstaff.

MILLS, JOHN E., and OSBORNE, CAROLYN.
1952. Material culture of an Upper Coulee rockshelter. Amer. Antiq., vol. 17, No. 4, pp. 352–359.

MOSIMAN, JAMES, and RABB, GEORGE B.
1952. The herpetology of Tiber Reservoir area, Montana. Copeia, No. 1, pp. 23–27. June 2.

MULLOY, WILLIAM.
1954. The McKean site in northeastern Wyoming. Southwestern Journ. Anthrop., vol. 10, No. 4, pp. 432–460.

NEUMAN, ROBERT W.
1957. Supplementary data on the White Rock Aspect. Abs., Proc. Nebraska Acad. Sci., pp. 3–4. April.
1960. The Truman Mound site, Big Bend Reservoir area, South Dakota. Amer. Antiq., vol. 26, No. 1, pp. 78–92. July.
1961 Excavations at four mound sites in the Oahe Reservoir. Plains Anthrop., vol. 6, No. 12, pt. 1, pp. 57–58.
1962. Field season, 1961. Plains Anthrop., vol. 7, No. 16, p. 81.
1962. Historic Indian burials, Fort Thompson, South Dakota. Plains Anthrop., vol. 7, No. 16, p. 95.
1963. Check-stamped pottery on the Northern and Central Great Plains. Amer. Antiq., vol. 29, No. 1, pp. 17–26.

OSBORNE, DOUGLAS.
1950. An archeological survey of the Benham Falls Reservoir, Oregon. Amer. Antiq., vol. 16, No. 2, pp. 112–120.
1953. Archeological occurrences of pronghorn antelope, bison, and horse in the Columbia Plateau. Sci. Month., vol. 77, No. 5, pp. 260–269.

OSBORNE, DOUGLAS; CALDWELL, WARREN C.; and CRABTREE, ROBERT H.
1956. The problem of Northwest coastal-interior relationships as seen from Seattle. Amer. Antiq., vol. 22, No. 2, pp. 117–128.

OSBORNE, DOUGLAS, and CRABTREE, ROBERT H.
1961. Two sites in the Upper McNary Reservoir. Tebiwa, Journ. Idaho State College Mus., vol. 4, No. 2, pp. 19–36.

OSBORNE, DOUGLAS; CRABTREE, ROBERT; and BRYAN, ALAN.
1952. Archeological investigations in the Chief Joseph Reservoir. Amer. Antiq., vol. 17, No. 4, pp. 360–373.

OSMUNDSON, JOHN, and HULSE, CHRISTOPHER.
1962. Preliminary report on an archeological survey of the Bruces Eddy Reservoir, north-central Idaho, 1961. Tebiwa, Journ. Idaho State College Mus., vol. 5, No. 1, pp. 11–29.

PECKHAM, STEWART.
1958. Salvage archeology in New Mexico, 1957–58: A partial report. El Palacio, vol. 65, No. 5, pp. 161–168. Santa Fe.

PENDERGAST, DAVID M., and MEIGHAN, CLEMENT W.
1959. The Greasy Creek site, Tulare County, Arizona. Univ. California, Ann. Rep. Archeol. Surv. Dept. Anthrop.-Sociol., pp. 1–9. Los Angeles.

PIERSON, LLOYD.
1957. A brief archeological reconnaissance of White Canyon, southeastern Utah. El Palacio, vol. 64, Nos. 7–8, pp. 222–230. Santa Fe.

PROCTOR, CHARLES C.
 1953. Report of excavations in the Eufaula Reservoir. Bull. Oklahoma
      Anthrop. Soc., vol. 1, pp. 43–59.

PURDY, WILLIAM M.
 1959. An outline of the history of the Flaming Gorge area. Univ. Utah
      Anthrop. Pap., No. 37.

ROBERT, FRANK H. H., JR.
 1948. A crisis in U.S. archeology. Sci. Amer., vol. 179, No. 6, pp. 12–17.
 1952. River Basin Surveys: The first five years of the Inter-Agency Archeo-
      logical and Paleontological Salvage Program. Ann. Rep. Smith-
      sonian Inst. for 1951, pp. 351–383.
 1955. The Inter-Agency Archeological and Paleontological Salvage Program
      in the United States. Pro Natura, vol. 2, pp. 213–218. (Series pub-
      lished by International Union for the Protection of Nature, Brussels.)
 1955. The Inter-Agency Archeological and Paleontological Salvage Program.
      Missouri Archeol. Soc. News Letter No. 96, pp. 7–10, November.

RUDY, JACK R., and STIRLAND, ROBERT D.
 1950. An archeological reconnaissance in Washington County, Utah. Univ.
      Utah, Anthrop. Pap., No. 9.

SCHOLTZ, JAMES A.
 1962. Salvage archaeology in Arkansas. Plains Anthrop., vol. 7, No. 16, p. 84.

SCHULTZ, C. BERTRAND, and FRANKFORTER, W. D.
 1948. Early man. Amer. Antiq., vol. 13, No. 3, pp. 279–280.
 1948. Preliminary report on the Lime Creek sites: new evidence of early
      man in southwestern Nebraska. Bull. Univ. Nebraska State Mus.,
      vol. 3, No. 4, pt. 2.
 1949. The Lime Creek sites. In Proc. Fifth Plains Conf. Archeol., Note
      Book No. 1, Lab. Anthrop., Univ. Nebraska, pp. 132–134.

SCHWARTZ, DOUGLAS W.
 1961. The Tinsley Hill site. (A late prehistoric stone grave cemetery in
      Lyon County, Ky.) Univ. Kentucky, Stud. Anthrop., No. 1.
 1962. The Driskill site; a Late Woodland occupation in the Lower Cumber-
      land River Valley. Trans. Kentucky Acad. Sci. vol. 23, Nos. 1–2;
      1–13.

SEARS, WILLIAM H.
 1950. Preliminary report on the excavation on an Etowah Valley site.
      Amer. Antiq., vol. 16, No. 2, pp. 137–142.

SHANE, RALPH M.
 1956. A short history of Fort Berthold [Indian Reservation]. 22 pp. Fort
      Berthold Indian Agency, Newtown, N. Dak.

SHARROCK, FLOYD W., ET AL.
 1963. 1961 excavations, Glen Canyon area. Univ. of Utah Anthrop. Pap.,
      No. 63 (Glen Canyon Series No. 18).

SHARROCK, FLOYD W.; ANDERSON, KEITH M.; FOWLER, DON D.; and DIBBLE,
  DAVID S.
 1961. 1960 excavations, Glen Canyon area. Univ. Utah, Anthrop. Pap.,
      No. 52, May. (With appendices by Don D. Fowler, and Christy G.
      Turner, II.)

SHARROCK, FLOYD W.; DIBBLE, DAVID S.; and ANDERSON, KEITH M.
  1961. The Creeping Dune Irrigation site in Glen Canyon, Utah. Amer.
    Antiq., vol. 27, No. 2, pp. 188–202. October.
SHARROCK, FLOYD W., and KEANE, EDWARD A.
  1962. Carnegie Museum collection from southeast Utah. Univ. Utah,
    Anthrop. Pap., No. 57. (Glen Canyon Ser., No. 160.)
SHINER, JOEL L.
  1952. The 1950 excavations at site 45BN6, McNary Reservoir, Washington.
    Amer. Antiq., vol. 17, No. 4, pp. 348–351.
SHIPPEE, J. M.
  1953. A Folsom fluted point from Marshall County, Kansas. Plains Archeol.
    Conf. News Letter, vol. 5, No. 4, p. 54.
SMITH, CARLYLE S.
  1949. Archeological investigations in Ellsworth and Rice Counties, Kansas.
    Amer. Antiq., vol. 14, No. 4, pp. 292–300.
  1949. Archeological research at the University of Kansas, 1946–1947. Proc.
    Fifth Plains Conf. Archeol., Note Book No. 1, Lab. Anthrop., Univ.
    Nebraska, pp. 29–30.
  1949. Field work in Kansas, 1949. Plains Archeol. Conf. News Letter, vol.
    2, No. 4, pp. 5–6.
  1950. Climate and archeology in Kansas. Proc. Sixth Plains Archeol. Conf.
    1948, Univ. Utah, Anthrop. Pap., No. 11, pp. 98–99.
  1951. Pottery types from the Talking Crow site, Fort Randall Reservoir,
    South Dakota. Plains Archeol. Conf. News Letter, vol. 4, No. 3,
    pp. 32–41.
  1953. Digging up the Plains Indian's past. Univ. Kansas Alumni Bull.
    December.
  1954. Cartridges and bullets from Fort Stevenson, North Dakota. Plains
    Anthrop., No. 1, pp. 25–29.
  1955. An analysis of the firearms and related specimens from Like-a-Fish-
    hook Village and Fort Berthold I. Plains Anthrop., No. 4, pp. 3–12.
  1959. Reconstructing a Plains Indian earth lodge. In Robert F. Heizer,
    "The Archaeologist at Work," pp. 131–133. New York.
  1959. The temporal relationships of coalescent village sites in Fort Randall
    Reservoir. Actas del XXXIII Congreso Internacional de Ameri-
    canistas, tomo II, pp. 111–123, figs. 1–3. San Jose.
SMITH, G. HUBERT.
  1953. Indian trade beads from Fort Berthold, North Dakota. Central Texas
    Archeol. No. 6. Waco.
  1954. Excavations at Fort Stevenson, 1951. North Dakota Hist., vol. 21,
    No. 3, pp. 127–135. July.
  1954. Archeological work at 32ML2 (Like-a-Fishhook Village and Fort
    Berthold), Garrison Reservoir area, North Dakota. Plains Anthrop.,
    No. 2, pp. 27–32.
  1957. Archeological salvage at historic sites in the Missouri Basin. Prog-
    ress, Missouri Basin Field Committee, pp. 49–50. January–March.
    Billings.
  1957. The present status of research on early historic sites of the Missouri
    Basin. Abs., Proc. Nebraska Acad. Sci., p. 3. April.
  1960. Historical archeology in Missouri Basin Reservoir areas: Current
    investigations. Plains Anthrop., vol. 5, No. 10, pp. 58–64.
  1961. Historic sites in the Oahe and Big Bend Reservoir areas. Plains
    Anthrop., vol. 6, No. 12, pt. 1, p. 57.

SMITH, JACK E.; LAFAVE, JACQUELINE M.; and WIRE, MARCIA V. V.
    1961. Archeological resources of Vaquero Reservoir. Univ. California, Dept.
        Anthrop. and Sociol., Los Angeles.

SOLECKI, RALPH S.
    1949. An archeological survey of two river basins in West Virginia. West
        Virginia Hist., vol. 10, No. 3, pp. 189–211, and No. 4, pp. 319–432.
    1952. Photographing the past. Progress, Missouri River Basin, Interior
        Missouri Basin Field Committee, pp. 1–9. September. Billings.
    1953. A Plainview point found in Marshall County, Kansas. Plains Archeol.
        Conf. News Letter, vol. 5, No. 4, pp. 52–53.

SPERRY, JAMES E., and KRAUSE, RICHARD A.
    1962. 1961 excavations at the Leavenworth site, 39CO9. Plains Anthrop.,
        vol. 7, No. 16, p. 80.

STALLARD, BRUCE.
    1957. Report on talk by Jim Garner concerning removal of Nespelem Indian
        burials from Chief Joseph Reservoir. Washington Archeol., vol.
        1, No. 8, p. 1.

STANTON, ROBERT B.
    1961. The Hoskaninni Papers: Mining in Glen Canyon, 1897–1902. Univ.
        Utah, Anthrop. Pap. No. 54 (Glen Canyon Ser. No. 15).

STEEN, CHARLIE R.
    1956. The archeological salvage program today. Archaeol., vol. 9, No. 3,
        pp. 175–181.

STEPHENSON, ROBERT L.
    1947. Archeological survey of Whitney Basin. Bull. Texas Archeol. and
        Paleont. Soc., vol. 18, pp. 129–142.
    1948. Archeological survey of McGee Bend Reservoir. Bull. Texas Archeol.
        and Paleont. Soc., vol. 19, pp. 57–73.
    1949. A note on some large pits in certain sites near Dallas, Texas. Amer.
        Antiq., vol. 15, No. 1, pp. 53–55.
    1949. Archeological survey of the Lavon and Garza-Little Elm Reservoirs.
        Bull. Texas Archeol. and Paleont. Soc., vol. 20, pp. 21–62.
    1949. A survey of the Whitney Basin in Hill and Bosque Counties, Texas.
        Proc. Fifth Plains Conf. Archeol., Note Book No. 1, Lab. Anthrop.,
        Univ. Nebraska, pp. 31–32.
    1952. The Hogge Bridge site and the Wylie Focus. Amer. Antiq., vol. 17,
        No. 4, pp. 299–312.
    1954. Salvage archeology. Bible Archeol. Digest, vol. 9, No. 2, pp. 2–11.
    1954. Taxonomy and chronology in the Central Plains—Middle Missouri
        River area. Plains Anthrop., No. 1, pp. 15–21. May.
    1954. The Stansbury site: An historic site in the Whitney Reservoir, Texas.
        Abs. Proc. Nebraska Acad. Sci. April.
    1957. Some research problems emerging out of Missouri Basin salvage. Ne-
        braska Acad. Sci., p. 4. April.
    1958. The Missouri Basin chronology program. Abs. Proc. Nebraska Acad.
        Sci., p. 4. April.
    1961. 1960 progress report, Missouri River Project. Plains Anthrop., vol. 6,
        No. 12, pt. 1, p. 55.
    1962. Three Smithsonian salvage sites. Plains Anthrop., vol. 7, No. 16, pp.
        80–81.
    1963. Administrative problems of the River Basin Surveys. Amer. Antiq.,
        vol. 28, No. 3, pp. 277–281.

STONEY, GEORGE.
    1950. Georgia's archeologists before the camera. Early Georgia, vol. 1,
        No. 2, pp. 18–21.

STRONG, WM. DUNCAN; JOHNSON, FREDERICK; and WEBB, WILLIAM S.
    1945. National archeological resources. Science, vol. 102, No. 2637, p. 44.
        July 13.

SWANSON, EARL H., JR.; TOUHY, DONALD R.; and BRYAN, ALAN L.
    1959. Archeological explorations in central and south Idaho, 1958. Idaho
        State College Mus., Occas. Pap., No. 2.

TREGANZA, ADAN E.
    1952. Archeological investigations in the Farmington Reservoir area in
        Stanislaus County, California. Univ. California Archaeol. Surv.
        Rep., No. 14.
    1954. Salvage archeology in Nimbus and Redbank Reservoir areas, central
        California. Univ. California Archaeol. Surv. Rep., No. 26.
    1958. Salvage archaeology in the Trinity Reservoir area, northern California.
        Univ. California Archaeol. Surv. Rep., No. 43, pt. 1.
    1959. Salvage archaeology in the Trinity Reservoir area, northern California,
        1958 field season. Univ. California Archaeol. Surv. Rep., No. 46.

TREGANZA, ADAN E., and HEICKSEN, MARTIN H.
    1960. Salvage archeology in the Whiskeytown Reservoir area and the Wintu
        Pumping Plant, Shasta County, California. San Francisco State
        College, Occas. Pap. Anthrop., No. 1.

TUNNELL, CURTIS D.
    1961. Evidence of a Late Archaic Horizon at three sites in the McGee Bend
        Reservoir, San Augustine County, Texas. Bull. Texas Archeol. Soc.,
        vol. 30 (for 1959) pp. 123–158.

TUOHY, DONALD R., and SWANSON, EARL H.
    1960. Excavation at Rockshelter 10–AA–15, southwest Idaho. Tibiwa, Journ.
        Idaho State Coll. Mus., vol. 3, Nos. 1 and 2, pp. 20–24.

WALLACE, WILLIAM J.
    1960. Archaeological resources of the Buena Vista Watershed, San Diego
        County, California. Univ. California, Ann. Rep., Archaeol. Surv.,
        Dept. Anthrop.-Sociol., pp. 277–294. Los Angeles.

WEAKLY, HARRY E.
    1961. Current developments in Plains dendrochronology. Plains Anthrop.,
        vol. 6, No. 12, pt. 1, p. 59.

WEAKLY, WARD F.
    1961. A site in the Fort Randall Reservoir, Brule County, South Dakota.
        Plains Anthrop., vol. 6, No. 14, pp. 230–241.
    1961. 1960 excavations at the Leavenworth site, 39CO9. Plains Anthrop.,
        vol. 6, No. 12, pt. 1, p. 58.

WEDEL, WALDO R.
    1947. Prehistory and the Missouri Valley Development Program; summary
        report on the Missouri River Basin Archeological Survey in 1946.
        Smithsonian Misc. Coll., vol. 107, No. 6.
    1947. The Missouri Basin Archeological Survey. Nebraska Hist., vol. 28,
        No. 1, pp. 32–40.
    1948. Prehistory and the Missouri Valley Development Program: summary
        report on the Missouri River Basin Archeological Survey in 1947.
        Smithsonian Misc. Coll., vol. 111, No. 2.

WEDEL, WALDO R.—Continued

1949. Some provisional correlations in Missouri Basin archeology. Amer. Antiq., vol. 14, No. 4, pt. 1, pp. 328–329.

1949. A summary of recent field work in central Plains archeology. Proc. Fifth Plains Conf. Archeol., Note Book No. 1, Lab. Anthrop., Univ. Nebraska, pp. 3–5.

1950. Missouri River Basin Survey 1948 season. Proc. Sixth Plains Archeol. Conf., Univ. Utah, Anthrop. Pap., No. 11, pp. 3–8.

1951. The use of earth-moving machinery in archeological excavations. *In* Essays on Archeological Methods, Univ. Michigan, Mus. Anthrop., Anthrop. Pap., No. 8, pp. 17–28.

1961. Historic man on the Great Plains. Univ. Oklahoma. (Contains information gathered by salvage operations.)

WEDEL, WALDO R., and GRIFFENHAGEN, GEORGE B.

1954. An English balsam among the Dakota aborigines. Amer. Journ. Pharmacy, vol. 126, No. 12, pp. 409–415.

WEDEL, WALDO R., and KIVETT, MARVIN F.

1956. Additional data on the Woodruff Ossuary, Kansas. Amer. Antiq., vol. 21, No. 4, pp. 414–416.

WENDORF, FRED; LUEBBEN, RALPH A.; BRUGGE, DAVID; and SCHROEDER, ALBERT H., with appendices by IRENE EMERY; EARL H. MORRIS; and ERIK K. REED.

1953. Salvage archeology in the Chama Valley, New Mexico. Monogr. School Amer. Res., No. 17.

WHEAT, JOE BEN.

1947. Archeological survey of the Addicks Basin: A preliminary report. Bull. Texas Archeol. and Paleont. Soc., vol. 18, pp. 143–145.

WHEELER, RICHARD P.

1950. Archeological investigations in Angostura Reservoir, Cheyenne River Basin, South Dakota. Abs. Proc. Nebraska Acad. Sci. May.

1951. The archeology of the Boysen Reservoir, Fremont County, Wyoming. Abs. Proc. Nebraska Acad. Sci. April.

1952. A note on the McKean lanceolate point. Plains Archeol. Conf. News Letter, vol. 4, No. 4, pp. 45–50.

1952. Plains ceramic analysis: a check list of features and descriptive terms. Plains Archeol. Conf. News Letter, vol. 5, No. 2.

1953. The distribution, cultural relationships and chronology of mounds and earthworks in the Dakotas. Abs. Proc. Nebraska Acad. Sci. May.

1954. Selected projectile point types of the United States: II. Bull. Oklahoma Anthrop. Soc., vol. 2, pp. 1–6. March.

1954. Two new projectile point types: Duncan and Hanna points. Plains Anthrop., No. 1, pp. 7–14.

1954. Check list of Middle Missouri pottery wares, types, subtypes. Plains Anthrop., No. 2, pp. 3–21.

1954. New contributions to the archeology of Oahe Reservoir. Abs. Proc. Nebraska Acad. Sci. April.

1955. Recent archeological salvage operations in the Missouri Basin. Progress, Missouri River Basin, Interior Missouri Basin Field Committee, October–December, pp. 65–73.

1957. Archeological field data and their interpretation. Abs. Proc. Nebraska Acad. Sci., p. 4. April.

1958. A bibliography of the Indian archeology of the Central and Northern Plains. Abs. Proc. Nebraska Acad. Sci. pp. 4–5. April.

WHEELER, RICHARD P., and SMITH, G. HUBERT.
    1953. The prehistory and early history of the Niobrara River basin. Missouri River Basin Project, Niobrara River Basin Development Plan, U.S. Dept. Int., Bur. Reclam., Reg. 7, Denver.

WHITE THEODORE E.
    1952. Observations on the butchering technique of some aboriginal peoples:
        I.   Amer. Antiq., vol. 17, No. 4, pp. 337–338.
    1952. Preliminary analysis of the vertebrate fossil fauna of the Boysen Reservoir area. Proc. U.S. Nat. Mus., vol. 102, No. 3296, pp. 185–208.
    1952. Suggestions on the butchering technique of the inhabitants at the Dodd and Phillips Ranch sites in the Oahe Reservoir area. Plains Archeol. News Letter, vol. 5, No. 2, pp. 22–28.
    1953. Studying osteological material. Plains Archeol. Conf. News Letter, vol. 6, No. 1, pp. 8–16.
    1953. Bison steaks and venison chops—the Flint-age way. Montana Farmer-Stockman, p. 8. September 15.
    1953. A method of calculating the dietary percentage of the various food animals utilized by aboriginal people. Amer. Antiq., vol. 18, No. 4, pp. 296–398.
    1953. Collecting osteological material, or how to get a block plastered. Plains Archeol. Conf. News Letter, vol. 6, No. 1, pp. 3–7.
    1954. Preliminary analysis of the fossil vertebrates of the Canyon Ferry Reservoir area. Proc. U.S. Nat. Mus., vol. 103, No. 3326, pp. 395–438.
    1954. Observations on the butchering technique of some aboriginal peoples, Nos. 3, 4, 5, and 6. Amer. Antiq., vol. 19, No. 3, pp. 254–264.
    1955. Observations on the butchering techniques of some aboriginal peoples, Nos. 7, 8, and 9. Amer. Antiq., vol. 21, No. 2, pp. 170–178.
    1956. The study of osteological materials in the Plains. Amer. Antiq., vol. 21, No. 4, pp. 401–404.
    1960. Plains quotes, "The Big Dogs of the Earth Lodge People." Plains Anthrop., vol. 5, No. 9, p. 35.

WILLIAMS, BOB.
    1953. The Ward site, Le Flore County, Oklahoma. Oklahoma Anthrop. Soc. Newsletter, vol. 1, No. 9, pp. 2–9.

WILMETH, ROSCOE.
    1956. The Payne site. Mus. News, W. H. Over Mus., Univ. South Dakota, vol. 18, Nos. 11–12, pp. 18–21.
    1958. Appraisal of the archeological resources of the Pomona and Melvern Reservoirs, Osage County, Kansas. Kansas State Hist. Soc.
    1958. Report of the investigation of the Payne site, 39WW302, Walworth County, South Dakota, 1956. Archeol. Stud., Circ. No. 8. Pierre.

WITHERS, ARNOLD.
    1950. Survey in eastern Colorado—University of Denver. Proc. Sixth Plains Archeol. Conf., Univ. Utah, Anthrop. Pap., No. 11, pp. 10–11.

WITTY, THOMAS A.
    1961. Excavations in the Wilson Reservoir area, Russell County, Kansas. Plains Anthrop., vol. 6, No. 12, pt. 1, p. 64.
    1962. Archeological salvage in the Milford and Council Grove Reservoirs. Plains Anthrop., vol. 7, No. 16, pp. 79–80.

Wood, W. Raymond.
  1953. Additional data on the La Roche Focus. Abs. Proc. Nebraska Acad.
      Sci., May.
  1954. Kipp's Post, 32MN1, Garrison Reservoir, North Dakota. Interim
      Report. State Hist. Soc., North Dakota.
  1958. Excavations of a village site in the Table Rock Reservoir. Missouri
      Archeol. Soc. News Letter, No. 119, p. 3. February.
  1961. 1960 field work at the Huff site, North Dakota. Plains Anthrop., vol.
      6, No. 12, pt. 1, p. 56.
  1961. The Pomme de Terre Reservoir in western Missouri prehistory. Mis-
      souri Archaeol., vol. 23, pp. 1–132. December.

Woodbury, Angus M., and Staff Members of the Division of Biological Sciences,
    University of Utah.
  1958. Preliminary report on biological resources of the Glen Canyon Reser-
      voir. Univ. Utah, Anthrop. Pap., No. 31.

Woodbury, Angus M.; Durrant, Stephen D.; and Flower, Seville.
  1959. Survey of vegetation in the Glen Canyon Reservoir Basin. Univ.
      Utah, Anthrop. Pap., No. 36.
  1962. A survey of vegetation in the Curecanti Reservoir Basins. Univ.
      Utah, Anthrop. Pap. No. 56 (Upper Colorado Ser., No. 6).

Woodbury, Angus M., et al.
  1961. Ecological studies of the flora and fauna of Navajo Reservoir Basin,
      Colorado and New Mexico. Univ. Utah, Anthrop. Pap., No. 55
      (Upper Colorado Ser., No. 5).

Woolworth, Alan R.
  1954. A search in the past [River Basin salvage in North Dakota]. North
      Dakota Outdoors, vol. 16, No. 9, pp. 6–7. (North Dakota State Game
      and Fish Dept.) Bismarck.
  1956. Archeological investigations at site 32ME59 (Grandmother's Lodge).
      North Dakota Hist., vol 23, No. 2, pp. 22–36.

Worman, Frederick C. V.
  1959. 1957 archaeological salvage excavations at Los Alamos, New Mexico:
      A preliminary report. El Palacio, vol. 66, No. 1. Santa Fe.

INDEX

Abraders, bone, 32
    cancellous tissue, 120 (fig.)
    faceted, 32, 59
    grooved, 32, 57, 59, 113, 114 (fig.)
    pumice, 209, 228
    sandstone, 209, 228, 356
    scoria, 60
    stone, 113, 305
Adenauer, Frank J., 327
Agate, 25, 27, 106
Agatized wood, 31
Agricultural Complex, trait list, 226
Akaska Focus, 130, 131
Aksarben culture complex, 328, 334, 337, 338, 342, 344, 347, 350, 353, 363, 366, 367, 368
Amphibia (*Rana* sp.), 233
Anderson, John, 146
Anderson, Sidney, 327
Andreas, A. T., 347, 348
Animals, 233–234
    effigies of, in baked clay, 24–25, 36 (figs.), 58
    hides of, 210, 223, 225
    remains of, 125 (list)
    sinews of, 223
    wild, 223
    See also Bones; names of specific animals.
Antelopes, 118, 125, 154, 212, 218, 234
Antler, bands of, 57, 59
    cylinder, 117 (fig.), 123–124, 133
    fragments, 219–220, 229
    miscellaneous shaped, 59
    sections, 219, 361, 366
    tines, 59, 60, 219
    work in, 45–48
Anvil, used in pottery making, 90, 161, 192, 224
Anvil stones, 208, 228, 300, 337
Archaic Component, 326, 328, 335, 337, 357, 360, 363, 366, 367
Archaic horizon, 223, 339, 347, 366
"Archaic Mandan" Period, 52, 58, 61
    sites, 57, 62
Archaic sites, 195
Archambault, George E., 73
Archer, figure of, 344
Architectural Complex, Hosterman site, 226
Arikara Indians, 208
    basketry, 125
    historic, 152
    sites, 56, 126, 132, 193
Arrowhead, 330
Arrow points, 34, 60, 61
    Hosterman site, 193–194
    miscellaneous, 194
Arrows, 348

Arrowshafts, 209, 314, 352
    smoothers, 286
    straighteners, 209–210, 228, 340
    wrenches, 223, 276, 287
Artifacts, 14–51, 78, 88–126, 147, 275, 283, 284–287, 288, 296
    antler, 117 (figs.), 119 (figs.), 123–124, 133
    basketry, 111 (figs.)
    bone, 45, 111 (figs.), 116–124, 132, 212–220, 229, 274, 284, 286–287, 305, 306, 353
    chipped stone, 105–112, 193–208, 304, 324
    ground stone, 109 (figs.), 113, 114 (figs.)–116, 208–211, 304–305
    lithic, 284, 285–286
    metal, 229, 277, 353
    pottery, 88–105, 160–193, 299–303, 306
    recent, 275, 277, 279, 282
    shell, 117 (figs.), 120 (figs.), 124, 221–222, 229, 284
    stone, 33 (fig.), 274, 279, 284, 286, 303–304, 306, 337, 340
    unidentified, 332, 341, 360
    wood, 111 (figs.)
Artiodactyles, 51 (list), 125, 233
Arzberger site, 96, 129, 130, 131, 132, 133, 134
Ash, white, 4, 7, 9, 22, 127, 151, 153, 154, 192, 278, 282, 283, 361, 366
Ash Hollow Cave, Nebr., 310
Atlatl, 367
Awls, bird long bones, 41 (fig.), 43, 59, 60, 119 (fig.), 121
    bone, 41 (fig.), 42, 43, 44, 45, 55, 59 (list), 120 (fig.), 121, 132, 209, 213, 217, 223, 224, 353, 361, 366
    fish spine, 41 (fig.), 43, 59
    mammal long bones, 40 (fig.), 42, 61, 120, 121–122
    mammal ribs, 41 (figs.), 43, 59 (list), 119 (fig.), 122
    miniature, 119 (fig.), 122
    neutral spine, 119 (figs.), 122, 132
    rough splinter, 218, 229
    scapula splinter, 121, 122, 213
    split metapodial bone, 219
Ax, grooved, 54, 208, 209, 223, 228, 336
    stone, 34, 58, 365
Azure, Lee, 295

Badger (*Taxidea taxus*), 125, 226, 233, 234
Badger Component (39LM238), 297, 308–314, 316 (list), 317
    discussion, 314–315
Badger Creek, *see* Good Soldier Creek.

Badwater site, 57
Baerreis, David, and Dallman, John E., 133
Bag, buckskin, 125, 134
Balls, cancellous bone, 218, 229
  stone, 210
Barka, Norman, 146
Barr, Robert P., xiii, 73
Bartos, Stanley, Jr., 309
Basalt, 112, 312
Baskets, 111 (fig.), 125, 134
Bastian, Tyler, 146
Bastions, 273, 274, 275, 276, 277
Beads, bone, 59, 212, 353, 361, 366
  ceramic, 25, 58
  copper, 222, 229
  disk, 48, 49 (figs.), 57, 59, 120 (fig.), 124, 229
  long bone, 38, 39 (figs.), 353
  shell, 12–13, 57, 120 (fig.)
  stone, 32, 59
Beans, charred, 127, 222, 223, 307
  kidney (Phaseolus vulgaris), 226, 232
  red, 125, 134
Bear, black, 226, 233
  head, model of, 25
  jaw, 147
Beaver, 51, 226, 233, 234
  incisor, 220, 229
  model of, 24
Beef, dried, 210
Belemnite, 212, 228
Bell, Robert E., and Baerreis, David A., 356, 357
Benthall, Joseph, 295
Berries, 208, 209, 210, 222
Bienville, Jean Baptiste Le Moyne, Sieur de, 344
Biesterfeldt Cheyenne site, 133, 134
Big Bend Reservoir, Lyman County, S. Dak., 271, 295
Birds, 51 (list), 125, 237
  bones of, 212, 217, 218
  sternum of, scored, 220
Bismarck, N. Dak., 1, 72
Bison, 51, 159, 226, 233, 234
  bones, 12, 32, 35, 38, 44, 45, 50, 56, 125, 151, 157, 158, 159, 212, 223, 235, 297, 299, 305
  bone tools, 111 (figs.), 116, 133
  chips, used for fuel, 151
  fat, 224
  incisor, grooved, 59
  kills, 158
  long bones, 216
  metapodial, 287
  radius, 219
  ribs, 214, 215, 218, 287, 296
    scored, 117 (fig.), 121
  scapulae, 212, 213, 214, 217, 223, 282, 287, 299, 305
  skulls, 11, 157, 158, 159, 220
  vertebrae, 299
Black Eagle Creek, 73
Black Hoop, David, tribal chairman, xiv

Black Partizan site (39LM218), 273
Blades, 342, 352, 356, 358, 364
  fragments of, 342, 351, 360, 366
  pyriform, 331, 336, 339, 340, 358, 364, 367
  trapezoidal, 276
  triangular, 352
Blake, Leonard, 231
Blum, Mark F., 73
Boatstones, limestone, 336
Bodkins, bone, 223
Boley, 57
Bone, fragmented, 78, 147, 308
  human, 85 (list)
  mineralized, 219, 229
  unmodified, 50, 51 (table)
  worked, 35–45, 37 (figs.), 39 (figs.), 41 (figs.), 43 (figs.), 59, 61, 353
  See also Artifacts; Tools; and names of animals.
Bones, animal, 12, 75, 212, 219, 223, 224, 225, 229, 276, 277, 279, 281, 283, 342
  mammal, 217, 306, 353
Bow and arrows, 158, 226, 342, 344, 367
Bower, John, 231
Bowers, Alfred W., 62, 63, 127
Boxelder, 125
Bracelets, antler, 119 (fig.), 124, 133
  bone, 119 (figs.)
Brazell Creek, 360
Brother-of-All, Eugene, 295
Brown, W. L., and Anderson, Edgar, 231
Brule County, S. Dak., 312
Buckbrush, 74, 75
Buffalo, see Bison.
Bull Creek, Lyman County, S. Dak., 306
Bulldozer, xiii, 3, 74, 78
Bullroarer, 215
Bureau of Indian Affairs, 295
Burials, 74, 315
  description of, 261–263
  human, 12–14
  primary, 310
  secondary, 309
Burin, angle, 205, 206, 228
Burinlike instruments, 205 (fig.), 205–206, 228
Burkitt, Miles Crawford, 206
Burned earth (F94), 7, 9, 151, 278, 281, 282, 283, 299, 308, 361

Caddoan group, 344, 350
Calcite, 34, 116, 310
Caldwell, Warren W., xiii, 73, 271, 281, 295
Canids, 125
Canis sp., 216
Cannonball Focus, 62
Cannonball River, 55
Carbon-14 age determination, 50, 63, 131, 306, 308, 309, 311, 314, 315
Carbon stains, 281
Carnivores, 51 (list), 125, 233
Carter, Hugh, 231
Cass Lake, Minn., 354

Catfish, 51, 125, 236, 237, 316
  blue, 236
  bones, 299
    spine, 42, 236
Catlinite, 211–212, 228
Cattail Creek, 3 (map)
Celts, 34, 58, 223, 336, 341, 342, 365
  diorite, 113, 114 (fig.), 286
  ground, 276
Cemetery, 12
Central Plains, 55, 56, 57, 71, 133, 161, 350
Cephalopod, extinct, 212
Chalcedony, 25, 60, 105, 110, 112, 193, 194, 196, 201, 203, 204, 207, 239, 240, 241, 242, 283, 285, 287, 304, 312, 313
  Badlands, 106
  vein, 110, 112, 204
Chalk, 35, 115
Chamberlain, S. Dak., 62, 272
Champe, John L., 62, 309, 310, 315
Charcoal, 7, 9, 50, 78, 80, 276, 281, 282, 283, 288, 306, 308, 315, 361
Charles Mix County, S. Dak., 309
Chase County, Kans., 324
Chatfield, D. William, 327, 354
Chert, black, brown, or gray, 25, 27, 29, 30, 31, 105, 106, 110, 112, 193, 194, 196, 201, 204, 207, 240, 241, 303, 324, 330, 331, 332, 335, 336, 337, 338, 339, 340, 341, 346, 351, 352, 356, 358, 360, 364, 365
  cream-colored, 356, 364
  Flint Hills, 330, 331, 332, 335, 336, 337, 338, 339, 340, 341, 345, 346, 351, 352, 356, 358, 360, 364, 365
  pink, 331, 335, 336, 337, 339, 340, 345, 346, 351, 352, 356, 358
  red, 335
  white, 60, 332, 340, 352, 358
Cheyenne River, 193
Chipped-stone Complex, Hosterman site, 227–228
Chippewa Indians, 56
Chisels, bone, 39 (fig.), 40, 59
  stone, 200, 223
  ulna, 111 (figs.), 123
Chokecherries, 222, 226
Choppers, 340
  biface, 203, 228, 286
  ovoid, 352, 365
  pyriform, 360
  stone, 30, 58, 112, 331, 336, 352, 360, 366, 367
  uniface, 286
Chordates, 51 (list)
Choutean Aspect, 129, 131, 132, 134, 307, 315
Clay, miscellaneous objects of, 24–25, 58 (list)
Clear Lake site, 311
Cleaver, scapula, 116, 117 (fig.), 132, 213–214, 223, 229
Cobbles, waterworn, 151
Cobblestone line, 299, 306
Collins, H. R., 205

Committee for Recovery of Archeological Remains, 324
Concretion, tubular, 286, 314
Coogan, Alan H., 296
Coogan, Alan H., and Irving, William N., 272
Cooper, Paul L., 71, 96, 130, 145, 192, 309, 311
Copper, 222
Cord, used on paddles, 92, 97, 99, 166, 170, 177
Cores, 340–341, 342, 346, 365
  pyriform, 337
Corn, 348
  braided, 134
  kernels, charred, 50, 124, 125, 134, 222, 223, 231 (table
  Northern Flint, 231
  stalks, 125
Corncobs, charred (*Zea mays*), 50, 125, 231, 282
Corson County, S. Dak., 71, 73
Cosner, Aaron J., 314
Coteau du Missouri, 245
Cottonwood, 151, 152, 323
Cottonwood formation, 324
Coyote (*Canis latrans*), 226, 233, 234, 316, 317
  skull, 299
Crane (*Grus canadensis*), 51, 125
Crane, H. R., and Griffin, James B., 310
Crow (*Corvus brachyrhynchos*), 51, 125
Crow Creek Indian Reservation, 295
Crystalline rock, 208
Cucurbita, 231, 232
Cupstones, 337, 338, 342, 346, 357, 365
Curtis, Norman, 353
Cylinders, antler, 133
Cyprinidae, 236

Dakota County, Nebr., 309
Dakota Indians, 208
Dalton gang, 353
Daly, Robert, 347
Danaczko, Edward A., 327
Dart points, stone, 54
Dawdles, clay, 191–192
Day, Adolph Burns, 295
Deer (*Odocoileus*), 51, 233, 234, 316, 317
  antlers, miscellaneous objects of, 46, 47 (figs.), 118, 219
  bones, 125, 212, 217, 218, 226
  footprints, pecked, 344
  leg bone, 353
  tines, worked, 46
Demery Component, 135
  pottery list, 105, 128, 129
Demery home, 74, 126
Densmore, Frances, 56
Dentry, Gordon, 146
Depressions, circular, 273, 276, 279
Deuder, Francis, 309
Dillenger culture, 311
Dinosaur National Monument, 316
Diorite, 34, 113, 209, 286
Disks, bone, 38, 39 (fig.), 56, 59
  sandstone, 114 (fig.), 115
  shell, 48, 49 (figs.), 57, 59, 61

Ditch, fortifying, 74, 146, 147, 148–149 (fig.), 225, 272, 273, 275, 276, 288
Dodd site, 55, 56, 132–133, 197, 213, 217, 220, 231, 235
Dog (*Canis familiaris*), 233, 234
    Canis sp., 51
    domestic, 226
    prairie (*Cynomys ludovicianus*), 226, 233, 234, 316, 317
Double Ditch (Bourgois) Mandan site, N. Dak., 1, 56, 57, 133, 175
Drills, expanding base, 106, 304, 329, 352
    stone, 29, 58 (list), 109 (figs.), 304, 329, 330–331, 335, 340, 342, 345, 352, 367
    tapered, 109 (fig.), 115
Dry Creek, 347, 353
Dry Creek Rockshelter (14WO224), 347–353, 366, 367
Ducks (size of teal and gadwill), 51
Dunkle, David H., 316
Dunlevy, Marion L., 133

Eagle, bones of, 118
    flesh eaten, 220
    tail feathers, 220
Eagle, golden, 51, 220, 233, 237
Eagle, Hobart, 295
Early Man sites, 195
Early Woodland cultures, 339
Earth lodge, 281
Effigies, baked clay, 36 (fig.)
Elk (*Cervus canadensis*), 51
    antlers, 219
    bones, 35, 125, 133, 305
    footprints, pecked, 344
    ribs, 215
    teeth, perforated, 46, 47 (fig.), 48, 56, 59
Ellsworth, Kans., 325
Elm trees, 323
Emetics, 56
End scrapers, 195–200, 249–255, 286, 312–313
    carinated, 200, 247–249
    chipped stone, 106, 109 (figs.), 331, 332, 336, 337, 342, 358
    irregular, 286
    keeled, 195, 197 (fig.), 244–246 (list)
    stone, 27, 28 (figs.), 29, 58 (list), 60, 61, 287, 303–304, 312–313
    teardrop, 250–251 (list)
    See also Scrapers.
Entryway, covered, 127
Epidemic, 288

"Face," miniature shell, 78, 120 (fig.), 124, 134
Fairbanks, Charles H., 226
Farming, 223
Faunal remains, 126 (list), 233–237
Feldspar, 90
Fence line, 283
Fenceposts, 279
Fenenga, Franklin, 54, 330
Fetish or trophy skull, 220, 229

Figures, human, 343–344, 346, 347, 350
Finger Creek, 241, 354
Fire Heart Butte, 2, 73
Firepit, 282, 283, 306, 307, 308
Fireplaces, 3, 4, 6, 7, 8 (map), 9, 12, 75, 78, 79, 80, 82, 85, 86, 127, 222, 361
Fish, 51, 125, 226, 235, 236, 237, 317
    bones, 316
Fisher, Richard, 327
Fishhook, bone, 38, 39 (fig.), 59, 118, 119 (figs.), 216, 229
    unbarbed, 216, 223
Fishing, 223
Flakers, bone, 214–215, 223, 229
    tine, 124
Flakes, stone, 31, 112, 338, 342
    worked, 314, 357
Flesher, metapodial, 282, 283, 286, 287
    serrated, 35, 37 (fig.), 55, 59, 133
Flint, Richard Foster, 145
Flint Hill region, Kans., 324
Flints, 196, 239, 308, 313, 334
Floyd, Edwin, 146
Fort Berthold Reservation, S. Dak., 56, 125
Forth, Michael, 295
Fortifications, 276–279
Fort Lincoln site (32SI4), 177
Fort Randall Reservoir, 130
Fort Thompson, 295
Fort Thompson Focus, 272
Fort Yates, 2, 71, 73
Fort Yates Focus, 62
Fort Yates site, XIII, 2, 3 (map), 62, 177
Fossils, shell, 48, 49 (fig.), 50 (table)
Four Bears site (39DW1), 186
Four Mile Creek, 3 (map), 50
Fowl, 316
Fowler, Melvin L., 311
Fox, 226
    gray (*Urocyon cinereorgentus*), 51, 226, 233
    kit (*Vulpes velox*), 220, 234, 316, 317
    model of, 25
    red (*Canis lupus*), 226, 233
Fraser, Dorothy E., 145, 146
Friedmann, Herbert, 237
Fritz, George, 327
Fruits, wild, 223, 226

Gaines Ranch, 57
Game pieces, stone, 109 (figs.), 115
Gannon, Craig, 73
Gastropods, 51 (list)
Gathering, 222, 223, 366, 367, 368
Gavins Point site (39YK203), 309
Geesefoot, 226
Gilmore, Melvin R., 125
Gipp, Robert F., XIII
Gipp, William C., 73
Glass fragment, 281, 282
Golden, Bernard, 271
Good Soldier Component (39LM238), 297–305, 306, 307, 315, 316 (list), 317

Good Soldier Creek, 296
Goose (*Branta canadensis*), 51
Gopher, pocket (*Geomys bursarius*), 226, 233
Gouges, 200, 201
Gourd, bottle (*Lagenaria*), 232
Grand River, S. Dak., 55, 89, 135
Grandmother's Lodge site (32ME59), 52, 54, 62
Grainers, bone, 224, 229
Granite, 30, 31, 34, 53, 90, 113, 115, 163, 192, 208, 209, 224, 286, 308
Gravers, 207, 256 (list), 331, 367
  tips of, 206, 208
Great Bend Culture Complex, 328, 334, 346, 347, 350, 353, 357, 367, 368
Great Plains province, 145, 306
Green stem fragments, 226
Greenwood County, Kans., 323, 324, 326, 328
Greenwood County sites (14GR201–218), 324
Grinders, hide, 215
  paint, 208
Ground stone, 113–116
  spheres, 31, 33 (figs.), 59
  tools, 208

Hackberry, 323
  seeds (*Celtis occidentalis*), 232
Hadleigh-West, Frederic, 71, 73
Hagen site, 177
Hairdress, figure of, 350
Haiser, George, 12
Hall, Robert L., 309
Hammer, 34, 113, 220
  antler, 229
Hammerstones, 31, 58, 113, 210, 223, 331, 337, 342, 346, 360, 365
  discoidal, 113
  ovoid, 286
  pebble, 113, 208
Hand County, S. Dak., 309
Handles, 184–186, 188 (figs.)
  lug, 183, 184–186, 192
  strap, 183–184, 186, 192
Handstones, 210, 228
Harding, Lester, 327
Havens site, 57, 60–61, 62
Hawk, 51, 125
Heart Butte campsite (32GT1), 175, 177
Heart Butte rockshelter (32GT5), 177
Hearth, 148 (map), 152, 153, 154, 306, 361
Heart River, 61, 62
Heath hen (*Tympanuchus cupido*), 51
Hecker, Thad. C., 1, 61
Hematite, 208, 211, 296, 299, 308, 360, 367
  and other paint substances, 211–212, 228
  Java Brown (8L10), 35, 115
  red, 192, 308, 332, 366
  siliceous, 341
Hensler site, 57
Hewes, Dr. Gordon W., XIII, 1, 4, 11, 12, 14, 19, 54, 63, 100, 175, 177
Hickey Ranch, 272

Hidatsa Indians, 133
  earth lodges, 126, 127
  sites of, 132
Hide grinders, 215, 229
Hide perforators, bone, 40, 45, 121
Hide scrapers, 212, 213, 214, 224, 229
Hill, A. T., and Wedel, Waldo R., 133
Hoard, Lyon J., 130
Hoes, scapula, 35, 36 (figs.), 44, 45, 55, 59 (list), 111 (fig.), 116, 132, 212–213, 216, 223, 229, 282
  stone, 341, 342, 346, 357
Hoffman, C. W., 56
Hold County, Nebr., 302
Homer, Dakota County, Nebr., 309
Hones, stone, 223
Hook and line, 226
Hopewell Complex, 325
Horse, figure of, 344, 346, 348, 353
Horticulture, 367, 368
Hosterman, John B., 145
House:
  depressions, 2, 11, 12, 60, 85, 127, 146, 271, 273
  entrance, 4, 7, 9, 51, 78, 81, 85, 126, 127, 152, 153, 154, 156, 222, 223, 306
  fill, 3, 12, 127, 128
  floors, 2, 3, 4, 7, 59, 81, 84, 127, 128, 148, 152, 153, 154, 156, 160, 223, 225, 279, 306
  midline, 51
  pits, 127, 147, 148 (map), 153, 222
  sites, 74, 306
  superstructure, 153
  walls, 4, 7, 12, 51, 52, 84, 128, 152, 153, 154, 155
Houses, 51, 61, 74, 78–85, 126, 151–154, 226
  circular, 75, 126, 151, 153, 215, 223
  conical, 127
  Demery site, 75, 78, 79 (map), 80–85, 92, 105, 124–128
  Havens site, 60
  oval, 128
  Paul Brave site, 2–11, 22, 51, 52, 58 (list)
  rectangular, 154, 222, 271, 283, 287, 306, 309
  Thomas Riggs site, 51, 58 (list)
Howard, J. Dan, 73
Howard, James H., 62, 124, 134, 288, 326, 327, 328, 330, 331
Howard, Mrs. James H., 327
Howe, Donald, 295
Hrdlička, Aleš, 261
Huff Focus, 129, 130, 131, 134, 135
Huff site (32MO11), 51, 63, 125, 129, 132, 133, 134, 288
Hughes County, S. Dak., 306
Human remains, 85–86, 221
Hunting, 222, 223, 226, 235, 366, 367, 368
  camp, 159
Hurt, Wesley R., Jr., 2, 35, 51, 52, 53, 56, 62, 96, 127, 130, 131, 132, 133, 171, 175, 179, 284, 287, 309
Huscher, Harold A., 295

Huscher, Harold A., and McNutt, Charles H., 295
Husks, 125

Ictaluridae, 236
Illinois River, 311
Incisor, grooved, 47 (fig.), 48
Indian dwelling, figure of, 353
Indian Knoll skeletons, 260
Insect remains, 238
Inter-Agency Archeological Salvage Program of the Smithsonian Institution, 295, 324
Irving village, 311

James, Edwin, 348
James, Jesse, 353
Jamison, Fred, 327
Jasper, 194, 196, 199, 201, 204, 239, 240, 241, 303, 313, 340, 351, 365
John Grass, Dakota chief, 73
John Grass Creek, 73, 76 (map), 127
Johnson, Alfred E., 324, 325, 326, 327, 330, 331, 334
Johnson, Elden, 309
Johnston, Francis E., 260
Jones, Hugh Carl, 146
Juniper, 152

Kanapolis Reservoir, 325
Kansa Indians, 323, 344
Kansas City Hopewell culture, 326, 328, 332, 367, 368
Kearney, Milo, 295
Keeler, Charles L., 259
Keith Focus, 310, 325, 326, 364, 366, 367
Kenel, S. Dak., 57
Kenel to Fort Yates road, 73, 76 (map)
Kettle, iron, 353
Kidder, A. V., 40, 121, 132
Kivett, Marvin F., 56, 310, 339, 364
Kleinsasser, Glenn, 14, 59, 284
Knife handles, bone, 37 (fig.), 44, 56, 59, 110, 111 (fig.), 118, 125, 134, 215, 229
    wood, 110, 111 (fig.), 118, 125
Knife River flint (chalcedony), 25, 27, 29, 30, 31, 60, 61, 105, 110, 112, 303
Knives, 41 (fig.), 44, 213, 283, 285–286, 287, 304, 313–314, 339–340, 352, 358
    asymmetrical, 108 (figs.), 112
    Badger Component, 313–314
    beveled, 366
    bifaced, 203, 204
    bone, 44, 56, 59, 116, 117 (fig.), 132, 212, 223, 224
    broad, 29–30, 58 (list), 110
    chipped stone, 108 (figs.), 224, 228
    flake, 30, 58, 61, 112, 204, 352
    four-edged, 203, 204
    Harahey, 340, 352
    hook-bladed, 56
    leaf-shaped, 285
    narrow, 30, 43, 54, 58 (list), 110
    oval, 110, 116
    ribbon flake, 204

Knives—Continued
    scrapula, 116, 117 (fig.), 132, 213, 229
    skinning, 196
    squash, 56, 116, 132
    stone, 28 (figs.), 54, 203–204
    thin-bladed, 204
    trapezoidal blade, 286
    vein chalcedony, 108 (figs.), 112, 203, 204
Knox County, Nebr., 302
Krogman, W. M., 258, 261

Lagomorpha, 233
Landes, Mr. and Mrs. Kenneth, 327
La Roche Focus, 130, 131
La Roche site, 97, 128, 129, 130, 133, 134, 179
Larson culture, 177
Larter site, 203
Later Heart River Period, 61
Lawrence, Russell B., xiii
Leaners, 52
Leather work, 134
Le Beau Focus, 171
Lehmer, Donald J., 1, 15, 44, 55, 56, 132, 152, 161, 197, 215, 284, 302, 317
Libby, Orin G., 56
Like-a-Fishhook Village, 127
Limestone, 314, 332, 341, 342
    Cottonwood formation, 336, 341, 346, 357, 360, 365
    Permian, 324
    slabs, 361
Limonite, 332, 366
Lincoln, Nebr., 162
Lindenmeier site, 206, 256 (list)
Lithic materials, 285–286
Little Missouri River, 54, 62
Little-Water-Man, supernatural being, 354
    petroglyph (14WO226), 347, 353–354
Livingston, Jerry, 295
Lodge, circular, 74, 126
    eagle-trapping, 127
    earth-covered, 52, 61, 282, 297, 306, 307
Log, charred, 281
Love, August, 327
Lower Brule, reservation town, 272
Lower Loup Focus, 133
Lyman County, S. Dak., 62, 214, 271, 272, 296, 306

MacNeish, Richard S., 196, 203
McDermott, John Francis, editor, 323
McKern, Thomas W., and Stewart, T. D., 260–261
McLaughlin, Jack, xiii
McNutt, Charles H., xiii, 301
Madison, Lee G., 271, 281
Maerz, A., and Paul, M. Rea, 35
Maize (Zea mays), 226
Mandan culture, 61, 63, 127, 131, 133, 134, 152, 220, 231
    sites, 55, 56, 61, 126, 132

Mandan-Hidatsa culture, 177
Mano, stone, 34, 55, 58, 115, 336–337, 341, 360, 365, 366
Maples Mill culture, 311
Marion County, Kans., 324
Marshno, Joseph, 327
Mason County, Ill., 311
Mauls, grooved, 31, 58 (list), 113, 208, 209, 224, 228
Mealing slab, 33–34, 55, 58, 115
Meat, dried, 208, 209, 223
Medicines, 337
Meleen, Elmer E., 130, 133, 134
Metcalf, George, 213, 214
Meyer, Winton, 231
Mica, 90, 116
Microblades, 194, 204, 227, 243–244
Middens, refuse, 60, 151, 152, 213, 223, 225, 275
Middle Missouri area, 1, 14, 15, 57, 62, 71, 126, 132, 133, 315
Middle Tent, Frederick, 295
Middle Woodland time level, 367
Miller, Carl F., 259
Miller, Loye, 50, 125
Miller, Ruth, 146
Mississippi Valley, 231
Missouri Basin Chronology Program, 306
Missouri Basin Project, Smithsonian Institution, 62, 71, 73, 131, 145, 146, 271, 273, 295, 327
Missouri Botanical Gardens, St. Louis, 231
Missouri Plateau section, 145
Missouri River, 2, 3 (map), 50, 52, 55, 60, 61, 63, 71, 73, 112, 127, 128, 129, 130, 134, 135, 145, 153, 222, 259, 271, 272, 295, 296, 306, 307, 311, 315
  drainage basin, 327
  flood plain, 2, 78
  terrace, 1, 296
Missouri River Valley, 1, 61, 62, 245
Mitchell Creek site, 56
Moat, protective, 147
Mobridge, S. Dak., 56, 132, 133
Mole, meadow, 233
Mollusks, 50, 51 (table)
Mongoloids, 258
Mooney, James, 344
Moorman, Edward H., 324, 326, 327
Morris County, Kans., 324
Morrison, Joseph P. E., xiii, 50, 221
Mortars, wooden, 152, 154
Motsiff site, 56, 57
Mullers, 115
Mulloy, William, 177
Muskrat, 51, 226, 233
Myers site, 130

Nakasa tribe (Caddoan group), 344
National Park Service, Dept. of Interior, xiii, 71, 295, 324, 327
Nebraska culture, 337
Needlelike tool, 215, 229
Needles, bone, 59, 352–353
Nelson, Wayne, 295

Neosho Focus, 356, 357
Neuman, Robert W., 73
Newell, H. Perry, and Krieger, Alex D., 89
Nickerson, Norton H., 316
Nickerson, N. H., and Hou Ding, 231
Niobrara River, Nebr., 89
North Cannonball sites, 57
North Dakota State Legislature, 71
Northern Plains tribes, 1, 56
Nuts, 209

Oahe Reservoir, N. Dak., xiii, 61, 71, 130, 259
Oak, blackjack, 347
  trees, 323
Obsidian, smoky, 112, 193, 194, 239, 241
Ocher, red, 34, 38, 166, 211
Ojibwa Indians, 354
Oldham site (39CH7), 309
Omaha Indians, 231, 310
On-a-Slant Mandan village, 133
One Mile Creek, 3 (map)
Oneota site, 133, 338
Orleans Aspect, 366, 367
Osage Indians, 323, 344
Osterholt, Dale, 146
Otter (Lutra canadensis), 226, 233
Outlaw Rockshelter (14WO225), 353
Over, H. R., and Thomas, C. S., 237
Over Focus Swanson site (39BR16), 51, 56

Paddle, 90, 128, 161, 165, 178, 192, 224, 300
  cord-wrapped, 53, 90, 92, 128, 161, 165, 177, 192
  grooved, 53, 128, 161
Paint, 332, 366
  brushes, 211
  red, 344
  stones, 208, 228
  See also Hematite.
Paint Creek culture, 334, 357
Paleo-Indian material, 366
Palisade, 150–151, 225, 272
  posts, 277
  wall, 275, 277
Pashe, H. W., 327
Paul Brave estate, xiv
Paul Brave site (32SI4), xiii, 1, 2, 3 (map), 4, 53, 54, 56, 57, 60, 61, 62, 63, 100, 104, 125, 132, 133
  See also Fort Yates site.
Pawnee Indians, 208
Payne site, 130, 131, 133, 224
Pebbles, unmodified, 34
  utilized, 210–211, 228
Pecking stones, 208
Pelecypods, 50, 51
Pelican, white, 125
Pemmican, 210, 224
Pendant, bone, 120 (fig.), 123
  rib, 59
  shell, 48, 49 (fig.), 59, 221, 222
  wapiti tooth, 229
Perforators or gravers, stone, 206–207, 228

Perfumes, 337
Petrified wood, 27, 30, 31, 106, 110, 112
Petroglyph, Little-Water-Man (14WO 226), 347, 353–354
Petroglyphs, 341, 342–344, 346, 347, 348–350, 353
  sites of, 326, 341–342
Phillips, George, 327
Phillips, Richard, 327
Phillips County, Kans., 326
Phillips Ranch site (39ST14), 55, 133, 231
Picks, bison radius, 111 (fig.), 123, 132, 219
  bone, 229
  stone, 365
  ulna, 111 (fig.), 123
Pierre, S. Dak., 133, 192, 257
Pigments, 35, 115, 189
Pine, scrub, 347
Pins, bone, 132
Pipe bowl, 211, 286
Pipes, baked clay, 58
  catlinite, 114 (fig.), 115, 211
  catlinite disk-bowl, 109 (fig.), 114 (fig.), 115
  fragments, 276
Pisces, 233
Pi-Sunyer, Oriol, xiii
Pits, 3, 78, 83, 297
  aboriginal, 283
  ash, 148 (map)
  basin-shaped, 4, 7, 9, 52, 75, 86, 127, 151, 153, 154, 157 (fig.), 158, 299, 308
  bell-shaped, 11, 52, 75, 80, 82, 84, 85, 86, 87, 124, 127, 148 (map), 152, 154, 156, 157 (fig.), 160, 223, 307
  borrow, 86, 156, 159
  cache, 3, 52, 148 (map), 151, 152, 154, 156–157 (fig.), 160, 190, 205, 209, 211, 212, 219, 220, 223, 238, 279, 283, 307
  circular, 151, 152, 159
  fire, 148 (map), 151, 152, 153, 154, 156
  irregular, 9, 52
  midden, 159–160, 192, 212, 214, 219, 221, 223, 225, 307
  oval, 80, 86
  quasi-rectangular, 159
  rectangular, 9
  rubbish, 52, 60, 75, 82, 152, 154, 156, 276
  saucer-shaped, 156, 159
  storage, 52, 156, 160, 223
  test, 11–12, 59, 74, 75, 78, 146, 276, 283, 296, 329, 330, 331, 332, 337, 348, 354, 357, 361
  undercut, 152
Plains Indian groups, 220, 348, 360
Plains Woodland Period, 315, 316, 328, 351, 358, 363, 364, 366, 367, 368
Plums, wild (Prunus americana), 222, 232, 342
Point Peninsula Focus, 221
Pomme blanche, 125

Possum Point site (14WO228), 327, 354–357, 355 (map), 366, 367, 368
Postholes, 3, 4, 6 (map), 7, 9, 12, 75, 79, 85, 127, 148, 151, 152, 155, 159, 160, 276, 277, 281, 297, 299, 306
Post molds, 277, 281, 282, 283, 297, 361
Posts, 78, 79 (map), 80, 82, 84, 125, 127, 154, 281, 283, 297
  cedar, 7, 11, 299
  charred, 9, 85
  Paul Brave site, 4, 52
  stockade, 150 (map)
  wall, 152, 222
Potsherds, 271, 277, 284, 296, 297, 299, 334, 346, 350, 354, 357
Potter County, S. Dak., 145, 259
Pottery, 92–105, 163–165, 211, 226, 284–285, 287, 299–303, 306, 308–311
  Aldren cord impressed, 55
  Anderson, 287, 288
  Anderson flared rim ware, 287
  Anderson low rim, 279, 284, 285
  appendages, 15, 17, 20, 21, 53, 90, 95, 97, 98, 100, 101, 102, 103, 161, 300, 302, 303
  Archaic Mandan, 20, 52, 58
  Arikara, 193
  Arzberger Group, 130, 131
  Arzberger horizontal incised, 130
  Arzberger opposed diagonal, 130
  Badger Component, 308–311, 314
  bases, 224, 300
  biconical perforations in, 24
  black painted, 188–189
  body sherds, 23–24, 60 (list), 89, 90, 91–92, 100, 162, 163 (list), 165–167, 285, 303, 329, 330, 334, 338, 344–345, 350–351, 356, 363
  brushed, 162, 163, 166, 171, 173, 177, 178, 224, 285
  Cadotte collared, 299, 301–302, 307
  Campbell Creek types, 132, 307
  Chamberlain incised triangle, 309
  check-stamped, 24, 53, 55, 58, 89, 92, 130
  color, 53, 90, 160, 165, 192, 224, 284, 285, 300, 301, 302, 309, 310, 330, 334, 338, 350, 351, 354, 363, 368
  cord-impressed, 103–105, 162, 166, 171, 173, 174, 175, 177, 178, 185, 192, 224–225, 308, 309, 310, 330, 334, 338, 342, 344, 347, 350, 363, 367
  cord-paddled, 315
  cord-roughened, 53, 55, 58, 60, 89, 92, 97, 99, 130, 131, 276, 285, 287, 288, 347
  corncob-impressed, 163, 167, 190
  Cowley plain type, 345, 350
  curvilinear-stamped, 162
  decoration, 17 (fig.), 18 (figs.), 19, 20, 21, 22, 23, 53, 55, 89, 92, 96, 97–98, 99, 100, 101, 102, 103, 104, 129, 162, 165, 167–171, 172 (fig.), 175, 224, 284, 285, 299, 300, 301, 302, 303, 356, 363, 367
  Demery site, 90–105, 128
  dentate stamping, 330, 332, 367

Pottery—Continued
Evans incised, 97
Evans indented, 302
fabric-impressed, 162, 167
finger-indented, 170, 171, 172 (figs.), 177, 283, 284
fingernail-pinched, 163, 192
firing of, 160
forms, 15, 16, 19, 20, 21, 22, 53, 89, 90, 93, 96, 98, 99, 100, 101, 102, 103, 104, 174, 175, 177, 300
Fort Rice cord-impressed, 100, 101, 105, 129
Fort Rice trailed, 101, 105, 129
Fort Yates cord-impressed, 20–21, 54, 55, 58, 59, 60, 100
Fort Yates Cross-Hatched, 19, 21, 54, 55, 58, 60
Fort Yates fine incised, 19
Fort Yates plain, 19
Fort Yates ware, 16, 20–21, 24, 53
fragments, 55 (list)
Geneseo plain type, 338, 345, 354
Geneseo red filmed, 334
geometric designs on, 182
grass-marked, 345, 356
Great Bend, 350, 357
Great Oasis, 309, 315
Grey Cloud horizontal-incised, 97, 131, 299, 300–301, 307
grit-tempered, 89, 163, 192, 300, 301, 302, 303, 309, 310, 330, 331, 338, 342, 344, 345, 346, 350, 363, 367, 368
handles, 24, 53, 90, 97, 161, 170, 183–186, 188 (figs.), 334
hardness, 90, 284, 285
Harlan cord-roughened, 310
herringbone incised, 168 (fig.), 170, 173, 174, 175, 177, 178, 179, 184, 185, 191, 299
horizontal parallel line patterns on, 179, 184, 190, 300, 301
horizontal stab and drag design on, 184
Hosterman cord-impressed, 177
Hosterman site, 160–193
Hosterman vertical rims, 177–178
Huff, 101
Hughes Group, 130, 131
incised or trailed, 58, 60, 89, 90, 91, 92, 162, 163, 168 (fig.), 170, 171, 173, 174, 178, 182, 192, 224, 302, 330, 363
Iona diagonal-incised, 307
Iona horizontal-incised, 97, 98, 132, 307
Iona indented, 296, 299, 300, 307
Iona S-rim, 307
Iona ware, 132
Le Beau cord-wrapped rod designs, 177
Le Beau finger-indented, 171
Le Beau horizontal cord-impressed, 175, 178
line-block zonal decorations, 176, 179, 186 (fig.), 187 (fig.)

Pottery—Continued
lip form, 90, 167, 168 (figs.), 169 (figs.), 171, 174, 175, 177, 284, 285, 300, 302, 309, 310, 350, 356
lip treatment, 167–171, 224, 284
making, technique of, 128, 224, 300
Mandan, 192
mat-impressed, 162
miniature vessels, 22–23, 161, 189–190 (figs.), 224
modeling tools, 44, 56, 59, 61, 119 (fig.), 122–123
Nordvold horizontal-incised, 131, 166 (fig.), 179
notched-stick decorations on, 310
painted, 53, 163, 182, 188–189
paste, 15, 24, 53, 89, 90, 99, 103, 104, 160, 163, 174, 177, 300, 311
Paul Brave, 14, 15, 53, 58 (list)
pinched ridged, 163
plain, 162, 163, 165, 168 (fig.), 171, 174, 175, 177, 178, 182, 192, 276, 279, 285, 299, 330
Plains, 301
polished, 90, 350, 351
punctated, 163, 168 (figs.), 170, 175, 177, 179, 182, 224, 301, 302
recurved rims, 101–103, 105
red-filmed, 89, 92, 166
Riggs cross-hatched rim, 19, 21, 55, 58, 60, 104, 105, 128, 129
Riggs flared rim, 279, 283, 284
Riggs incised rim, 19–20, 53, 55, 58, 60
Riggs pinched rim, 20, 55, 58, 60
Riggs plain rim, 16, 17 (figs.), 18 (figs.), 53, 54, 55, 58, 59, 60
Riggs punctate, 54, 55, 58, 59, 281, 282, 283, 284
Riggs straight rim, 104, 105, 128, 129
Riggs ware, 16–20, 24, 53, 58 (list), 284, 287, 288
Riggs wavy rim, 54
rim decoration on, 175–180 (figs.), 224
rim form, 15, 23, 53, 71, 90, 91 (figs), 92, 129, 162, 173, 174, 177, 284, 285, 300, 356
rim sherds, 128, 162, 283, 284–285, 287, 300, 301, 302, 306, 307 (list), 308, 310, 329–330, 334, 338, 350, 354, 361–363
rim types, 89, 91 (figs.), 93 (figs.), 94 (figs.), 129, 173, 174 (table), 363
Rio Grande glaze paint, 334
rocker-stamped, 330, 332, 367
Russel plain rim, 301
Russell ware, 301
Rygh rainbow corded, 175, 177, 178
S-shaped rim decorations, 172 (figs.), 173, 174 (table), 175, 177, 185 (fig.), 192
sand-tempered, 354
shapes, 53, 161
shell-tempered, 89, 342, 344
shoulder decorations on, 183, 184 (fig.), 224

Pottery—Continued
  shoulder elements on, 93 (figs.), 94
    (figs.), 95 (figs.), 97, 99, 100, 101,
    161
  shoulder treatment, 182–183, 300
  simple-stamped, 23, 53, 55, 58, 59,
    60, 89, 90, 91, 92, 98, 128, 130, 161,
    162, 163, 165, 173 (fig.), 177, 182,
    183 (fig.), 192, 224, 285, 297, 299,
    306
  smoothed, 58, 59, 60, 90, 92, 128, 161,
    334, 338, 344, 345, 346, 367
  Stanley braced rim ware, 302, 307
  Stanley tool impressed, 299, 302, 307
  surface finish, 15, 53, 89, 90, 97, 98,
    99, 100, 101, 102, 103, 104, 165,
    174, 177, 192, 284, 285, 300
  Talking Crow brushed types, 179
  Talking Crow straight rim, 91
    (figs.), 92, 96, 105, 129, 131, 132,
    299, 301, 307
  Talking Crow ware, 301
  tempering, 53, 90, 160, 224, 284, 285,
    300, 334, 354
  texture, 90, 160, 164, 284, 285, 300
  ticked-line, 180–182 (fig.)
  tool impressed, 171, 182 (list), 301,
    302
  Twelve Mile black-on-gray, 55, 58
  unclassified, 16, 21–22, 58, 60, 61
  Valley cord-roughened, 310
  vertical rim sherds, 178 (table)
  vessel shape, 15, 177, 186–188
  Weaver ware, 311
  Wheeler horizontal-incised, 96, 131,
    132, 179
  Wheeler incised-triangle, 132
  Wheeler plain rim, 96
  Wheeler ridged, 96
  with flaring rims, 96, 97, 99, 105,
    130, 297
  Woodland, 100
Prairie chicken (Tymfanuchers ameri-
    canus), 24
Pre-Arikara group, 208, 226
Preceramic remains, 325
Prehistoric Omaha, 309, 315
Pre-Mandan group, 226
Projectile points, 239–242 (list), 276,
    285, 297, 303, 311–313, 329, 330,
    332, 334–336, 338–339, 340, 342,
    345, 351, 354, 356, 358, 360, 363–
    364, 366
  chipped stone, 54, 105–106, 107
    (figs.), 193–194, 223, 225, 227
  expanding stem, 342, 345, 347, 351,
    356, 357, 358, 367
  fragments, 106, 330, 332, 335, 352,
    357, 358, 363
  large point, 335, 339, 345, 352, 356,
    357, 367
  late horizon, 335, 339, 356
  plain lanceolate, 25, 27
  plain triangular, 27
  small point, 335, 345, 352, 356, 367
  stone, 25, 26 (figs.), 27, 58 (list),
    224, 357

Pottery—Continued
  triangular, basal notched, 303
  triangular, corner-notched, 312
  triangular, straight base, 303, 311–
    312
  triangular blade, concave base, 106,
    285, 303
  triangular blade, straight base, un-
    notched, 106, 303, 351
  triangular blade, two side notches,
    106, 285
Pronghorns (Antilocapra americana),
    212, 216, 226, 233
  metapodial bone, 216, 217, 219, 229
Prunus americanus, 317
Pumice, 209, 223, 228
Pumpkin, sugar, 232
Pumpkin seeds, charred, 50, 231
Punches, antler, 219
  bone, 45, 59, 215–216, 224, 229
Quartz, 30, 31, 90, 303, 304, 312
Quartzite, 30, 31, 106, 110, 112, 113, 193,
    194, 196, 201, 204, 207, 208, 239,
    240, 241, 242, 286, 303, 312, 313,
    314, 331, 341, 364
  Bijou Hills, 30, 112, 282, 283, 285,
    304, 314
Quill flatteners, 44, 282, 287
Rabbit, 226, 317
  cottontail (Sylvilagus floridanus),
    51, 125, 233, 234, 316
  jack (Lepus townsendii), 51, 125,
    233, 234
Radiocarbon dating, 63
Rafters, 222
Redbird Focus, 97, 130, 133
Reed, Erik K., 327
Ree Heights, Hand County, S. Dak., 309
Ree Heights Buffalo Kill site (39HD3),
    309
Reid, Russell, XIII, 71
Reptiles, 51, 125
Ribs, cut, 215, 229
  fragments of, perforated, 229
  notched, 215, 229
  tip of, slotted, 45, 59, 117 (fig.), 119
    (fig.), 122, 133
Rice County, Kans., 334
Ridgepole, 52
Rifle, 344
Rim sherds, 59, 60
Ritchie, William A., 221
River Basin Survey, XIII, 324, 326, 327
Roberts, Frank H. H., Jr., 206, 327
Robert Zahn site (32S13), 57–60, 62
Robinson, Stephen W., XIII, 73
Rock fragments, 297
Rocks, fire-cracked, 308
Rockshelter, Dry Creek, (14WO224),
    347–353, 349 (map), 366, 367
  Outlaw (14WO225), 353
  Walleye (14WO222), 326, 341–347,
    343 (map), 366, 367
Rodentia, 233

Rodents, 51 (list), 125
Roof, dirt, 222
  poles, 127, 152
  supports, 127, 151, 154, 222
Roots, 125, 223
Rough-stone Complex, Hosterman site, 227
Rubbing stones, 208, 228
Rubbing tools, bone, 45, 59
Rutherford Mound, 311
Ryan site (25DK2), 309

Sample, Mark, 327
Sandstone, 31, 32, 33, 55, 57, 113, 114, 115, 209, 286, 323, 336, 337, 341, 342, 344, 346, 348, 352, 354, 357, 360, 365
Sátwa, Arikara work basket, 125
Scalp Creek, 97
Scalp Creek site, 130, 132, 133, 179
Scapula, worked, 216, 229
Scapula spines, 213, 214, 229
Scheans, Daniel J., 62
Schist, gray micaceous, 336, 341
Scoops, horn core and frontal, 59
  split metapodial, 37, 38, 59
Scoria, 32, 60, 113, 304
Scraper-burin combination, 205
Scrapers, 195–203, 227–228, 286, 329, 367
  bone, 212, 223
  bowshaft, 340
  circular, 195
  elliptical, 195
  end, 195, 196, 197–201, 205, 207, 228, 244–247 (list), 248–255, 282, 283, 286, 314, 340, 345–346, 366
  flake, 112, 195, 198, 282, 331, 336, 337, 338, 340, 342, 346, 352, 360, 365, 366, 367
  ovate, 195
  ovoid, 203
  planoconvex, 195, 198
  pointed oval, 196
  scapula, 214
  shell, 117 (fig.), 124, 134, 221
  side, 194, 195, 198, 201–203, 228, 244 (list), 314
  single edged, 195
  snub-nosed, 223
  stone, 225
  subtriangular, 195
  teardrop, 195, 198
  thumbnail, 195, 199
  turtleback, 364–365
  unifaced, 195
Screen, 153
Seeds, 208, 222, 226
Setzer, H. W., 233
Shaft scrapers, 340
Shaft smoothers, 32, 33 (fig.), 59, 114 (fig.), 115, 223, 282, 304, 342, 352
Shaft wrenches, 59, 117 (fig.), 118, 215, 229
Shale, 113
Shannon Focus, 129, 130, 131, 307, 315
Sharpening stone, 352
Sha-we, Mandan women's game, 56

Shells, 134, 221 (table)–222, 277
  Anodonta grandis plana, 51, 221, 226
  deposits of, 146
  "*Goniobasis*" *nebrascensis*, 49 (fig.), 50
  Lampsilis cardium, 51
  L. siliquoidea, 51
  Lasmigona complanata, 51, 221
  L. sp., 222
  Lioplax nebrascensis, 48, 49 (fig.) modified, 120 (fig.)
  Nucula planimarginata, 50
  Olivella biplicata, 221
  Oyxtrema insculpta, 49 (fig.), 50
  snail, 57, 59
  Succinea grosvenori, 221
  Tancredia americana, 50
  unmodified, 50, 51 (table)
  unworked, 221, 229
  Viviparus leidyi, 49 (fig.), 50
  V. retusus, 49 (fig.), 50
  work in, 48–50, 59 (list)
Sherds, 12, 147, 161, 224, 274, 277, 278, 281, 283
  See also Pottery.
Sheyenne-Cheyenne site, 56
Shotwell, J. Arnold, 50, 125
Sickles, bone, 212, 223
  scapula, 214, 229
Siltstone, 31, 55
Siouan tribes, Thegiha-speaking, 323
Skeletons, analysis of, 261
Skulls, 220, 229, 235
Skunk (*Mephitis hudsonica*), 51, 226, 233, 234
Slabs, grooved sandstone, 57
  limestone, 361
Slant site (32MO26), 56, 57, 133
Slaughtering or butchering areas, 157–159
Slow, Horace, 295
Smith, Carlyle S., 62, 96, 129, 132, 162, 180, 301, 306, 307, 325, 327
Smith, Carlyle S., and Grange, Robert T., Jr., 96, 98, 129, 130, 131, 133, 296, 299, 300, 301, 306, 307
Smith, G. Hubert, 295
Smoky Hill River, 325
Smoothers, stone, 223
Solecki, R., 205
Southern Cult items, 134
Sower, J. E., 327
Spain site (39LM301), 96, 98, 130, 131, 133, 300, 306, 307
Spaulding, Albert C., 89, 96, 130, 132, 133, 134, 197, 337
Spatula tip, bone, 38, 39 (fig.), 59
Spears, 158
Sperry culture, 177
Spinden, Herbert J., 1
Spokeshaves, 218
Spoons, brass, 353
  shell, 221
Spotted Bear site, 127, 133
Squash, 226
  seeds, charred, 50, 222, 223, 231

Squirrel, ground (*Citellus* sp.), 51, 125, 226, 233, 234
Standing Rock Indian Agency, 71
Standing Rock Indian Reservation, XIV, 73
Standing Rock Tribal Council, XIII, XIV, 73
Standing Soldier site (32S18), 62
Stanek, James J., 295
Stanton, N. Dak., 57
Stanton Ferry, 57
State Historical Society of North Dakota, XIII, XIV, 53, 56, 57, 59, 60, 71, 73, 74, 125
Steamboat Creek site (39PO1), 186
Steen, Charlie R., 327
Steinbrueck, Emil R., 57
Stephenson, Robert L., XIII, 73, 131, 295, 327
Stewart, Evelyn B., 295
Stewart, T. D., 261
Stockade trench, 146, 147, 279
Stone, fragments of, 332
    problematical object of, 314
    unworked, 116, 276, 277, 281, 332, 341
    worked 25–35, 58 (list), 59 (list), 60–61
Stringers, wooden, 127
Strong, William D., 56, 192, 193
Structures, ceremonial, 12
    discussion of, 51–52, 126–128
Swan, whistling (*Cygnus columbianus*), 51
Swan Creek site (39WW7), 130, 131, 171, 186, 217, 224
Swanson site, 309
Swanton, John R., 344
Talking Crow site (39BF3), 96, 132, 301
Tanner, Lloyd, 327
Tattoo designs, 344, 350
Taylor, William, 236
Tazewell County, Ill., 311
Teeth, beaver, 220
    elk, 46, 47 (fig.), 48, 56, 59
    human, 85, 221, 229
    wapiti, 221
    worked, 220–221, 229
Tefft, Gaylord S., 327
Thomas Riggs Focus, 62, 63, 85, 89, 104, 105 (list), 128, 129, 130, 131, 133, 135, 288
Thomas Riggs site (39HU1), 2, 14, 51, 52, 53, 54, 55, 57, 62, 63, 132, 284, 287, 306
Thong stretchers, bone, 35, 59, 212, 213, 214, 216, 229
Timbers, charred, 75
    milled, 281
Tines, deer, 46
Tipsina (*Psorales esculenta*), 125, 134
Tissue abraders, cancellous, 118
Tony Glas site (32EM3), 62
Tools, antler, 352
    bone, 12, 212, 229, 352
    digging, 123, 212, 213
    flake, lamellar, 207–208, 228
    flaking, 366

Tools—Continued
    flint, 12, 223
    ground and pecked stone, 208–211, 228
    lamellar flake, 207–208, 228, 255 (list)
    needlelike, 215
    pentagonal-shaped, 216–217
    scapula, 132
    sharpening, 346
    wooden, 352
Toronto, Woodson County, Kans., 323, 347
Toronto Dam, 323, 324
Toronto Reservoir, 323, 324, 325, 326, 327, 328, 347, 366, 368
Toronto Reservoir sites, 368 (tabulation)
Trade goods, European, 334, 347
    southwestern, 334
    White, 315
Tree ring dating, 63
Trench, exploratory, 147, 148, 275, 283
    Paul Brave site, 11, 52
    stockade, 146, 147
    test, 275–276, 361
Tribal Council, Standing Rock Indian Reservation, 73
Trotter, Mildred, and Gleser, Goldine C., 258, 261
Tubers, 223
Tubes, bone, 37 (fig.), 40, 56, 59, 118, 119 (fig.), 212, 217, 229
Tulsa District, Kans., 323
Turkey, 24, 226
    bones, 212
Turtle, 51, 125
Twelve Mile Creek site, 56
Two Teeth site (39BF204), 301, 307
Underwater Panther, mythical figure, 348
University of California, 125
University of Kansas, 62, 306, 307, 324, 327
University of Michigan, 63, 308, 309
    radiocarbon laboratory, 63, 131
University of Minnesota, 309
University of Nebraska, 131, 309
    laboratory of anthropology, 309
    State Museum of, 327
University of North Dakota, XIII, XIV
University of Oregon, 125
Upper Plains, 191
Upper Republican, 56, 133, 222, 325, 326, 337
Upper Sanger, 57

Valley Focus, 310
Vegetal remains, 50, 231–232, 317, 342
Verdigris River, 323, 332, 337, 341, 360, 361
Vertebrae, 235
Vessels, bowl shaped, 338
    exotic, of possible Caddoan extraction, 190–191
    globular, 189, 297, 306
    miniature, 9, 22–23, 92, 189–190 (figs.), 191 (table)

Vessels—Continued
    Plains Woodland, 310
    pottery, 12, 80
    soot deposit on, 187, 224
    two-spouted, 191 (fig.)
    See also Pottery.
Villages, area of, 74, 129, 226
    farming-hunting, 306
    Paul Brave site, 58 (list)
    Thomas Riggs site, 58 (list)
    unfortified, 61
Vole, meadow, 226

Wallace, Wayne O., 327
Walleye Rockshelter (14W0224), 326, 341–347, 343 (map), 366, 367
Walls, 222, 281
    posts for, 11, 52
    wattle-and-daub, 52
Wapiti tooth (*Cervus canadensis*), 221, 229
Waterfowl, 226
Watermelons, 146
Webb, Albert, 327
Webb, George, 327
Wedel, Waldo R., 44, 55, 56, 132, 133, 208, 332, 334, 338, 345, 350, 357
Wedel, Waldo, and Kivett, Marvin F., 310, 326, 354
Weeks, Richard, 257
Weinreich, Bernard, xiii, 72
Wellington, J. W., xiv, 71
Wheeler, Richard P., 44, 56, 146, 161
Whetstones, 209
Whistle, bone, 38, 39 (fig.), 59

White, Theodore, 159, 233, 235, 316, 317
White River, 62
Whitlocks Crossing, Missouri River, 145, 257
Wichita culture, 334
Wichita Indians, 344, 357
Wilford, Lloyd A., 309, 315
Will, George F., 1, 61, 63, 187
Will, George F., and Hecker, Thad. C., 1, 2, 20, 51, 52, 57, 60, 61, 62, 63, 74, 175
Will, George F., and Spinden, H. J., 55, 57, 61, 133, 175, 225
Will, Oscar H., 125
Willey, Gordon R., 129
Willow, black, 125
Wilmeth, Roscoe, 130, 131, 133, 179
Wilson, Gilbert L., 127
Wilson, Ione, 295
Winona, 3 (map)
Wood, W. Raymond, 50, 56, 71, 97, 125, 129, 130, 133, 134, 302
Wood, charred, 342
    See also Petrified wood.
Woodland Indians, 348
Woodland Pattern, 326
Woodland remains, 325, 347, 357, 363
Woodruff Ossuary, Kans., 310, 326
Woodson County, Kans., 323, 326, 328, 347
Woodson County site, 324
Woolworth, Alan R., 52, 54, 62, 71

Yankton County, S. Dak., 309
Yellow Back, Junior, 295

O

Thomas Riggs site, 58 (list)
unfortified, 01
Vole, meadow, 220

Wallace, Wm.,
Walleye Hook site (14W0221), 328.
341-347847 (map), 366, 367
Walls, 322, 331
posts for, 11, 52
wattle-and-daub, 52
Wapiti tooth (Cervus canadensis), 221,
220
Waterfowl, 220
Watermelons, 140
Webb, Albert, 327
Webb, George, 327
Wedel, Waldo R., 14, 55, 56, 122, 158,
204, 322, 334, 335, 348, 350, 367
Wedel, Waldo, and Kivett, Marvin F.,
310, 326, 354
Weeks, Richard, 327
Wellington, J. W., xiv, 71
Wetstones, 208
Whalife, bone, 85, 89 (fig.), 50

White River, 62
Whitlocks (Crossing, Missouri River,
145, 207
Wichita culture, 321
Wichita Indians, 311, 327
Wilford, Lloyd A., 306, 315
Will, George F., 1, 61, 85, 157
Will, George F., and Hecker, Thad C.,
1, 2, 20, 51, 52, 57, 60, 61, 62, 68,
74, 176
Will, George F., and Spinden, H. J., 62

Willey, Gordon
Willow, black, 140
Wilmeth, Roscoe, 189, 131, 193, 170
Wilson, Gilbert L., 127
Wilson, Ione, 205
Winona, B (map)
Wood, W. Raymond, 50, 56, 71, 97, 124,
120, 130, 132, 134, 302
Wood, charred, 312
See also Petrified wood.
Woodland Indians, 348
Woodland lithics, 328
Woodland remains, 328, 341, 357, 368
Woodruff Ossuary, Kans., 310, 326
Woodson County, Kans., 323, 326, 328,
347
Woodson County site, 321
Woolworth, Alan R., 52, 54, 02, 71

Yankton County, S. Dak., 300
Yellow Bear, Junior, 208